DATE DUE

DEMCO 38-296

THE ROMAN NEAR EAST

31 BC – AD 337

✦

Based on

Carl Newell Jackson Lectures

THE ROMAN NEAR EAST

31 BC – AD 337

✦ ✦ ✦

FERGUS MILLAR

HARVARD UNIVERSITY PRESS

CAMBRIDGE, MASSACHUSETTS

LONDON, ENGLAND

1993

This book has been supported by a grant from the National Endowment
for the Humanities, an independent federal agency.

This book is printed on acid-free paper, and its binding materials have been
chosen for strength and durability.

Library of Congress Cataloging-in-Publication Data

Millar, Fergus.
The Roman Near East, 31 B.C.–A.D. 337 / Fergus Millar.
p.   cm.
Includes bibliographical references and index.
ISBN 0-674-77885-5
1. Middle East—History—To 622.
2. Rome—History—30 B.C. –476 A.D.
I. Title.
DS62.25.M53   1993
939.4—dc20

93–18174
CIP

For Susanna

CONTENTS

II. REGIONS AND COMMUNITIES

PREFACE

The subject of this book can be defined in three different ways: geographically, chronologically and linguistically. In geographical terms I mean by 'the Roman Near East' all those areas which lie between the Taurus Mountains and Egypt, and which were, or came to be, under Roman rule. The region concerned overlaps the territories of eight modern states: Turkey, Iraq, Syria, Lebanon, Jordan, Israel, Egypt and Saudi Arabia. To the west it is of course bounded by the Mediterranean, and to the north, somewhat less clearly, by Mount Amanus and the foothills of the Taurus. To the east and south the eventual limits of Roman military occupation did not correspond with any very definite geographical boundaries. The middle Euphrates, which for long served as a symbolic boundary between the empires of Rome and of Parthia, ceased to do so in the course of the second century. With that great change, to which I will come back many times, the Roman Empire in the east expanded decisively beyond the Mediterranean seaboard, with consequences of immense significance. By the end of the third century Roman control extended to, and in some not very clear sense beyond, the upper-middle Tigris. In the south-west of the area, similarly, the Roman military presence has left traces in part but not all of the Hedjaz, the barren mountain-range running along the eastern side of the Red Sea. What seems to be the furthermost Roman outpost here is Medain Saleh, a little over 300 km north of Medina.

The area concerned thus represents a large section of the Fertile Crescent; its definition as fertile reflects the fact that all of it shades off into what is often called desert, but is in fact at almost all points not desert but a flat, largely dry and often very stony steppe, in places coloured dark-grey or black from the presence of volcanic rock. To emphasise the fact that the zone along whose margins a great line of Roman roads and forts, from the Red Sea to the Tigris, eventually stretched was not a 'desert' of sand-dunes, I have consistently used the word 'steppe'. How we should understand the mutual relations of the Roman government, the settled population and the peoples of the steppe—*skēnitai* ('tent-dwellers'), *nomades, Arabes,* or *Saraceni*—is precisely one of the major problems which the book attempts to confront.

In chronological terms, as its sub-title indicates, the book starts from the moment of the battle of Actium and ends with the death of Constantine. It might reasonably have begun a little further back, with the arrival of Pompey's forces in Syria in the mid-60s BC. But the complex narrative of events in the late Republic would have either taken up too much space or failed to reveal much about the Near East itself, or most probably both. But some evidence, above all from Strabo's *Geography,* which relates to that period has been used.

Similarly, it could have been reasonable to end with the treaty of 298 or 299 which gave Rome firm control of the upper-middle Tigris; or, even more reasonably, to take as the terminal point the moment when, after the death of Julian in 363, Jovian was forced to cede Nisibis and the eastern part of the Mesopotamian shelf to the Persians. As it is, the book deliberately stops just when two related but separate major developments in religious history began; first, the formal recognition of the Christian Church by Constantine, and the construction of churches as visible, public features of the urban landscape; and second, something of perhaps equal significance in the evolution of Christianity: the ascetic movement, which so far as the Roman Near East is concerned began simultaneously in the south-western corner of the region, around Gaza, and in its north-eastern corner, around Nisibis, both in the early years of the fourth century.

Long ago, I imagined that I might write a social history of the Near East which would cover the whole period from Alexander to Mahomet. But the Hellenistic period has its own problems, which I tried to explore in a chapter in A. Kuhrt and S. Sherwin-White, *Hellenism in the East* (1987). As for the period of precisely three centuries from the death of Constantine to the first Islamic conquests, that must represent a major challenge for someone else. For a book on these centuries would have to embrace the great conflicts with Sasanid Persia which broke out again in the sixth century, and of course provided the context of the Islamic invasions of the seventh; late paganism and the definitive Christianisation of the region; the great Christological controversies and the flowering of Syriac Christian literature; the beginnings of Armenian Christian literature; pagan and Christian Antioch as a major political and cultural centre; Judaism—including the compilation of the 'Jerusalem' Talmud, contacts with Babylonia, and influence in the Hedjaz in the time of Mahomet; the Samaritans as an important community, capable of major revolts; and the significant role played by newly Christianised Arab peoples in the unsettled steppe zone between Rome and Persia.

It is thus very easy to see why no such overall history of the late-Roman and early-Byzantine Near East has ever been attempted; why one now does require to be written; and why it was beyond my powers at any rate to embrace these centuries along with the earlier period of nearly four centuries.

Even so, it was impossible to deny myself all hindsight, or all use of the vivid testimony of Ammianus Marcellinus, Theodoret and Sozomenus for the social history of the Near East, or of the *Notitia Dignitatum* for the structure of the 'desert frontier' as it had evolved by the end of the fourth century. Nonetheless there were very good historical and technical reasons for treating the period from the mid-first century BC to the mid-fourth century AD as a distinctive phase. First, from the point of view of Roman Imperial history, the step-by-step advance of Roman direct control demonstrates that, in the Near East at least, the idea that Roman imperialism and expansionism died out after the early Empire is simply false. More important, however, is the fact that these centuries saw the main flowering of the 'epigraphic habit' as expressed in the Near East. It should be stressed here that inscriptions represent the fundamental material on which the book is based. I have of course used all the literary evidence that I could find, among which the works of Josephus play an important role. I have also tried to make sense, for myself and the reader, of the complex geography of the region, with its very distinctive sub-regions. Thus, while the long first part is designed to give a conception of evolution over time, it is also intended as an introduction to the geography of the region. The various different sub-regions and local areas are then treated in the core of the book, the even longer second part. To make each section intelligible by itself, there has been some deliberate repetition at particular points.

In all this I have of course also used archaeological and iconographic evidence, though what follows is in no way an adequate study of the physical evidence. The book is primarily based on inscriptions, for two linked reasons: political structures, and language. First, my approach is essentially about politics and 'ethnicity'; about what political formations, including the Empire itself, were present in the region, and how people identified themselves and whatever wider political community they conceived of themselves as belonging to. The book is thus concerned with 'imagined communities' in the sense used by Benedict Anderson. For that, inscriptions are all-important. The Christian epigraphy of the late Empire, in Greek, more rarely in Syriac and (very occasionally) in Arabic, reflects a different outlook and a much-changed world. It is in the first few centuries, as is well known, that the 'epigraphic habit' does most to reveal political and communal structures.

It is this which then brings me to the third way in which the 'Roman Near East' can be defined: by language. The 'Near East' is, on this definition, that area of the Roman Empire where Greek (rather than Latin) co-existed with a family of Semitic languages. There is no simple way of listing these without being misleading. Nabataean, Palmyrene and Syriac are to be seen as dialects of Aramaic, written in the same alphabet, but with slightly different scripts. But that leaves us without a parallel term for the Aramaic used by Jews (and probably gentiles) in Judaea, or later 'Syria Palaestina', or that used by gentiles in the broad zone between the Jordan and the steppe, and north of the Nabataean kingdom. Greek observers tended to speak of all these languages or dialects, without distinction, as 'the language of the *Suroi*', and to refer to people using it (or them) as speaking *Suristi*.

Then there was Phoenician, written in the same alphabet of twenty-two letters, and only very slightly attested, on coin-legends and a couple of inscriptions, in our period; and Hebrew, normally written in the square Aramaic script, but for which the ancient 'Palaeo-Hebrew' script could be re-deployed for nationalistic reasons. Then, out in the steppe, but also attested at places in the settled zone, for instance at Dura and in Palmyrene territory, there are many thousands of graffiti written in 'Safaitic'—a mere nickname borrowed from the volcanic steppe called the Safa east of the Jebel Hauran. Finally, there is Arabic itself, attested on only two documents from our period—but that it is so attested is still a fact of the greatest importance.

One of the prime purposes of the book is to use the surviving inscriptions to draw a geographical and chronological map of the places and times where and when these various languages or dialects are attested, and to give some initial impression (it cannot be more) of how they were used and how they related to Greek. Latin too plays a significant part, above all (obviously) in military contexts and in the 'colonial' zone of Berytus and the Bekaa Valley. The reader will also find many instances of how the Greek actually used in this region, always the predominant language, was shot through with Latin words and proper names on the one hand, and with Semitic words and proper names on the other.

However limited their content, inscriptions have the overwhelming advantage for the historian of being tied to place and time: that is, of being found (generally speaking) where they were set up, and of being either explicitly dated or (at worst) broadly datable. A geography of language—or at least of *public* language—is thus attainable. But in the Near East the evidence of inscriptions is also, now, being ever more fully supplemented by documents on perishable materials, that is, papyrus or parchment: the priceless collection from Dura-Europos; the documents in Hebrew, Aramaic and Greek from the

Judaean Desert, largely but not wholly relating to the Bar Kochba war; the 'archive of Babatha', of which the Greek items, sadly without their Nabataean and Aramaic counterparts, were admirably published in 1989 by Naphtali Lewis; and the remarkable Greek and Syriac archive of the third century from the middle Euphrates, still in the course of (very rapid) publication by Javier Teixidor, Denis Feissel and Jean Gascou.

How to represent this profusion and interplay of languages (in which a Syriac, Nabataean or Palmyrene text may contain a transliteration of a Greek transliteration of a Latin word) in an English text is an insoluble problem, in which true consistency simply cannot be achieved. This problem is paralleled by the equally insoluble problem that there is no agreed transliteration of modern Arabic place-names. As for the latter, so far as possible I have used the simplified forms which the reader will find on modern English maps of the Near East, sometimes giving variants where this seems necessary. But this hardly solves the problem, since there is no modern English map which gives more than a tiny proportion of village names. The text of the book tries above all to make sense of where places are in functional relation to each other.

The maps provided in the book follow approximately the sequence of regions discussed in Part II. They try to set at least a selection of the places named into an intelligible geographical context. It should be stressed that there are no cross-references to the maps in the main body of the text. The first map covers the whole area and indicates the sub-regions to which the following maps relate. No attempt has been made to list all the sites which can be identified or to give a consistent picture of what place-names were officially in use at any one moment; for one of the themes of the book is precisely how malleable these names were. The aim is to provide an intelligible guide to location. The maps, especially map II, are based on the excellent one in D. L. Kennedy and D. Riley, *Rome's Desert Frontier from the Air* (Batsford, 1990), p. 25. Map IX, which for obvious reasons of geography has to be on a smaller scale than the others, is based on the map in G. W. Bowersock, *Roman Arabia* (1983), facing p. 1. I am very grateful to Mrs. A. Wilkins of the Institute of Archaeology, Oxford, for drawing the maps included here.

As regards the use of Greek in the book, some rather short quotations in the Greek alphabet are given when necessary in the notes. Otherwise everything is transliterated, in particular with the intention of reproducing as accurately as possible the precise form of local rustic Greek, whether formally 'correct' or not; and, more important, of showing the exact spelling of place-names (often inconsistent in the original) and of Semitic or Latin terms or proper names in Greek transliteration. The long vowels *omega* and *eta* have been indicated as 'ē' and 'ō'. Outside quotations, I have largely used Latin forms, for instance 'Antiochia' (or 'Antioch') and 'Aurelius'; but in quotations from Greek, 'Antiocheia' and 'Aurēlios'. The inevitable inconsistency is emphasised by leaving such terms in whatever form they appear when I have used published translations. It will do no harm if this too serves to remind the reader that 'representing' the ancient world in an English text involves choices at every level.

As regards ancient Semitic scripts, I have adopted the device of using the same standard transliteration into capitals for all the Semitic languages involved. This may sometimes look odd, as with extracts from literary texts in Syriac, or even more so with rabbinic texts in Hebrew. But it has the practical merit of avoiding the presentation of material printed right-to-left within an English text; and it has the much more important function of instantly distinguishing transliterations from Semitic texts from those from texts in Greek; of exhibiting the widespread adoption of Greek (and some Latin) loan-words into these languages; and of revealing how close, as languages, they are to each other.

I should make explicit what will be instantly obvious to many readers, that I am not a Semitist by training. As is clear throughout, the book represents an expedition by a Classical ancient historian into Near Eastern territory. Whether this makes it a more or a less reprehensible example of 'Orientalism' in Edward Said's sense is not for me to say. On the other hand the deployment of Semitic languages here is not based on pure ignorance. I have a reasonable reading knowledge of Biblical Hebrew, and hence a basic grasp of the grammar of the languages concerned, other than Arabic. I need the assistance of modern works in approaching these various texts. But in the case of whatever is quoted, I would claim to have understood not merely what it means but why it means it.

If the book serves, by its manifest imperfections, to goad some Semitists into acquiring a wider historical training, or some Graeco-Roman historians into gaining a wider linguistic base, so much the better.

My concern with the Near East as it was in the Classical period goes back some quarter of a century, and should have been given expression in book form long since. But the stimulus to bring it to whatever fruition I could was provided by the very welcome invitation to deliver the Carl Newell Jackson lectures at Harvard University, which I gave in the spring of 1987. The hospitality of Albert Henrichs and his colleagues in the Department of Greek and Latin has left the happiest of memories of the week which my wife and I spent in Cambridge. With no disrespect to colleagues of my own generation, one particular privilege of the occasion was the presence of persons then in retirement: from Harvard itself Sterling Dow, John Finley and Mason Hammond; and from outside it Naphtali Lewis and Meyer Reinhold.

As will be obvious, even a Cambridge audience could not have supported the ordeal of hearing the whole text as it now is, or anything like it. It has taken another five years to deal with the subject in a way which I hope is not too inadequate; and in the course of that time the length of the text has increased far beyond what the benevolent editors of Harvard University Press would have wanted. I can only plead that I think the subject is important, and that even now the choice of ancient evidence and modern works to be referred to is at all points ruthlessly selective.

That selection itself could have been carried out, at least by myself, only with the unique resources of the Ashmolean Library and its Near Eastern wing, the Griffith Institute; of the Oriental Institute just next door; and of the Bodleian Library, in particular the Oriental Reading Room. It is above all when one attempts a topic which crosses some established boundaries that one realises just how remarkable this combination of resources is. But my 'base' has been, as always, the Ashmolean Library, and everything is owed to the help of Brian McGregor and his staff. It was thus there that during a sabbatical year in 1990–91 this book was at last written.

After prompt and helpful critiques from two readers appointed by Harvard University Press, a final revision was carried out in June 1992. Even those unacquainted with my handwriting will appreciate that preparation of the text was an extremely demanding task. So I am very grateful to Priscilla Lange for the efficiency and good humour with which it was done.

It will be clear that such a book, even with its many imperfections, would have been a great deal worse but for the guidance of friends and colleagues. My greatest single academic debt is to Sebastian Brock, who not only translated for me some recondite Syriac material when no printed help was to hand, but answered a long series of questions, some of them on points so elementary that he must have felt amazed that anyone could both be puzzled by them and have the temerity to write on these subjects at all. Not content with that, he kindly read the whole of Chapter 12, on the Euphrates and Mesopotamia, and saved me from many further errors. Martin Goodman also added to his many burdens as the newly appointed Reader in Jewish Studies at Oxford University by reading the whole text, with immense benefit to its clarity and accuracy. Of his predecessor, Geza Vermes, I need only state the obvious, that this book is in many ways the inheritor of our two decades of joint work on the new edition of Schürer's *History of the Jewish People;*

and from him too I learned an immense amount both during the writing of this book and long before.

This is not the place for a review of the names of the great figures, from Ernest Renan onwards, who have worked on the history of the Near East in the Classical period. But it would be improper, at the moment of the disappearance of the Soviet Union, not to mention Michael Rostovtzeff; apart from his years of work on Dura-Europos, his paper 'La Syrie romaine' in *Revue historique* (1935) remains the most brilliant brief portrait of the area. Then there is Henri Seyrig, whom I was fortunate to meet in Princeton in 1968, and whose work sums up the profound French involvement in the exploration of ancient Syria in the twentieth century. This involvement is reflected also in two major recent works, of which the earlier receives very inadequate reflection in what follows, and the later none at all: J.-M. Dentzer and W. Orthmann (eds.), *Archéologie et histoire de la Syrie* II (1989); and M. Sartre, *L'Orient romain: Provinces et sociétés provinciales en Méditerranée orientale d'Auguste aux Sévères (31 J.-C.–235 après J.-C.)* (1991), an invaluable work which covers Achaea, Macedonia, Asia Minor and Egypt, as well as the Syrian region (but not as such Mesopotamia).

Of contemporaries, I would particularly like to thank Peter Fraser; if in reality I have always seen Rome and its Empire from a Rostovtzeffian perspective, in other words from the Greek East, it is due to his influence when I was at All Souls in 1958–1964. As for others on whose generous help I have depended, I would like to name Jean-Charles and Jeanine Balty, Glen Bowersock, Hannah Cotton, Hazel Dodge, Han Drijvers, Denis Feissel, Michal Gawlikowski, David Graf, Chris Howgego, Ben Isaac, David Kennedy, Nikos Kokkinos, Sam Lieu, Michael MacDonald, David Potter, Jean-Paul Rey-Coquais, Maurice Sartre and Javier Teixidor.

Hazel Dodge and David Kennedy also provided valuable practical guidance before a visit to Jordan and Syria in 1986. During that visit I had very generous assistance from the Syrian Archaeological Service, and in particular from Dr. Adnan Bounni. It is not fortuitous that the book begins by implicitly recalling the many hours which I spent examining the marvellous collections in the National Museum in Damascus, not least the reconstruction there of the synagogue at Dura-Europos. During that trip I also spent a wonderful day on a taxi-journey from Homs to the remote site of Baetocaece (which proved extremely difficult to find), and then over the Jebel Ansariyeh to the Orontes Valley and Apamea, where the welcome from the Baltys and their team remains an indelible memory.

In 1989 I also had the greatest good fortune in being able to make a car-journey with Chris Lightfoot of the British Institute in Ankara, from Ankara through the Taurus to Cilicia, the Amanus, Antioch, Urfa, Nisibis, Amida (Diyarbakir), Commagene with Samosata and Nemrud Dag, and back via Malatya (Melitene). If in the course of it I gained a deeper understanding of why Caracalla had needed to step aside on the journey from Urfa to visit the temple of the Moon-Goddess at Carrhae/Harran, it was still an absolutely essential and invaluable experience, which would never have been possible without such expert guidance. I am very grateful to the British Academy and the Craven Committee for grants to assist this journey.

As one who has visited Israel many times (including in 1969 an adventurous trip with Zvi Yavetz up to the snowbound peak of Mount Hermon) and who has also looked out from ancient Gadara over the Sea of Galilee, the Plain of Jezreel and Mount Tabor, as well as down the Bekaa Valley from Tell Nebi Mend (Laodicea ad Libanum, just on the Syrian side of the Syrian-Lebanese border), it is impossible not to hope that these years will bring peace, and an opening of borders, to all of the haunting landscapes of the Near East. By down-playing, as it explicitly does, the significance, and even the reality, of any coherent 'Arab' identity in the period in question, this book might seem to take one side in the profound religious and communal tensions of the modern world. It does not. Religious affiliations, mythical origins and ethnic identities are human constructs, and we simply falsify history by fathering on peoples in the past identities which they did not construct, or had not yet constructed, for themselves. If anything, this book will serve to suggest how new, how profound and original and how totally unexpected in its effects the message of the Prophet was to be; but also, in its appeal to the Old Testament, to the inheritance of Abraham, Hagar and Ishmael, how much Islam was to owe to the Judaeo-Christian tradition:

> Say you: 'We believe in God, and in that which has been sent down on us and sent down on Abraham, Ishmael, Isaac and Jacob, and the Tribes, and that which was given to Moses and Jesus and the Prophets, of their Lord; we make no division between any of them, and to Him we surrender'. (*Koran, Sura* II, trans. A. J. Arberry)

At the point where this book stops, Islam still lay three centuries in the future. But all three versions of the Religion of the Book were formed in or on the borders of the Roman and late-Roman Near East.

Brasenose College   FERGUS MILLAR
Oxford

ABBREVIATIONS

AAAS	*Annales archéologiques arabes syriennes* (1966–)
AAES	*Publications of an American Archaeological Expedition to Syria 1899–1900.* I, *Topography and Itinerary* (1914), by R. Garrett; II, *Architecture and Other Arts* (1903), by H. C. Butler; III, *Greek and Latin Inscriptions* (1908), by W. K. Prentice; IV, *Semitic Inscriptions* (1904), by E. Littman
AAS	*Annales archéologiques de Syrie* (1951–1965)
ADAJ	*Annual of the Department of Antiquities of Jordan*
AE	*Année épigraphique*
AHS	J.-M. Dentzer and W. Orthmann (eds.), *Archéologie et histoire de la Syrie* II, *La Syrie de l'époque achéménide à l'avènement d'Islam* (1989)
AJA	*American Journal of Archaeology*
Anal. Boll.	*Analecta Bollandiana: Bruxelles, Société des Bollandistes*
Anat. Stud.	*Anatolian Studies*
Anc. Hist. Bull.	*The Ancient History Bulletin*
ANRW	*Aufstieg und Niedergang der römischen Welt. Geschichte und Kultur Roms im Spiegel der neueren Forschung*
Ant. Class.	*L'antiquité classique*
Arch. Anz.	*Archäologische Anzeiger*
Arch. f. Or.	*Archiv für Orientforschung*

Avi-Yonah, *Gazetteer*	M. Avi-Yonah, *Gazetteer of Roman Palestine* (*Qedem* 5, 1976)
BA	*Biblical Archaeologist*
Baldus, *Uranius Antoninus*	H. R. Baldus, *Uranius Antoninus: Münzprägung und Geschichte* (1971)
Barnes, *New Empire*	T. D. Barnes, *The New Empire of Diocletian and Constantine* (1982)
BASOR	*Bulletin of the American Schools of Oriental Research*
BASP	*Bulletin of the American Society of Papyrologists*
BCH	*Bulletin de correspondance hellénique*
BE	*Bulletin épigraphique*, published in *Revue des études grecques*
BES	*Bulletin d'épigraphie sémitique*, published in *Syria*
Beth She'arim II	M. Schwabe and B. Lifshitz, *Beth She'arim II: The Greek Inscriptions* (1974)
Beyer, *AT*	K. Beyer, *Die aramäischen Texte vom Toten Meer* (1986)
BGU	*Aegyptische Urkunden aus den Staatlichen Museen zu Berlin, Griechische Urkunden*
Bidez-Cumont	J. Bidez and F. Cumont, *Les mages hellénisés: Zoroastre, Ostanès et Hystaspe, d'après la tradition grecque* (1938)
Birley, *Septimius Severus*	A. R. Birley, *The African Emperor: Septimius Severus* (1988)
BMB	*Bulletin du Musée de Beyrouth*
BMC Arabia	G. F. Hill, *Catalogue of the Greek Coins of Arabia, Mesopotamia and Persia in the British Museum* (1922)
BMC Mesopotamia	G. F. Hill, *Catalogue of the Greek Coins of Arabia, Mesopotamia and Persia in the British Museum* (1922)
BMC Palestine	G. F. Hill, *Catalogue of the Greek Coins of Palestine in the British Museum* (1914)
BMC Phoenicia	G. F. Hill, *Catalogue of the Greek Coins of Phoenicia in the British Museum* (1910)
BMC Roman Empire	H. Mattingly, et al., *Coins of the Roman Empire in the British Museum* (1910–)
BMC Syria	W. Wroth, *Catalogue of the Greek Coins of Galatia, Cappadocia, and Syria in the British Museum* (1899)

Bonn. Jahrb.	*Bonner Jarhbücher des Rheinischen Landesmuseums in Bonn und des Vereins von Altertumsfreunden im Rheinlande*
Bowersock, *Roman Arabia*	G. W. Bowersock, *Roman Arabia* (1983)
BSOAS	*Bulletin of the School of Oriental and African Studies*
Cantineau, *Inv.*	J. Cantineau et al., *Inventaire des inscriptions de Palmyre* (1930–)
Cantineau, *Le Nabatéen* II	J. Cantineau, *Le Nabatéen* II (1932)
Cantineau, *RES*	J. Cantineau, *Répertoire d'épigraphie sémitique* I–VII
Cavenaille, *CPL*	R. Cavenaille, *Corpus Papyrorum Latinarum* (1958)
CCID	M. Hörig and E. Schwertheim, *Corpus Cultus Iovis Dolicheni* (1987)
CIS	*Corpus Inscriptionum Semiticarum*
CPh	*Classical Philology*
CRAI	*Comptes-rendus de l'Académie des Inscriptions*
CSCO	*Corpus Scriptorum Christianorum Orientalium*
Dam. Mitt.	*Damaszener Mitteilungen*
Dentzer, *Hauran*	J.-M. Dentzer (ed.), *Hauran: Recherches archéologiques sur la Syrie du sud à l'époque hellénistique et romaine* I.1–2 (1985–1986)
Devijver, *PME*	H. Devijver, *Prosopographia militiarum equestrium quae fuerunt ab Augusto ad Gallienum* I–IV (1976–1987)
DHA	*Dialogues d'histoire ancienne*
Dial. di Arch.	*Dialoghi di Archeologia*
DJD	D. Barthélemy et al., *Discoveries in the Judaean Desert* (1956–)
Doc. Masada	H. M. Cotton and J. Geiger, *Masada* II, *The Yigael Yadin Excavations 1963–1965, Final Reports: The Latin and Greek Documents* (1989)
Donner and Röllig, *KAI*	H. Donner and W. Röllig, *Kanaanäische und aramäische Inschriften* I–II (1962)
DOP	*Dumbarton Oaks Papers*
Drijvers, *Inscriptions*	H. J. W. Drijvers, *Old-Syriac (Edessean) Inscriptions* (1972)

Dunand, *Musée de Soueida*	M. Dunand, *Le musée de Soueida* (1934)
Dunant, *Baalshamin* III	C. Dunant, *Le sanctuaire de Baalshamin à Palmyre* III, *Les inscriptions* (1971)
Dura Report	P. V. C. Baur and M. I. Rostovtzeff (eds.), *The Excava-* *tions at Dura-Europos, Preliminary Report* I–IX.2 (1929–1946)
EAEHL	*Encyclopaedia of Archaeological Excavations in the* *Holy Land* I–IV (1975–1978)
Edelstein and Kidd	L. Edelstein and I. G. Kidd (eds.), *Posidonius* I, *The* *Fragments* (1972)
Epig. Anat.	*Epigraphica Anatolica*
Feissel and Gascou, "Documents"	D. Feissel and J. Gascou, "Documents d'archives ro- mains inédits du Moyen-Euphrate (IIIe siècle après J.-C.)", *CRAI* (1989), 535
FGrH	F. Jacoby, *Die Fragmente der griechischen Historiker*
FHG	C. Müller, Th. Müller et al., *Fragmenta Historicorum* *Graecorum* I–V (1853–1870)
Fitzmyer, *PAT*	J. A. Fitzmyer and D. J. Harrington, *A Manual of Pales-* *tinian Aramaic Texts* (1978)
Freeman and Kennedy, *DRBE*	P. Freeman and D. L. Kennedy (eds.), *The Defence of* *the Roman and Byzantine East* (BAR Int. Ser 297, 1986)
Frey, *CIJ*	J.-B. Frey, *Corpus Inscriptionum Iudaicarum* I–II (1936–1952)
Gawlikowski, *Temple palmyrénien*	M. Gawlikowski, *Le temple palmyrénien* (1973)
GCS	*Die Griechischen Christlichen Schriftsteller der ersten* *drei Jahrhunderte*
Géog. admin.	T. Fahd (ed.), *La géographie administrative et politique* *d'Alexandre à Mahomet* (Colloque de Strasbourg 1979, 1983)
Géog. hist.	P.-L. Gatier, B. Helly and J.-P. Rey-Coquais (eds.), *Géographie historique au Proche-Orient (Syrie, Phéni-* *cie, Arabie grecques, romaines, byzantines)* (1988)
Gerasa	C. H. Kraeling (ed.), *Gerasa: City of the Decapolis* (1938)

Goodman, *Ruling Class*	M. D. Goodman, *The Ruling Class of Judaea: The Origins of the Jewish Revolt against Rome, AD 66–70* (1987)
GRBS	*Greek, Roman and Byzantine Studies*
Hajjar	Y. Hajjar, *La triade d'Héliopolis/Baalbek* I–III (1977–1985)
Halfmann, *Itinera*	H. Halfmann, *Itinera Principum: Geschichte und Typlogie der Kaiserreisen im römischen Reich* (1986)
HSCPh	*Harvard Studies in Classical Philology*
HThR	*Harvard Theological Review*
HUCA	*Hebrew Union College Annual*
Hüttenmeister, *Synagogen*	F. Hüttenmeister and G. Reeg, *Die antiken Synagogen in Israel* I (1977)
IEJ	*Israel Exploration Journal*
IG	*Inscriptiones Graecae*
IGLS	L. Jalabert, R. Mouterde et al., *Inscriptions grecques et latines de la Syrie* (1929–)
IGR	R. Cagnat et al., *Inscriptiones Graecae ad Res Romanas Pertinentes*
I.K. Ephesos	*Inschriften griechischer Städte aus Kleinasien: Ephesos*
ILS	H. Dessau, *Inscriptiones Latinae Selectae*
INJ	*Israel Numismatic Journal*
Ins. Didyma	*Didyma* II, *Die Inschriften*, ed. A. Rehm and R. Harder (1958)
IRT	J. M. Reynolds and J. B. Ward Perkins, *The Inscriptions of Roman Tripolitania* (1952)
Isaac, *Limits*	B. Isaac, *The Limits of Empire: The Roman Army in the East* (1990; 2nd ed. 1992)
Ist. Mitt.	*Istanbuler Mitteilungen*
Jahrb. f. Ant. u. Chr.	*Jahrbuch für Antike und Christentum*
Jahrb. f. Num. u. Geldg.	*Jahrbuch für Numismatik und Geldgeschichte*
JAOS	*Journal of the American Oriental Society*
JJS	*Journal of Jewish Studies*
JNES	*Journal of Near Eastern Studies*

Jones, *CERP*²	A. H. M. Jones, *The Cities of the Eastern Roman Provinces*, revised by M. Avi-Yonah et al. (1971)
JQR	*Jewish Quarterly Review*
JRA	*Journal of Roman Archaeology*
JRS	*Journal of Roman Studies*
JSJ	*Journal for the Study of Judaism in the Persian, Hellenistic and Roman Period*
JSS	*Journal of Semitic Studies*
JThSt	*Journal of Theological Studies*
Kennedy, *Explorations*	D. L. Kennedy, *Archaeological Explorations on the Roman Frontier in North-East Jordan* (BAR Int. Ser. 134, 1982)
Kennedy and Riley, *RDF*	D. L. Kennedy and D. Riley, *Rome's Desert Frontier from the Air* (1990)
Kettenhofen, *Kriege*	E. Kettenhofen, *Die römisch-persischen Kriege des 3. Jahrhunderts n. Chr.* (1982)
Krencker and Zschietzschmann, *Römische Tempel*	D. Krencker and W. Zschietzschmann, *Römische Tempel in Syrien* I–II (1938)
Le Bas-W.	P. Le Bas and W. H. Waddington, *Inscriptions grecques et latines recueillies en Grèce et en Asie Mineure* III.1 (1870)
LIMC	*Lexicon Iconographicum Mythologiae Classicae* (1981–)
Mém. Ac. Ins.	*Mémoires présentés par divers savants à l'Académie des Inscriptions et Belles Lettres*
Meshorer, *City Coins*	Y. Meshorer, *The City Coins of Eretz-Israel and the Decapolis in the Roman Period* (1985)
du Mesnil du Buisson, *Inventaire*	du Mesnil du Buisson, *Inventaire des inscriptions palmyréniennes de Doura-Europos* (1939)
Millar, "Empire"	F. Millar, "Empire, Community and Culture in the Roman Near East: Greeks, Syrians, Jews and Arabs", *JJS* 38 (1987), 143
Millar, *ERW*	F. Millar, *The Emperor in the Roman World* (1977)
Millar, "Hellenistic Syria"	F. Millar, "The Problem of Hellenistic Syria", in A. Kuhrt and S. Sherwin-White (eds.), *Hellenism in the East* (1987), 110

Millar, "Phoenician Cities"	F. Millar, "The Phoenician Cities: A Case-Study of Hellenisation", *Proc. Camb. Philol. Soc.* 209 (1983), 55
Millar, "Roman *Coloniae*"	F. Millar, "The Roman *Coloniae* of the Near East: A Study of Cultural Relations", in H. Solin and F. M. Kajava (eds.), *Roman Policy in the East and Other Studies in Roman History* (1990), 7
Mitchell, *Armies and Frontiers*	S. Mitchell (ed.), *Armies and Frontiers in Roman and Byzantine Anatolia* (BAR Int. Ser. 156, 1983)
Moretti, *IAG*	L. Moretti, *Iscrizioni agonistiche greche* (1953)
Moretti, *IGUR*	L. Moretti, *Inscriptiones Graecae Urbis Romae* I–III (1968–1979)
Mus. Helv.	*Museum Helveticum*
MUSJ	*Mélanges de l'Université St. Joseph*
NC	*Numismatic Chronicle*
NPNF	*Nicene and Post-Nicene Fathers*
OGIS	W. Dittenberger, *Orientis Graeci Inscriptiones Selectae* I–II
PAES	*Syria: Publications of the Princeton University Archaeological Expedition to Syria in 1904–1905 and 1909.* I, *Geography and Itinerary* (1930), by H. C. Butler, F. A. Norris and E. R. Stoever; II.A–B, *Architecture* (1919–1920), by H. C. Butler; III.A–B, *Greek and Latin Inscriptions* (1921–1922), by E. Littman and W. K. Prentice; IV.A–D, *Semitic Inscriptions* (1914–1949), by E. Littman
Parker, *Roman Frontier*	S. T. Parker (ed.), *The Roman Frontier in Central Jordan: Interim Report on the Limes Arabicus Project, 1980–1985* I–II (BAR Int. Ser. 340, 1987)
PBSR	*Papers of the British School at Rome*
P. Dura	C. Bradford Welles, R. O. Fink and J. Frank Gilliam, *The Excavations at Dura-Europos: Final Report* V.1, *The Parchments and Papyri* (1959)
PEFQSt	*Palestine Exploration Fund Quarterly Statement*
PEQ	*Palestine Exploration Quarterly*
Pflaum, *Carrières*	H.-G. Pflaum, *Les carrières procuratoriennes équestres* I–III (1960–1961)
PG	J.-P. Migne, *Patrum Graecorum Cursus Completus*
Philol.	*Philologus*

PIR²	*Prosopographia Imperii Romani²*
P. Lond. inv.	F. G. Kenyon et al., *Greek Papyri in the British Museum* (1893–)
PLRE	*The Prosopography of the Later Roman Empire* I, A.D. 260–395, ed. A. H. M. Jones, J. R. Martindale and J. Morris (1971)
P. Mich.	C. C. Edgar, A. E. R. Boak, J. G. Winter et al. (eds.), *Papyri in the University of Michigan Collection* (1931–)
Poidebard, *Trace*	A. Poidebard, *La trace de Rome dans le désert de Syrie: Le limes de Trajan à la conquête arabe: Recherches aériennes (1925–1932)* I–II (1934)
Potter, *Sybilline Oracle*	D. S. Potter, *Prophecy and History in the Crisis of the Roman Empire: A Historical Commentary on the Thirteenth Sibylline Oracle* (1990)
P. Oxy.	B. P. Grenfell, A. S. Hunt et al. (eds.), *The Oxyrhynchus Papyri* (1898–)
P. Yadin	N. Lewis, *The Documents from the Bar-Kochba Period in the Cave of Letters: Greek Papyri* (1989)
P. Zenon	C. C. Edgar, *Papyri in the University of Michigan Collection* I, *Zenon Papyri* (1931)
RAC	*Reallexikon für Antike und Christentum*
RAO	C. Clermont-Ganneau, *Recueil d'Archéologie Orientale* I–VIII (1888–1924)
RB	*Revue biblique*
RE	Pauly-Wissowa, *Realencyclopädie der classischen Altertumswissenchaft*
REL	*Revue des études latines*
RES	*Répertoire d'épigraphie sémitique* I–VII (1900–1950)
Rev. arch.	*Revue archéologique*
RN	*Revue numismatique*
RPC I	A. M. Burnett, M. Amandry and P. P. Ripollès, *Roman Provincial Coinage* I.1–2, *From the Death of Caesar to the Death of Vitellius (44 BC–AD 69)* (1992)
Sartre, *Trois etudes*	M. Sartre, *Trois études sur l'Arabie romaine et byzantine* (1982)
SBFLA	*Studii Biblici Franciscani, Liber Annus*
SC	*Sources chrétiennes*

Schürer, *HJP*	E. Schürer, *History of the Jewish People in the Age of Jesus Christ (175 BC–AD 135)* I, ed. G. Vermes and F. Millar (1973); II (1979); III.1–2, ed. G. Vermes, F. Millar and M. Goodman (1986–1987)
SCI	*Scripta Classica Israelica*
SDB	*Supplément au Dictionaire de la Bible*
SEG	*Supplementum Epigraphicum Graecum*
Segal, *Edessa*	J. B. Segal, *Edessa, 'the Blessed City'* (1970)
Segal, *Town Planning*	A. Segal, *Town Planning and Architecture in Provincia Arabia: The Cities along the Via Traiana Nova in the 1st–3rd Centuries C.E.* (*BAR* Int. Ser. 419, 1988)
Spijkerman, *Coins of the Decapolis*	A. Spijkerman, *Coins of the Decapolis and Provincia Arabia* (1978)
Starcky and Gawlikowski, *Palmyre*²	J. Starcky and M. Gawlikowski, *Palmyre*² (1985)
Stern, *GLAJJ*	M. Stern, *Greek and Latin Authors on Jews and Judaism* I–III (1974–1984)
TAPhA	*Transactions of the American Philological Association*
Wagner, *RET*	J. Wagner, *Die Römer an Euphrat und Tigris* (*Antike Welt, Sondernummer,* 1985)
Wenning, *Nabatäer*	R. Wenning, *Die Nabatäer—Denkmäler und Geschichte: Eine Bestandaufnahme des archäologischen Befundes* (1987)
YCS	*Yale Classical Studies*
ZDMG	*Zeitschrift der Deutschen Morgenländischen Gesellschaft*
ZDPV	*Zeitschrift des Deutschen Palästina-Vereins*
ZPE	*Zeitschrift für Papyrologie und Epigraphik*

THE ROMAN NEAR EAST

31 BC – AD 337

✦

PROLOGUE:
IN SEARCH OF THE ORIENT

The visitor to the National Museum of Damascus, confronted by the products of five thousand years of Near Eastern history, might be forgiven for not noticing a small stone altar standing in a corner of the room called the Hall of Dura-Europos. But if the visitor were interested in the history of this region while it was under Roman rule in the early centuries of our era, this altar would repay his or her attention. The altar is inscribed on the front face with eight brief lines in Greek, which not only tell us a great deal about the Near East as it was in the period of Roman domination, but also serve to illustrate how ambiguous much of our evidence is. Our difficulty in studying the ancient Near East is not only that modern Europeans approaching it cannot help doing so with a host of confused and half-formed preconceptions about the 'Orient'. Nor is it merely that the evidence which we have—archaeological remains, inscriptions, papyri, coins, allusions in ancient literary works—is scattered, inadequate and often difficult to relate to any intelligible context. The greatest problem is precisely that the more explicit and informative an item of evidence apparently is, the more it is likely to embody its own preconceptions. But it will still be valuable, provided that we read it not as a simple report about the society which we are trying to approach, but as the expression of a viewpoint or interpretation of that society, whether from inside or outside.

It is time to turn to the little altar from Dura-Europos itself, and the brief dedication in Greek inscribed on it:

To the Ancestral God, Zeus Betylos, of those by the Orontes, Aurēlios Diphilianos, soldier of the legion IV Scythica Antoniniana, has offered (this) in fulfilment of a prayer.[1]

1. *Dura Report* IV (1933), 68, no. 168 (Pl. XV, 1); SEG VII, no. 341: Θεῷ πατρῴῳ / Διὶ Βετύλῳ / τῶν πρὸς τῷ / Ὀρόντῃ Αὐρ(ήλιος) / Διφιλιανὸς στρα(τιώτης) / Λεγ(εῶνος) Δ΄ Σκυ(θικῆς) Ἀντ(ωνεινιανῆς) / εὐξάμενος / ἀνέθηκεν.

That the dedication should have been in Greek is no surprise. But for that very reason we may fail to underline its significance, from two different but related aspects. If we think of the cultural and social history of the Near East, Greek had been in widespread and fully established use there since the conquests by Alexander, the setting-up of the Seleucid dynasty there at the end of the fourth century BC and the extensive foundation, especially under Seleucus I, of Greek cities and settlements.[2] Dura-Europos itself, situated on a promontory overlooking the middle Euphrates from the west, had been one of these settlements.

Aurelius Diphilianus, however, does not identify himself as a citizen of Dura, but as a soldier in a Roman legion, the IV Scythica, which had been stationed in Syria since the middle of the first century AD. His presence thus reflects the long and gradual step-by-step extension of Roman direct rule in the Near East, which had begun with the arrival of Pompey's forces in the 60s BC, and was to reach its greatest extension at the end of the third century AD; for two-thirds of a century, until the defeat of Julian in 363, it was to cover not only all of northern Mesopotamia but some territory east of the Tigris.

Dura itself, after three centuries of Parthian rule, had been captured and garrisoned by the Romans in the 160s. Diphilianus will have made his dedication at some point between then and the destruction of the town by the forces of the new Persian Empire in the 250s. Most probably he did so in the last decades of the town's life, when his legion had earned the extra name 'Antoniniana' from one of the Emperors, perhaps M. Aurelius Antoninus (AD 211–217), for whom we tend to use the contemporary nickname 'Caracalla'.

Diphilianus may have owed the fact that he was a Roman citizen to Caracalla's grant of Roman citizenship to all the free inhabitants of the Empire. At all events his typical Romano-Greek name, 'Aurelius Diphilianus', shows that the citizenship will not have been acquired by him, or perhaps by a previous generation of his family, earlier than the reign of Marcus Aurelius (AD 161–180). The form of his name is only one small sign of a complex range of Roman influences which profoundly affected the social structure, culture and economy of the Near East in the first four centuries of Roman rule. Looked at from Rome, the Near East gained an ever-increasing significance in terms of the extension of territory, the acquisition of tribute revenue and the deployment of military force. At the time when Aurelius Diphilianus made his dedication, his legion, the IV Scythica, was one of two stationed in this province, now called Syria Coele (northern Syria); there was also one in southern Syria, for which the Romans had revived the name 'Syria Phoenice', as well as two in 'Syria Palaestina' (Judaea), one in the province of 'Arabia' and two in the

2. See now J. D. Grainger, *The Cities of Seleukid Syria* (1990).

newly acquired province of Mesopotamia. Together with the two stationed to the north in Cappadocia, this meant that, out of thirty-three Roman legions in all, ten were stationed in the east. Whether one should think of them as a frontier force deployed for defence, as an occupying army or as an imperialist force still poised for further conquests is a profound question, recently raised in challenging form, to which we will return.[3]

Since the perspective of this book cannot in any event fail to be a Western one, the approach adopted has been to make this starting-point explicit; that is to say, to define the region, or series of linked regions, with which it will be concerned as those areas between the Taurus Mountains and the Red Sea which were progressively subjected to Roman direct rule. That will serve to provide a chronological and geographical framework, to be set up in the first part of the book. But although any definition of a region involves an element of arbitrary decision, such a choice is not merely a matter of convenience. There are also other, not wholly arbitrary, criteria by which the area concerned can be defined. One is that it is that region of the Near East which fronts directly on the eastern coast of the Mediterranean. Another is that it is the western and northern part of the Fertile Crescent, the area of cultivable land closely tied to mountain-chains which linked the Mediterranean and Egypt with Babylonia, Iran and the head of the Persian Gulf. The third is that as an area of cultivable land it merges at all points into what is usually called desert, but is more precisely a dry, stony steppe with volcanic outcrops and one mountain ridge, that which stretches from near Damascus to the north-west of Palmyra. Only in the far south, where Roman-controlled territory extended into the northern Hedjaz, do we come at all close to the true sand desert which has so captivated the European imagination.

The area where Roman forces exercised control was therefore a cultivable arc of territory structured by mountains and shading off into a wide steppe. With the conquests of the 160s this area, which previously stopped at the upper-middle Euphrates, came to extend down the river to the region of Dura-Europos, and with those of the 190s came to include the Chabur River, which flows into the Euphrates from northern Mesopotamia. Both rivers, which might look on the map as if they marked definable frontiers, in fact functioned more as routes of communication, and as affording narrow strips of cultivable land bisecting the steppe.

The area concerned could alternatively be defined, at least approximately, as that part of the Near East which fell to the Islamic invaders of the seventh century, who never succeeded in occupying permanently any of Anatolia over the Taurus Mountains. A retrospective view can be highly misleading. But

---

3. My whole approach to this area owes much to the stimulus of the work of Ben Isaac; see now *The Limits of Empire: The Roman Army in the East* (1990; 2nd ed., 1992).

the fact that this whole area was to become, three to four centuries later, a predominantly Arabic-speaking world whose ruling population were followers of Islam cannot but raise questions about the Roman period itself.

First, what was the relevance, in military, social, religious or cultural terms, of relations between the generally settled, cultivable areas controlled by Rome, and the inhabitants, whoever they were, of the steppe? As we will see, Roman military installations were placed almost all along the edge of the steppe, and sometimes deep within it, and still offer highly evocative remains, above all when photographed from the air.[4] But whether we should think of these as representing a 'desert frontier', which might have to deal with a significant threat from nomadic or migratory peoples, or as police-posts lining roads is a more difficult question. In either event both documentary and literary items of evidence show beyond question that the steppe was not uninhabited: nomad peoples dwelt there whom Graeco-Romans called *Arabes* or *skēnitai*, or later progressively *Saraceni*, who belonged to groups we may as well call tribes, who might pose at least localised threats to the settled population or to travellers, and at least some of whom spoke a language which can be called Arabic. Within the last few years indeed, the earliest evidence of written Arabic has moved back from AD 328 (a famous inscription from en-Nemara on the fringe of the steppe south-east of Damascus) to about AD 100, when two lines of verse in Arabic appear in the middle of a Nabataean inscription from the Negev.[5]

The extensive evidence now available raises the question of how far the apparent 'frontier' created by Roman forces along the fringe of the steppe was really porous; of how far, in other words, we should see the apparently settled region as being open to nomadic groups, either moving around within it or crossing the 'frontier' itself. More important, how far did the inhabitants of the settled region share a culture or customs, or sets of religious beliefs, with the 'Arab' tribes of the marginal zone? How far indeed were such ethnic or 'tribal' groupings divided between nomadic or pastoral components and settled, agricultural ones, while still maintaining a group identity? Many of these questions have also been reassessed in recent years.[6]

Arabic apart, there is ample evidence that a number of Semitic languages

4. See the brilliantly suggestive book of D. Kennedy and D. Riley, *Rome's Desert Frontier from the Air* (1989).

5. The reference is to ll. 4–5 of the Nabataean inscription published by A. Negev, "Obodas the God", *IEJ* 36 (1986), 56; the inscription is in Nabataean script and the remaining four lines are in Nabataean. But these two lines represent a personal affirmation by the dedicator. See now J. A. Bellamy, "Arabic Verses from the First/Second Century: The Inscription of 'En 'Avdat", *JSS* 35 (1990), 73. See further 11.2 below.

6. See above all D. Graf, "Rome and the Saracens: Reassessing the Nomadic Menace", in T. Fahd (ed.), *L'Arabie préislamique et son environnement historique et culturel* (1989), 341.

were spoken, and mostly also written, in the Roman Near East: Aramaic, Hebrew, Phoenician, Nabataean, Palmyrene and Syriac, as well as the language known as 'Safaitic' attested mainly by large numbers of graffiti from the outer edges of the steppe region.[7] That too raises an important question: should we see the speakers of all these Semitic languages as being united by something more than language, that is, by customs, beliefs, religious practices or some sense of mutual identity? Should we, in a word, see them all as 'Semites'?

While there are obvious and well-founded reasons for a reluctance to use this term, it would at least be important to know whether any related terms were used in antiquity to describe the inhabitants of this region as a group. It might indeed have been so, for the conception owes its origin to the mythical account of the origins of peoples in Genesis 9–10, and the description of certain peoples as the descendants of Shem. How then was this grouping interpreted in our period? It is important that there is an answer, and that it is to be found in the *Jewish Antiquities* of Josephus. This work, written in Rome in the later first century AD, is of the greatest significance, not merely for its attempt at a continuous history of the Jewish people from the Creation to AD 66, but as the only surviving history of any Near Eastern people to link their past in the ancient Orient with their present under Roman rule, and in doing so to link the past and the present of those non-Jewish peoples with whom the Jews had had contact in the course of their history. This question of ascribed identity, of belonging or not to some identifiable group persisting through time, is of crucial importance to what the population of the Roman Near East 'was'. The question is not a factual one, of actual biological descent (which is both wholly unanswerable and of limited importance anyway), but of identity, or 'ethnicity'.[8]

It also brings us back again to Aurelius Diphilianus, the soldier dedicating an altar in Dura-Europos in the third century AD. The deity to whom he dedicated the altar was 'the ancestral god, Zeus Betylos, of those by the Orontes'. The original publication offers a translation of the initial words which is bold to the point of embodying a far-reaching interpretation: 'to (his) national god . . .'. But whether Diphilianus actually was a native of the Syrian region we do not know; precisely one of the crucial ambiguities of this unusually explicit dedication is that we do not know whether we are reading the words

7. For the best surveys see R. Schmitt, "Die Ostgrenze von Armenien über Mesopotamien, Syrien bis Arabien", in G. Neumann and J. Untermann (eds.), *Die Sprachen im römischen Reich* (Beih. Bonn. Jahrb. 40, 1980), 187, and H. P. Roschinski, "Sprachen, Schriften und Inschriften in Nordwestarabien", ibid. 151.

8. For recent works on this question, see for example E. Gellner, *Nations and Nationalism* (1983); B. Anderson, *Imagined Communities* (1983); A. D. Smith, *The Ethnic Origins of Nations* (1986).

of an 'insider' who happened also to be a Roman soldier or of an outsider paying his respects (as Roman soldiers can be found doing throughout the period) to a local, or regional, deity. How he actually described the deity will concern us later. For the moment it is significant, in either case, that he thought of that deity as being the ancestral one 'of those by the Orontes'. Making his dedication by the banks of the Euphrates, did he mean to distinguish 'those by the Orontes' from the community in which he now found himself? Or (as seems much more probable) did he intend to use the Orontes, which flows from the Bekaa Valley northwards behind a mountain-chain, and then turns west to Antioch and the Mediterranean, as the geographical symbol of the population of the whole region? If the latter, he was indeed claiming an ancestral cult common to them all.

So far as we know, Aurelius Diphilianus thought up this conception for himself; at any rate it has no parallel in the literature or documents available to us. Nor indeed can we find any sense of a common past uniting the contemporary populations of the region and identifying them with the life of the cities of the ancient Orient, or with the experience of the Assyrian, Babylonian or Persian Empires. Nor indeed, except among the Jews, and perhaps in Phoenicia, can we find, in individual areas, any sense of a continuity linking communities to their more remote past. If the tells covering the remains of ancient cities which dominated (for instance) Samosata on the Euphrates, Laodicea ad Libanum at the mouth of the Bekaa Valley or Scythopolis in the Jezreel Valley provided a sense of historic identity for those who lived there, or even provoked curiosity, there is nothing to show it. So far as our evidence goes (an important qualification), a noteworthy 'amnesia' marked the historical consciousness of the inhabitants of the Near East in this period.[9] If the pagan inhabitants of Scythopolis had listened at all to their Jewish neighbours and fellow-inhabitants, they could hardly not have known that their tell was that of the ancient Bethshan, where the Philistines had once hung up the bodies of Saul and his sons: 'on the walls of the city of Bethshan, which is now called Scythopolis', as Josephus recorded it.[10] Was it *because* of this non-Greek past or in ignorance of it that the citizens of Scythopolis described themselves, in a Greek inscription of the second century, in terms which emphatically asserted the Greek character of the place? They addressed the ruling Emperor as 'lord of the Nysaeans also called Scythopolitans, (a city which is) holy and inviolate, (one of) the Greek cities of Coele Syria'.[11] They might

9. The expression is borrowed from W. Witakowski, *The Syriac Chronicle of Pseudo-Diony-sius of Tel-Maḥrē: A Study in the History of Historiography* (1987), 76.

10. Josephus, *Ant.* VI, 14, 8 (374).

11. G. Forster and Y. Tsafrir, "Nysa-Scythopolis—A New Inscription and the Titles of the City on Its Coins", *INJ* 9 (1986–87), 53. Note that they were using 'Coele Syria' in a way which did not at all correspond to the official designation of a province used from the 190s onwards.

indeed have been aware, from the Bible of their Jewish neighbours, of the pre-Greek past of the city. If so, they were consciously disassociating themselves from it.

Equally, it is theoretically possible, Aurelius Diphilianus might have known from the Jewish community of Dura-Europos of a mythical past in which many of the peoples of the Near East and beyond belonged within a single descent-group. But it is more than unlikely. A common past which had the Near East as its focus was to become part of a general world-view only when Christianity triumphed. For the moment it was only a Jew, Josephus (writing in Greek, in Rome), who in setting out his version of Genesis 9–10 could link Shem and his sons to the present inhabitants of the Near East and its neighbouring regions:

> Shem, the third of Noah's sons, had five sons, who inhabited Asia as far as the Indian Ocean, beginning at the Euphrates. Elymus had for his descendants the Elymaeans, ancestors of the Persians. Assyras founded the city of Ninus, and give his name to his subjects, the Assyrians, who rose to the height of prosperity. Arphaxades named those under his rule Arphaxadaeans, the Chaldaeans of today. Aramus ruled the Aramaeans, whom the Greeks term Syrians ... Of the four sons of Aramus, User founded Trachonitis and Damascus, situated between Palestine and Coele Syria ... Arphaxades was the father of Selez and he of Heber, after whom the Jews were originally called Hebrews.[12]

Even if an ethnic categorisation based on attributing peoples to different branches of descent from Noah had come to be more widely used in antiquity, it would not have done much to suggest to anyone that 'Semites' would be the right designation for all the peoples living either west or immediately east of the Euphrates. For one thing Josephus himself had already, earlier in the same book, listed some of the nearer neighbours of the Jews among the descendants not of Shem but of Ham:

> The children of Ham held the countries branching from Syria and the mountain-ranges of Amanus and Libanus, occupying all the district in the direction of the sea and appropriating the region reaching to the ocean ... Chananaeus, the fourth son of Ham, settled in the country now called Judaea and named it after himself, Chananaea ... Chananaeus also had sons, of whom Sidonius built in Phoenicia a city named after him, still called Sidon by the Greeks, and Amathus founded Amathus, which the inhabitants to this day call Amathe, though the Macedonians renamed it Epiphaneia after one of Alexander's successors.[13]

12. Josephus, *Ant.* I, 6, 4 (143–145).
13. Josephus, *Ant.* I, 6, 2 (130–138); Loeb trans.

However confusing it may be, Josephus' attempt to offer a categorisation of the peoples found in Genesis in terms of known groups to be found in the long-since Hellenised Near East of the Roman Empire is of great interest, and would deserve further study; it owes much of course to the Greek tradition of portraying the 'origins of peoples' in terms of descent from mythical founders, the subject of a justly famous paper by Elias Bickerman.[14]

This form of categorisation can also be extended by Josephus to the Arab peoples of the region, for he sees them as the descendants of Ishmael, the son of Abraham and Hagar. Once again he brings his picture of their immediate mythical descendants into relation with peoples currently to be found in the Near East:

> When the child (Ishmael) reached manhood, his mother (Hagar) found him a wife of that Egyptian race from which she herself had originally sprung; and by her twelve sons in all were born to Ishmael, Nabaioth(es), Kedar, Abdeel, Massam, Masmas, Idum(as), Masmes, Chodam, Thaiman, Jetur, Naphais, Kadmas. These occupied the whole country extending from the Euphrates to the Red Sea and called it Nabatene; and it is these who conferred their names on the Arabian nation and its tribes in honour both of their own prowess and of the fame of Abraham.[15]

Josephus has thus both embraced all the Arab tribes of the steppe and desert between the Red Sea and the Euphrates in the category of the descendants of Ishmael, and introduced for that region the name 'Nabatene', which is not in the Septuagint text of Genesis 25, and was the name of the contemporary kingdom with its capital at Petra. The designation of contemporary Arabs as the descendants of Ishmael was later to be of momentous significance. For by the mid-fifth century Sozomenus, the Church historian and a native of Gaza, not only repeats the story of the descent of Saracen tribes from Ishmael and Hagar, but claims that some of them had come to accept this tradition themselves: 'Some of their tribe afterwards happening to come in contact with the Jews, gathered from them the facts of their true origin, returned to their kinsmen, and inclined to the Hebrew customs and laws'. If there is any truth in this, its potential relevance to the origins of Islam is very considerable.[16]

Josephus' ascriptions of ethnic identity and relationship are thus highly significant. But what his words will not do is to offer any support at all for

14. *"Origines Gentium"*, *CPh* 47 (1952), 65.

15. *Ant.* I, 12, 4 (220–221); Loeb trans.

16. Sozomenus, *HE* VI, 38, 10–13, trans. C. D. Hartranft in *NPNF.* For a striking and controversial view of the origins of Islam, in which self-identification as 'Ishmaelites' or 'Hagarites' plays a central role, see P. Crone and M. Cook, *Hagarism: The Making of the Islamic World* (1977). This passage is also highlighted in M. Cook, *Muhammad*, (1983), 80ff.

the modern notion of 'Semites' as some sort of racial category embracing the different population-groups of the Near East; for to him some of them descended from Ham.

Josephus is, however, very conscious of the impact of Hellenisation on place-names, ethnic terminology and political structures in the Near East. His sweeping analysis of this is worth quoting:

> Of the nations some still preserve the names which were given them by their founders, some have changed them, while yet others have modified them to make them more intelligible to their neighbours. It is the Greeks who are responsible for this change of nomenclature; for when in after ages they rose to power, they appropriated even the glories of the past, embellishing the nations with names which they could understand and imposing on them forms of government, as though they were descended from themselves.[17]

Josephus thus offers here a vivid (and it seems unique) 'insider's' view of the transformations which had overtaken the region since the conquests by Alexander just over four centuries previously. But he also, in the passage quoted earlier, asserts an identity of the ancient city of Hama on the Orontes with the Hellenistic foundation of Epiphania, named after the Seleucid king Antiochus Epiphanes.[18] More important still, he appears to claim that the inhabitants (better 'locals' or even 'natives'—*enchōrioi*) still used the ancient name for it. If 'locals' means the people of that precise area, that raises a different question; for, as we will see later, the Orontes Valley is one of the few regions of the Near East where there is to date no documentary evidence of the use of any Semitic language in the Roman period.

In this context, the categorisation of languages, the use of the term 'Semitic' is harmless and unavoidable; the mutual resemblances in vocabulary and grammatical form, the identity of alphabet and the similarities of script of all the languages concerned are unmistakable;[19] and the contrast and interplay between them on one hand and Greek (and Latin) on the other in the Near East is one of the most clearly definable features of the cultural history of the period. The fact that the region concerned is one in which a group of Semitic languages was in use can therefore serve as one further non-arbitrary means of defining it. But even in this respect, language, it should be stressed that the currency of this language-group received very little attention from 'insiders' and even less from 'outsiders'.

17. *Ant.* I, 5, 5 (121); Loeb trans.
18. See Grainger, op. cit. (n.2), 138–139.
19. For the Semitic languages as a group, no overall history has replaced E. Renan, *Histoire générale et système comparé des langues sémitiques*⁵ (1878). But see, e.g., S. Moscati et al., *An*

Josephus, who, as we saw, identifies the Aramaeans of the Bible as those 'whom the Greeks call Syrians', does, however, note the relationship of language and script as between Aramaic and Hebrew. Significantly indeed, he alters a passage in his source, the Hellenistic *Letter of Aristeas*, giving a legendary account of the translation of the Bible into Greek in the third century BC, to assert as much a resemblance as a contrast between Hebrew and Aramaic:[20] 'The character of their writing seems to resemble the distinctive form of the Syrian letters and the language sounds similar to theirs, but it is in fact distinct'.

Josephus of course, for all that he wrote his entire surviving works in Greek and while living in Rome, was an 'insider', for whom the national tradition carried by writing in Hebrew and Aramaic was of central significance. Others, on the other hand—that is, persons writing in Latin or Greek from outside the Near East—paid very little attention to the scripts and languages of the region, and hardly help us to define in what terms ethnic and cultural groupings there should be identified. There seems, for instance, to be no single allusion anywhere in Classical literature to the language and script of Palmyra. But Diodorus, in a much-quoted passage, attributes to the Nabataeans of the late fourth century BC the ability to write a letter 'in Syrian characters',[21] as their (later) inscriptions and papyri show that they did. More generally, Strabo, quoting and adapting Posidonius, speaks of the resemblance in language, culture and physical type between Armenians (whose then homeland lay not in the Caucasus but just beyond the upper-middle Tigris), Syrians and Arabs:

> For the nation of the Armenians and that of the Syrians and Arabians betray a close affinity, not only in their language, but in their mode of life and their bodily build, and particularly wherever they live as close neighbours . . . Indeed Poseidonius conjectures that the names of these nations also are akin; for, says he, the people whom we call Syrians are by the Syrians themselves called Arimaeans and Arammaeans.[22]

Even though Strabo (or Posidonius) here comes closer than other commentators to suggesting common racial or physical characteristics for at least some of the peoples of the Near East, enough has been said to indicate that any single term used in the modern world to denote them all, whether 'Semites' or

---

Introduction to the Comparative Grammar of the Semitic Languages (1964), or G. Garbini, *Le lingue semitiche: Studi di storia linguistica* (1972).

20. *Ant.* XII, 2, 1 (15), adapting *Letter of Aristeas* 2/11.

21. Diodorus XX, 96, 1.

22. Strabo, *Geog.* I, 2, 34 (41–42), Loeb trans. = Posidonius, FGrH 87, F.105a = Edelstein and Kidd, F.280.

any other, would represent a purely arbitrary choice, with no basis in ancient terminology.[23]

'Semitic' in this book will be used solely to refer to the family of languages concerned, whose mutual resemblances are a matter of observable fact. But even if we abandon the use of racial terminology, the question remains open of how far and in what senses there was a common culture, pattern of religious customs or sense of mutual identity or relationship among the peoples of the Near East who spoke Semitic languages. Given the fundamental importance of language to the emergence of nationalism in the modern world, it is natural that we should pose the question, provided that we remain aware that it may embody completely inappropriate preconceptions.

Such questions will be pursued throughout this book, and cannot be answered fully at this point (or indeed, given the limits of our evidence, at all). But they do need to be posed in a preliminary way, above all in the sphere of religious practice. 'The Religion of the Semites', of which Jewish cult-practices, as portrayed in the Old Testament, are to be conceived of as one aspect, has long been the subject of scholarly enquiry.[24] Even if this were conceded to be a legitimate term, it would not follow that common characteristics of religious practice, perhaps with a particular compatibility with Jewish observances, were still to be found in this region in the Hellenistic or Roman Imperial periods. But in fact there are some indications, however partial and unsatisfactory, that this was indeed the case. Take for example the custom of circumcision. Here again Josephus relates Jewish and Arab practice, and puts the resemblance in the context of their supposed common descent. Speaking of Isaac, he says: 'Eight days later they promptly circumcised him; and from that day forward the Jewish practice has been to circumcise so many days after birth. The Arabs defer the ceremony to the thirteenth year, because Ishmael, the founder of their race, born of Abraham's concubine, was circumcised at that age'.[25] Josephus' comment about the age of circumcision among the Arabs is his own addition to the Biblical account, and is in the present tense. We have to take it that he intends to refer to the contemporary world of the first century AD. If confirmation is needed, it is provided by an important work to which we will return, Bardesanes' *Book of the Laws of Countries,* written in Syriac in the first part of the third century, and perhaps the only rival to Josephus' *Antiquities* as a contribution to the anthropology of the Roman Near East. Giving instances of the fact that customs can

23. It follows, as will be clear, that I cannot accept the logical basis of an approach such as that of S. Moscati, *The Semites in Ancient History: An Inquiry into the Settlement of the Bedouin and Their Political Establishment* (1959).

24. I refer above all of course to the classic volume of W. Robertson Smith, *The Religion of the Semites* (1894).

25. *Ant.* I, 12, 2 (214).

change, and are not determined immutably by the stars, he says:[26] 'Recently the Romans have conquered Arabia and have done away with the old laws there used to be, particularly circumcision, which was a custom they used'. Given that 'Arabs' were to be found in the steppe bordering all of the Fertile Crescent, it is quite unclear whether he means to refer back to the acquisition of Nabataea in AD 106, to the conquest of Mesopotamia in the 190s or to some other event. But the point, and its relevance to the Roman Imperial period, remains.

More essential still is the question of whether the Near Eastern region was characterised in any general way by the avoidance of images, or the worship of cult-objects which were distinct from the anthropomorphic images typical of Graeco-Roman antiquity. The proposition that this was so in the Hellenistic period formed the core of the revolutionary approach to the crisis of Judaism in the 170s and 160s BC, put forward by Elias Bickerman.[27] On this view the cult which was set up in the Holy of Holies in 167 BC was not an example of Hellenisation, that is to say, an anthropomorphic Greek cult instituted by Antiochus Epiphanes. Instead it was a reforming adoption of 'Syrian' cult-practices, in which the altar itself became the object of worship. This brilliant hypothesis cannot be proved, and runs counter to the fact that our best evidence distinguishes a phase of Hellenisation within Judaism from a succeeding phase of overt intervention by the Seleucids.[28] More problematic for Bickerman's view, but more relevant for the present discussion, is the fact that all the evidence cited for the worship of altars in particular or for aniconic cults in general, usually of large stones, comes not from the Hellenistic but from the Imperial period.[29] We will return later to the hill-top temples of the limestone massif in northern Syria, built in the Roman Empire,[30] which include one of Zeus Bōmos, 'Zeus (the) Altar', paralleled a few miles away by the temple of 'Zeus Madbachos and Selamanes, the Ancestral Gods'; here the adjective for this local Zeus clearly derives from the Aramaic root DBK, or Hebrew ZBK, meaning 'sacrifice': this Zeus too was a 'Zeus (the) Altar'. The only literary evidence which can be cited for the concept of the altar as itself the object of worship again comes from the Imperial period, namely the fascinating work *On Abstinence from Living Things* written by Porphyry, a native

---

26. *The Book of the Laws of Countries: Dialogue on Fate of Bardaisan of Edessa*, ed. and trans. H. J. W. Drijvers (1965), 56–57. See further 12.5 below.

27. E. Bickerman, *Der Gott der Makkabäer* (1937), esp. 90ff.

28. So F. Millar, "The Background to the Maccabean Revolution: Reflections on Martin Hengel's 'Judaism and Hellenism'", *JJS* 29 (1978), 1.

29. See F. Millar, "The Problem of Hellenistic Syria", in A. Kuhrt and S. Sherwin-White (eds.), *Hellenism and the East* (1987), 110, on p. 131.

30. 7.3 below.

of Tyre, in the later third century. The reference in this case is purely incidental, for he is in fact assembling instances of human sacrifice. But among these
he adds: 'And the Doumatēnoi of Arabia used each year to sacrifice a boy
whom they buried beneath an altar, which they treat as a cult-statue *(xoanon)*'.[31] The place referred to is of great interest for other reasons, for it is
Dumatha, present-day Jawf, at the far end of the Wadi Sirhan, a wide depression which carries a route from Damascus south-east into the Empty Quarter
and eventually to the Persian Gulf. Scattered epigraphic evidence from there
shows it to have been just within the limits of both Nabataean and later Roman control.[32] Whether, again, we should read Porphyry, an important Neo-
Platonist philosopher and pupil of Plotinus, as an 'insider', even as an 'Oriental', when he speaks of customs at different locations in the Near East is a
question to which we will have to return.[33] It is more than unlikely that he
ever visited Dumatha, which lies over 500 km south-east of Damascus. Nonetheless it was not a wholly remote and fabulous place, but on a route visited
by Roman soldiers. It is also noticeable that Porphyry speaks of human sacrifice there in the past tense, but of the status of the altar there as a cult-object
in the present.

The evidence for this precise form of aniconic cult in the Near East, while
it exists, is thus very slender and hardly offers much support for Bickerman's
typically brilliant hypothesis. But in a wider form, the use of a non-
representational object, usually a large stone, in place of a cult-statue is very
well attested, by literary, epigraphic and visual evidence, both on coins and
on relief-carvings. We even gain from Herennius Philo of Byblos, writing his
Phoenicica early in the second century AD, a glimpse of how such sacred
stones might have been understood. For in the course of his exposition of
Phoenician beliefs he makes the brief statement, without further elaboration:
'moreover Theos Ouranos thought up *baitulia,* having devised stones invested
with life'.[34] This allusion, unfortunately for us, presumes rather than does
much to illuminate the role of large stones as cult-objects, which is attested
on the coins of various Phoenician cities, and is known also elsewhere in the
Near East.[35] Beyond this, the word 'Symbetylos' or 'Symbaitylos' appears
once or twice as the name of a god in the Greek inscriptions from the villages
of the limestone massif in northern Syria, and seems to mean 'the one who

31. Porphyry, *De abst.* II, 56, 6: καὶ Δουματηνοὶ δὲ τῆς Ἀραβίας κατ᾽ ἔτος ἕκαστον ἔθυον
παῖδα, ὃν ὑπὸ βωμὸν ἔθαπτον, ᾧ χρῶνται ὡς ξοάνῳ.

32. See 11.1 below.

33. See 8.5 below.

34. Quoted by Eusebius, *Praep. Ev.* I, 10, 23 = Jacoby, *FGrH* 790, F.2 (23): ἐξενόησε Θεὸς
Οὐρανὸς βαιτύλια, λίθους ἐμψύχους μηχανησάμενος. On Philo see further 8.4 below.

35. See 8.4, 9.2 and 11.4 below.

shares the betyl', or cult-object.[36] But here immediately, as so often in the Near East, we enter the area of where linguistic, cultural and religious speculations interact, and the conclusion which emerges is all too likely to represent above all the presuppositions of the investigator. Nonetheless, it seems difficult to set aside the long-established view that Greek words using the root 'betyl' or 'baityl' reflect variant transliterations of the Semitic-language term 'bethel' (BT'L), meaning 'house of El (god)'. This conception in itself gains some force from the fact that the term seems now to be attested on an Aramaic inscription from the Roman Imperial period, found at the village of El-Mal in southern Syria, some 40 km south-west of Damascus.[37] The inscription, which dates from 7/6 BC, seems to record that someone 'built a house of god' (BNH BYT 'LH), that is, a temple. Though there were Jewish settlements in this region, bordering on Gaulanitis (the Golan Heights), the context is surely pagan. However, it is clear that what is referred to here is not a 'betyl' as understood by Philo, and taken as a general conception by moderns, that is, a stone housing a divine spirit, but a building, no doubt one of those small rural sanctuaries so well attested over large parts of the Near East.

As so often, if we try to generalise too confidently when confronted with the intermingling of languages, cultures and forms of religious belief and practice which we encounter in the Near East, the evidence will not quite fall into the patterns we would like. This is indeed partly because, when and if literary or documentary evidence from the period is particularly explicit, or offers some wider characterisation or interpretation of the culture or cultures of the region, it in itself may constitute an observer's interpretation, not a report which can be taken at face value.

It is precisely for these reasons that the dedication inscribed by Aurelius Diphilianus on the little altar which he put up at Dura-Europos is of such significance. The context is one where papyri, parchments and inscriptions in a number of different languages, like the iconography, sculpture and architecture of the town, demonstrate the co-existence of an extraordinary variety of cultures and religious systems,[38] just as newly discovered papyri and parchments of the third century, mainly relating to an area not far up the Euphrates from Dura, also reveal a bilingual world to which until now we have hardly had any access.[39] There can be no question therefore that Aurelius Diphilianus, in dedicating his altar in Greek 'to the Ancestral God, Zeus Betylos, of those by the Orontes', was making an affirmation which was intended to be

---

36. *IGLS* II, no. 376 (Kafr Nabo); 383 (Qalota). For a detailed discussion see *Dura Report* IV, 69ff.

37. See J. Naveh, "An Aramaic Inscription from El-Mal—a Survival of 'Seleucid Aramaic' Script", *IEJ* 25 (1975), 117. Cf. J. Teixidor, *BES* (1976), no. 167. See further 11.1 below.

38. See more fully 12.2 and 12.4 below.

39. See esp. 4.2 below.

significant at the time, and demands our attention now. He clearly saw the object of his dedication both as inherited from previous generations (though whether *his* ancestors or others' is a different question) and as being worshipped by the population of a wider geographical region. We might even suppose that he intended 'those by the Orontes' to refer to all the pagan inhabitants of the Syrian region.

However, the divine appellation he used, 'Zeus Betylos', remains unique in our evidence. It does not even seem clear whether 'betylos' here is an adjective ('Betylian Zeus') or a noun, as in 'Zeus Bōmos'. In the latter case it would be 'Zeus (the) Betyl' which Diphilianus claims to have been the long-standing object of worship of a wider population. That in its turn *may* mean that he conceived of this deity as being embodied in a stone. Furthermore, as we will see, one contemporary writer, the historian Herodian, clearly asserts that the stone which represented the god Elagabal at Emesa was imagined to have fallen from heaven. His words provide a clear example of how a Classical writer of the Imperial period may put that same distance between himself and the customs of the 'Orient' as the modern European observer tends to do: 'There was no actual man-made statue of the god, the sort Greeks and Romans put up; but there was an enormous black stone, rounded at the base and coming to a point at the top, conical in shape and black. This stone is worshipped as though it were sent from heaven'.[40] Whether the stone actually was a meteorite we cannot know; what is significant is the conception. But it is almost inevitable that speculation should lead one to think of a possible connection between the patterns of cult-practice visible here and the central role which Mahomet was to give to the black stone built into the Kaaba in the new cult he instituted at Mecca; this was one element which he took over from the existing pagan worship there.[41]

Enough has been said to give some impression of the diversity and richness of the evidence which is potentially available for any attempt to understand the society and culture of the Near East in the period when Roman rule steadily extended to reach its furthest limits. But, while the evidence is indeed rich and diverse, and steadily becoming more so, it is also very scattered, cannot yield anything approaching statistics, or even orders of magnitude, and above all leaves the economic basis of society there in almost total obscurity. What, for instance, was the role of long-distance trade in forming Near Eastern society in this period? The question is of much more than purely economic significance. For if there were indeed important trade-routes by land through the Hedjaz, as (perhaps) in the time of Mahomet; through the Wadi Sirhan to

40. Herodian V, 3, 5, Loeb trans. See further 9.2 below.

41. See now the highly sceptical account of the origins of Islam in Mecca by P. Crone, *Meccan Trade and the Rise of Islam* (1987), 192.

the Persian Gulf; or via Palmyra to the Euphrates, or via the Fertile Crescent to the Tigris, continuing to Babylonia or Central Asia, then we may have to see the region which was incorporated in the Roman Empire as belonging not just geographically but in some more profound sense to the 'Orient'. For example, were the Jews of Judaea the only speakers of a Semitic language in the Roman Near East who maintained active and continuous contacts with a related community in Babylonia?

Modern views of the economy of the ancient world tend strongly to mini-mise the dependence of any community on long-distance trade.[42] But ancient observers, from Strabo at the beginning of our period to Pliny the Elder and to Ammianus Marcellinus in the fourth century, strongly affirm the impor-tance of long-distance trade on all the routes mentioned above, if less clearly in the case of that through the Wadi Sirhan. Should we then see at least some of the cities of the Near East as striking and significant exceptions to a general rule, as having been, in Rostovtzeff's phrase, 'caravan cities'? He used the term of Petra, of Dura-Europos, of Jerash (Gerasa) and above all of course of Palmyra.[43] But while no one can doubt that 'caravans' (*synodiai* in Greek) did go from Palmyra to the east, a study of what seems as if it would be the best evidence for Palmyrene trade, the bilingual customs-law from the reign of Hadrian, shows that it actually deals mainly with products coming into the city from its surrounding territory, which was far from being mere desert, or even (as above) steppe, but included a large number of small settlements or villages.[44]

Both the cultural and the economic importance of long-distance trade will have to be discussed further below. So will the contrasting element in eco-nomic and social life mentioned above, the smaller settlements and villages of the region. For if there is a single feature of Near Eastern society which emerges more clearly than any other from the mass of isolated and enigmatic items of evidence—archaeological finds, inscriptions, papyri and parchments, and literature, whether pagan, Christian or Jewish, and whether written in Latin, Greek or a variety of Semitic languages—it is the life of the dense net-work of villages and small settlements which can be shown to have covered large parts of the region. This is of course not equally true of all areas. The extent of settlement and cultivation along the fringes of the steppe has always been acutely dependent on political and military factors; but it is quite clear

---

42. See, above all, M. I. Finley, *The Ancient Economy* (1973; 2nd ed. 1985)—qualified in P. Garnsey, K. Hopkins and C. R. Whittaker (eds.), *Trade in the Ancient Economy* (1983).

43. M. I. Rostovtzeff, *Caravan Cities* (1932). Note the important review by D. Schlumberger, *Gnomon* 11 (1935), 82.

44. J. F. Matthews, "The Tax Law of Palmyra: Evidence for Economic History in a City of the Roman East", *JRS* 74 (1984), 157, a study to which this book is very much indebted.

that the Empire represents, in comparative terms, a period of the very wide extension of cultivation, hardly paralleled until the present day.

On the other hand it has never been sufficiently clearly acknowledged that within the Roman Near East there are mountainous areas which have never been seriously examined for archaeological and documentary remains. One, on the north-east fringe of the region, is Mount Amanus; here almost the last village community we can encounter in our evidence is the fortified village called Pindenissum, which Cicero spent fifty-six days besieging in 50 BC.[45] Second, there is the chain of mountains between the middle Orontes Valley and the Mediterranean, stretching south from Antioch and terminating at the gap between Emesa and the sea formed by the river Eleutheros (Nahr el Kebir). These limestone hills rising to some 1500 m, the ancient Mons Bargylus or present Jebel Ansariyeh, inhabited by an Alawi population since the Middle Ages, have never been open to archaeological investigation, and remain an almost complete blank in the archaeological and social map of the region.[46] Yet there is cultivable land, formed into small fields, up to the very summit of the ridge; and the great temple of Baetocaece near the south end of the chain, and lying at some 1000 m above sea-level, itself suggests that there was a significant population here under the Empire.[47] Paradoxically, in the much higher Mount Lebanon chain, stretching south of the Eleutheros River as far as the Leontes (Litani) River, a whole series of rural sanctuaries are known, though not the villages which must have been not too distantly associated with them.[48] But above all, at the very heart of the region, there is the great mass of Anti-Lebanon, reaching some 2400 m, and its southern extension, Mount Hermon, which attains just over 2800 m. The entire mountain-chain extends some 230 km from the north-east, where it almost touches on the steppe, to the south-west, where it reaches the Golan Heights, the headwaters of the Jordan and the hills of Galilee; and it is some 30 km wide between the Bekaa Valley and Damascus. Investigations of the south-western end of this chain in recent years have shown the same widespread traces of cultivation and settlement as elsewhere, not to speak of olive-presses found at heights of up to 1200 m.[49] Our literary and documentary evidence for the social history of the region hardly takes us beyond references to raiding by the Ituraean population of these mountains in the early Roman period, and

45. Cicero, *ad fam.* XV, 4, 10.

46. For a study of this region, see J. Weulersse, *Le pays des Alaouites* I–II (1940).

47. On Baetocaece see further 8.3 below.

48. See the remarkable survey by D. Krencker and W. Zschietzmann, *Römische Tempel in Syrien* I–II (1938). Note the map in vol. II, Taf. 1. In fact, with the exception of Baetocaece, most of the temples surveyed lie in the territory of present-day Lebanon, a few on Anti-Lebanon and Mount Hermon being just on the Syrian side of the border.

49. S. Dar, "The History of the Hermon Settlements", *PEQ* 120 (1986), 26.

expeditions against them under Augustus.[50] But here above all we ought to think of both an inner 'frontier', possibly more real than that which lay along the fringes of the steppe, and a major reserve of population whose history and culture are still virtually unknown.

The stress just laid on extensive rural settlement, which would be valid also on either side of the Euphrates and its tributary the Chabur, which runs south from northern Mesopotamia, is important for several reasons. One is that we ought to be open to the possibility that the region as a whole contained a far larger population than comparison with most more recent periods would suggest. Second, it means that those places which ancient evidence and modern treatments label as 'cities' (poleis) have to be seen in the context of a network of other settlements, which in sum will have been far more important in terms of overall population, while taken individually they may have been indistinguishable from small poleis. It should not indeed be presumed in advance that the distinction between city (polis) and village (kōmē) was always entirely clear. The fact that Josephus can use polis of various settlements in Galilee (for instance Gischala and Jotapata) which we would not list as 'Greek cities', and can even use sometimes the one term and sometimes the other for the same place there, is not necessarily just carelessness.[51] Nor is it in the least certain that the whole region was neatly divided up among territories (chōrai) dependent on recognised poleis. At the very least it is clear in several regions, the Hauran in southern Syria above all, that villages could conduct their own communal lives without any apparent reference to a polis under whose authority they lived.

Of course in our period, beginning three centuries after the conquest by Alexander, the central role of cities, whether Hellenistic foundations or ancient cities (like Damascus or Tyre) which had evolved into Greek cities, is undeniable. Moreover the number of places which 'became' Greek cities in this period is considerable (for instance Flavia Neapolis, present-day Nablus). Such transformations continue throughout the period. Even within the few years covered by the important new Greek and Syriac archive from the middle Euphrates region, from the 230s to the 250s, the settlement of Appadana turns into another Greek city called Neapolis, duly equipped with town-councillors (bouleutai).[52] A few decades later, under the Tetrarchy, the village of Sakkaia in the northern Hauran was to emerge as the Greek city of Maximianopolis, named after one of the Emperors; and later still, in the 320s, the port of Gaza, Maioumas, was to be made a city with the title Constantina.[53]

50. 2.1 below.

51. See M. Goodman, *State and Society in Roman Galilee, AD 132–212* (1983), 27.

52. D. Feissel and J. Gascou, "Documents inédits du Moyen Euphrate (IIIᵉ siècle après J.-C.)", *CRAI* (1989), 535, on pp. 541–542.

53. Eusebius, *VC* IV, 38–39; Sozomenus, *HE* V, 3, 6–8.

But the very ease with which these transformations could apparently be effected raises a major question about the culture of the region. It is natural to think of 'the Greek city' as an alien importation, a form of colonisation and domination over a 'native' population; and indeed there is some truth in this view for the early Hellenistic period.[54] But centuries had passed; many villages in the region bore more than a mere outward or physical resemblance to Greek cities. And if it is appropriate to think in terms of a contrast between 'Greek' on the one hand and 'native' or 'Semitic' or 'Oriental' elements in the culture and social structure of the region on the other, it is by no means clear that any such contrast coincides with a division between city and country. As newly published documents make ever clearer, the life of villages in this region could be marked by complex property-relations; by private legal transactions carried out with the use of documents in Greek; and by direct exchanges with representatives of the state.

Take for example the marriage-contract agreed in AD 128 in the village of Maoza in the district of Zoara, which lies in the deep depression, the Wadi Arabah, which extends beyond the south end of the Dead Sea. Both families concerned were Jewish, and one came from Engedi in the province of Judaea. But Maoza formed part of the new province of Arabia, created in AD 106 by the absorption of the kingdom of Nabataea. The marriage-contract comes from the 'archive of Babatha', found in a cave in the Judaean Desert and now published by Naphtali Lewis. It is written in Greek and begins in a style which emphatically recalls the attachment of this rural world to a wider power-structure:

> In the consulship of Publius Metilius Nepos for the 2nd time and Marcus Annius Libo on the nones of April, and by the compute of the new province of Arabia year twenty-third on the fifteenth of month Xandikos, in Maoza, Zoara district, Judah son of Eleazar also known as Khthusion, gave over Shelamzion, his very own daughter, a virgin, to Judah surnamed Cimber son of Ananias son of Somalas, both of the village En-gedi in Judaea residing here.[55]

Both the families define themselves by village and province, and one by the attachment of their village to the district of Zoara (literally 'around Zoara'); no Greek *poleis* come into the picture at all. But the fact that the people con-

54. See esp. P. Briant, "Colonisation hellénistique et populations indigènes: La phase d'instal-lation", *Klio* 60 (1978), 57 = *Rois, tributs et pasteurs: Ètudes sur les formations tributaires du Moyen-Orient ancien* (1982), 227.

55. N. Lewis, *The Documents from the Bar-Kochba Period in the Cave of Letters: Greek Papyri* (1989), no. 18 (henceforward *P. Yadin*). G. W. Bowersock, "The Babatha Papyri, Masada and Rome", *JRA* 4 (1991), 336, on p. 339, argues that the transliterated Latin word should be *libellarius*, not *librarius*.

cerned could have the very detailed provisions of the contract set out in Greek does not mean that they were fluent Greek speakers or writers. On the contrary, the document was written by a scribe, Theënas son of Simon, who identifies his role, somewhat oddly, by using the transliterated Latin word *librarius*. And when the parties come at the end of the document to give their subscriptions in their own hands, they do so in Aramaic: 'Yehudah son of Elazar Khthusion: I have given my daughter Shelamzion, a virgin, in marriage to Yehudah . . .' (YHWDH BR 'L'ZR KTWŠN HQHT YT ŠLMṢYN BRTY BTWLH LYHDH . . .).

But the most striking feature of the document must be the visible presence in it of the wider Roman Empire. In this case the name of the Emperor himself (Hadrian) does not appear. But the 'new province' of Arabia does. So does a Roman system of dating, and the names of the two consuls holding office in Rome. Both of the new archives, from the Judaean Desert and from the middle Euphrates, give a powerful and unexpected impression of the significance in private life, in relatively remote country districts, of belonging to the Empire. That from the middle Euphrates, which incorporates some documents from the cities of northern Mesopotamia, also reflects another aspect of the transformation which cities underwent in this period: that is, the rapid spread, from the 190s onwards, of the conferment of the Roman status of *colonia,* which was no mere title but involved the restructuring of the city magistracies and (at least in principle) the use of Latin in public transactions.[56] In this new archive, Nisibis, Carrhae and Edessa in Mesopotamia all appear as *coloniae;* and by that time the same title had been conferred on Jerusalem (now Aelia Capitolina) in Judaea (now Syria Palaestina) and on Bostra and Petra in Arabia. It was also, almost certainly, enjoyed by Dura-Europos, where Aurelius Diphilianus erected his altar to Zeus Betylos.

For however evocative, if baffling, is the designation which Diphilianus gave to this deity, the most significant fact about his dedication may still be the very simple one that it represents the self-expression of a Roman legionary soldier writing in Greek. The fact that he construes his 'Zeus Betylos' as the ancestral god of those by the Orontes must be taken, as we have seen, as reflecting some awareness of a distinct culture, characteristic of this region. We can also accept that 'Betylos' is a loan-word from Aramaic or one of its dialects, and (less certainly) that it embodies the concept of an aniconic cult-object, a 'stone invested with spirit', as Philo of Byblos had put it. Did that in its turn reflect a system of belief native to this region, which offered, as a contrast to the multiplicity of gods portrayed in the cult-statues of Graeco-

---

56. F. Millar, "The Roman *Coloniae* of the Near East: A Study of Cultural Relations", in H. Solin and M. Kajava (eds.), *Roman Policy in the East and Other Studies in Roman History* (1990), 7.

Roman paganism, a fundamental preference for monotheism and for the conception of a single deity who could not be represented in human form? If so, it can have been no more than a tendency, for the array of distinctive divine images, to which we can often attach no mythology, and sometimes not even a name, for instance at Palmyra or in Nabataea, is precisely one of the most difficult problems for the religious history of the region.[57] But it may still be claimed, as it has been in a major modern work on the popular religion of the Near East in this period, that this tendency to monotheism made the Near East fertile ground both for attraction to Judaism and for the spread of Christianity, and later of Islam.[58] We should be very careful before importing any such presumptions.

The spread of Christianity must indeed be taken as the single most important development which occurred in the period from the reign of Augustus to the death of Constantine. By that moment a Christian literature in a Semitic language, Syriac, had been in existence for at least a century. Churches had been built everywhere, from Mesopotamia to Antioch, Tyre, Jerusalem or southern Syria (while the only known pre-Constantinian house-church had been obliterated when the Persians captured Dura-Europos in the 250s). Pilgrimage to Biblical sites and to the magnificent new churches of the Holy Land was already well established.

But *had* the Near East really offered a distinctively favourable cultural and religious setting for Christianity since the time of Jesus? Had there been in this region gentile Christian communities using Aramaic or a dialect of it? The Jewish community of Dura-Europos had certainly used Aramaic, as well as Greek. But had the Christian community nearby? Even if we do not treat the question as a purely linguistic one, was there, as so many modern books presume, a distinctive 'Syrian' Christianity using Greek, which owed its character to its regional environment? If so, what would that mean? Of which of the many sub-regions of the Near East are we talking, and what are the criteria of 'Syrian' Christianity?

These questions will have to be discussed later, and some may prove unanswerable. But if such issues remain baffling, what is abundantly clear is the influence of the Roman Empire, as mediated in the first instance through common Roman soldiers like Aurelius Diphilianus. It would be illegitimate, because circular, to claim that it was Roman rule which created the unity of the region, from the Red Sea to the Tigris and the Taurus Mountains. For the

57. See now the major surveys by M. Gawlikowski, "Les dieux de Palmyre", *ANRW* II.18.4 (1990), 2605, and "Les dieux des Nabatéens", ibid., 2660.

58. J. Teixidor, *The Pagan God: Popular Religion in the Ancient Near East* (1977), 17: 'But the increasing emphasis on such beliefs is evidence of a trend towards monotheism, namely toward the exclusion of other gods' existence. In the Near East of Greco-Roman times this trend facilitates the spread of Judaism, Christianity and Islam'.

(eventual) extension of Roman rule has been taken here as defining the area in question. But what is indisputable is that nearly all the forms of expression of the culture of this region, or its sub-regions—architecture; sculpture; wall-paintings; inscriptions in Greek, Latin (occasionally) and a variety of Semitic languages, including Arabic—themselves came into existence within the framework of the Roman Empire or of its dependent kingdoms. So far as our evidence goes, the preceding Hellenistic period has left us almost nothing which can count as the expression of a regional or local pagan culture. Whatever may have been the case at the time, those aspects of the local culture or cultures of the Near East which survive for us to encounter came into existence in the Roman Empire. To claim that they actually owed their existence, or their capacity to flourish and find self-expression, to Roman rule would be to go further than can be proved. For we can never know what the region would have been like if Roman rule had not been imposed. But it is suggestive that in the later second century the bishop Melito of Sardis acknowledged that it had been by divine providence that Christianity, beginning among *barbaroi,* had coincided with the foundation of the Imperial monarchy *(basileia)* by Augustus. Since that time the power of the Empire had grown, and Christianity had flourished with it.[59]

At the time of Jesus it could not necessarily have been expected that Roman soldiers and officials would leave traces of their activities deep into the Hedjaz, far into the Jordanian steppe and down the Wadi Sirhan as far as Jawf; through the steppe from Damascus via Palmyra to the Euphrates; along the Chabur, in northern Mesopotamia and on the Tigris, where the walls of Amida (Diyarbakir), which Ammianus was to describe, were to be created under Constantine.[60] By that time the Parthian Empire which had confronted Rome across the Euphrates in the first two centuries had been replaced by a Persian Empire in the 220s, and northern Mesopotamia had become an endlessly contested battleground between the two powers. Roman direct rule had been substituted for a whole series of dependent kingdoms, among them Judaea, Commagene, Emesa, Nabataea and Osrhoene.

But it was not only that the Emperors now ruled a solid block of territory, which extended to the limits of cultivable land and stretched along the edge of the steppe continuously over a distance of some 750 km. It was also that, whether we conceive of the army in this region as being devoted primarily to conquest, to defence or to occupation, it represented a large proportion of the forces of the Empire. More significant still, the confrontation with Parthia and then with Persia had given the northern part of this region a prime role as a field for the activities of the Roman Emperors in person. A whole series

59. Eusebius, *HE* V, 26, 7–8.
60. Ammianus XVIII, 9, 1.

of third-century Emperors had died or been captured in the Near East, or en route to or from it: Caracalla (217), Macrinus (218), Gordian (244), Valerian (260), Carus (282). It was entirely appropriate in symbolic terms that the end of the period with which we are concerned should be marked by the death of Constantine in 337, when preparing for yet another campaign against the Persians.

One effect of that obsession with campaigns in the East was the steadily increasing use of Antioch as an Imperial residence and military headquarters, and its clearly established status as a permanent Imperial capital in the Tetrarchic period.[61] With the reign of Maximinus as 'Caesar' and then 'Augustus' in 306–311, an Emperor was for the first time to be found continuously resident in this region, and visiting not only Antioch but some of the other major cities. The last phase of pagan Imperial rule as expressed in the Near East is aptly summed up in Eusebius' vivid portrait of Maximinus, while present in Caesarea (now officially a Roman *colonia*) in AD 306/307, presiding in person at wild-beast shows (one of the most distinctive of Roman importations to the Greek East), and having Christian martyrs executed in the arena before him.[62] Christianity was to triumph only a few years later, with churches being built everywhere, and Jerusalem (officially Aelia Capitolina, another Roman *colonia*) becoming a recognised place of pilgrimage. But that itself was yet another expression of the Imperial will, and of the power of the Roman state. If the social and cultural history of the Near East between Augustus and Constantine can be understood at all, it is only within the framework created by that Imperial power.

61. See F. Millar, *The Emperor in the Roman World* (1977), esp. 48–50 (henceforward *ERW*); T. D. Barnes, *The New Empire of Diocletian and Constantine* (1982), 65–66.
62. Eusebius, *Mart. Pal.* 6–7.

I

· · ·

EMPIRE

CHAPTER

2

THE BRIDGEHEAD AND THE
DEPENDENT KINGDOMS,
31 BC–AD 74

2.1. FROM THE BATTLE OF ACTIUM TO THE DEATH
OF HEROD THE GREAT

When the news spread of the victory of Actium in 31 BC, which brought the
Roman civil wars to an end and enabled Octavian, the future Augustus, to
exercise effective sole power, Rome possessed no more than a bridgehead in
the Near East. The province of 'Syria' had been established by Pompey only
three and a half decades before.[1] By 58 BC it had become a consular province
and a base for ambitions for conquest both southwards, to Ptolemaic Egypt,
and eastwards, to Parthia. But at the same time, even the restricted territory
which Rome occupied directly—in effect the Phoenician coast, along with the
Orontes Valley and northern Syria, the main area of Hellenistic settlement—
had been ravaged by local dynastic rivalries, by wars fought by Roman armies
against each other, and by a major Parthian invasion in 40 BC.

It is not necessary to retail the events of these years in detail. It is enough
to recall that even without the Parthian invasion (which no one could have
known was to be the last which would ever be successfully mounted) Roman
control was tenuous and erratic, and did little or nothing to reduce the long-
standing insecurity of the region. Thus when Julius Caesar passed rapidly
through Syria in 47 BC, on his way from Alexandria to Asia Minor, he could
exercise diplomacy only in satisfying the communities and dynasts of the region as best he could:

1. For a sketch of its history see Schürer, *HJP* I, 243ff. For the situation of the region in this
period, and after, see the important survey by J.-P. Rey-Coquais, "Syrie romaine de Pompée à
Dioclétien", *JRS* 68 (1978), 44, to which this whole book owes much.

Stopping in almost all those cities which were of greater prestige, he gave rewards to those who deserved it, both individually and collectively, and held jurisdiction and issued decisions on long-standing controversies. As for kings, tyrants and dynasts neighbouring on the province, who had all hastened together to him, he received them into his trust on condition of protecting and defending the province, and dismissed them as being now the most loyal friends of himself and the Roman people.[2]

A couple of years later, in 45 and 44 BC, Caecilius Bassus, a follower of Pompey, had been able to seize the Greek city of Apamea on the Orontes and hold out against two successive Roman armies from the Caesarian side. As so often, our best account of the area in the first century BC, and our most vivid impression of the dynamics of the highly disturbed power relations between different groups, comes from the *Geography* of Strabo, written in the last part of Augustus' reign:

> Caecilius Bassus, with two cohorts, caused Apameia to revolt and, though besieged by two large Roman armies, strongly resisted them for so long a time that he did not come under their power until he voluntarily put himself in their hands upon his own terms; for the country supplied his army with provisions, and he had plenty of allies, I mean the neighbouring chieftains, who possessed strongholds; and among these places was Lysias, which is situated above the lake that lies near Apameia, as also Arethusa, belonging to Sampsiceramus and his son Iamblichus, chieftains of the tribe of the Emeseni; and at no great distance, also, were Heliopolis and Chalcis, which latter was subject to Ptolemaeus the son of Mennaeus, who possessed Massyas and the mountainous country of the Ituraeans. Among the allies of Bassus was also Alchaedamnus, king of the Rhambaeans, who were nomads this side of the Euphrates River; and he was a friend of the Romans, but upon the belief that he was being treated unjustly by the Roman governors he retired to Mesopotamia and then went into the service of Bassus as a mercenary.[3]

In the Triumviral period which followed, when the Near East all fell under the rule of Marcus Antonius, if Roman armies no longer fought each other in the region, major local kings, in Commagene, in Judaea (where Herod was formally recognised as king in 40 BC) and in Nabataea, gained considerable power; the Parthians invaded in 40 BC, being repelled fully only in 37; and large parts of the coast and some of the inland territory in the south were granted to Cleopatra of Egypt. At the time of the battle of Actium, the forces of Herod of Judaea were on campaign, on Antonius' orders, against those of

2. [Caesar], *Bell. Alex.* 65, 4.
3. Strabo, *Geog.* XVI, 2, 10 (752–753), Loeb trans.

Malichus I of Nabataea, who had not paid the tribute due for the territory given to Cleopatra.[4] Nonetheless Malichus had sent forces to join Antonius, as had Mithridates II of Commagene, the builder of the last of the series of great dynastic monuments there.[5]

Some very immediate consequences of the victory can be traced in our sources. The most immediate is the letter which Octavian wrote from Ephesus towards the end of 31 BC in response to an embassy from the little city of Rhosus, situated on the coast on the northern side of the Amanus Mountains. Acknowledging the crown *(stephanos)* sent in recognition of his victory, and referring to the merits of a naval captain *(nauarchos)* from there named Seleucus, who had served with him in his wars, Octavian promises benefits for the city when he comes to the area.[6] He did indeed do so very soon, as we will see. But the document, significant on the one hand of the involvement of smaller communities also in the civil wars, and of the new relationship to an unchallenged single ruler, is also important in a quite different way. For the Near East proper, beginning, as defined here, on the other side of the Amanus Mountains, cannot compare with Asia Minor for the wealth of documents which would from now on illustrate relations between the subject communities and Rome, or the Emperor.

Thus, if we can reconstruct the impact of Rome in the Near East, or the role of the Near East within the Empire, it is from a variety of other sources, always partial and inadequate. For instance one of the most crucial steps in the strategic shape of the Empire in the Near East seems almost certainly to have been taken as an immediate consequence of Actium. Since 64 BC Seleucia on the Euphrates, the main crossing of the river—and hence known more often as Zeugma, 'the bridge'—had been part of the kingdom of Commagene; one of the sanctuaries of the royal cult was located there.[7] Now, in spite of his support of Antonius, Mithridates II was evidently confirmed in his kingdom by Octavian—but at the price, as it seems, of yielding Zeugma to Rome. No evidence explicitly says so; but coins of Seleucia/Zeugma under the Roman Empire use an era going back precisely to 31 BC.[8] If that is so, then it was at this moment that the middle Euphrates became the accepted boundary of the Roman and Parthian Empires, a fact repeatedly symbolised in diplo-

4. Schürer, *HJP* I, 580.

5. Plutarch, *Ant.* 61.

6. *IGLS* III, no. 718, iii = R. K. Sherk, *Roman Documents from the Greek East* (1971), no. 58, iii. Even though the area immediately north of the Amanus may have formed part of the province of Syria, as argued by H. Taeuber, "Die syrisch-kilikische Grenze während der Prinzipatszeit", *Tyche* 6 (1991), 201, it is not treated here as part of the Near East.

7. See the sketch-map of the monuments of the royal cult on p. 189 of the fundamental paper by J. Wagner, "Dynastie und Herrscherkult in Kommagene", *Ist. Mitt.* 33 (1983), 177.

8. See J. Wagner, *Seleukeia am Euphrat/Zeugma* (1976), 64.

matic meetings in the course of the first century. But the role of Zeugma as a legionary base came only later.[9] Under Augustus and Tiberius the legions of Syria were to be disposed internally, as an army of occupation.[10]

It may also have been at this moment that the cult-centre of Doliche, some 40 km west of Zeugma, became part of the provincial territory. But for this period we have no significant evidence about it, or about the large triangle of fertile land, between the Euphrates and the Taurus, which formed the kingdom of Commagene itself. A couple of episodes reflecting dynastic strife are no substitute for a social history of this region.[11] We can only recall that it was there, flanking the province proper on the north, as other dependent kingdoms did to the south.

If the consequences of Actium for the northern part of Syria have to be deduced indirectly, the situation is quite different for the southern part of the region, above all because of the two major historical works of Josephus, the *Jewish War* and the *Antiquities*. The importance of these works for Jewish history in the Classical period needs no emphasis. The significance of the *Antiquities* as representing the only 'insider's' history of any Near Eastern people to carry through from the second millennium to the Roman Empire has also already been stressed, as has the importance of that narrative for our view of the neighbouring peoples.[12] The same is true, however, of these two narratives as offering a view of the structure of the Roman Empire in this region and of the working of power-relations, up to where the *Jewish War* stops, in AD 74. Again the light cast extends far outside the area of Jewish settlement; if what it primarily illuminates is the region of southern Syria and Nabataea, in the end it returns to Commagene, to offer the best available account of the forcible provincialisation of a dependent kingdom.[13]

It is thus from Josephus that we know that Herod reacted to the news of Actium by setting off to meet Octavian on the island of Rhodes in 30 BC. Laying aside his royal diadem as a sign of submission, the king argued that his loyalty to Antonius should be construed as a sign of his prospective loyalty to Octavian. Whether convinced by these arguments or not, Octavian duly assented.[14] Herod, thus confirmed as king, escorted Octavian through Syria on his way to Egypt, entertained him lavishly at Ptolemais and provided supplies for the crossing of the desert; and on Octavian's return after the conquest

9. 2.7 and 3.1 below.

10. 2.2 below.

11. For Doliche see 7.2 below. Episodes of dynastic strife: Dio LII, 43, 1 (29 BC); the succession of Mithridates (III) in 20 BC: LIV, 9, 3. See R. D. Sullivan, "The Dynasty of Commagene", *ANRW* II.8 (1977), 733, on pp. 775ff.

12. Ch. 1 above.

13. 3.1 below.

14. Josephus, *BJ* I, 20, 1–3 (386–393); *Ant.* XV, 6, 6–7 (187–193).

of Egypt, he escorted him north as far as Antioch. In between, he had been to see Octavian in Egypt, and received additions to his kingdom in the form of Hippos on the eastern shore of the Sea of Galilee; Gadara beyond the Jordan; Jericho in the Jordan Valley; Samaria; and a line of small places on the coast, Straton's Tower, Joppa and Anthedon.[15]

What matters about these exchanges is not the exact details, some of which are uncertain, but the structures of power revealed, which show a fluency and changeableness which was to continue for many decades. The new ruler, Octavian, operates by personal contact and favour, arbitrarily transferring places from Roman direct rule to royal control (or, apparently, in the opposite direction, as with Zeugma). He can march his forces through royal territory, taking the land route to Egypt and back, just as Herod can escort him in either direction through Syria, and offer lavish entertainments at Ptolemais, a city which was never under his control, and must therefore have been thought of as part of the Roman province of Syria.

Exactly what the boundaries of that province were (if indeed the problem should be stated in those terms) can be left aside for the moment. To understand the nature of Roman control in the region, it is necessary, first, to recall the well-known truth that the term *provincia* meant both a sphere of operation and a geographically defined area. Second, the Roman presence in the Near East at this moment consisted of a single 'provincia' called Syria. Third, under the constitutional arrangements made in Rome in January 27 BC Syria became what Strabo, the best contemporary witness, called a province of Caesar as opposed to a province of the Roman people. The difference was essentially that the governors of the 'provinces of Caesar' were to be appointed by the Emperor (Augustus, as he had now been officially named), and were called *legati,* envoys; in the provinces of the Roman people the governors still were appointed by the archaic procedure of using the lot, and were called *proconsules.*[16]

These details of the new Roman structure are of some importance, for the broad principle of the distinction was in theory (and largely in practice) that the 'provinces of Caesar' were the military areas. In terms of the workings of the Roman Empire, Syria, like all the other provinces subsequently acquired in the Imperial period, was a military area, and one in which at all times comparatively large military forces were stationed. A second consequence was that all the higher officials who operated in this region were throughout,

15. Schürer, *HJP* I, 289.

16. See F. Millar, "The Emperor, the Senate and the Provinces", *JRS* 56 (1966), 156, with some corrections as regards terminology in "'Senatorial' Provinces: An Institutionalised Ghost", *Ancient World* 20 (1989), 93. The long-established proposition that 'sphere of operation' represented the original meaning of *provincia* is challenged by J.-M. Bertrand, "A propos du mot provincia", *Journal des savants* (1989), 191.

without exception, personal appointees of the Emperor, serving until recalled.

'All the higher officials' might give a false impression. In fact they were very few indeed. The most important was the *legatus* of the province of Syria. The position was held to be of major importance, and all holders whose careers are known were ex-consuls, the highest senatorial rank. Under them were the senatorial commanders of the legions, also called *legati,* and in the established Imperial system normally of ex-praetor rank. In the latter part of the reign of Augustus there seem to have been three legions in Syria.[17] If we assume (as a guess) a complement of five thousand men each, that meant a garrison of fifteen thousand citizen legionaries, with an unknown number of auxiliaries.

The significance of these figures lies in the fact that they represent a conscious decision at the centre of power about the apportionment of force within the Empire. Whatever else might have occurred by accident or oversight, or as an imperceptible development to which no attention was paid, the disposition of the legions between provinces was a matter of deliberate choice. It was one of the matters on which Augustus' successor, Tiberius, regularly consulted the Senate; and it is Tacitus' account of Tiberius' report to the Senate in AD 23 which reveals that by then the number of legions in Syria had risen to four.[18]

The second level of significance of such figures for the legions lies in the fact that they represent almost the whole of the Roman presence in the region. As elsewhere in the Roman provinces, what we might be tempted to think of as civilian administration remained at a very restricted level. Outside the structure just described—a consular *legatus* of the province, and three praetorian *legati* of the legions, with under them six military tribunes and sixty centurions for each legion—the only civilian official who can be attested for this period is a *procurator* of equestrian rank whose duties will have been concerned with the raising of taxation and the payment of the troops. The only one of these whom we can see at work under Augustus is the Sabinus whom Josephus shows intervening to secure the royal treasures in Jerusalem after the death of Herod in 4 BC.[19]

In terms of personnel employed by the Roman state, these legionaries, an unknown number of auxiliaries and the officers of each, under the overall command of the *legatus* of Syria, *were* the Empire as expressed in this early

17. The number is not certain; but Josephus, *BJ* II, 3, 1 (40); 5, 1 (67); *Ant.* XVII, 10, 9 (286), firmly states that in 4 BC there were three in all. Since his narrative relies at least in part on Nicolaus of Damascus, a contemporary who was closely involved in the events in question, he is likely to be correct.

18. Consultation of the Senate: Suetonius, *Tib.* 30; Tiberius' report of AD 23; Tacitus, *Ann.* IV, 5.

19. See below.

period in the Near East. There is nothing to suggest, and no reason to believe, that there was any strictly civilian administration. Least of all was there a pyramid of local Roman administrators culminating in the *legatus,* or any bureaucratic hierarchy. In essence, therefore, Syria was still a military 'province', or sphere of operations, where the Roman state *was* its military forces, whose role was to confront Parthia across the Euphrates on the one hand, and to keep at least a potential control of dependent kingdoms and to impose order internally on the other hand.

Military relations with Parthia are not as such the subject of this book. The relevance here of the often-discussed confrontations which took place at intervals over the first two and a half centuries of the Empire is only in the conception of where the 'eastern frontier' of the Empire lay; in the way that the Roman forces were disposed; and in the degree to which Rome relied on the forces which could be provided by the dependent kings of the region.

As for the frontier, Zeugma, the main crossing of the Euphrates, seems to have passed from Commagene to Rome immediately after the battle of Actium. That the Euphrates, or rather this section of it, was now conceived of as the symbolic frontier between Rome and Parthia is made clear by Strabo: 'The Euphrates and the land beyond it constitute the boundary of the Parthian empire. But the parts this side of the river are held by the Romans and the chieftains *(phylarchoi)* of the Arabians as far as Babylonia, some of these chieftains preferring to give ear to the Parthians and others to the Romans'.[20] That is to say, where the river traversed the Fertile Crescent there was a clear frontier. But in the wide steppe zone to the south it was a matter of unstable alliances and diplomatic relations. The role of the river as a frontier was in any case clearly symbolised in AD 1, when Augustus' grandson, and adopted son, Gaius, met Phrataces, the king of Parthia, on an island in the Euphrates, watched by their armies on either bank.[21]

In this early period it is impossible to say where the three, and then four, legions of Syria were regularly stationed, or even whether it is right to assume that each had a regular station and was kept together as a strategic unit; or indeed to gain any impression at all of how a legion and the surrounding population interacted in normal times. It is only in AD 18/19 that passing references in Tacitus' narrative reveal the 'winter-quarters' *(hiberna)* of the Xth legion, at the Greek city of Cyrrhus in the broad fertile region in the north of the province, bordering on Commagene, and on the route between Antioch and Zeugma; and also that of the VIth legion at Laodicea on the coast.[22] It is quite likely that a legion will have been there on a regular basis.

20. Strabo, *Geog.* XVI, 1, 28 (748).
21. Velleius II, 101.
22. Tacitus, *Ann.* II, 57, 2; 79, 3.

But that, if accepted, should lead to no presumptions about any more precise relationship between each city and the camp; it is only later, and only at certain specific places (Bostra, Dura-Europos, Palmyra) that we can actually see such a relationship in concrete form.

The stations, or camps, of the other legions in Syria under Augustus and Tiberius are normally given as Antioch for III Gallica and Raphaneae in the Orontes Valley for XII Fulminata.[23] Even if the assumption that they had regular stations is correct, the evidence for this period is very slight. But, to put it simply, there were not many other places where they could have been. The area directly occupied by Rome consisted of the coast and the mountain-ranges behind it as far south as Ptolemais; the hilly but fertile region stretching from the Amanus Mountains across to the Euphrates; and the Orontes Valley as far south as its source in the Bekaa Valley. But even in the Orontes Valley, where the tableland to the east of the river shades off gradually into barren steppe, Roman direct rule was not continuous. For at Emesa (Homs) the local dynasty of Sampsigeramus and Iamblichus, the 'phylarchoi of the tribe *(ethnos)* of the Emiseni', whom we saw in the 40s BC in control also of a small place called Arethusa to the north, persisted through most of the first century AD.[24] In the early years of Tiberius another Sampsigeramus was in power there, for he is named along with Germanicus (hence in AD 18/19) in a Palmyrene inscription from the temple of Bel. Here he seems to be described as 'great king', as he is in retrospect in a Latin inscription (calling him *rex magnus*) put up at Heliopolis to honour his son.[25]

This dynasty, and its forces, will reappear several times; but its relevance here is that its territory, however restricted, must have represented a zone which the Roman forces did not occupy, and where the Roman Empire did not raise taxes. How far this territory stretched to the west we do not know; but to the east it seems to have been very extensive. A boundary-marker inscribed in Latin shows that one point on the boundary between Emesene and Palmyrene territory was Qasr el Hair, 60 km west-south-west from Palmyra, and some 90 km south-east from Emesa.[26]

This boundary-marker is one of several indications that Palmyra itself was also firmly within the Roman sphere of influence. It itself is not dated. But another, found at Khirbet el-Bilaas, 75 km north-west of the city, shows that the 'boundaries of the *regio Palmyrena*' had been established under Creticus

23. So, e.g., J. Wagner, *Die Römer an Euphrat und Tigris* (*Die Antike Welt*, Sondernummer, 1985), 26, an important study to which the whole of this part of the book is greatly indebted.

24. For the dynasty see R. D. Sullivan, "The Dynasty of Emesa", *ANRW* II.8 (1977), 198.

25. J. Cantineau, "Textes palmyréniens provenant de la fouille du temple de Bêl", *Syria* 12 (1931), 116, on p. 139, no. 18, l.6: [ŠM]ŠGRM MLK [HMṢ ML]K' RŠY'. *IGLS* VI, no. 2760 (Heliopolis).

26. *AE* (1939), no. 180.

Silanus, *legatus* of Syria in AD 11–17. The tax-law of AD 137 also quotes a regulation made by Germanicus, evidently when in Syria in AD 18/19; and at the same time, as it seems, a *legatus* of the legion X Fretensis put up a Latin dedication to Tiberius, Drusus and Germanicus, found in the temple of Bel.[27] There is no reason to suppose that Roman troops were regularly stationed there at this early period. But the city probably paid tribute, and should be seen as part of the Empire.

To reach southern Syria or Judaea, as they on occasion did, Roman forces must, as it seems, either have had to march through the territory of the kings of Emesa or have taken the coastal route through Berytus and Tyre to Ptolemais. There is nothing surprising in that in itself. But it does serve to emphasise that it was only in the north that Roman direct control was firmly established. As soon as we look south, to the Mount Lebanon chain, the Bekaa Valley, Anti-Lebanon, Mount Hermon and then the territory to the south of Damascus, a much more complex picture of the interplay of Roman and local forces presents itself.

There is no simple way of representing this interplay, but the best may be to outline its main features area by area, moving southwards. The contrast between the zone of settled Roman control in the valley of the Orontes on the one hand and police or military operations in the mountainous territory on the other is in fact perfectly caught in the famous Latin inscription recording the career of an Augustan military officer named Q. Aemilius Secundus.[28] Under Sulpicius Quirinius as *legatus Caesaris Syriae,* so around AD 6, he had conducted a census in the *civitas Apamena* and recorded 117,000 persons. Leaving aside this crucial datum for the moment, we may note that he also says he had been sent by Quirinius against the Ituraeans of Mount Lebanon and had captured a *castellum* of theirs. Full-scale military operations were therefore still going on in southern Syria in the early years AD, some seventy years after the formation of the province.

A further picture of these Ituraeans of the mountain zone, and their relations with the Bekaa Valley (the Massyas Plain) and the coast, is provided, as always, by Strabo:

> After Macras one comes to the Massyas Plain, which contains also some mountainous parts, among which is Chalcis, the acropolis, as it were, of the Massyas. The beginning of this plain is the Laodiceia near Libanus. Now all the mountainous parts are held by Ituraeans and Arabians, all of whom are robbers, but the people in the plains are farmers; and when the latter are harassed by the robbers at different times they require different

27. For this evidence see H. Seyrig, "L'incorporation de Palmyre à l'empire romain", *Syria* 13 (1932), 266; Starcky and Gawlikowski, *Palmyrez* (1985), 37.
28. *ILS*, no. 2683.

kinds of help. These robbers use strongholds as bases of operation; those, for example, who hold Libanus possess, high up on the mountain, Sinna and Borrama and other fortresses like them, and, down below, Botrys and Gigartus and the caves by the sea and the castle that was erected on Theuprosopon. Pompey destroyed these places; and from them the robbers overran both Byblus and the city that comes next after Byblus, I mean the city Berytus, which lie between Sidon and Theuprosopon.[29]

Later we will come back briefly to this region and to Strabo's idea that the population of Mount Lebanon could be classified as 'Ituraeans and Arabians'.[30] What is clear is that Strabo sees some relationship between raiding from the mountain to the plain and the coast and what he then goes on to record, the foundation of a *colonia* at Berytus, with a territory stretching to the sources of the Orontes in the Bekaa Valley. Here again it will be necessary to return later to the complex consequences of the settlement of the veterans of two legions in this area in 15 BC;[31] this colony, Colonia Iulia Augusta Felix Berytus, not only was the sole colonial settlement in the Near East under Augustus, but represented by far the most profound and long-lasting Roman, or Latin, intrusion into the culture of the region in the entire Roman period.

Strabo moves on from there to record the security situation on the southern side of Anti-Lebanon and Mount Hermon, where lay the ancient city of Damascus:

> The city of Damascus is also a noteworthy city, having been, I might almost say, even the most famous of the cities in that part of the world in the time of the Persian empire; and above it are situated two Trachones, as they are called. And then, towards the parts inhabited promiscuously by the Arabians and Ituraeans, are mountains hard to pass, in which there are deep-mouthed caves, one of which can admit as many as four thousand people in times of incursions, such as are made against the Damasceni from many places. For the most part, indeed, the barbarians have been robbing the merchants from Arabia Felix, but this is less the case now that the band of robbers under Zenodorus has been broken up through the good government established by the Romans and through the security established by the Roman soldiers that are kept in Syria.[32]

It is not quite clear exactly what sub-regions Strabo is referring to, and whether he is distinguishing the slopes of Mount Hermon and Anti-Lebanon from the very distinctive zone which lies south-east of Damascus, and was

29. *Geog.* XVI, 2, 18 (755), Loeb trans.
30. 8.3 below.
31. 8.4 below.
32. Strabo, *Geog.* XVI, 2, 20 (756).

normally called Trachonitis: not a mountain at all, that is, but a plate of broken lava, now known as the Leja, lying on the plain and measuring some 50 km north-south and 30 km east-west. Its very broken terrain made it a natural stronghold, and a base for robbery directed to the surrounding plains of the Damascene territory and the northern Hauran (Auranitis).

Whether Strabo, who speaks in rather general terms here, is right to think of traders from Arabia Felix (the Yemen) coming up by land as far north as this is an important question. Nor is it clear whether he is right to suppose that it had been Roman soldiers who had imposed order in this region. Josephus, in his detailed account of Herod the Great, tells a more complex story. According to him the Zenodorus referred to by Strabo had leased territory in this area from Cleopatra, and had subsequently encouraged the inhabitants of Trachonitis in raids on the territory of Damascus. They had then complained to the *legatus* of Syria, and he had reported to Augustus. Acting on Augustus' instructions, the *legatus,* Varro, 'made an expedition', cleared out the robbers and deposed Zenodorus. As such, this is a perfect example of the episodic use of force by the Romans in the outlying, perhaps indeed geographically separate, part of the province south of the major mountains. The story strongly suggests that no Roman forces at all were permanently stationed in the Damascus region.[33]

The area concerned is described by Josephus as Trachonitis (the lava plate), Auranitis (the Hauran) and Batanea, which borders on the Hauran to the north-west. After the police-action by Varro, it was now, in 23 BC, added to Herod's territory, which already included Galilee and, as we have seen, Hippos and Gadara to the east and south-east of the Sea of Galilee. Three years later, as Josephus records, Augustus paid a visit to Syria, in fact in 20 BC, and is described as granting to Herod Trachonitis (again), Ulatha (the area round Lake Huleh) and Paneas, which had belonged to Zenodorus and lay on the southern slope of Mount Hermon above the Golan Heights.[34] There is no need to pretend that the details of all this are clear. But the total effect was to be very important for the history of the districts immediately to the south of the mountains for more than a century. For they were to remain under the rule of members of the Herodian dynasty almost (though not quite) continuously until the end of the first century AD. Damascus, one of the major cities of the Roman province, was thus bounded by the territory of the dynasty of Emesa to its north on the route along the east side of Anti-Lebanon; by Palmyrene territory to its north-east; and by Herodian royal territory immediately to its south. Only to the west (if at all) does it appear from the story of a boundary-dispute recorded by Josephus that its territories bordered that

---

33. Josephus, *BJ* I, 20, 4 (398–400); *Ant.* XV, 10, 1 (343–348).
34. *BJ* I, 20, 4 (399–400); in much more detail, *Ant.* XV, 10, 3 (354–364).

of another city under Roman direct rule, namely (and very surprisingly) Sidon on the coast.[35] But if so, as a glance at the map will show, this can have been only at some point on Mount Hermon or at the southern end of the Bekaa Valley, between Herodian territory (including Paneas) to the south and the two small tetrarchies of Abila, on the road between Damascus and the Bekaa Valley, and Chalcis, somewhere in the southern half of the valley.[36] In a real sense, therefore, Damascus and its surrounding oasis, fed by water running off the mountains, was an enclave which Rome ruled in principle but where it seems to have intervened only on occasion.

Further south the interplay of power and geography was equally complex. Mention has been made of Auranitis, which Augustus transferred from Zenodorus to Herod. But before this, Zenodorus, according to Josephus, had leased it to 'the Arabs', that is to say, the Nabataean kingdom. The area concerned is the northern Hauran, both the plain (the Nuqra) and the hillcountry or Jebel Hauran, more recently called the Jebel Druse or Jebel Arab. If this area was indeed ever under Nabataean rule, it was thus only for a few years before 23 BC, perhaps 30–23 BC. But from then on it was almost continuously under the Herodian kings. The point has some significance, which we will come to much later. For this region, with its Aramaic inscriptions and major cult-centre at Sia', and the town of Kanatha, has a quite distant history from that of the properly Nabataean area immediately to the south, with the important city of Bostra.[37]

The Nabataean kingdom now stretched as far north as Bostra. At the same time the Herodian kingdom covered Idumaea, Judaea, Samaria, Galilee, and now also Batanea, Auranitis and Trachonitis, as well as a stretch of territory on the east of the Jordan and the Dead Sea, extending as far south as the fortress of Machaerus, and known as Peraea. In 20 BC Augustus also agreed to give this area to Herod's brother Pheroras as a separate tetrarchy.[38]

One consequence of the Roman recognition, and in the Herodian case extension, of these two major kingdoms was to raise the question of the relation to them of the Greek cities of the so-called Decapolis which had grown up in the Hellenistic period. Apart from Scythopolis, in the Plain of Jezreel, all of them lay on the fertile Transjordanian plateau. The question of the urban character of these cities and of their culture and identity as Greek cities will

35. Josephus, *Ant.* XVIII, 6, 3 (153–154).

36. For these tetrarchies see the sketchy details available in Schürer, *HJP* I, App. I.

37. See J. Starcky, "Les inscriptions nabatéennes et l'histoire de la Syrie du Sud et du Nord de la Jordanie", in Dentzer, *Hauran* I.2, 167, and J.-M. Dentzer, "Conclusion: Développement et culture de la Syrie du Sud dans la période préprovinciale (1er s. avant J.-C.–1er s. après J.-C.)", ibid. I.2, 387. See further 11.1 below.

38. Josephus, *BJ* I, 24, 5 (483); *Ant.* XV, 10, 3 (362).

have to be considered later.[39] For the moment it is enough to recall that when Pompey had acquired the area for Rome in the 60s, he had made a deliberate point of liberating all those cities in this area which had been under Jewish rule (following conquests by the Hasmonaeans), and had made them part of the province of Syria.[40] Where the 'boundaries', if indeed that term is applicable, of the Nabataean kingdom, Herod's kingdom and the provincial territory lay at successive stages in the later first century BC is often very obscure, and not all of the problems need be pursued here. For instance, shortly before Actium Herod had fought a battle against the Nabataeans near Philadelphia (Amman). It is quite uncertain whether the city was then under his control, or under Nabataean rule, or was regarded as part of the province of Syria, or was effectively isolated.[41]

Moreover, especially in view of what was to happen after Herod's death, it is important to note that the question of whether a city belonged to one of the kingdoms or to the province arose in acute form already in 20 BC. For at the same moment as other decisions, already mentioned above, were being taken, Josephus gives a highly coloured report of how, when Augustus visited Syria in 20 BC, the people of Gadara made accusations against Herod, alleging above all robbery and destruction of temples, in the hope of gaining liberation from his kingdom and attachment to the province. The scene ended when Augustus' favour to Herod was seen to be unchanged.[42] Gadara and Hippos therefore remained within the kingdom, as did Kanatha in the Hauran. But a number of cities which were normally included in the (fluctuating) list of the cities of the Decapolis—for instance Scythopolis, Pella, Abila, Dium, Adraa, Gerasa and Philadelphia—formed a block of Roman provincial territory entirely surrounded by the two kingdoms. How, and to what extent (if indeed at all), Roman authority was exercised here in the early Imperial period is a mystery. Certainly there is nothing to indicate that any Roman forces were stationed here. The complex political map of this area forms the background to the important changes in the late first and early second century, when both the kingdom of Herod's grandson, Agrippa II, and that of the Nabataeans came under Roman direct rule.

The relative weakness of Roman control in this whole southern area in this period was to be dramatically illustrated in 9 BC, when a war broke out between the two kingdoms. Again we are entirely dependent on the narrative of Josephus, based on a much fuller contemporary narrative by Nicolaus of

---

39. 11.3 below.
40. Schürer, *HJP* I, 240.
41. Josephus, *BJ* I, 19, 5 (380). See further 11.3 below.
42. *Ant.* XV, 10, 3 (354-359).

Damascus, who himself acted as Herod's envoy to defend his actions before Augustus.[43] In brief, the conflict developed as follows: In 12 BC, while Herod had been absent, the Nabataeans had encouraged the inhabitants of Trachonitis, now under Herod's rule, to revert to brigandage, and had given asylum to forty of their 'bandit-chiefs' *(archilēstai)*. Using a base provided for them in Nabataean territory, they raided not only Judaea but 'Coele Syria', which in this case must mean the Decapolis. Herod could and did repress resistance in Trachonitis, but as regards those operating from Nabataean territory, he could only appeal to 'the governors of Caesar, Saturninus and Volumnius'—in fact the consular *legatus,* Cn. Sentius Saturninus, and the *procurator* of the province. No question of Roman military intervention seems to have arisen. They merely decided that the Nabataeans should pay a debt due to Herod, and that refugees on both sides should be restored. Only when this was not done did they give Herod permission to invade Nabataea. After a successful invasion and a minor battle, Herod settled a colony of three thousand Idumaeans to control Trachonitis, and wrote to the Roman officials explaining his actions.

The affair was further complicated by the death of Obodas, the king of Nabataea, and the accession, without Augustus' permission, of Aretas IV; as will be seen later, it seems to have been in his long reign that the major monuments of Petra were built.[44] It is significant for the workings of the Imperial system as it affected dependent kingdoms that all the matters in dispute were decided at a hearing before Augustus in person, at which Nicolaus spoke, accusing Syllaeus, the chief minister of the Nabataean court, of being responsible for all the wrongs done. Augustus, after interrogating Syllaeus, who was present, accepted the defense of Herod, and momentarily thought also of giving him Aretas' whole kingdom. But he was then deterred by news of conflicts between Herod and his sons, accepted gifts sent by Aretas, and confirmed him as king.

These episodes, for which we have what is in effect a contemporary, if of course partial, account, is immensely revealing of what the Roman Empire in the Near East at this period was. All decision-making depended very immediately on representations made to the Emperor in person in Rome, as well as on letters addressed to him. Problems of time and distance, often very important to the role of the Near East within the Empire, do not play any visible part. By contrast the Roman officials in Syria on the one hand depended closely on the Emperor, and on the other relied equally on personal and writ-

---

43. Josephus, *Ant.* XVI, 9, 1–4 (271–299); 9, 8–9 (335–355). There is a brief excerpt of Nicolaus' autobiography, written in the third person, referring to these events, *FGrH* 90, F.136(5). For the episode see G. W. Bowersock, *Roman Arabia* (1983), 50–53.

44. 11.2 below.

ten communications in exercising a rather limited influence on events in the southern region. No Roman forces were involved at any point.

Some similar features are visible after Herod died in the spring of 4 BC, having made a final will in which he named three of his sons as his heirs: Archelaus as king, and Herodes Antipas and Philip as tetrarchs.[45] Antipas was to rule Galilee and Peraea, and Philip was to have Gaulanitis, Trachonitis, Batanea and the city of Paneas. That was in the end how the territories were disposed. But the manner in which the Roman state now operated, both in Rome and in the Near East, again casts a flood of light on what type of system the Empire at this stage was.[46] Again we can depend both directly and indirectly, through Josephus, on a contemporary narrative by Nicolaus; in the modern historiography of the Roman Imperial system at this formative stage the contemporary evidence of Nicolaus has hardly played the role that it should.

Only the broadest lines of the complex events which followed need be mentioned, and many will belong rather to the internal history of the Jewish community.[47] In Judaea itself Archelaus had to call out the entire royal forces before managing to repress a popular revolt, prior to leaving for Rome to argue his claims before Augustus. At Caesarea, before embarking, he encountered both Sabinus, the *procurator* of Syria, who had come to take possession of the royal treasuries, evidently because Herod had left vast sums to Augustus in his will, and also Quinctilius Varus, the *legatus* of Syria, to whom Archelaus had appealed, and who forbade Sabinus to take over the treasuries, and returned to Antioch. The initial Roman intervention was thus very limited. Once Varus had gone, Sabinus, however, disobeyed instructions and took steps to possess himself of the treasuries all the same, as well as writing to Augustus to make charges against Archelaus.

Letters were also sent by Varus to Augustus, to report a general uprising by the Jews. On what seems to have been a second visit, he had brought a legion to Jerusalem, and had left it there to collaborate with the royal forces in repressing the revolt. But letters from Sabinus in Jerusalem reported that the forces there were in danger of complete destruction. Varus' response serves to illustrate both the structure of Roman military resources in the region at this moment and even more clearly their limits. Josephus is quite explicit in saying, as mentioned earlier,[48] that there were only three legions in all in Syria, and that the fact that Varus brought two more with him meant

45. Josephus, *BJ* I, 33, 7 (664); *Ant.* XVII, 8, 1 (188–190).
46. For the available narratives see Nicolaus, *FGrH* 90, F.136(8)-(11); Josephus, *BJ* II, 1–6 (1–100); *Ant.* XVII, 9–11 (206–323).
47. 10.1–2 below.
48. See n.17 above.

that the entire legionary garrison of the province was now operating in Judaea. Along with these two remaining legions he brought four *alae* of cavalry
'and whatever allied forces kings or tetrarchs could provide'. Varus evidently
passed down the coastal route to Ptolemais, the southernmost city on the
coast which was still within the province, where the allied forces were instructed to gather. For as he passed through the *colonia* of Berytus, the inhabitants provided fifteen hundred soldiers. As Isaac has rightly argued,[49] this
does not mean that we should see such a *colonia* as having a long-term military function; it had been founded only eleven years before, with the veterans
of two legions, so at this time it could still produce trained ex-soldiers for
an emergency. This was, however, the only occasion on which the *colonia* is
recorded as having performed this function; its later military role was to be
quite different, as providing a long series of individual soldiers and officers
for the Roman army.[50] Only one of the dependent kings and tetrarchs who
sent troops is named, Aretas IV of Nabataea, who sent a considerable force
of both cavalry and infantry. The revolt was now repressed without difficulty;
but Varus still left one whole legion in Jerusalem, returning again to Antioch.
Though Josephus does not say so, presumably the third legion returned to
Syria when Archelaus came back from Rome, duly confirmed as king by
Augustus.

Not for the last time, an outbreak of Jewish popular resistance had demonstrated just how fragile Roman military control of the Near East still was.
Not for the last time either, the process of restoring control in one region was
aided by allied royal forces from another. A combination of different royal or
popular forces in a common effort against Rome was hardly to be feared—
though, as we will see, a *legatus* of Syria was later, in the 40s AD, to feel alarm
at just such a prospect.[51] Moreover, looking farther ahead, we cannot quite
discount the possibility that the abortive coup d'état of a *legatus* of Syria,
Avidius Cassius, a native of Cyrrhus, in AD 175 had some ethnic or regional
basis;[52] or, more seriously, that the brief empire of Palmyra in the mid-third
century did not draw on some sense of regional or cultural identity.[53]

But if for the moment, and throughout the first century, dependent kings
and tetrarchs could be relied upon to use their forces in support of Rome,
that does not disguise the fact that the *legatus* had had to commit his entire
forces to repress a popular revolt in one region. Had there been simultaneously a threat from Parthia, or even disturbances in Commagene, the military
situation would have been extremely precarious.

49. Isaac, *Limits*, ch. 7.
50. See Millar, "Roman *Coloniae*", 16; and 8.4 below.
51. 2.3 below.
52. 3.4 below.
53. 4.3 and 9.4 below.

The crucial decisions were again taken in Rome, and by the device, characteristic of the very personal rule of the Emperors, of a hearing before Augustus, sitting with his advisers in at least two successive sessions, of which the second was held in public at the new temple of Apollo next to his house on the Palatine.[54] Here again the medium of persuasion was competing speeches by representatives of different parties, among them Nicolaus of Damascus himself, speaking successfully in support of the claims of Archelaus. What is striking and crucial in this particular episode is the number of different interests making conflicting claims: not only Archelaus, Herodes Antipas and Philip, but other unsatisfied relatives, a Jewish embassy of fifty persons asking for *autonomia*, meaning the end of royal rule, and also the Greek cities which had been under Herod. They demanded if possible to be 'under Caesar', that is, to be part of the province, or if not to be under 'the younger brother' (apparently Philip). In his *Autobiography,* giving many details which Josephus omits, Nicolaus describes how he defended Archelaus successfully first against his relatives and then against the Jews. But he advised him not to resist the demands of the Greek cities for freedom nor to oppose his brother.[55] Augustus duly awarded Archelaus half of Herod's kingdom, with the title of ethnarch (promising to make him a king if he showed himself worthy), and made both Philip and Antipas tetrarchs. Nicolaus does not make clear which, or how many, Greek cities had joined in this claim, and a number in fact remained under Herodian rule. But Josephus duly notes (without explaining how or why) that Gadara and Hippos were now attached to Syria (thus joining the provincial enclave of the Decapolis), as was Gaza on the coast. The effect was therefore to produce yet another enclave, with no geographical connection to the rest of the province; and also, as will be seen, to offer an opportunity for the raising of taxes for Rome from the trade which reached Gaza from Arabia Felix.[56] Two small steps had thus been taken towards the extension of Roman direct rule over the whole of the Near East.

2.2. FROM THE DEATH OF HEROD THE GREAT TO THE END OF TIBERIUS' REIGN

Herod's death thus led to a radical reorganisation of the royal territory in the south of the region, with three separate units, one an ethnarchy and two called tetrarchies, replacing the former kingdom. But two other, apparently very minor, changes were perhaps of greater significance in the long run. For

---

54. For hearings before the Emperor, for which Josephus' narratives provide some of the best evidence from the first century, see Millar, *ERW*, passim, and esp. 375ff.

55. Nicolaus' account: *FGrH* 90, F.136 (8)–(11).

56. 3.2 and 13.1 below.

Gadara and Hippos now escaped from Herodian rule and joined the enclave of provincial cities in Transjordan, while Gaza formed another provincial enclave on the coast. The consequence must have been that these places now paid tribute to Rome, and that Roman indirect taxes were collected there. But there is nothing to suggest that any Roman forces were stationed in either region; whether the *legatus* of Syria, or any other official, ever visited them remains uncertain. In spite of the apparent weakness of Roman control here, the changes are still very significant. For they represent the first of a long series of extensions of Roman direct rule in the Near East which were to continue for another three centuries.[1]

A much more decisive change was, however, to occur ten years later, in AD 6, with the deposition of Archelaus and the creation of the province of Judaea. Whether we see this change from the point of view of the structure of the Roman Empire or of its effects on the Jewish community and the Temple, or of the origins of Christianity, its significance can hardly be exaggerated.

It came about in a manner which itself is indicative of the way that the Empire worked, as a personal monarchy of a strikingly primitive type. Provoked by the brutality of the regime, both the Jews and the Samaritans (whatever organisation they may have had) sent embassies to complain to Augustus, who deposed Archelaus and sent him into exile.[2] As so often, a formal hearing before the Emperor, whatever delays or problems of travel it involved, was assumed to be the normal way that a problem could be resolved.

The consequence was not merely that the wide area ruled by Archelaus (Idumaea, Judaea and Samaria) became provincial territory, but that the evidence allows us to follow the installation of a quite new type of province: that is to say, a second-rank province with auxiliary units but no legions, and governed by a *praefectus* of equestrian rank, not by a senator. Other such provinces were formed, but at indeterminate dates, under Augustus and Tiberius. But Judaea, whether or not it was actually the first, is the only one where we can see this new aspect of the Roman Imperial state coming into existence. Moreover the Gospels reflect, if in an erratic way, the royal rule of Herod down to 4 BC, the regime of Archelaus between 4 BC and AD 6, Galilee and Peraea as they were under the tetrarchy of Herodes Antipas, the territory of Philip, and above all Jerusalem under Roman direct rule.

---

1. I am not persuaded by the interesting suggestion of G. W. Bowersock, *Roman Arabia* (1983), 54ff., arguing, on the basis of Strabo XVI, 4, 21 (779), of a gap in coinage of Aretas IV in 10–3 BC and also some reports of Gaius Caesar's activities in the East, that Nabataea was briefly a province in 3 BC–AD 1. For Gaius' possible involvement in Nabataea, see F. E. Romer, "Gaius Caesar's Military Diplomacy in the East", *TAPhA* 109 (1979), 199.

2. Josephus, *BJ* II, 7, 3 (111–113); *Ant.* XVII, 13, 2–3 (342–344). For the Samaritans see 10.1 below.

The structure of that rule may be briefly sketched.[3] The *praefecti* were appointed and dismissed by the Emperor, and stayed in office as long as he chose. It seems clear that from the beginning their normal residence was not Jerusalem itself but the city of Caesarea on the coast, which had been re-founded with that name by Herod. But Roman troops were stationed, prob-ably permanently, in Jerusalem, and used both the fortress called Antonia next to the Temple, which Herod had built, and probably also the palace of Herod in the upper city, the so-called Citadel. To our knowledge, direct garrisoning of a provincial city was very rare in the early Empire. But the explanation in this case is not in doubt, namely the importance of the Temple and the danger of major disorders at the main annual festivals, Passover above all.

To a very remarkable degree the entire structure of the governor's activity was determined by that of the dynasty which he had replaced. It is probable that in Caesarea too these *praefecti* used royal buildings as their headquarters. At any rate Acts reveals a Roman governor of a few decades later using 'the *praitōrion* of Herodes' to detain a prisoner in.[4] More important, it seems that at least some of the auxiliary units under the *praefectus'* command were simply the royal units recruited from Sebaste and Caesarea, the two main cities founded by Herod.[5] This cannot be quite certain, since the direct evi-dence for such a transfer relates to the period after AD 44. But it would fit with all the other evidence.

Perhaps the most striking of the roles inherited by these Roman *praefecti* from Herod and Archelaus was the appointment and dismissal of the High Priests. Thus all the High Priests whom we see in the Gospel narratives were Roman appointees, chosen from within a restricted circle of priestly families, a fact which has a considerable bearing on the politics of the time.[6] Beyond that, the *praefecti* also inherited the role of guarding the high-priestly robes, as Herod and Archelaus had done before them. Josephus' account records a unique element in the history of Roman provincial government:

> After him, when the Romans took over the government, they retained con-trol of the high priest's vestments and kept them in a stone building, where they were under the seal both of the priests and of the custodians of the treasury and where the warden of the guard lighted the lamp day by day. Seven days before each festival the vestments were delivered to the priests

---

3. For full details see Schürer, *HJP* I, 357–382.

4. Acts 23, 35.

5. For Herod's forces see M. H. Gracey, "The Armies of the Judaean Client Kings", in Free-man and Kennedy, *DRBE* II, 311. See now I. Shatzman, *The Armies of the Hasmonaeans and Herod* (1991), esp. 170ff.

6. For the list of these appointees see Schürer, *HJP* II, 230. More fully in 10.2 below.

by the warden. After they had been purified, the high priest wore them; then after the first day of the festival he put them back again in the building where they were laid away before. This was the procedure at the three festivals each year and on the fast day.[7]

The 'three festivals' were Passover, Pentecost and Tabernacles, and 'the fast day,' the Day of Atonement. So far as we know, although individual Roman soldiers can be found observing many local cults throughout the Near East, there is no parallel to this deep official involvement in the annual cycle of festivals of a local community.

If many features of the government of Judaea as a Roman province were thus highly localised, one at least was not: the imposition of the census and the raising of tribute. It is important to stress that the taking of a census of this type, the counting of a provincial population and the assessment of their property for the purpose of the payment of tribute, was not a long-standing feature of Roman government, but an innovation by Augustus. The earliest ever attested is that taken by Augustus in Gaul in 27 BC;[8] in Gaul the imposition of the census was to provoke disturbances and resistance in the course of Augustus' reign.[9] So it did also in Judaea, where religious factors added a more profound motive for resistance. It is not surprising, therefore, that the moment when the census was imposed was long to be remembered. Its most famous reflection is of course in Luke's Gospel: 'It came to pass in those days that an edict went out from Caesar Augustus, that the whole world should be registered'.[10] Given that such a census was an innovation, Luke's allusion to it, though too dramatic in implying that at this moment there was single *edictum* applying to all provinces, is not fundamentally misleading. The use that he makes of it—in order to reconstruct how Jesus, as the promised Messiah, will have been born in Bethlehem—is, however, wholly misleading and unhistorical. For no Roman census was imposed in Galilee, where he represents Jesus' family as living, or could have been. For there was no moment in the lifetime of Jesus when Roman tribute was raised in Galilee, which was part of the tetrarchy of Herodes Antipas.[11] The contrast between Galilee, under the tetrarchy, and Jerusalem, under Roman rule, is vital to any understanding of the Gospels.

7. Josephus, *Ant.* XVII, 4, 3 (93–94).

8. See F. Millar, "State and Subject: The Impact of Monarchy", in F. Millar and E. Segal (eds.), *Caesar Augustus: Seven Aspects* (1984), 37, on p. 43.

9. For the imposition of the census in Gaul, and the resistance which it provoked, see Livy, *Epit.* 134 and Dio LIII, 23, 5 (27 BC); Livy, *Epit.* 139 (12 BC); Tacitus, *Ann.* I, 31, 2 (AD 14).

10. Lk 2, 1.

11. For an exhaustive analysis of all the problems relating to the census and the reference to it in Luke, see Schürer, *HJP* I, 399ff.

Luke, whom some moderns manage to see as a real 'historian', is hardly more successful when he makes Gamaliel, addressing the Sanhedrin in (in our terms) the 30s, allude first to Theudas, a prophet and popular leader who belongs in the 40s, and then to the census: 'After him there arose Judas the Galilean, in the days of the census, and roused up the people behind him. He too was destroyed, and all those who believed in him were scattered'.[12] Here again, though the context is hopelessly confused, certain essentials are preserved: above all the underlying presumption that popular movements would typically be opposed by the ruling group in Jerusalem, and be repressed. So indeed it had been in AD 6, where Josephus' accounts, scattered at various points in his two major works, provide a glimpse of a classic rural resistance-movement, directed as much or more against collaborators as against the occupying power.

Josephus' narratives make clear that at this moment of renewed crisis the *legatus* of Syria, now Sulpicius Quirinius, again marched south to intervene in person, accompanied by Coponius, who was to be the first *praefectus*. When the census was imposed, the Jewish authorities urged compliance, but Judas 'the Galilean' (or 'Gaulanite') and a pharisee named Saddok argued that submission was a form of slavery, and that Heaven would assist the fight for freedom.[13] This is not the place for an analysis of what Josephus calls the 'fourth philosophy', which saw political freedom as a religious duty, or of his claim that there was a sequence of events leading from this moment to sacrilegious internal strife, to the loss of divine favour and to the destruction of the Temple. It is more important, while analysing what Empire meant in the Near East, to turn to a passage later in the *Jewish War* where he makes a direct link between the Sicarii who occupied Masada during the great revolt and the resistance in AD 6, as well as giving a more concrete picture than elsewhere of what resistance had meant in terms of internal conflict:

> This fortress was called Masada; and the Sicarii who had occupied it had at their head a man of influence named Eleazar. He was a descendant of the Judas who, as we have previously stated, induced multitudes of Jews to refuse to enrol themselves, when Quirinius was sent as censor to Judaea. For in those days the Sicarii clubbed together against those who consented to submit to Rome and in every way treated them as enemies, plundering their property, rounding up their cattle, and setting fire to their habitations; protesting that such persons were no other than aliens, who so ignobly sacrificed the hard-won liberty of the Jews and admitted their preference for the Roman yoke.[14]

12. Acts 5, 37. For the real Theudas, as recorded by Josephus, see *Ant.* XX, 5, 1 (97–99).
13. *Ant.* XVIII, 1, 1 (1–10); less fully in *BJ* II, 8, 1 (117).
14. *BJ* VII, 8, 1 (252–255), Loeb trans.

Nothing is said by Josephus about either the arrival of Roman forces from Syria or the role of the royal forces, which (as it seems) passed directly under the control of the new *praefectus*. All that is said otherwise of Quirinius' actions while in Jerusalem is that he sold off the property of Archelaus, and, because the High Priest Joazar had been opposed by the people, dismissed him and appointed Ananus (or Annas) instead.[15] This man was to remain in office for some ten years, and only three brief tenures separated his period from the long occupation by Joseph Caiaphas, who John's Gospel (alone) says was his son-in-law; and John's Gospel is also alone in recording that Jesus when arrested was taken first to the house of Annas and then to that of his son-in-law Caiaphas, the High Priest then in office.[16]

By contrast with the events of 4 BC, the disturbances of AD 6 seem to have represented a more profound and ultimately insoluble problem for Rome. The census was evidently completed, however, and tribute began to be paid. The facts that this new structure came into being, that the two aspects of it were closely connected in the popular imagination, and that the tribute was thought of as a payment 'to Caesar' are all reflected in the different versions of a dialogue between Jesus and some Pharisees and 'Herodians', which all three Synoptic Gospels correctly set in Jerusalem.[17] The point of the dialogue, as need not be argued, is that it was impossible to give a straight answer to the question of whether 'the census' should be paid or not. For to say that it should would be to risk losing the role of a popular religious leader; and to say that it should not would expose one to accusations of inciting revolt (a charge which Luke's Gospel, though not the others, claims was actually brought when Jesus appeared before Pilate).[18]

It had apparently been mere accident that accusations against Archelaus had led to the provincialisation of Judaea at the time when, as we saw, Quirinius was conducting a census in the existing province of Syria.[19] That the impact of taxation was felt in both provinces is attested by a passing allusion in Tacitus under the year AD 17: 'the provinces of Syria and Judaea, exhausted by impositions, petitioned for a reduction of tribute'.[20] Somewhat typically, Tacitus fails to say how, or by whom or to whom the petition was presented, or even whether it was accepted or rejected.

Given that our evidence largely consists of later narratives, we cannot ex-

---

15. *Ant.* XVIII, 2, 1 (26).

16. Jn 18, 12–28. For the importance of this narrative, and arguments to suggest that it should be preferred to those of the Synoptics, see F. Millar, "Reflections on the Trials of Jesus", in P. R. Davies and R. T. White (eds.), *A Tribute to Geza Vermes* (1990), 355.

17. Mk 12, 13–17; Mtt 22, 16–22; Lk 20, 20–26 (not identifying the interlocutors).

18. Lk 23, 2: τοῦτον εὕρομεν διαστρέφοντα τὸ ἔθνος ἡμῶν, καὶ κωλύοντα Καίσαρι φόρους διδόναι . . .

19. 2.1 above.

20. Tacitus, *Ann.* II, 42, 7.

pect to form a real conception of how the direct taxation of Syria and Judaea really worked; or, looking at it from outside, how it fitted into the wider framework of the Empire. As regards the impact on individuals, the second century provides far better evidence, including extremely important new papyri reflecting the first few decades of the province of Arabia, formed in AD 106.[21] So that aspect may be left aside until later. But the whole problem of the extraction of value from a subject population, its deployment within the region in which it was levied as taxation, or its possible export either to Rome or elsewhere in the Empire, presents fundamental difficulties which need to be faced.[22]

First, was Roman tribute raised predominantly in coin or in kind? If in kind (as was certainly the case at least in part, as the archive from the early years of the province of Arabia will show), how did the Romans use what was paid over? The possibilities are: delivering it to the units garrisoning the province for immediate consumption; accepting cash in lieu; or exporting it to Rome or elsewhere. So far as can be determined, there is precisely no evidence even to illustrate any of these possibilities.

If, however, we think of the global 'profit' gained by Rome from the provinces of the Near East, perhaps predominantly in coin, a serious problem arises. Were these provinces in fact profitable? The issue presents itself because the predominant current model of how the Empire worked as a financial system suggests that a surplus of tribute was raised in certain rich and lightly garrisoned provinces; the province of 'Asia' (western Turkey), where there were no legions and only a few auxiliaries, would be a prime example. This surplus was then continuously transferred, in cash (for we know of no system which could have effected paper transfers), to Rome and to the more heavily garrisoned provinces. On the guess that some 10 percent of the overall product of the Empire was taken in taxation, these movements of tribute cash will have been sufficient to have had a marked effect on the economy of the Empire, producing a relatively integrated system in which inflows of tribute were matched by outflows of cash in private trade.[23] Whether the effects of

---

21. 3.2 below.

22. For recent discussions of these complex questions, for which the evidence is wholly inadequate, see P. A. Brunt, *Roman Imperial Themes* (1990), ch. 15 and addenda, revising "The Revenues of Rome", *JRS* 71 (1981), 161; and R. Duncan-Jones, *Structure and Scale in the Roman Economy* (1990), ch. 12, "Taxation in Money and Taxation in Kind". The pattern of minting, in both silver and bronze, mainly with Greek legends, but some Latin, in Antioch in the first century of the Empire is extremely complex, and I have been unable to draw from it any clear conclusions as to the financial system of the province. See now the essential work of A. Burnett, M. Amandry, and P. P. Ripollès, *Roman Provincial Coinage* I.1–2 (1992); on Antioch, pp. 606ff.

23. For this model see K. Hopkins, "Taxes and Trade in the Roman Empire", *JRS* 70 (1980), 126. The more sophisticated discussion by R. W. Goldsmith, "An Estimate of the Size and Structure of the National Product of the Early Roman Empire", *Review of Income and Wealth* 30 (1984), 263, would suggest a 'national product' which was considerably larger, but a share taken

the circulation of tribute were so immediate and significant within the overall economy can be, and has been, questioned.[24] But two major problems arise on any interpretation of the system. First, if large quantities of coin arising from tribute were regularly moved out of these (or any other) regions of the Empire, how was this done? Silver (the Roman *denarius*) is the most likely medium. We should not underestimate the purely physical problems involved. On a purely schematic calculation, the entire tribute of the Empire, if moved at one moment in silver, would have required over 1600 heavy waggons and over 6000 draught animals. If we suppose, simply for the sake of argument, that in the first century AD the two Near Eastern provinces of Syria and Judaea provided 10 percent of the tribute revenue of the Empire, that would have meant, if it were all exported elsewhere, the use of a total of over 160 waggons and over 600 animals.[25]

But of course it was not all exported. On the contrary, the Near East always remained a heavily garrisoned area, and the proportion of the Roman army which was required for it steadily increased. On the model proposed above, it cannot even be quite certain *a priori* that it was not a net tribute-importing region. It is not an impossible notion that the Roman Empire expended more there than it raised in revenue. In the only survey of the provinces and (in outline) their 'profitability' which we have, that by Appian in the preface to his *Roman History,* the idea that Britain cost more than it contributed is clearly expressed.[26]

Although no figures on which we can rely are available, some relevant statements are made by our sources and at least deserve mention; and some schematic calculations can be made which can serve to create a framework within which we can pose questions. The revenue of the Empire under Augustus, for example, has been calculated at roughly 112 million silver *denarii.*[27] The model discussed above would give a rather higher estimate for the period with which we are concerned at this moment, the early first century AD, namely something over 200 million *denarii.*[28] That is quite sufficient to put some figures which Josephus gives us for Judaea and its surrounding regions into some sort of perspective.[29] According to these figures Herod's king-

---

by Imperial taxation which was considerably smaller, producing a more or less comparable (hypothetical) tax-revenue.

24. See Duncan-Jones, op. cit. (n.22), ch. 2, "Trade, Taxes and Money".

25. See F. Millar, "Les congiaires à Rome et la monnaie", in A. Giovannini (ed.), *Nourrir la plèbe, actes du colloque tenu à Genève . . . en hommage à D. van Berchem* (1991), 143.

26. Appian, *Hist. Rom., praef. 7.*

27. Tenney Frank, *Economic Survey of the Roman Empire* V (1940), 7 (450 million *sesterces*).

28. Hopkins, op. cit. (n.23), 119.

29. See E. Gabba, "Le finanze del re Erode", *Clio* 15 (1979), 6; idem, "The Finances of King Herod", in A. Kasher, U. Rappaport, and G. Fuks (eds.), *Greece and Rome in Eretz Israel: Col-*

dom at its fullest extent had provided the king with a revenue equivalent to 5.4 million *denarii per annum* (plus whatever had earlier been paid by Ga-dara, Hippos and Gaza). For the revenues of the ethnarchy of Archelaus and the tetrarchies of Antipas and Philip, at the moment when they received them in 4 BC, were the equivalent of 3.6 million, 1.2 million and 600,000 *denarii* respectively.[30] There is no self-evident way of knowing whether the Roman state would expect, or achieve, a higher or lower revenue from a given area than a dynast ruling the same region. But some increase of revenue is apparent. When, as we will see, all of Herod's kingdom was briefly re-unified under his grandson, Agrippa I, in AD 41–44, his total revenues are given as 12 million *drachmai*, or *denarii*.[31]

That re-unification is itself an example of the flexibility between direct rule and dynastic rule visible during the first century, and there is no doubt that such changes in either direction did have effects on the taxation of the population. We can see this in Josephus' brief but extremely revealing account of the taxation-history of a colony of Babylonian Jews whom Herod settled at a place called Bathyra in Batanaea, on the edge of Trachonitis. The colony was led by a Jew called Zamaris, and was designed to improve security in the area:

> And so his land became very populous because of its immunity from all taxation—a state of things which lasted so long as Herod lived. But when his son Philip succeeded to the kingship, he subjected them to taxation, though it was not much and only for a short time. Agrippa the Great, however, and his son of the same name did indeed grind them down and yet were unwilling to take their freedom away. And the Romans, who have succeeded these kings as rulers, also preserved their status as free men but by the imposition of tribute have completely crushed them.[32]

The story covers approximately a century, and anticipates events to which we will come, the rule of Agrippa I and then his son Agrippa II, and the final provincialisation of his territory, which preceded by a few years the provincialisation of Nabataea to the south, and is highly relevant to it.[33] But it also manages to omit two brief interludes of Roman direct rule: after the death of

---

lected Essays (1990), 160; cf. A. Gara, "Il mondo greco-orientale", in M. H. Crawford (ed.), *L'impero romano e le strutture economiche e sociali delle province* (*Biblioteca di Athenaeum* 4, 1986), 87, on p. 91.

30. Josephus, *Ant.* XVII, 11, 4 (318–320). The figures are given in talents (600, 200, and 100). At 6000 *drachmai* = *denarii* to the talent, these revenues come out therefore at a total of 5.4 million.

31. Josephus, *Ant.* XIX, 8, 2 (352).

32. *Ant.* XVII, 2, 2 (27–28), Loeb trans.

33. 3.2 below.

Philip in AD 33/34 his territory had been made part of Syria before being given to Agrippa I in AD 37; and after the latter's death in AD 44 Batanaea and Trachonitis were not given to Agrippa II until AD 53.[34] On the first of these occasions, however, the attachment to the province of Syria seems to have been regarded as temporary; for Josephus records, somewhat enigmatically, that Tiberius 'ordered, however, that the tributes which were collected in his (Philip's) former tetrarchy should be stored up'.[35] There seems to be a clear implication both that these revenues would otherwise have been shipped out elsewhere and that a rough equivalence between Roman and dynastic tribute revenues could be assumed. We can indeed see this balance being taken into account in Rome in AD 17, when King Archelaus of Cappadocia was accused in Rome and committed suicide, and his kingdom was made a *provincia;* Tiberius explained, evidently addressing the Senate, that its revenues would allow the 100th-part sales tax levied elsewhere to be reduced to a 200th-part one.[36] Cappadocia was a large area, which in the event had only an auxiliary garrison, so a net surplus could be expected; even so, the level of taxation was somewhat reduced, to make Roman direct rule more acceptable to the population.[37]

If we may take the attested royal or dynastic revenues as roughly equivalent to what might be expected from Roman taxation, some meaning can be given to the available figures. The cost of whole legions is very difficult to calculate, because we cannot construct an adequate model of the pay of the pyramid of ranks between ordinary footsoldiers and centurions. But we know that in this period the ordinary soldier received 225 *denarii* per year. So 12 million *denarii* would have provided pay for something over fifty thousand Roman common soldiers, that is, those of some ten legions.[38] Thus whatever calculations we make about other expenses, or the pay of higher ranks (and, later at least, *procuratores* would receive between 15,000 and 50,000 *denarii* a year, and a consular *legatus* presumably something like a proconsul, namely 250,000 *denarii*), the total revenues of the Syrian region should have meant that the area was at least self-supporting in terms of Imperial finance.

But, as has already been indicated, the region continued through most of the first century to be subject to considerable fluctuations between Roman and dynastic rule. One important instance concerned Commagene, whose king Antiochus III died in AD 17; Tacitus notes briefly that Commagene, like Cilicia, whose king had also died, was in turmoil 'because most preferred

34. Text to n.45; and 2.3 below.
35. *Ant.* XVIII, 4, 6 (108).
36. Tacitus, *Ann.* II, 42, 4.
37. Tacitus, *Ann.* II, 56, 4.
38. For some useful calculations see R. MacMullen, "The Roman Emperors' Army Costs", *Latomus* 43 (1984), 571.

Roman, but others royal rule'. As he notes a little later, Commagene was in fact provincialised, though this time he says nothing of the financial aspect. But a contemporary, the geographer Strabo, making what must have been one of the last additions to his work, attaches to his description of this small but fertile country, with its fortified royal capital, Samosata, the note 'but now it has become a province'.[39] As such, it too seems to have come under the *legatus* of Syria, but only for some twenty years. For in AD 38 Gaius restored the throne to Antiochus' son, Antiochus IV, who was to rule until the early 70s. With that period, as will be seen, we enter a quite new phase, when in four and a half decades all the dependent kingdoms west of the Euphrates were successively swept away.

For the moment we are still in a phase when kings played a very significant part in the Near East, in terms of territories and populations ruled, or of armies supplied; and also in terms of the context in which the higher Roman officials operating in this area functioned. The highest of all these officials was Germanicus, the nephew and adopted son of Tiberius, who in AD 17–19 was invested with the rank of *proconsul* and sent to take charge of all the eastern provinces. The formal record of his role embodied in the decrees passed by the Senate after his death in AD 19 in Antioch clearly expresses the combination of provinces and kingdoms which made up the Roman Empire in this area: 'sent as proconsul to the provinces across the sea with the function of putting them and the kingdoms of that region *(tractus)* in order, in accordance with the *mandata* of Tiberius Caesar Augustus'.[40] His mission embraced also regions other than the Near East as defined here. But the narrative of his actions there captures many features of the structure of the area at this moment. Coming back from Armenia in AD 18, he met Calpurnius Piso, the *legatus* of Syria, and a personal enemy, at Cyrrhus, 'the winter quarters of the Xth legion'. It was perhaps there also that 'the king of the Nabataei' (Aretas IV), who had evidently travelled north to pay his respects, gave a dinner to both, and caused further offence by offering heavy gold crowns to Germanicus and his wife Agrippina, and lighter ones to Piso and the other guests.[41] Meanwhile ambassadors from Artabanus of Parthia arrived to confirm the current friendship of the two empires, and offered Germanicus the honour that the king should meet him at the Euphrates.[42] After a visit to Egypt Germanicus returned to Antioch, the chief city of Syria, fell ill, and temporarily recovered. When prayers were offered by the city for his recovery,

---

39. Tacitus, *Ann.* II, 42, 7; 56, 2. Strabo, *Geog.* XVI, 2, 3 (749).

40. *AE* (1984), no. 508, Fr. I (the *Tabula Siarensis*). See now W. Lebek, "Der Proconsulat des Germanicus und die Auctoritas des Senats: Tab. Siar. Frg. I, 22–24", *ZPE* 87 (1991), 103.

41. Tacitus, *Ann.* II, 57.

42. *Ann.* II, 58; on the Euphrates as the symbolic frontier, 2.1 above.

Piso's lictors broke up the ceremony, with its sacrificial animals, the attendants and the crowd in festal clothing. The scene is a small reminder that the primary context of the activity of Roman officials in the East was that of the communal life of the Greek cities. Piso then left Syria, embarking from Seleucia Pieria on the coast, another of the major foundations of Seleucus I, and due later to play an important part in the structure of the Empire in the Near East.[43]

When Germanicus died, whether by poison or otherwise, his body lay in state in the forum (or rather *agora*) of Antioch before being cremated, while Piso, hearing the news, turned back to regain control of Syria, collecting some irregular forces from deserters (apparently from the Syrian legions), camp-followers *(lixae)* and a detachment of legionary recruits on the way to Syria, and also writing to the minor dynasts of Cilicia to supply forces. One of his friends landed at Laodicea, another of Seleucus' major foundations, and tried to reach the quarters of the VIth legion, which were evidently located there.[44]

The minor civil war which followed in Cilicia need not be described here. It is more important to stress the complexity of the relations which this odd episode revealed, between the Imperial house, which was later to be more and more frequently represented in this region, the Roman officials of the province, the legions, the population of Antioch and the kings. The casual reference to deserters from the legions who could be found and collected together on the coast of Asia Minor is also striking.

The role of the kings was to become temporarily more important in the following years, above all during the reign of Germanicus' son Gaius (Caligula) in 37–41. In 33/34, it is true, the tetrarch Philip had died, and his territory was provisionally added to Syria.[45] Also in the 30s, Herodes Antipas became involved in complex dynastic and border conflicts with Aretas IV of Nabataea, which resulted in a regular war, fought without Roman knowledge or permission, in which Antipas was defeated. Rome became involved only when Herodes wrote to Tiberius (now on his notorious retreat in Capri), and he sent instructions to Lucius Vitellius, the *legatus* of Syria, to intervene by force against Aretas.[46]

This intervention was all the more significant in that in these years the primary Roman concern was relations with Parthia. Lucius Vitellius, the father of the future Emperor, had been sent as *legatus* in AD 35, with a mission to support a pretender to the Parthian throne, Tiridates. He therefore marched with a force of legions and auxiliaries 'to the bank of the Euphrates',

43. *Ann.* II, 69; on Seleucia Pieria see 3.1 below.
44. *Ann.* II, 78–79.
45. Text to n.34 above.
46. Josephus, *Ant.* XVIII, 5, 1 (109–115).

presumably at Zeugma. A bridge of boats was made, and the Roman army crossed the river, to be joined by Ornospades, the Parthian commander of Mesopotamia (who had earlier gained the Roman citizenship for military service with Tiberius), and two local dynasts, Sinnaces and Abdagaeses. The later Roman involvement in Mesopotamia was thus clearly foreshadowed. But at this period the Euphrates still functioned as a frontier, and the Roman army crossed back into Syria. Tiridates, however, advancing further in 36, enjoyed some success, winning over the Greek cities of Nicephorium on the Euphrates, Anthemusia in Mesopotamia and even Seleucia on the Tigris. But before long he was driven out. This brief episode is still significant as a sign of the surviving Greek influence in the Parthian Empire, and as a foretaste of later Roman ambitions.[47]

In 36, however, Vitellius was occupied elsewhere. For in that year, following complaints by the Samaritans, he deposed the long-standing *praefectus* of Judaea, Pontius Pilatus, and sent him to Rome to stand trial. On this occasion Vitellius in fact came to Jerusalem in person; while there he remitted taxes, deposed a High Priest, Joseph Caiaphas, and appointed Jonathan son of Ananus instead. But, much more important, he made the diplomatic concession of restoring to Jewish control the custody of the high-priestly robes, which the *praefecti* had retained since the formation of the province.[48] If we follow the account which Josephus gives elsewhere of the same visit, he made the concession only after writing to Tiberius to ask permission.[49]

It was in the spring of 37 that Vitellius was forced, as mentioned above, to intervene in the southern region again, in order to take military action against Aretas IV. These measures involved approximately half the Roman forces in Syria, two legions accompanied by infantry and cavalry auxiliaries. As was evidently normal, they took the coastal route southwards to Ptolemais, and would apparently have marched through Judaea but for entreaties saying that images carried there would be a religious offence. So the army marched through the Plain of Jezreel, intending to cross over to the Transjordanian plateau. Meanwhile Vitellius made a visit to Jerusalem to take part in a festival, which must have been Passover. For while he was there, news came of the death of Tiberius on March 16, AD 37. On receiving this news, he abandoned the campaign and returned to Antioch. The intention to use force against Aretas was simply dropped.[50]

Many different items of evidence from around these years tend to suggest how comparatively tenuous and uncertain Roman control of the southern

47. For L. Vitellius and Tiridates see Tacitus, *Ann.* VI, 32–37; 41–44.

48. Josephus, *Ant.* XVIII, 4, 1–3 (85–95).

49. *Ant.* XV, 11, 4 (404–405).

50. *Ant.* XVIII, 5, 3 (120–125).

region was, and how much it depended on diplomacy and on the erratic effects of personal presence. It should of course be stressed that the only continuous narratives are provided by Josephus, and therefore tend to highlight this
area; we have no comparable view of power-relations in northern Syria. But,
as regards the southern area, it is worth noting that Herodes Antipas left his
tetrarchy to accompany Vitellius to Jerusalem, an aspect of the diplomatic
relations between dynasts and governors which we can see repeated many
times. While in Jerusalem, Vitellius again assumed the powers normally exercised by the *praefectus,* greatly his inferior in rank, deposing one High Priest
and appointing another.

This time it was Jonathan son of Ananus who was deposed in his turn as
High Priest, after only a year, to be replaced by his brother Theophilos.[51] With
that name we reach a moment when some very different strands in our
complex and erratic web of evidence intersect. For this High Priest, with his
Greek name transliterated, appears on the newly published Hebrew ossuary-
inscription of his granddaughter: TPLOS HKHN HGDL, 'Theophilos the
High Priest'.[52] His successor, however, was to be appointed by a Jewish king,
one sign of the very rapid changes in the shape of the Roman Near East over
the next few years.

2.3. FROM THE REIGN OF GAIUS TO THE OUTBREAK
OF THE JEWISH WAR

The accession of Gaius in March AD 37 began a series of changes in the structure of Roman rule in the Near East which were to have important effects
over the following decades. In essence this period represents the last flowering
of the system of dependence on kings and dynasts, before its rapid repression
towards the end of the century.

In the south the interplay of events and personalities again illustrates the
unstable and vacillatory nature of Roman control in this period. In the later
30s the regions in southern Syria previously ruled by the tetrarch Philip were,
as we saw, provisionally attached to the province. In the spring of 37, the
Roman army dispatched to repress Aretas IV of Nabataea went back to Syria
on hearing of the death of Tiberius. As before, there is nothing whatever to
suggest that any Roman forces were present in the Decapolis, in the former
territories of Philip, or even in Damascus. It may even be that in this period
of flux, towards the end of Aretas' long reign, the Nabataeans gained some
measure of control in Damascus. There must at least have been some degree

51. *Ant.* XVIII, 5, 3 (123).

52. D. Barag and D. Flusser, "The Ossuary of Yehoḥanah, Granddaughter of the High Priest
Theophilos", *IEJ* 36 (1986), 39. See further 10.2 below.

of power vacuum there. For unless we reject the entire narrative of Acts and its account of the conversion of Paul, we have to accept the surprising information that a High Priest (we do not know which) in Jerusalem could send an emissary to Damascus, a city in the Roman province of Syria, to arrest Jewish converts to Christianity and bring them back to Jerusalem.[1] But while Paul was there the danger in which he found himself came not from any representatives of the Roman state or even from the city magistrates, but (in the story as told by Acts) from the Jewish community there, after his own conversion, and on his own account from 'the ethnarch of Aretas the king'.[2] If that means that Damascus was now actually under Nabataean control, the unnamed ethnarch must have been in a position something like that of Pheroras, when he was made ethnarch of Peraea in 20 BC, while his brother Herod was king of Judaea.[3]

But in fact there is no information on either the formal or the actual circumstances of Damascus in these years, and for that matter we cannot tell what year is referred to, except that it cannot be later than AD 40, when Aretas died, to be succeeded by his son Malichus II. His rule in Nabataea, and that of his son Rabbel II, in AD 70–106, was to provide one element of continuity, hardly matched elsewhere in the region.

Early in his reign Gaius reversed the temporary attachment of Trachonitis and its neighbouring regions to the province of Syria, and gave them, in principle, to a grandson of Herod, Agrippa I, who had gained his favour in the last years of Tiberius. Along with that went the little-known 'tetrarchy of Lysanias', located on Anti-Lebanon, straddling the road between Damascus and the Bekaa Valley.[4] As there was a common boundary between the territory of Damascus and that of Sidon on the coast,[5] it seems clear that Agrippa's new domains represented two geographically separate areas. In any case it was not until the autumn of the year 38 that he came back from Rome to begin his rule. As he passed through Alexandria on his way, the sight of his bodyguard, with their armour inlaid in gold and silver, is said by Philo, a contemporary witness, to have aroused the resentment both of the city mob and of the prefect of Egypt, Avillius Flaccus.[6] This view of the relations of king and prefect is not a triviality, for such questions of prestige, precedence

1. Acts 9, 1–25; 22, 3–16; 26, 12–20.

2. 2 Cor 11, 32.

3. 2.1 above. *RPC* I, 663, accepts the view that the gap in the dated coinage of Damascus between AD 33/34 and 65/66 reflects Nabataean domination, a theory which remains to be proved.

4. Josephus, *Ant.* XVIII, 6, 10 (237). For the fragmentary information available on this tetrarchy, referred to by Lk 3, 1, see Schürer, *HJP* I, 569–571.

5. 2.1 above.

6. Philo, *Flacc.* 5/29–35.

and diplomacy were integral to the unstable relations between Roman governors and local dynasts.

The same point can be illustrated by contemporary events elsewhere in the region. At the beginning of Gaius' reign Herodes Antipas was still ruling Galilee and Peraea as tetrarch, and it seems to have been under Gaius, in AD 37 or 38, that he took care to be present at a meeting between Vitellius and Artabanus of Parthia, who had just driven out the Roman-backed pretender Tiridates. As on earlier occasions, the meeting took place on the Euphrates, evidently at Zeugma, and both sides were feasted by Herodes in a tent erected on the bridge itself. According to Josephus, he also sent news of these events to the Emperor, forestalling the messengers sent by Vitellius.[7]

But personal conflicts and jealousies affected the dynasts as well as Roman officials. According to an elaborate story in Josephus, Herodes Antipas was urged by his wife Herodias, Agrippa's sister, to go to Italy to petition Gaius for the status of king, to equal his brother-in-law. But while he was there, letters came to Gaius from Agrippa alleging, among other things, that Herodes was in league with Artabanus of Parthia and had weapons in store sufficient for seventy thousand men. Herodes was unable to deny this, and was exiled. His tetrarchy was added to the area ruled by Agrippa.[8] The figure of seventy thousand may seem fantastic but is consistent with the level of forces which Josephus claims (at one point) that he later raised in Galilee in the Jewish revolt.[9] It deserves some stress; the Romans were attempting, with a degree of success, to control a densely populated area at arm's length, from their base in northern Syria, the fertile region between the Mediterranean and the Euphrates settled in the early Hellenistic period—and still, after a whole century, the same area which they had occupied in the 60s of the first century BC.

How difficult that control might be was graphically illustrated in AD 39/40, when major disturbances were created in Judaea itself, at this time still under direct rule. A conflict in Jamnia between the Jewish inhabitants and some gentile ones who provoked them by setting up an altar to the Emperor led to Gaius' order (in itself entirely untypical of Roman attitudes) that a statue of himself should be set up in the Holy of Holies. The order went to the *legatus* of Syria, who was once again to take half his legionary force, that is, two legions, and march south. Both in the early summer of AD 40 at Ptolemais (the normal point of entry) and again in the autumn at Tiberias, the city founded by Herodes Antipas in Galilee, he was confronted by vast, non-

7. Josephus, *Ant.* XVIII, 4, 5 (101–105). Josephus believed that these events took place under Tiberius. For the (probable) chronology see Schürer, *HJP* I, 351.

8. *Ant.* XVIII, 7, 1–2 (240–254).

9. 2.4 below.

violent demonstrations by the Jewish population. In the end Petronius, having bought as much time as possible, openly asked Gaius by letter to revoke the order. The reply to that is recorded to have been a letter ordering him to commit suicide; but it was overtaken en route by another in which Gaius agreed to abandon the plan, having been persuaded by Agrippa I, already back in Rome at court. In any case the murder of Gaius on January 24, AD 41, brought this whole episode to an end.[10]

The richly coloured narratives of Philo and Josephus on which we depend for these events do nonetheless serve to illustrate further the indirectness of Roman control. Not only did any significant effort to exert force in the southern region entail marching a large proportion of the legionary garrison of Syria down the coast to Ptolemais and beyond, but all decisions ultimately depended on the Emperor in Rome, who could be reached only by letter. The three months it took Gaius' letter ordering his suicide to reach Petronius were indeed exceptional. But abundant evidence shows how communications depended on the unreliable sea-route which functioned counter-clockwise from Rome to Alexandria and then up the Phoenician coast; it then went westwards along the coast of Asia Minor for the return journey to southern Italy. The effective integration of the Near East into the Empire was not going in the end to depend on this sea-route, but first on land-communications across Asia Minor and second on an ever more frequent direct Imperial presence.

For the moment, however, the tendency was the opposite, a swing back to indirect control through kings. In 37 Gaius restored the son of Antiochus III to the throne of Commagene: a Roman citizen, like the Herodians, he had as his full name Gaius Iulius Antiochus Epiphanes. The territory he received included also a large part of Cilicia, and Suetonius claims that he was also given back reserves of 100 million *sesterces*, or 25 million *denarii,* accumulated since the death of his father in AD 17. While we can hardly take these figures literally, they suggest on the face of it that Commagene produced a tax-revenue of something over one million *denarii* per year. Antiochus IV seems to have been deposed again by Gaius, only to be restored finally by Claudius on his accession in AD 41.[11] The kingdom was to play an important role until its destruction in AD 72.

The successive phases of royal rule in Judaea and southern Syria were even more complex. As soon as Claudius came to the throne, he rewarded Agrippa I, who had been in Rome and had helped in the dramatic and complex process of his accession, by giving him Judaea and Samaria, thus not only restoring the whole kingdom as it had been under Herod the Great, but giving up an established Roman province which had had its own governor. Indeed, since

---

10. For the details, and the chronology followed here, see Schürer, *HJP* I, 394–398.
11. For the details see *PIR2* I, 149.

the tetrarchy of Lysanias was included, the boundaries of Agrippa's kingdom were wider, including some (quite undefinable) territory on or around Anti-Lebanon. As a significant element in the structure of the Roman Empire in the Near East, it presents a few well-known but crucial features, which need to be put in context here.

First, the armed forces of the kingdom continue (as it seems) to illustrate the remarkable ease of the transference, in either direction, between Roman and dynastic rule. As we have seen, it is only a very probable inference that the units recruited from Sebaste and Caesarea had passed into Roman service on the deposition of Archelaus in AD 6.[12] But it is beyond question that such units were found in Agrippa's army in AD 41–44, and that they passed into Roman service on the king's death. Josephus describes vividly how the people of Sebaste and Caesarea rejoiced at the king's death, and how Claudius had intended to punish the cavalry *ala* and the five infantry *cohortes* recruited from these cities by transferring them to Pontus, replacing them from the units (presumably auxiliary units) stationed in Syria. But they (the units or the cities?) sent an embassy to Claudius and obtained the cancellation of the transfer. Thus, Josephus claims, they were able to contribute to the conflicts leading up to the Jewish revolt, and the transfer took place only under Vespasian.[13]

Second, various aspects of the reign serve to illustrate how such kings could still attempt to operate an independent foreign policy. At a local level we find the king, as represented in the one chapter of Acts where he appears, receiving embassies from the Tyrians and Sidonians, who have incurred his anger, and who beseech his favour because they depend economically on the royal territory.[14] A glance at the map will show that indeed a large part of the hinterland of both cities was under his rule. Whatever the nature of the dispute, it is striking that it is conducted with no reference to the (normally distant) *legatus* of Syria.

The *legatus* in fact still intervened in this southern region only when forced by circumstances. On occasion the intervention could be indirect. Thus, as Josephus also records, when some Greek youths set up a statue of the Emperor in a synagogue at Dora in southern Phoenicia, Agrippa went to appear before Petronius, who was still *legatus;* and he wrote to the 'first men' of the city ordering them to hand over the guilty parties to a centurion, who would bring them for trial before himself. The implication seems to be that

---

12. 2.2 above.

13. *Ant.* XIX, 9, 1–2 (356–366).

14. Acts 12, 20. Agrippa appears here as 'Herodes' (12, 1), a name which no other source gives him. As a Roman citizen his name was Iulius Agrippa. There is no doubt, however, of the identity of the king concerned.

the little town *(polis)* of Dora, lying between Ptolemais and Caesarea, and south of Mount Carmel, was within the bounds of the province. But Agrippa could still exercise influence with the *legatus* over the protection of Jewish rights there.[15]

More ambitious plans on his part were met with a more repressive attitude. When the king began the construction of a new north wall for Jerusalem, the new *legatus* of Syria, Domitius Marsus, wrote to Claudius, and he wrote in turn to Agrippa, instructing him to stop the work.[16] More significantly, Agrippa was visited at Tiberias, evidently at his invitation, by four other kings: two from Asia Minor, Cotys of Armenia Minor and Polemo of Pontus, and three from the Near East, Antiochus IV of Commagene, Sampsigeramus of Emesa and his own brother Herod of Chalcis. By accident or otherwise, Marsus also arrived at Tiberias at this moment. The diplomatic gesture on Agrippa's part of taking the four other kings with him in his carriage to greet Marsus on his approach had the opposite effect from that intended: 'To Marsus their concord and such a degree of mutual friendship was suspect, for he took it that the meeting of minds of such important dynasts was not to the advantage of the Romans'. So they were ordered to return at once to their kingdoms.[17]

When Agrippa died in AD 44, his son, the later Agrippa II, was at Rome being brought up at the court of Claudius. According to Josephus, the Emperor's first inclination was to give him his father's kingdom. But his freedmen and friends persuaded him that the 'boy' (now sixteen) was too young. So the whole area reverted to being a province, with an equestrian official, now with the title *procurator,* to govern it.

Whether the motivation recorded by Josephus is correct or not, which we obviously cannot know, the result was as he said. So far as Judaea was concerned, it would be only in two periods of rebellion that in the future the area would not be under Roman direct rule. A century later, after the second of those rebellions, the province would be given a new name, 'Syria Palaestina', from which all reference to the Jewish character of its population was lacking; it would have a garrison of two Roman legions and be the location of two Roman *coloniae,* Caesarea and Aelia Capitolina (Jerusalem). The long hesitation of Roman rule was over, with consequences which would be felt in full only when the Emperors themselves became Christian and saw the country as the Holy Land.

A similar hesitation was far from over, however, as regards the north-

---

15. *Ant.* XIX, 6, 3 (300–311). No reliance should be placed on the text of the letter or edict of Petronius as quoted by Josephus. For Dora see further 8.2 below.

16. Josephus, *Ant.* XIX, 7, 2 (326–327).

17. Josephus, *Ant.* XIX, 8, 1 (338–341).

eastern regions, and indeed part of Galilee, which had belonged to Agrippa's kingdom. While all of Galilee for the moment became part of the province of Judaea, what of Batanaea, Trachonitis and Auranitis? As it happens, a convenient series of Greek and Aramaic inscriptions duly reflects the changing overlords of the latter area: a statue-base at Si' dedicated in Greek to 'King Herodes' (unfortunately the statue itself is missing) is followed by the dedication of an altar there in the year 33 'of the lord Philip' (LMRN' PLPS), and then by the record of the construction of a gate at Hebran in the year 7 of Claudius Caesar (LQLDYS QYSR); but then Herodian rule reappears, with datings by years 16 and 21 of 'King Agrippa, (our?) lord' in a Greek inscription from Sanamayn.[18] The north-eastern parts of the kingdom had first, therefore, been made part of a province, and presumably (though it is nowhere explicitly stated) of Syria rather than Judaea, briefly recreating a geographical unity of provincial territory in that area. The arrangement did not last long, and reversion to Herodian rule went in parallel with a series of developments in Judaea which added a unique degree of complexity to the structure of power there. Again, the history of Judaea between AD 44 and 66 is exceptionally well known, for the period is that of the education and early manhood of Josephus (born in AD 37/38), who by the end of it was a central figure in the Jewish ruling class. Consequently only certain features bearing on the exercise of power there need be isolated here.

Direct rule of the area from Idumaea in the south to Galilee in the north, and including Peraea across the Jordan, reverted, as we have seen, to a Roman *eques*, now with the title *procurator*. But when the first of these, Cuspius Fadus, demanded the restoration to him of the custody of the high-priestly robes, held by the earlier *praefecti* from AD 6 to 36,[19] the Jewish authorities petitioned him, and also the new *legatus* of Syria, Cassius Longinus, for the right to retain them. Josephus notes, in a way which will now be familiar, that Longinus had come to Jerusalem with a large force in case Fadus' demands provoked resistance. In the event, the Jewish leaders were allowed to send an embassy to Claudius in Rome; and he, influenced by the younger Agrippa, who was in Rome, by the elder Agrippa's brother 'King Herod' and by the latter's son Aristobulus, agreed to the request.[20] The significance of royal dynasties in this period did not lie only in the extent of 'Roman' territory which they actually ruled, but in the decision-making at the centre, where personal influence could play a crucial role.

18. Herod: Le Bas-W., no. 2364 = *IGR* III, no. 1243: [Βα]σιλεῖ Ἡρῴδει Ὀβαίσατος Σαόδου ἔθηκα τὸν ἀνδρίαντα. Philip: *RES*, no. 2117 = *PAES* IV, p. 78, no. 101. Claudius: *CIS* II, no. 170: BYRḤ TŠRY ŠNT ŠB' LQLDYS QYSR (building of a gate at Hebran). Agrippa: see Schürer, *HJP* I, 473, n.8.

19. 2.2 above.

20. *Ant.* XX, 1, 1–2 (6–14).

'King Herod', as Josephus goes on to explain, was currently the ruler of Chalcis (an undefinable small territory based in the southern part of the Bekaa Valley). This too was a result of royal influence, for Agrippa I had asked it of Claudius for his brother.[21] Herod now asked for the favour which was to produce a crucial anomaly in the functioning of power in Judaea for the two decades up to the revolt, namely that he should have authority not only over the Temple and its funds but over the selection of High Priests, a right which he immediately used.[22] The High Priests were thus no longer, as in AD 6–41, Roman nominees; and Judaea experienced the concurrent, and conflicting, exercise of the governor's and a king's power at the same time.

The complications thus created increased steadily with the progressive extension of the territory and rights given to Agrippa the younger.[23] In AD 50, as it seems, when his uncle died, he was given his kingdom of Chalcis as well as the 'care of the Temple', which was evidently accompanied by the right to depose and appoint the High Priests. Consequently six of the last seven of the long line of eighty-three High Priests, which Josephus regarded as having been continuous from the time of Aaron, were appointees of Agrippa II; there remained only the last of all, appointed as part of a popular movement during the revolt.[24]

In AD 53 Claudius took back the small kingdom of Chalcis, which presumably was added to the province of Syria, and gave Agrippa the former tetrarchy of Philip—the ill-defined neighbouring districts called Gaulanitis, Batanaea, Trachonitis and Auranitis—as well as the 'tetrarchy of Lysanias' (based on Abila, between Damascus and the Bekaa Valley) and 'the former tetrarchy of Varus', which seems to have been somewhere in Ituraea. Certainty as to the geography here (which is wholly unattainable) is less important than the visible ease with which these areas of Mount Lebanon and Anti-Lebanon could be transferred from one dynast to another; as they had from the beginning, those high mountainous areas remained an anomalous and ill-controlled zone, of considerable extent, at the heart of 'Roman' Syria. It is very significant too that the extensive districts which lay between Mount Hermon and Damascus on the one hand and the provincial Greek cities of the Decapolis on the other now passed, for at least forty years, out of Roman direct rule. By the moment, in the early second century, when these areas, divided between the provinces of Syria, Arabia and Judaea, became solidly integrated into the Roman provincial system, they had been under Roman overall control for more than a century and a half, while Auranitis and its

21. *Ant.* XIX, 5, 1 (277).
22. *Ant.* XX, 1, 3 (15–16).
23. For the details see Schürer, *HJP* I, 471ff.
24. For Josephus' survey, *Ant.* XX, 10, 1–5 (224–251); see Schürer, *HJP* II, 227–236.

attached areas had been under Herodian direct rule almost continuously for over a century. What has been called the pre-provincial phase in the history of the Hauran and the other districts of present-day southern Syria was both long and of considerable significance.[25]

In narrative terms, however, we know very little of events here (as in Nabataea) in the second half of the first century. Our only available narrative evidence is represented by the two major historical works of Josephus, which naturally enough touch on the history of other groups only when they became involved in some way with the Jews. Thus for instance the first of the *procuratores* had to deal with violent conflicts between the Jewish inhabitants of Peraea (part of his *provincia*) and those of Philadelphia (Amman) over the boundaries of a village called Zia. By luck we know the precise location of this village, which Josephus says was 'full of warlike men'. The *Onomasticon* of Eusebius, a priceless source for the social geography of the region, shows that it lay fifteen Roman miles (some 20 km) west of Philadelphia, hence on the boundary between the plateau and the great depression through which the Jordan runs.[26] The episode can be seen as a small foretaste of the communal conflicts which were to break out in AD 66 all round Judaea; and also as another small indication of the way in which the demography of the region was dominated by large villages.

Most of the conflicts which Josephus describes in this period belong to the internal history of the Jewish community, and did not affect the structure of the Roman Near East as a whole. But one of them involved not only open conflicts between Jews and Samaritans but the intervention of the *legatus* of Syria, a judicial hearing before Claudius in Rome and the condemnation of the *procurator*. In that sense it illustrates very clearly the means by which a local conflict, once again involving villagers from different groups, could make its way through the entire decision-making structure of the Empire. It *may* also have provided the context for the creation of the second Roman *colonia* of the region, Ptolemais, which followed immediately after.

In outline, the issue, which seems to belong to AD 51 or 52, arose from conflicts between Jewish travellers from Galilee, on their way to Jerusalem for a festival, and the Samaritan inhabitants of a village on the border between Samaria and the Plain of Jezreel. Getting no satisfaction from the *procurator,* Ventidius Cumanus, the Galilean Jews called in a brigand from the mountains and sacked various Samaritan villages. Cumanus reacted by deploying a cavalry *ala* of Sebastenes and four infantry cohorts, arming the Samaritans and launching an assault on the Jews (of Galilee, as seems clear).

25. 11.1 below.
26. Josephus, *Ant.* XX, 1, 1 (2–4); Eusebius, *Onom.* (ed. Klostermann) 94, 3 (calling it Ζία).

The 'leaders of the Samaritans' (whose communal structures are quite unknown) then went to appear before the *legatus* of Syria, Ummidius Quadratus, who was at that moment at Tyre. Having heard them, Quadratus came to Judaea and held further hearings in Samaria and at Lydda ('a village of a size no less than that of a *polis*', as Josephus describes it). Having put various persons to death, he sent the leaders of both the Samaritans and the Jews (the High Priest Ananias and the 'Captain of the Temple', Ananus) to the Emperor, along with Cumanus himself and a tribune named Celer. He himself visited Jerusalem to see that all was quiet, and returned to Antioch.

In Rome the influence of Agrippa II (who was still there, just before the decisive extension of his domains) ensured that the Samaritan leaders were condemned and put to death, Cumanus exiled and Celer, very remarkably, brought back to Jerusalem, dragged round the city and publicly executed.[27]

Although the episode illustrates again the extreme difficulty which was presented by trying to keep order among the very large armed population of the villages, there is nothing in Josephus' account to indicate that Quadratus brought any significant forces with him from Syria. No legions are known to have been stationed as far south as Tyre, and he may have been there on the normal judicial circuit of a Roman governor. Nonetheless, it is clear that Ptolemais will once again have been the point from which a *legatus* of Syria entered Judaea to impose order; and this fact may serve to explain why in the last couple of years of Claudius' reign the city was refounded as a Roman *colonia,* with the title 'Colonia Claudia Stabilis Germanica Felix Ptolemais'. The very fragmentary evidence is just enough to make it certain that veterans were in fact settled there, and seem to have come from all four of the legions of Syria. The refoundation was therefore clearly not simply a grant of status and privileges to an existing city, of a sort which was to become very common later.[28] Its significance is further emphasised by a Latin inscription from AD 56 recording the building of a road along the coast southwards 'from Antiochia to the new *colonia* of Ptolemais'. This inscription, from a point just south of Beirut, is the earliest Roman milestone so far discovered in the Near East.[29]

It cannot be claimed that this foundation of the only *colonia* of the Julio-Claudian period in the Near East, with its explicitly related road, is entirely intelligible. But both serve to suggest the importance of concern directed

27. *BJ* II, 12, 3–7 (232–246); *Ant.* XX, 6, 1–3 (118–136).

28. For Ptolemais as a *colonia* see Millar, "Roman *Coloniae*", 23–26, and the very full discussion by S. Applebaum, "The Roman Colony of Ptolemais—'Ake and Its Territory", in his *Judaea in Hellenistic and Roman Times* (1989), 70.

29. See R. G. Goodchild, "The Coast-Road of Phoenicia and Its Roman Milestones", *Berytus* 9 (1948–49), 91; Th. Bauzou, "Les routes romaines de Syrie", in *AHS*, 205.

southwards, to the ever-troubled area of Judaea. This becomes all the more significant when it is realised that the early 50s saw the beginnings of a major confrontation in the opposite direction, across the only real 'frontier', the Euphrates.

The complexities of the endless rivalries for the Parthian and Armenian thrones in this period do not concern us here, except as revealing the structure of the Roman Empire in the Near East. Throughout, the Euphrates—and particularly the main crossing at Zeugma—continued to be treated as the boundary. So, in AD 49, the *legatus* of Syria, Cassius Longinus, had escorted a pretender to the Parthian throne, Meherdates, as far as Zeugma and entrusted him to leading Parthians and 'the king of the Arabs, Acbarus', who escorted him to Edessa.[30] It would be over a century before the little kingdom of Osrhoene, whose capital was at Edessa, entered the Roman orbit, while in the meantime giving birth to a new literary language, Syriac. Meherdates was soon defeated and betrayed to the Parthian king.

A quite new level of crisis came by AD 54, at the beginning of Nero's reign, when the throne of Armenia was claimed by Tiridates, the brother of the king of Parthia. For the first time it is possible to see what resources the Romans had in the Near East and how they would be disposed. The first step was to levy soldiers in the neighbouring provinces (exactly which, Tacitus does not say), to place the legions in relation to Armenia and to order 'the long-established kings Agrippa and Antiochus to send forces for the invasion of Parthia'.[31] Tacitus might have noted that the heart of Antiochus' kingdom was Commagene, while its capital was Samosata, which overlooked Parthian territory across the Euphrates. By contrast it would have been understandable if he had felt the difficulty, shared by moderns, of stating what Agrippa II's territory actually consisted of. At any rate he passes over the fact, recorded by Josephus, that about now Nero added to it part of Galilee, with the cities of Tiberias and Tarichaeae, and of Peraea, with Abila and Julias.[32] It is, however, a reflection of the very considerable extent and population of Agrippa's domains that his forces were thought relevant to operations across the Euphrates. Bringing them to Zeugma involved a march of some 400–450 km from his nearest border.

In fact the arrangements now made, since they primarily concerned Armenia, lying beyond the upper Tigris, foreshadowed those that were to be made permanent by Vespasian in the 70s. The forces 'of the East' (that is, Syria) were divided, on the basis that two legions and auxiliaries remained with

30. Tacitus, *Ann.* XII, 12.

31. *Ann.* XIII, 7.

32. Josephus, *BJ* II, 13, 2 (252); *Ant.* XX, 8, 4 (159). For topographical problems see Schürer, *HJP* I, 473.

Ummidius Quadratus in Syria, while two, along with newly brought auxiliaries and those already there, were put under Domitius Corbulo in Cappadocia to the north. Nothing more is then reported in Tacitus' narrative until AD 58, when Corbulo is found training his legionaries, long unaccustomed to discipline, receiving extra recruits from Galatia and Cappadocia, and an extra legion 'from Germany, along with auxiliary *alae* and *cohortes*'.[33] In fact what happened was that the legion IV Scythica was moved from Moesia (not Germania), perhaps already a year or two earlier, to Syria (not Cappadocia), where it was to form part of the permanent garrison for the whole of our period.[34] Its arrival thus marks one more small stage in the very slow evolution of an integrated provincial system in the Near East. In the established system of the eastern frontier, IV Scythica was to be the permanent garrison of Zeugma on the Euphrates.

In AD 62, with the arrival of yet another legion from Moesia, the V Macedonica, we can see a further redistribution of forces on the frontier. For a campaign in Armenia, Caesennius Paetus was to have the V Macedonica, IV Scythica and XII Fulminata, and auxiliaries from Galatia and Cappadocia, while the III Gallica, VI Ferrata and X Fretensis, along with normal auxiliaries stationed in Syria, stayed there with Corbulo, who concentrated on protecting the crossing at Zeugma, advancing only very slowly, and too late, to rescue Paetus' force in Armenia from accepting conditions and retreating.[35]

Finally, in 63, when it became clear in Rome that the Parthians had successfully occupied Armenia, Corbulo was given command of all the forces on the eastern frontier, without the governorship of any province.[36] A further legion, the XV Apollinaris, was brought from Pannonia. The transfer of legions from the Danube, either from Pannonia or earlier from Moesia, was presumably carried out by marching them via Byzantium and across Anatolia. If so, we are beginning to see the functioning of the land-route which was with the passage of time to represent the means by which the Near East was firmly integrated, so far as time and distance allowed, in the military structure of the Empire.

Tacitus continues by listing all those officials or dynasts who were placed under Corbulo's orders: 'Letters were written to the tetrarchs and kings, to *praefecti* and *procuratores* and to whatever *praetores* were governing the neighbouring provinces instructing them to obey Corbulo's orders'.[37] The ref-

33. *Ann.* XIII, 35.
34. *RE* XII, *s.v.* "Legio", 1558ff.
35. Tacitus, *Ann.* XV, 1–17.
36. *Ann.* XV, 24–31.
37. *Ann.* XV, 25, 6.

erence, which is far from clear, must be mainly to Asia Minor. In the Near East there were, of Roman officials, only the *legatus* of Syria and the *procurator* of Judaea.

The legions IV and XII were left in Syria, under the *legatus*, Cestius Gallus, while Corbulo crossed the Euphrates frontier at Melitene in Cappadocia, taking legions III, VI and XV as well as detachments from the Balkans and Egypt, a number of auxiliary *alae* and *cohortes* and forces provided by kings (which kings is not stated). But when it came to the point, a diplomatic settlement was easily reached, by which Tiridates would be king of Armenia, but receive his crown from Nero. In this period such large-scale concentrations of force in the East were not intended to achieve permanent conquest, and left undisturbed the presumption that the frontier of the two empires lay on the middle Euphrates.

No source offers any description of how the legions now based in Cappadocia and operating in Armenia were then re-grouped for normal garrison duties. What is certain at least is that none were to be permanently stationed in Cappadocia until the 70s, under Vespasian. Nor was any legion stationed in Judaea on a regular basis until after the Jewish War. So the legionary garrison of the Near East was still in the latter years of Nero confined to Syria. It seems clear that there were again four legions here: the IV Scythica, which had come from Moesia and now remained permanently, having already been left there during Corbulo's last campaign; the XII Fulminata, also left in Syria at that time; and the VI Ferrata and X Fretensis, which had been with Corbulo.

The III Gallica, previously in Syria, which had been in Armenia under Corbulo, was transferred to Moesia towards the end of Nero's reign,[38] returning to Syria only in the 70s; where it had been in the mid-60s is not known. Nor does there seem to be any information as to how or where, within Syria, these legions were disposed in the few years between the end of Corbulo's operations and the outbreak of the Jewish War.

In the first century, by comparison with later periods, documentary evidence, for the army as for civilian life, is extremely scarce. It is for that reason that in this period any conception which we can gain of the structure of the Empire in the Near East is still heavily dependent on the accidents of what subjects or areas are touched on by the available narratives. Once again, therefore, for these years the only viewpoint we have is that provided by Josephus.

The Roman preoccupation with Armenia and Parthia may perhaps explain why, in spite of ever-increasing unrest and violence in Judaea, no intervention by the *legatus* of Syria or his forces is attested by Josephus until Pass-

38. Suetonius, *Vesp.* 6; Tacitus, *Hist.* I, 79; III, 24.

over of AD 66. The complex power-structure of Judaea remained as described earlier: a *procurator* with his auxiliary forces, largely drawn from the gentile inhabitants of Caesarea and Sebaste; successive High Priests, now appointed by Agrippa II, whose territory now included part of Galilee and Peraea; and the king himself, who came frequently to the province, maintained a palace in Jerusalem and could summon the Sanhedrin.[39]

The complexity of government in these years is in fact perfectly illustrated by the narrative in Acts of Paul's return to Judaea in the later 50s, and his experiences there: the riot in Jerusalem when he was thought to have brought a gentile into the Temple; his detention and beating by the 'tribune of the cohort'; his appearance before the Sanhedrin, and his despatch with an escort of no less than two-hundred soldiers to the *procurator* in Caesarea; then a trial there, with an accusation brought by the High Priest, Ananias, represented by a rhetor called Tertullus. The two opposed speeches encapsulate in miniature the politics of jurisdiction in a Roman province. Then Paul is detained for two years in the '*praitōrion* of Herod', until (probably in AD 60) the *procurator* Felix is replaced by another, Festus. In accordance with diplomatic convention, Agrippa II and his sister Berenice come to greet him, and when they and Festus jointly examine Paul, the two royal persons make their entry to the audience-chamber 'with a great display *(phantasia)*', and the hearing is joined by Roman tribunes and by 'leading men of the city (Caesarea)'. But Paul has appealed to the Emperor in Rome, and is sent off under escort on the long sea voyage up the Phoenician coast and along the southern shore of Asia Minor, arriving only several months later.[40]

The deployment of the local auxiliary forces in Judaea, essentially in a police role, is very evident in the vivid narrative of Acts, as it is in Josephus' narratives of these years. But it was only in AD 66 that major forces from Syria were again deployed there. As a first step, we find Cestius Gallus, the *legatus,* visiting Jerusalem at Passover and being surrounded by a vast crowd complaining of the misgovernment by the then *procurator,* Gessius Florus. Gallus spoke to the crowd, promised that Florus would exercise more restraint in future and returned to Antioch.[41] But such diplomacy had no long-term effect. When Gallus returned later in the year, it was with a whole legion and substantial other forces. But by then the great revolt was under way, and Rome was faced with something almost unparalleled in the history of the Empire, a full-scale popular rebellion. Its beginning was to be marked by the routing of a whole legion by irregular forces drawn from a civilian population.

39. For Agrippa see Schürer, *HJP* I, 471–483.
40. Acts 21, 17–27, 1.
41. Josephus, *BJ* II, 14, 3 (280–281).

2.4. THE JEWISH WAR AND ITS AFTERMATH

It would be impossible to exaggerate the significance, from many different points of view, of the great revolt which broke out in Judaea in AD 66 and did not end until the suicide of the defenders of Masada in 74. Within the Jewish community it was marked by internal conflicts of unparalleled ferocity, and led to the destruction of the Temple, the disappearance of sacrifice as a central element in Jewish religious practice and the ending of the long line of High Priests. In terms of historiography, it gave rise to by far the most important historical works written in the first century AD, the *Jewish War, Antiquities* and *Autobiography* of Josephus, a leading Jerusalemite who himself acted as the Jewish commander in Galilee in 66/67, was captured and spent the rest of his life as an Imperial protégé in Rome, where all of his works were written. That both his own role and standpoint and his curiously elusive account of how the revolt really started were and remain acutely controversial does not alter the fact that the *Jewish War* offers the fullest available account of any event in the entire Roman Empire in the first century.[1] At this point, however, we must leave aside its significance for Judaism and Christianity, and to a large degree also the light it throws on the social history of the gentile Near East, to concentrate very strictly on its relevance to the resources which the Roman Empire had for the exercise of force in the Near East, and the way in which they were deployed. Only the barest outline of the very complex military history of the war is possible here. It remains curious that, with the exception of the ultimately disastrous campaign of Cestius Gallus and the legion XII Fulminata in the autumn of 66, no strictly military study has been devoted to this war.[2] Yet it represents by far the best-attested series of operations by the Roman army in the entire history of the Empire.

A partial exception is provided by studies devoted to the siege of Masada by the Romans. For with that we reach what is almost the earliest physical evidence for the presence of the Roman army in the Near East, in the form of the Roman camps and siege-mound;[3] and also, equally important, recently

1. For the complexities of Josephus' personal standpoint, I note here only a few essential recent works: S. J. D. Cohen, *Josephus in Galilee and Rome* (1979); T. Rajak, *Josephus: The Historian and His Society* (1983); M. Goodman, *The Ruling Class of Judaea: The Origins of the Jewish Revolt against Rome, AD 66–70* (1987). For a detailed narrative of the war, Schürer, *HJP* I, 484–513.

2. See M. Gichon, "Cestius Gallus's Campaigns in Judaea", *PEQ* 113 (1981), 39; for a more general analysis of Josephus' evidence on the Roman army, idem, "Aspects of a Roman Army in War according to the *Bellum Judaicum* of Josephus", in Freeman and Kennedy, *DRBE*, 287.

3. See the classic paper by I. A. Richmond, "The Roman Siege-works of Masada, Israel", *JRS* 52 (1962), 142. See also Kennedy and Riley, *RDF*, 95ff., illustrating also the very slight traces of Roman siege-works around Machaerus.

published documentary evidence from Masada emanating from the army during the siege and then during its occupation of the fortress itself.[4] In a curious way, from the point of view of our evidence from the Roman Near East, the end of the Jewish War represents the moment when we lose the only major historical narratives written from inside, those of Josephus, and begin to gain a steadily denser network of documentary and archaeological evidence, for both military and (in far greater depth) general social history.

After initial conflicts in 66 between the Jewish population in Jerusalem and the auxiliary forces stationed there, outside military intervention began in a way not attested before, with the despatch by Agrippa II of 2000 cavalry to Jerusalem (the equivalent, that is, of four Roman cavalry *alae*), recruited from Auranitis, Batanaea and Trachonitis.[5] But after the Roman soldiers in Jerusalem had been massacred and Agrippa's forces had withdrawn, the long-established pattern of large-scale intervention from Syria was again repeated. Cestius Gallus, the *legatus* of Syria, marched from Antioch with the legion XII Fulminata, 2000 men from each of the other three Syrian legions, six *cohortes* of infantry and four *alae* of cavalry. He was accompanied also by quite significant royal forces, which Josephus gives as follows: from Antiochus IV of Commagene, 2000 cavalry and 3000 archers on foot; from Agrippa II the same number of footsoldiers and rather fewer cavalry; and from, Sohaemus of Emesa 1000 cavalry and 3000 infantry, mainly archers. At something like 13,000 men in all, the royal forces were, in numbers, equivalent to between two and three legions, or twenty-six of the normal auxiliary units of 500 men. Gallus also raised large irregular forces (which Josephus called *epikouroi*) from the cities, including the *colonia* of Berytus, who made up for their lack of training by their hatred of the Jews.[6] The army took the now traditional route via Ptolemais and Caesarea to Antipatris, Lydda and Jerusalem. There, while Josephus claims that with determination Gallus could have captured the whole city, after some fighting he chose to withdraw. While the army was doing so, its retreat was forced into headlong flight with the loss of 5300 infantry (effectively the equivalent of a whole legion) and 480 cavalry (the equivalent of a whole cavalry *ala*).[7] There is no other example of a comparable defeat of Roman regular forces by the population of an established province.

Nero's reaction was to appoint one ex-consul, Licinius Mucianus, as the regular *legatus* of Syria and another, Flavius Vespasianus, to take charge of

---

4. See now H. M. Cotton and J. Geiger, *Masada* II, *The Yigael Yadin Excavations 1963–1965, Final Reports: The Latin and Greek Documents* (1989), abbreviated as *Doc. Masada*.

5. *BJ* II, 17, 4 (421).

6. *BJ* II, 18, 9 (499–502).

7. *BJ* II, 19, 4–9 (527–555).

the war in Judaea. Once again the military and administrative arrangements of a later period were foreshadowed. There were, however, in the winter of AD 66/67, no significant Roman forces left in Judaea, so Vespasian had inevitably to start with those of Syria. Once again, therefore, we see a Roman *legatus* marching south from Antioch to Ptolemais (now a Roman *colonia*) before entering Galilee. Given the evident extent of the crisis, the occasion offers even clearer evidence of what military resources could be deployed.

Vespasian's forces consisted of three whole legions. One, the XV Apollinaris, which had earlier in the 60s been engaged in the Armenian campaign,[8] had since been moved to Alexandria and was now marched from there to Ptolemais by Vespasian's son Titus. The others were the V Macedonica, also earlier in Armenia, but where it had been since is unknown; and the X Fretensis, also earlier engaged in Armenia, but from the established garrison of Syria.[9]

The significance of these details is the accumulation of force in the Near East which they represent. For three of the four legions of Syria remained there, and six whole legions, out of an Empire-wide total of twenty-six, were now divided between Syria and Judaea; therefore just under a quarter of the total.

The legionary forces were accompanied by twenty-three auxiliary *cohortes* and six *alae* of cavalry, presumably drawn largely from Syria. The total is very substantial (in principle, at full strength, some 14,500 men), but at this period we still do not have the evidence to identify any of the units. It is not until the later 80s that the *diplomata* given to their soldiers on discharge begin to detail the auxiliary forces of Syria and Judaea.[10]

Along with these there were forces provided by four dependent kings. Antiochus IV of Commagene, Agrippa II and Sohaemus of Emesa each sent 2000 infantry archers and 1000 cavalry, and 'the Arab' Malchus (Malchus II of Nabataea) also 1000 cavalry, but as many as 5000 infantry, mainly archers.[11] These totalled some 18,000 men, roughly a third of the whole force. The Jewish War is notable also, in the military history of the Roman Empire, as being the last moment of significant dependence on royal forces.

So substantial a deployment of force was necessary, for even the most northerly area of Jewish settlement, Galilee, contained a very large population mainly grouped in villages which were easily made defensible, and which each contained, so Josephus claims, at least 15,000 inhabitants.[12] That must be an

8. 2.3 above.
9. *BJ* III, 4, 2 (64–65).
10. 3.1 below.
11. *BJ* III, 4, 2 (68).
12. *BJ* III, 3, 2 (43).

exaggeration, as is no doubt his claim that the army which he, as the Jewish commander in Galilee, raised in 66/67 amounted to 100,000 men.[13] But Rome nonetheless faced a major task.

In fact Galilee was reconquered relatively easily in the course of 67, and Josephus himself surrendered at the end of the siege of Jotapata, ensuring his survival and his future role as a historian by proclaiming to Vespasian that the king whom the people mistakenly believed would now arise in the East was Vespasian himself.

In 68 the Roman forces effectively completed the reconquest of all of Peraea and Judaea, except Jerusalem itself, before the campaign was halted on the news of the death of Nero on the June 9. Operations were suspended for almost a year, before resuming in the summer of 69. At this stage Jewish resistance was already confined only to Jerusalem itself and the areas dominated by three fortresses built by Herod the Great—Herodium, Masada and Machaerus.

It was at this point, however, that Vespasian was brought news of the successful claim to the position of Emperor by Vitellius, and, supported by Licinius Mucianus in Syria and Tiberius Iulius Alexander, the *praefectus* of Egypt, determined on a bid for power on his own part. It may well be, as Tacitus claims, that the initial proclamation of Vespasian as Emperor was made in Egypt, on the first of July, 69.[14] But it is certain, and of some significance for the future, that it was at Caesarea in Judaea that Vespasian in person was first hailed as Emperor by his troops.[15] Caesarea had been his main base throughout; and this is surely relevant to the fact that early in his reign it gained the status of *colonia*, with the title 'Colonia Prima Flavia Augusta Caesarea'.[16] At both a local and a more general level it is significant too that the earliest document of his reign should be a milestone (the earliest Roman milestone from Judaea) put up in his name in the Jezreel Valley by Ulpius Traianus, the *legatus* of X Fretensis. Lacking the full Imperial titulature, for which the decree of the Senate was required, the milestone must date to the second half of 69. It proves also, what had not been known before, that Traianus was still there to support Vespasian's coup; and it helps to explain both his important role as *legatus* of Syria a few years later[17] and how his son came to have the chance, at the end of the century, to become Emperor himself.[18]

13. *BJ* II, 20, 5 (576).

14. Tacitus, *Hist.* II, 79, 1.

15. Tacitus, *Hist.* II, 80, 1; see, in graphic detail, the account, written during Vespasian's reign, in Josephus, *BJ* IV, 10, 2–6 (592–620).

16. Millar, "Roman *Coloniae*", 26–28.

17. 3.1 below.

18. B. H. Isaac and I. Roll, "A Milestone of AD 69 from Judaea: The Elder Trajan and Vespasian", *JRS* 66 (1976), 15.

On a wider basis, the proclamation of Vespasian marks a significant stage in the political integration of the Near East in the Roman Empire, and in the long and gradual process by which Antioch in particular was to emerge as a secondary Imperial capital. Political integration was vital in the short term also. From Caesarea Vespasian travelled north to Berytus, 'where many embassies from Syria, and many also from the other provinces met him, bearing crowns *(stephanoi)* from each city, and congratulatory decrees. Mucianus, the *legatus* of the province, was also present, reporting the enthusiasm of the different peoples and the oaths taken in each city'.[19] Before this Mucianus had confirmed the loyalty of the Syrian legions and had also made sure to go to the theatre in Antioch, 'where it is their custom to hold meetings', and to address the people in passably good Greek style. He also appealed to both the legionaries and the civilian population, with which they had by now many personal connections, by suggesting that Vitellius intended to make the Syrian and the German legions change places. Vespasian was also supported by Sohaemus of Emesa 'with no inconsiderable forces' and Antiochus of Commagene, 'the richest of the dependent kings', as well as by Agrippa II, who hastened back from Rome.

As Tacitus describes it, a council of war was now held at Berytus, attended by Mucianus and his officers, select elements of the Judaean army and 'the kings competing between them'. A levy of soldiers was ordered, veterans recruited, the richest cities required to manufacture arms, and a mint set up at Antioch. Titus was to have charge of Judaea, while Vespasian went to secure Egypt, and Mucianus set off towards Italy, overland through Asia Minor; his forces were the VI Ferrata and detachments from the other legions amounting to thirteen thousand men.[20] Josephus perfectly expresses at this point the reasons why it was this land route (and not, as the map might suggest, the interior sea-route provided by the Mediterranean) which was to tie the Near East steadily more closely into the Imperial structure: 'Being wary of the sea voyage because it would be the height of winter, he led the army through Cappadocia and Phrygia'.[21]

The further story of the campaigns which led to the recognition of Vespasian as Emperor in the winter of 69/70 need not concern us, except to note the significant role of the legion III Gallica. Stationed in Syria since the very beginning of the Empire, and then under Corbulo in Cappadocia and Armenia, it had been transferred to Moesia on the lower Danube at the very end of Nero's reign. In the confusion of the civil war, elements of this legion, now

19. Josephus, *BJ* IV, 10, 6 (620–621).
20. Tacitus, *Hist.* II, 80–83.
21. Josephus, *BJ* IV, 11, 1 (632).

at Aquileia, persuaded other forces to support Vespasian, whose merits they knew.[22] But beyond that we find in Tacitus' narrative the *tertiani* ('the men of the third legion'), during the civil war, saluting the rising Sun 'as is the custom in Syria'.[23] We seem, as so often, to be granted a general insight from an outside observer. But, as we will see, the notion of a typical custom of Sun-worship in Roman Syria is somewhat deceptive.[24] As so often, an observer's generalisation, which might seem to give a key to what was distinctive about the culture of the region, will seem too simple when we encounter the detailed evidence available from the area and its sub-regions.

If the successful conclusion of the Roman civil war was Vespasian's major objective, the capture of Jerusalem still remained an immense task, which absorbed a high proportion of the total forces of the Empire. This role was left to Titus, who in the winter of 69/70 marched back from Alexandria along the coast and, once again, made Caesarea his main base.[25] His forces, listed by both Tacitus and Josephus,[26] consisted of the same legions as had been under his father, the V Macedonica, X Fretensis and XV Apollinaris, as well as one further legion from Syria, the XII Fulminata, the same one which had been routed in 66 at the beginning of the revolt. Added to these were detachments of the two legions stationed in Egypt, the III Cyrenaica and XX Deiotariana, twenty infantry *cohortes* and eight mounted *alae*, as well as forces from Agrippa II, Sohaemus of Emesa and Antiochus IV of Commagene, and (in Tacitus' words) 'a strong force of Arabs imbued with the hatred of the Jews customary between neighbours'. Josephus adds that the detachments from Egypt amounted to two thousand men. But he also says that the gaps in the number of legionaries were made up by 'three thousand of the guards *(phylakes)* from the Euphrates'. The reference must be to legionaries, and if it both is to be taken literally and is correct, it would mean that a legion must already have been brought to Zeugma. On some views indeed this may already have happened under Tiberius. If that cannot be proved, Josephus clearly states that the X Fretensis had been there before joining Vespasian in 66/67; it had presumably now been replaced there by the IV Scythica.[27] Three thousand men represented half the strength of a legion. Finally, Josephus mentions

---

22. Suetonius, *Vesp.* 6. See Tacitus, *Hist.* II, 74.

23. Tacitus, *Hist.* III, 24: 'undique clamor, et orientem solem (ita in Syriae mos est) tertiani salutavere'.

24. See H. Seyrig, "Le culte du Soleil en Syrie à l'époque romaine", *Syria* 48 (1971), 337, and 13.1 below, text to n.117.

25. Josephus, *BJ* IV, 11, 5 (658–663).

26. Tacitus, *Hist.* V, 1; Josephus, *BJ* V, 1, 6 (41–42).

27. See Wagner, *RET,* 31, 40. For the X Fretensis on the Euphrates in the 60s, see Josephus, *BJ* VII, 1, 3 (17).

again that a large number of irregulars *(epikouroi)* came from Syria. Since these were neither Roman nor royal forces, they must have been provided, as before, by the various communities (but which, is not stated).

The details of the siege of Jerusalem need not concern us. What is significant is that it took this very substantial force, representing roughly one-seventh of the whole Imperial army, five months, from April to September of AD 70, to complete the capture of the city. Nothing could have served to emphasise more clearly the degree to which the coherence of the Empire depended on at least passive acquiescence by the provincial populations, or at the very least the absence of any coherent local or regional nationalisms which might offer a challenge to Rome.

The most immediate lesson drawn by Rome was that Jerusalem, even though now largely destroyed, required to be garrisoned. Consequently, the X Fretensis was left there (to remain in fact for some two centuries) along with some cavalry *alae* and infantry *cohortes*.[28] Though Josephus reports this only as a narrative detail in his description of Titus' actions, it in fact represented the first step in a long-term change in the position of Judaea within the Empire. Now that the province had a legion as its garrison, it required a governor of senatorial rank, and the status of ex-praetor.[29] His dual function, as governor of the province and commander of the legion, is reflected in the elaborate title found on inscriptions: *leg(atus) Augusti leg(ionis) X Fret(ensis) et leg(atus) pr(o) pr(aetore) provinciae Iudaeae.* The change was closely accompanied by other alterations in the disposition of force in the east of the Empire, which were indeed to do with the role of the Near East as a 'frontier'.[30] But in the case of Judaea this was unquestionably not so. The deployment of increased force followed on a major rebellion, and the province had no external frontier. In Judaea at least the Roman garrison must be seen as an army of occupation.

In the first few years of the new-style province it also had to act still as an army of conquest, for major strongholds—Herodium, Machaerus and Masada—remained in rebel hands. Herodium and Machaerus were taken by Lucilius Bassus, the first governor sent out as such to the new province. The latter, on its great hill overlooking the Dead Sea from the east, and heavily fortified by Herod the Great, required all the troops from the province for the siege, which ended by surrender.[31] Some traces remain also of the Roman

28. Josephus, *BJ* VII, 1, 2 (5).

29. For the known governors, Schürer, *HJP* I, 514ff.

30. 3.1 below.

31. Josephus, *BJ* VII, 6, 1–4 (163–209). For the fortress of Machaerus see V. Corbo, "La fortezza di Macheronte", *SBFLA* 28 (1978), 217.

siege-works, a circumvallation-wall, some small siege-camps and an assault-ramp, never completed.[32]

This episode has of course always been overshadowed, both in Josephus' narrative and now in the archaeological record, by the siege of Masada under the next *legatus*, Flavius Silva, in AD 73 or more probably 74.[33] Once again the siege required the concentration of all the forces available in the province; and as is well known, the circumvallation-wall, the seven Roman siege-camps and other installations and above all the siege-ramp on the west side of the rock remain clearly visible to this day.[34] None of these, however, has been excavated. For a reflection of the presence of the Roman army on this remote site beside the Dead Sea, we need to turn to the newly published papyri and other documents from Masada itself.[35] Evidently deposited while a Roman garrison occupied the fortress after the suicide of the defenders, some of the papyri had in fact been written earlier. Thus a Latin papyrus probably dated to AD 72 preserves the pay-record of a legionary cavalryman evidently serving in the X Fretensis and identified as 'C(aius) Messius son of C(aius), (of the Roman tribe) Fabia, Berytian'—hence one of many recruits to the Roman army from this Latin-speaking *colonia*.[36] Another, a list of medical supplies, may (somewhat hypothetically) be related to the military hospital *(valetudinarium)* identified among the Roman siege-installations.[37] A garrison seems to have remained on Masada for some decades, until the early second century. Fragmentary as they are, the documents which the Roman army left there, found along with others from earlier periods, are vivid reflections of a presence which as time went on was to be more and more clearly felt in this region. One potential form of cultural influence was, however, to be no more than abortive, that of Latin literature. It is still curiously evocative that among the documents from Masada should be a single line of Vergil's *Aeneid* (IV, 9), symbolically matching that from a few decades later found at Vindolanda in Cumbria, at the opposite corner of the Empire, and some 4000 km distant.[38]

---

32. See esp. A. Strobel, "Das römische Belagerungswerk um Machärus: Topographische Untersuchungen", *ZDPV* 90 (1974), 128, with the folding plan opposite p. 184, and Kennedy and Riley, *RDF*, 99–101.

33. Josephus, *BJ* VII, 8, 1–9, 2 (252–406). See Schürer, *HJP* I, 511–513.

34. See n.3 above.

35. See n.4 above.

36. *Doc. Masada*, no. 722.

37. *Doc. Masada*, no. 723.

38. *Doc. Masada*, no. 721 (Pl. I). The editors date the text (not later than) AD 73/74, on the hypothesis (pp. 18–20) that all the varied material in the 'locus of the scrolls' was gathered together at the initial stage of the occupation of the fortress itself. If this hypothesis is correct, the papyrus becomes the earliest witness to the text of the *Aeneid*. For the line found in the auxiliary

The aspect of Roman culture which impressed itself on the inhabitants of the cities of the Near East in the immediate aftermath of the Jewish War was a rather different, and less refined, one, namely gladiatorial combats and wild-beast shows. For it was in these two forms of public show, distinctively Italian and in no way native to the Greek world, that Titus made a point of celebrating his victory before the gentile populations of the region. Dangerous as it had been to the Empire, the Jewish revolt had at no point been supported by the non-Jewish populations of the surrounding area, and had not represented to even the smallest degree the beginning of a general uprising by the Semitic-language populations of the region. On the contrary, the beginning of the revolt in 66 had been marked by fierce communal conflicts between gentiles and Jews in a whole series of Near Eastern cities and areas: Caesarea first of all, and then Philadelphia, Esbous, Gerasa, Pella, Gadara, Hippos and Gaulanitis, as well as in the territory of Tyre, and at Ptolemais, Gaba in Galilee, Sebaste, Ascalon, Anthedon, Gaza, Scythopolis and Damascus. Josephus notes that only at Antioch, Sidon and Apamea had the gentiles refused to kill or imprison any of their Jewish fellow-inhabitants.[39] Some aspects of these communal conflicts will need consideration later, not least because they raise the question of the ethnic identities of the city—and village—populations concerned.[40] At this point it need only be stressed that collaboration in the repression of the revolt was not due only to dependent kings or other persons in authority. As Tacitus noted, the Arab forces who served under Titus were imbued with 'the hatred characteristic of neighbours'.

It was therefore not surprising, but is still striking and significant, that Titus should have made an emphatic point of celebrating the victory in a number of different cities in the area. It is notable that he began by taking at least some of his forces to the main city of Agrippa II's kingdom, Caesarea Philippi, at the foot of Mount Hermon, founded by the tetrarch Philip. There some of the Jewish prisoners were thrown to wild beasts (that is, used for the Roman spectacle known as *venatio*) and others made to fight each other like gladiators.[41] His next step was also of considerable symbolic significance: 'After this Caesar went to Berytus; this is a *colonia* of the Romans in Phoenicia. Here he made a more extended stay, displaying a greater lavishness in the celebration of his father's birthday, both in the variety of shows and in the arrangement of other expenditures. A mass of captives perished in the same

---

fort at Vindolanda (*Aen.* IX, 473), see A. K. Bowman and J. D. Thomas, "New Texts from Vindolanda", *Britannia* 18 (1987), 125, on p. 130, no. 1 (Pl. XVA).

39. Caesarea: Schürer, *HJP* I, 465ff.; communal hostilities elsewhere: Josephus, *BJ* II, 18, 1–6 (457–486); Damascus II, 20, 1 (559–561).

40. 10.1–2 below.

41. Titus' shows in Caesarea Philippi: *BJ* VII, 2, 1 (23–24); 3, 1 (37–38).

manner as before'. From there he went on to Antioch 'providing lavish displays in all the cities of Syria through which he passed, and using the Jewish
captives to demonstrate their own destruction'.[42] He no doubt did so at Antioch also, though Josephus does not explicitly say so. Instead, he concentrates
on two episodes. First, he recounts Titus' excursion to Zeugma to receive an
embassy bearing a gold crown from Vologaeses of Parthia and to entertain the
emissaries at a dinner. Second, and in much more detail, he describes Titus'
reception by the people as he approached Antioch, and a petition for the expulsion of Jews from the city. At this he agreed to do as Mucianus had done
earlier, and address the assembly in the theatre, but once again only to refuse
the petition.[43] It may even be, as is claimed in the sixth-century *Chronicle* of
the Antiochene John Malalas, that Vespasian set up in Antioch the Cherubim
from the Temple and built a theatre at Daphne near Antioch with the Latin
inscription *ex praeda Iudaeae,* 'from the spoils of Judaea'.[44] But whether that
is historical or not, it is clear that elaborate steps were taken to associate the
other communities of the Near East with the repression of the revolt. The
prolonged displays there thus formed a sort of prelude to the great triumph
held in Rome in 71, and still portrayed on the Arch of Titus there.[45] It was in
fact the only triumph ever to celebrate the subjugation of the population of
an existing province.

42. Josephus, *BJ* VII, 3, 1 (39–40); 5, 1 (96), Loeb trans.
43. Josephus, *BJ* VII, 5, 2 (100–111).
44. Malalas, *Chron.* X, 260–261.
45. For the triumph, Josephus, *BJ* VII, 5, 3–7 (121–157). For the arch, M. Pfanner, *Der Titusbogen* (1983).

CHAPTER

3

IMPERIALISM AND EXPANSION, AD 74–195

3.1. VESPASIAN: A NEW NEAR EASTERN EMPIRE

Looked at as a whole, the development of the provincial system in the Near East and the transformation of Roman military dispositions there in the late first century give every impression of representing an integrated plan, conceived in Rome and thought out with the aid of a map. Judaea, as we have seen, became a one-legion province governed by a senator of praetorian rank. Commagene ceased to be a dependent kingdom and became part of the province of Syria, as (it seems clear) did the kingdom of Sohaemus of Emesa, straddling the upper Orontes and stretching out a considerable distance into the steppe; and Palmyra, whatever its relation to the province before, was now clearly tied within it. But, most important of all, it is natural to see these developments in connection with the transformation of Cappadocia into a major military province, with two legions stationed at Melitene (Malatya) and at Satala, and a senatorial governor of ex-consul status. It was at this moment, in the 70s, that after nearly a century and a half the Roman presence in the Near East ceased to be a bridgehead and came to resemble an integrated provincial and military system.

It is at this moment too that documentary and archaeological evidence begins to play a fuller part; that has its own dangers of course, for we can never fully account for the logical gap between the first attestation of something which happens, perhaps by mere accident, to appear in our evidence, and the claim that that was when the pattern now attested first came into existence. Nonetheless the cumulative effect of all the evidence is such as to make it impossible to deny a radical transformation at this stage.

Whether it represented a plan, and if so, who formed it, where and when, is a more difficult question. The major step, which Suetonius attributes to Vespasian, and which Tacitus also alludes to, was the stationing of two legions in Cappadocia.[1] One of these was almost certainly the XVI Flavia, newly created and named after the Emperor, and stationed at Satala, 40 km west of the upper Euphrates.[2] Exactly how soon the legion was raised, and where, is not known, nor precisely when it arrived at Satala; but it certainly existed by the mid-70s.[3] The other legion to go to Cappadocia was the XII Fulminata, at Melitene; and it would be natural to see both dispositions as part of the creation, for the first time, of an extended 'Euphrates frontier' from the upper Euphrates through Commagene to Zeugma. But in fact Josephus attributes this displacement to Titus, distributing rewards and punishments to his army immediately after the end of the siege of Jerusalem in September 70, while Vespasian was already in Italy: 'Recollecting too that the twelfth legion had under the command of Cestius succumbed to the Jews, he banished them from Syria altogether—for they had previously been quartered at Raphanaeae—and sent them to the district called Melitene, beside the Euphrates, on the confines of Armenia and Cappadocia.'[4] One could not guess from the nature of this report, from a well-placed observer, that the move was part of a major strategic plan; still less, of course, that the legion was to stay there for several centuries and construct a permanent camp which would receive a detailed description from Procopius in the sixth century.[5] Nor was the central element of the 'Euphrates frontier' yet in place, as Commagene was still a dependent kingdom. For an account of how it came to an end, we are again indebted to Josephus, by now in Rome living in a house provided by Vespasian: no longer an eyewitness on the spot, therefore, but close to the Imperial court. Here too there is nothing on the surface of the account to suggest any overall plan. Whatever its limits, Josephus' narrative represents the most detailed description we have of the provincialisation of a dependent kingdom.

In Vespasian's fourth year, so 72 or 73, Caesennius Paetus, the *legatus* of Syria, wrote to Vespasian to say that Antiochus IV and his son Epiphanes had connections with Parthia, which should be forestalled before serious trouble began. Vespasian, thinking particularly of the strategic position of Samosata on the Euphrates, gave permission to Paetus to act as he thought fit. (We can

---

1. Suetonius, *Vesp.* 8; Tacitus, *Hist.* II, 81.

2. For this area and the new legion see T. B. Mitford, "Some Inscriptions from the Cappadocian *Limes*", *JRS* 64 (1974), 160, on pp. 164ff.; idem, "The Euphrates Frontier in Cappadocia", *Studien zu den Militärgrenzen Roms* II (1977), 501, and "Cappadocia and Armenia Minor", *ANRW* II.7.2 (1980), 1169. The creation of the legion by Vespasian is recorded by Dio LV, 24, 3.

3. Text to n.34 below.

4. Josephus, *BJ* VII, 1, 3 (18), Loeb trans.

5. See *Not. Dig., Or.* 38, 4; Procopius, *Aed.* III, 4, 15–18.

assume that this exchange will have taken at least several weeks, depending as it will have done on messengers travelling in both directions.)[6] Paetus then invaded, taking the VI Ferrata, some *cohortes* and some *alae* of cavalry; with them once again were two kings with their forces, Aristobulus of Chalcis— not heard of before, and whose kingdom cannot even be securely located[7]— and Sohaemus of Emesa, marking the last appearance of his dynasty. There was no popular resistance; but Antiochus' two sons, Epiphanes and Callinicus, led the royal forces in a drawn all-day battle with the Roman troops. Resistance was ended only by Antiochus' determination to surrender.[8] Once again, as with Judaea and Galilee, we are concerned with an extensive, very fertile area which could support a large population, and which represented more than a trivial military problem.

The newly acquired area was also, in military terms, a genuine frontier zone. For both sides of the river, Commagene, now Roman, with its capital, Samosata, right on the banks of the river, and on the other side Osrhoene, with its capital at Edessa, still under Parthian control, were part of the Fertile Crescent and the location of significant settled populations. It is even possible that the earliest example of Syriac literature, the *Letter of Mara bar Serapion*, which refers to people being driven out of Samosata by the Romans, and to others going to Seleucia (that is, perhaps, Zeugma), reflects the moment of the Roman takeover.[9]

What form the Roman occupation immediately took is not clear. As Josephus records, a detachment was sent to Samosata during the campaign. Then very soon after, in 73, a Latin inscription from the bank of the Euphrates at Ayni, slightly over halfway from Samosata to Zeugma, records that Vespasian and Titus had had constructed an *opus cochliae* (a screw to raise water from the river), in the legateship of Marius Celsus. The very ruined sculptural representation of the personified Euphrates which adorned the work is accompanied by another Latin inscription naming the III Gallica.[10] There can be no doubt, therefore, of the Roman occupation of the right bank of the river between Zeugma and Samosata. There is also no doubt that a road-system was constructed in the interior of Commagene, west of the Euphrates. For on the perfectly preserved Roman bridge over the Chabinas River, reconstructed un-

---

6. See F. Millar, "Emperors, Frontiers and Foreign Relations, 31 BC–AD 378", *Britannia* 13 (1982), 1.

7. For what little can be conjectured about this Aristobulus, see Schürer, *HJP* I, 573.

8. Josephus, *BJ* VII, 7, 1–3 (219–245).

9. See 12.3 below.

10. *IGLS* I, nos. 65–66 (Ayni). See F. Cumont, *Etudes Syriennes* (1966), 248ff.; H. Hellenkemper, "Der Limes am nordsyrischen Euphrat. Bericht zu einer archäologischen Landesaufnahme", *Studien zu den Militärgrenzen Roms* II (1977), 461, with sketch-map on p. 462.

der Septimius Severus, just enough of a fragmentary Latin inscription survives to show that a first bridge was built under Vespasian.[11] But whether there was immediately a line of posts along the Euphrates, and what force, if any, occupied Samosata itself, is not clear. It may be that a legion, perhaps III Gallica, was stationed here already in the Flavian period, but there seems to be no concrete proof. It is rather more probable, however, that IV Scythica was again stationed at Zeugma.[12] In between, the water-lifting screw installed at Ayni suggests at least a small fort on the river. North of Samosata, at Tille, there may also have been an auxiliary fort as early as this period.[13] Further south, at Tell el Hajj, Latin inscriptions mentioning a Cohors Secunda Pia Fidelis and the Cohors Prima Milliaria Thracum (attested in Syria between 88 and 124) suggest that there may have been a fort there.[14] The site lies on the Euphrates almost due south of Hierapolis.

How far to the south Roman control extended at any time before the 160s is quite uncertain, but it must have been considerably further than this. For, as has always been recognised, a very important clue to the extension of Roman active control in the direction of the Euphrates is provided by the well-known milestone erected in AD 75 at Arak (or Erech), some 27 km east-north-east of Palmyra, by M. Ulpius Traianus, the *legatus* of Syria in the mid 70s.[15] Unless we are to believe that this represents an abortive project, it must reflect the existence of a Roman road leading in the direction of Oresa (Tayibeh), continuing either to the Euphrates in the area of its confluence with the Balikh, that is, at Sura or Nicephorium/Callinicum, or even, alternatively or simultaneously, eastwards from Oresa to the confluence of the Euphrates and the Chabur at Circesium. At the least, therefore, we may suppose that Roman occupation now extended down the Euphrates to its confluence with the Balikh. These considerations of course presuppose that a Roman road marked out east of Palmyra would necessarily have gone as far as the Euphrates, which cannot be quite certain. In this period, before Roman occupation extended down to the lower-middle Euphrates and Dura-Europos, that is, from the 160s onwards, Dura itself was firmly Parthian; but Palmyrene outposts were established on the river further down. In other words what the famous

11. *IGLS* I, no. 38.

12. Hellenkemper, op. cit. (n.10), 468–469.

13. See J. G. Crow and D. H. French, "New Research on the Euphrates Frontier", in W. S. Hanson and L. J. F. Keppie (eds.), *Roman Frontier Studies 1979* III (1980), 903; D. H. French, J. Moore and H. F. Russell, "Excavations at Tille 1979–1982", *Anat. Stud.* 32 (1982), 161.

14. Ph. Bridel and R. A. Stucky, "Tell el Hajj, place forte du limes de l'Euphrate", in J. C. Margueron (ed.), *Le Moyen Euphrate* (1980), 349.

15. *AE* (1933), no. 205: see G. W. Bowersock, "Syria under Vespasian", *JRS* 63 (1973), 133; M. Gawlikowski, "Palmyre et l'Euphrate", *Syria* 60 (1983), 53, on p. 60.

milestone of Ulpius Traianus shows for certain is the firm integration of Palmyra within the provincial system of Syria; what it tells us about that system's relation to the eastern steppe and the Euphrates is less clear.

This process seems to have been accompanied by the disappearance of the dependent kingdom of Emesa, and its incorporation into the province. The evidence is no more than circumstantial. Sohaemus of Emesa makes the last appearance in history by any member of the royal dynasty in 72, assisting the Roman forces to suppress the dynasty of Commagene.[16] Then, in 78/79, a Greek epitaph from a funerary pyramid at Emesa (finally blown up about 1911 to make way for a petrol store) records a 'Gaios Ioulios Samsigeramos' of the Roman tribe Fabia, also called Seilas, son of Gaius Iulius Alexion, who constructed the tomb during his lifetime.[17] He may be a relative of the dynasty, and the text gives the impression (though no more than that) of reflecting a provincial rather than a royal context; no dynastic or other position is indicated. It thus cannot be proved at what moment the dynasty ceased, or under what circumstances. Coinage of Emesa as a city, with no king, begins only under Antoninus Pius.[18] It is, however, significant that in the Parthian war fought by Trajan in 114–116 no Roman dependent kings are recorded as providing forces.

The Roman Empire in the Near East had by that time entered a quite new phase, with the end both of the extensive kingdom of Agrippa II and of Nabataea. It is thus quite likely that the kingdom of Emesa had indeed disappeared in the 70s. If so, it would at any rate fit with two other items of evidence for the evolution of Roman control in this period. First, the milestone of Ulpius Traianus from a road going east from Palmyra would tend to imply the marking-out of Roman roads in the area further west. What happens to be preserved in our evidence is of course largely accidental. But it does so happen that there is another milestone of Traianus, dating to 75, from a site called Qorsi, some 75 km south-east of Apamea in the direction of Palmyra. The milestone might alternatively relate to a route running north-south through the steppe, between Chalcis (or Beroea) in the north and Emesa to the south.[19]

Second, although Roman forces were always able to, and did, traverse the

16. Text to n.7 above.

17. *IGLS* V, no. 2212. See R. D. Sullivan, "The Dynasty of Emesa", *ANRW* II.8 (1977), 198.

18. *BMC Syria*, 237ff.

19. J. Balty and J. C. Balty (eds.), *Apamée de Syrie, Actes du Colloque 1972* (1972), 108, no. 9 = *AE* (1974), no. 653. Qorsi is described as lying north-east of Sabbura, near which modern reconstructions of the road-network (not necessarily 'Roman roads') show the two routes mentioned as crossing. So R. Mouterde and A. Poidebard, *Le limes de Chalcis* I (1945), 47; for a more extensive plan, D. Kennedy and S. Gregory, *Sir Aurel Stein's Limes Report* I (1985), folding map at end.

territories of dependent kingdoms, the normal route they had taken when intervening in Judaea or Nabataea had always been, as we have seen repeatedly, along the coast through Berytus, Tyre, Ptolemais and Caesarea. It cannot be a complete accident that three of these places were now *coloniae* (and were listed as such by Pliny the Elder, writing in the late 70s).[20] If the territory of Emesa were now provincial, we would expect increased official traffic to have gone along the Orontes Valley, whether to diverge east of the mountain massif to reach Damascus or to continue down into the Bekaa Valley, into the inland territory of the *colonia* of Berytus, around Heliopolis.

It is thus wholly appropriate that the inscription which gives the most vivid and detailed reflection of the impact of Roman rule in this area towards the end of the first century should have been put up at Hama/Epiphania in the reign of Domitian (81–96) and should have to do with the demands of Roman official travellers. Epiphania, which as we saw will have gained its Greek name under Antiochus Epiphanes (175–164 BC),[21] and in the Empire was a very minor place (a *polis?*) which never minted coins, lies on the Orontes some 45 km north of Emesa and 50 km south-east of Apamea. There under Domitian an extract from the Imperial instructions *(mandata)* given to the *procurator* (financial manager) of the province was somehow acquired, translated into Greek and put up in public, in what context is not known. Whatever the process of transmission of the text, the fact of its having been inscribed publicly can be confidently attributed to local initiative. Hence it is certain that the issues set out in it were of acute local concern. The text runs as follows:[22]

> From instructions of Imperator [Dom]itianus Caesar, son of Augustus, Augustus. To Claudius Athenodorus, procurator: Among items of special importance that required great attention by my father, the god Vespasianus, I know that he gave great care to the cities' privileges. With his mind fixed on them he ordered that neither by the renting of beasts of burden nor by the distress of lodging should the provinces be burdened, but, nevertheless, by conscious decision or not, deliberate neglect has set in and this order has not been observed, for there remains up to the present an old and vigorous custom which, little by little, will progress into law if it is not obstructed by force from gaining strength. I instruct you to see to it that nobody commandeers a beast of burden unless he has a permit from me. For it is most unjust that, either by the favour or prestige of certain people, requisitions should take place which nobody but myself can grant.

20. Pliny, *NH* V, 17/38 (Berytus); 17/75 (Ptolemais); 13/69 (Caesarea).
21. Ch. 1 above.
22. *IGLS* V, no. 1998, trans. R. K. Sherk, *The Roman Empire: Augustus to Constantine* (1988), no. 95.

Therefore, let there be nothing which will break my instructions and spoil my intent, which is most advantageous to the cities, for to help the weakened provinces is just, provinces which with difficulty have enough for the necessities of life. Let no force be used against them contrary to my wish, and let nobody commandeer a guide unless he has a permit from me, for, when farmers are torn from their homes, the fields will remain without their attention. You, either using your own beasts of burden or renting them, will act best [———]

There is, however, yet more striking evidence for the increased investment by the Roman state in the Near East in this period, which has to do with the role of Seleucia and Antioch as the arrival-points of Roman communications by sea, and their interconnection with land-routes.[23] First, a cylindrical stone in the form of a milestone, found just north-east of modern Antakya, near the site of the hippodrome of Roman Antioch, records that under Traianus as *legatus*, in AD 75, a stretch *(ductus)* of three Roman miles of what is described as the 'Dipotamia(e?) flumen', with bridges, had been constructed by soldiers of various units.[24] 'Dipotamia(e?) flumen', an expression mixing Latin and transliterated Greek, must mean something like 'double river'. The only reasonable interpretation is that of D. van Berchem: the reference is to a canalisation of the combined course of the two rivers, the Orontes from the south and the Kara Su from the north, which meet a few kilometres above Antioch.

The fact that the Roman army was so heavily involved in the work probably implies that the canalisation served some Imperial purpose and was not purely for local benefit. It is true that the inscription shows that 'Antiochenses' were also involved, but whether as civilian labour or as soldiers is unclear. Two long and important Greek inscriptions from Antioch, however, also dated by the legateship of Traianus, show that work was simultaneously being carried out on an extensive water-channel for use by fullers, that is, for local civilian use. In this instance the labour-force was secured by corvée from the different quarters of the city, and Traianus is recorded as having merely 'supervised' the work.[25]

23. What follows is entirely dependent on the major paper by D. van Berchem, "Le port de Séleucie de Piérie et l'infrastructure logistique des guerres parthiques", *Bonn. Jahrb.* 185 (1985), 47.

24. On the units concerned, see p. 89. The Latin inscription, first published by van Berchem in *Mus. Helv.* 40 (1983), 185, is *AE* (1983), no. 927, as revised in van Berchem, op. cit., 85–87. Translated in Sherk, op. cit. (n.22), no. 85a.

25. D. Feissel, "Deux listes des quartiers d'Antioche astreints au creusement d'un canal", *Syria* 62 (1988), 77.

If it was in the Imperial interest to invest large quantities of military labour in a canalisation of the Orontes above Antioch, this was surely to prolong the navigability of the river, perhaps even to, and hence across, the lake of Antioch (which is now dry). Strabo in the *Geography* already records that one could travel by boat from the sea to Antioch in a day.[26] But this route, through a narrow gorge, must always have been difficult (and today no traffic at all uses the river). Hence it is no surprise to find that Pausanias records that major works had been needed, under an Emperor whom he does not name: 'The Syrian river Orontes does not flow throughout its whole course to the sea on level ground, but tumbles over a precipitous ledge of rock. Wishing, then, that ships should sail up the river from the sea to the city of Antioch, the Roman Emperor had a navigable canal dug with much labour and at great expense, and into this canal he diverted the river.'[27]

From the evidence given earlier it must be reasonable to suppose that the Emperor concerned is Vespasian, and very likely that military labour was used on the river below as well as above Antioch. This becomes all the more likely when we find military labour being used under Vespasian in a closely related but separate project at Seleucia, on the coast. On a small-scale map, Seleucia might look as if it lay almost at the mouth of the Orontes, and was literally a port for Antioch, some 25 km inland up the river. But in fact, while the Orontes reaches the sea at the south end of the coastal plain, at the foot of Mount Casius, Seleucia lies at the north end of the shore-line, below Mount Coryphaeus (a spur of Mount Amanus), some 10 km away. Its artificial harbour, dug out of the plain, remains clearly visible, as is (even more so) the well-known cutting and tunnel made in the side of Mount Coryphaeus under Vespasian to divert a stream from the port and thus prevent it from being silted up. The project was a major one, 1300 m in length and with a maximum depth of 50 m; apart from the building of roads and frontier installations, it would be hard to find in the Roman provinces examples of construction projects undertaken by the Empire on a scale comparable to those on the Orontes and at Seleucia.[28] Latin inscriptions with the names of Vespasian and Titus (and no doubt originally Domitian) make it certain that this work too was carried out by soldiers. This is confirmed by Greek inscriptions, from the earlier phases of the project, recording that work was done in sections, in one case under a centurion of IV Scythica and in another a ship-captain (*nau-*

26. *Geog.* XVI, 2, 7 (751).
27. *Graec. Descrip.* VIII, 29, 3, trans. J. G. Frazer.
28. See still the classic article by R. MacMullen, "Roman Imperial Building in the Provinces", *HSCPh* 64 (1959), 207; S. Mitchell, "Imperial Building in the Eastern Roman Provinces", *HSCPh* 91 (1987), 333.

archos). Other inscriptions record further work, by soldiers of IV Scythica
and XVI Flavia Firma, under Antoninus Pius in about 149.[29]

Both projects, separate but closely comparable, thus represent a quite exceptional investment of effort and labour by the Empire. That labour, as
noted before, was largely provided by soldiers. The Latin inscription of 75
recording the construction of a *dipotamiae fluminis tractus* lists four legions—the III Gallica, IV Scythica, VI Ferrata and XVI Flavia—and twenty
infantry *cohortes.* From just this period, because of the developing use of
individual bronze *diplomata* issued to discharged auxiliaries, we can begin to
have a fuller picture of what these units were. The earliest *diploma* issued to
an auxiliary soldier from Syria dates to 88, and (as they normally do) reflects
a mass grant of rewards after twenty-five or more years of service (so going
back to the early 60s). In this case three mounted *alae* and seventeen infantry
cohortes are listed.[30] As most auxiliary units bore the names of the ethnic
groups from which they were originally recruited, we seem at first sight to be
granted an insight into the varied geographical composition of the auxiliary
part of the Roman army: the groups mentioned come both from within the
Near East—Ascalonites, Sebastenes and Ituraeans—and from far outside it—
Pannonians, Gauls, Numidians, Thracians, Bracaraugustani from Spain and
so forth. This impression is indeed valid as regards the original raising of such
forces, and hence is of immense value. If we think only of units originally
raised in the Near East, *diplomata* of the following few decades show a *cohors*
of 'Damasceni' from which discharges are being made in 90 (hence in service
by the 60s), and of 'Antiochenses' in 93, an *ala* of Ituraeans in Pannonia in
98, Tyrians in Moesia Inferior (the lower Danube) in 99, and, very significantly, the second Cohors Flavia of Commagenians in 100, with another,
listed as 'the first', in 105.[31] Recruitment of auxiliaries had thus begun in
Commagene immediately after the fall of the kingdom.

As is well known, however, it would be quite misleading to see the ethnic
names of these units as proving the continued ethnic composition of the soldiers who served in them. The individual who received the *diploma* of 88 was
Bithus son of Seuthus, a Breucan, who took the *diploma* back with him to his
native Thrace; but he had been serving in a *cohors* of Musulamii, a people
from North Africa. In other words, the presence of the various types of unit
of the Roman army was very important as contributing to a complex process
of mutual cultural influence, which it would be an over-simplification to call
'Romanisation'; but the ethnic names of the auxiliary units concerned will in

---

29. The inscriptions are *IGLS* III, nos. 1131–1140, discussed by van Berchem, op. cit., pp.
53–61.

30. *CIL* XVI, no. 35.

31. *CIL* XVI, nos. 36; 39; 45; 46; 50.

most cases give clear evidence of the origins of the soldiers who served in them only at the moment of the initial raising of the unit. Nonetheless we would have a much clearer conception of the relevance of the army to the cultural and social history of the Near East if we knew how the *alae* (at least three) and *cohortes* (at least twenty) of the province were distributed; and at a more local level, whether they lived in camps, or occupied parts of towns or were billeted on the civilian population.

We gain a comparable (and equally partial) conception of auxiliary forces in Judaea from a *diploma* of 86, found in Hungary, to which it had been brought back by the recipient, a cavalryman named Seuthes son of Trabai-thus, from an ethnic group called the Cololetici, who was serving in a *cohors* of Thracians.[32] The list of units from which discharges had been made includes *alae* of Gaetuli, from North Africa, and of Thracians; and *cohortes* of Lusitanians, Thracians and Cantabrians. The Sebastenes and Caesareans, originally raised as local royal forces, had, as Josephus noted, evidently been moved elsewhere by Vespasian.[33]

If we return to the important Latin inscription recording the construction of the *dipotamiae fluminis ductus* above Antioch, considerable importance attaches to the names of the four legions whose soldiers contributed to the work. The date of the inscription (though not necessarily of all the work) is 75. The four are III Gallica, which may already have been at Samosata; IV Scythica, which was probably already at Zeugma; VI Ferrata, which had taken part in the conquest of Commagene, and whose regular station is unknown; and XVI Flavia. As we have seen, this last legion had been created by Vespasian; the inscription from Antioch is in fact the earliest documentary evidence for its existence. Everything suggests that it either still was or at any rate until recently still had been in Syria. The building-up of Cappadocia as a two-legion province under a consular *legatus* was therefore, it seems, a process completed only in the mid-70s, and Josephus was not necessarily wrong to see Titus' despatch of XII Fulminata to Melitene as an isolated step of late 70. The first consular governor of Cappadocia is in fact attested in 76,[34] and the second legion, certainly the XVI Flavia, must have arrived there by then. If we look at the 'eastern frontier' as a whole, the diffusion of a permanent legionary garrison both southwards to Judaea and northwards to Cappadocia was thus a process which took place in two stages, but separated by only a few years. The two stages taken together, both within the reign of Vespasian, represent a considerable change in the strategic shape of the Empire.

If, alternatively, we look towards the Mediterranean, the reign of Ves-

32. *CIL* XVI, no. 33.

33. 2.3 above.

34. B. E. Thomasson, *Laterculi Praesidium* I (1984), 264.

pasian *may* also represent, as van Berchem suggests, the moment of the creation of the 'Syrian fleet' *(classis Syriaca)* attested in the second century; but it cannot be proved.[35] What is clear is that this period, the 70s, produces a quite new level of evidence on the ground for the presence and impact of the Roman Empire in this region. This process is visible from the coast to the Euphrates, in the interior of Commagene, in the steppe on either side of Palmyra, on the middle Euphrates, and also of course in Judaea itself, where a legion now occupied part of the ruins of Jerusalem, and a detachment left behind some of its documents on the top of Masada. Fragmentary as our evidence is, we can observe both an intensification and a considerable geographical expansion of the Roman presence. An important aspect of both was the replacement of royal rule (as well as royal taxation and the maintenance of royal forces) by Roman provincial rule. Two further stages of this process were soon to follow: the absorption of the kingdom of Agrippa II and then that of Nabataea.

3.2. TRAJAN: EXPANSION AND REARRANGEMENT IN THE SOUTHERN NEAR EAST

With the absorption of Commagene the province of Syria had reached a natural 'frontier', in the sense not only of the upper-middle Euphrates itself but of the mountains of the Kurdish Taurus, round which the Euphrates sweeps through gorges in a great eastward bend between Melitene and Samosata. No route could follow the river through the gorge; and troops moving, like XII Fulminata in 70 or 71, from Syria to Melitene will have crossed the mountains further west.[1] In the southern part of the province, the kingdom of Emesa, on the upper-middle Orontes and stretching far out into the steppe, seems clearly to have been absorbed in the 70s, while Roman roads now extended to and beyond Palmyra. Only in the far south did there remain a complex pattern of royal and provincial territory, some of the latter still forming an enclave geographically separate from the rest of the province. By the mid-second century Gaza, on the coast, had certainly ceased to be an enclave separate from the province of Syria, and became part of Syria Palaestina (as Judaea was by then called). When this happened is not certain; but probably as soon as Judaea was put under a senatorial governor in the early 70s, for Pliny

35. So also M. Reddé, *Mare Nostrum* (1986), 236ff.

1. See the remarkable description of this area and the gorge in T. B. Mitford, "The *limes* in the Kurdish Taurus", in W. S. Hanson and L. J. F. Keppie (eds.), *Roman Frontier Studies 1979* III (1980), 913.

the Elder, writing in the 70s, describes the long trade-route from Arabia Felix as ending in Gaza 'in Judaea'.[2]

A far more complex pattern is presented by the central mountain region of Lebanon, Anti-Lebanon and Mount Hermon, the territories to the south belonging to Agrippa II (including part of Galilee and Peraea) and then Nabataean territory. The absorption of Agrippa's territories, whatever these precisely were, represented the logical preliminary to the takeover of Nabataea in 106, and its conversion into the province of 'Arabia'. But we cannot state either exactly what Agrippa's territories consisted of or whether this absorption belongs in the 90s under Domitian or in 100 under Trajan.[3] It cannot indeed be certain that the process took place all at once.

In brief, since 53 Agrippa had ruled Batanaea, Trachonitis and Auranitis; the 'tetrarchy of Lysanias', apparently based on Abila, on the pass between Damascus and the Bekaa Valley; and the 'territory of Varus', of unknown location and extent, but apparently on Mount Lebanon. Nero had added considerable parts of Galilee (with the cities of Tiberias and Taricheae) and Peraea. Agrippa may have also have received further territory under Vespasian. At any rate as Titus marched back up the coast in the autumn of 70, he passed near a town called Arcea of the kingdom of Agrippa, lying between Berytus and Raphaneae in the Orontes Valley; this is the small place Arca or 'Caesarea ad Libanum', at the north end of Mount Lebanon whence the Emperor Severus Alexander was later to come.[4] It thus seems clear that Agrippa's domains were not geographically continuous.

All that is certain is that by the time Josephus was coming to the end of his *Antiquities,* completed in 93/94, Batanaea had become provincial territory. For we have already seen Josephus' sketch of the history of the colony of Babylonian Jews there, settled by Herod and later under the tetrarch Philip, Agrippa I and Agrippa II, but by now crushed by the tribute imposed by Rome.[5] Josephus might seem to imply that Agrippa was now dead. Reliance has often been placed on the statement in the *Bibliotheca* of Photius, compiled in the ninth century, that Agrippa died in the third year of Trajan, so 100.[6] Documentary evidence, however, makes clear that Batanaea and the surrounding area will have become provincial just about the time when Josephus was completing his *Antiquities* and writing the pendant to it, his *Autobiogra-*

2. Ptolemy, *Geog.* V, 16, 6, ed. Nobbe. See C. A. M. Glucker, *The City of Gaza in the Roman and Byzantine Periods* (1987), 41 (where the word 'not' is evidently a slip), Pliny, *NH* XII, 32/64.

3. For the complex issues involved, see Schürer, *HJP* I, 471–483. The full evidence will not be cited here.

4. Josephus, *BJ* VII, 5, 1 (97). See 3.4 and 9.2 below.

5. Josephus, *Ant.* XVII, 2, 2 (26–28), quoted in 2.2 above.

6. Photius, *Bib.* 33.

phy, where indeed he speaks of Agrippa as no longer living. The latest known document of Agrippa's reign is a Greek inscription from Sanamein in Batanaea dated by the double era of Agrippa to the years 37 and 32, so 92/93.[7] But some three years later local datings show that royal rule was over, and that the area was provincial. In the remarkable collection of antiquities, largely in the local basalt, in the museum of Suweida (Souedias/Dionysias) there is an inscription carved on a basalt grave-*stele,* and dated by the sixteenth year of Domitian, 96.[8] Within a year or so we have another dating in Greek by the first year of Nerva, 96/97, from southern Trachonitis.[9]

Whatever the precise personal history of Agrippa II, therefore, it is indisputable that the central area of his kingdom had become provincial territory before the end of Domitian's reign. As must already be clear, nothing whatsoever is known of the circumstances. But the most reasonable conclusion is that he died in about 92/93, and that his varied territories became provincial at that moment.

The southern area was in any case the most important, for it was that which bordered on Nabataean territory. In the short term all of this region presumably became part of Syria, with the effect that for the first time the land-area of the province was continuous into the Decapolis. It is perhaps relevant that an equestrian officer is recorded by an inscription as exercising some functions in 'the Decapolis of Syria' at some point under Domitian, probably around 90;[10] and that an inscription shows that the south theatre at Gerasa, or some of it, was dedicated in 90/91 'in accordance with a decree of Lappius Maximus, *legatus Augusti pro praetore*'.[11] Whether this is an accident of our evidence or not, no earlier evidence attests a governor's decision in this outlying region. Galilee and Peraea may now have reverted to Judaea; nothing is known. For a picture of a complete transformation of this whole area, we have to await the acquisition of Nabataea in 106.

Again, nothing is known of the circumstances. No conflicts with Rome are recorded in the long reign of the last king, Rabbel II, described in Nabataean documents as 'he who has given his people life and deliverance' (DY ḤYY WŠYZB 'MH).[12] His reign lasted from 70 to 106, and the latest record of it

7. *OGIS*, no. 426 = *IGR* III, no. 1127.

8. M. Dunand, *Le Musée de Soueida* (1934), p. 49, no. 75. See 11.3 below.

9. *IGR* III, no. 1176, from the site described variously as Aeritae, 'Ahireh and Ariqah. See, e.g., the map in Dentzer, *Hauran* I.1, p. 138.

10. B. Isaac, "The Decapolis in Syria, a Neglected Inscription", *ZPE* 44 (1981), 67.

11. J. Pouilloux, "Deux inscriptions au théâtre sud de Gérasa", *SBFLA* 27 (1977), 246. See further 11.3 below.

12. Fuller details on Rabbel in Schürer, *HJP* I, 584–585 (with some errors); Bowersock, *Roman Arabia*, 72–75.

comes from his thirty-sixth year, so immediately before the Roman conquest.[13]

All that we know of the moment of conquest, or acquisition, is a single sentence of Cassius Dio: 'About this time also Palma the governor of Syria subjugated Arabia around Petra and made it subject to the Romans'.[14] Speculation on motives, whether simply the occasion of the king's death, or local disputes or (improbably) an interest in trade-routes, is fruitless. This occasion, significant though it is, can contribute nothing to any discussion of the reasons for continued Roman expansionism in the Near East. All that is certain is that no alleged motive of the sort concerned in the suppression of Commagene—royal connection with a neighbouring power—can have played any part. For Nabataea bordered only on the steppe, except where it extended into the mountain-chain of the Hedjaz stretching down the east coast of the Red Sea. Complex as is the problem of the relations of the Nabataean area and its population to the unsettled peoples of the steppe, there is nothing to suggest that any large-scale military threat was felt from that direction.

If neither the decision-making process which lay behind it nor the campaign itself (if there was any real campaign) can be understood, by contrast the multiple effects of the annexation are very clearly reflected in our evidence. In strategic terms we know that, as Dio records, the operation was conducted from Syria, not from Judaea, and by the *legatus* of *circa* 104/105–107/108, A. Cornelius Palma, who duly earned triumphal *ornamenta*, a statue in the Forum of Augustus in Rome and a second consulate in 109.[15] What forces he took from Syria we do not know. All that is clear is that as early as 107 a governor of Arabia, Claudius Severus, was already in office. The same structure had been created as in Judaea, whereby a senatorial governor of ex-praetor rank was simultaneously the *legatus* of the province and of the one legion which was stationed there. The legion was the III Cyrenaica, which had been brought from Egypt, reducing its legionary garrison to one.

All this and more appears with great clarity in the famous papyrus letter of a soldier in III Cyrenaica written to his father in Egypt in March 107 from Bostra, to which he had just been moved. Since he explains that Bostra is an eight days' journey from Petra, the major city of the kingdom, it is probable that he had previously been stationed there. Strikingly, he also records that merchants were arriving from Pelusium in Egypt every day. The distances were considerable: certainly well over 300 km along the coast and across the

---

13. H. Jaussen and R. Savignac, *Mission archéologique en Arabie* I (1914), 217, no. 321.
14. Dio LXVIII, 14, 5.
15. *ILS*, no. 1023.

Negev to Petra, and some 260 km from Petra to Bostra in the southern Hauran.

In both this and a later letter from February 108 the soldier, Iulius Apollinaris, describes how, as a result of promotion, he can go around doing nothing while others toil all day cutting stones.[16] The reference may be to the most conspicuous landmark of the Roman occupation, the Via Nova Traiana, which ran from the Hauran down to Aila at the head of the Red Sea: as milestones of 111–117 put it in triumphal terms, Trajan 'after Arabia had been reduced to the form of a province opened and paved a new road from the borders of Syria to the Red Sea through C. Claudius Severus, *legatus Augusti pro praetore*'. Even these words hardly capture the dramatic impact of the road as visible from the air today, stretching along the Jordanian plain and then across the great Wadi Mujib (the ancient Arnon), which runs into the Dead Sea.[17] The total volume of stone-cutting must have been prodigious.

Iulius Apollinaris, writing from Bostra, may alternatively have been talking of the construction of a camp. For what seems to be beyond question the outline of a Roman camp (a rectangular enclosure of *circa* 463 m by 363 m) can be seen from the air attached to the north side of Bostra, whose plan as both a Nabataean and a Roman provincial town is clearly visible from the air and on the ground.[18] If this is correct, it is a rare case when we can give some meaning to the statement that a legion was stationed 'at' a particular town.

So profound a transformation of the region could hardly fail to register with the population living there. In Avdat in the Negev someone dated a building by 'year two of the province', using the Greek word *eparcheia* in transliteration: ŠNT TRTYN LHPRKY'.[19] A year later at Madaba someone dated a tomb in Greek 'in the third year of the province', but in Nabataean in a slightly different way, 'in the third year of the province (i.e., the provincial regime at?) Bostra': BŠNT TLT LHPRK BṢR'.[20] The expression may reflect a consciousness that that was where the main Roman base was. It will not, however, mean that Bostra was the 'capital of the province', for Roman provinces did not have capitals. By 114 an inscription on a Roman arch erected

---

16. *P. Mich.*, nos. 466 (107) and 465 (108). See, for this archive and other details of the early military occupation, K. Strobel, "Zu Fragen der frühen Geschichte der römischen Provinz Arabia und zu einigen Problemen des Imperium Romanum zu Beginn der 2. Jh. n. Chr.", *ZPE* 71 (1988), 251.

17. P. Thomsen, "Die römischen Meilensteine der Provinzen Syria, Arabia und Palaestina", *ZDPV* 40 (1917), 1, sect. xx; Kennedy and Riley, *RDF*, 85–88.

18. Kennedy and Riley, *RDF*, 124–125.

19. A. Negev, "Nabataean Inscriptions from 'Avdat (Oboda)", *IEJ* 13 (1963), 113, p. 117, no. 11.

20. J. T. Milik, "Nouvelles inscriptions nabatéenes", *Syria* 35 (1958), 227, p. 243, no. 6.

at Petra (as it seems, the earliest Greek monumental inscription from the Nabataean region) records Petra as a metropolis ('mother-city')—apparently, for the text has a gap, 'mother-city of Arabia'. That has no significance for the misdirected question of whether Petra or Bostra was 'the capital': the governor will have given jurisdiction at either, for Roman governors were peripatetic, and they certainly did give jurisdiction at times at Petra. On November 17, 130, one of the documents in the priceless 'archive of Babatha' shows someone summoning her to appear before Haterius Nepos, the then *legatus,* 'at Petra or elsewhere in the province'. But in the following year, faced with a summons by someone else to appear at Petra, she issued a counter-summons to her opponent to appear first before the governor at Rabbathmoab.[21]

Auxiliary units were also transferred to the new province. So the Ala veterana of Gaetuli, which we saw in Judaea in 86, was later in Arabia, and its cavalrymen left graffiti, in highly erratic Greek, at Medain Saleh in the Hedjaz, the southernmost known Roman outpost, 900 km from Bostra.[22] Similarly the Cohors I Hispanorum and Cohors I Thebaeorum, recorded in 105 as having been transferred from Egypt to Judaea, may have gone on to Arabia; if so, then perhaps accompanying the legion III Cyrenaica. As for other units, their presence is even more speculative, or attested only later.[23] Certainty is not essential, for we could assume in any case that a number of auxiliary units arrived; the role of some of them in the inscriptions of the later second century and after will be discussed below. But the wider issue is important, for it involves the problem of what the army in this area was for, and in what sense the outermost area of Roman occupation represented a 'frontier'.

For the moment it is more important to stress that the acquisition of Arabia involved some reshaping of the provincial structure south of Mount Hermon. For a start, two or three cities of the Decapolis which had been part of the enclave belonging to the province of Syria now found themselves in Arabia: from south to north, Philadelphia (Amman), Gerasa and possibly Adraa.[24] The new order is perfectly expressed in the dedication to Trajan

21. Bowersock, *Roman Arabia,* 84, n.28; *AE* (1982), no. 904. *P. Yadin,* nos. 23 and 25.

22. See J. Bowsher, "The Frontier Post of Medain Saleh", in Freeman and Kennedy, *DRBE* I, 23. I cannot follow the view that at least for a time the southern part of the kingdom (the Hisma and Hedjaz) continued as a dependent kingdom under Malichus, a son of Rabbel. So J. W. Eadie, "Artifacts of Annexation: Trajan's Grand Strategy and Arabia", in J. W. Eadie and J. Ober (eds.), *The Craft of the Ancient Historian: Essays in Honor of Chester G. Starr* (1985), 402.

23. See M. P. Speidel, "The Roman Army in Arabia", *ANRW* II.8 (1977), 687, esp. on pp. 705 and 711–712; reprinted in Speidel, *Roman Army Studies* (1984), 229. On the garrison see also F. Zayadine and Z. T. Fiema, "Roman Inscriptions from the Siq at Petra", *ADAJ* 30 (1986), 199.

24. For the very complex issues involved, not worth discussing in detail here, see M. Sartre, *Trois études sur l'Arabie romaine* (1982), ch. 1, "Les frontières de l'Arabie romaine".

from the North Gate at Gerasa, on the part of the 'Antiochenes by the Chrysorhoas, the former Gerasenes, to their own saviour and (?)founder', put up under Claudius Severus, still there as *legatus* in 115.[25] A new boundary between 'Arabia', as a Roman province, and Syria thus now ran east-west through the Hauran to the north of Bostra and probably of Adraa also. What the situation was on the western edge of the Jordanian plateau (for instance with the city of Gadara, formerly in Syria or along either side of the Jordan) is remarkably unclear. It has to be admitted that this area might have been either in Arabia, or in Judaea or in Syria; Judaea is the most probable. Certainly the area of Scythopolis, in the Plain of Jezreel west of the Jordan, which had been part of Syria, seems now to have belonged to Judaea; for an inscription attests the presence there of an *ala,* earlier stationed in Syria, which by 139 at least was certainly part of the garrison of that province.[26] Similarly the Babatha archive (once again) shows that another auxiliary unit which had earlier been in Syria was by 124 stationed in Engeddi in Judaea, on the west shore of the Dead Sea. For in that year Judas son of Elazar, a resident of Engeddi, acknowledged receipt of a loan from Magonius Valens, centurion of the Cohors prima milliaria Thracum. What is more, the property which he pledged was located to the west of a military headquarters (*praesidium,* transliterated in Greek). The intensified presence of the Roman army could not be more clearly illustrated.[27]

'Arabia', as a province, certainly extended across the Wadi Arabah into the Negev and Sinai, and we have seen that at Avdat (Oboda) people began immediately to date by the new province. So far as is known, 'Arabia' did not reach to the Mediterranean, and the question of how real a presence Rome was able to establish in either the southern Negev or the vast expanses of the Sinai peninsula cannot be answered. But, as we will see when we look at the military structure of the Near East as it was at the end of the second century, Roman outposts are attested not only at Medain Saleh in the northern Hedjaz but at Dumatha (Jawf) in the Wadi Sirhan. The total area of the new *provincia,* if we think of it in the older sense of an area of military activity, was enormous, stretching over hundreds of kilometres.

The presence of Roman legionary and auxiliary soldiers will have been the most immediately perceptible aspect of the arrival of provincial organisation. Its counterpart was the raising of auxiliary troops, perhaps (it is not known) by a takeover of some or all of the royal forces. What is certain is that Nabataean troops entered Roman service immediately as regular auxil-

---

25. C. H. Kraeling, *Gerasa, City of the Decapolis* (1938), ins. no. 56/57 (C. B. Welles).
26. R. Last and A. Stein, "Ala Antiana in Scythopolis: A New Inscription from Beth-Shean", *ZPE* 81 (1990), 224.
27. *P. Yadin,* no. 11.

iary units. A diploma of AD 139 records men of the fourth and sixth cohorts of Petraeans being discharged in what was by then called Syria Palaestina; they should thus have entered service no later than 114. As another *diploma,* of 156, shows, all these *cohortes* (at least six, so three thousand men) raised in Arabia will have borne the formal title 'Cohors Ulpia Petraeorum', after the Emperor Ulpius Traianus, under whom their region became a province.[28] All the discharged auxiliaries gained the Roman citizenship, only one of the many complex changes in local society which Roman rule brought, and which will need to be considered later.

As we have seen on several occasions, in Syria and Judaea in AD 6, and in Batanaea in (probably) the early 90s, the most distinctive feature of Roman rule in a new area would be the imposition of the census and of direct taxation. For Arabia we do not have to envisage this impact through narrative reports written later, for two newly published papyri present the nature of the exchanges between the settled population and the new occupying forces in concrete detail. One of the documents forms part of the Babatha archive; the other may well have been found originally in the same desert area to the west of the Dead Sea. Both relate to a small area already mentioned, the village of Maoza in the district of Zoara, lying in the great depression south of the Dead Sea. Like the marriage-contract quoted much earlier,[29] these two papyri illustrate the use of written documents in Greek in a rural society remote from any town. The only town mentioned in them is Rabbathmoab on the Jordanian plateau, some 37 km away as the crow flies—and, more realistically, at an elevation of some 1000 m higher.

Both documents (and probably fragments of a third) are returns of land for the census of 127 under the *legatus Augusti pro praetore* of Arabia, Titus Aninius Sextius Florentinus.[30] The well-preserved document from the Babatha archive will be used to illustrate the new relationships involved in the census. There is nothing to indicate how many previous Roman censuses had been conducted before the current year: 'according to the compute of the new province of Arabia year twenty-second'. If a census had first been imposed in (say) 107, there may have been a ten-year cycle, with an intervening one in about 117. The document begins with the attestation of its being a copy of that posted in the *basilica* at Rabbathmoab. The declaration itself follows, starting with the dating: by Hadrian, the two consuls and the year of the province. Then comes Babatha's sworn statement:

28. *CIL* XVI, no. 87 (AD 139); 106 (AD 156).

29. Ch. 1 above.

30. (a) *P. Yadin,* no. 16 (quoted in part below, trans. N. Lewis); (b) N. Lewis, "A Jewish Landowner in Provincia Arabia", *SCI* 8/9 (1985/1988), 132. I cannot follow the interesting suggestion of A. Wasserstein in *JQR* 80 (1989), 93, that the expression τῆς νέας ἐπαρχείας Ἀραβίας in *P. Yadin,* no. 18, also used here, refers to a province called Arabia Nova in southern Palestine,

> As a census of Arabia is being conducted by Titus Aninius Sextius Florenti-
> nus, legatus Augusti pro praetore, I, Babtha daughter of Simon, of Maoza
> in Zoarene [district] of the Petra administrative region, domiciled in my
> own private property in the said Maoza, register what I possess (present
> with me as my guardian being Judanes son of Elazar, of the village of En-
> gedi in the district of Jericho in Judaea, domiciled in his own private prop-
> erty in the said Maoza), viz. within the boundaries of Maoza a date or-
> chard called Algiphiamma.

The text continues with more details, some very difficult to understand, but
enough to make clear that each plot paid a fixed tax, calculated both in produce (dates) and in coin.

The document concludes with a record of the 'subscriptions' (formal statements 'written below' a document) made by Babatha herself and the *praefectus alae* stationed at Rabbathmoab. Nothing could more perfectly exem-
plify the role of Greek as the common language of the eastern Mediterranean
and as the medium of communication between the Roman Empire and its
Semitic-language subjects. For this paragraph translates into Greek both the
oath made by Babatha in Aramaic and the subscription of the *praefectus* in
Latin:

> Translation of subscription: I, Babtha daughter of Simon, swear by the
> *genius* of our lord Caesar that I have in good faith registered as has been
> written above. I, Judanes son of Elazar, acted as guardian and wrote for
> her. [Second hand] Translation of subscription of the prefect: I, Priscus,
> prefect of cavalry, received (this) on the day before the nones of December
> in the consulship of Gallicanus and Titianus.

To complete our impression of the meeting of languages, the document has
on the back the names of five witnesses who have signed in Nabataean; the
first is ''Abdu son of Moqimu, witness' ('BDW BR MQYMW ŠHD).

As hinted above, we cannot possibly say how far down the great new road
to Aela, or into the Hedjaz or into the Negev or Sinai the Romans could find
any settled population, or bring them within the operations of the census. But
it should be stressed that only a series of accidents, in the ancient and the
modern world, led to the discovery of these documents in the 'Cave of Letters'
on the side of the Naḥal Ḥever between Engeddi and Masada. We can confidently assume that similar declarations were made all over the settled area of
the former kingdom, at least from Petra in the south through the Decapolis
and the area to the east of it shading off into the steppe, to Bostra and the

---

distinct from 'Arabia'; (c) H. M. Cotton, "Fragments of a Declaration of Landed Property from
the Province of Arabia", ZPE 85 (1991), 263.

Hauran in the north.[31] The area of the Near East to which Roman direct rule, Roman jurisdiction, and the Roman census and taxation were applied, widening stage by stage, and never possible to calculate accurately, will approximately have doubled since the battle of Actium in 31 BC. More significant than that, it had now stretched decisively outside those areas—northern Syria, the Phoenician coast and the Decapolis—where Greek cities were, or seemed to be, the predominant social form. It had at the same time, though the two processes are not to be equated, removed all the dependent kingdoms west of the Euphrates and substituted its own tax-gathering, military occupation and military conscription. It could also have been thought to have reached its natural geographical limits: all of the mountain-chain from the Taurus to the northern Hedjaz, all of the cultivable land between the mountains and the steppe, and all of the upper-middle Euphrates from where it emerges from the Taurus gorge to where the Fertile Crescent stops and the river turns south-east through the steppe. The reign of Trajan thus does indeed represent a sort of culmination. But the campaign which he fought in the second decade of the second century represented not only the first in the Near East in which royal forces could play no part, but the first which a reigning Emperor led in person, and the first which aimed at the permanent occupation of territory across the Euphrates.

3.3. THE ROMAN PRESENCE, AD 114–161

With the Parthian war fought by Trajan in the last years of his reign, the relation of the Near East to the Empire again entered a quite new phase, which was to last to and beyond the end of the Parthian Empire in the 220s, and its replacement by a new Persian Empire. Its features included Roman campaigns beyond the Euphrates, not merely from Cappadocia into Armenia but from Syria into northern Mesopotamia; the aim, achieved in the 190s, to make northern Mesopotamia into Roman provincial territory; and the conduct of these campaigns by Emperors in person. The eastern wars of the 350s and 360s, in which Ammianus Marcellus was to participate as an officer and of which he was later to write the history, went back, in their context and objectives, to Trajan's war. It was a continuity of which Ammianus himself was fully conscious; for he recalls Trajan's siege of Hatra, mentions the town called Ozorgadana on the Euphrates, where Trajan's *tribunal* was still pointed out; and reproduces Julian's speech to his soldiers reminding them of the victories in Mesopotamia of Trajan, Lucius Verus and Septimius Severus.[1]

31. See further 11.1 below.
1. Ammianus XXV, 8, 5 (Hatra); XXIV, 2, 3 (Ozogardana); XXIII, 5, 17 (victories). See above all J. Matthews, *The Roman Empire of Ammianus* (1989), 130ff. My view of these events

As is well known, the two, or perhaps three, provinces formed by Trajan across the Euphrates were immediately given up. But if we take a longer-term view of this abortive project, it acquires a far greater significance. Exactly such a view is provided by the *Breviarium* of Rufius Festus, a brief survey of Roman expansion written in the 360s, some three decades after our period ends:

> At last under the principate of Trajan the diadem was taken from the king of Greater Armenia, and through Trajan Armenia, Mesopotamia, Assyria and Arabia were made *provinciae* and the eastern frontier was established on the banks of the Tigris. But Hadrian, who succeeded Trajan, jealous of Trajan's glory, voluntarily returned Armenia, Mesopotamia and Assyria, and wished the Euphrates to be the boundary between the Persians *(sic)* and the Romans. But afterwards under the two Antonines, Marcus and Verus, also Severus, Pertinax (?) and other Roman Emperors, who fought with varying fortunes against the Persians, Mesopotamia was four times lost and four times recovered. Then in the time of Diocletian, after the Romans had been defeated in a first campaign, and in a second battle king Narses was worsted ... and when peace was made Mesopotamia was restored and the frontier was re-formed along the banks of the Tigris, in such a way that we gained the overlordship of five peoples settled across the Tigris.[2]

What matters about this passage is not the details in it, but first its perspective and second its implication for the continuity of Roman imperialist ambitions in the East from Trajan onwards. Nor need the controversial details of the Parthian war itself be explored.[3] What matters here is that Trajan, hearing that the Parthians had crowned a king of Armenia without his consent, came to the Near East in person (the first reigning Emperor to do so since Augustus), leaving Rome in autumn 113 and spending 114 on the establishment of Armenia as a province. The year 115 seems to have seen the creation of the province of 'Mesopotamia', a term which now (as later under Severus) meant the north-Mesopotamian shelf as far as Nisibis and Singara; the frontier may perhaps have been envisaged as running down the river Chabur from near Singara to its confluence with the Euphrates. It will have been the acquisition of these two new provinces about which Trajan sent a 'laurelled letter' to the Senate which arrived in February 116; for coins of 116 celebrated 'Ar-

---

owes everything to the paper by C. S. Lightfoot, "Trajan's Parthian War and the Fourth-Century Perspective", *JRS* 80 (1990), 115.

2. See J. W. Eadie, *The Breviarium of Festus* (1967); the passage quoted is sect. 14.

3. For the chronology I follow the conclusions of F. A. Lepper, *Trajan's Parthian War* (1948), with adjustments by Lightfoot, op. cit. (n.1).

menia and Mesopotamia subjected to the power of the *populus Romanus*'.[4]
It was probably in the same year that the kingdom of Adiabene, lying mainly
beyond the Tigris, was conquered; if (as is improbable) there ever was a
short-lived Trajanic province of 'Assyria', it will have been here.[5] Then,
after a winter (115/116) in Antioch marked by a great earthquake, in 116
Trajan marched down the Euphrates to Ctesiphon, the Parthian capital,
and then to the head of the Persian Gulf. There Cassius Dio describes him
looking longingly at a merchant-ship setting off for India, and wishing that
he were as young as Alexander.[6] This motive is by no means irrelevant to
the growing Imperial preoccupation with the East. But then a general revolt
broke out, and Trajan was forced to return, and to recognise the Parthian
dynasty. He himself fell ill, and died, back on Roman territory, in Cilicia
in 117.

Whatever else is unclear about this poorly recorded sequence of events, it
is certain that *provinciae* of Armenia and Mesopotamia were indeed formed,
before being given up by Hadrian on his accession in 117. For both a senatorial governor and a *procurator* of Armenia Maior are recorded on inscriptions;[7] and in 116 another Latin inscription, from Artaxata in Armenia,
shows building being undertaken by soldiers of the legion IV Scythica, probably stationed at Zeugma.[8] At about the same time at least one Roman road
was being constructed in Mesopotamia. For a milestone whose Latin inscription gives Trajan's titles as of 116 was found 15 km north-west of Singara, at
a point where a pass leads over the Jebel Sinjar in the direction of Nisibis.
(Nusaybin).[9]

This city, which eight decades later would find itself with the rank of a
Roman *colonia,* played a key part in Trajan's campaign. For his route took
him across northern Mesopotamia to the Tigris, and a bridge of boats was
constructed by cutting wood in the forests around Nisibis and transporting it
(about 100 km) to the river on waggons.[10] The reference must be to the foothills of Mount Masius (the Tur Abdin), just below which modern Nusaybin

4. *BMC Roman Empire* III (1936), 221–222.

5. See Dio LXVIII, 26, 4[1], equating Adiabene and 'Assyria'. There is no contemporary evidence for a province called Assyria, and no source earlier than the fourth century claims that
there had been one. See, however, A. Maricq, "La province d'Assyrie créée par Trajan", *Syria* 36
(1959), 254, identifying Babylonia proper as the province of 'Assyria'. But see Lightfoot, op.
cit. (n.1).

6. Dio LXVIII, 29, 1.

7. *ILS*, nos. 1041 and 1338; see Pflaum, *Carrières*, no. 95 (Armenia Maior).

8. *AE* (1968), no. 510. For the legion's probable station at this point, see 3.1 above.

9. *AE* (1927), no. 161. See D. Oates, *Studies in the Ancient History of Northern Iraq*
(1968), 71–72.

10. Dio LXVIII, 26, 1–2.

lies. At some point Trajan's forces besieged Hatra, in the steppe west of the Tigris and some 120 km south of Singara, no more successfully than Severus later, as Dio notes.[11] But in the 230s this place, encircling its famous temple of the Sun, was to be the furthest point to the south-east occupied by Roman troops.[12]

Roman forces also, as we have seen, advanced down the middle Euphrates, in the campaign of 116. They certainly remained at Dura-Europos long enough for the legion III Cyrenaica to erect an arch in honour of the Emperor to the north of the town.[13] They did not stay, however, and the place reverted to Parthian control. One citizen of the place duly recorded on a Greek inscription how he had restored a shrine there: 'and the original doors were taken away by the Romans, and after their departure from the city I made anew other doors for the same *naos* at my own expense, and outer doors also'. His inscription was dated to the Seleucid year 428, so between October 116 and September 117.[14] The evacuation need have no connection with Hadrian's abandonment of the provinces of Mesopotamia and Armenia. From the 160s onwards, when Dura was occupied by the Romans, it would belong to the province of Syria.[15]

The Parthian war was of great significance as a demonstration of the continued vitality of Roman imperialism—reflected not only in narrative accounts but in contemporary documents—and also as the first sign of a strategic commitment which would last for centuries, until the Islamic conquests, and which meant that Syriac literature would evolve largely within the bounds of the Empire. It also meant, in the shorter term, a renewal of relations with dependent, or potentially dependent, kings, of a type which, west of the Euphrates, had for the time being disappeared. When Trajan reached Antioch in the winter of 113/114, he was greeted by an embassy from 'Augaros the Osrhoenian'—that is, Abgar the king of Edessa—who sent expressions of friendship but did not appear himself, in the hope of remaining neutral. It was only when he reached Edessa itself that he met Abgar, along with 'Mannos, the *phylarchos* of the neighbouring part of Arabia, and Sporakes, *phylarchos* of Anthemousia'. Abgar laid on a banquet for the Emperor and, knowing Trajan's personal tastes, had his good-looking son dance 'in barbaric fashion' during the meal.[16] The dynasty of Edessa, which was to figure in a number of late-Roman and medieval Syriac chronicles, thus makes another

11. Dio LXVIII, 31.

12. 4.1 below.

13. *Dura Reports* IV, 57–65; VI, 480–482.

14. *Dura Reports* VII/VIII, 128–134, no. 868, trans. C. B. Welles.

15. See M. I. Rostovtzeff, "Kaiser Traian und Dura", *Klio* 31 (1938), 285. Fronto, *Principia Historiae* 10, the source closest in time to the event, confirms that Hadrian gave up *provinciae*, but does not say which, or how many.

16. Dio LXVIII, 18, 1; 21, 1–3.

of its sporadic appearances in Graeco-Roman narratives. It may indeed
be that when Parthian control was restored, there was an interregnum for a
couple of years.[17]

The partial nature of our evidence for these major campaigns means that
we cannot assess in detail which legions from which provinces participated;
and more generally the evidence for the movements and numbers of legions
in these years presents complex problems which are not worth exploring here.
It is clear at least that IV Scythica, probably from Zeugma, was in Armenia,
and that some or all of III Cyrenaica was briefly at Dura. The XVI Flavia
Firma from Satala naturally took part, as did the VI Ferrata, perhaps from
Samosata, which is found operating in the mountains, evidently in Armenia;
for a fragment of Arrian shows its *legatus*, Bruttius Praesens, equipping his
men with snowshoes in local style.[18] The X Fretensis from Jerusalem also took
part (there is as yet no concrete evidence of a Jewish revolt in Judaea, parallel
to that in Egypt, Cyrene and Cyprus, at this moment).[19] More significant is
the fact that a *tribunus militum* of the legion XI Claudia, stationed in Moesia
Inferior (along the lower Danube), led cavalry detachments from that province and Dacia to take part in 'the Parthian expedition'.[20] For we begin at this
point to have evidence of the importance of the land-route from the Balkans
through Asia Minor via Ancyra (Ankara) and the Cilician Gates to Syria, and
its role as one of the crucial links which made the Empire, for all the limitations imposed by space and time, a unitary organism in military terms.[21] From
Ancyra itself at this time we have the honorific inscription of a local magnate
who had 'received' (that is, supplied) the forces wintering in the city and had
'sent forward (with supplies again) those on their way to the war against
the Parthians'.[22]

Yet the sea-route to northern Syria, though it certainly never carried
troops en masse, nor could have, remained significant. Trajan himself had
travelled through the province of Asia and then Lycia, arriving by sea at Seleucia.[23] It was in the second century, if not for certain before, that we can see
Seleucia emerging as an established naval base. The Latin epitaphs of officers

17. For the eighth-century *Chronicle of Zuqnin* see App. C.

18. *ILS*, no. 2660 (XVI Flavia Firma); Arrian, *Parthica*, Fr. 85; *AE* (1950), no. 66 (Bruttius
Praesens as *legatus*); *ILS*, no. 2726. See R. Syme, *Roman Papers* IV (1988), 306–307.

19. *ILS*, no. 2727. See Schürer, *HJP* I, 429–434.

20. *ILS*, no. 2723. See R. Saxer, *Untersuchungen zu der Vexillationen des römischen Kai-
serheeres von Augustus bis Diokletian* (1967), 26.

21. For the road itself and its milestones, D. H. French, *Roman Roads and Milestones of
Asia Minor* I. *The Pilgrim's Road* (1981); see S. Mitchell, "The Balkans, Anatolia, and Roman
Armies across Asia Minor", in S. Mitchell (ed.), *Armies and Frontiers in Roman and Byzantine
Anatolia* (1983), 131.

22. *IGR* III, no. 173 = *OGIS*, no. 544.

23. Dio LXVIII, 17, 3.

and sailors, from both the 'Syrian fleet' (now named as such for the first time) and those of Misenum and Ravenna, inscribed at Seleucia, reflect its importance in communications and represent a small island of Romanisation, and the use of the Latin language.[24] So we find at Seleucia Pieria in 166 an *optio* of the Misenum fleet making a contract, in Latin and Greek, for the purchase from a sailor of the same fleet of a slave-boy 'from across the river [*transfluminianum*]', called Abba or also Eutyches.[25] Then, as in 114–116, Roman armies were operating beyond the river Euphrates, captives will have been available in larger than normal numbers, and ships from other fleets will have come to Seleucia. D. van Berchem may well be right to suggest that we need to envisage a network of communications and supplies stretching from the Mediterranean through Seleucia to northern Syria and the Euphrates. That would explain why one of the very rare Latin honorific inscriptions from Syria was erected to a prefect of the Misenum fleet, Marcius Turbo, in about 114, precisely at Cyrrhus, on one of the two main routes from Antioch to Zeugma.[26] Whether we would think of supplies, rather than forces, travelling over such distances is uncertain; but in later campaigns we do know that supplies were shipped from southern Asia Minor to Syria for the armies;[27] and, while we must resist too confident a reconstruction of a supply network, an inscription from Caria does record an equestrian officer who had been 'in charge of supplies in the Parthian war on the bank of the Euphrates'.[28]

If the Parthian war marks a notable step in the evolution of the Empire in the Near East, and a significant foretaste of future strategic commitments, the very fact that a reigning Emperor was now resident there for some three years was also important. First, there was the simple fact that it was possible; that the Empire was not such that it had to be ruled from Rome. Whatever an Emperor needed to do by way of the civilian government of the Empire could be done from his stopping-points on a journey, or in the intervals of campaigning.[29] But in so stark a form this too was a sign of the future rather than of established practice; not since Augustus, more than a century before, had any Emperor spent so long a continuous period in (or beyond) the provinces. What this meant for the Empire is perfectly expressed by Dio in recounting the consequences of the great earthquake which struck Antioch when Trajan was there in December 115:

24. *IGLS* III, nos. 1155–1182.

25. *P. Lond. inv.*, no. 229 = Cavenaille, *CPL*, no. 120.

26. *AE* (1955), no. 225; for the prefect, Q. Marcius Turbo Fronto Publicius Severus, see *PIR²* M 249. For this interpretation, D. van Berchem, *Bonn. Jahrb.* 185 (1985), 47, esp. 77ff.

27. 4.2 below.

28. *ILS*, no. 9471; cf. L. Robert and J. Robert, *La Carie* II (1954), 180, no. 78.

29. For this theme, Millar, *ERW*, passim.

While he was staying in Antioch an extraordinary earthquake took place. Many cities suffered from it, but Antioch was the most unfortunate. For as Trajan was wintering there, and many soldiers had gathered there as well as many civilians, whether for judicial hearings or on embassies or as traders or out of curiosity, there was not a province or a community which remained unharmed, and thus in Antioch the whole world under the Romans suffered disaster.[30]

The slowly emerging role of Antioch as a secondary Imperial 'capital' is vividly captured. Trajan escaped on this occasion, to die of natural causes while sailing back from Syria along the Cilician coast in August 117. Whether he had intended it or not, the succession went to a son of his cousin, P. Aelius Hadrianus, well placed as *legatus* of Syria, who heard the news within days and proclaimed himself Emperor 'in Antioch, the metropolis of Syria'.[31] Setting off from there, and sending some forces before him, he took the land-route across Asia Minor, through Ancyra, Iuliopolis and Nicomedia, to the Balkans, arriving in Rome nearly a year after his proclamation, in July 118.[32]

His reign, as is well known, was to be unique in that so much of it was spent on systematic journeys through the provinces, with both civilian and military ends in view. But the military aspect arose largely not from the necessities of campaigns but from a desire to inspect the army. The fact that his journeys included the Near East is thus not distinctive in itself. What is distinctive is first the strongly local colouring of the documentary evidence which happens to reflect his presence there; then the second of the two great Jewish revolts, under Bar Kokhba or Ben Kosiba, in 132–135, against which the Emperor took command in person; and finally his foundation of the last 'real' *colonia* in the history of Rome, Aelia Capitolina, Jerusalem.

Hadrian may have been in Syria in 123, but the period when his visit left the clearest traces in our evidence seems to be from the autumn of 129 to the summer of 130. Much of any possible reconstruction depends on later sources and may be left aside. For instance the fact that there were 'Hadrianic Baths' in Antioch is now made certain by the new archive of the third century from the middle Euphrates.[33] But whether, as Malalas records in the sixth century, Hadrian ordered the construction of these baths himself, as well as of other

30. Dio LXVIII, 24, 1–2.
31. Dio LXIX, 2, 1.
32. R. Halfmann, *Itinera Principum* (1986), 188ff. For refinements see R. Syme, "Journeys of Hadrian", *ZPE* 73 (1988), 159 = *Roman Papers* VI (1991), 346; T. D. Barnes, "Emperors on the Move", *JRA* 2 (1989), 247.
33. D. Feissel and J. Gascou, *CRAI* (1989), 535, no. 1: a subscription posted in 245, ἐν ταῖς Ἀδριαναῖς θερμαῖς. See further 4.2 below.

public buildings, or did so while present in person, is quite uncertain.³⁴ What matters is the very vivid documentary evidence of his presence in certain areas. Perhaps the most distinctive is the earliest documentary record of an Imperial visit to Palmyra, which in this reign gained the Greek title 'Hadrianē Palmyra'. It comes from a bilingual honorific inscription from the temple of Ba'alshamin recording that a man called Males had been secretary *(grammateus)* of the city during the visit of Hadrian, had provided oil for strangers and citizens and had seen to the reception of the troops. In the Palmyrene text Hadrian is 'our lord Hadrian, (the) god: [MR]N HDRY[N'] 'LH'.³⁵ The inscription dates the dedication of the statue of Males to 130/131, but does not of course serve to date the exact moment of the visit. Nonetheless it is highly significant that the Imperial entourage and escort troops did visit Palmyra at this time, when it was reaching the summit of its architectural development; on the other hand there is nothing whatsoever in the literature of the second century to suggest that the culture of Palmyra had been registered as something of particular interest to intellectual circles elsewhere in the Empire.

Probably on the same journey Hadrian also travelled south to the province of Arabia. A Greek inscription put up in his honour by Gerasa, 'the city of the Antiochenes by the Chrysorhoas, the former Gerasenes', seems to refer to the whole period of his stay, and to his having held jurisdiction while there, and dates to 130. It is matched by a Latin dedication on his behalf by some of his escort troops, his *equites singulares* who had wintered 'at Antiochia by the Chrysorhoas, also called Gerasa, sacred, inviolate and autonomous'. The triumphal arch which stands to the south of Gerasa was dedicated by the city on behalf of the Emperor at the same time, 130.³⁶ Here, too, no Emperor had ever been before. It is very likely that the Emperor did give jurisdiction while there, as Caracalla was later to do in Antioch.³⁷

We would have known anyway that Hadrian visited Arabia, for contemporary coins record ADVENTUS AUG ARABIAE, as they do ADVENTUS AUG IUDAEAE. But precise connections between his presence, the plan to found a new *colonia* at Jerusalem, with a temple to Iuppiter Capitolinus, and the outbreak of the great revolt in 132 cannot be established. There is, however, no good reason to disbelieve the implications of Cassius Dio's account, according to which it was this plan, involving the settlement of a gentile population, which provoked rebellion (a reported ban on circumcision may also have been rele-

34. For his alleged constructions, some perhaps simply deduced from the fact that buildings were named after the Emperor (as was very common throughout the Empire), see Malalas, *Chron.*, 277–278.

35. *CIS* II, no. 3959 = Cantineau, *Inv.* I, no. 2 = C. Dunant, *Le sanctuaire de Baalshamin à Palmyre* III: *Les inscriptions* (1971), no. 44.

36. *Gerasa*, ins. no. 30 *(equites singulares)*; 58 (arch); 144 (visit).

37. 4.2 below.

vant). According to Dio, fighting did not break out while Hadrian was in Egypt or again in Syria, but only when he was far away.[38]

Hadrian certainly visited Gaza in 130, was in Egypt over the winter of 130/131 and may have sailed up the Phoenician coast before spending the winter of 131/132 in Athens. So it is not unreasonable to regard the plan for a new *colonia,* with the title 'Colonia Aelia Capitolina', reflecting the name of the Emperor, P. Aelius Hadrianus, as a product of his personal initiative while there. Whether it was planned before that cannot be known. All that is clear is that Judaea was transferred from being a one-legion province, under a *legatus* of ex-praetor status, to being a two-legion province under an ex-consul, not after the revolt, as we might expect, but before it. If this change did not take place, as had been argued, under Trajan,[39] it had certainly occurred by the 120s, when first the legion II Traiana (before going to Egypt) and then, on a permanent basis, the VI Ferrata were stationed there.

At this point no details of the revolt itself are needed except to emphasise that it lasted some three and a half years, saw the foundation of a regular administration in the areas free of Roman control and again required a major concentration of force by the Roman army. The contemporary documents which reflect life in the Jewish-held area belong in the social history of Judaea; they strongly suggest that the revolt began in the spring of 132 and continued until the autumn of 135.[40] Even for the Roman army it is enough to recall that apart from X Fretensis and VI Ferrata, III Cyrenaica from Bostra and (at least) IV Gallica from Syria took part; as the consular *legatus* of Syria left the province to confront the uprising in Judaea, probably other units from Syria came too. Moreover, the tribune of a legion in Pannonia was appointed by Hadrian to bring detachments for the war.[41] More significant still, it can be taken as certain that the Emperor took command in person, at least for a time; inscriptions recording military honours now granted by the Emperor describe the campaign as an *expeditio Iudaica,* one on which the Emperor was present.[42] The revolt thus left Judaea as a major, and on the surface a highly Romanised, element in the structure of the Empire: two *coloniae,* Caesarea and Aelia; an ex-consul as governor with two legions each under a praetorian *legatus;* and a substantial number of auxiliaries. A *diploma* of 139 shows that there were then at least three cavalry *alae* and twelve *cohortes* in

38. Dio LXIX, 12, 1–2. The ban on circumcision is reported directly only by HA, *v. Had.* 14, 2, given more weight by the permission for it granted by Antoninus Pius, as recorded by Modestinus in *Dig.* XLVIII, 8, 11. See Schürer, *HJP* I, 534–543, and A. Linder, *The Jews in Roman Imperial Legislation* (1987), no. 1.

39. W. Eck, "Zum konsularen Status von Iudaea im frühen 2. Jh.", *BASP* 21 (1984), 55.

40. 10.3 below, and for a catalogue App. C.

41. For the details see Schürer, *HJP* I, 547, n.150.

42. So R. Syme, *ZPE* 73 (1988), 166–167 = *Roman Papers* VI (1991), 353–554.

the province.[43] No other province with no external frontier had so large a garrison. But what the *diploma* of 139 also shows is that the name 'Iudaea', with its ethnic reference, had already disappeared, to be replaced by a new name, 'Syria Palaestina'.

With these changes the evolution of the structure of the Empire in the Near East west of the Euphrates was almost complete. If we look at it in very local terms, we can see that it consisted of a spread of major legionary bases: from Samosata (XVI Flavia Firma) and Zeugma (IV Scythica) in the north overlooking the Euphrates, to the Orontes Valley, where III Gallica seems to have been at Raphaneae, to Syria Palaestina, where X Fretensis was at Aelia and VI Ferrata at Caparcotna in the Jezreel Valley; and III Cyrenaica at Bostra in Arabia, where, as we have seen, the camp is still visible from the air, attached to the north side of the city. Even here we are hardly in a position to assess the complex mutual influences and relationships between the civilian population and these large masses of soldiers. Still less is this the case with auxiliary units, whose long-term locations, if they had them, are hardly ever known. One place where a few such sidelights are available, however, is Palmyra, where the earliest evidence for the presence of Roman auxiliary units belongs to the middle of the second century. Typically, what little we know is a product of the 'epigraphic habit', and specifically of the habit of putting up honorific inscriptions. So Greek inscriptions from the temple of Bel at Palmyra show us the *praefectus* of the Ala Herculiana of Thracians, Iulius Iulianus, in 167; and around the same period a different *praefectus*, Vibius Celer, who had also become a town-councillor *(bouleutēs)* of the city; he is described as 'the prefect of the *ala* (stationed) here', presumably the same one.[44]

How the different units of the army were distributed across the landscape, how they were housed and supplied and what functions they performed, for instance as a police-force, in relation to the civilian population are questions impossible to answer in general terms. There is no way in which the impact or presence of the Roman state in the Near East can be adequately assessed. Its more profound, longer-term effects, for instance the spread of the Roman citizenship or the transformation of collective identities (in what sense did any Commagenian or Nabataean identity survive the imposition of provincial status?) must be reserved for a closer look at the different sub-regions of the area. But it is still relevant to pick out, by way of illustration, a few features of the presence of the Roman state which we can discern from our scattered evidence.

One, which cannot have escaped anyone, was the construction of roads. Though a road might be anything from a fully paved construction, like the

43. *CIL* XVI, no. 87.
44. Cantineau, *Inv.* IX, no. 22 (= *ILS,* no. 8869), no. 23.

much-photographed section still visible between Antioch and Beroea, or a track from which stones had been systematically cleared, or just a track, milestones bearing the name of the Emperor, wherever they were placed, will have been an unmistakable sign of the Imperial presence. For instance, still clearly visible from the air and from the ground is the road linking Damascus to Bostra cut, in the middle of the second century, directly across the Leja, the plate of broken volcanic rock known as Trachonitis, once part of Herodian domains.[45] The road is lined with watch-towers and milestones, one of which records that in 185/186 the road was restored 'from Phaena to Aerita', that is, from the northern edge of the rock plate at Phaena (Mismiyeh) almost to the southern edge at Aerita (Ahire or Ariqah). Here a Greek inscription from above a surviving gate, dating to 169/170, perfectly exemplifies one form of interaction between Empire and subjects. For the gate was built at his own expense by a man from Aerita with a perfectly Roman name, T. Claudius Magnus, a veteran (*ouetranos*, transliterated), and the work was supervised by a centurion of III Gallica. The same centurion, as well as one from XVI Flavia Firma, appears engaged in building at Phaena.

Most of the inscriptions from Phaena come from a monumental construction, finally destroyed in 1890, which may have been a temple or some sort of official building.[46] Its most striking feature is a letter, engraved beside the main entrance, of Iulius Saturninus, *legatus* of Syria in 185–187:

Iulius Saturninus to the Phaenesians, *mētrokōmia* of Trachōn, greeting. If anyone imposes himself on you by force, whether a soldier or a private person, send to me and you will have justice. For you do not owe any contribution to strangers, and having a guest-house you cannot be forced to receive strangers in your houses. Put up this letter of mine in a prominent place in your *mētrokōmia*, so that no one may be able to excuse himself on grounds of ignorance.[47]

This letter thus takes its place, along with the extract from the *mandata* of Domitian from Hama/Epiphania, in a long list of documents illuminating the most contentious area of friction between the state and its subjects. The use of a distinctive local term, *mētrokōmia* ('mother-village'), as well as the fact that the *legatus* addresses this community directly, also illustrates the city-like function of the major villages of this region. Whether the change was for good or ill, no one there could mistake the fact that since the disappearance of

45. See M. Dunand, "La voie romaine du Ledgâ", *Mém. Ac. Ins.* 13 (1930), 521; Th. Bauzou, "Les voies de communications dans le Hauran à l'époque romaine", Dentzer, *Hauran* I, 137; Kennedy and Riley, *RDF,* 78–79.

46. Le Bas-W., no. 2438 (Aerita); *IGR* III, nos. 1113–1118 (Phaena). See S. Hill, "The Praetorium at Musmiye", *DOP* 29 (1975), 349.

47. Le Bas-W., no. 4551 = *IGR* III, no. 1119 = *OGIS*, no. 609.

Agrippa II some decades before, they belonged to a wider and quite different state-system.

As we have seen in the cases both of the colony of Babylonian Jews established in Batanaea by Herod the Great and of the villagers of Maoza when Nabataea became the province of Arabia, it would have been equally impossible to ignore the imposition of Roman taxation and the Roman census.[48] Yet, as elsewhere in the Empire, our documentation for the Near East hardly allows us to gain any conception of this process, or even to be sure whether direct taxation was paid predominantly in cash or in kind.[49] What we do know, or are told, about this in our sources manages to combine sweeping assertions with a lack of concrete detail. So, for instance, Appian, writing in the middle of the second century, mentions in passing that for 'Syrians' and 'Cilicians' there is an annual tax, at 1 percent of their census-rating.[50] That would imply a total valuation of landed property, as a basis for the payment; and it also implies a very high level of taxation. For if we suppose that land yielded 7 percent per year on its capital value, the rate of taxation would have been something like 15 percent on income. But the two known census-returns from Judaea show no trace of any such system—each piece of property has a conventional rate of taxation, in cash or kind, attached to it.[51] Nor do we gain any conception of how taxation of property related to taxation of individuals, the 'head-tax', or *tributum capitis*. So the most important of the Roman lawyers of the early third century, Ulpian, a citizen of Tyre, writes of the *census*: 'It is necessary to record a person's age in the census-return, because certain groups gain exemption by reason of age; for example in Syria males are liable to the *tributum capitis* from 14 years, females from 12, until the 65th year'. We have to assume that both a land tax *(tributum soli)* and a 'head-tax' were payable. For the jurist Paulus, a contemporary of Ulpian, notes that when Vespasian made Caesarea a *colonia,* he remitted only the *tributum capitis;* but his son Titus exempted their land *(solum)* also.[52] Babatha, making her census-return in the province of Arabia in 127, makes no reference to her own age, however, or to anyone else as being resident on the properties concerned.[53]

In other words the realities of the process by which the Roman state lived off its subjects, in this as in other areas, escape us. Almost equally fragmentary evidence survives for the collection of tolls *(portoria)* by contractors *(publicani)* on the main routes. The complex question of long-distance trade

48. 2.2 and 3.2.
49. See 2.2.
50. Appian, *Syr.* 50/253.
51. 3.2 above.
52. *Dig.* L, 15, 3 *pr.* (Ulpian); L, 15, 8, 7 (Paulus).
53. 3.2 above.

will concern us later;[54] so it is sufficient here to mention the collection of tolls at Gaza on the caravan-trade coming up from the Yemen (Arabia Felix), and the 'quarter-collector' *(tetartōnes),* attested (again) on an honorific Greek and Palmyrene inscription from the agora at Palmyra put up in 161. The honorand, Marcus Aemilius Marcianus Asclepiades, was a town-councillor of Antioch, and was honoured by 'the traders who had come up from Spasinou Charax' at the head of the Persian Gulf. It is accompanied by another, of 174, which honours another *tetartōnes,* and is one of the very few known trilingual inscriptions, in Latin, Greek and Palmyrene—brief as it is, a perfect expression of the complex cultural framework created by the extension of Roman power into the steppe.[55] A quite different perspective is offered by a scene in Philostratus' historical novel the *Life of Apollonius of Tyana,* written in the early third century: when Apollonius and his party are about to cross the Euphrates into Mesopotamia, the *telōnēs (publicanus)* stationed at Zeugma takes them to a board on which standard charges for various items are listed.[56]

This work, set in the later first century, properly takes no account of the great changes and upheavals which occurred in the later second century and early third. These events were to give Syria a new and unexpected centrality in the functioning of the Empire, and to extend Roman rule both far down the middle Euphrates and across northern Mesopotamia to the Tigris.

3.4. EMPERORS AND PRETENDERS IN THE NEAR EAST FROM LUCIUS VERUS TO SEPTIMIUS SEVERUS: THE CONQUEST OF MESOPOTAMIA

For a quarter of a century after the end of the Bar Kochba revolt, no significant changes took place in the shape of the Empire in the Near East. When they did come, it was again the result, so our Roman sources relate, of Parthian ambitions:[1] for Vologaeses IV of Parthia, taking advantage of the accession in 161 of two new joint Emperors, Marcus Aurelius and Lucius Verus, installed Pacorus, a member of his family, as king of Armenia. The early fighting took place on the upper Euphrates and involved the defeat and suicide of the *legatus* of Cappadocia. The subsequent Roman reaction was of

54. 13.1 below.

55. Cantineau, *Inv.* X, nos. 29 and 113. A further trilingual inscription referring to the same man is published by Kh. Al-As'ad and J. Teixidor, *Syria* 62 (1985), 279, no. 9.

56. Philostratus, *V. Ap.* I, 20.

1. For a detailed and perceptive account of these events, on which I draw for those details relevant to the Near East in the sense used here, see A. Birley, *Marcus Aurelius: A Biography*[2] (1987), 121–126; 128–131. On Vologaeses (IV), see now A. Pennachietti, "L'iscrizione bilingue greco-partica dell'Eracle di Seleucia", *Mesopotamia* 22 (1987), 169, on pp. 181–182.

great significance for the nature of the Imperial system for centuries to come. One Emperor, Marcus Aurelius, stayed in Rome, while the other, Lucius Verus, travelled (slowly and luxuriously, it was said) to Antioch to conduct the campaign, apparently arriving in 162 or 163. In the event, when the Romans took the initiative, first in 163 and then decisively in 165, it proved possible to place a Roman nominee on the throne of Armenia and to march all the way to the centre of the Parthian Empire, capture Ctesiphon and sack the major Greek city of Seleucia on the Tigris.

As such, these campaigns are perhaps most significant for having been the subject of a satire by a native of Samosata with the Hellenised Latin name of Loukianos, or Lucian, whose *How History Should Be Written* mocks panegyrical and ill-informed contemporary accounts. What it meant that a major Greek writer should come from the ancient capital of Commagene must be discussed later.[2] But his contemptuous analysis of the instant histories produced to celebrate the event, written already in 166, is enough to confirm the facts of fighting in northern Mesopotamia, around Edessa and Nisibis, as well as the currency of fantastic reports of how the third legion (III Gallica) and some auxiliaries, under 'Cassius', had even crossed the Indus.[3] Documentary evidence shows movements not much less remarkable than that: one legion was moved from Bonn and came with other detachments through the Orient to Osrhoene and Anthemousia, and another from the lower Danube.[4] In fact the river which Avidius Cassius, the *legatus* of III Gallica, will have crossed will have been the Tigris; and it will have been his advance into Media which earned Lucius Verus the title 'Medicus'. But the image of Alexander was not an unreal or insignificant element in Roman thinking about military glory in the East.

What if anything really changed as a result of the Mesopotamian campaign is quite unclear. What seems certain at least is that the king, Mannus, of Osrhoene took the Roman side and was temporarily exiled to Roman territory. For two years as it seems (approximately 162/163–164/165), a Parthian-backed king ruled there. The coinage of Edessa in fact begins with issues showing Vologaeses IV on the obverse and 'Wael the king', named in Syriac (W'L MLK'), on the reverse. But then there came issues either with 'Ma'nu the king' in Syriac (M'NW MLK') or with members of the Antonine dynasty on the obverse, and 'King Mannos, friend of Romans' *(Basileus Mannos Philorōmaios)*, on the reverse. The coins, very remarkably, fit exactly with the report by an eighth-century Syriac chronicler—admittedly placing these

2. See H. Homeyer, *Lukian, Wie man Geschichte schreiben soll* (1965); C. P. Jones, *Culture and Society in Lucian* (1986), esp. ch. 6. See 12.3 below.

3. Lucian, *Hist.* 15 (Nisibis); 22 (Edessa); 31 (Indus).

4. Birley, op. cit. (n.1), 130; *ILS*, no. 1098; *CIL* III, no. 6169.

events more than two decades earlier—that a king Ma'nu ruled for twelve years after being in exile in Roman territory for two.[5]

Rome had thus, after an interval of more than half a century, acquired another dependent kingdom, and one of considerable importance in cultural and religious history. Whether any of Mesopotamia was now actually occupied by Roman soldiers remains uncertain. Certainly such an occupation took place to the north, in Armenia, where a Roman nominee, Sohaemus, was installed as king, and Roman forces were left at a newly named capital, Kainepolis ('new city'). Two Latin inscriptions duly attest detachments of the Cappadocian legions stationed at Echmiadzin just south of Mount Ararat.[6] If this is indeed Kainepolis (or even if not), it represents a remarkably deep penetration of Armenia, for it lies the best part of 400 km east of Satala. Over mountainous territory this must have meant a march of twenty days or more. In the light of that remarkable example of imperialism, it may seem less improbable that garrisons, or outposts, were also left in eastern Mesopotamia, at Nisibis. But our only evidence to suggest that possibility is that in the 190s troops loyal to the *legatus* of Syria, Pescennius Niger, were besieged there by the Adiabenians (to the east) and the Osrhoenians (to the west).[7] If there was a Roman protectorate of Mesopotamia, we do not know what form it took; certainly there is no reason to think of a dependent king having been supported at Nisibis.

If the situation in that area remains obscure, a considerable advance down the Euphrates is quite certain. Lucian refers to a battle near Sura on the Euphrates, which may have been the point at which Roman control had previously stopped.[8] Another contemporary, Fronto, writing to Verus about the glory won by his campaigns, refers to the storming not only of Artaxata (in Armenia) but of Dausara and Nicephorium.[9] He does not need to say that these were on the Euphrates, that Dausara in fact lay upstream from Sura or that Nicephorium (also called Callinicum) lay at the confluence of the Balikh and the Euphrates. More important still, however, Lucian speaks several times of a great battle at Europos, in which one panegyrical historian claimed that over seventy thousand men had been killed. Another thought that Europos was in Mesopotamia.[10] But even Lucian does not make clear that this meant a great extension of Roman control down the river (over 250 km as the river runs), and above all that it took Roman occupation southwards past

5. See further 12.5 below, and App. B.

6. *ILS*, nos. 394 and 9117. See M. G. Angeli Bertinelli, "I romani oltre l'Euphrate nel II secolo d.C.", *ANRW* II.9 (1976), 3, on p. 27.

7. Dio LXXV, 1, 2–3.

8. Lucian, *Hist.* 29. See 3.1 above.

9. Fronto, *Ad Verum Imp.* 2, 1 (Loeb ed. II, 132).

10. Lucian, *Hist.* 20, 24, 28.

the confluence of the Euphrates and the Chabur at Circesium, which would later be heavily fortified by Diocletian.[11]

The Romans had thus regained what may have been the key element in the 'frontier' of Trajan's short-lived province of Mesopotamia;[12] and if there were now some sort of occupation of Mesopotamia, the route following the Chabur up to the region of Nisibis may have been important. But both the line of the Euphrates and that of the Chabur were in any case routes, narrow strips of cultivated territory, rather than frontiers.

In terms of area, even as regards the zone to the west of the Euphrates, this substantial advance thus added less to Roman territory than a map conceived in terms of regions bounded by 'frontiers' might suggest. It did have the quite accidental effect of transforming the volume and nature of what we now can hope to understand of the Near East under Roman rule. For, first, as we will see in more detail later, the newly available archive of documents dating between the 230s and 250s relates primarily to the life of the villages on the west side of the Euphrates between the Balikh and just below the Chabur, a region of whose culture and social life virtually nothing was previously known.[13] Second, what has been known of it, or of areas near it, has until recently depended on the vast mass of evidence of all kinds revealed by the excavations of Dura-Europos in the 1920s and 1930s.[14] This small Macedonian settlement on its spur overlooking the Euphrates had been in Parthian occupation since the later second century BC and was to remain in Roman hands from the 160s until its destruction by the Persians in the 250s. Because the archaeological and documentary evidence from here is wholly out of proportion to that from anywhere else; because it was for so long 'Parthian'; and because the evidence was heavily over-interpreted when first found and has not all been published in final form even yet, Dura presents the most acute problems for any overall interpretation of the 'Roman' Near East. For the moment, however, what concerns us is the presence of the Roman army there, and only in its first phase, until the major changes of the 190s.

The Roman military presence is illuminated by a considerable range of documents, both inscribed and perishable (parchments and papyri), though none of the latter belong to this first phase.[15] A considerable series of Palmyrene inscriptions from Dura (the first dating to 34/33 BC and hence almost the earliest known) shows that there had been close connections across

11. 5.1 below.

12. 3.3 above.

13. For this archive, ch. 1 above, and 4.2 and 12.5 below.

14. See, as a preliminary, C. Hopkins, *The Discovery of Dura-Europos* (1979).

15. For all that follows see J. F. Gilliam, "The Roman Army in Dura", in C. B. Welles, *The Excavations at Dura-Europos, Final Report V.1, The Parchments and Papyri* (1959), introduction, ch. 4, reprinted in J. F. Gilliam, *Roman Army Papers* (1986), 207.

the steppe throughout the period; and it may just be that a military role on the part of the Palmyrenes persisted from the Parthian to the early Roman period. At any rate one Palmyrene dedication to Yarhibol from the Parthian period was made by the 'Bne Mita, the archers' (BNY MYT' QŠṬ')—which does not, however, have to imply a regular military presence.[16] Such a presence *is* clearly implied by a Palmyrene inscription of 168/169 made by an 'officer' (the Greek word *stratēgos*, transliterated as 'ṢṬRṬG'), 'who is in command of the archers who are at Dura' (DY 'L QŠṬ' DY BDWR'), as well as a second inscription in Greek, of 170/171, naming a Palmyrene as '*stratēgos* of the archers'.[17] No other evidence of a Palmyrene military presence reappears until 208, when the unit concerned was a regular Roman auxiliary cohort;[18] speculation on this early phase can be taken no further. At least by the reign of Commodus (180–192) an auxiliary unit from the garrison of Syria, the Cohors II Ulpia Equitata, which had been involved in operations in Mesopotamia in Verus' Parthian war,[19] had moved to Dura. Very typically, in various ways, the evidence comes from an altar dedicated in Latin to the Genius of Dura by two *decuriones* of the cohort, for the safety of Commodus.[20] The *cohors* was still there in 194, at a time of civil war and considerable changes, when an *actuarius* of the cohort was, in all apparent innocence, involved in putting up a dedication 'for the safety and victory' of Emperor Septimius Severus and his fellow-consul of the year (and later defeated rival), Clodius Albinus.[21]

How this inscription relates to the rise and fall of the other rival Emperor of that year, Pescennius Niger, the *legatus* of Syria itself, is quite unclear. But before that we need to put in context various aspects of these decades, which clearly illustrate the growing importance of the Near East within the Imperial military and political system.

The first focus of attention must be the personality and career of C. Avidius Cassius, whom we have seen as *legatus* of III Gallica winning glory in Verus' Parthian war.[22] On the surface his background and very prominent career now present few problems. He came from Cyrrhus in northern Syria

16. *Dura Reports* VII/VIII, 279, no. 909 = du Mesnil du Buisson, *Inventaire des inscriptions palmyréniennes de Dura-Europos (32 avant J.-C. à 256 après J.-C.)* (1939), no. 33.

17. *Dura Reports* VII/VIII, 83–84, nos. 845–846. The Palmyrene one is Mesnil du Buisson, op. cit. (n.16), no. 19.

18. 4.1 below.

19. *ILS*, no. 2724; see Devijver, *PME* V 17 (M. Valerius Lollianus).

20. *Dura Reports* I, 42–44.

21. *Dura Reports* V, 226, no. 561.

22. See M. L. Astarita, *Avidio Cassio* (1983), and above all R. Syme, "Avidius Cassius: His Rank, Age and Quality", *Bonner Historia-Augusta Colloquium 1984/1985* (1987), 207 = *Roman Papers* V (1986), 689.

and was the son of a well-known orator, Avidius Heliodorus, who was *ab epistulis* (in charge of letters—almost certainly Greek letters) of Hadrian, and later prefect of Egypt. Since, when he proclaimed himself Emperor in 175, Avidius Cassius was to refer to Alexandria as his 'paternal city', he was almost certainly born there while his father was in the entourage of Hadrian. He himself will then have entered the Senate in the mid-150s, and would (as was normal) have been an ex-praetor when he commanded III Gallica in Verus' campaign.

So far what we see is an example of the classic pattern of the integration of the Greek upper classes into the highest orders of the Roman system. First the Roman citizenship; then a career, by the father, in equestrian posts, gaining advantage also from a reputation for rhetorical skills; then the son enters the Senate. This pattern, with many variations, has been much studied and needs no comment.[23] But it is much less well attested for the Near East than for Anatolia, especially if we leave out the direct descendants of kings on the one hand, and citizens of Roman *coloniae* on the other.[24] Even if this disparity is a product of a comparable disparity in the number of inscriptions set up in the cities of the two regions, a Roman senator from Cyrrhus, beginning his career in the middle of the second century, remains a noteworthy phenomenon.

What followed his success in the Parthian war was more noteworthy still: a suffect consulship, perhaps already in 166, and held in absence; and then very soon, perhaps even immediately, the consular post of *legatus* of Syria. A long series of inscriptions, including those from Phaena and Aerita already mentioned, reflect his role there between 169 and 175. All describe him in the normal terminology, *legatus Augusti pro praetore,* or in Greek, *lamprotatos hypatikos* (translating *clarissimus consularis*).[25] But two Greek writers of the first half of the third century, Cassius Dio and Philostratus, both state that he was given also some general command, either of 'all of Asia' or of 'the East'.[26] Apart from an expedition to crush a rebellion in Egypt, there is no precise sense which we can attach to this.

In 175, when it was thought that Marcus Aurelius, now sole Emperor,

23. The classic presentation is still A. Stein, "Zur sozialen Stellung der provinzialen Oberpriester", *Epitumbion Swoboda* (1927), 311. See now, for all the evidence, H. Halfmann, *Die Senatoren aus dem östlichen Teil des Imperium Romanum* (1979).

24. See G. W. Bowersock, "Roman Senators from the Near East: Syria, Judaea, Arabia, Mesopotamia", in S. Panciera (ed.), *Epigrafia e ordine senatorio* II (1982), 651.

25. For the full references, B. E. Thomasson, *Laterculi Praesidum* I (1984), 312–313. In *AE* (1937), no. 167 = C. Dunant, *Le sanctuaire de Baalshamin à Palmyre* III, *Les inscriptions* (1971), no. 48a, παρὰ Ἀουίδιῳ Κασσίῳ τῷ διασημοτάτῳ ὑπά[ρχ]ῳ; the last word should be ὑπα[τικ]ῷ.

26. Dio LXXXI, 3, 1: τῆς Ἀσίας ἁπάσης ἐπιτροπεύειν. Philostratus, *V. Soph.* II, 1, 32: ὁ τὴν ἑῴαν ἐπιτροπεύων.

and with only the thirteen-year-old Commodus left to succeed him, had died, Avidius Cassius proclaimed himself Emperor; Cassius Dio believed that Marcus' wife Faustina encouraged him to do so. In the event, little is known of the three-month 'reign' of Avidius except that he gained the allegiance of the Near East and Egypt. It ended with his murder, while Marcus was still on the Pannonian front. But although the *legatus* of Cappadocia took immediate control of Syria, Marcus still came in person, making peace with the barbarian tribes beyond the Danube, some of whom now supplied troops. Many aspects of the Empire as it was developing are reflected in the honorific inscription of an equestrian officer from Pannonia who at this moment was 'placed in charge of cavalrymen of the peoples of the Marcomanni, Naristae and Quadi on their way to the punishment of the eastern uprising'.[27] Marcus, as we would expect, took the established land-route through Asia Minor to the Cilician Gates. But no contemporary evidence, literary or documentary, reflects Marcus' presence in the Near East. According to the late biography of him in the *Historia Augusta,* he passed directly on to Alexandria, where he seems to have spent the winter of 175/176, and visited Antioch only on his return journey. But he perhaps visited Syria in 175 and went by land from there to Egypt. For Ammianus records him on a journey through Palestine complaining of the turbulence of the Jews: 'O Marcomanni, O Quadi, O Sarmatae, at last I have found others more restless than you!'. In the immediate context the remark is, in a certain limited sense, intelligible. Whether any of the barbarian soldiers accompanying him overheard it is not recorded. Nor do we know what disturbances among the Jewish population of Syria Palaestina, three decades after the end of the Bar Kochba war, prompted this exclamation—or why it had been in his account of Marcus' reign that Ammianus, in a lost book, had first given an account of the *Saraceni.*[28]

Whether, as the *Historia Augusta* claims, Marcus really prohibited all shows and public meetings at Antioch as a punishment, and whether, as Malalas might suggest, there was a restoration of the games at Antioch under Commodus, need not be decided.[29] But the episode must have served to emphasise the potential role of Antioch as a secondary capital city, and with that the relationship between the *legatus,* or self-proclaimed Emperor, and the population of the main city of his province. Furthermore, it does also seem to have raised a wider question of regional identities and regional loyalties. For Cassius Dio, a Greek from Bithynia, who entered the Senate in the late 180s, both describes Avidius Cassius as 'a Syrian, from Cyrrhus' and includes in his *History* a speech of Marcus Aurelius, addressed to his soldiers, in which

27. *AE* (1956), no. 124; Pflaum, *Carrières,* no. 181 *bis.*
28. Ammianus XXII, 5, 4–5 = Stern, *GLAJJ* II, no. 506 (Jews); XIV, 4, 2 (Saracens).
29. HA, *M. Ant.* 25, 9–17; Malalas, *Chron.* 283–290.

he derides the forces under Cassius as being 'Cilicians, Syrians, Jews and Egyptians'. More significant, Dio records that it was then laid down that no one should govern the province from which he himself came.[30] If 'Syrian' means simply 'inhabitant of the Roman province of Syria', there is no problem, though there is very little to suggest that in the Empire a person's province served as a sort of ethnicity. We would far more naturally suppose that it was a person's city or community which did that. Moreover, in what sense an inhabitant of a Greek city in Syria, and a Roman senator, would have accepted a description of himself as a 'Syrian' is a major problem. So is the implication of Marcus' measure, that such an origin would have attracted a degree of regional loyalty throughout the province.

Such regional loyalties proved in any case not to be a necessary condition for a *legatus* of Syria to proclaim himself Emperor, or to attract widespread support. For within two decades such a proclamation was made, in 193, by Pescennius Niger, *legatus* since 190 or 191. The civil war which followed and Pescennius' defeat by Septimius Severus, Emperor in 193–211, were to have fundamental consequences for the Near East—and ones whose origins, nature and effects themselves raise difficult questions of how communal and regional identities were understood then or should be analyzed now. In this instance the whole shape of the region and of the Roman presence in it was transformed by external and civil wars, and by decisions made by an individual monarch whose relations to that region were of the most complex kind. Certain aspects of Severus' biography are therefore essential to note if these changes are to be understood.[31]

Severus had been born in 145 at Lepcis Magna in Tripolitania, now (since 112) a Roman *colonia*, but as a city a distant product of the Phoenician colonisation of North Africa, and still a region where a Semitic language (Neo-Punic) was current alongside Latin. That the Phoenician origins of Lepcis are relevant to the reshaping of the Near East is no mere novelistic fantasy. For perfectly clear documentary evidence from this period shows that the historic role of Tyre in Phoenicia as the 'mother-city' of Lepcis was still publicly celebrated. Precisely this is reflected in a second-century dedication, in Latin and Greek, put up in Tyre by the *colonia* of Lepcis and honouring Tyre as its *mētropolis*.[32] Severus, coming from a prominent local family including Roman senators, entered the Senate himself, and in about 180, as an ex-praetor, was sent to Syria as *legatus* of the legion IV Scythica at Zeugma. For anyone

30. Dio LXXI, 22, 2: Σύρος μὲν ἐκ τῆς Κύρου ἦν; 24–26 (Marcus' speech); 31, 1.

31. As will be obvious, what follows depends on A. Birley, *The African Emperor: Septimius Severus* (1988).

32. See J. P. Rey-Coquais, "Une double dédicace de Lepcis Magna à Tyr", in A. Mastino (ed.), *L'Africa Romana* IV (1986), 597, and Millar, "Roman *Coloniae*", 35–36. AE (1987), nos. 958–959.

who has looked across the Euphrates from the acropolis of Zeugma to the rolling, fertile territory on the other bank, it is hard to reject altogether a connection between this appointment and Severus' later claim that Mesopotamia, now conquered, would serve as a bulwark for Syria. In fact we know nothing of any military or other role of Severus at this time. It was only later recorded that before becoming Emperor, he had consulted the oracle of Bel at Apamea on the Orontes (evidently while *legatus*), and had received in reply two lines of the *Iliad* describing Agamemnon. The appearance in this major Greek city of a god with a Babylonian name is another puzzle, to which we will return.[33] But for the moment, if we may believe the biography of Severus in the *Historia Augusta,* it was another aspect of divine agency, a horoscope, which a few years later, while he was *legatus* of Lugdunensis, persuaded him to marry a lady from Emesa, Iulia Domna.[34]

Whether the story was fiction or not, the marriage is a fact. On the surface at least, it could be seen as a marriage-connection typical among the provincial aristocracies who had risen into the higher ranks of the Imperial service. Whether Iulia Domna's family had any connection with the dynasty of Emesa which had come to an end, apparently, in the 70s is pure speculation. It may equally be speculation when a fourth-century source records that the father of Iulia Domna and her sister Iulia Maesa was Bassianus, priest of the Sun, 'whom the Phoenicians, from whom he sprang, called Heliogabalus'.[35] That description masks profound problems, as will be seen later. If there is truth in the report, Bassianus must, from the names of his daughters, have been a Roman citizen, Iulius Bassianus; and the family's citizenship must indeed have gone back to the early first century AD. Iulia Domna's sister, Iulia Maesa, married an *eques* who later rose to the Senate, the Iulius Avitus Alexianus from Emesa who as *legatus* of Raetia about 200 was to dedicate an altar to 'his ancestral Sun God Elagabal'.[36] By 193 he will have been settled in his equestrian career, and it was probably Severus who made him a senator. Their daughter Iulia Sohaemias, perhaps born in the early 180s, will have been married around 200 to Sextus Varius Marcellus, an equestrian official who, as we learn from Cassius Dio, was from the same province (the undivided 'Syria' of before 194), being from Apamea. It is Dio too who goes on to say that Maesa's other daughter, Iulia Avita Mamaea, was married to Gessius Marcianus,

33. Dio LXXVIII, 8, 5–6. See 7.4 below.

34. HA, *v. Sept. Sev.* 3, 6.

35. *Epit. de Caes.* 21, 1; 23, 2.

36. *PIR*[2] I 192. For the identification see H.-G. Pflaum, "La carrière de C. Iulius Avitus Alexianus, grand'père de deux empereurs", *REL* 57 (1979), 298; H. Halfmann, "Zwei syrische Verwandte des severischen Kaiserhauses", *Chiron* 12 (1982), 212. For the whole family nexus, Birley, op. cit., App. 2. The family is also treated, in the context of the history of Emesa, in 9.2 below.

also 'a Syrian', from Arca (also called Caesarea ad Libanum), an equestrian *procurator*.[37]

The sons of these two marriages, born in about 203 and 209, were to be the youthful Emperors of 218–222, M. Aurelius Antoninus, or 'Elagabal', and of 222–235, Severus Alexander. In itself it must be an open question as to whether these provincial, or regional, connections had any significance. But the fact that a prominent contemporary, Dio, stresses them cannot be ignored. The integration of these products of Syrian cities into the equestrian service would be of some significance even without the accession of Severus in 193, and the further promotions to the Senate which followed.

The murder of Commodus on the last night of 192 led to the brief regimes in Rome of Helvius Pertinax and then Didius Julianus, ended by the entry of Septimius Severus' troops from Pannonia Superior, where he had been *lega-tus*. But even before he began his march, in April 193, he may have heard that Pescennius Niger had proclaimed himself Emperor in Antioch. Herodian's *History*, written towards the middle of the third century, provides a model of how such a proclamation, made in a major Greek city, would take place.[38] Niger began by summoning some officers and getting them to spread the rumour of a possible proclamation. Popular response soon followed:

> Syrians, being characteristically erratic people, are always ready to upset established rule. But they also had a real affection for Niger because he had been a mild governor to everyone, and frequently used to join in the celebration of their festivals. The Syrians are naturally fond of holidays, which applies particularly to the citizens of Antioch, the largest and most flourishing city. In Antioch they celebrate festivals practically the whole year round, either in the city or in the surrounding district. Because Niger had given them a succession of shows (about which they are particularly enthusiastic), and had granted them licence to have feasts and celebrations, which he knew were popular, he was obviously respected.

He is then represented as making a speech to the soldiers, with a civilian crowd also present:

> After such a speech the entire army and the assembled crowd at once proclaimed him emperor and hailed him with the title of Augustus. They also put the purple cloak of an emperor on him and provided him with all the other tokens of imperial dignity made out of makeshift materials, including the carrying of fire before him in processions. After conducting him to the temples of Antioch they installed him ceremoniously in his own house,

37. Dio LXXVIII, 30, 2–3.
38. Herodian II, 7, 7–8, 6, Loeb trans.

which was now regarded as the imperial court and no longer a private house. Outside it was decorated with all the insignia of office.

Embassies then came from all the neighbouring provinces, as well as messages from 'satraps' and kings beyond the Euphrates and Tigris.

In 193/194, however, Severus' forces marched east, while Niger remained inactive; both the forces and the Emperor himself, following later, took the established route through Asia Minor, and by 194 Severus was in control of Syria. In 195 he was campaigning in Mesopotamia (where there may already have been some Roman forces),[39] marching back through Asia Minor in early 196. After the defeat of another rival Emperor, Clodius Albinus, the *legatus* of Britain, he set off in summer 197 to Syria (this time via Brundisium), and invaded Parthia in 197/198, capturing Ctesiphon (perhaps in January 198). In the rest of 198 he seems to have been in Syria; and then, apparently in 199, there came a further expedition, during which he failed to take Hatra. After that he returned, and travelled through Syria Palaestina to Egypt. How long he stayed there is uncertain; but he then returned to Syria, where he and his son (now called M. Aurelius Antoninus, better known by his nickname Caracalla) entered on the consulate of 202 in Antioch. After that they marched back by the normal route across Asia Minor, passing through Ancyra and Nicaea.[40]

The details of these movements are important. For, first, the government of the Empire could be and was conducted by and from the Emperor's travelling entourage. Second, the sheer stretch of time involved is a sign of how the Empire was evolving. When Severus celebrated the beginning of the tenth year of his reign in Rome in 202, he had spent at least half of it either in Syria or on campaigns across the Euphrates. Third, to enter on a joint consulate in Antioch was deliberately to emphasise that the institutions of the Roman *res publica* could be deployed in the East. Within two decades, two different pretenders and two established Emperors had, for varying periods, ruled from there. And fourth, it was in the 190s, in the aftermath of the civil war, that major changes took place in the Near East, both internally in the shape of the provinces and externally in the level of military commitment.

The first step was to divide the province of Syria into two; looking back, Herodian was later to emphasise that Pescennius Niger had governed the whole of Syria, a vast province covering Phoenicia and all the territory up to the Euphrates.[41] That was of course the point; looked at from Rome, it was too large. So the region now became two provinces: the northern half, with two legions, became (against all previous usage) 'Syria Coele', or 'Hollow

39. 3.3 above.
40. See Halfmann, *Itinera*, 216–221, and T. D. Barnes, *JRA* 2 (1989), 255–256.
41. Herodian II, 7, 4.

Syria';[42] the southern part, with one legion, was to be 'Syria Phoenice'. Latin inscriptions leave no doubt that this (not 'Phoenicia') was its title; but 'Phoenice' (like 'Coele' indeed) is not a normal Latin adjective, but a straight transliteration from Greek. As such, it is even declined as in Greek. So milestones from the road through Trachonitis, mentioned above, record their establishment by Manilius Fuscus, the first *legatus,* described as 'praesidem Syriae Phoenices'.[43] The use of this term can have been intended only as a historical reminiscence, emphasising the importance of the cities of Phoenicia.

This newly devised province was not confined to areas which anyone would previously have thought of as 'Phoenician', for the 'border' between it and Syria Coele ran all the way from the Mediterranean across to the Euphrates. On the coast the city of Arados and its territory belonged to Syria Phoenice; so did Raphaneae, the camp of III Gallica, Emesa and its territory, Damascus and Palmyra, with its vast zone stretching to the Euphrates. But Dura-Europos, as abundant evidence shows, belonged to Syria Coele. In spite of the conquest of northern Mesopotamia, the (now) two legions of Syria Coele seem to have remained where they had been before, on the Euphrates at Samosata and at Zeugma;[44] if so, they now faced provincial territory across the Euphrates and were over 300 km from the southernmost part of the province where it reached the river.

The reason for the division can be regarded as certain, namely to limit the forces available to any one *legatus* in the Near East to not more than two legions. The *legati* of Syria Coele, with their two remaining legions, were still of ex-consul rank, while those of Phoenice were of ex-praetor status, as commanding only one legion; that it remained at Raphaneae in the Orontes Valley, not far from Emesa, is made quite clear by events in the civil war of 218.[45] In what sense if at all Syria Phoenice should be thought of as a *frontier* province remains to be seen when we look at the evidence for the Severan frontier as a whole. But certainly many aspects of security remained in the hands of the Palmyrenes, whose role in the protection of caravans going across the steppe to the Euphrates is best attested in this period. That fact, and the relation of Palmyra to the early governors of the new province (whom they still flatteringly called *hypatikoi—consulares*), is clearly reflected in a bilingual Palmyrene inscription of 198 in honour of one Aelius Bora, 'placed in charge of keeping the peace by the *hypatikoi* Manilius Fuscus (194–197?) and Veni-

---

42. On this see the typically brilliant article by E. Bickerman, "La Coelé-Syrie: Notes de géographie historique", *RB* 54 (1947), 256. The term had been used, very inconsistently, for various regions in *southern* Syria, including the Bekaa Valley and the Decapolis. See also M. Sartre, "La Syrie Creuse n'existe pas", *Géog. hist.,* 15.

43. M. Dunand, "La voie romaine du Ledjâ", *Mém. Acad. Ins.* 2 (1930), 1, on pp. 22–37.

44. So Wagner, *RET,* 65; but cf. 4.1 below.

45. 4.2 below.

dius Rufus (198?) and by his native city, and having shown great determination and courage and having acted as *stratēgos* several times and having retained the same courage and manhood, and having been honoured for these qualities by Iarhibol the ancestral god, and by the governors and by the decrees of his native city'. What this meant is made more explicit by a decree of the following year, 199, honouring someone else 'who by his continued commands against the nomads had come to the aid of the merchants and afforded safety to the caravans *(synodiai)'.*[46]

If our evidence were better, we might well think that the most significant feature of Phoenice as a province, perhaps even as a military command, was the two great mountain-chains of Lebanon and Anti-Lebanon with Mount Hermon, which occupied a large proportion of its western part. The proportion may have been made even greater in the early third century by the loss of some territory in the Hauran and Trachonitis to Arabia, for unknown reasons and with not very clear consequences, except that Canatha and other small places now fell within the area of activity of the legion III Cyrenaica stationed at Bostra.[47]

The fact of the creation of a new province has naturally led historians on the vain search for its 'capital' (Tyre, Sidon, Damascus?) and the seat of its governor. That is a misapplied question. But, by contrast, what is very well attested arc thc drastic changes imposed by Severus by way of reward and punishment for the different attitudes taken by cities in the civil war.[48] Herodian records that while Antioch, as we have seen, supported Pescennius Niger, Laodicea on the coast supported Severus, and was sacked by Niger's forces; similarly Berytus supported Niger, and Tyre Severus, and Tyre was also sacked by Niger's troops. Herodian then claims that after Severus' victory Antioch lost the formal status of a city altogether, and became a village *(kōmē)* in the territory of Laodicea—which if true lasted only a few years.[49] What is certain, and very well attested in various types of evidence, is that the Greek title 'metropolis' ('mother-city') and the Roman status of *colonia* were liberally distributed by the Emperor. The clearest case is Laodicea, which became a metropolis immediately in 194, and a *colonia* with *ius Italicum* in 198—'on account of its services in the civil war', as the contemporary Roman jurist Ulpian, a native of Tyre, records. He is not so explicit about his own city, preferring to speak in general terms of its loyalty to the Roman state; but it certainly was for that reason that Tyre appeared on its now Latin coinage

---

46. H. Ingholt, "Deux inscriptions bilingues de Palmyre", *Syria* 13 (1932), 278 = *SEG* VII, nos. 138–139; the second = Cantineau, *Inv.* X, no. 44. See J. Starcky and M. Gawlikowski, *Palmyrez* (1985), 78–79.

47. See Bowersock, *Roman Arabia*, 114–115.

48. For what follows see Millar, "Roman *Coloniae*", 31ff.

49. Herodian III, 3, 3; 6, 9 (Antioch as *kōmē*).

from Severus' reign as 'Septimia Turus Metropolis Colonia'. Ulpian felt no equal reserves about the case of Heliopolis, which since 15 BC had been part of the territory of the *colonia* of Berytus. Now, 'on the occasion of the civil war', it gained the rank of *colonia*, becoming the 'Colonia Iulia Augusta Felix Heliopolis'. This island of Romanness and the Latin language in the Near East thus became two independent cities, a punishment (as is clear) for Berytus' support of Niger. No such explanation is available for Severus' other grant of this status, to Sebaste (Samaria), founded by Herod the Great—unless we use the item offered by the *Historia Augusta*, that the people of Flavia Neapolis, the neighbouring city, had also displeased him by taking Niger's side, and lost their status.[50]

These arbitrary changes of name, of constitutional status (for all the inhabitants of the new *coloniae* will have become Roman citizens) and of mutual precedence, absurd though they may seem, are of considerable significance. From one point of view they are merely another example of the remarkable malleability of communal 'identities' in the Near East; from another, the local rivalries which they reveal suggest how dubious any notion of a *regional* identity or solidarity would be; from yet another, they are a clear reflection of the intensification of the Imperial presence and of Imperial attention in this period; and finally they mark the beginning of a period when, at least on the surface, the Near East became 'Roman' in a way of which there had been little trace before.

But that process applied also—and even more suddenly—to the newly conquered territory across the Euphrates. If the level of Roman involvement here in the period from 165 to 195 is uncertain, there can be no doubt about the drastic nature of the transformations which now took place. Nor can there be any doubt about the significance of this step as a deliberate product of Roman imperialism. For Cassius Dio records both the justification for it offered by Severus and his own doubts about the long-term strategic consequences: 'Severus . . . used to say that he had gained a very extensive territory and had made it a bulwark for Syria. But it is demonstrated by the facts as being the source of continual wars for us and of great expenditures. For it provides very little, and consumes very much, while we having advanced as far as the nearer of the Medes and Parthians are always as it were fighting on their behalf'.[51] This passage will almost certainly have been written after the fall of the Parthian Empire in the 220s and the rise of the new Persian dynasty, which offered a much more active threat to Rome. On the other hand, with two brief exceptions in the 250s, all of the endless Roman-Persian wars were to be fought east of the Euphrates, on what the Romans now claimed as provincial territory. But in essence Dio was correct.

50. HA, *v. Sept. Sev.* 9, 5, a possibility raised in Millar, "Roman *Coloniae*", 38.
51. Dio LXXV, 3, 2–3.

New evidence shows just how quickly at least part (and probably all) of the new provincial framework was established east of the Euphrates. For a Latin inscription dating to 195, the year of Severus' first campaign, records how C. Iulius Pacatianus, *proc(urator) Aug(usti),* established boundaries between the 'provincia Osrhoena' and the kingdom of Abgar.[52] The boundary lay a mere 40 km west of Edessa, and new light is cast on what we knew already, the fact that the kingdom survived as an enclave after the Roman conquest. We will come back later to the complex evidence for Edessa in the time of Abgar, whose reign probably lasted from 177 until 212.[53] For the moment it is more important to note how small the geographical area of the kingdom seems to have been, and that it was surrounded or bordered by a new Roman province for which the name 'Osrhoena' had been taken over. There was naturally a provincial garrison, and in 197 we find a detachment of the legion IV Scythica, from Zeugma, building a *castellum* in the northwest of the new province, on the route across it between Zeugma and Samosata. Eight years after that, in 205, we find another *procurator* of the new province, L. Aelius Ianuarius, recorded on another Latin inscription, from the same place as the boundary-marker, as having been the Imperial agent for the construction of a road for forty-eight Roman miles (70 km) 'from the Euphrates to the boundary of the kingdom of Septimius Abgar'.[54]

It is thus certain that as early as 195 the area east of the Euphrates included the small dependent kingdom of Abgar and a minor province called Osrhoena, under an equestrian *procurator.* Within a few years there was also a major province further east, called Mesopotamia, with two legions; it was not, as would have been normal, placed under a *legatus* of ex-consul rank, but, like Egypt since the beginning, came under a *praefectus* of equestrian status. The change can have been no accident, and is an important step in the evolution of the Imperial system away from its roots in the Republican past.

Just how soon this major new province was organised is not quite certain, but it surely cannot have been later than 198 or 199, during Severus' second period of campaigning there.[55] An inscription from Bithynia records that Ti. Claudius Subatianus Aquila, before being prefect of Egypt (in 206–211), had been 'the first prefect of Mesopotamia'. For the reasons mentioned above, the point was worth making. Even with our fragmentary evidence, several differ-

52. *AE* (1984), no. 919. This, like the following inscriptions, was published by J. Wagner, "Provincia Osrhoenae" *(sic),* in Mitchell, *Armies and Frontiers,* 113.

53. 12.5 below, and App. C.

54. *AE* (1984), no. 918 *(castellum);* 920: '(Severus, Caracalla and Geta) viam ab Euphrate usque ad fines regni Sept. Ab<g>ari a novo munierunt, per L. Aelium Ianuarium proc. Aug. prov. Osrhoenae m.p. XXXXVIII'.

55. For what follows see D. L. Kennedy, "Ti. Claudius Subatianus Aquila, 'First Prefect of Mesopotamia'", *ZPE* 36 (1979), 255; and "The Garrisoning of Mesopotamia in the Late Antonine and Early Severan Periods", *Antichthon* 21 (1987), 57.

ent features of the new provincial and military structure are clear. First, Severus created three new legions (an increase of 10 percent in the legionary establishment of the Empire), called the I–III Parthicae, of which I and II were stationed in Mesopotamia. Exactly where I was stationed is not known; but II Parthica was in the south-east corner of the province at Singara, on the southern slopes of the Jebel Sinjar: 'which legion is at Singara in Mesopotamia by the river Tigris', as a legionary's tombstone from Aphrodisias in Caria was to record, exaggerating a little.[56] Moreover, at least two cities in the new province found themselves transformed, already in Severus' reign, into Roman *coloniae*. In the cases of Nisibis and Carrhae/Harran (only 50 km from Edessa but evidently outside the remaining *regnum* of Abgar) this is certain. It is quite likely also in two other cases, Reshaina and Singara, both of which later in the century had titles including the words 'Septimia colonia'.[57] Mesopotamia, whose greatest extension was yet to come, presents the clearest possible example of continuing Roman military expansionism from the later Imperial period. But for a fuller appreciation of that expansionism we need to look not just at the contested frontier with Parthia, but at the whole borderland of Roman control, from Mesopotamia to the Red Sea, over much of which Roman forces confronted not the army of a rival kingdom but the little-known peoples of the steppe.

56. J. Reynolds and M. Speidel, "A Veteran of I Parthica from Carian Aphrodisias", *Epigraphica Anatolica* 5 (1985), 31 = *AE* (1985), no. 800. The creation of these two legions by Severus, and the fact that they were stationed in Mesopotamia, is recorded by Dio LV, 24, 4.

57. Millar, "Roman *Coloniae*", 38–39.

ROME AND MESOPOTAMIA:
FROM PARTHIA TO PERSIA

4.1. THE SEVERAN NEAR EAST AS
A MILITARY STRUCTURE

The military history of the Near East, as of any other region, cannot be separated from its social history. For a start, the life of the units of the Roman army, distributed across the immensely varied landscapes of the Near East, is itself an aspect of social and economic history. It is also, in many important ways, an aspect of cultural and religious history. The soldiers, drawn from many different parts of the Empire, may often have brought their own cults with them. But what we actually see much more clearly, from Hatra in Iraq to Dura-Europos, or from Dumayr between Damascus and Palmyra to the great temple of Baetocaece high up in the mountain-range behind Arados, is how soldiers of the Roman army made dedications to local deities, and thus (as in so many other ways) integrated themselves into the life of the region. The approach to the Near East adopted here began with the dedication which a soldier of IV Scythica made at Dura-Europos in the first half of the third century, in honour of 'the ancestral god, Zeus Betylos, of those by the Orontes'. An even more complex example is provided by the dedication of a statue of 'Iuppiter Optimus Maximus Heliopolitanus', made, probably in the second half of the second century, by Sextius Rasius Proculus, *praefectus* of the Cohors II Thracum Syriaca. It comes from a place of some significance, namely Suhneh (Suknah), on the road north from Palmyra to Sura on the Euphrates, and where a road may have diverged east to reach the river at Circesium. As it happens, this is one of only two explicitly labelled representations of the Iuppiter of Heliopolis. But it will not in fact help with the controversial question of the god's iconography; for Proculus simply used a statue of purely Palmyrene local workmanship.[1]

But does the making of a Latin dedication at this place by a Roman *praefectus* mean that his unit, which we know to have been stationed in Syria, occupied a post on this strategic road?[2] An aerial photograph reveals a rectangular structure of *circa* 110 m by 80 m there, which may have been a small auxiliary fort.[3] But if this and perhaps other forts, lying within the zone of Palmyrene settlement and occupation in the steppe and along the Euphrates, were occupied by Roman units, how did this military presence work in relation to Palmyrene police activity and the protection of caravans against the nomads? Was this route, going northwards, in fact a trade-route at all?

A sketch of some of the more salient features of what little we know of the army in the decades before and after AD 200 will of course reveal how erratic our evidence is, and how rarely we can prove that a military presence anywhere was continuous over more than a very short period. But we should not yield too readily to scepticism. Even our fragmentary evidence reflects great changes and an extension of the Roman military presence over vast areas where in the first century AD it had been quite unknown.

It was of course in Mesopotamia that the changes, already discussed, had been most dramatic. If we cannot be sure where the legion III Parthica was stationed, perhaps Nisibis,[4] it is certain that I Parthica was at Singara, where it still appears in Ammianus' narrative of events in 360. By then Singara was a fortified city, defended both by its inhabitants and by two of the now smaller Roman legions, but through lack of water had been captured several times already, as it was again now.[5] The line of the Roman fortifications, of uncertain date, is still visible from the air.[6] The normal construction of roads also followed (broadly reproducing the abortive process under Trajan a century earlier), and a Roman milestone of 231/232 has been found some 5 km southwest of Singara;[7] given its position, it might perhaps indicate a road leading towards the Chabur and then down the Euphrates. Roman outposts will very probably have extended also to the Tigris; it was probably in the early third century that a Roman veteran *(ouetranos)* put up beside the Tigris a bilingual

---

1. For the inscription (*AE* 1911, no. 124) and the statue see Y. Hajjar, *La triade d'Héliopolis-Baalbek* I (1977), 211, no. 186 and Pl. LXX.

2. The unit is listed on a *diploma* of 157, *CIL* XVI, no. 106.

3. Kennedy and Riley, *RDF*, 143–144.

4. So Kennedy, *Antichthon* 21 (1987), 61.

5. Ammianus XX, 6, 1–8.

6. Kennedy and Riley, *RDF*, 125–131.

7. J. N. Fiey, "A Roman Milestone from Sinjar", *Sumer* 8 (1952), 229; see A. Maricq, *Syria* 34 (1957), 294, and D. Oates, *Studies in the Ancient History of Northern Iraq* (1968), 73.

dedication to Zeus, in Greek and Aramaic.[8] But our most vivid evidence for the limits of Roman occupation comes from Hatra, some 115 km south-east of Singara. All that we know from narrative sources is that both Trajan and Severus had failed to capture this walled city with its great temple of the Sun. An aerial photograph again brings out with remarkable clarity the roughly circular line of walls, the street-plan and the oblong enclosure of the temple at the centre.[9] By the 230s Roman forces were there. Again the evidence comes from dedications, one to the local deity: of three Latin inscriptions from there, contrasting with a long series of several hundred Aramaic ones,[10] one gives the date 235; one is a dedication to Hercules by a tribune of I Parthica, apparently also tribune of Cohors IX Maurorum Gordiana (so in the reign of Gordian, 238–244); and one, by the same man, is to the 'Unconquered Sun God' ('Deus Sol Invictus') of Hatra.[11] Whether this was an alliance or an occupation, and when it began, is not known. But it is certain that Hatra was captured by the Persians in about 240, and it seems never to have been retaken.[12]

Hatra was thus a mere outpost, which did not stay long in Roman hands. If there was a 'frontier' of Mesopotamia other than the Tigris, it should have lain along the Chabur River, running south-west down to the Euphrates. But there is no specific evidence, datable to this period, to tell us whether there was a line of forts, or a road, along the river. As soon as we come within the range of the evidence provided by either the papyri and parchments of Dura-Europos or the newly available ones from the middle Euphrates, our ability to catch at least some glimpses of the system is restored. Indeed one contribution from the new documents is precisely to suggest regular connections between the zone of villages near the middle Euphrates, above and below its confluence with the Chabur, and the cities of Osrhoene and Mesopotamia: Edessa, Marcopolis, Nisibis, Carrhae, Singara.[13] To give two precise examples, two separate sales of slaves conducted at Beth Phouraia on the Euphrates refer back to previous sales of the same slaves at Nisibis; and in

8. See D. L. Kennedy, "A Lost Latin Inscription from the Banks of the Tigris", *ZPE* 73 (1988), 325. The reality of this inscription is doubted by C. S. Lightfoot and J. F. Healey, "A Roman Veteran on the Tigris", *Epig. Anat.* 17 (1991), 1, publishing the very significant bilingual inscription, on which see further 13.1 below.

9. Kennedy and Riley, *RDF,* 106–107.

10. See F. Vattioni, *Le iscrizioni di Hatra* (1981); see H. J. W. Drijvers, "Hatra, Palmyra and Edessa", *ANRW* II.8 (1977), 799. As Hatra was so briefly under Roman occupation, it will not be considered further in this chapter.

11. See A. Maricq, "Les dernières années d'Hatra: L'alliance romaine", *Syria* 34 (1957), 288; *AE* (1958), nos. 238–240.

12. 4.2 below.

13. 4.2 and 12.5 below.

one of these cases the seller had been the wife of a centurion of the legion I Parthica.[14] Again it is important that we can now at least glimpse the economic and social integration of the soldiers into local society.

Both the middle Euphrates and Dura lay within the new province of Syria Coele, whose two legions, the XVI Flavia Firma and the IV Scythica, may or may not have kept as their main bases Samosata and Zeugma far to the north. It is not known when they moved south to the stations where they are found at the end of the fourth century: XVI at Sura and IV at Oresa (Tayibeh) on the road to Palmyra.[15] Nor is there any inscriptional or archaeological evidence for the Roman posts along the Euphrates between the Balikh and the Chabur, and below the Chabur as far as Dura, in the third century. But there was a line of posts above and below Dura, even though this was now not a frontier facing hostile territory. It was both a narrow strip of cultivable land and an important military and civilian route. When the Persians invaded in the 250s, they were to move not across but along it, destroying a long series of small places as they went.

Although there is no evidence on the ground datable to this period, the evidence from the new archive from the middle Euphrates and from the extensive military archives from Dura can combine to give a real impression of the military presence. It will be worth listing a few examples.[16] For instance we find that a villager living at Birtha Okbanon had complained (without effect) to a centurion stationed there, saying that his vineyard had been occupied by a neighbour. Another, from a village called Magdala, complained in 243 to the centurion 'in charge of public order in Sphoracene' about a murder and robbery; when the complaint was laid at Appadana, testimony was given by a veteran and a serving soldier of XVI Flavia Firma. Both a place called Birtha and one called Magdala appear in the Dura archives as posts to which small detachments were sent out; and Birtha Okbanon and Sphoracene appear in the list of his conquests in the 250s set up by the Persian king Shapur I.

The soldier of legion XVI, testifying as a private person, is matched by the one from the same legion with the historic name 'Aurelius Corbulo', who is recorded in a document of 232 as making a contract at Beth Phouraia, a village on the Euphrates in the territory of Appadana; Aurelius Corbulo was a pilot *(gubernator)* in legion XVI, and was selling a boat (in bad repair) located on the river. Finally we find a soldier from a *numerus* of Palmyrenes

---

14. See D. Feissel and J. Gascou, "Documents romains inédits du Moyen-Euphrate (IIIᵉ s. après J.-C.)", *CRAI* (1989), 559, nos. 8 and 9. See more fully 4.2 below.

15. *Not. Dign., Or.* 33, 28 (Sura); 23 (Oresa).

16. Feissel and Gascou, op. cit., 557–558, nos. 2 and 5 (complaints); 559, no. 11 (sale of boat); 560, no. 14 (settlement of debt).

making a formal agreement at Appadana to regard as settled a debt due to him from a woman living at Dusaris (*perhaps* the place Dausara far to the north near Callinicum).

These views of local society and the role (both official and private) of soldiers within it are closely paralleled, for just this area, by the documents from Dura-Europos. One of the most notable documents from there is a Greek deed of sale of AD 226, drawn up in the winter-quarters (*paracheimasia*) of the Cohors III Augusta Thracum at a village called Sachare. The purchaser was a veteran of the same cohort living in the area; and the land, consisting of vineyards and orchards, was bounded by the Chabur River on the one side and a canal on the other. Five serving soldiers signed as witnesses, four in Latin and one in Greek. The village of Sachare may have lain some 25 km up the Chabur from the Euphrates. But the document is beyond price in revealing that there were auxiliary camps on this river also, and in saying so much about the economy of the strip along the river.[17]

In such a document we see the role of military units and individual soldiers as it were from below, from within local society. The military archives proper from Dura of course give a different impression. But they too show how small detachments were strung along the Euphrates in this period, as well as illustrating how detachments from the two legions of the province, IV and XVI, could be present as far south as this. The best impression of how the river functioned as a route, lined with military posts, is provided by the letter which the *legatus* of Syria Coele, Marius Maximus, wrote in 207 or 208 about provisions for a Parthian envoy on his way to or from the court of Severus and Caracalla. It was addressed to the *tribuni* and *praefecti* and the *praepositi* of *numeri,* and ended by listing five places on the river, in order from north to south: Gazica (near the confluence with the Chabur), Appadana, Dura, Eddana and Biblada.[18] Appadana in particular appears many times in the Dura documents as a place to which detachments were sent, and we can assume that there were military posts at all these places.

The history of Dura as a garrison town from the 190s to its end in the 250s is very well attested, and can be briefly summarised here.[19] Detachments of legions IV and XVI are found building a shrine to Mithras in 209, and ones of IV and III Cyrenaica (from Bostra in Arabia) an amphitheatre in 216. References to XVI continue in the 220s, and almost the last document of Roman Dura is a Greek divorce-deed of 254, involving a soldier of legion IV, now called IV Scythica Valeriana Galliena. Three years earlier two Greek

17. *P. Dura,* no. 26.

18. *P. Dura,* no. 60B. See M. L. Chaumont, "Un document méconnu concernant l'envoi d'un ambassadeur parthe vers Septime Sévère (P. Dura 60B)", *Historia* 36 (1987), 423.

19. See J. F. Gilliam, op. cit. (3.4, n.15).

dedications show that an auxiliary unit with the title 'Cohors II Paphlagonum Galliena Volusiana' was also at Dura.[20]

But these passing mentions cannot of course be made into a history of the garrison. The stable element, which is very fully attested, is the XXth cohort of Palmyrenes, perhaps raised first in the 190s; whether it had any connection with the Palmyrene archers who were there before is not known. It is first recorded at Dura in 208, and seems to have been there to the end. Of the vast range of detail revealed about military life, we may pick out, first, the hints of the rather strikingly detailed control exercised by the *legatus*, from northern Syria, by letter. One document reveals soldiers sent with letters 'to the headquarters of the governor', and two others contain letters of the *legatus*, Marius Maximus, assigning horses to individually named soldiers; one is written from Hierapolis and one from Antioch.[21] Second, of some ten *tribuni* or *praepositi* of the cohort whose names are known, one, Iulius Terentius, holding his post in the late 230s, has achieved a particular fame. For it is he who is represented, and named, in the well-known wall-painting from the temple of Bel showing him leading his men in a sacrifice to the *Tychai* (personified Fortunes) of Palmyra and Dura and to three other gods who may be Palmyrene.[22] Once again, a member of the Roman army can be seen paying his respects to local deities. It is certain that the Iulius Terentius who is identified on the mural is a tribune of this cohort, for he is named also in the Greek verse epitaph which his wife put up to him when he died in battle.[23] The occasion was perhaps the moment in April 239 when 'the Persians descended upon us', as a graffito records.[24]

Third, since its excavation Dura has always been regarded as providing the major case where we can see the occupation of a whole quarter of a walled town by the army, and its physical reconstruction to serve the needs of the army. Thus one building with a number of Latin inscriptions is interpreted as a *praetorium* (headquarters-building) with a 'house of the prefect' beside it; and a brick wall which can be traced for some distance through the city is taken to mark the boundary of the new military quarter.[25] Other buildings

20. *P. Dura*, no. 32; *Dura Report* IX.3, 110–114, nos. 971 and 972.

21. *P. Dura*, no. 82, col. ii, l. 7; 56B–C (Marius Maximus).

22. Published by F. Cumont, *Fouilles de Dura-Europos* (1926), 89ff. (where the temple is still called the temple of the Palmyrene gods); A. Perkins, *The Art of Dura-Europos* (1973), 42ff. and Pl. 12 (now in Yale University Art Gallery); cf. M. A. R. Colledge, *The Art of Palmyra* (1970), 228–229. See further 12.4 below.

23. See C. B. Welles, "The Epitaph of Julius Terentius", *HThR* 34 (1941), 79; *Dura Report* IX.1, 176, no. 939.

24. *Dura Reports* IV, 110, no. 233B.

25. *Dura Reports* V, 201–237.

(baths, the Mithraeum, an amphitheatre) in whose construction soldiers took part are also held to be part of this development. Most controversially of all, one elaborate building with a portico overlooking the Euphrates has been labelled 'the Palace of the Dux Ripae'. But the evidence for the identification consists of two painted inscriptions in Greek from this building, commemorating slaves of Domitius Pompeianus, who in one of these is called *dux ripae*.[26] This identification, and the excavators' conception of the military takeover of the whole quarter, may be correct. But it is all very uncertain, and cannot be used for historical purposes. What is certain is (in general) no more than the clear evidence for the close integration of the army into the life of the town. But a more particular point which these and other documents do establish is that the late-Roman military rank of *dux,* not a technical term in the High Empire, had come into use at Dura in the first half of the third century.[27] But *dux ripae*—'commander of the bank or frontier' (transliterated in Greek as *doux tēs reipēs*)—appears only in the one painted inscription just mentioned. Until there is clearer evidence, too much effort should not be devoted to constructing a picture of his regional military responsibilities—or to admiring the luxury of his residence.

For our conception of the military structure of the Empire, it would be more important to know how much further down the Euphrates below Dura Roman military occupation extended, and how it related to Palmyrene control. As we have seen, there were certainly Roman outposts at places called Eddana and Biblada; the latter *may* be the little fort of the Severan period which looks out over the Euphrates at Ertaje, from the east bank.[28] Not far below that, we come to the island of Ana, or Anatha, which Julian was to capture from the Persians during his invasion of 363.[29] In the late 250s, however, it is listed first by Shapur I in his record of the places captured in his third invasion, and we would thus take it to have been then a Roman outpost.[30] But Palmyrene inscriptions of 132 and of around 200 show that Palmyra kept a cavalry force there (or in the latter case 'at Gamla and 'Ana'). More important, another Palmyrene inscription, of AD 225, mentions a '*stratēgos* at 'Ana and Gamla' ('STRTG 'L 'N' WGML'). What is significant about this inscription is above all its location, at Umm es Selabeikh, some 120 km west-

26. *Dura Reports* IX.3, *The Palace of the Dux Ripae and the Dolichenum* (1952): for the inscriptions 30ff., nos. 945 (ὁ Δομιτίου [Πο]μπηιανοῦ τοῦ ἁγνοῦ καὶ δικαίου δουκὸς τῆς ῥείπης θρεπτός) and 946.

27. Gilliam, op. cit. (3.4, n.15), 23, and idem, "The Dux Ripae at Dura", *TAPhA* 72 (1941), 157.

28. Kennedy and Riley, *RDF*, 224–225.

29. Ammianus XXIV, 1, 6–10.

30. 4.3 below.

south-west of Palmyra on the road crossing the steppe to the lower-middle Euphrates.[31]

There can be no doubt therefore that even after Roman occupation extended to this area of the Euphrates, the Palmyrenes continued to exercise some military or police role on the route across the steppe, and on the river itself. How did that relate to the Roman presence there, if any? Equally significant (and perhaps more so than might appear at first sight) is the question of whether any Roman troops stationed on this stretch of the river belonged to Syria Coele (as did those at Dura) or to Syria Phoenice, with its one legion some 300 km away at Raphaneae. The fact that the Palmyrenes retained a force at Ana even in the 220s might suggest that Biblada was the last outpost of Syria Coele, and that the lower stretch of the river belonged to Syria Phoenice, and was militarily dependent on Palmyra.[32] If so, that would fit perfectly with the discovery of a Palmyrene inscription of the late second century some 20 km south of Ertaje which seems to say that the person commemorated 'came to the limit of the frontier' in the *stratēgia* (B'ṢṬRṬGWT) of Iarhai.[33] However, archaeological evidence (coins, and graffiti in Greek) from the settlement of Kifrin, which lies below Ana, on the left bank of the river, might suggest a Roman occupation there in the first half of the third century. *If that is so*, and if Kifrin is the place called Bechuphrein to which troops were occasionally posted from Dura,[34] then the notion of two clearly distinguished military/provincial zones is not valid.

Archaeological evidence (pottery, Imperial coins and some fragmentary graffiti in Palmyrene, Aramaic and—a single name—Latin) also suggest a Roman, or Romano-Palmyrene, occupation of the island of Bidjan, 150 km downstream from Dura, in the first few decades of the third century, without allowing any greater precision.[35] But, as we will see, Shapur's record of his victories in the 250s identifies no place downstream from Ana, or Anatha, and there is no known evidence for either a Roman or a Palmyrene military

31. For the Palmyrene inscriptions referring to Ana see A. Northedge, A. Bamber and M. Roaf, *Excavations at 'Āna, Qal'a Island* (1988), 6–7; for the road see A. Poidebard, *La trace de Rome dans le désert de Syrie* I (1934), 105–114, and Kennedy and Riley, *RDF,* 80–81.

32. So M. Gawlikowski, "The Roman Frontier on the Euphrates", *Mesopotamia* 22 (1987), 77, on p. 78.

33. J. Starcky, "Une inscription palmyrénienne trouvée près de l'Euphrate", *Syria* 40 (1963), 47.

34. See, e.g., A. Invernizzi, "Kifrin and the Euphrates Limes", in Freeman and Kennedy, *DRBE,* 357. In *P. Dura,* no. 46, a soldier mentions in a letter that he has been on campaign to Βηχχουφρείν, and in the rosters of the Cohors XX Palmyrenorum 'Becchuf(r)' appears several times; see nos. 82, 100, 101.

35. So M. Gawlikowski, "L'île de Bedjan, forteresse assyrienne et romaine", *Archéologia* 178 (May 1983), 26; "Bejan Island", *Arch. f. Or.* 29/30 (1984), 207; "Bijan in the Euphrates", *Sumer* 42 (1985), 15.

presence, for instance at Haditha, or at Hit, towards which the road from Palmyra through Umm es Selabeikh seems to have led. Nonetheless, the relative fragility of the Roman hold on this area and the importance of Palmyra for the whole eastern zone of Syria Phoenice have a considerable bearing on the events of the 260s and the brief Palmyrene Empire.

It is thus very significant that there is nothing in our evidence to suggest that the legion III Gallica, or detachments of it, either guarded the lower-middle Euphrates or policed the steppe against the *nomades;* resisting their attacks on caravans was, as it seems, a purely Palmyrene function. Yet this state of affairs was evidently compatible with what seems to have been an established presence of auxiliary units (perhaps not more than one at a time) at Palmyra itself.[36] We have already encountered the inscription in honour of Vibius Celer, 'prefect of the *ala* (stationed) here' in the second half of the second century.[37] For most of the century the units attested were all mounted *alae;* one, the Ala Vocontiorum, apparently just arrived from Egypt, is found constructing a *campus* (training-ground) in 183.

A garrison also continued after Severus' division of Syria, but in the form of a part-mounted cohort, the Cohors I Flavia Chalcidenorum equitata, which is mentioned on inscriptions from there in 206/207 and in the reign of Philip (244–249).[38] This raises the question of the Roman military presence, not east of Palmyra, but south-west of it, in the direction of Damascus. For before this period the same unit is recorded on a Latin inscription of 162 found built into the wall of a surviving Roman *castellum* at Maqsura.[39] The location is important, 5 km to the east of Dumayr, the site of a major temple of Zeus. Dumayr itself lies 45 km east of Damascus on the main route towards Palmyra. This was where there was to be, in the Tetrarchic period, the major Roman route, lined with *castella* or guard-posts, called the Strata Diocletiana. It is not in the least certain that what this *cohors* was building in 162 was precisely the large *castellum* still visible in the modern period. But they were clearly building something, and with that we therefore have the earliest evidence for this route as the site of Roman construction and military activity. It was of course a sign, and a product, of the integration of both Palmyra and Damascus into the Imperial military system; and (as we will see) it relates also to the integration of the area south of Damascus, effectively

36. For a survey of the known evidence see H. Seyrig, "Textes relatifs à la garrison romaine de Palmyre", *Syria* 14 (1933), 152, with corrections and additions by M. Speidel, "Numerus ou ala Vocontiorum à Palmyre", *Syria* 49 (1972), 494 = (in English) *Roman Army Studies* I (1984), 571.

37. 3.4 above.

38. *AE* (1969–70), nos. 610–611 (206/207); 1933, no. 216 (238/244).

39. *CIL* III, no. 6658 = Le Bas-W., no. 2562d. On the *castellum*, R. E. Brünnow and A. von Domaszewski, *Die Provincia Arabia* III (1909), 187ff.; Poidebard, *Trace*, 43.

possible only after the absorption of the kingdom of Agrippa II. As so often, so it seems, the development of the Roman military system went in parallel with civilian development. Thus at the major temple of Dumayr itself, at an indeterminate date in the later second or third century, a *strator* of a *praefectus* of the Ala Vocontiorum contributed to building-work out of his own pocket. This was, however, a mixed case, for the man belonged to this place, whose ancient name was Thelsea, and identified himself as a 'Thelseēnos'.[40] In this local context this was no insignificant claim. For the temple of Zeus there was a major local centre, and was to be the subject, in 216, of a case heard before Caracalla in person; and the '*mētrokōmē*' ('mother-village') of the Thelseēnoi' is a classic instance of those important villages which are so characteristic of the Near East, and hardly seem to have 'depended' on any city.[41]

If Thelsea had depended on a city (and it may in theory have done so), it would surely have been Damascus. Earlier characterised by apparent isolation from the main part of the then single province of Syria, Damascus was now, at least in some sense, solidly embedded in provincial territory, and must have been relatively prominent among the cities of Syria Coele. The very limited evidence surviving from this continuously inhabited place, however, makes its history as a city in the Roman period remarkably mysterious;[42] and since as always so much of our evidence for military and for civilian history depends on honorific or building inscriptions, our conception of the Roman military presence here is also very limited.

As we have seen, the Severan period shows at least the beginnings of a Roman military presence along what would later be the 'Strata Diocletiana' linking Damascus to Palmyra and the Euphrates. But in geographical terms the large oasis of Damascus, formed by the run-off of rivers from the mountain massif behind, was also a frontier zone; for as soon as the very rich oasis area stopped, some 30 km east of Damascus, the steppe began. Whatever reasons lay behind the clearly attested extension of Roman forts into the steppe both north-east and (as we will see) south-east of Damascus in this period should have applied to the oasis also. But so far the only evidence for that is an unpublished Latin inscription from Gaslaniye, south-east of Damascus, showing the Ala I Pannoniorum equitata engaged in building-work in the 180s.[43] Indeed these reasons ought to have applied more strongly here. For if the *nomades* of the steppe needed to be watched or controlled, so had in the

---

40. See N. Ehrhardt, "Die ala Vocontiorum und die Datierung des Tempels von Dmeir", *ZPE* 65 (1986), 225.

41. 9.3 below.

42. 9.3 below.

43. J.-P. Rey-Coquais, *JRS* 68 (1978), 68, n.332 = *AE* (1978), no. 818.

past the inhabitants of Trachonitis to the south of Damascus, and also the Ituraeans of the mountain massif behind the city.

But the fact is that we know virtually nothing of the Roman military system, if there was one, in this area in the Severan period. It is quite unclear whether military observation of the mountain massif, as a sort of inner frontier, was still required. The one certain aspect of the military presence is the road which now ran from Damascus across Trachonitis (the Lejja) to Bostra, already discussed.[44] What would be significant would be to know if in this period, as certainly later under the Tetrarchy, there were Roman forts or routes in the steppe zone east of Trachonitis and the Jebel Hauran, which linked up with the roads and forts which we know for this period in the Jordanian steppe to the south. The sole evidence datable (broadly) to this period is provided by Greek and Latin graffiti which seem to make clear that Roman soldiers at least visited a small oasis in the steppe some 50 km east of the northern Jebel Hauran, at a place called en-Namara: the fragmentary inscriptions there reveal a *dromedarius,* a non-commissioned officer *(dekadarchos),* and a cavalryman of the legion III Cyrenaica stationed at Bostra.[45] It thus seems clear that the steppe zone fell within the province of Arabia. This site becomes of immense importance later, because of the inscription which an Arab king was to put up there in 328.[46] But for the whole borderland of the steppe, from the Damascus–Palmyra route in the north to the southern fringes of the Jebel Hauran, a distance of some 130 km, we have to confess that there is no evidence as to whether there were any established Roman forts or not in the Severan period.

For the steppe region south of the Jebel Hauran, however, there is significant evidence.[47] The fact that it is (as always) fragmentary and subject to the accidents of discovery, and that it is never possible in principle to prove that something attested at a certain date first began at that date, should not blind us to the fact that until now there has been no evidence earlier than the late second century for a Roman military presence in this region. The salient items of evidence may be briefly noted. First, at Qasr-al-Hallabat, some 30 km north-east of Amman, the remains of a Roman fort include an inscription of

44. 3.3 above.

45. Le Bas-W., nos. 2264–2285. See Poidebard, *Trace,* 61–62.

46. 11.5 below.

47. For this region, from which only a few salient items of evidence are picked out here, see D. L. Kennedy, *Archaeological Explorations on the Roman Frontier in North East Jordan* (1982); D. L. Kennedy and H. I. MacAdam, "Some Latin Inscriptions from the Azraq Oasis", *ZPE* 65 (1988), 231; S. T. Parker, *Romans and Saracens: A History of the Arabian Frontier* (1986); idem, "The Roman *Limes* in Jordan", in A. Hadidi (ed.), *Studies in the History and Archaeology of Jordan* III (1987), 151.

212 recording that a 'new fort' *(castellum novum)* had been built by the soldiers of four auxiliary cohorts.[48]

More significant still is the cluster of evidence from the area of the Azraq oasis, lying in the true steppe made up of a vast field of dark stones and, more important, on the route to the Wadi Sirhan, leading south-east into Arabia proper. Whether this was, as has been suggested, a major trade-route leading to the Persian Gulf will have to be discussed later.[49] But the fact that it was a route is beyond question. Azraq lies some 80 km east of Amman, and military occupation in this area was eventually to be significant in relation not only to the Wadi Sirhan but to a Roman road leading north towards Damascus. For the Severan period, however, what we know for certain is that there was road-building here under Severus, though in what direction is uncertain (the milestones recording it are not in position); and that some 14 km south-west of Azraq, at Qasr el Uweinid, a detachment of III Cyrenaica constructed a *castellum et praesidium Severianum* in 205.[50]

This activity would be of some interest even if there were no probable connections to the Wadi Sirhan. But in fact from Jawf, some 400 km down the Wadi from Azraq, there is a Latin inscription of a centurion of III Cyrenaica, dedicated 'for the safety of our (two) lords the Augusti' to Iuppiter Optimus Hammon and a deity called Sanctus Sulmus.[51] The date should certainly be the early part of the third century.[52] There is nothing to show whether a permanent post was established here; but given the vast distances involved, even occasional patrols would reflect a Roman involvement in this area which would have been unimaginable in the first century. Dumatha (Jawf) was also, it may be recalled, the place whose people, according to Porphyry, had carried out human sacrifice and still conceived of an altar as being itself an object of worship.[53]

Much—indeed everything—is speculative about how the Roman army operated in such a context, and what it was intended to achieve. But what is certain is that, as on the Euphrates and Chabur, it must represent a line of movement through an area, not a 'frontier' held as a line against a putative enemy attacking from the side. Much the same will be true of the military presence in the central and southern part of Arabia, where the traceable evidence of the Roman army never appears far from the Via Nova Traiana, built in the first few years of the province. From Bostra the road ran south-east to

48. Kennedy, *Explorations*, 39, no. 3.

49. 13.1 below.

50. Kennedy, *Explorations*, 169–175 (milestones); 113ff. (Qasr el Uweinid).

51. Kennedy, *Explorations*, 190; see Bowersock, *Roman Arabia*, App. 2.

52. See M. Speidel, "The Roman Road to Dumata (Jawf in Saudi Arabia)", *Historia* 36 (1987), 213.

53. Ch. 1 above.

Amman (Philadelphia) and then south along the border between the cultivated plateau of Moab and the steppe proper, then to descend a steep escarpment to reach the Red Sea at Aila. In fact, however, to say that is simply to
repeat in effect what is claimed on milestones of the reign of Trajan, found
(only) on the northern part of the road, between Bostra and Philadelphia;
other milestones of later reigns can be found in considerable numbers both in
that area and further south, as far as Petra. But for the stretch between Petra
and Aila there is no precisely datable physical evidence, though stretches of
the road, with associated small forts, are visible.

Though the line of the road across the southern desert, the Hisma, to Aila
(Aqaba) has some milestones, no inscriptions have been read on these, so
nothing definite can be said on dating. While it need not be doubted that
Trajan's Via Nova did reach Aqaba, we cannot identify anything more than
a road, with side-roads westwards, and watch-towers.[54] Why it was built at
all, whether it had some relation to trade from the Red Sea, and how occupation in this area in the Roman period compared with that in the preceding
Nabataean period are all uncertain.

What is certain, however, is that a Roman official and military presence
did not stop at Aqaba, but followed the earlier Nabataean presence at least
as far as Medain Saleh in the northern Hedjaz.[55] For from the region of Medain Saleh—some 900 km from Bostra and the main camp of the legion III
Cyrenaica—there are graffiti in a mixture of Greek and Latin in Greek transliteration (as well as other Nabataean ones), which reveal Roman *dromedarii*
and cavalrymen of an *ala* of Gaetuli; and a roughly inscribed *stele* contains a
Greek dedication to the Fortune of Bostra by a painter with the legion III
Cyrenaica.[56] It is worth reflecting that the march back to the legionary base
at Bostra would have taken at least a month.

As so often, we do not know how permanent the Roman presence here
was. Certainly there is nothing to suggest a regular military occupation; once
again we seem to be concerned with a route, for we know from Pliny the
Elder, writing in the 70s, that there was a land-route from Arabia Felix
(Yemen) which passed through this area, needing sixty-five camel-stages to
reach Gaza.[57]

54. For a sceptical view of the extent of the Roman military presence in the southern area,
see J. Eadie, "The Evolution of the Roman Frontier in Arabia", in Freeman and Kennedy, *DRBE*
I, 243. See also Isaac, *Limits,* 122ff.

55. The essential evidence here is well known, and again I merely pick out the salient points.
See Sartre, *Trois Etudes,* 30–38; Bowersock, *Roman Arabia,* 95–98.

56. See H. Seyrig, "Postes romains sur la route de Médine", *Syria* 22 (1941), 218: for example Φολσκιανὸς Σεουερος ἔκυυης ἄλε Γετουλῶν. For the painter, Bowersock, op. cit., 96 = *AE*
(1977), no. 835: Τύχη Βόστρων Ἀδριανὸς ζωγράφος σὺν λεγ. III Κυ.

57. Pliny, *NH* XII, 32/64–65. See 13.1 below.

We can hardly expect to gain any clear conception of the peoples of this region, or of their culture and social structure. But the Romans were of course aware of a large number of different peoples in the Arabian peninsula, for instance the 'Tamudaei' or 'Thamudēnoi' to whom Pliny and Ptolemy refer.[58] It could be assumed that the *legatus* of Arabia would have had to conduct some diplomatic relations with such peoples. But it could hardly have been expected that at Ruwwafa, some 200 km north-west of Medain Saleh, we should have available a formal record of such relations, inscribed in Greek and Nabataean on a temple dedicated on behalf of Marcus Aurelius and Lucius Verus, in the later 160s. The group which erected the temple is described in Greek as 'the *ethnos* of the Thamoudēnoi' and in Nabataean as ŠRKT TMWDW, perhaps 'confederation (of the) Thamud'. The governor, Antistius Adventus ('NṬSṬYS 'DWNTS HGMWN' in Nabataean), is described as having made peace among them.[59]

Neither the inscription nor the temple to which it refers will necessarily indicate that either of the two governors who are mentioned, Adventus and his apparent successor, Claudius Modestus, in whose time the temple was dedicated, actually came to Ruwwafa in person. Nor is it worth asking whether this place was within the frontiers of the province; for there may well have been no such defined frontier. What is certain is that this place, used by the Thamud to erect a temple, was within the sphere of influence both of the Roman governor and of Graeco-Nabataean culture. We are not, however, yet in the period when independent Arab tribes had treaty-relations with Rome; nor, so far as is known, had units drawn from these yet entered regular Roman service. It is only in the late fourth century that we know that the Roman army included units of 'Equites Saraceni Thamudeni'.[60]

It has even been suggested that the word ŠRKT, supposed to mean 'federation', is the origin of the term 'Saracen' itself; that is, that the term was borrowed in Greek and Latin to refer to Arab tribal federations. That seems far-fetched.[61] As it happens, the earliest attested use of the term comes from Ptolemy's *Geography*, of the mid-second century: here a people called Sarakēnoi are listed immediately before those called Thamudēnoi.[62] But nonetheless, for a whole complex of reasons, the relations, both political and cultural, on display in the bilingual inscription of Ruwwafa were of momentous consequence for the future.

58. Pliny, *NH* VI, 32/157; Ptolemy, *Geog.* VI, 7, 21, ed. Nobbe.

59. G. W. Bowersock, "The Greek-Nabataean Bilingual Inscription at Ruwwāfa, Saudi Arabia", in *Le monde grec: Hommages à Claire Préaux* (1975), 513 = *AE* (1977), no. 834.

60. *Not. Dign., Or.* 28, 17.

61. See M. P. O'Connor, "The Etymology of *Saracen* in Aramaic and Pre-Islamic Arabic Contexts", in Freeman and Kennedy, *DRBE* II, 603.

62. Ptolemy, *Geog.* VI, 7, 21, ed. Nobbe.

No Roman of the second or third century, or indeed for long after, would have imagined that it would be from this direction that the dominance of Graeco-Roman civilisation in the Near East would one day be destroyed, and by a major invasion. Contemporaries were, however, conscious that Imperial expansion had brought them into significant contact with persons whom they called Arabs. Contemporaries of Septimius Severus indeed could not have failed to be aware of 'Arabs' as political or actual enemies. For 'Arabicus' appeared among Imperial victory-titles, for the first time ever, under Severus and his son Caracalla: so for instance 'Arabicus Adiabenicus Parthicus Britannicus Maximus'. But the allusion was not to any frontier wars fought in what Romans called Arabia, but to the conquest of Mesopotamia. However we interpret the function or purpose of the long line of Roman roads and occasional legionary fortresses, as well as auxiliary forts and guard-posts, which in the Severan period has left traces over a distance of some 1250 km from the middle Tigris to Aqaba, and whether we want to call it a 'frontier' at all, the significant fact is that it was now *there,* approximately covering the limits of regularly cultivable land, and bringing Roman forces along its whole length into contact with non-sedentary peoples whom they called indiscriminately Arabs, and began in the second and third centuries to call Saracens. To emphasise the scale and (by comparison with the first century) the novelty of this involvement is neither to imply that this 'frontier' had been created as a defence against large-scale invasion nor to suggest that nomadic communities, brigands and essentially unsubdued peoples did not exist also within the provinces. It is striking, for instance, that Severus' contemporary Ulpian describes Palmyra as 'located near barbarous *gentes* and *nationes*'.[63] The modern notion of symbiosis between nomads and settled populations, while no doubt objectively valid for the steppe zone of the Roman Near East, was not shared by Graeco-Roman observers. The threat of a potential invader was not a necessary condition for there to be a major and complex problem of security, in which military and police functions might be largely indistinguishable. But in any case continued Roman imperialism in Mesopotamia was soon to be confronted with just such a perceived threat.

4.2. EMPERORS ON CAMPAIGN, FROM CARACALLA TO PHILIP THE ARAB

That the third century was a period of intense stress for the structure of the Empire needs no emphasis. But as regards the history of the Near East, certain more specific points need to be underlined: that the presumption that all major campaigns should be led by the Emperor in person was by now well estab-

---

63. *Dig.* L, 15, 1, 5.

lished; that many of these campaigns brought Emperors to the Near East, and to Mesopotamia in particular; and that it was thus in this period that the effects of Severus' conquest of Mesopotamia, profoundly altering the strategic balance of the Empire, first became clear.

This phase, beginning just after the decisive Roman advance across the Euphrates, ended with a peace imposed on Persia which extended Roman domination across the Tigris. In between came a succession of campaigns, including in the 250s the only major Persian invasions of Roman territory west of the Euphrates before the sixth century. A considerable variety of narrative accounts, in various languages, often written much later, might seem to allow a year-by-year reconstruction of the military history of the area.[1] But the space and effort required would be immense, and the results few and uncertain. What follows, in this chapter and the next, will therefore be, in narrative terms, a mere outline, while attempting to make clear, where possible, the significance of these events both for the evolving structure of the Empire and for the Near East itself. More important, however, it will be based above all on contemporary documents, many only newly available, which for some decades serve to put the sequence of events in a quite different light.

That the Near East was now central to the concerns of Emperors (even indeed crucial to any successful claim to be an Emperor) must have been clear to any observant inhabitant of the Empire. It will at least have been known in Ephesos, where an inscription honouring a man who went on repeated embassies to the Emperors vividly reflects the travels and campaigns of those Emperors in the first two decades of the century. The man honoured had been, on behalf of Ephesos, to the following places: Rome, Britain, Upper Germany, Sirmium, Nicomedia, Antioch and Mesopotamia. The series begins under Severus and Caracalla in 202–208, and ends with successful representations before Macrinus and his son Diadumenianus in Mesopotamia in 217/218.[2] Severus' long campaigns in the East had thus been followed, after a spell in Rome, by his expedition to Britain in 208–211, and then by his son Caracalla's campaigns in Germany in 213. Thereafter his military concerns lay in the Near East. Abundant contemporary evidence makes perfectly clear that Caracalla's imitation of Alexander was no superficial whim but the determining factor in his actions as Emperor. It is surely relevant also to his historic proclamation that the entire population of the Empire should become Roman citizens.[3]

---

1. See now the invaluable collection of sources in translation by M. H. Dodgeon and S. N. C. Lieu, *The Roman Eastern Frontier and the Persian Wars (AD 226–363)* (1991). I have not been able to cross-refer to this work in the chapters which follow.

2. *I. K. Ephesos* III, no. 802 (*SEG* XVII, no. 505).

3. For Caracalla as Alexander and the relevance of his policy, see most recently K. Bouraselis, Θεῖα Δωρεά. Μελετὲς πάνω στὴν πολιτικὴν τῆς δυναστείας τῶν Σεβηρῶν καὶ τὴν *Constitutio Antoniniana* (1989), 38ff.

Emulation of Alexander is certainly relevant to the fact that in 214 Caracalla took the long-established route to Syria via Asia Minor, passing the winter of 214/215 at Nicomedia, and arriving at Antioch in 215, as it is to his visit to Alexandria in 215/216.[4] But by May of 216 he was back in Antioch; for it was there that he agreed to hear a dispute about the priesthood of the temple of Zeus at Dumayr—the clearest proof of the importance of this temple and of the 'mother-village of the Thelseēnoi' on the road between Damascus and Palmyra. The verbatim report of the hearing, inscribed on the wall of the temple, makes quite clear that advantage had been taken of the Emperor's presence to gain direct access to him, against the normal rules.[5] In a more than superficial sense the Roman state had come to the region and integrated it with itself. Of course not all of the complex features of that integration were distinctive to the Near East. Others, however, were. One possible, but very ambiguous, sign of an integration between Empire and city in this specific region is the appearance under Caracalla, from 214 onwards, and again under Macrinus, of large numbers of silver tetradrachms evidently minted in the Near East and circulating there. But the idea that we can identify a long list of cities—in Mesopotamia, Syria Coele, Syria Phoenice and Syria Palaestina—which were given the honour (or burden?) of producing these large-value silver coins is pure speculation.[6] For it depends on nothing more than resemblances between the images and symbols on the normal (if intermittent) bronze issues of these cities, and those found on this sudden flood of silver coins. But not a single city is actually named on these coins. The only legends on them are the names and titles of the two Emperors, written in Greek. In that sense they do exhibit, like the continuous presence of these two successive Emperors in the Near East, a coming-together of Imperial and regional elements.

On the other hand the fact that all the inhabitants of the Near East were now made Roman citizens was something which they shared with the population of all the other provinces.[7] What was not equally common to all areas was the granting of the status of Roman *colonia*.[8] Caracalla followed his father's grants by giving this status to Antioch itself, and to Emesa, the native city of his mother. Whether it was he or Severus who made Palmyra a *colonia* is not clear. But the grant certainly came no later than his reign, and thereby

4. For Caracalla's movements see H. Halfmann, *Itinera Principum* (1986), 223–230.

5. See 4.1 above and 9.3 below.

6. For a very over-confident identification of 'the mints' which produced these coins, written before it was demonstrated that the same workshop could and did produce coins for different cities, see A. R. Bellinger, *The Syrian Tetradrachms of Caracalla and Macrinus* (*Numismatic Studies* 3, 1940).

7. See most recently Bouraselis, op. cit. (n.3).

8. See Millar, "Roman *Coloniae*", 39ff. The meaning of this change in the case of each place will be discussed more fully later in this chapter.

not only introduced a radically new constitution, but greatly complicates any analysis of what third-century Palmyra 'was', and of the unique role played by Palmyra in the 260s and 270s. Third-century Palmyra was to be 'Oriental', 'Greek' and 'Roman' all at once.

So also was Edessa in Osrhoene, which on Caracalla's accession in 211 was still the capital of the little kingdom of Abgar. He was probably succeeded by another king Abgar in 211 or 212, and it was therefore probably this Abgar who was summoned by Caracalla in 212 or 213 and deposed, on the grounds that he had been mistreating his subjects in order to force them to adopt Roman customs.⁹ If he had, he was in a curious way to be justified after the event. For it is certain that his city, now absorbed into the surrounding province of Osrhoene, also became a Roman *colonia* in 212/213. As will be apparent later, it is possible for us to understand something of the social and cultural context in which this change of status was introduced. But if we think only of the Imperial aspect, the newly conquered territory across the Euphrates was now divided between two provinces, Osrhoene and Mesopotamia; it had two new legions stationed in it; and it contained five Roman *coloniae*: Edessa, Carrhae, Reshaina, Singara and Nisibis.

Caracalla's conception, however, went beyond a revitalisation of Roman imperialism, for his emulation of Alexander extended to ideas of eastern conquest, and to marriage with the daughter of the Parthian king—or rather with the daughter of one of the two claimants, Artabanus V. A campaign in 216 took the Roman forces as far as Arbela beyond the Tigris. The winter of 216/217 may have been spent without returning west of the Euphrates; at any rate it was when travelling between Edessa and Carrhae in April 217 that the Emperor was murdered by a member of his escort, having got off his horse to relieve himself.¹⁰

This trivial, even absurd, episode was of momentous consequence for the future structure of the Empire. For the first time an Emperor had died while with his troops on campaign, and had been replaced from within his entourage. His successor, reluctantly recognised by the Senate in Rome, was Opellius Macrinus, the Praetorian Prefect, and the first non-senator to become Emperor. His brief reign in 217/218 was spent entirely in the Near East, and may serve to illustrate the progressive detachment of the Imperial structure from its roots in the institutions of the city of Rome. In this case, as with Pescennius Niger, we also see how the role of Emperor could be played in a Syrian context, primarily Antioch; but also, in the very special circumstance of the origins of Caracalla's mother, Iulia Domna, in Emesa, how regional loyalties, partly embracing the army as well, could bring forward a successful rival.

9. So Dio LXXVII, 12, 1ᵃ–1². For the complex issues involved here see 12.5 below.
10. Dio LXXVIII, 5, 4.

After his proclamation Macrinus marched back towards Antioch; crossing the Euphrates at Zeugma, he was met by his young son Diadumenianus, brought from Antioch, who was then proclaimed as 'Caesar' by the troops. Once securely in power, Macrinus remained mainly in Antioch, and Herodian offers a description of him holding audiences there, and spending more time than he should have at public shows.[11] In 217, however, there was a campaign in Mesopotamia, for Artabanus demanded a Roman withdrawal, and defeated Macrinus' forces at Nisibis. But peace was then made on payment of a large sum by Rome, and Mesopotamia remained a province.[12]

Macrinus' overthrow came not from any movement at Rome or in one of the other main military regions, but as a direct product of the close relations of the previous Imperial house, and the army, to local society in Syria. The sister-in-law of Septimius Severus, Iulia Maesa, had now returned from court and was living near Emesa as a wealthy landowner. Her two daughters, Iulia Soaemias and Iulia Mamaea, as we have seen, were both married to prominent *equites* who came from cities in Syria: Sextus Varius Marcellus from Apamea and Gessius Marcianus from Arca, also called Caesarea ad Libanum.[13] As we have noted before, this could be seen simply as a characteristic process of the integration of local landowning families into the upper orders of the Imperial system. But the fact that Caracalla's murder took place in the Near East gave more purely local factors a greater importance. For both the sons of these marriages, Varius Avitus Bassianus, born about 203, and his younger cousin, Gessius Alexianus Bassianus, born about 209, served as priests of the cult of Elagabal at Emesa. The problems of the nature of this cult, whose object was the large black stone portrayed on coins of the city, will need to be discussed later.[14] The crucial factor in this instance, however, as in so many other attested cases, was that the soldiers of the legion III Gallica, the only legion in Syria Phoenice, stationed at Raphaneae in the Orontes Valley, frequently visited the city and the temple—and were also said to admire the beauty of the elder boy. Given that, and the claim that he was in reality an illegitimate son of Caracalla, it was easy to persuade them to admit him to the camp and proclaim him Emperor, in May 218. Officially, he assumed at once the name 'M. Aurelius Antoninus', borrowed from the Antonine dynasty, and used also by 'Caracalla'; but posterity was to know him by the nickname borrowed from the name of his deity, 'Elagabal'.[15]

Macrinus' reaction, after some delay, was to move south to Apamea, the major city in that part of the Orontes Valley which belonged to Syria Coele,

11. So Herodian V, 2, 3–6.

12. Dio LXXIX, 26, 2–27, 3.

13. For the family, see 3.4 above.

14. Herodian's classic description is in V, 3, 2–8. See already ch. 1 above, and further 9.2 below.

15. Herodian V, 3, 9–12; Dio LXXVIII, 30, 2–33, 1.

to proclaim the young Diadumenianus as 'Augustus', and to celebrate the event by distributing money to the soldiers and giving a dinner to the whole population.[16] Once again an apparently trivial detail of narrative history reveals important features of the structure of the Empire. First, as at Antioch, the population of major cities needed to be carefully cultivated. But, more important, the soldiers concerned are described by Dio as 'the Albanioi and the others wintering in this region'. Very considerable forces had been brought by Caracalla for his eastern campaign; legionary detachments from Africa, Pannonia, Raetia and possibly Germany are attested, as well as at least one praetorian cohort.[17] But the significant element is the reference to 'the Albanioi'. For this was a way of referring to the second of the three *legiones Parthicae* formed by Septimius Severus. While legions I and III were stationed in Mesopotamia, II had its base at Alba, south of Rome, and was the first legion of the Imperial period to be stationed in Italy. While the concept of a mobile strategic reserve is perhaps anachronistic, the facts show clearly that this legion did participate repeatedly in distant campaigns under Imperial command.

More important still, however, recent dismantling of a third-century tower in the city-wall of Apamea has produced large numbers of grave-*stelai* of soldiers of this legion, whose cemetery must have been nearby.[18] The inscriptions now available in fact reflect three separate periods of the presence of this legion at Apamea: 215–218; 231–233 under Severus Alexander; and 242–244 under Gordian III. Moreover, grave-*stelai* of auxiliaries show some of these units there at another crisis-point, 252.[19] It is possible to distinguish those which belong in this first period, for the legion was then entitled 'II Parthica Antoniniana'. It must for instance have been during the legion's initial journey to Syria that one of the soldiers died at Aegeae in Cilicia and was buried at the next stopping-point, Catabolon; but his epitaph was put up by his fellow-soldiers when the legion reached its intended base, Apamea. Another is recorded as having died at Immae, a place on the road between Antioch and Beroea, not far from where a route turns south down the Orontes. This must be a reference to the defeat of Macrinus in June 218 by the forces of 'Elagabal', which Dio says took place near a village in Antiochene territory, 180 stades (about 35 km) from the city.

16. Dio LXXVIII, 34, 1–3.

17. *RE s.v.* "Legio", XII, 1321–1323.

18. For these important new documents, not yet formally published, see J.-C. Balty, "Apamée (1986): Nouvelles données sur l'armée romaine d'Orient et les raids sassanides du milieu du IIIᵉ siècle", *CRAI* (1987), 213; "Apamea in Syria in the Second and Third Centuries AD", *JRS* 78 (1988), 91. A few already known military epitaphs from the site are published in *IGLS* IV, nos. 1357–1362.

19. 4.3 below.

The new Emperor entered Antioch the next day, and remained there for several months before taking the now established route across Asia Minor to Nicomedia, where he spent the winter of 218/219, and then through the Balkans, to arrive in Rome in July or August of 219. It was five years since a reigning Emperor had been seen there. This time, however, the Emperor's return had a special character, for every effort was made to advertise the exotic and 'Oriental' nature of the cult of his god Elagabal; if it made a deep (and hostile) impression on contemporaries, this was, for modern observers, only to multiply the ambiguities involved in trying to understand religious belief and practice in the Near East. At a less problematic level the interdependence between the elements of the Roman state present in Syria and the different groups within local society had been clearly demonstrated. But if 'Elagabal' could exhibit himself deliberately as an 'Oriental' in Rome, he still followed the practice of Caracalla and Septimius Severus in 'Romanising' cities in the Near East: for it was in his reign that the status of *colonia* was granted to Arca or Caesarea ad Libanum, the home-city of his uncle by marriage, Gessius Marcianus; to Sidon, also in Syria Phoenice; and to Petra in Arabia.[20] By now this was hardly more than a mere title among others. But it was a *Roman* title, with a long history, and these continued grants are thus another sign of the complexity of cultural exchanges in this period.

When an Emperor next reappeared in the Near East, it was in 231, and military relations there had been transformed. For in the 220s the Parthian Empire had been overthrown and replaced by a Persian dynasty from Fars in present-day Iran. The complex background of the establishment in power of Ardashir I need not detain us.[21] What mattered for the provinces of the Roman Near East was, first, his immediate attack on Hatra, and second, his proclaimed ambition to regain the entire territory of the ancient Persian dynasty of the Achaemenids. This new challenge forms part of the deeply pessimistic conclusion of Cassius Dio's *Roman History,* which ends in 229:

> He was indeed a source of fear to us, menacing not only Mesopotamia and Syria, but threatening to regain everything that the ancient Persians had occupied, as far as the Hellenic (i.e. Aegean) sea, as being an ancestral possession. Not that he himself seems so formidable, as that the attitude of our military forces is such that some are liable to go over to him and others are not willing to resist him. For they exhibit such luxury, licence and ill-discipline that those in Mesopotamia dared to kill their governor, Flavius Heracleo.[22]

20. Millar, "Roman *Coloniae*", 50–52.

21. See R. N. Frye, *The History of Ancient Iran* (1983), 287ff. For the complex narrative sources in various languages, many very late, see Dodgeon and Lieu, op. cit. (n.1), 9ff.

22. Dio LXXX, 3, 4; see Herodian VI, 2, 1.

There can be no doubt that a profound change in the nature of the situation on the eastern frontier was now felt in Rome. Equally, whatever the content of successive treaties, it is clear that the Sasanid dynasty never accepted the loss of Mesopotamia; hence in the repetitive military history of the next century and a half the same place-names recur again and again, above all Nisibis, Carrhae and Edessa. But there were to be only two occasions, in 252/253 and 260, when Persian forces in fact crossed the Euphrates into Syria. As we will see, even the record of his victories put up by Shapur I, the second Sasanid king, after these invasions makes quite clear that they were simply destructive raids. Though they did extend into eastern Anatolia, even as raids they never approached the Aegean. And even in Roman Mesopotamia itself no secure Persian occupation was ever established until Iovian was forced to give up Nisibis and the eastern part of the Mesopotamian shelf in 363.

The treaty then made had the effect of dividing in two a largely Christian population in which Syriac was the main language of literary expression.[23] But the accentuated rivalry between two empires which began immediately with the accession of Ardashir might have meant something of great importance, a conflict of loyalties for the peoples of the Roman Near East itself. For instance, as speakers of a group of Semitic languages of which related dialects were also used in the Persian Empire, they might have felt the rise of the Sasanid Empire as a source of potential liberation from Rome, as representing a culture or tradition which was more truly theirs. If so, then the events of the 220s would have been of even more profound significance for the history of the region.

These possibilities are raised here only to stress that, so far as our evidence can tell us, the rise of the Sasanids had no such significance, even in Mesopotamia itself, which had been until very recently under Parthian rule. Iranians speaking an Iranian language (Pehlevi, or Middle Persian), the Sasanids ruled a multilingual and multicultural empire just as did the Romans; there is almost nothing to suggest that identification with Persia or its history played any part in the mentality of anyone in the Roman Near East (one set of anecdotes about a pro-Persian from Antioch will be mentioned later).[24] To say that is of course to leave open the question of what part was played by identification with Rome or with Graeco-Roman culture; or indeed the question of whether wider political loyalties, rising above attachment to a city (or, in the Near East, a village), were a significant factor at all.

So far as we can tell, therefore, the rise of Ardashir, and the continuing conflict between Persia and Rome, was of purely military importance. It

23. See J. B. Segal, "Mesopotamian Communities from Julian to the Rise of Islam", *Proc. Brit. Acad.* (1955), 109.
    24. 4.3 below.

meant above all that Mesopotamia, and to a lesser extent the Euphrates Valley, became a repeated battleground. That said, only the broadest lines of the very confused sequence of these battles will be set out here; the emphasis will be on changes brought about, and on the occasional items of contemporary evidence which illuminate their consequences.

In the 220s Persian forces certainly attacked Hatra and failed to take it, though whether it was then held by Roman or by Parthian forces is not clear. They also invaded Roman Mesopotamia towards 230, but there is no good evidence that they crossed into Syria. As was by now established, the situation demanded the intervention of the Emperor in person. This was now the younger cousin of 'Elagabal', brought up as Gessius Alexianus Bassianus, the son of Gessius Marcianus from Caesarea ad Libanum and Iulia Avita Mamaea from Emesa. As Emperor, after the murder of his cousin in 222, he was officially called M. Aurelius Severus Alexander, thus combining elements drawn from the Antonine and Severan dynasties with the name of Alexander—the only time that it was ever used by a Roman Emperor.

When he marched eastwards, certainly in 231, he took the normal route through the Balkans and Asia Minor to Antioch,[25] which was then his main base for two years. With him came at least part of the legion II Parthica from Alba, now called Parthica Severiana Alexandriana, some of whose soldiers were buried at Apamea.[26] The effects of the Imperial presence were felt widely, as always. Supplies for the army were requisitioned from as far away as Pamphylia, presumably being brought by sea to Seleucia.[27] It was surely also now that Iulia Mamaea sent soldiers from her escort to bring the great Christian scholar Origen (probably already established at Caesarea in Palestine) to expound his faith to her at Antioch.[28] We can assume that Antioch acted, as so often before, as a temporary capital, attracting people from all over the Empire. But the campaigns still allowed the Emperor to visit other parts of Syria, a process vividly reflected in one of the most important documents of Palmyra as a Roman *colonia*. Like other such documents, it is bilingual, in Greek and Palmyrene. As we will see more fully later, Palmyra as a *colonia* had a new constitution, with a pair of chief annual magistrates, called *duumviri* in Latin or *stratēgoi* in Greek. One of these was Iulius Aurelius Zenobius, also called Zabdilas, who may have been the father of Zenobia, and who is described on an honorific inscription from the Great Colonnade as 'stratēgos of the colonia during the presence of the deified Alexander Caesar' ('ŚTRṬG LQLNY' BMYTWYT' DY 'LH' 'LKSNDRWS QSR).[29] Severus Al-

---

25. Herodian VI, 4, 3.
26. Text to n.19 above.
27. *AE* (1972), nos. 625–628.
28. Eusebius, *HE* VI, 21, 3–4.
29. *CIS* II, no. 3932 = Cantineau, *Inv.* III, no. 22.

exander seems at least to have intended to visit Egypt (as Caracalla had), and it may have been in that connection that Bostra joined the ranks of Near Eastern *coloniae*. It now become officially 'Colonia Bostra N(ova?) Tr(aiana) A(lexandrina?)' as its coins show, sometimes also calling it by the Greek title 'mētropolis'.[30]

The main purpose of Alexander's presence was, however, a counter-attack against Persia.[31] Herodian's vague account makes clear only that the Roman forces were divided into three groups, with one entering Armenia, one going south (apparently down the Euphrates towards its convergence with the Tigris) and one in the centre commanded by the Emperor, evidently operating in the classic battleground of northern Mesopotamia. All that we know for certain is that in 232 the Romans were able to build a road leading from Singara towards Carrhae (so nearly all of Roman Mesopotamia, if lost, must have been regained), and that by 235, the year of Alexander's death, Roman forces were at Hatra, where they still were (or were again) in the first two years of Gordian's reign (238–240), before it was finally taken by Shapur I in about 240.[32] The relatively brief campaign thus seems to have regained whatever territory Rome had lost, and Alexander returned to Rome in 233 to celebrate his victory and then to move to the northern frontier, where he was killed by his own troops at Mainz in 235.

It is possible, as Syncellus records, that the Persians captured Nisibis and Carrhae under Maximinus (235–238),[33] but the first clear evidence of major conflicts breaking out comes from 239. As we have seen, in that year the Persians 'descended' on Dura, perhaps the occasion of the death in battle of the tribune of the XXth cohort of Palmyrenes, Iulius Terentius.[34] But they certainly did not occupy the middle Euphrates, which the new archive from there shows was Roman until the mid-250s.[35] The major conflicts began elsewhere, with the capture of Hatra by Ardashir. For the now famous miniature codex with a text incorporating a later Greek version of Mani's own account of his preaching shows that he dated his call to preach, on April 18/19, 240, as having come in the year in which Ardashir subjugated Hatra, and in which his son Shapur assumed the diadem; the fall of Hatra might thus belong either

30. For the intended visit to Egypt, Halfmann, *Itinera,* 232; Bostra: Millar, "Roman Co-loniae", 52.

31. Herodian VI, 5, 1–6, 6.

32. See A. Maricq, "Les dernières années d'Hatra", *Syria* 34 (1957), 288.

33. Syncellus, *Chron.,* 681. For a very detailed account of the events of these years, and the difficult sources for them, see X. Loriot, "Les premières années de la grande crise du IIIᵉ siècle: De l'avènement de Maximin le Thrace (275) à la mort de Gordian III (244)", *ANRW* II.2 (1975), 657.

34. 4.1 above.

35. 4.1 below.

to 239/240 or to 240/241.[36] With that, so far as we know, a very distinctive local centre, ruled by a line of vassal kings under Parthian suzerainty, renowned for its temple of the Sun, and producing several hundred Aramaic inscriptions, came to an end. At any rate, when Roman forces reached it during their retreat up the Tigris in 363, it was 'an old town located in the middle of the desert, and long since deserted'.[37]

In Roman terms, however, Hatra was only an outpost, even if it deserves some note as the furthest point south-eastward ever continuously occupied by Roman forces. A major conflict did not break out until Ardashir had died, in 241 or 242, and Shapur became sole king, while 242 was the year in which Gordian III (238–244) came to campaign on the eastern front. In the meantime strange transformations had been taking place in Edessa, and must have had some relation to political tensions in Mesopotamia.[38] In 212/213, with the deposition of its king, Edessa had become a *colonia*, and its coin-legends (all in Greek) show that it remained so under the following reigns, though no coins are known from that of Maximinus (235–238). But then, under Gordian III, the city reverts to calling itself by its Syriac name, Orhai ('WRHY), and a king linked directly to the previous dynasty reappears. As he is described in a document from the new archive from the middle Euphrates, he is 'Aelius Septimius Abgar, king, son of Manu PṢGRYB' ('crown-prince'), son of Abgar, king'. The date is December 18, 240, and it is year 2 of the king and year 3 of 'Autokrator Kaisar Markos Antoninos Gordianos' (all transliterated into Syriac). The king's first year was therefore the Seleucid year October 239–September 240, and his second 240/241. But this was not on the face of it a revolt against Rome; for Gordian is mentioned also in the heading of the document, and in any case coins of Edessa/Orhai show 'Abgar the king' *(Abgar basileus)* offering Gordian a statuette. At Edessa alone, among all Roman *coloniae*, there had evidently been a dynasty in waiting since 212/213. The period of twenty-six years is exactly the length of reign which an eighth-century Syriac chronicle gives to a king Manu; but our new Syriac document makes clear that he had not in fact been a reigning king but an 'heir-apparent' or 'crown-prince' (PṢGRYB').

We cannot tell whether the Emperor had actually approved this change or (more likely) had been forced to tolerate a fait accompli. If so, toleration did

36. For the Cologne Mani Codex, containing a Greek version written in the fourth or early fifth century of an original thought to have been in eastern Aramaic, see L. Koenen and C. Römer, *Der kölner Mani-Kodex* (1985), Fr. 18, 1–6. See the translation by R. Cameron and A. J. Dewey, *The Cologne Mani Codex* (1979). See S. N. C. Lieu, *Manichaeism in the Later Roman Empire and in Medieval China*2 (1992), 37ff.

37. Ammianus XXV, 8, 5. See 4.1 above.

38. For what follows see Millar, "Roman *Coloniae*", 46–50, and more fully 12.5 below and App. C.

not last long. For another Syriac document from the same archive shows that by October 242 the king had disappeared, and the local dating is given as year 30 'of the liberation of Antonina Edessa, the renowned Colonia Metropolis Aurelia Alexandria' (DḤRWR' D'NTWNYN' 'DYS' NSYḤṬ' QLWNY' MṬRPWLS 'WRLY' 'LKSNDRY'), just as it is in the following year (31, that is, April/May 243) in the famous Syriac contract of sale found at Dura. Though Syriac is still used (a notable fact), the place has lost its Syriac name, Orhai, and the king has vanished. We have no evidence as to how these successive transformations occurred; but they must at least suggest that a Roman, or Graeco-Roman, identity was something less well established here than west of the Euphrates. At any rate, the coins show that under Decius (249–251) Edessa still counted as a Roman *colonia,* as also (as shown in documents from the new archive) did Nisibis and Carrhae.

Not long after that, however, Roman Mesopotamia was to endure major convulsions, set out for us most clearly in the trilingual record of his victories which Shapur I had carved at Naqsh-e Rustam near Persepolis, the capital of the ancient Persian dynasty.[39] This part of the inscription divides into three sections: a campaign into Babylonia by Gordian III, in 242–244, and his death and replacement by Philip; an invasion of Syria and Cappadocia by Shapur, following on a wrong done by an unnamed Roman Emperor, which, as it now seems, belongs to 252; and an invasion of Roman Mesopotamia by Shapur, evidently in 260, in which Valerian was captured, and after which Persian raids spread into Syria, Cappadocia and Cilicia.

Shapur thus makes no claim to any military operations in Roman Mesopotamia until 260, and (as we will see) no claim any time to have advanced further south up the Orontes than Arethusa. Apart from places along the Euphrates, Syria Phoenice, including Palmyra, as well as Syria Palaestina and Arabia, remained outside these major combats. That is not to say that events, and changes of Emperor, at the centre were not reflected at the furthest corners of the Empire, in the Near East as elsewhere. Thus in June 238, after the accession of Gordian III, a centurion at Sakkaia in the northern Hauran erected a statue, made in the local black basalt, of the 'Great Fortune of Sakkaia', dedicating it 'on behalf of the safety and [victory of our lord?] the Emperor [M. Antonius Gordianus] Augustus'. The name of the Emperor was subsequently erased.[40] For the loyal centurion was not then to know that six

39. See A. Maricq, "Res Gestae Divi Saporis", *Syria* 35 (1958), 295; English translation in R. N. Frye, *The History of Ancient Iran* (1983), App. 4. The most detailed historical study, on which what follows greatly relies, is E. Kettenhofen, *Die römisch-persischen Kriege des 3. Jahrhunderts n. Chr.* (1982; henceforward, Kettenhofen, *Kriege*). See also E. Winter, *Die sasanidisch-römischen Friedensverträge des 3. Jahrhunderts n. Chr.* (1988).

40. M. Sartre, "Le *dies imperii* de Gordian III: Une inscription inédite de Syrie", *Syria* 61 (1984), 49.

years later Gordian would be murdered on the Euphrates, and replaced by Iulius Philippus, who came from a place a short distance from Sakkaia, which then became a splendid new town with the name 'Philippopolis'.

It was in 242 that Gordian III set off on his *expeditio Orientalis;* the term is used on an inscription from Misenum which records the participation of the fleets from Misenum and Ravenna. But the Emperor probably took the normal route through the Balkans and Anatolia to Antioch, again accompanied by at least detachments of the legion II Parthica, once again to be stationed at Apamea.[41] What circumstances then prevailed in the Near East is not certain. We know only that the Persians had raided the Dura area in 239 and taken Hatra in about 240. Given that date, the claim by two Byzantine chronicles that Nisibis and Carrhae had been captured by the Persians under Maximinus (so by 238), and were not retaken by Gordian, must be dubious.[42] At any rate documents of Gordian's reign in the new archive from the middle Euphrates show no interruption of Roman rule there in 239–244;[43] so the Persian raid of 239 had no lasting consequences in that area. Mesopotamia proper, against which the Persians would normally have advanced up the Tigris, is of course another matter. But it is clear that Edessa, or Orhai, both as a restored kingdom in 239/240 and 240/241 (and perhaps 241/242?) and obviously as a re-established *colonia* from 242 onwards recognised the suzerainty of Gordian III; so it was therefore not under Persian control.

It is, however, clear that the first objective of Gordian's campaigns was Mesopotamia, and that a battle took place on Roman provincial territory, near the *colonia* of Reshaina, at which Shapur was defeated.[44] It is thus possible that Nisibis and Carrhae, respectively some 100 km to the east and the west of Reshaina, had been taken by the Persians (but probably after the fall of Hatra), and were now recovered. If so, Singara is likely to have been captured before Nisibis, but may also have been recovered at some point. What is certain is that both Carrhae and Nisibis were functioning as Roman *coloniae* in the reign of Decius (249–251).[45]

Gordian's Mesopotamian campaign must belong to 243, and it was certainly in this year that the influential Praetorian Prefect Timesitheus, his father-in-law—accompanying the Emperor on campaign as a Praetorian Prefect

41. See Halfmann, *Itinera*, 233–234, and *ILS*, no. 9221. For II Parthica, 4.2 above.

42. See 4.1 (Dura) and text to n.36 above. The report is, however, accepted in the important new study of this period by D. S. Potter, *Prophecy and History in the Crisis of the Roman Empire: A Historical Commentary on the Thirteenth Sibylline Oracle* (1990), 189ff. (Henceforward Potter, *Sibylline Oracle.*)

43. See Feissel and Gascou, "Documents", 557ff., nos. 16 (*circa* AD 239–241, Euphrates region); 14 (AD 241, Appadana); 13 (AD 243, Beth Phouraia); 12 (AD 244, Beth Phouraia).

44. Ammianus XXIII, 5, 17.

45. Text to n.52 below.

normally did—died and was replaced by M. Iulius Philippus, an equestrian officer or official from the Hauran, whose post before that moment is not known. His brother, C. Iulius Priscus, already held the other of the two posts as Praetorian Prefect.[46] The choice was to have important consequences. For in the following year the Roman forces went over to the offensive and reached close to the heart of Persian territory before being defeated at Misikhe on the Euphrates, over 200 km in a straight line from the nearest Roman outposts on the middle Euphrates, and not far from Ctesiphon on the Tigris. How the army reached there, whether directly from Mesopotamia down the Chabur or from Syria, is not known.

It is with this campaign and its defeat that Shapur's account of his conflicts with Rome opens:

> When at first we had become established in the Empire, Gordian Caesar raised in all of the Roman Empire a force from the Goth and German realms and marched on Babylonia [Assyria] against the Empire of Iran and against us. On the border of Babylonia at Misikhe, a great 'frontal' battle occurred. Gordian Caesar was killed and the Roman force was destroyed. And the Romans made Philip Caesar. Then Philip Caesar came to us for terms, and to ransom their lives, gave us 500,000 *denars,* and became tributary to us. And for this reason we have renamed Misikhe Peroz-Shapur.[47]

Shapur thus omits the earlier phase of Persian initiative, perhaps because he wants to record only events while he was sole king. He also flatly contradicts the Roman version of the sequence of events which led to the proclamation of Philip as Emperor. For in this version it was only after the Roman army had retreated up the Euphrates to near Circesium that Gordian was assassinated, and Philip took his place.[48] What is certain at least is that a tomb was built for Gordian at a place called Zaitha near Circesium, where Ammianus saw it during Julian's expedition of 363.[49]

This first phase of unsuccessful invasions by both sides was followed, perhaps surprisingly, by several years of peace. Whether or not Shapur is truthful in reporting that Philip acknowledged his suzerainty and made a payment of money as a sign of that, peace evidently was concluded; and Philip departed for Rome, apparently (as usual) via the Balkans.[50] Peace in this area indeed seems to have lasted until 252, and therefore also through the otherwise

46. PIR2 I 461 (Philippus); 484 (Priscus).

47. See n.39 above; trans. Frye, op. cit. (n.39), 371.

48. For the very complex narrative traditions, see X. Loriot, op. cit. (n.33 above), 770ff.

49. Ammianus XXIII, 5, 7.

50. For a revised chronology see D. E. Trout, "Victoria Redux and the First Year of the Reign of Philip the Arab", *Chiron* 19 (1989), 221.

troubled reign of Decius, who in 251 was to die in battle against the Goths (whether he was the first of all Roman Emperors to die in battle depends on whether Shapur's version or the Roman version of events in 244 is correct).

Our evidence does now allow us to gain some glimpses of this phase of established Roman rule in the Near East. Indeed, slight as this evidence is, it is enough to suggest that, contrary to what one might suppose, we could see this decade as representing the height of overt 'Romanisation' in this region. It was now, for instance, in the reign of Philip 'the Arab', that the last known grants of the status of *colonia* were made. The best-known instance was of course Philippopolis itself, where the grant of colonial status accompanied its foundation as a city. But even the modest little garrison-town of Dura seems by now to have gained this status, as did Damascus and Flavia Neapolis.[51] In Mesopotamia the famous contract of sale found in Dura, dating to 243, expresses in Syriac the colonial character of the town at that moment; while documents from the new archive include, for instance, a contract of sale of 250 from Carrhae—'in Aurelia Carrhae Colonia, Metropolis of Mesopotamia'—another, of 251, refers back to a previous contract made at Nisibis, also in 250—'in Septimia Colonia Metropolis Nesibis'.[52]

The first of the new documents to be fully published also reflects the same status as now enjoyed by Antioch, while shedding a vivid light both on the structure of Roman government in the region and on the limits of its effectiveness.[53] This is the petition *(libellus)* of some villagers from Beth Phouraia, a village owned by the Emperor and situated on the Euphrates in the region of Appadana, itself located, as we have seen, just below the confluence of the Euphrates and the Chabur.[54] The reply 'written under' their petition (hence called *subscriptio,* or in Greek *hypographē*)—and perhaps also the petition itself—had been posted at Antioch in 245: 'In the consulship of the Emperor Caesar Marcus Iulius Philippus Augustus and of Messius Titianus, the 5th day before the Kalends of September, in the year 293 (of Antioch), the 28th of the month Lōos, at Antioch, *colonia* and *mētropolis,* in the Hadrianic Baths'. As elsewhere, the wider structure of the Empire with its usually distant Emperor, his fellow-consul holding office, and even the Roman calendar-system, are all visibly present in the document.

The petition was addressed to the most senior Roman official in the region, Iulius Priscus, the brother of the Emperor, here described as *praefectus (eparchos)* of Mesopotamia, and as 'holding the *hypateia*', an expression which seems to indicate his overall command of the region. That peasants

51. Millar, "Roman *Coloniae*", 52–55.

52. Feissel and Gascou, "Documents", 559, nos. 10 (Carrhae) and 8 (Nisibis). See Millar, "Roman *Coloniae*", 39.

53. Feissel and Gascou, "Documents", no. 1.

54. 4.1 above.

from a village in a remote corner of the Empire could address so high an official in person is a very significant fact. Nonetheless, the outcome from their point of view had been, and was evidently to remain, very disappointing: 'Having, Lord, a dispute with our fellow-villagers over land and other matters, we came up here to seek justice before your Goodness, and having waited eight months . . .'. Even then, however, the case had been only half heard, and they now asked for orders to be given to Claudius Ariston, the *procurator* resident at Appadana, to take immediate steps. The reply was minimal: 'Ariston, *vir egregius,* will examine your petition'. Even so, it is striking that the villagers had felt able to refer to 'the Imperial orders, which you revere', which allowed the current possessors of land in dispute to remain in occupation until the case was settled. A sense of belonging to a wider legal system informs the whole document, however erratic its application might be in practice.

In a different way a sense of belonging to the wider Imperial system is also expressed very clearly by a man from the *colonia* of Heliopolis, L. Trebonius Sossianus, who served as a legionary centurion.[55] In Rome, under Gordian, he made a dedication to Iuppiter Optimus Maximus Heliopolitanus, '*conservator* of the imperium of our lord, Gordianus'. And a few years later he put up a Latin dedication to Iulius Priscus, the brother of the Emperor Philip, at their place of origin, now a city (and *colonia*) with the name 'Philippopolis' on the north-west tip of the Jebel Hauran, some 80 km south-south-east of Damascus. The sudden creation of an elaborate new Graeco-Roman city, built in the local black basalt and named after the Emperor, was a significant moment in the history of the area, characterised in general by large villages.[56] In the present context it is relevant that Sossianus described Priscus by a title which seems to explain the odd expression *hypateia* in the petition, namely '*Praefectus Praetorio* and *rector Orientis*'. He must mean some overall command of the East, as indeed Zosimus was later to record: 'appointed to rule the provinces there (in the East)'.[57] It should perhaps be noted that this inscription seems to be the first occasion on which 'Oriens' is used to refer to 'the Near East' in the sense employed here.

Zosimus reports that Priscus' rule was oppressive, and both he and Aurelius Victor say that someone called Iotapianus now led a revolt in the East. A few coins with Latin legends and giving Iotapianus Imperial titles are enough to confirm that there really was such a short-lived pretender in Syria. But we know effectively nothing about him.[58] The information would be totally

55. See Millar, "Roman *Coloniae*", 34.
56. See 11.4 below.
57. *ILS,* no. 9005; Zosimus I, 20, 2.
58. *PIR*² I, 49. See Potter, *Sibylline Oracle,* esp. 248–249.

insignificant if it were not for the real importance of other Near Eastern pretenders over the following couple of decades. For the moment, however, far
from being in general a period of disturbance in the Near East, the later 240s
after the defeat and death of Gordian and the retreat and departure of Philip
might be seen as a period of solidly established Roman government and of
the celebration of the 'Romanness' of the cities and of the ruling class of the
region. Such at any rate might well be the impression given by a statue-base
put up at Tyre about this time and inscribed in Greek as follows: 'Septimios
Odainathos, *lamprotatos,* Septimia Col(onia) Tyros the *mētropolis'.*[59] The
city's self-description, of course, reflects its acquisition of the status of *colonia*
under Septimius Severus. The honorand is described as *lamprotatos,* the
Greek for *clarissimus,* that is to say, the conventional status-designation of a
Roman senator. The person concerned, still apparently no more than another
example of a local dignitary who has risen to senatorial rank, is Septimius
Odenathus from Palmyra, which itself was now another Roman *colonia.* The
date is not certain, but is probably the 240s. If so, the rise to prominence of
the family, which was briefly to give Palmyra a quite exceptional role in the
Empire, was not long delayed. For by 251 Septimius Airanes (Hairan), the
son (as it now seems) of Odenathus, was already a senator himself, and had
also gained the position of '*exa*[*rchos?*] of the Palmyrenes' (or 'head of
Tadmor' in Palmyrene—RŠ TDMWR). He is honoured as such by a soldier
of the legion III Cyrenaica (expressed in Palmyrene as 'who is in the legion
at Bostra'—DBLGYWN' DY BṢR), and who calls him his *patronus.*[60] The
importance of the family was perhaps beginning to be felt even before the
major Persian invasion of 252. Nonetheless, it is now clear that there is no
reason to see the prominence of Septimius Odenathus, a Roman senator from
a Roman *colonia,* as reflecting the importance of an established 'dynasty' at
Palmyra. The wholly exceptional role which the family played was to be a
product of very special circumstances, and of the provincial and military
structure of the region, and lasted just two decades.

That already in 251 Septimius Odenathus' son, Septimius Airanes, had
the rank of senator (and hence should in principle have been at least twenty-
five) and the position of '*exarchos*(?) of the Palmyrenes' (RŠ TDMWR), and
have been honoured by a centurion from another province, suggests a real
prominence of the family. As it happens, his father seems to have had the
same title, as a newly published inscription of 252 reveals.[61] But what could
such a title, held in a Roman *colonia* by a father and son who were both

59. For the honorific inscription from Tyre, see Millar, "Roman *Coloniae*", 37, following
M. Gawlikowski, "Les princes de Palmyre", *Syria* 62 (1985), 251.

60. So Gawlikowski, op. cit., 258–260.

61. Gawlikowski, 257, no. 13.

senators, have meant? Is it, as often supposed, a sign of an emerging military command separate from the Roman army proper? Perhaps so. On the other hand the term *exarchos* can be used in Imperial Greek to describe a Roman priesthood.[62] It might seem equally likely that a senator from Palmyra, with his son, who was perhaps really only a boy of senatorial rank *(clarissimus)*, held an office of this type in his native *colonia*. Among the functions performed by senators in their native cities, in the Greek East as elsewhere, priesthoods are very prominent.[63] As for RŠ, we will see later that in contemporary Aramaic it could be used in a phrase whose Greek equivalent meant simply 'leading citizen'.[64]

What was really implied by the two not very common terms *exarchos* and RŠ, neither of which had an established technical meaning, thus cannot be ascertained. Neither can be used to demonstrate an emerging independent military role for Palmyra, a whole decade before our narrative sources suggest any such thing.

The power of established Roman rule in the Near East was, however, also to be felt in quite a different way in these years. For under Decius the question of the worship of the pagan gods became an issue in a way that it had never been before. It was he who in the first winter of his reign (249/250) issued a general order, communicated by *edicta* posted in the provinces, that every inhabitant of the Empire should sacrifice to the gods, and obtain a certificate of having done so. But the very full evidence available for elsewhere for the 'Decian persecution' is matched for the Near East only by a brief report by Eusebius (born about ten years later) of the martyrdom of Alexander, bishop of Jerusalem (formally Aelia Capitolina); of the death in prison of Babylas, bishop of Antioch; and of the prolonged torture suffered by Origen, now long since resident at Caesarea in Syria Palaestina, who died not long after.[65] The lack of evidence is certainly just an accident; for this, the first of the general persecutions, was felt in the Near East as elsewhere. Thus the author of the *XIIIth Sibylline Oracle,* probably from Emesa, and writing his pseudo-prophetic narrative only a few years later, records of Decius' reign: 'immediately there will be spoliation and murder of the faithful'.[66] The impact of Decius' edict, of immense significance as a precursor of what was to come, was unmistakable. But it is important to stress that in military terms the years up to and just after the mid-century were ones of peace and established Ro-

62. H. J. Mason, *Greek Terms for Roman Institutions* (1974), 43.

63. See W. Eck, "Die Präsenz senatorischer Familien in den Städten des Imperium Romanum bis zum späten 3. Jahrhundert", in W. Eck, H. Galsterer and H. Wolff (eds.), *Studien zur antiken Sozialgeschichte* (1980), 283.

64. 4.3 below.

65. Eusebius, *HE* VI, 39.

66. *Sib. Or.* XIII, 87–88, trans. Potter.

man rule in the Near East, from the Mediterranean to the middle Euphrates and across northern Mesopotamia almost to the Tigris. The next few years would be very different.

4.3. SHAPUR'S INVASIONS AND THE EMPIRE OF PALMYRA, AD 252–273

In 252 the city of Apamea on the Orontes again witnessed a concentration of troops: not on this occasion the legion II Parthica, but mounted auxiliary units transferred there from Pannonia. One was the Ala I Ulpia Contariorum, as we know from the grave-stele of a *signifer* who died there on April 252, the consulship of the Emperors Gallus and Volusianus. Another was the Ala I Flavia Augusta Britannica. At least ten men from these units are now known to have died at Apamea in 252, enough to suggest that major military conflicts had taken place already in that year.[1] This and other items of evidence are enough also to support a re-dating to 252, rather than 253, of the second of the three great conflicts described by Shapur, which will thus have begun in the brief reign of Trebonianus Gallus and his son Volusianus, in 251–253.[2] This is indeed what the narrative of Zosimus claims, while Zonaras relates the invasion to a dispute over Armenia in the same reign.[3] Gallus will thus have been the unnamed (because so short-lived?) Emperor who, according to Shapur, 'again lied and did wrong with regard to Armenia'.

Shapur's account of the battles then fought when he invaded, and the places ravaged, is a priceless document, even if it is not laid out in the sort of geographical sequence which would allow troop movements to be followed with complete confidence on the map.[4] But the broad lines are certain. First, it is clear that, unusually, the Persian advance was directed up the Euphrates, and was aimed at Syria, not at Roman Mesopotamia. The major battle, at which Shapur claims that a Roman force of sixty thousand was destroyed, took place at Barbalissos, on the Euphrates above its confluence with the Chabur. But then (as seems clear) the king turns to the forts and cities *(kastelloi* and *poleis)* 'which we burned and ravaged and captured'. He begins with Anatha, the island of Ana on the lower-middle Euphrates where there was a

---

1. For the relevant arguments, not repeated here in detail, see J.-C. Balty, "Apamée (1986)", *CRAI* (1987), 228ff., abbreviated in idem, "Apamea in Syria", *JRS* 78 (1988), 102–103. See Zosimus I, 27, 2, and Zonaras XII, 21A.

2. For Shapur's *Res Gestae*, A. Maricq, *Syria* 35 (1958), 295; trans. R. N. Frye, *History of Ancient Iran* (1984), 371ff.

3. Zosimus I, 27, 2; Zonaras XII, 21.

4. For such a map, making as good a reconstruction as is possible, see Kettenhofen, *Kriege,* map 2.

Roman garrison;[5] then BYRT' 'KWPN or 'RWPN, mentioned only in the Parthian text, but surely the same as the small place in the region of Appadana named Bertha Okbanōn in the new archive from the middle Euphrates. Unfortunately we have no exact date for the petition in this archive in which someone from 'Bertha Okbanōn' claims to have fled before the Persians, only to find that someone else had then occupied his vineyard and refused to give it up.[6] Next, in Shapur's account, comes 'Bertha Aspōrakou', surely the district on the Euphrates called Sphōrakēnē, which also appears in the archive.[7] The little places which lay along the middle Euphrates thus begin to emerge into the light.

They had not been Shapur's objective, however, and we cannot even be certain whether the 'Doura' and 'Kourkisiōn' mentioned quite separately in Shapur's list are or are not 'the' Dura and Circesium on the Euphrates. What is clear is that Shapur took first Sura on the Euphrates, then Barbalissos itself, and then advanced into Roman Syria proper, west of the river. The places listed make a clear geographical sequence: Hierapolis, Beroea, Chalcis, Apamea, Raphaneae. The geographical picture then becomes very confused, but the list at any rate includes Antioch and Seleucia, and a sequence of places in northern Syria and Commagene, including Zeugma, Doliche, Germanicia, Nicopolis, Gindarus and Cyrrhus. The invasion thus took the Euphrates route up to the western part of the Fertile Crescent, skirting round the steppe; there is no mention of Palmyra.

As we have seen, however, some Persian forces moved southwards up the Orontes Valley as far as Apamea and Raphaneae. A separate brief list shows that they continued further south, taking three small places between Apamea and Emesa: 'Sinzara' (Larissa), 'Chamath' (Epiphania—'which', as Josephus had said, 'the *epichōrioi* call Hama') and 'Aristē' (Arethusa, which had once been under the *phylarchoi* of the Emesēnoi).[8] No claim is made as to any conquest of Emesa itself. But a combination of items of evidence allows us to accept that in fact the Persian forces did advance on Emesa, and were defeated.[9] The sixth-century chronicler John Malalas records how a priest of Aphrodite from Emesa, called Sampsigeramus, gathered a force of peasants to resist Shapur, engineered his death by a trick and put his army to flight. The story must be at least partly legend, because Shapur did not die. But a closely comparable picture of local resistance to the Persians is given by a

5. 4.1 above.

6. See Feissel and Gascou, "Documents", 553. no. 2.

7. Feissel and Gascou, op. cit., 542–543.

8. See 2.1 above. For Shapur's allusions to places in this region see Kettenhofen, *Kriege,* 68ff.

9. For a summary of this evidence, depending essentially on H. R. Baldus, *Uranius Antoninus: Münzprägung und Geschichte* (1971), see Millar, "Empire", 158–159. See now also Potter, *Sibylline Oracle,* 323ff.

contemporary work, the *XIIIth Sibylline Oracle*. Given its pseudo-prophetic character, the narrative is of course in the future tense: 'Then there will be a rout of the Romans; but immediately thereafter a priest will come, the last of all, sent from the sun, appearing from Syria, and he will do everything by craft; the city of the sun will arise, and around her the Persians will endure the terrible threats of Phoenicians'.[10] The anonymous author had by this point moved on to the brief reign as Emperor of Aemilianus in 253, and it is quite possible that the Persian advance up the Orontes took place then. There must in any case be some connection between the resistance led by Sampsigeramus, the role of the priest 'sent from the sun' in leading Phoenicians against the Persians and the series of coins issued by Emesa, in bronze, silver and gold, all apparently in 253, which name a pretender to the position of Emperor: 'Auto(kratōr) Soulp(ikios) Antonōninos Se(bastos)' in Greek, or (in the fullest version) 'L. Iul(ius) Aur(elius) Sulp(icius) Ura(nius) Antoninus' in Latin. But whether this man is to be *identified* with the priest (and whether there is any connection here with Iulia Domna's family, or even with the earlier dynasty of Emesa) is the purest speculation. It does remain significant that local resistance, by a city in Syria Phoenice which was also a Roman *colonia*, did—as it seems impossible to deny—lead to a claim to Imperial rank by a local notable.

Equally mysterious is the representation in the *Oracle* of a Syrian who acted (or, in the pseudo-prophecy, will act) like a brigand in Syria and Cappadocia—apparently under Decius (249–251)—before fleeing back across the Euphrates to join the Parthians. Coming from a contemporary source, this account must reflect some reality; but whether the unnamed figure can be equated with the pro-Persian citizen of Antioch called Mariades or Cyriades who appears in various later accounts as associated with the capture of the city (but which capture?) is again a matter of speculation. The story deserves a mention only to recall the possibility that the Persian challenge to Rome *may* have found some popular support in the Near East. Some lines later, when recounting the reign of Gallus (251–253), the *Oracle* says that 'Syrians joined with Persians will destroy the Romans'. Whether the author means to identify these two episodes is unclear.[11]

More serious is the question of whether it was now or a whole decade later that the independent military role of Palmyra under Odenathus began. The sole evidence that it did begin now is provided by Malalas, continuing his story of the Persian defeat at Emesa: 'There confronted them (as they passed) through the *limes*, fighting on behalf of the Romans, "Enathos", king of the barbarian Saracens, the ruler of the Arabian land, who had a wife, Zenobia

10. *Or. Sib*. XIII, ll. 150–154, trans. Potter.

11. *Or. Sib*. XIII, 89–102 and 110–112, with Potter, op. cit., 268ff. and 297–298, who argues for the identification of Mariades, and discusses all the evidence in detail.

by name, the Saracen queen. And Enathos, king of the Saracens, destroyed all the Persians in the forces of Shapur'.[12] Malalas takes this story from a historian called Domninus, adding another account from a different historian, Philostratus, which tallies very closely with Shapur's account of his third campaign (in 260)—except that 'Enathos' kills Shapur. The odds are very strong that both stories belong to 260 and after. There is in any case no documentary evidence that Odenathus took the title of 'king' at any time up to his death in 267; as we will see, it was only posthumously that the Palmyrenes began to call him 'king of kings'. By 257/258, as contemporary documents show, he had advanced only to the purely Roman title of *hypatikos*, literally *consularis*, which *may* mean simply that he was the then governor of Syria Phoenice.[13] The known independent military role of Palmyra was on any interpretation wholly exceptional and striking. But it may be suggested that it came only in the 260s, after even more drastic events than those just mentioned.

What the consequences of this first major Persian raid were, and how soon Roman control was restored and where, are questions which can hardly be answered. Even Dura, where there is a mass of evidence, presents very complex problems. The Persians must at least have marched past it in 252; but the 'Doura' which Shapur claims to have ravaged may or may not be this one. What is certain is that Roman auxiliary forces were still in occupation in late summer 251, when the Cohors II Paphlagonum Galliana Volusiana (named after Gallus and his son Volusianus) was there.[14] It was also in Roman hands in 254, for the latest dated document from the city is a Greek divorce-deed for a soldier of the legion IV Scythica Valeriana Galliena, drawn up 'In the consulship of our lords, the Emperors Valerian (for the second time) and Gallienus, on the day before the Kalends of May [. . .], year 565, in the *Kolōneia* of the Eurōpaioi of [Seleukos] Neikatōr, the sacred, inviolate and autonomous'.[15] Nothing could more emphatically underline both the Hellenistic past and the present Roman status of the city. But it seems from graffiti in Pehlevi that it had in fact been in Persian hands in the early 250s, perhaps 252/253.[16] Its final capture and destruction seems to have come in 256 or 257, hence outside the context of either of the two major invasions recorded by Shapur.[17]

A similar picture of Roman occupation, which must have been interrupted

12. Malalas 297, ll. 4–10. Cf. also the translation by E. Jeffreys, M. Jeffreys and R. Scott, *The Chronology of Malalas* (1986), pp. 162–163.

13. Text to n.28 below.

14. *Dura Report* IX.3, 110ff., nos. 971–972; Balty, *CRAI* (1987), 237.

15. *P. Dura*, no. 32, see ch. 6 and 12.4 below.

16. So Balty, op. cit., 237–238.

17. For a vigorous critique of the evidence, arguing against the idea of an initial capture in 253, and for a (final) capture in 257, see D. MacDonald, "Dating the Fall of Dura-Europos", *Historia* 35 (1986), 45.

at least briefly by Shapur's invasion of 252/253, is presented by the new archive from the middle Euphrates above Dura. One document records the purchase of a female slave at Beth Phouraia on the Euphrates in June 252, in the consulship of Gallus and Volusianus. The Persian army either had not yet arrived or had already passed by, leaving life to go on as before. At some time after this, but presumably before 256/257 (the destruction of Dura), or perhaps before 260 (Shapur's third invasion), the same purchaser, Abi(d)samtas son of Abidierdos, reappears with the title *bouleutēs* (town-councillor) of Neapolis—in the interval, it seems, Appadana has been formally recognised as a *polis,* perhaps as a reward for loyalty. Abi(d)samtas is addressing a complaint to Iulius Proculus, *praefectus, praepositus praetenturae,* a local military official. But if the deduction that this petition is later than 252 is correct, then this is the latest document from the new archive.[18] And with that our evidence stops, and we hardly hear more of the middle Euphrates until Ammianus' account of Julian's march in 363.

There is no evidence at all as to the after-effects of the Persian invasion (indeed no evidence as to how long their occupation lasted in the various areas it reached), nor as to the dispositions of the Roman army, or any rearrangement which may have followed. What we do know is that the minting of Imperial coins began again at Antioch in 253/254. Moreover, it is certain that the new Emperor, Valerian, will have arrived in Syria in the course of 254; for on January 18, 255, he wrote a letter from Antioch to the city of Philadelphia in Lydia.[19] Antioch was thus once again serving as an Imperial 'capital'. Syria therefore also had to draw resources from other parts of the Empire: thus in 253–256 we find villages in Egypt taking an oath to the Emperors Valerian and Gallienus (his son) that they will deliver thirty-six ploughing-oxen to Syria, 'wherever it may be commanded'.[20] The broad relevance to army supplies is clear, as is the implication that a need for supplies for more than one year is anticipated. According to Zosimus, Valerian and a newly appointed praetorian prefect also saw to the rebuilding of Antioch, evidently in the mid-250s.[21]

How long Valerian stayed in the Near East is not known. Zosimus' very episodic and abbreviated narrative would suggest that he left only for an abortive campaign into Cappadocia, in the face of Scythian invasions of Asia

18. Feissel and Gascou, "Documents", 568, nos. 3–4 (two copies), compared with 559, no. 9 (252).

19. See Baldus, op. cit. (n.9), 259–261; the letter of Valerian is *SEG* XIII, no. 528. For a good survey of the problem, revealing that the only certain gap in Imperial coin-production at Antioch is in the reign of Aemilianus (253), coinciding perhaps with Shapur's occupation, see K. W. Harl, *Civic Coins and Civic Politics in the Roman East, AD 180–275* (1987), App. 2.

20. *P. Oxy.* no. 3109.

21. Zosimus I, 32, 2.

Minor, before returning to Antioch to confront Shapur's invasion of 260. There is indeed no certain proof that Valerian ever left the East in the period from 255 to 260.[22] Hence we may accept that the reply given by Valerian to a lady called Theodora, whose bigamous 'husband' was trying to recover gifts made to her, was indeed issued at Antioch in May 258.[23] It was surely also while Valerian was in Syria that he issued, in the name of himself, his son Gallienus as joint Augustus and his grandson, the 'Caesar' Saloninus, a *subscriptio* about the privileges of the great temple of Zeus of Baetocaece, in the mountain-range behind Arados.[24] The date must be 258–260, and the nominal involvement of the two other Emperors is highly significant. For in these years Gallienus and Saloninus will both have been on campaign in Europe. The 'Tetrarchic' system, of a college of Emperors, each operating in different geographical regions, had already arrived. None of them was in Rome. Valerian's residence in the East will also serve to explain why his instructions to the Senate in Rome about the persecution of 258 came in the form of a letter.[25]

Though, as we have seen, the archaeological evidence suggests that the life of Roman Dura ended abruptly in 256 or 257, this must have been the result of a minor conflict. Shapur claims no campaign between his second, in 252/253, and his third, in 260. So far as our evidence goes, therefore, the second half of the 250s was a period of general peace in the Near East, and of established rule, by the senior Augustus, from Antioch. The mere three martyrdoms which Eusebius can record as having taken place at Caesarea in Palestine under Valerian will have seemed to the pagan majority to represent due order rather than its opposite.[26]

Almost no evidence survives to illuminate the relation of the cities and communities of the Near East to the Roman government in this period; the inscriptions of this area, never as extensive or detailed as those of the Greek cities of Asia Minor, become very few at this time. One exception is provided by the city of Adraa in Arabia, where a series of Greek inscriptions, beginning in the 250s, shows construction of walls and towers by the 'gift' of the Emperor, and supervised by military personnel.[27] A more important exception is provided by Palmyra; and it is only a seeming paradox that the integration of

22. Zosimus I, 36. Note, however, J. Reynolds on C. Roueché, *Aphrodisias in Late Antiquity* (1989), no. 1, a fragmentary letter of Valerian and Gallienus apparently written from Cologne.

23. *Cod. Just.* V, 3, 5, and IX, 9, 18 (extracts from the same text): 'Accepta XV id. Mai. Antiochiae Tusco et Basso conss'.

24. *IGLS* VII, no. 4001. See 8.3 below.

25. Cyprian, *Ep.* 80. See G. W. Clarke, *The Letters of St. Cyprian of Carthage* IV (1989), *ad loc.*

26. Eusebius, *HE* VII, 12.

27. H.-G. Pflaum, "La fortification de la ville d'Adraha d'Arabie (259–260 à 274–275) d'après les inscriptions récemment découvertes", *Syria* 29 (1952), 307.

the Palmyrene ruling class into the Imperial system is most clearly displayed—as always, in the form of honorific inscriptions—precisely in the decade before Odenathus led its ascent to independent power. Septimius Odenathus himself, already attested as a Roman senator, appears in 257/258 with the further title *hypatikos*. If we could attach a precise meaning to this term, it would be of crucial significance. But the word, the standard Greek equivalent of *consularis* (a man of ex-consul rank), seems to have come (like *consularis* itself) also to mean 'governor', and by the normal inflation of titles could be used of the governor of a one-legion province like Syria Phoenice, even though he would not be an ex-consul.[28] It is thus possible, but not certain, that when inscriptions from Palmyra in 257/258 call Odenathus *hypatikos* (HPTYK'), he was then the *legatus* of Syria Phoenice.[29] If so, it should be noted that the rule made after the proclamation of Avidius Cassius in 175 had been forgotten, and that he was governing the province from which he himself came.[30] At any rate what is certain is that the title is a Roman one, and that no more is heard of his being *exarchos*(?) or 'head of Tadmor' (RŠ TDMWR), whatever these unusual titles had meant a few years before. One of the four trade-associations which put up honorific inscriptions to him in 257/258 does indeed call him 'master' (*despotēs* in Greek, MRN in Palmyrene); but the other three, in Greek only, use *patrōn*, borrowing the Latin term *patronus*. The inscriptions are thus evidence of a relationship between Odenathus and trade-associations in the city, but not of some overall domination of the city by him.

Odenathus was not the only Palmyrene to be honoured in Roman terms in this period. In 258/259 Aurelius Vorodes (WRWD), of whom more below, was described as *hippikos* (that is, *eques*) and town-councillor, *bouleutēs* (in Palmyrene transcription HPK' WBYLWT' TDMRY'). For a Roman *colonia* this mélange of languages was of course very distinctive, though no more so than in the *coloniae* of Mesopotamia. But if we take the dated evidence in order, there is still no concrete evidence of any distinctive role on the part of the city, or any status within it on the part of Septimius Odenathus beyond what we would expect of (apparently) the only person from there to rise to high rank in the Roman Senate.

We could thus see the later 250s also as a period of established, or re-

---

28. Cf., however, B. Rémy, "Ὑπατικοί et *consulares* dans les provinces impériales prétoriennes au IIᵉ et IIIᵉ siècles", *Latomus* 45 (1986), 311, arguing that the title was used only when the person had gained a consulate in absence or been adlected *inter consulares*.

29. See M. Gawlikowski, "Les princes de Palmyre", *Syria* 62 (1983), 251, and Potter, *Sibylline Oracle*, App. 4, "The Career of Odenathus", an important discussion which takes a different view from that offered here: that Odenathus was not a governor, but did occupy a formal position of dominance at Palmyra.

30. 3.4 above.

stored, Roman rule in the Near East, marked above all by the almost continuous presence of the senior Augustus. All this, however, was to be violently disturbed by the last of Shapur's three invasions, which led to the capture of Valerian himself in Mesopotamia in 260. We must begin with Shapur's own version:

> During the third invasion, when we set out against Carrhae and Edessa and were besieging Carrhae and Edessa, Valerianus Caesar came against us . . . And beyond Carrhae and Edessa there was a great battle between us and Valerianus Caesar and we gained possession of Valerianus Caesar . . . And we burned and devastated and took captives from and conquered the province of Syria and the province of Cilicia and the province of Cappadocia.[31]

The first objective had therefore been western Mesopotamia, and after this there follows a long list of the places ravaged, confirming that the invasion did reach far into Cilicia and Cappadocia. Of places in Syria which are, or may be, mentioned, only Samosata is certain. For the 'Antiochia' which Shapur names is listed along with other small places in Cilicia. If we took this list as our main guide (as in principle we should), we could not be sure if even Carrhae and Edessa (or Nisibis, which is not mentioned) were actually taken; and we might reasonably conclude that the Persian army moved directly westwards from Samosata to Cilicia, and did not enter the central area of northern Syria at all. There is no mention of Zeugma, Cyrrhus, Beroea or Seleucia. For the established notion of a second capture of Antioch, under Valerian, we are entirely dependent on Greek and Latin sources of the fourth century and later.[32]

Even if we accept, as on balance we probably should, that Antioch was captured for a second time in 260, there is no question but that the weight of the Persian invasion was directed against Mesopotamia, and then Commagene, Cilicia and Cappadocia. How the Persian army reached the area of Carrhae and Nisibis is not known (whether by the Euphrates and Chabur, or more probably by the Tigris); nor is there any clear indication of what effects the invasion had in eastern Mesopotamia. If we follow the quite varied details provided in a series of much later narratives (and we have nothing better), it is far from certain even that Edessa was taken. Two Byzantine chroniclers, Georgius Syncellus and Zonaras, record that Roman forces under Callistus

31. For the *Res Gestae*, see 4.2, n.39. For discussion see again Kettenhofen, *Kriege*, 97ff., and map 3.

32. So Jerome, *Chron.*, ed. Helm, p. 220; Zosimus III, 32, 5 (a later summary of Roman–Parthian/Persian relations, inadvertently making Valerian's campaign a *reaction* to the capture of Antioch); Syncellus, *Chron.* I, p. 715; Zonaras XII, 23 (the fullest account, and the one which corresponds best with Shapur's *Res Gestae*). The question of Antioch is well discussed in Potter, *Sibylline Oracle*, 337ff.

finally mounted an effective counter-attack in Asia Minor, and that Shapur then retreated; and another says that on his retreat Shapur bribed the Roman troops occupying Edessa not to attack his army.[33] The story, like all these accounts, may be fanciful. But it is noteworthy that even Shapur makes no claim actually to have captured Carrhae or Edessa.

Insofar as we can gain any impression of the effects of this last Persian invasion, which left most of the Roman Near East wholly untouched, it is from the equally unreliable accounts of the restoration of Roman power, inextricably confused with narratives of the rise of Odenathus of Palmyra, and his confrontation with two other Roman pretenders, the short-lived Roman Emperors Macrianus and Quietus. The contemporary evidence, apart from a vague and allusive few lines, apparently added on subsequently, at the end of the *XIIIth Sibylline Oracle,* which refer to Valerian, Gallienus and Odenathus,[34] consists almost entirely of honorific inscriptions from Palmyra. The inevitable limitations of such evidence show up all the more clearly when the crucial items expressing Odenathus' role and status turn out, though broadly contemporary, to be posthumous, put up under the much more ambitious rule of his widow Zenobia and his son Vaballathus after 267.

Nonetheless it is possible to set out at least the broad outlines of the history of the Near East in the exceptional period of twelve years, 260–272, during which no recognised Emperor came there; the first was to be Aurelian, leading the campaign which brought about the defeat and reconquest of Palmyra in 272. The aftermath of the capture of Valerian in 260 did lead to a brief usurpation, when Macrianus, a high equestrian official on Valerian's campaigns, proclaimed as Emperors his two sons, Macrianus and Quietus, who reigned in 260/261; they were recognised in Egypt before Macrianus was killed in the Balkans, and Quietus was killed while being besieged by Odenathus in Emesa. No evidence survives to illustrate their rule in the Near East, where they will surely have been recognised in at least some provinces.

Among these provinces Syria Phoenice may or may not have been included. For it is at this point that the independent military role of Palmyra begins. We would of course see it in a quite different light if we could be certain that Odenathus, when described as *hypatikos* in an inscription of 257/258, had in fact been the *legatus* of the province, and even more so if in 260 he still were. In the long list of provinces from which Shapur claims that Valerian's forces in 260 had been drawn, all those of the Near East are included: Syria (Coele), Phoenice, Judaea (as he still calls it), Arabia and Mesopotamia. But whatever legionary detachments or auxiliary units had served under Valerian, it is relevant that Syria Phoenice was the nearest province

---

33. Syncellus, *Chron.* I, p. 716; Zonaras XII, 23; Petrus Patricius, Fr. 11 (*FHG* IV, p. 187).
34. *Sib. Or.* XIII, 155–173. See Potter, *Sibylline Oracle,* 151; 328ff.

which had in no way been touched by the invasion, and from which direct routes led across the steppe to the Euphrates, and from there either north to Roman Mesopotamia or south to Babylonia. Active Palmyrene contacts with Babylonia continued until this period. The latest dated 'caravan-inscription' (that is, an honorific inscription for someone involved in the protection of caravans) which actually names a destination in Persian territory, Vologaesias, comes from 247; but there is one of 257/258, and another which seems certainly to belong to the 260s.[35] The dating depends on identifying the honorand, Septim[ius Vorodes]—this part of the name is missing—with an important figure of the 260s, Septimius Vorodes, of whom more later, who may have adopted the name 'Septimius' and be in fact the same as the 'Aurelius Vorodes' whom we saw honoured as a *hippikos* and *bouleutēs* in 258/259.[36] In the inscription (probably) of the 260s he is honoured as a *procurator ducenarius* of the Emperor, as the holder of a long series of city offices and as having 'brought back the caravans *(synodiai)* at his own expense'. He must either have provided an escort or, perhaps equally likely, have paid off potential nomad raiders. We would not know from this inscription that anything at all had changed as regards the integration of the *colonia* of Palmyra into the Roman Empire.

What is significant in the immediate context, however, is that the Persian military advance up the middle Euphrates does not seem to have stopped the caravan traffic across the steppe (which would always enter Persian, and earlier Parthian, territory at some point); and that whatever forces remained in the western part of Syria Phoenice had not been confronted by a Persian invasion since 252/253. But what is much less clear is how easily any regular Roman units could be, or now were, moved along the routes over the steppe to the Euphrates.

Our greatest problem, which seems at the moment insoluble, is thus to know whether we should see Odenathus' actions in response to Valerian's capture as those of a Roman governor with regular forces on the one hand, or of a local notable with local forces on the other. But even in the latter case it should be recalled that Palmyra was now, and remained, a *colonia* under *duumviri/stratēgoi*.

The initial phase of the rise of Odenathus to a major role in the Near East took the form of a military reaction against the retreating Persian forces and against the usurpation of Macrianus and Quietus, and was followed in 260 or soon after by recognition of Gallienus, who was occupied in Europe throughout his reign, and had no co-Emperor.[37] No clear sequence of events

35. Cantineau, *Inv.* III, no. 21 (247); 13 (257/258); 7 (260s).
36. See above, p. 165.
37. For treatments of this controversial and uncertain sequence of events see, e.g., F. Millar, "Paul of Samosata, Zenobia and Aurelian: The Church, Local Culture and Political Allegiance

can be established, but we find in our varied narratives that Odenathus besieged Quietus at Emesa, whose people then killed him;[38] that he recovered Mesopotamia, including the cities of Nisibis and Carrhae (if they had really been taken by the Persians, we do not know when); and that at some point his forces advanced as far as Ctesiphon. It would help if we had any conception of the disposition of Roman forces at this time. But we do not, and our highly coloured narratives tend to speak of Odenathus' own forces as being Syrian peasants.[39] What then was the relation of Odenathus, and of Palmyra, to the Roman Empire between 260 and his murder in 267/268? First, the little evidence that we have shows a normal regime in operation in the other provinces of the Near East. At Adraa in Arabia, for instance, towers and walls were built under successive governors in 262/263 and 263/264, using military supervisors, and were dedicated 'on behalf of the safety (and victory) of our lord Imperator Gallienus Augustus'.[40] In Syria Palaestina, even after the general edict of toleration issued by Gallienus, Eusebius reports an isolated but striking case of a martyrdom before the governor, Achaeus; the victim, a centurion named Marinus, was given a magnificent tomb by a local Christian dignitary of senatorial rank named Astyrius.[41] It is patent that this episode belongs in a normal provincial context, governed by a distant Emperor. But in any case we hardly need such incidental evidence. For normal minting at Antioch continued in the name of Gallienus until his death in 268, as it did for Claudius Gothicus until 269. It was in this period, probably in the autumn of 268, that the heretical bishop of Antioch, Paul of Samosata, was finally deposed by a synod which met there. The long-established notion that Paul had been a *protégé* of Zenobia, and had even served as a *ducenarius* under her, has no foundation. On the contrary, one of the misdeeds of which his fellow-bishops accused him was that of behaving in public *like a ducenarius*. The point was included in the letters which they sent to Dionysius, the bishop of Alexandria, and Maximus, the bishop of Rome.[42] The episode reflects not Palmyrene power, but established Roman rule in Syria Coele.

The structure of government in Syria Phoenice would be even more relevant, but on that we have no evidence beyond the narrative detail that Odenathus besieged Quietus in Emesa. For the position of Odenathus himself we

---

in Third-Century Syria", *JRS* 61 (1971), 1, on pp. 8ff.; Starcky and Gawlikowski, *Palmyre*, 59ff.; Potter, *Sibylline Oracle,* 341ff. and App. IV.

38. Petrus Patricius, *FHG* IV, p. 195; Zonaras XII, 24.

39. So, e.g., Festus, *Brev.* 23: 'collecta Syrorum agrestium manu'; Jerome, *Chron.*, ed. Helm, p. 221: 'collecta agrestium manu'; Orosius, *Hist.* VII, 22, 12: 'collecta agresti manu'.

40. H.-G. Pflaum, *Syria* 29 (1952), 312–313.

41. Eusebius, *HE* VII, 13 (edict of toleration); 15–16 (Marinus and Astyrius).

42. The essential evidence is contained in Eusebius, *HE* VII, 27–30. For the complex arguments involved see Millar, op. cit. (n.37).

are dependent either on repeated statements by the late-fourth-century (and acutely unreliable) *Historia Augusta* that he received the *imperium* of the Orient, or even the title 'Augustus'; on reports by two Byzantine chroniclers that he was made *stratēgos* (general or military commander) of the East;[43] or on contemporary documents. But the only two contemporary documents which record his position, a milestone and a statue-base, both come from the reign of his widow Zenobia and his son Vaballathus, when the entire situation had changed. Both call him retrospectively 'king of kings' (MLK MLK'), while the second, a statue-base dedicated by two Palmyrene generals in 271, calls him also MTQNN' DY MDNḤ' KLH, 'restorer of the whole East'.[44] How this would have been expressed in Latin or Greek is uncertain; nor is it necessarily a reference to an established *position* rather than a laudatory allusion to his victories in the early 260s.

If we cannot trace any clear evolution of the position of Odenathus himself, the inscriptions honouring Septimius Vorodes do at least provide some check. They suggest for instance that, unlike Edessa in 239–241,[45] Palmyra did not cease in the 260s to call itself a Roman *colonia*. This is certainly true of an inscription honouring Vorodes as *epitropos (procurator)* of the Emperor, put up in 262 by a *stratēgos* of the *colonia*.[46] The strongly Roman overtones continue on an inscription of 267, again calling Vorodes *epitropos* of the Emperor, put up by Iulius Aurelius Salmes, who describes himself as 'Roman *eques*'—*hippeus Rōmaiōn*, or HPQ'. Something does change in this period, however, for in this same inscription, and in others, a new official title appears, 'argapet' (*argapetēs* or 'RGBṬ'), a word of Iranian origin taken to mean 'governor (of the city)'.[47] But about this time, in the undated inscription mentioned earlier, Vorodes is also described as 'giver of justice', or 'judge' *(dikeodotēs)* of the *mētrokolōneia*. The hybrid Latin-Greek term has evidently been borrowed from *mētropolis* to indicate a *colonia* of higher standing than others.[48] No dated inscription from Palmyra of 267 or before would lead us to suppose that the city was not still fully integrated in the Imperial system.

However, we need not argue away the clear implications of our sources that a very distinctive and unusual role had been achieved, in the context of at least a relative power-vacuum in the Roman Near East. The clearest sign

43. So Syncellus, *Chron.* I, p. 716; Zonaras XII, 24.

44. *CIS* II.3, no. 3971 (milestone); *CIS* II.3, no. 3946 = Cantineau, *Inv.* III, no. 19 (statue-base). I cannot see what conclusions should be drawn from the very fragmentary honorific inscription, *Inv.* III, no. 10, beginning with the words [B]ασιλεῖ βασιλέων.

45. 4.2 above.

46. Cantineau, *Inv.* III, no. 10.

47. Cantineau, *Inv.* III, no. 6 (267); cf. no. 8 (265); no. 9 (264 or 267).

48. Cantineau, *Inv.* III, no. 7.

of this is the fact that both Odenathus' widow Zenobia and his son Vaballa-thus could rapidly advance to much more exceptional positions following his murder in 267/268, said by one source to have occurred at Emesa.[49]

But how immediate an acquisition of an exceptional status, and what personal status, is again uncertain. For that we would need evidence datable to the period between 267 and 269 or 270, when a decisive break occurred and Palmyrene forces advanced into neighbouring Roman provinces, possibly first through Arabia to Egypt, and subsequently to Antioch, and from there north-west into Asia Minor. Vaballathus *may* have enjoyed some formal Roman title from the moment of his father's death. But our evidence is either retro-spective or not dated. So for instance the undated bilingual inscription on the stone in the form of a milestone mentioned above, from west of Palmyra on the road to Emesa or Damascus, calls Zenobia 'queen' *(basilissa)*, and Vaballathus 'king of kings', as well as 'PNRṬ' DY MDNH' KLH—'*epanorthōtes* (transliterated) of the whole East'.[50] The term should be the equivalent of the Latin *corrector*—but this word itself had no precisely defined application. However, the absence of all strictly Imperial titles here does suggest that the inscription dates from before Palmyra's expansion. All our other evidence clearly does come from the period of the geographical extension of Palmyrene power. In Arabia there are milestones in Latin from along Trajan's Via Nova, between Bostra and Philadelphia, recording Vaballathus as (for instance) 'L. Iulius Aurelius Septimius Baballathus Athenodorus, Rex, co(n)s(ul), Impera-tor, Dux Romanorum'.[51] Another, from the same road, goes in for a fine dis-play of Imperial victory-titles: 'Imp(erator) Caesar L. Iulius Aurelius Septim-ius Vaballathus Athenodorus, Persicus Maximus, Arabicus Maximus, Adiabenicus Maximus, Pius Felix Au[gustus]'.[52] These inscriptions are enough to indicate beyond doubt that what was now claimed was the position of Roman Emperor, and no co-Emperor is named. But the papyrus documents reflecting Palmyrene rule in Egypt are different: for there Aurelian is named first as Emperor, and Vaballathus follows. So we have texts dated by the sec-ond year of Aurelian (272) and the fifth year of Vaballathus: 'Iulius Aurelius Septimius Vaballathus Athenodorus, the most illustrious king, Consul, Impe-rator, Stratēgos of the Romans'.[53]

Detailed examination of titles will not in reality help us, for they were

49. So Zosimus I, 39, 2.

50. *CIS* II.3, no. 3971.

51. See Th. Bauzou, "Deux milliaires inédits de Vaballath en Jordanie du Nord", in Freeman and Kennedy, *DRBE*, 1.

52. *ILS*, no. 8924.

53. *P. Oxy.*, no. 1264; cf. *BGU*, no. 946. See above all the documents relating to the corn-dole at Oxyrhynchus in the late 260s and early 270s published by J. R. Rea, *Oxyrhynchus Papyri* XL (1972); table of datings by Aurelian and Vaballathus on p. 16.

being made up in an unprecedented and fluid situation. They are enough to
suggest that the milestone from west of Palmyra should be relatively early, for
no Imperial titles appear on it; that with the expansion from 269/270 onwards Vaballathus began to claim Imperial rank, in a variety of ways; that
his public posture was that of co-Emperor with Aurelian; and that eventually
'Augustus', the most distinctive of Imperial names, is used also, as 'Augusta'
can be for Zenobia. Palmyrene 'Imperial' coinage struck at Antioch tells the
same story: first joint coining in the names of Vaballathus, calling himself
'Re(x), Im(perator), D(ux) R(omanorum)', and of Aurelian; then, at the very
last moment, Aurelian's name disappears, and the coins name 'Imp(erator)
C(aesar) Vhabalathus *(sic)* Aug(ustus)' and 'Zenobia Augusta'.[54]

What this brief and violent episode meant for the Near East can hardly
now be recovered. A mere few fragments of evidence serve to recall its effects:
for instance a temple of Zeus Hammon at Bostra, repaired after being damaged by 'the Palmyrene enemies'.[55] Or, from more than two decades later,
there is a subscript of Diocletian and Maximian, addressed to someone called
Agrippa in 293, and now preserved in the *Codex Justinianus*: 'Since you say
that your freeborn relative, made a captive so to speak during the domination
of the Palmyrene faction, has been sold, the governor of the province will see
to it that his freeborn status is restored to him'.[56] Otherwise, some features
of the situation emerge from the only relatively satisfactory account of Aurelian's reconquest, that by Zosimus, though even here it must be recalled that
what we read is part of an overall narrative of Imperial history written in
about AD 500.[57]

In Zosimus' account, Aurelian brought his forces along the normal route
through Asia Minor, retaking Ancyra and Tyana, and defeated the Palmyrene
army near Antioch (other sources add that this was at Immae, precisely where
Elagabal's forces had defeated those of Macrinus).[58] Entering Antioch, he
published edicts to reassure the population that they would not be punished
for having supported Zenobia. His army then marched up the Orontes Valley
via Apamea, Larissa and Arethusa, and encountered the Palmyrene forces
again at Emesa (geography thus dictated an almost exact repetition of Shapur's invasion in 252/253).[59] Zenobia then retreated to Palmyra, while Aurelian was welcomed at Emesa. The *Historia Augusta* adds at this point an item
of great importance, if true: that Aurelian celebrated his victory by worship-
ping at the temple of Elagabalus at Emesa; and later also, as a memorial of his

54. H. Seyrig, "Vhabalathus Augustus", *Mélanges Michalowski* (1966), 659.
55. *IGLS* XIII.1, no. 9107.
56. *CJ* VII, 14, 4.
57. Zosimus I, 50–60.
58. Immae: Festus, *Brev.* 24; Jerome, *Chron.*, ed. Helm, p. 222. See 4.2 above.
59. Text to nn.8–9 above.

victory, built his well-known temple of the Sun at Rome.[60] Rightly or wrongly, therefore, the author says that the temple of the Sun-God in Rome was a borrowing made by Aurelian from Emesa. Aurelian then advanced to Palmyra, and Zosimus tells a colourful story of Zenobia being placed on a camel and reaching the Euphrates, in the hope of taking refuge with the Persians, before being captured. The city was taken, and a garrison left there. On his way back to Europe Aurelian heard of a renewed uprising in Palmyra, which he returned to suppress. According to Zosimus, the leader of the revolt first tried to persuade Marcellinus, the governor of Mesopotamia, to revolt; if the story has any substance, it suggests that normal Roman government had been restored there also.[61]

What this extraordinary and unparalleled episode meant in terms of the role of Palmyra as between the Empire and Persia, and in terms of its cultural and ethnic identity as a place on the fringes of Greek culture, will need to be discussed later.[62] In strictly military terms, and in terms of the structure of force in the Roman Near East, it is indeed hardly intelligible. For we can discern neither whence the Palmyrenes gained their forces, nor what Roman troops remained either to join or to oppose them, nor how the mass of the civilian population reacted. Nor is there any way of knowing whether the Palmyrenes themselves, the other communities of the Near East or the Roman forces stationed there saw this as a local ethnic movement against Rome or as a breakaway Roman regime reacting to a power vacuum and the Persian invasion. These Persian invasions, however brief, were also quite exceptional. It would not be until the sixth century that Persian forces again crossed the Euphrates. Mesopotamia would be a different matter, and would remain a battleground. But there as elsewhere the military structure of the Roman Near East does not become (relatively) clear again until the Tetrarchic period.

60. SHA, *Aurel.* 25, 5–6.
61. Zosimus I, 60, 1.
62. 9.4 below.

THE TETRARCHY AND
CONSTANTINE

5.1. THE TETRARCHY: PERSIAN WARS
AND FORTIFIED LINES

For just over a decade after Aurelian's reconquest of Palmyra, we have effectively no evidence at all about the Roman Near East. Almost all that can be offered is a few inscriptions from Arabia, of the 270s and early 280s, showing governors supervising the building of walls and possibly other structures at Adraa and Bostra. But even these are sufficient to illustrate one of the major changes in the structure of the Empire which began step by step in the middle decades of the third century, and were taken much further in the period of the Tetrarchy and Constantine. That is to say, in broad terms, that the Imperial structure moved almost entirely away from its roots in the Republican system, based on the Senate and the holding of major offices by senators. Thus these inscriptions from Arabia show that the governors, who had previously been senators of ex-praetor rank, *legati Augusti pro praetore*, were now men of equestrian rank with the title *praeses* (*hēgemōn* in Greek).[1] What we call the late Empire is already coming into being.

Beyond that, in the Tetrarchic period, from 284 onwards, there came rearrangements of provincial boundaries; a new taxation-system; what seems to have been a more active and positive attitude on the part of government (reflected in this period in a long series of boundary-decisions in the name of the Emperor); the appearance of a new tier of regional government, the twelve

---

1. *SEG* XVI, nos. 813–814 (274/275, Adraa), Flavius Aelianus, *praeses*—ἡ(γεμόνος); *IGLS* XIII.1, no. 9108 (278/279, Bostra), Aur. Petrus, τοῦ δια[σημοτάτου ἡμῶν] ἡγεμ(όνος); 9109 (282/283, Bostra), Aemilius Aemilianus, *hēgemōn*.

'dioceses', each embracing a number of provinces; and above all the formalisation of the geographical division of the Empire between (eventually) four Emperors: two senior *Augusti* and two *Caesares*. It was within that framework that the repeated role of Antioch as an Imperial residence was in effect transformed into that of a regular capital. It was also in this period, in 298/299, that a treaty with Persia gave the Empire in the Near East its greatest-ever extension, to and apparently across the Tigris. Moreover, virtually all along the zone between the settled area and the steppe literary evidence, inscriptions and the physical remains of Roman forts and roads combine to provide the most detailed picture we have for any period of a Roman 'desert frontier'.

It was perhaps merely an accident that the much more active and interventionist attitude of the state in this period was to be expressed also in the form of the last great persecution of Christians—and then, after the conversion of Constantine in 312, by equally active support of Christianity and vigorous Imperial efforts to enforce unity in the Church. This transformation of internal structures, and then the later phase, after 312, will need separate treatment. But, both for the military aspect (which will come first) and for these others, it is of profound significance for our understanding that we can again rely on the view provided by a contemporary, Eusebius, bishop of Caesarea, who was born soon after 260 and died in 339.[2] Unlike Josephus, the last 'native' of this region on whom we could depend for a connected narrative of events and an understanding of them from within, Eusebius remained resident there throughout the entire period. Our best narrative evidence for the entire half-century of the Tetrarchy and Constantine thus comes from a Near Eastern perspective. Eusebius' narratives, in the later books (VIII–X) of his *Ecclesiastical History,* in the *Martyrs of Palestine* and in *On the Life of the Blessed Constantine,* all show us events unfolding as they were seen from the viewpoint of Caesarea in Palestine. His *Onomasticon,* a work on place-names in the Bible, also happens to give a priceless snapshot of social structures and military dispositions as they were in these same places towards the end of the third century.[3] It is from this work, and this alone, that we know that the legion X Fretensis (or at least a detachment of it) had already moved down from Jerusalem to its new station at Aila at the head of the Gulf of Aqaba: 'Ailam: on the borders (of Palestine), lying next to the southern desert and the Red Sea which is next to it, sailed by both those crossing from Egypt and those from India. Stationed there is the Tenth legion *(tagma)* of the Romans.

2. For Eusebius, I depend throughout on T. D. Barnes, *Constantine and Eusebius* (1981).

3. For the work and its date see Barnes, op. cit., 106ff. The question of the date is controversial, but I believe Barnes's early dating to be correct. The strongest argument for such a date is the absence of any reflection of established Christianity.

It is now called Aila'.[4] This region, as we will see later, was now part of 'Syria Palaestina', not as before 'Arabia'; and Trajan's construction of his Via Nova had been followed at last by a large-scale military investment. The fact that we have this information, from this date, is in a sense accidental. But a writer from outside the region, however interested in Biblical sites, might not have been able to add this detail. Moreover, a focus on Biblical sites was a relatively new feature of Christianity in this period, and was to be reinforced on a vast scale by Constantine. In these senses, important enough, the fact that Eusebius' perspective on his time is a regional one is more than just an accident of biography. But whether there is more to it than that, whether he or anyone else represents a distinctive 'Syrian' Christianity, is quite another matter.[5] If that issue is more complex than it may seem, we do have unambiguously regional perspectives on the Tetrarchic Empire from rabbinic writings on the one hand,[6] and from Syriac martyr-acts, narrating martyrdoms in Edessa, on the other.[7] With the ever deeper implantation of the Roman state in the Near East, it and the world of rabbinic learning could come into very close contact. Witness the rabbinic ruling that a *cohen* who incurred defilement (through contact with a corpse) could be excused because he had walked over graves in order to see the Emperor Diocletian at Tyre.[8]

Diocletian had become Emperor in circumstances which were of great significance as illustrating the continued relevance of Roman imperialism in this region, and the importance of the Near East as a military zone. For he had been in the entourage of the Emperor Carus and his son Numerianus on their campaign into the heart of the Persian Empire in 283, when both Ctesiphon and Seleucia on the Tigris were captured.[9] Carus seems to have died there, and by March 284 Numerianus may have been back in Syria, at Emesa.[10] But after that he took his forces on the established route across Asia Minor. It must have been on that journey that he was murdered, and his death then concealed during several days' march. For it is certain that it was at

4. Eusebius, *Onom.*, ed. Klostermann, p. 6. It was to be there throughout the fourth century, see *Not. Dign., Or.* XXXIV, 30: 'Praefectus legionis decimae Fretensis, Ailae' (under the Dux Palaestinae).

5. See 13.1 below.

6. See esp. S. Lieberman, "Palestine in the Third and Fourth Centuries", *JQR* 36 (1945–46), 329; 37 (1946–47), 31 (both, however, highly speculative).

7. See 12.6 below.

8. *Jerusalem Talmud, Berachoth* 3, 1 (trans. M. Schwab, *Le Talmud de Jérusalem* I [1871], 58; trans. ed. J. Neusner, *Talmud of the Land of Israel* I [1989], 119). For the impact of Diocletian's visit here, as reflected in the Talmud, see now also J. C. Greenfield, "An Aramaic Inscription from Tyre from the Reign of Diocletian Preserved in the Palestinian Talmud", *Atti* II. *Cong. Int. Studi Fenici e Punici* II (1991), 499.

9. SHA, *Car.* 8, 1; Zonaras XII, 30. See Halfmann, *Itinera*, 242.

10. So *CJ* V, 52, 2 (but in the names of Carus, Carinus—his other son—and Numerianus).

Nicomedia, on November 20, 284, that Diocles, an equestrian officer, was proclaimed Emperor, subsequently taking the name 'Imperator Caesar C. Aurelius Valerius Diocletianus'.

It was he who inaugurated the Tetrarchic system, taking first a 'Caesar' and then a co-'Augustus', Maximian, and subsequently in 293, two junior 'Caesares', Constantius (the father of Constantine), who reigned in the West under Maximian, and Galerius, who was active in the East under Diocletian himself. The fact that the senior Augustus took the East as his area is itself a clear indication of the way that strategic priorities had become established. But 'the East' in this sense means the whole eastern half of the Empire, up to the Danube. In 287 Diocletian achieved some sort of submission from the Persians, involving the sending of gifts, including animals; but whether he himself was actually then on campaign in the Near East is not certain. It is not until 290 that he can be shown for certain to have been in Syria, issuing rulings in May from Antioch, from Emesa to the *praeses* of Syria (Phoenice) and probably from Laodicea. More important, a panegyrist, addressing Maximian at Trier in 291, alludes briefly to a recent victory over 'the Saracen'—as it seems, the first occasion on which this word was ever used to describe a defeated Imperial enemy: 'I pass over the Saracen oppressed by the shackles of captivity'. He clearly means to speak of peoples living near Roman Syria, for later he makes another allusion: 'that laurel (won) from the conquered *nationes* bordering Syria'.[11] The speaker probably had even less of an idea than we as to where precisely these *Saraceni* might have been located. Like all such terms, it could be used of peoples who might be found anywhere from Mesopotamia to Aila on the Red Sea. But, given Diocletian's movements and the extensive military investment in what was to be called the Strata Diocletiana, running from the Hauran to Damascus and then through Palmyra to the Euphrates,[12] it was probably in that area, hence in Syria Phoenice or the northern part of Arabia, that the action took place. One of the very last old-style senatorial *legati Augusti pro praetore* of the province of Syria Phoenice is found making a Latin dedication at Heliopolis about this time to Diocletian as 'the liberator of the Roman world, the bravest and most dutiful and most unconquered'.[13]

During this period the Persian front was quiescent, and it was not until perhaps 295, and more certainly from 296 onwards, that major campaigns began again.[14] In brief, Galerius was first defeated by the Persian king Narses in a battle in Mesopotamia ('between Callinicum and Carrhae', so apparently

---

11. Barnes, *New Empire*, 51. *Pan.* III (11), ed. Galletier, 5, 4; 7, 1.

12. Text to nn.22ff. below.

13. *IGLS* VI, no. 2771.

14. For the complex issues of Imperial chronology in this period see T. D. Barnes, "Imperial Campaigns, AD 285–311", *Phoenix* 30 (1976), 174.

somewhere on the river Balikh). In 297 he collected new forces from the Balkans, and in 298 fought a successful campaign further north, in Armenia, and then marched south along the Tigris as far as Ctesiphon (once again), finally returning by the route up the Euphrates. According to Ammianus, when Julian's forces reached the fortified post of Anatha (now Persian) in 363, they found among the captives a Roman soldier left behind during Galerius' retreat; the implication is clearly that the invasion had not served to reimpose Roman control on the lower-middle Euphrates.[15] Diocletian's occupation of the Euphrates stopped at Circesium, at its confluence with the Chabur.[16]

The major consequence of this victory was the recapture of Nisibis (though how long it had been lost seems quite unclear). More important still were the terms of the peace now imposed on Narses, and the role of Nisibis as expressed in them. It was either in 298 or 299 that Diocletian joined Galerius there and sent an envoy to Narses to dictate terms. Five districts, described as Intelene, Sophene, Arzanene, Carduene and Zabdikene, were to be held by the Romans, while the Tigris would be the frontier between the two empires.[17] What this means is far from clear, for these districts lie largely on the far bank of the Tigris; it is possible that in this zone across the river Rome now gained some recognised hegemony, without military occupation. What is important, however, is that the treaty led to a firm Roman occupation of a region to the north-east of the existing province of Mesopotamia, along the upper-middle Tigris, where it flows first eastwards behind the Mons Masius (the Tur Abdin) and then south-east to enter the Mesopotamian plain. This stretch would (at least within a few decades) contain the major Roman strongholds of Amida (Diyarbakir) and Bezabde.[18] Although reports of this treaty speak of Rome gaining regions 'across the Tigris',[19] it seems clear that it was in fact on the right bank of the river that the Roman defences would be built. There was thus a real extension of Roman military occupation to the Tigris, and one in which a heavy investment would be made. In geographical terms it was not large; but this advance into a remote and little-known area along the Tigris deserves some attention. For it was yet another step in the continuing

15. Ammianus XXIV, 1, 10.

16. Text to n.25 below.

17. Petrus Patricius, Fr. 14 (*FHG* IV, p. 189). See E. Winter, "On the Regulation of the Eastern Frontier of the Roman Empire in 298", in D. H. French and C. S. Lightfoot (eds.), *The Eastern Frontier of the Roman Empire* II (1989), 555.

18. For this area see the illuminating discussion by J. Matthews, *The Roman Empire of Ammianus* (1989), 41ff.

19. Festus, *Brev.* 25: 'Persae ... Mesopotamiam cum Transtigritanis regionibus reddiderunt'.

forward movement of Roman forces, which in the Near East was to last beyond our period. This particular advance could be seen as the preliminary to the partition of Armenia, directly across the river, in 387; in the Roman part of Armenia major fortifications were still being undertaken in the sixth century.[20]

The provisions relating to Nisibis were also of great significance. In spite of reported objections by Narses, it was laid down that commercial exchanges between the two empires would take place there. For over sixty years, until it was surrendered after Julian's campaign in 363, Nisibis was to be the commercial and military centre of the eastern part of Roman Mesopotamia. Like Edessa, it was also to be one of the major centres of Christian Syriac literature. The greatest of all Syriac writers, Ephrem, was born there a few years after the treaty, and left it only when it was abandoned to the Persians in 363.

Diocletian seems to have been based largely in Antioch in the years 300–302, with a journey to Egypt, on which he travelled through Palestine, and Eusebius for the first time set eyes on the young Constantine, who was in the Emperor's entourage.[21] In 302 Diocletian returned to his main capital, Nicomedia, where the great persecution was instituted in February 303. In 305, with the abdication of Diocletian and Maximian, Galerius became the 'Augustus' of the eastern half of the Empire, resident mainly in the Balkan peninsula, while his nephew (C. Galerius Valerius) Maximinus became the 'Caesar', then being proclaimed 'Augustus' by his troops in 310. As was noted before, his rule between 305 and 311 represents a notable phase in the integration of the Near East into the Imperial system. For he was resident there continuously throughout that period, perhaps primarily at Antioch, but also on occasion at Caesarea in Palestine. The military history of these years, if there was one, is entirely unknown, though a victory against the Persians is celebrated in 310. With the death of Galerius in 311, a quite new phase opened, and Maximinus moved rapidly to secure Nicomedia, returning to Antioch in 312, when a campaign was fought, for unknown reasons, in Armenia. In 313 he returned to the Balkans, was defeated by Licinius, then the 'Augustus' of that area, and committed suicide after retreating to Tarsos. With that again a new phase opens. But the years 311 and 312 are chiefly notable as the last phase of active persecution of the Christians, renewed even after Galerius' deathbed edict of toleration

---

20. See J. D. Howard-Johnston, "Procopius, Roman Defences North of the Taurus and the New Fortress of Citharizon", in D. H. French and C. S. Lighfoot (eds.), *The Eastern Frontier of the Roman Empire* II (1989), 203.

21. Eusebius, *VC* I, 19; Barnes, *New Empire*, 55.

in 311. How this phase worked out is closely bound up with the interplay of relations between the emperor and the still pagan communities of the Near East, the city of Antioch above all. Before that it will be necessary to look at how the Empire in the Near East, viewed as a military structure, had developed over the previous three decades.

Later writers were in no doubt that the reign of Diocletian had seen a massive programme of fortification all along the frontiers, including particularly the eastern one.[22] To Zosimus, writing in about AD 500, this was a valuable measure, subsequently undone by Constantine: 'For, as the Roman Empire, everywhere along its frontiers, had by the foresight of Diocletian . . . been equipped with cities and forts and towers, and the whole army was stationed there, passage into it was impossible for the barbarians'.[23] Malalas, writing some decades later, sums up the implementation of this on the eastern frontier: 'Diocletian also built fortresses on the *limes* from Egypt to the Persian borders, and stationed *limitanei* in them, and he appointed *duces* for each province, to be stationed further back from the fortresses with a large force to ensure their security'.[24] What Malalas says is partly anachronistic (the term *limitanei* for frontier troops belongs later, and *duces* were not yet to be found in each province), and partly contradicts the general thrust of Zosimus' conception. Nonetheless they both share the impression of a major phase of fortification-building. It is more significant that the same view is shared by a much better qualified observer, Ammianus Marcellinus, who was born towards 330 in Antioch and served on the eastern frontier in the 350s and 360s. To him, Diocletian's fortification of the small town of Circesium, on the Euphrates, was part of a wider policy:

> The Emperor (Julian) marched at quick step to Cercusium, a very safe and skilfully built fortress, whose walls are washed by the Abora (Chabur) and Euphrates rivers, which form a kind of island . . . This place, which was formerly small and exposed to dangers, Diocletian, alarmed by a recent experience (one of the Persian invasions of the mid-third century), encircled with walls and lofty towers, at the time when he was arranging the inner lines of defence on the very frontiers of the barbarians, in order to prevent the Persians from overrunning Syria.[25]

The expression 'the inner lines of defence' *(interiores limites)* should not be taken to imply the idea of a double line of frontier installations, outer and

---

22. For what follows see the classic work of D. van Berchem, *L'armée de Dioclétien et la réforme constantinienne* (1952), esp. 3ff., and the useful recent survey by A. Lewin, "Dall' Eufrate al Mar Rosso: Diocleziano, l'esercito e i confini tardo-antichi", *Athenaeum* 78 (1990), 141.

23. Zosimus I, 34, 1.

24. Malalas 308, trans. E. Jeffreys, M. Jeffreys, and M. Scott.

25. Ammianus XXIII, 5, 1–2, Loeb trans.

inner. It means 'the border-districts further inland'.[26] But Ammianus' conception of the importance of a fortified frontier, in this case directed to defence against Persia, is quite clear. Similar defences, in Ammianus' view, were needed also against other neighbours: so he describes Arabia as filled with strong camps *(castra)* and forts *(castella)* 'for repelling the raids of neighbouring *gentes*', and as containing major cities—Bostra, Gerasa and Philadelphia—all defended by mighty walls.[27]

It is quite likely that this work of fortification went on in the early fourth century along the newly acquired stretch of the Tigris, at Nisibis after its recapture and at Singara, where two of the now smaller late-Roman legions, the I Flavia and (still) the I Parthica, were stationed in 363.[28] But there is no precise evidence until later, under Constantine. Nor can any Roman forts of this period be securely identified anywhere along the Chabur River. But the area where there is ample evidence to illustrate the validity of later views of Diocletian's activity is along the line from the Euphrates at Sura across the steppe to Palmyra and Damascus, and then south to Aila on the Gulf of Aqaba: 'from Egypt to the Persian frontier', as Malalas said.

In relation to that line Circesium itself was an outpost, some 150 km down the river. There must presumably have been some Roman forts along this stretch, over which Julian's forces marched in 363, that is to say, between Callinicum, which Ammianus calls 'a strong fortress and most welcome because of the wealth of supplies on sale', at the confluence with the Balikh, and Circesium, at the confluence with the Chabur. But even Ammianus, who was there, says nothing of this area. The great fortress of Zenobia (Halebiyeh) on the right bank, 50 km above Circesium, was built only later, by Justinian.[29] But Procopius may well be right in saying that Diocletian built three forts in this region, including one called Mambri, not far from Zenobia (which he thought had been built by Zenobia of Palmyra, and then abandoned).[30] In effect, however, the military and social history of this stretch of the river, briefly illuminated by the new documents of the 230s to 250s, remains, for this period, wholly obscure.

By contrast, the route across the steppe from Sura towards Damascus, lined with forts, is very well known. The legion XVI Flavia Firma, or a section of it, may already have been at Sura, where the route left the Euphrates, and the IV Scythica (or a section) at Oresa (Tayibeh), where they are listed by the

---

26. See B. Isaac, "The Meaning of the Terms *limes* and *limitanei*", *JRS* 78 (1988), 125.

27. Ammianus XIV, 8, 13.

28. Ammianus XX, 6.

29. For the fortress, and this stretch of the Euphrates, see J. Lauffray, *Halabiyya-Zenobia: Place forte du limes oriental et la Haute-Mésopotamie au VIe siècle* I (1983), with the excellent map in fig. 1.

30. Procopius, *Aed.* II, 8, 7–8. On this piece of historical fiction see further 11.5 below.

late-fourth-century *Notitia Dignitatum*. Documentary evidence of the early fourth century suggests that the legion I Illyricorum was already at Palmyra, and confirms that the III Gallica was at Danaba between Palmyra and Damascus, the stations where the *Notitia* locates them.[31]

Few places show the impact of Tetrarchic military occupation more vividly than Palmyra. The reconquest by Aurelian had not meant the destruction of the city, though it was reduced in size. A new, much more restricted circuit of city-walls seems to date from this period. At least some of its major temples remained, as the great temple of Bel with its *temenos* still does. So apparently did the temple of Baalshamin. For a Greek inscription of AD 302 from there shows (once again) a Roman soldier making a dedication to a local deity; but Baalshamin had become a colourless 'Zeus the Highest who listens' (*Zeus Hypsistos* and *Epēkoos*).[32] The temple of Allat, however, at the far end of the Great Colonnade from the temple of Bel, was enveloped in a complex of Roman military headquarters buildings which rose up a hill on the west of the city, looked directly across to the temple of Bel and was surrounded by an angle of the new wall.[33] At the highest point lay the *principia,* facing down the *via praetoria,* crossed by the *via principalis.* The complex was clearly designed as a whole, and was built in the Tetrarchic period, between 293 and 305. For within the *principia* the highest, and focal, point of the whole ensemble is formed by the 'temple of the standards', on whose lintel a Latin inscription proudly proclaimed the completion of the work: 'The Repairers of their world and Propagators of the human race, our Lords Diocletianus and Maximianus, the most unconquered Imperatores, and Constantius and Maximianus (*i.e.,* Galerius), the most noble Caesares, have successfully founded the camp *(castra),* under the care of Sossianus Hierocles, *vir perfectissimus,* governor *(praeses)* of the province, devoted to their *numen* and *maiestas*'.[34] No other document expresses more perfectly the triumphalism of the Tetrarchic period, when in the East the Roman Empire had just reached its greatest-ever extent.

The builders evidently conceived of the whole complex as belonging to

---

31. *Not. Dign., Or.* XXXIII, 23: 'Praefectus legionis quartae Scythicae, Oresa'; 28: 'Praefectus legionis sextaedecimae Flaviae Firmae, Sura'; XXXII, 30–31: 'Praefectus legionis primae Illyricorum, Palmira; Praefectus legionis tertiae Gallicae, Danaba'. From Herodian V, 3, 9, it is clear that the III Gallica had been moved from Raphaneae before 238, and it may have been one of the legions moved by Severus Alexander 'to locations more suitable for preventing the raids by barbarians', so Herodian VI, 4, 7. *CIL* III, no. 755 (Nicopolis), of the late third or early fourth century, shows that the legion was already at Danaba.

32. C. Dunant, *Le sanctuaire de Baalshamin à Palmyre* III, *Les inscriptions* (1971), no. 31.

33. See M. Gawlikowski, *Palmyre* VIII, *Les principia de Dioclétien, 'Temple des Enseignes'* (1984), esp. 62ff.

34. *CIL* III, no. 6661 = Cantineau, *Inv.* VI, no. 2.

the category of *castra,* conventionally translated 'camp' (hence these structures are often called the camp of Diocletian). But whether the forces now in Palmyra were all quartered there or were lodged in the city is not clear. Strictly speaking, our only documentary evidence to suggest that the Legio I Illyricorum was already stationed there is inscriptions recording detachments of it and the III Gallica operating jointly in Egypt in 315/316 and 322/323.[35] But we do not know how large a 'legion' of this period was. There can hardly have been less than a thousand men in any case, and it most likely that the *castra* really functioned as a headquarters, while the soldiers lived in the city. The activities of the *praeses,* Sossianus Hierocles, and the names of the Tetrarchs were evident there too. For in the same period a Greek inscription records that the Diocletianic Bath *(Dioklētianon Balanion)* was completed by Hierocles 'for the safety and victory of our lords the Emperors and Caesars'; the reference seems in fact to be to a portico, with columns of Egyptian red granite, fronting on the Great Colonnade.[36]

It is not necessary to survey all of the remarkable line of forts which now marked the route from the Euphrates at Sura to Damascus.[37] Suffice it to emphasise that the term 'Strata Diocletiana' appears on milestones from a series of stretches of the road: between the Euphrates and Palmyra, between Palmyra and Damascus, and on the branch which left the road near Dumayr and ran south along the edge of the steppe, passing along the east side of the Jebel Hauran and (as we will see) joining the route to Azraq and then Jawf (Dumatha) beyond the end of the Wadi Sirhan.[38] What matters is not whether we can date when a road, or route, came into use (which we cannot), but the conception, clearly visible in the documents, of a unified system named after the Emperor, a conception which necessarily imposed itself on any user of the road.

The route was lined with a whole series of forts, of which some are still standing and others visible on aerial photographs. So far as can be determined, none of them has produced a dated building-inscription. But their Roman character, and their connection with the Strata Diocletiana, is beyond

35. See *ILS,* no. 8882, and Gawlikowski, op. cit., 63.

36. H. Seyrig, *Syria* 12 (1931), 321, no. 4. See H. Dodge, "Palmyra and the Roman Marble Trade: Evidence from the Baths of Diocletian", *Levant* 20 (1988), 215.

37. See R. Mouterde, "La Strata Diocletiana et ses bornes milliaires", *MUSJ* 15 (1930), 221 and 339; M. Dunand, "A propos de la Strata Diocletiana", *RB* 40 (1933), 227 and 529; A. Poidebard, *La trace de Rome dans le Désert de Syrie* I–II (1934); van Berchem, op. cit. (n.22 above); Kennedy and Riley, *RDF,* passim.

38. From north of Palmyra, e.g., *CIL* III, no. 6179: 'strata Diocletiana a Palmyra Aracha'; from Palmyra-Damascus, e.g., *MUSJ* 15 (1930), 226, nos. 7–8. From the branch-road towards Azraq, e.g., *AE* (1931), no. 101 (near Sa'neh). See Th. Bauzou in Dentzer, *Hauran* I.2, p. 153 (and map on p. 138).

doubt. The best preserved, Khan al Hallabat, a small fort of some 47 m square with corner towers, 31 km south-east of Palmyra, is likely to be the place called Veriaraca which is named on one of the milestones, and which appears in the *Notitia Dignitatum* as the station of the Ala Nova Diocletiana.[39] It would be carrying scholarly caution too far not to see all this as an integrated system of the Tetrarchic period. But to say that implies that we have extensive evidence of a set of physical structures stretching through the steppe, not that we understand exactly how it was intended to work, or whether it in fact did achieve its purpose.

A glance at the map would suggest that if protection against Saracens from the steppe were the objective of this system, Damascus should have been its focus, both from its central position along the Strata Diocletiana and because it was the major city most exposed to the steppe zone. In fact, as earlier, the nature of the Roman military presence in Damascus and its region remains a mystery. Malalas, supported by the *Notitia,* states that Diocletian established an arms-factory there, 'having in mind the raids of the Saracens'. Modern studies of the city also tentatively suggest, without direct evidence, that a Roman camp occupied the north-west corner of the city, in the area of the present Citadel. But we have no better contemporary evidence of the Roman military presence in Damascus than Eusebius' report of how in 311/312 a '*stratopedarchēs,* whom the Romans call *dux*', tortured women there to give false evidence against the Christians.[40]

As for the Strata Diocletiana, a branch-road marked by milestones now diverted south from near Dumayr, to pass along the eastern edge of the Jebel Hauran. If this road was first marked out at this time (which cannot be certain), that might help to explain why the prominent village of Sakkaia, on the north-eastern edge of the Jebel Hauran,[41] now found itself elevated to the rank of a city with the name 'Maximianopolis'. It will in fact have been named after Galerius as 'Caesar' in this region. For his full name was C. Galerius Valerius Maximianus, and literary sources often (confusingly) call him Maximianus. The place first appears with this name on one of the numerous Tetrarchic boundary-regulation inscriptions which are so prominent a feature of the Near East in this period.[42] Half-way between the south end of the Jebel Hauran and Azraq oasis (an area already occupied by the army in the Severan period),[43] the road was joined by another coming from Bostra in the Hauran plain.

39. *MUSJ* 15 (1930), 226, no. 7; *Not. Dign., Or.* XXXII, 34.

40. Malalas, *Chron.,* 307–308, see *Not. Dign., Or.* XI, 20; for the hypothetical camp, D. Sack, "Damaskus, die Stadt *intra muros*", *DM* 2 (1985), 207, plan on p. 210. For the *stratopedarchēs,* or *dux,* Eusebius, *HE* IX, 5, 2.

41. See

42. *SEG* VII, no. 1055; see App. A, no. 35.

43. See 4.1 above.

Before that point, on the outer road, there lies (to take only one example) the major Roman fort of Deir el-Kahf, still standing to a height of several metres when surveyed in the early years of this century. A Latin inscription naming the 'Augusti and Caesares' of 306 probably comes from the lintel of a gateway.[44] It will of course serve to show that some construction took place there in that year, not that there was no fort there previously. But combined with the evidence of other forts and Tetrarchic milestones in this area, it is enough to confirm the impression of consistent activity in the border-zone between cultivated land and the steppe.

New evidence, in the form of a Latin inscription from Azraq, serves both to show how the road-system all the way from Bostra to Dumatha was envisaged and to demonstrate a very surprising level of military investment here:

> [The Emperor built?] through his very brave soldiers of the legion XI Cl(audia) and VII Cl(audia) and I Ital(ica) and IV Fl(avia) and I Ill(yricorum) linked by manned posts *(praetensione coligata)* to his soldiers from the legion III Cyr(enaica). From Bostra to Basien(s)es 66 miles, and from Basien(s)es to Amat(a) 70 and from Amata to Dumata 208 miles.[45]

The involvement of these four legions becomes all the more surprising when one realises that they (or detachments of them) had come from Moesia on the Danube. The date is almost certainly the 290s, when detachments of these same legions are found in Egypt.

The distances and places are also significant. The total of 344 Roman miles would give a distance of almost 500 km. There are many puzzles here, not the least being exactly what is meant by *praetensione coligata*: the reference to a line of manned posts is no more than a serious hypothesis. But it is certain that both Bostra and Dumat(h)a are mentioned. Hence some military link is being envisaged between these places, which are in fact almost 500 km apart. From the intervals given, it may well be that 'Basiensis' is the name of Azraq oasis itself, where the inscription was found. If that is so, it is almost certain that the same place is named on a very revealing Latin inscription of 334, found roughly half-way between Azraq and Bostra:

> When Vincentius the *protector,* on duty at 'Basie', saw that many of the peasants while carrying water for their own use had been ambushed and killed by the Saraceni, he constructed a water-tank from the foundations, in the consulship of Optatus and Bassus.[46]

If Vincentius, named also on a fragmentary Latin building-inscription from Azraq, dating to 333, was indeed stationed at Azraq/Basiensis(?), the water-

---

44. For the fort see *PAES* IIA, 145ff.; for the inscription, *PAES* IIIA, 126, no. 228.

45. See now M. P. Speidel, "The Roman Road to Dumata (Jawf in Saudi Arabia) and the Frontier Strategy of *Praetensione Colligare*", *Historia* 36 (1987), 213.

46. *AE* (1948), no. 106; see Kennedy, *Explorations*, 184, and Speidel, op. cit., 217.

tank itself will clearly have been constructed near where the inscription was found.

The wider context seems just about intelligible. There seem to have been military operations against 'Saracens', apparently dating to 290, and perhaps covering much of the area along which the Strata Diocletiana would be constructed, and even following the line of penetration into the Wadi Sirhan. But that apart, the significant development is marked by roads and forts stretching along the edge of the steppe, and at certain points across it. It was not a 'frontier', least of all one designed to repel a major invasion or migration of peoples, which no one could have expected or had any reason to expect. But it does seem to have accompanied an extension of cultivation into the steppe zone, and to have been designed against attacks by 'Saracens'.

Similar forts certainly existed further south near the edge of the Jordanian steppe, and could now be found some distance to the east of Trajan's road.[47] Only a few need be mentioned here. One is the quite large rectangular fort, measuring some 160 m by 140 m, at Umm-er Resas, lying a few kilometres east of the Via Nova, and just north of the Wadi Mujib. By good fortune an inscription of AD 785 seems to give the name of the place, Kastron Mefaa. It must surely therefore be the same place as one which Eusebius mentions in his *Onomasticon*: 'Mēphaath: of the tribe of Benjamin; and there is another beyond the Jordan, where a garrison of soldiers is posted beside the desert'.[48]

Another is the even better preserved fort called Qasr Bshir situated some 25 km to the south-east. Both lie to the north or east of the Wadi Mujib, in a cultivable semi-arid zone well to the west of the present Desert Highway from Amman to Aqaba. Qasr Bshir is much smaller, an irregular rectangle of 50–60 m, and stands to a height of several metres. But what is important is that its Latin building-inscription is still in place on the lintel over the main entrance. Few documents proclaim more clearly the message that even a small outpost like this is to be seen as the product of the Imperial political and military system:

> To our Best and Greatest Emperors, Gaius Aurelius Valerius Diocletianus
> Pius Felix Invictus Augustus and Marcus Aurelius Valerius Maximianus

---

47. For this area see S. T. Parker, *Romans and Saracens* I–II (1987), and idem (ed.), *The Roman Frontier in Central Jordan* I–II (1987).

48. See Kennedy and Riley, *RDF,* 189–193. Eusebius, *Onom.*, ed. Klostermann, 128. Also mentioned in *Not. Dign., Or.* XXXVII, 19: 'Equites Promoti Indigenae, Mefa'. See, however, Y. Elitzur, "The Identification of Mefa'at in View of the Discoveries from Kh. Umm er-Resas", *IEJ* 39 (1989), 267, questioning the identification. This is nonetheless secure; see M. Piccirrillo, "L'identificazione storica delle rovine di Umm er-Rasas—*Kastron Mefaa* in Giordania", *Biblica* 71 (1990), 527.

Pius Felix Invictus Augustus, and Flavius Valerius Constantius and Galerius Valerius Maximianus the most noble Caesars, the *castra* of the *praetorium Mobenum* (which) from the foundations Aurelius Asclepiades,
praeses of the province of Arabia, carried through to completion.[49]

Whatever the precise intended function of a small fort like this, it is a
mere outpost compared with the large rectangular camp, of 242 m by 190 m,
situated a few kilometres to the south-west, near the head of the Wadi Mujib,
and still called Lejjun *(legio)*. No inscription survives to give a date, but
the archaeological evidence shows that it too is Tetrarchic.[50] The camp
would not have held a legion of the earlier size, some 6000 men; but it is
thought that it could have taken 1000–1500, quite appropriate for the
smaller, or sub-divided, legions of the late Empire. The odds are that this
is the place called Bethorum, where the *Notitia Dignitatum* places a legion,
the IV Martia. This newly formed legion will have been stationed here in
the Tetrarchic period.

These and other small forts lie in the cultivable region of the Moab plateau, drained by the 'Grand Canyon' of Jordan, the Wadi Mujib, the ancient
Arnon, which runs into the Dead Sea. The area, with all these forts, lies well
within the 200-mm-rainfall limit for dry-farming. Here again Eusebius shows
himself aware of the presence of Roman posts. For he speaks of the gorge
called Arnonas, north of 'Areopolis of Arabia', 'in which military garrisons
are on guard on all sides, because of the dangerousness of the area'.[51] He can
hardly be speaking of the terror which still grips the modern traveller whose
vehicle begins the precipitous descent down the King's Highway into the
gorge. The reference can only be either to robbers using hideouts along the
wadi or, much more probably, to the possibility of raids from the steppe, only
a few kilometres away.

Even further south, along Trajan's road down to Aila on the Red Sea,
there were military installations, for instance at Udruh to the east of Petra
(which may possibly have been another legionary camp) and at Humeima,
half-way between Petra and Aila.[52] Neither the line of the road nor the forts
associated with it should be thought of as a true frontier. Rather, the road was

49. For a detailed description see V. A. Clark, "The Roman *Castellum* of Qasr Bshir", in
S. T. Parker, op. cit. (n.47) II, 457. The building-inscription is *CIL* III, no. 14149.

50. See J. C. Groot, "The Barracks of el-Lejjun", in Parker, *Roman Frontier* I, 260; and
B. de Vries, "The Fortification of el-Lejjun", ibid., 311; Kennedy and Riley, *RDF,* 131. See *Not.
Dign., Or.* XXXVII, 22: 'Praefectus legionis quartae Martiae, Betthoro'.

51. Eusebius, *Onomasticon*, ed. Klostermann, 10: ἐν ᾧ καὶ φρούρια πανταχόθεν φυλάττει
στρατιωτικὰ διὰ τὸ φοβερὸν τοῦ τόπου.

52. For Udruh see A. Killick, "Udruh and the Southern Frontier", in Freeman and Kennedy,
DRBE, 431. For Humeima, Kennedy and Riley, *RDF,* 146–148.

a means of communication, and the forts represented essentially the limits of policing, for which no Imperial employees were available except the army. No clear distinction can thus be drawn between frontier functions and police ones; and although, as we have seen, the evidence is perfectly clear in representing Roman troop-placements on the fringe of the steppe as being intended for protection against 'Saracens', non-sedentary populations of a similar character existed also within the 'frontier', above all in the Negev and Sinai. It is thus significant from both points of view that our evidence for the Roman military presence in this period seems to show an increased level of 'internal' policing also. The random selection of allusions to Roman military posts (usually called *phrouria*) provided by Eusebius' *Onomasticon* is particularly valuable: apart from the 'frontier' installations already mentioned, he speaks of posts at Thamara on the road between Hebron and Aila; on the road down from Aelia (Jerusalem) to Jericho; near Zoara, just below the south end of the Dead Sea; ten Roman miles (15 km) north of Hebron; a village called Thaima, about fifteen Roman miles (22 km) from Petra (direction not stated); another in Gebalene (the area north of Petra); and Chermel, 'a very big village' to the south of Hebron.[53]

Eusebius was of course not conducting a survey of Roman military posts, but making incidental mention of them in listing Biblical place-names, and relating them to contemporary settlements. For that very reason, the scatter of Roman forts *(phrouria)* which he mentions must be impressive. One at Zoara south of the Dead Sea (where we earlier saw some persons making their census-returns under Hadrian)[54] may perhaps be especially significant. For it is possible that a Roman road with forts ran down the Wadi Arabah, the great depression which continues the Jordan and Dead Sea valleys, as far as Aqaba. Eusebius' *phrourion* at Zoara might be the enclosure, 84 m square and fed by an aqueduct, which is visible from the air and is known as Qasr el Feifeh.[55] Then 25 km south of the Dead Sea is the small fort at el Telah, with a reservoir fed by an aqueduct and (surprisingly) fronting a regular network of ditches, indicating cultivation; it must be the place called Toloha, where the *Notitia Dignitatum* locates the Ala Constantiana; similarly, Gharandal, some 80 km further south, where there is another small fort, should be 'Arielda', where the *Notitia* lists the Cohors Secunda Galatarum.[56]

These of course are in effect police posts, not frontier defences. But these

53. Eusebius, *Onomasticon*, ed. Klostermann, 8, 24, 42, 50, 96, 142, 172. I. Roll, op. cit. (n.57, below) identifies Thamara, a day's journey south of Mampsis, with Hazeva (see his excellent map on p. 254).

54. 3.2 above.

55. Kennedy and Riley, *RDF*, 144–145.

56. Kennedy and Riley, *RDF*, 205–208.

little outposts, situated in a dramatic and desolate landscape, are evidence of the steadily growing Roman military investment in this southern area leading to Aila and the Red Sea. Moreover, new evidence continues to accumulate for this investment, and precisely from the Tetrarchic period. Thus further south along the wadi, at Yotvata or Ghadyan, 40 km north of Aila, a Roman fort of some 40 km square has been excavated. What makes it significant is the Latin building-inscription found on the site.[57] Not wholly intelligible, it nonetheless speaks the familiar language of Tetrarchic imperialism: 'For perpetual peace Diocletianus Augus(tus) and Maximianus Augus(tus) and Constantius and Maximianus (i.e., Galerius) the most noble Caesars erected the wing with the gate (?) by the *providentia* of Priscus, *praeses* [of ?]'. Which province will have been named where the text breaks off will be discussed later.[58] It is not quite clear what was being built, or whether the inscription does not refer rather to the establishment of an *ala* (wing) in the sense of a mounted unit, at this point. But the message and function of the inscription are clear; and the Arabic name of the place, 'Ghadyan', will reflect that of the known Roman site of Ad Dianam.[59]

Finally, from Aila itself we now have fragments of an official Latin inscription, which may date to the second or third decade of the fourth century.[60] No precise conclusions can be drawn from it; but it is enough—along with a remarkable density of other evidence on the ground— to make it reasonable that later narrative sources were not wrong, and that 'from Aila to the Persian frontier' there was an unprecedented level of military construction in the period of Diocletian. In the central area this direct Roman military presence may well reflect the disappearance of Palmyra as a military power, exercising a widespread police function. But the evidence, of various kinds, over the whole length of the 'frontier' is too consistent for us to doubt that, in a way not attested before, this activity reflected concern about the threat from the 'Saracens'. This conclusion would be misleading only if it led us to suppose that comparable problems of security and the military policing of roads, caused (in some areas) by the presence of non-sedentary 'Arab' or 'Saracen' populations, did not exist also far within the 'frontiers' which we can now draw on the map. The force of a rapidly changing Roman Imperial state was felt in this period also within the existing provinces.

57. See Z. Meshel, "A Fort at Yotvata from the Time of Diocletian", *IEJ* 39 (1989), 228; I. Roll, "A Latin Imperial Inscription from the Time of Diocletian Found at Yotvata", ibid., 239. Roll's article constitutes an important survey of the entire Tetrarchic road-and-fortification-system in this region.

58. 5.2 below.

59. So already Bowersock, *Roman Arabia*, 179–181.

60. H. I. MacAdam, "Fragments of a Latin Building Inscription from Aqaba, Jordan", *ZPE* 79 (1989), 163; *AE* (1989), no. 750.

5.2. THE NEAR EAST IN THE TETRARCHIC EMPIRE, AD 284–312

The line of forts, many carrying grandiose inscriptions in Latin, which now stretched along the borders of cultivable land, and the milestones of the Strata Diocletiana remain the most obvious expressions in the Near East of the new Tetrarchic order. Many other changes seem to have taken place also: but in some cases their dating and real nature remain uncertain, and in others there is no relevant evidence to illustrate their application in this region. Presumably, for instance, Diocletian's extraordinarily ambitious *edictum* of 301, laying down the maximum prices which could be charged for a vast range of goods and services, was applied in these provinces. It certainly lists many products whose names imply that they originated from towns in this region.[1] But as to how (or even, strictly speaking, whether) it affected the life of the Near East we have no evidence at all.

By contrast, the course and effects of the last great persecution of the Christians, between 303 and 312, are more fully known for this region than for any other. Moreover, our evidence, almost all provided by Eusebius of Caesarea, makes it possible to discern a parallel development in the impact of the state on its subjects, in the form of the census and new types of direct taxation. This in its turn can be related to the remarkable series of boundary-decisions, often attributed to officials called *censitores* (transliterated in Greek as *kēnsitores*), which can be found in various areas of the Near East—and are themselves some of our best evidence for the names of communities and the nature of social formations there.[2]

These and other developments in the nature of the state and its relations with its subjects seem to have taken place within the framework of two other profound changes in the structure of the state, both of which culminated in the Tetrarchic period, after a slow evolution through the third century: the sub-division and rearrangement of provinces, and the progressive (and not easily traced) separation of civilian and military functions. Viewed from Rome, the latter was of immense significance. For the evolution not merely of separate posts but of whole career-patterns in Imperial service into civil and military meant implicitly the abandonment of the preconception on which the whole history of Rome and its Empire had been based: the unity of military and governmental responsibilities and capacities on the part of members of the office-holding class. It accompanied another change which represented a

---

1. On the prices edict and the products named in it, see S. Lauffer, *Diokletians Preisedikt* (1971). For the distribution of epigraphic copies, M. H. Crawford and J. Reynolds in *JRS* 65 (1975), 160, and J. Reynolds in C. M. Roueché, *Aphrodisias in Late Antiquity* (1989), ch. 12.
    2. Text to nn.12ff. below and App. A.

profound rupture with the Roman past, the loss both of military functions and of many governorships by members of the Senate in Rome.

Viewed from below, from the standpoint of the inhabitant of the Near Eastern provinces, these changes were both gradual and probably of no very profound significance. They were not invisible, however: we have seen already how inscriptions recording building and other activities by governors of Arabia reflect a change of title, from the senatorial *legatus Augusti pro praetore* to the non-senatorial term, gradually established for all governors, *praeses* (*hēgemōn* in Greek);[3] along with that came a change from the standard senatorial status-term *vir clarissimus* (*lamprotatos* in Greek) to *vir perfectissimus* (*diasēmotatos*). As all the provinces of the Near East had always been 'Imperial' (that is, their governors had been nominated by the Emperor), no governors with the title 'proconsul' had ever served there. Now the title *legatus* disappeared also, being last attested (in the evidence which we happen to have) on the inscription from Heliopolis in which L. Artorius Pius Maximus, *v(ir) c(larissimus)*, honoured Diocletian sometime between 285 and 297.[4]

It is by no means equally certain that a general division into military and civilian functions had already been carried out by this period. Indeed, in the case of the construction of the *castra* of the *praetorium Mobenum* by Aurelius Asclepiades, *praeses* of Arabia between 293 and 305, it clearly had not; for the building is distinctly military, but the term *praeses* was—or was becoming—the regular title for a civilian governor.[5] Nonetheless, the emergence of the Latin term *dux* as a regular expression for a military commander did not go unnoticed. (Before the third century it had not been an official term at all, but is found at Dura-Europos, and had therefore come into use by the 250s.)[6] For, as we have seen, Eusebius talks of a '*stratopedarchēs* (literally "camp-commander"), whom the Romans call *dux*', conducting examinations at Damascus during the persecution of 311/312.[7]

Eusebius must be referring to the same function when he speaks of another *stratopedarchēs* executing Christian martyrs who were already serving sentences in the copper mines at Phaeno in 309/310. In this case, moreover, Eusebius does portray a division of civilian and military functions. For it is the governor (here called *archōn*) of the province who consults the Emperor (Maximinus) about the Christians, and the *stratopedarchēs*, or *dux*, explicitly described as 'placed in charge of the forces there', who carries out the execu-

3. 5.1, text to n.4.
4. *IGLS* VI, no. 2721; 5.1, text to n.13.
5. *CIL* VI, no. 14149; 5.1 above.
6. 4.1 above.
7. Eusebius, *HE* IX, 5, 2: ἕτερος στρατοπεδάρχης, ὅν δοῦκα Ῥωμαῖοι προσαγορεύουσιν.

tions.[8] The late-Roman structure of the state was visibly coming into being.

This same report by Eusebius also implies the only major rearrangement of provinces in the Near East which certainly took place under the Tetrarchy. For he describes the mines at Phaeno, which lie to the east of the Wadi Arabah and to the north of Petra, as being in 'Palestine'. Equally, Eusebius in his *Onomasticon* sometimes calls Petra a city 'of Arabia' (its traditional designation), and sometimes a city 'of Palestine'.[9] This and later evidence makes it certain that under the Tetrarchy, probably in the 290s, the southern part of the Roman province of Arabia, including the southern Negev, Sinai and the area east of the Wadi Arabah, from Aila north to roughly a line from the southern tip of the Dead Sea eastward into the steppe, became part of the province of Syria Palaestina. The effect—and quite possibly the intention—was to leave in 'Arabia' part of the Roman forces along the edge of the steppe zone, in particular the legion III Cyrenaica, still at Bostra, and the IV Martia at Bethorum, almost certainly Lejjun. But Udruh, if it was a legionary base, was now in 'Palaestina', as was the legion X Fretensis, now moved forward from Aelia (Jerusalem) to Aila on the Gulf of Aqaba. The transfer of this legion thus took place within the now much-enlarged province (usually called just Palaestina in the fourth century); and the forces stationed along the steppe zone will have been divided roughly in half (or in equal thirds, if we think also of those along the Strata Diocletiana in Syria Phoenice); or into four roughly equal segments, if we include the two legions which the *Notitia* records at Sura and Oresa, in the province of Syria Coele.

This transfer of a large territory represents the only certain rearrangement of provinces made at this time. There is no documentary evidence from this period for a province called Augusta Libanensis (later to be detached from Phoenice) or for a 'Euphratensis' along the river and embracing Commagene, or part of it.[10] As for the territory across the Euphrates, we do not even know whether there was now only one province, Mesopotamia, or also another, Osrhoene. When there are contemporary documents, they sometimes make confusion worse. Thus a papyrus reveals a man calling himself 'Aurelius Malchus from the confines of Eleutheropolis of the New Arabia', who presented a petition to a governor in Egypt in about 314–318. The place must be the city of Eleutheropolis in Idumaea, south-west of Jerusalem, and (until now at least) part of Syria Palaestina. The idea that while much of 'Arabia' became part of 'Palaestina', part of 'Palaestina' formed a short-lived province called

8. Eusebius, *MP* 13, 1–3. On the mines see below.

9. Eusebius, *Onom.*, ed. Klostermann, 36, 13; 112, 8; 144, 7 (still listed as of 'Arabia'). For Aila and X Fretensis see above. See Y. Tsafrir, "The Transfer of the Negev, Sinai and Southern Transjordan from *Arabia* to *Palaestina*", *IEJ* 36 (1986), 7.

10. For these issues see T. D. Barnes, *The New Empire of Diocletian and Constantine* (1982), 223–224.

'New Arabia' seems odd even for an inventive period like the Tetrarchy. But no better solution has been proposed, and the question must be left open.[11]

What is called here the Near East will certainly have been in the 290s part of one of twelve wholly new groupings of provinces known as dioceses. The one in question was called Oriens, but embodied a much wider area than 'the Near East' in this sense, namely the whole region from south-eastern Anatolia round through Egypt to Libya. As these 'dioceses' emerge into the light in the course of the fourth century, they appear as regions each with their own civilian governor, with largely judicial functions, normally called the *Vicarius* (meaning a deputy of the Praetorian Prefects), and with their own financial officials. But there is no evidence to show how this superstructure affected the provinces of the Near East in the Tetrarchic period. In any case the almost continuous presence there of an *Augustus* or a *Caesar* was far more significant.

That is not to say that the weight and authority of the Imperial state was not felt as such, or that being part of it was simply an unchanging and accepted framework for ordinary life. On the contrary, the most detailed and localised of possible evidence shows that the demands and decisions of the state in this precise period penetrated into the most remote of country districts. The evidence that we have seems to be a reflection of the fundamental reform of taxation which Diocletian and Maximian proclaimed in 297. We know it best from the edict which the Prefect of Egypt issued in that year:

> Our most provident Emperors, the eternal(?) Diocletian and Maximian, Augusti, and Constantius and Maximian, most noble Caesars, having learned that it has come about that the levies of the public taxes are being made haphazardly, so that some persons are let off lightly and others overburdened, have decided to root out this most evil and baneful practice for the benefit of their provincials and to issue a deliverance-bringing rule to which the taxes shall conform. Accordingly, the levy on each aroura according to classification of the land, and the levy on each head of the peasantry, and from which age to which, may be accurately(?) known to all from the [recently] issued divine (i.e., Imperial) edict and the schedule annexed thereto, copies of which I have prefaced for promulgation with this edict of mine. Accordingly, seeing that in this, too, they have received the greatest benefaction, the provincials should make it their business in conformity with the divinely issued regulations to pay their taxes with all speed and by no means wait for the compulsion of the collector; for it is proper to fulfil most zealously and scrupulously all the royal obligations, and if anyone should be revealed to have done otherwise after such

11. See Ph. Mayerson, "P. Oxy. 3574: 'Eleutheropolis of the New Arabia'", *ZPE* 53 (1983), 258.

bounty, he will risk punishment. The magistrates and council presidents of every city have been ordered to send out to every village and every locality a copy of the divine edict together with the schedule, and also of this (edict) as well, in the interest of having the munificence of our Emperors and Caesars come speedily to the knowledge of all.[12]

Whether the population of the Empire really shared the view that the proposal to tax them and their property more efficiently represented an act of munificence *(megalodōria)* on the part of the Emperors may be doubted. Nor does the complex evidence on late-Roman taxation really allow us to go much beyond what is implied here: that the new system would relate both to each head of population and to each item of agricultural property 'in accordance with the character of the land'. What this meant was that different types of land, from vineyards to pasture-land, would be assigned different taxation-values. As it happens, the only relatively clear explanation of how this calculation was made comes from a text preserved in Syriac; whether that implies that the system which it describes was based on practice in the Syrian region (or, more precisely, Mesopotamia) is not clear. At any rate this text, part of the so-called Syro-Roman Law Book, composed in Greek in the later fifth century and apparently translated very soon into Syriac, includes the only available description of how different categories of land were to be assessed and then calculated in terms of a common land-taxation unit, the *iugum* (hence the Latin term for this process, *iugatio*):

> The *iugum* was measured in the days of the Emperor Diocletian and became fixed. Five *iugera,* which make 10 *plethra,* of vineyard were established as 1 *iugum;* 20 *iugera* of seed land, which make 40 *plethra,* provide *annonas* of 1 *iugum* . . . So, too, land which is of poorer quality and is reckoned as second quality: 40 *iugera,* which make 80 *plethra,* pay 1 *iugum;* if, however, it is reckoned or assessed as third quality, 60 *iugera,* making 120 *plethra,* provide 1 *iugum.*[13]

Any system of land-taxation ought in principle to have been based on unambiguous information as to the ownership of the land in question and the boundaries between different properties or different communities. There is abundant evidence through the Near East to show that a particular effort was

---

12. A. E. R. Boak and H. C. Youtie, *The Archive of Aurelius Optatus (P. Cair. Isidor.)* (1960), no. 1, trans. N. Lewis and M. Reinhold, *Roman Civilisation*[3] II (1990), 419.

13. For the 'Syro-Roman Law Book' see, e.g., A. Baumstark, *Geschichte der syrischen Literatur* (1922), 83. The translation is taken from N. Lewis and M. Reinhold, *Roman Civilisation*[3] II (1990), 420, with extensive revisions very kindly provided by Sebastian Brock, using revised texts published by E. Sachau, *Syrische Rechtsbücher* I (1907), and by A. Vööbus, "The Syro-Roman Law Book", *Papers Est. Theol. Soc. in Exile* 36 (1982), 39.

made by the state in the Tetrarchic period to clarify these questions and record the results on inscriptions erected *in situ.* This operation may well have been conducted throughout the whole region. But the surviving records which we happen to have come mainly from two areas: from the villages of the limestone massif between Antioch and Beroea, and from a wide zone from Galilee across the Golan heights (Gaulanitis) to the Hauran and the new city of Maximianopolis, and as far south as Souedias. It thus involved at least four provinces: Syria (Coele), Palaestina, Phoenice and Arabia.

Many of the inscriptions are fragmentary, and most involve complex problems of topography and local nomenclature. It will be sufficient here to give a few examples (a complete catalogue is provided later).[14] Most are dated merely by the Tetrarchs of 293 to 305. But those with more precise dates show that the operation was indeed conducted at the same moment, 296/297, when Diocletian and Maximian were announcing their new taxation-system. One such text comes from near the famous Christian shrine of Qalaat Seman in the limestone massif:

> For the safety and victory of our Lords Diocletianus and Maximianus, the *Augusti,* and Constantius and Maximianus, the most noble *Caesares,* there were established the boundaries [of the village] of the Kaprokēroi, under the supervision of Iulius Sabinus the most distinguished *(lamprotatos) kēnsitōr* (year 345, Panemos 8).[15]

The era is that of the city of Antioch, and the year is 296/297.

Inscriptions reflecting the same operation further south tend to adopt a different formula. Thus, for example, one found north of the Sea of Galilee reads as follows:

> Diocletianus and Maximianus, the *Augusti,* (and) Constantius and Maximianus [the *Caesares*], ordered (this) stone to be set up, marking the boundary of the fields of the village of Dēra and (those of) Ōsea, under the supervision of Aelius Statilius the *perfectissimus.*[16]

The same formula is used in a newly published inscription from the southern Golan, giving the boundaries of the *kōmē* of Kapar Haribos.[17] It appears also

14. For surveys of the evidence then available see A. Déléage, *La capitation du Bas-Empire* (1945), 152–157; cf. also W. Seston, *Dioclétien et la tétrarchie* I (1946), 374. For the full list now known see App A.

15. J. Jarry, "Inscriptions arabes, syriaques et grecques du massif du Bélus en Syrie du Nord", *Annales Islamologiques* 7 (1967) 139, on p. 158, no. 33 = *AE* (1968), no. 514; see below, App. A, no. 10.

16. *SEG* XIX, no. 901; App. A, no. 29.

17. P. Porat, "A New Boundary Stone from the Southern Golan", *SCI* 10 (1989–90), 130; App. A, no. 21.

further east, in the inscription recording a similar boundary-marker, which serves also as the earliest evidence for the elevation of Sakkaia in the northern Hauran to be the city of Maximinianopolis:

> Our Lords Diocletianus and Maximianus, the *Augusti,* and Constantius and Maximianus, the most noble *Caesares,* ordered (this) stone to be set up marking off (the territory of the?) village of the Oreloi (and the) boundary of Maximianopol(is), under the supervision of Lucius and Acacius, *kēnsitores.*[18]

More examples need not be given here. These inscriptions, of which there must originally have been hundreds (if not more), are important first as yet further evidence of the way in which the Emperors made their names and their measures literally visible even in quite remote country districts. The connection with the census, and hence with taxation, is perfectly evident both from the involvement of state officials on so systematic a basis and from their title, *censitor.* In all cases the boundaries determined are, however, not those of private properties, but of the territories of collectivities, whether villages or cities. The implication must be that villages had a collective responsibility at least for the land-tax due from their area (and perhaps for the *capitatio* also). Whether, if a village lay within the territory of a city, such as Antioch, its tax-payment was in some way mediated through that city remains uncertain. But on any construction the long list of village-names appearing on these boundary-inscriptions set up by Roman *censitores* represents further evidence of the primary role of villages in the structure of society in this region.

Regular taxation was not the only form of payment which the state might exact from its subjects. The familiar area of conflict represented by exactions for transport services is reflected again in a letter from Diocletian and Maximian to Charisius, evidently an official and possibly the Charisius who was *praeses* of Syria in 290: 'Let no one of the rural plebs, which, situated outside the walls (of any city), pays its *capitatio* and provides the appropriate *annona* (land tax?), be called away to perform any other duty nor be forced by a *rationalis* (financial official) of ours to undertake the provision of mules or horses for public service'.[19] In rather different language, and with a concrete reference to regular taxation, the thought is precisely that which Domitian had expressed in his *mandata* to a financial official, and which the public had been able to see on a Greek inscription at Hama.[20] If the date is indeed around 290, the word *capitatio* had already come into use for what had earlier been

18. *SEG* VII, no. 1055 (incomplete). Full text in M. Dunand, *Le musée du Soueida* (1934), 75, no. 160. App. A., no. 35.

19. *Cod. Just.* XI, 55, 1; Charisius as *praeses Syriae* in 290, IX, 41, 9.

20. 3.1 above.

called *tributum capitis;* and the use of *annona* (supplies) for the other form
of obligation due strongly suggests that the land-tax was payable in kind. It
is indeed certain that some direct taxation on the land was payable in kind in
this period, and delivered to the army and officials in the form of supplies.
But how the system really worked is a question of acute controversy which
will not be pursued here.

That the 'rustic plebs' of the countryside was liable for both a personal
tax and a land-tax is clear. But whether what Diocletian and Maximian say
implies that city-populations were exempt from both is not: for the context
is that of the demands of official travellers, and specifically of the provision
of transport-animals. Nonetheless it is quite clear that the question of the
census of city-populations was a controversial one at this period, and one on
which successive Emperors took different views.[21] Eusebius' account of the
second phase of the persecution, as it was conducted in Caesarea in 305/306,
clearly implies that the authorities either already had, or compiled there and
then, lists of all the inhabitants of the city, and used these to compel universal
sacrifice.[22] In one version he uses the term *apographē,* the normal Greek expression for a census-return (already used by Luke's Gospel). But if this is
indeed enough to show that city-dwellers were now liable to *capitatio,* five
years later, when Maximinus was competing for power after the death of
Galerius in 311, the situation seems to have changed. For when he arrived to
take control in Bithynia, where Nicomedia lay, in that year, he is reported to
have curried popular favour by suppressing the census. That probably means
the census of city-dwellers. For Eusebius' description of a general famine in
the same year distinguishes city-dwellers from those who lived 'in the fields
and villages'; and he claims that it was the high death-rate among these *agroi-
koi* which meant that the census-lists *(apographai)* were almost empty.[23] This
may well be the real context for an Imperial letter preserved (under 313) in
the *Theodosian Code* and addressed to the *praeses* of Lycia and Pamphylia:
'Let the *plebs urbana,* as is the custom also in the *Orientales provinciae,* by
no means be enrolled in the censuses in respect of its *capitatio,* but in accordance with this order of ours let it be regarded as immune, as the same *plebs
urbana* had been immune under our lord and parent Diocletianus, the senior
Augustus'.[24] Though certainty is impossible, the tone and context of the letter

21. For these questions see T. D. Barnes, *The New Empire of Diocletian and Constantine*
(1982), 226ff.

22. Eusebius, *Mart. Pal.* 4, 8 (long recension): ὀνομαστὶ χιλιάρχων [ἀπ'] ἀπογραφῆς ἕκαστον
ἀνακαλουμένων. The short recension reads: χιλίαρχοι . . . κατ' οἴκους καὶ ἄμφοδα παριόντες ἀνα-
γραφὰς τῶν πολιτῶν ἐποιοῦντο. For a general census under Galerius, including land and both
rustic and city populations, see Lactantius, *de mort. pers.* 23, 1–2.

23. Lactantius, *de mort. pers.* 36, 1; Eusebius, *HE* IX, 8, 5.

24. *Cod. Theod.* XIII, 10, 2, following the arguments of Barnes, op. cit., 232.

would fit perfectly the circumstances of an Emperor (Maximinus) arriving (in 311) from the *Orientales provinciae* to seize power in Asia Minor, and seeking to win general favour where it mattered, among the urban population whom he would directly encounter. It might, however, belong a year later, in 312, in the context of equally complex exchanges between Maximinus and his subjects, over what position (if any) Christians were to occupy within the still predominantly pagan communities of these provinces. To see those exchanges in context, we need to go back to the history of the persecutions in the Near East, as they had evolved since 303.[25]

Indeed even the preliminary stage which preceded the first general persecution ordered by Diocletian belongs in the Near East. For it was while he was in 'the Oriental region', and before moving to Nicomedia for the winter of 302/303, that Diocletian found that a sacrifice which he was conducting was nullified by a Christian sign placed on the animals by one of his attendants; and in reaction to this he ordered sacrifices on the part of all those serving in the palace, and of all soldiers.[26]

The record of the successive Imperial orders which followed in the years 303–312, and their enforcement in Palestine and the neighbouring provinces, as witnessed by Eusebius in Caesarea, constitutes the best evidence we have for the working of the Tetrarchic state and its relation with its subjects. Only some particularly relevant details need be picked out here. The earlier phases followed the terms of Imperial orders, in edict or letter form, issued from Nicomedia, and their enforcement depended entirely on the governor *(praeses)* in each province. The first edict was posted at Nicomedia on February 24, 303, and a copy reached Palaestina in March or April. Among other provisions it ordered that churches be destroyed, and copies of the Bible burned. Eusebius names the *praeses* of Palaestina, Flavianus, in office at the time, but reports no measures on his part to enforce it.[27] Soon after came other orders, first that the leaders of the Church be imprisoned and then that they be compelled to sacrifice.[28] Under this order Eusebius records that the first martyrdom at Caesarea was that of Procopius from Scythopolis, on June 7, 303. It is particularly significant that the long recension of Eusebius' *Martyrs of Palestine* (known from a Syriac translation contained in a manuscript of AD 411) describes how Procopius originated from Aelia (Jerusalem), but served the church at Scythopolis as a reader, as an interpreter from Greek into Aramaic (LŠN' YWNY' L'RMY' MTRGM) and as an exorcist. For this pass-

25. For the view that *Cod. Theod.* XIII, 10 , 2, belongs in 312, see S. Mitchell, "Maximinus and the Christians in AD 312: A New Latin Inscription", *JRS* 78 (1988), 105, on which all of the following discussion of the persecution heavily depends.

26. So Lactantius, *de mort. pers.* 10.

27. Eusebius, *HE* VIII, 2, 4; *Mart. Pal., praef.* 1.

28. *HE* VIII, 5; *Mart. Pal., praef.* 2.

ing reference is the first indication we have that the predominantly Greek-speaking churches of Palaestina also had members who were speakers of a Semitic language. Procopius was brought from Scythopolis to Caesarea, testified before the governor and was executed.[29] Eusebius then gives the examples of Zacchaeus, a deacon from Gadara (evidently now part of Palaestina), and Alphaeus, from Eleutheropolis in Palaestina, a reader and exorcist at Caesarea.[30] A brief reference also confirms the existence of a separate military structure in Palaestina, for he describes the *stratopedarchēs* (that is, *dux*) enforcing sacrifice among the soldiers.[31]

In terms of the structure and working of the Empire, the persecution in the Near East was still being conducted at second hand, through the medium of written orders transmitted to the governors by the Emperors.[32] This remained the case in the second year of the persecution, 304/305, when Urbanus was *praeses* of Palaestina, and orders arrived that the whole population be compelled to sacrifice. The long recension of the *Martyrs* again conveniently serves to mark out some of the borders of the province of Palaestina as it then was, for it describes the martyrdom of Timotheos from Gaza, in the presence of Urbanus, as taking place in the context of a pagan festival, including plays, horse-racing and exposure of victims to wild beasts. The setting seems (the manuscripts vary) to be Gaza itself.[33] But even if it were in fact Caesarea, the context would be the same, for both cities were now *coloniae*, and the mass public entertainments listed represented some of the most distinctive Roman imports into the popular culture of the Greek East. It would not be surprising if the *praeses* had in fact attended public spectacles at a major city on the borders of his province.

A similar scene is also recorded by Eusebius at Tyre 'of Phoenice', which he says he witnessed in person; no governor is explicitly mentioned, but the *praeses* of Phoenice must have been there, for all executions and martyrdoms were conducted by governors. Once again the context is that of wild-beast shows *(venationes)* before a large crowd, in a city which had for a century been a Roman *colonia*.[34] Looking more widely, Eusebius speaks of martyrdoms in Egypt, Cappadocia and Pontos; but also—within the Near East—in

---

29. *Mart. Pal.* 1 (long recension). The Syriac text was published and translated by W. Cureton (1861). For the ms of AD 411, the earliest dated ms in Syriac, see also 12.3 below.

30. Ibid., 5b–d.

31. *HE* VIII, 4, 3–4. See ch. 1 above.

32. Note, however, the puzzling account in the long recension of *Mart. Pal.* of how at this time Romanus, a deacon and exorcist from Caesarea, went to Antioch, appeared before the governor there, and was martyred while Diocletian was in the city. The attested movements of Diocletian make this most unlikely; Barnes, *New Empire*, 56.

33. *Mart. Pal.* 3, 1.

34. *HE* VIII, 8.

Arabia, at Antioch and in Mesopotamia. Going into rather more detail, naturally enough, as regards the neighbouring province, he mentions martyrdoms
within the province of Phoenice of bishops and priests from Tyre, Sidon and
Emesa.[35] His accounts are notable for two fundamental aspects of the Roman
Imperial system: the conduct of their business by governors in public in the
context of the life of the cities, and of their public spectacles and ceremonials;
and the gruesome repertoire of forms of physical degradation and execution
now deployed by the state. Eusebius' account also makes clear that another
instrument of punishment had by now been added to this repertoire: condemnation to the mines. But that is best examined in the context of the much-
intensified phase which followed the appointment of Maximinus as *Caesar* in
305, and his continued residence in the Near East.[36]

In the first instance renewal of persecution again took the form of letters
distributed throughout the region in 305/306. Their content was the same,
that all should sacrifice; but their enforcement was to employ new means, the
involvement of city officials, proclamations by heralds, active searches of each
city-quarter by soldiers and (as we have seen) the use of census-lists.[37] The
impact of Maximinus' orders was followed by his arrival in person. Eusebius'
description of the shows given by the Emperor at Caesarea to celebrate his
birthday in November 306 might be taken to mark the high point of the integration of a Near Eastern city, and Roman *colonia*, into the pagan Imperial
state:

> In the fourth year of the persecution against us, on the twelfth day before
> the Kalends of December, that is, on the twentieth of the month Dius, on
> the day before the Sabbath, a thing was done in this same Caesarea,
> in the presence of the tyrant Maximin himself, who was lavishing upon
> the multitudes spectacles in honour of his birthday, as it is called, which
> is truly worthy of being placed on record. Hitherto it was the custom that,
> when emperors were present, spectacles on a lavish scale should provide
> more excellent entertainments for the spectators than on any other occa-
> sion, and that new and strange shows should take the place of the usual
> programme. Sometimes it would be animals brought from India or Aethi-
> opia or somewhere else; or perhaps men who amaze and divert the minds
> of the onlookers by a display of certain skilful bodily exercises. On that
> occasion also, since the emperor was providing the exhibition, it was abso-

35. *HE* VIII, 9, 1–13, 4.

36. The significance of the change is heavily emphasised in *Mart. Pal.* 3, 5ff., but obscured
in *HE*.

37. *Mart. Pal.* 4, 8.

lutely necessary that in some way the lavish display should include some unusual and extraordinary item.[38]

It might be quite difficult to find, in the entire literature of the Empire, a passage in which so many different strands of cultural history come together. For a start there is the dating-system employed, which combines elements from the history of the Church, the Roman calendar, the Macedonian months and the Jewish week. Then there is the Roman importation of the wild-beast shows, with the Emperor able to provide animals from far outside the Empire. But Roman as the content of the show is, the ideology of display is explicitly seen as only a grander version of what would be expected in a Greek city. The word translated as 'lavish display' is *philotimiai*, meaning at root 'love of reputation', now used concretely, and in the plural, for the shows put on, at their own expense, by the leading personalities of Greek cities.

The following episode, however, reveals that the Roman state in Palaestina had also developed in quite a different direction; for it contains the first explicit reference to condemnation to hard labour in 'the mines *(metalla)* of copper at Phainō of Palaistinē'.[39] The allusion is a painful reminder of how far our understanding is limited by what our sources happen to be interested in saying. For we have no evidence at all as to how long such mines had been in operation, or how they came to be in Imperial possession; but many references in Eusebius show that condemned Christians (and presumably others) carried out hard labour there, shackled, often mutilated and living under military guard. Nonetheless, Eusebius' account shows that by 309/310 the confessors working in the mines had achieved a high degree of liberty, and had even constructed buildings to serve as churches. But the then governor, arriving on a visit, consulted the Emperor, and the superintendent of the mines had these Christians either dispersed elsewhere or executed by the *dux*.[40] The earlier history of condemnation to the mines or quarries (for the word *metalla* covers both) can hardly be written; the institution begins to be visible from about the end of the first century AD. As regards these particular copper-mines, located at Fenan, east of the Wadi Arabah, between the south end of the Dead Sea and Petra, if they had been at Imperial disposition

38. *Mart. Pal.* 6, 1–2 (long recension), trans. Lawlor and Oulton.

39. *Mart. Pal.* 7, 2.

40. *Mart. Pal.* 13, 1–3. For the background see F. Millar, "Condemnation to Hard Labour in the Roman Empire, from the Julio-Claudians to Constantine", *PBSR* 52 (1984), 124. For detailed accounts of the workings at Fenan see H. D. Kind, "Antike Kupfergewinnung zwischen Rotem und Totem Meer", *ZDPV* 81 (1965), 56, and A. Hauptmann and G. Weisberger, "Archaeometallurgical and Mining-archaeological Investigations in the Area of Feinan, Wadi Arabah (Jordan)", *ADAJ* 31 (1987), 419.

earlier (which we do not know), they would have been in the province of Arabia. But with the eastward and southward extension of Palaestina they now formed part of the means of repression under the control of the *praeses* of that province.

In this period above all, a governor in this region was not a free agent, and operated under the shadow of the Emperor himself. So Eusebius can report with some satisfaction that Urbanus, still *praeses,* and accustomed to his high *tribunal,* to his escort of soldiers and to sharing the table of 'the tyrant', suddenly found himself condemned to death by Maximinus, who delivered the sentence at Caesarea.[41]

With his successor, Firmilianus, we see yet another aspect of the deployment of force by the state. For at a city which the Syriac version of the *Martyrs* calls 'in Syriac Lud, but in Greek Diocaesarea'—a mistake, for the current name of Lydda was Diospolis—he held a mass trial of three hundred confessors sent from Egypt, conducted in public in front of the largely Jewish population of the town, with the herald calling out the Biblical names, like 'Elijah' and 'Daniel', which the Egyptian Christians bore. Firmilianus, perhaps on his normal judicial circuit, may have been unaware of the competing claims to the Biblical heritage which these names represented. But from Eusebius' Christian view, the point was unmistakable: 'the Jews were greatly amazed, while they themselves were despised for their wickedness and apostasy'.[42]

The last phase of persecution before the great changes of 311 also saw Maximinus trying to bring into effect both the resources of the state and those of the cities. In 308 Imperial orders were again circulated, commanding not only universal sacrifice but that pagan temples be reconstructed, that food on sale in the *agora* be sprinkled with libations and that sacrifices be demanded of those using the public baths. The normal features of ancient city life, long since a problem for Jews, were thus to be invested with an explicit religious meaning. The orders went to Imperial officials, the *praeses* and *dux,* but also to the magistrates of each city. In listing those concerned—*logistai (curatores), stratēgoi* (the normal Greek for the *duumviri* of a *colonia*) and *taboularioi* (a Latin term transliterated into Greek)—Eusebius must surely be using the example of his own *colonia,* Caesarea.[43] These measures have to be seen as a foreshadowing of the much more radical attempt at a revival of city paganism which Maximinus was to make in 311/312.

It must be this later stage which Eusebius is referring to in the *Ecclesiasti-*

41. *Mart. Pal.* 7, 7 (some details only in the long recension).

42. *Mart. Pal.* 8 (long recension). See A. Oppenheimer, "Jewish Lydda in the Roman Period", *HUCA* 69 (1988), 115, on pp. 134–135.

43. *Mart. Pal.* 9, 1–3.

cal History, when he says that along with temple-building and reconstruction, Maximinus appointed priests in each place and a High Priest for each province, giving each a military escort.[44] Maximinus had by then, after the death of Galerius, taken possession of Asia Minor and the Tetrarchic 'capital', Nicomedia. According to Eusebius, he subscribed to the formal edict of toleration issued by Galerius in 311 only to the extent of giving verbal orders to governors, and leaving it to his Praetorian Prefect to send round letters ordering the end of active persecution, telling them to write in turn to city and local officials.

At the same point in 311/312 Maximinus, now in control of both the Near East and Asia Minor, began to reverse the measures of toleration for Christians, taking steps of some sort to prevent their meeting in their cemeteries. But the fuller expression of his anti-Christian attitude came only after exchanges between himself and the communities he ruled, which are strikingly indicative of the real nature of the state in this period. In the view of both the two main Christian witnesses of this period, Eusebius and Lactantius, Maximinus was responsible for instigating the presentation to himself of anti-Christian petitions from the cities and leagues of these two regions.[45] Two of the most significant petitions were presented by the two 'capital' cities of the regions he ruled, Nicomedia and Antioch. So, in a letter of his which Eusebius quotes, written towards the end of 312, Maximinus says that at some point in the previous year, thus 311, when he arrived in Nicomedia, people had come before him bearing images of the gods and requesting that Christians be no longer permitted to live there. But at that time he had taken no steps, and would not do so until pressed by further petitions from both Nicomedia and other cities. Perhaps the most significant of these cities was Antioch, where the citizens (allegedly prompted by Maximinus himself) demanded as an Imperial favour that Christians no longer be allowed to live there.[46] The movement was led, according to Eusebius, by a citizen of Antioch called Theotecnus, who symbolised the pagan revival by erecting a cult-statue of Zeus Philios, instituting an array of ceremonials and purifications and inventing suitable oracular responses to please the Emperor.[47] Eusebius thought that Theotecnus was at that point *curator (logistēs)* of Antioch, and later states that he obtained a governorship *(hēgemonia)* from the Emperor—in fact of Galatia Prima, where he was again active in persecution.[48] The inte-

44. *HE* VIII, 14, 8–9.
45. Eusebius, *HE* IX, 2; Lactantius, *de mort. pers.* 36, 3.
46. *HE* IX, 9a, 4–6 (letter to Sabinus, probably Praetorian Prefect).
47. *HE* IX, 2–3.
48. *HE* IX, 2; 11, 5–6. S. Mitchell, "The Life of Saint Theodotus of Ancyra", *Anat. Stud.* 32 (1982), 93, on pp. 107–108.

gration of city magistracies and Imperial office-holding was becoming steadily closer, along with the physical presence of the Imperial court in these provincial cities.

The course of the persecution in these years was thus determined by a close inter-relation between the court and the cities; but nothing clearly distinguishes the pattern in the Near Eastern provinces from that in Maximinus' other area of control, Asia Minor. Eusebius tends of course to record specific events in the Near Eastern provinces: the arrests made by the '*stratodeparchēs* whom the Romans call *dux*' at Damascus 'of Phoenice'; martyrdoms at Emesa, 'a city of Phoenice' (conveniently demonstrating that no separate province of 'Augusta Libanensis' yet existed); and the trial and martyrdom of a major theologian, Lucian, a presbyter at Antioch, who was taken to Nicomedia for the purpose.[49] But when he generalises, what he says relates to both regions: 'As priests of the idols in each city, and above them High Priests *(archiereis)*, there were appointed by Maximinus himself those who had particularly distinguished themselves in city affairs and had achieved a reputation in all these offices. They were filled with a special zeal in the service of the gods they worshipped'.[50] The last active phase of persecution was thus a close alliance between city and court, expressing values which were common to the Graeco-Roman cities of any region. Indeed even what might have seemed one of the most distinctive products of this phase, Maximinus' letter to Tyre about that city's and his own devotion to the gods, turns out—as a new inscription shows—to be a standard letter which Maximinus addressed also to communities in Asia Minor. Even the fact that it was inscribed in Latin at Tyre, and then translated into Greek by Eusebius for inclusion in his *Ecclesiastical History*, proves not to be a product of Tyre's status as a *colonia*; for (surprisingly) the same text, as sent to a small community in Lycia and Pamphylia, is also in Latin.[51]

In the meantime, however, Constantine, ruling in the West, had declared himself publicly as a Christian, had gained control of Rome in 312 and towards the end of the year met at Milan with Licinius, then in control of the Balkan region; they agreed on a proclamation of toleration of Christianity, and restitution of Christian property. Licinius invaded Maximinus' area in spring 313, and a final proclamation of toleration by Maximinus did nothing to avert his defeat, and his suicide at Tarsos. The declaration of toleration and restitution issued by Licinius from Nicomedia in June 313, in the name of Constantine and himself, was the historic document often later to be la-

49. *HE* IX, 5, 2; 6, 1; 6, 3.
50. *HE* IX, 4, 2.
51. See Mitchell, op. cit. (n.25 above).

belled 'the edict of Milan'. A new era had dawned in the religious and communal life of the Empire, in the Near East as elsewhere.

In a significant sense what is important about the record of the Near East in the Tetrarchic period is precisely that in cultural and religious terms it was not distinctive. Apart from rabbinic works in Aramaic, whose date is often very uncertain, and a couple of martyr-acts in Syriac, relating events at Edessa, only the slightest of epigraphic evidence explicitly reveals the presence of a population, within and beyond the 'frontier', speaking Semitic languages. Even the Greek culture of the region gives the strong impression of having become, under the pressure and influence of the state, more truly a Graeco-Roman one, in which Roman and Latin elements are very prominent. The physical record of the Roman forces, erecting grandiloquent Latin inscriptions, is more evident than ever before. Even the form in which many of the martyrs of the region met their death was itself a Roman importation, the wild-beast show: so for instance the three martyrs at Emesa in Maximinus' last year became 'food for beasts'.[52] Within pagan culture only one city in the region acted as a major centre of education, drawing young men from other provinces: the Latin 'island' of Berytus, where one could follow liberal studies and (in particular) Roman law. Such young men might come, like the future martyr Apphianus, who receives a brief biography from Eusebius, from a prominent family in Lycia.[53] But others came, for instance, from the province of Arabia, to devote themselves at Berytus to *liberalia studia* and the *professio iuris*.[54]

Opportunities for preferment in the Imperial service were all the more obvious partly because the Roman state had so visibly implanted itself in the region and had expanded its functions there. We catch an odd glimpse of that in Eusebius' report about Dorotheus, a priest at Antioch under the bishop Cyrillus, in 281–303: because he was a eunuch by birth, he won the favour of the Emperor, who placed him in charge of the dye-works at Tyre.[55] As with the mines at Phaeno, we have no evidence as to how long the Roman state had operated any such establishments. But one such now existed, and with it a post for the Emperor to confer as a favour. Merely being *procurator* of a dye-works was, however, a relatively modest office. Higher posts were open also, and all the more so as a result of the repeated physical presence of the Emperor, his court and his armies. Even senatorial status could become quite common among the upper classes of an Imperial 'capital' like Antioch. That

---

52. *HE* IX, 6, 1.
53. Eusebius, *Mart. Pal.* 4–5.
54. *Cod. Just.* X, 50, 1. See Millar, "Roman *Coloniae*", 16–17, and 8.4 below.
55. *HE* VII, 32–33.

at least is the implication of a muddled passage in Malalas' *Chronicle,* which seems both to conflate the Emperors Maximianus and Maximinus, in talking of an Emperor's return from an Armenian campaign (apparently Maximinus' campaign in 312), and to confuse the diplomatic gesture of exchanging Imperial dress for the robe of a president at the city's Olympic games with a real act of abdication. But at all events Malalas records how both children and young men of Roman senatorial status performed at the games at Antioch in front of the Emperor. We know that Maximinus did fight an Armenian campaign in 312, and did return to Syria after it, for the winter of 312/313.[56]

The increased opportunities for civilian and military rank in the Imperial system might not have created fundamental problems for the cities if the Emperors themselves had not, precisely in this period, made a series of rulings which profoundly affected the tripartite relationship of individuals, their cities and the state.[57] In essence the Emperors chose to reward those in Imperial service with immunity from city obligations, not *e   efore* merely during their service, but for life, as a privilege of rank. It was thus these decisions which created the characteristic tension visible in the fourth century, whereby Imperial service became a prized escape-route which the Emperors themselves made repeated efforts to control. The effects had been felt immediately, however. The *Codex* of Justinian contains the fragmentary record of a hearing before Diocletian in person, in which the issue of rank and exemption was evidently raised by a deputation from Antioch. The two main figures, Firminus and Apollinarius (perhaps the *duoviri/stratēgoi* of the *colonia?*), are named, with the other leading citizens *(principales)* in attendance. It is thus probable, but not certain, that the hearing took place in Antioch itself. A speech in Greek, of which only fragmentary traces remain, was made on behalf of the deputation by one Sabinus. Diocletian then replied: 'To certain ranks *(dignitates)* exemption *(indulgentia)* from city and personal obligations *(munera)* has been granted by us: that is, to those who are ex-*praefecti* or ex-*praepositi*. These therefore will not be summoned to perform personal or city *munera*'.[58] The deputation must have been laying claim to the services of citizens of Antioch who had risen to these military ranks and then retired. They received a negative answer which, along with similar rulings relating to other posts and ranks, was dramatically to reduce the pool of local property-owners on whom the cities could depend. The closer integration of state and city—or the competition of state and city for the services of individuals—thus had consequences almost as profound as those of the fluctuating efforts of the

56. Malalas, *Chron.* 311, 12ff.; see Eusebius, *HE* IX, 8, 2; 4 (Armenian war).
57. For what follows see F. Millar, "Empire and City, Augustus to Julian: Obligations, Excuses and Status", *JRS* 73 (1983), 76.
58. *Cod. Just.* X, 48, 2.

state in first persecuting the Church and then restoring it. The Christianised Near East which would rapidly emerge in the following decades, with bishops privileged by the support of Emperors and their officials, churches for the first time rising as public buildings, and Aelia Capitolina transformed into a centre of Christian pilgrimage, adorned with monuments built by the Emperor, would itself be a function of the increased ambitions and ever more visible presence of the Imperial state.

5.3. LICINIUS AND CONSTANTINE, AD 313–337: RETROSPECT FROM A CHRISTIANISED EMPIRE

There was perhaps no period when the impact of the Roman state, or more precisely of the will of successive Emperors, was felt more acutely in the Near East than in the quarter of a century which followed Licinius' proclamation of 313, in the name of Constantine and himself, that Christianity would be tolerated, and Christian property restored. Licinius' first step was to come to Antioch and torture to death Theotecnus, the leader of the pagan revival under Maximinus.[1] Yet what we know of the government of the Near East in this period is largely confined to the consequences of that proclamation, its partial reversal in the later years of Licinius and its decisive reinstatement by Constantine after his defeat of Licinius in 324. Even more clearly, a strictly military history of the period cannot be written. We have nothing more than Imperial victory titles to suggest that Licinius may have fought a campaign on the eastern front in 313 or 314;[2] from then on, so far as we know, there was a standstill in fighting until near the end of Constantine's reign. It was only just before his death that an invasion of the eastern provinces, of which we know no details, was reported to the Emperor at Constantinople; and he was preparing an expedition against the Persians when he died near Nicomedia in 337.

Looked at in a longer perspective, that unfulfilled intention can be seen both as the culmination of a tendency which had shown itself ever more clearly over the preceding centuries and as a foretaste of the repeated campaigns and mutual invasions which were to mark the following decades. For the account in Eusebius simply presupposes the long-established rule that major campaigns required the presence of the Emperor in person. Moreover, for all the Christian colouring of his depiction of the role of Emperor as Constantine interpreted it, Eusebius still incorporates within it one of the most vivid of all expressions of Roman imperialism, and one which by implication

1. Eusebius, *HE* IX, 11, 5–6.
2. Barnes, *New Empire*, 81.

expresses as clearly as anything else in our evidence the Imperial claim to the heritage of Alexander:

> About this time ambassadors from the Indians, who inhabit the distant regions of the East, arrived with presents consisting of many varieties of brilliant precious stones, and animals differing in species from those known to us. These offerings they presented to the emperor, thus allowing that his sovereignty extended even to the Indian Ocean, and that the princes of their country, who rendered homage to him both by paintings and statues, acknowledged his imperial and paramount authority. Thus the Eastern Indians now submitted to his sway, as the Britons of the Western Ocean had done at the commencement of his reign.[3]

But now of course a quite different element could also enter the language of Imperial diplomacy. For some time earlier—when is not clear—Constantine had replied to an embassy from Shapur II (309–374) by writing a letter in which he represented himself as the protector of the Christian communities in Persia.[4] In spring 337 a further embassy arrived, on hearing of Constantine's preparations for his campaign, offered terms and, if we may believe Eusebius, had them accepted.[5]

If peace was then made, it was not to last long. For war broke out immediately after, and these exchanges were in reality the beginnings of the repeated conflicts which were to dominate the middle decades of the fourth century, and to form one of the central subjects of Ammianus' great *History*. But if the ambition for eastern conquests was something which went back even before the Imperial period, to the campaigns of Lucullus and Pompey, the military structure of the Roman Empire in the East, as Ammianus was to describe it, was almost exactly that which had reached its culmination in the Tetrarchic period. That is to say, an army stretched out, in relatively small units, perhaps none of more than some fifteen hundred men each, and occupying fortified cities, fortresses and small forts on a line from the Tigris to the Red Sea at Aila.

So far as we know, this system altered very little under the rule of Licinius and Constantine. The only real changes that are recorded belong at the very end of Constantine's reign, in the period from 335 or 336 when his son Constantius, as *Caesar*, was in command of the East to confront Persian raids; he seems, as we would expect, to have used Antioch as his capital. It was from

---

3. Eusebius, *VC* IV, 50, trans. E. C. Richardson in *Nicene and Post-Nicene Fathers* ser. 2, vol. I (1890).

4. Eusebius, *VC* IV, 8–13. See T. D. Barnes "Constantine and the Christians of Persia", *JRS* 75 (1985), 126.

5. Eusebius, *VC* IV, 57 (chapter-heading); see Barnes, op. cit., 132.

there that he returned on hearing of the last illness of Constantine in the spring of 337.[6]

It was in this context that the last attested phase of the fortification of the frontier took place, along the upper Tigris in the area gained by the treaty of 298 or 299. One place concerned was the hitherto small town of Amida, on the right bank of the Tigris, and north of the Tur Abdin. Ammianus describes Constantius' measures:

> This city was once very small, but Constantius, when he was still a Caesar, in order that the neighbours *(accolae)* might have a secure place of refuge, at the same time that he built another city called Antoninupolis, surrounded Amida with strong walls and towers; and by establishing there an armoury of mural artillery, he made it a terror to the enemy, and wished it to be called after his own name.[7]

It is very likely that a Roman circuit does indeed underlie the massive medieval walls of Amida (Diyarbakir). But there is no other evidence that it was called Constantia or Constantina. That may be a confusion with the other place which he mentions, surely the same as the 'Tela, formerly called Antipolis' (perhaps 'Antoninopolis'), which the sixth-century *Chronicle of Edessa* says was built by Constantius; but whether it was also the same place as the 'Maximianopolis of Osrhoene' which Malalas says that Constantine rebuilt and called Constantina, we can hardly decide.[8] The place concerned, perhaps now called Constantia or Constantina, may well be Viransehir, on the road along the Mesopotamian shelf from Edessa to Nisibis, for a late-Roman circuit of walls is still visible there. In any case Ammianus' whole narrative presents the defensive system of Roman Mesopotamia as depending on fortified cities or towns: Amida, Bezabde near the Tigris, Nisibis, Singara.[9] But Ammianus, as we have seen, also conceived of the rest of the frontier—Circesium on the Euphrates, fortified by Diocletian, and the walled cities of Arabia—in the same terms.[10] Ammianus, a Roman officer and a native of Antioch, born towards 330, must be our best witness to this final stage of the evolution of the military structure of Roman Mesopotamia, before the loss of its eastern section in 363. If we were to depend on his testimony, we would see Constantius' measures as *Caesar* under his father Constantine not as a reversal but as the culmination of Diocletian's fortification of the frontier.

So far as the Near East is concerned, therefore, there is nothing to support the hostile generalisation later made by Zosimus: that Constantine over-

6. Zonaras XIII, 4.

7. Ammianus XVIII, 9, 1, Loeb trans.

8. For the *Chronicle of Edessa* see 12.3 and App. C below; Malalas, *Chron.* 323.

9. See J. Matthews, *The Roman Empire of Ammianus* (1989), esp. 51ff.

10. See 5.1 above.

turned Diocletian's policy of putting his forces in fortified cities along the frontiers, and withdrew them into the interior.[11] Though the earliest document distinguishing between troops who were *comitatenses* (serving in a field-army) on the one hand and *ripenses* (frontier-soldiers) on the other belongs to 325,[12] there is no evidence to illustrate any corresponding division of function on the ground in the Near East in this period. Nor can other generalisations made by Zosimus be confirmed. For instance, on his view it was Constantine who created the regional military commanders, called *magistri militum,* or *equitum* or *peditum* ('master of the soldiers', or 'of the cavalry' or 'of the infantry'). But none happen to be attested in the East until the 350s.

Zosimus saw that change as a function of another, whereby the Praetorian Prefects lost their military commands (which in fact they had never had, in the sense of commanding whole armies), became responsible only for taxation and military supplies and had their responsibilities divided on a regional basis.[13] But again he seems to be retrojecting arrangements which did in fact come into being in the middle of the fourth century, but were only in their initial stages under Constantine. Even at the end of Constantine's reign only the provinces of Africa were under a genuine regional Praetorian Prefect. The four other Praetorian Prefects known to have been in office at this time seem all to have been serving with one or another of the Emperors: with Constantine himself as *Augustus,* and with the then *Caesares,* Constantius, Constantinus, Constans and Dalmatius. The Praetorian Prefect who was with Constantius in the East, apparently based at Antioch, may perhaps have been a Christian from Crete of humble birth, Flavius Ablabius. There are many uncertainties. But as it happens, we know that there were five of them in 336, for the whole group is recorded in a Greek inscription on a statue-base from Antioch erected in that year and representing the *Caesar* Constantinus: Papius Pacatianus (probably with Constans), Flavius Ablabius, Valerius Felix, Annius Tiberianus (the father of Saint Ambrose, then in Gaul with the *Caesar* Constantinus) and Nestorius Timonianus. But whether it was he or Ablabius who was serving with Constantius, and if so who (if anyone) was with Constantine himself, remains mysterious.[14]

In spite, or perhaps even because, of such puzzles, this document is not an unsuitable symbol of the stage in the evolution of the late-Roman system which had been reached by 336, as seen from Antioch. For if some of the details it conveys remain unclear, it still offers a snapshot of the highest level

11. Zosimus II, 34.

12. *Cod. Theod.* VII, 20, 4.

13. Zosimus II, 33.

14. D. Feissel, "Une dédicace en l'honneur de Constantin II César et les préfets du prétoire de 336", *Travaux et mémoires* 9 (1985), 421. *AE* (1985), no. 823; *SEG* XXXV, no. 1484.

of the late-Roman administrative hierarchy at a moment when it was still in the course of formation; and it represents itself as the product of a college of five Prefects, all with senatorial rank, without making it explicit that they were scattered over the different regions of the Empire. But in another sense it is a perfectly typical product of the public life of a Greek city, in being a statue-base inscribed in Greek and carrying a representation of a distant Emperor.

Though the structure of the Empire was thus in the process of transformation, the pattern of the civil government of the provinces of the Near East, like the military dispositions there, seems to have remained in the form established by the Tetrarchy. Again, we can see that structure, as it was a few decades later, in a brilliant sketch offered by Ammianus.[15] By then, and perhaps already under Constantine, Osrhoene was a province separate from Mesopotamia (both arrangements appear at different points in the third century); and the north-eastern part of Syria Coele, along the Euphrates, had by Ammianus' time become the province of 'Euphratensis', which included the two major cities of Hierapolis and Samosata. Ammianus' vivid description of the eastern provinces then lists 'Syria', with Antioch as its most famous city, but also with Laodicea, Apamea and Seleucia (thus the city foundations by Seleucus Nicator, to whom Ammianus has just referred, still dominant in the area). Next comes the province of Phoenice 'lying against Mount Lebanon', and containing the cities of Tyre, Sidon, Berytus, Emesa and Damascus (a division into 'Phoenice'—paradoxically the eastern part—and 'Phoenice Libani' or 'Augusta Libanensis', present in some lists, is unknown to Ammianus). Then comes Palaestina, with Caesarea, Eleutheropolis, Neapolis, Ascalon and Gaza (Jerusalem is mentioned only as having been taken by Pompey); and finally Arabia, with the walled cities of Bostra, Gerasa and Philadelphia. This to Ammianus was the *Orientis limes,* 'the frontier-zone of the East', starting in the north at Mount Amanus, stretching from the Euphrates to the neighbourhood of the Nile, and bordered on one side by the *Saracenae gentes* and on the other by the sea. Though, in true Graeco-Roman fashion, he saw the presence of Greek cities as the primary characteristic of any area, he was nonetheless aware of other and older elements in the culture of the region: he notes that Damascus had been 'founded in ancient times'. Just before, he also gives a vivid general account of Seleucus' city-foundations and their relation to the present:

> For by taking advantage of the great number of men whom he ruled for a long time in peace, in place of their rustic dwellings he built cities of great strength and abundant wealth; and many of these, although they are now called by the Greek names which were imposed on them by the will of

15. Ammianus XIV, 8, 5–13, Loeb trans.

their founder, nevertheless have not lost the old appellations in the Assyrian tongue which the original settlers gave them.

Ammianus' view was, from our standpoint, a doubly retrospective one, set in his narrative of the 350s, but written at least three decades later. Contemporary evidence for the early decades of the century can provide no comparable picture (and above all the regime here of Licinius is hardly known at all). What evidence we have shows how the operations of the state were informed by quite new priorities: hostility to pagan practice, the enforcement of Christian morality and the glorification of the Christian Church.

Only a few illustrations will be needed here; a closer look at what the innovations and conflicts of Constantine's reign can tell us about the culture of the region belongs much later. But few inhabitants of the region can have been left unaware of the new uses to which the apparatus of the state was now being put. Some pagans might subsequently have felt that they envied the man and wife, from families with mixed Greek and Semitic names, who erected an elaborate tomb for themselves at a village in the limestone massif, north of Apamea:

> In year 636, on the 21st of Artemisios, Abedrapsos son of Dionysios and Amathbabea daughter of Eupolemos, his wife, finished the tomb, having shared life cheerfully, and they paid their vows to their ancestral gods. Be of good cheer, soul; no one is immortal![16]

The tomb was completed in May 325, the year after Constantine's victory over Licinius—and exactly at the moment when several hundred bishops were meeting for the Council of Nicaea. What Constantine's triumph was to mean was proclaimed in the greatest detail throughout the eastern provinces. A general letter to the provincials, declaring the Emperor's personal mission as a Christian, and the restoration of Christian persons and property, was followed by another denouncing the errors of idolatry, though commanding mutual tolerance.[17] The resources of the state were placed at the disposition of the bishops for the building and adornment of churches: Eusebius himself, at Caesarea, like other bishops, received a letter instructing him to draw the necessary materials 'from the governors (that is, the *praesides*) and the praefectural staff' (the office of the *Vicarius* of Oriens).[18] The new, two-level structure of civilian administration is visible again when Eusebius describes how Constantine instructed Macarius, the bishop of Jerusalem, to set about the construction of the Church of the Holy Sepulchre: 'And as regards the construction and adornment of the walls, be informed that the responsibility has

16. *IGLS* IV, no. 1409, cf. 1410–1411.
17. Eusebius, *VC* II, 24–44; 48–60.
18. *VC* II, 46.

been entrusted by us to our *amicus* Dracilianus, the *Vicarius* of the Prefects, and to the *praes* of the province'.[19] Dracilianus' predecessor was perhaps the Maximus who in 325 received instructions on the conditions under which town-councillors might be allowed to enter the army, posted at Antioch in July of that year;[20] in the autumn he received another, substituting, as a punishment for criminals, service in the *metalla,* instead of the 'bloody spectacles' of being forced to fight as gladiators. This was posted at Berytus on the first of October 325.[21] The motivation for the ban was clearly Christian, and in this still very Roman *colonia* the prohibition will have been particularly relevant.

Equally appropriate, but in a quite different way, were the orders which Constantine gave to have the practice of castration banned in Mesopotamia: any slave who had suffered this was to be confiscated from his owner, along with the property where it had been carried out. The order was addressed, at an unknown date, not to a civil governor but to the *dux* of Mesopotamia— as it happens, the only *dux* in office in the Near East in these years who can be identified.[22] The practice cannot have been wholly unrelated to that of self-castration, which a king Abgar had banned in Edessa in the Severan period, perhaps as part of a policy of compelling his subjects to follow Roman customs.[23] If so, Christian and traditional Roman ideals and norms for once tended in the same direction, as applied to this predominantly Syriac-speaking region.

In general, however, Constantine's Christianising measures and legislation constituted a revolutionary reversal of the previous values and objectives of the state. This is not the place for a reassessment of the wider impact on pagan society and pagan cults of Constantine's Christian mission; many aspects of this—above all, the intended scope and the actual effectiveness of his attested ban on sacrifice—remain in any case highly controversial. Nor is it relevant here to follow the complex history of the Arian question as it affected the churches of this region, or the almost equally complex issues surrounding the bishopric of Antioch. But three aspects of the fundamentally changed nature of the relations of state and subject, as they unfolded in this region, do deserve mention.

The first is the Council of Nicaea in 325, not only because of its historic significance, but because it followed so closely on Constantine's defeat of Licinius, and meant the sudden elevation of a long list of local bishops to the

---

19. VC III, 30–32.
20. *Cod. Theod.* XII, 1, 10.
21. *Cod. Theod.* XV, 1, and *Cod. Just.* XI, 44, 1.
22. *Cod. Just.* IV, 42, 1.
23. 3.4 above and 12.5 below.

visible status of Imperial favourites. In view of the conflicts which had always arisen over the demands of official travellers, it will have been one of the most deeply felt symbols of change that the letter summoning the bishops to Nicaea gave them the right to use the Imperial transport-service.[24] We should not underestimate the significance of this. For the list of bishops who came from the Near Eastern provinces provides a roll-call of the urban communities of the region (as well as raising the question as to whether all the places named can really have been independent *poleis*).

The list, though incomplete and subject to many problems, may nonetheless give an impression of what the Roman Near East 'was' in 325. The following places were represented:[25]

From Syria Coele: Antioch, Seleucia, Laodicea and Apamea (Seleucus Nicator's four major foundations); Hierapolis, Samosata, Neocaesarea (apparently a small place on the Euphrates), Doliche and Zeugma in the Commagenian region; Balaneae and Gabala on the coast; Larissa, Epiphania (Hama), Arethusa and Raphaneae (apparently now detached from Phoenice) in the Orontes Valley; Cyrrhus, Gindarus and Germanicia in the north, as well as an unidentifiable place whose name is transmitted as Arbocadama.

From Phoenice: Antaradus, Tripolis, Berytus, Sidon, Tyre and Ptolemais on the coast; Emesa in the Orontes Valley; Caesarea Paneas and Damascus; and Palmyra (as well as an unidentified place given as Alassius).

From Palaestina: Jerusalem, Neapolis, Sebaste, Caesarea, Ascalon, Nicopolis (Emmaus), Iamnia, Eleutheropolis, Maximianopolis (the former legionary camp of Caparcotna), Lydda, Azotus and Gaza; Jericho in the Jordan Valley; Scythopolis, Capitolias and Gadara, cities of the 'Decapolis'; Zabulon(?); and, as a reflection of the recent large southward expansion of the province, Aila at the head of the Red Sea.

From Arabia: Philadelphia, Esbous (Heshbon), Sodom(?), Bostra, Souedias (Dionysias), as well as a couple of unidentifiable places.

From Osrhoene and Mesopotamia only Edessa and Nisibis seem certain— and in general all these lists, reconstructed from a variety of later sources, can be taken only as roughly indicative. But as a visible symbol of the changed priorities of the state, it is impossible to exaggerate the importance of the summoning of scores of bishops to make their way from these provinces across Asia Minor to Nicaea, using official transport-services. Ammianus was later to claim that under Constantius the official transport-system had almost

24. Eusebius, *VC* III, 6, 1; cf. Millar, *ERW*, 327 and 595.
25. For this list I have simply used A. von Harnack, *Die Mission und Ausbreitung des Christentums*4 II (1924), 660ff. (Coele Syria); 655ff. (Phoenice); 641ff. (Palaestina); 699ff. (Arabia); 678ff. (Osrhoene and Mesopotamia). See also D. S. Wallace-Hadrill, *Christian Antioch: A Study of Early Christian Thought in the East* (1982), App. I, "Eastern Representation at Nicaea".

broken down under the weight of squads of bishops hurrying hither and thither to attend synods.[26] The impression made on observers in 325 will have been just as powerful.

Equally impressive symbolic changes were shortly to follow. One was the use of the resources of the state to build churches. We would miss the full impact of this unless we realised that, for all the respect paid by the Emperors of the previous three and a half centuries to the major pagan shrines of the provinces, actual construction of new temples by them—except in Rome itself—had been almost unknown.[27] Naturally, even now churches constructed on Imperial orders represented only a few key elements in a wave of construction, normally dependent on local initiative, which had begun already in the years following the proclamation of toleration in 313. Thus the sixth-century *Chronicle of Edessa* reports that in 312/313 Bishop Qona built a church there;[28] and the major literary monument of this hopeful phase in the early years under Licinius is the sermon which Eusebius himself delivered at the dedication of the Christian basilica of Tyre.[29] Nonetheless, the orders from Constantine for the repair of the existing churches and if necessary the construction of new ones, with resources to be provided by the provincial governors and the 'prefectural staff' (of the *Vicarius* of the diocese), represented a quite new phase in the nature of the state.

In deploying the resources of the state to advertise his own commitment to Christianity, Constantine's priorities were naturally shaped by the political geography of the pagan state itself. Apart from his new capital, Constantinople (placed at the central point of the route between the Danube and the Euphrates), his major Christian buildings were erected in Rome itself and in the Tetrarchic capitals of Nicomedia and Antioch: in Eusebius' words, 'that metropolis of the East which derived its name from Antiochus, in which, as the head of that portion of the empire, he consecrated to the service of God a church of unparalleled size and beauty'. This was the great Octagon, or Golden House, begun in 327 and dedicated in 341.[30]

By contrast, Constantine's building in and around Jerusalem imported a new element into Imperial priorities. A Christian conception of particular places and sites as being in themselves holy, and as worthy objects of pilgrimage, is attested even in the second century; and Eusebius' own *Onomasticon* reflects a heightened interest in the historical topography of Biblical history.

26. Ammianus XXI, 16, 18.

27. See S. Mitchell, "Imperial Building in the Eastern Roman Provinces", *HSCPh* 91 (1987), 333.

28. See 12.3 below.

29. The text is reproduced by Eusebius in *HE* X, 4.

30. Eusebius *VC* III, 50; *Or. Triac* 9, 15. See G. Downey, *A History of Antioch in Syria, Seleucus to the Arab Conquest* (1961), 342ff.

But Constantine's ambitions and elaborate constructions, at the Holy Sepulchre, on the Mount of Olives and at Bethlehem, gave—or began to give—Jerusalem and its neighbourhood a centrality in Christian conceptions which it had never had before.[31] The record of his journey to and from the Holy Land in 333 left by a pilgrim from Bordeaux represents a new moment in Christian consciousness, and a new place for the Holy Land in the conceptual map of the Empire. The local details of that map had been marked out by lavish constructions erected on the Emperor's orders and using the resources of the state: the Bordeaux Pilgrim records the new Imperial basilicas which he saw at the Holy Sepulchre, the Mount of Olives, Bethlehem and the terebinth at Mambre near Hebron.[32]

This last also represented another very novel aspect of the role and ambitions of the state: the deliberate repression of pagan cult-activities at certain selected sites, sometimes accompanied by the actual destruction of temples. In the case of the Holy Sepulchre, a temple of Venus was destroyed to make way for the new church; and it should be stressed just how deliberate and visible a reversal of priorities this was. Whether or not tradition accurately recalled the location of Jesus' tomb, the site was one which had duly lain outside the walls of early first-century Jerusalem, as was required for a burial. The temple of Venus will have been a feature, along with the temple of Capitoline Juppiter, of the new Roman *colonia* of Aelia Capitolina, created by Hadrian; its boundaries extended further north than those of the previous city. The temple thus destroyed was therefore no mere local shrine, but a Roman temple deriving from the last real colonial foundation in the history of Rome.

Rather different considerations applied to the oak, or terebinth, of Mambre near Hebron, for it owed the Imperial attention given it to the tradition that it was there that God had first appeared to Abraham. But the site was now, as Constantine's mother Helena reported, disfigured by pagan idols and an altar. The removal of these, and the erection of a church, was thus simultaneously a blow against idolatry and a Christian claim to the inheritance of the Old Testament.[33] It is also a reminder of how complex a pattern of coexistence between different religious communities might mark this region. Eusebius' *Onomasticon* itself had identified different villages in Palaestina as being inhabited by either Jews, Christians or Samaritans. But he also notes, for instance, that near a large village between Jerusalem and Diospolis there

---

31. See E. D. Hunt, *Holy Land Pilgrimage in the Later Roman Empire* (1982), esp. ch. 1; P. W. L. Walker, *Holy City, Holy Places? Christian Attitudes to Jerusalem and the Holy Land in the Fourth Century* (1990).

32. *Itin. Burdig.* (CSEL XXXIX), 589–599.

33. Eusebius, *VC* III, 52–53. See further 10.1 below.

had been a spring with an idol beside it 'worshipped by the natives'.[34]

The deliberate acts of destruction of pagan cult-centres ordered by Constantine were not confined to Palaestina and to sites rendered sacred by the Bible. But those that we know of were almost entirely restricted to the Near East as defined here; as so often, however, we cannot tell whether our knowledge simply reflects the limitations of Eusebius' perspective. The fact remains that he reports no case further away than Aegeae in Cilicia, on the other side of Mount Amanus. There, in a way never paralleled in the earlier history of the Empire, a detachment of soldiers destroyed the temple of Asclepius, 'whom thousands regarded with reverence as the possessor of saving and healing power'.[35]

That apart, the only two other places where we know that Imperial action was taken against pagan shrines were both in Phoenice. The first was something very characteristic of the Near East, a remote cult-centre at Aphaca on Mount Lebanon. Eusebius' words vividly evoke the special features of its location: 'This was a grove and temple, not situated in the midst of any city, nor in any public place, as for splendour of effect is generally the case, but apart from the beaten and frequented road, at Aphaca, a part of the summit of Mount Lebanon, and dedicated to the foul demon known by the name of Aphrodite'.[36] To Eusebius, what attracted Constantine's destruction of the temple, again carried out by a detachment of soldiers, was the homosexual intercourse and ritual prostitution practised there. His report serves to raise profound questions about the religious culture of the region. For should we see this cult-centre, whose remains lie high up on Mount Lebanon, at the source of the river Adonis (Nahr Ibrahim), as a surviving 'Oriental' or Semitic 'high place'? As everywhere, its architecture is of the Imperial period, and it is never mentioned in our sources until the third century.[37]

As we will see in many contexts, it is precisely Christian evidence which, for obvious reasons, first gives explicit accounts of many aspects of society and culture in this region. Precisely because it is Christian, it is not to be read as embodying mere reports, but as an interpretation of the hostile pagan universe of idols, 'demons', sacrifices and cult-practices with which the Christians found themselves confronted. Our difficulty in knowing what perspective to adopt is nowhere clearer than in the last instance which Eusebius gives, namely Constantine's repression of what seems also to be represented as ritual prostitution at Heliopolis: 'We may instance the Phoenician city Heliopolis, in which those who dignify licentious pleasure with the appellation of

34. Eusebius, *Onom.*, ed. Klostermann, 8.
35. Eusebius, VC III, 56, trans. Richardson.
36. VC III, 55, 2, trans. Richardson.
37. See 8.4 below.

Aphrodite, had permitted their wives and daughters to commit shameless for-nication'.[38] Unlike later Christian writers, Eusebius does not in this case say that force was used, or any temple destroyed. Instead he says that Constantine wrote to the city to forbid the continuation of such practices, and built what was apparently the first church there, manned by a bishop, a presbyter and deacons.

But 'Heliopolis of Phoenice' was in fact a Roman *colonia,* settled by veter-ans as part of the foundation of the *colonia* of Berytus under Augustus, and transformed by Septimius Severus into an independent city: 'Colonia Iulia Augusta Felix Heliopolis'.[39] The deity to whom Eusebius refers as 'Aphrodite' can hardly be other than the 'Venus Heliopolitana' celebrated on Latin in-scriptions from Heliopolis and Berytus, as are the two other best-attested gods of Heliopolis, Iuppiter Optimus Maximus Heliopolitanus and Mercur-ius. Had the worship of Venus there always been simply a Latinised expres-sion of a pre-existing worship of a female deity with a Semitic name, perhaps Atargatis? If so, had an 'Oriental' custom of ritual prostitution simply been taken over by the settlers? Or had the descendants of the original Roman veterans only gradually succumbed to the demoralising influences of their Oriental environment, to the point where their city could be perceived as 'Phoenician' in more than a purely geographical sense? Or, on the contrary, did Constantine's very circumspect approach in merely writing a letter (pre-sumably to the magistrates and council of the city) and building a church reflect a Roman status which the city still embodied? Eusebius' brief account raises in acute form the question of what sort of city early-fourth-century Heliopolis really was.

That question, like many others, must remain for the moment unan-swered; and, as with many others which relate to the culture of the Near East under Roman rule, we may have to accept that no unambiguous answer is possible. For the value of surveying the history of this region, and the progres-sive steps by which it came under Roman direct rule, does not lie in the pre-sumption that such an approach, or any other, will necessarily take us far in determining whether there were distinctive common characteristics of the civilisation of this region, and if so what these were. Rather, a military and geographical survey, following the evolution of Roman rule step by step in chronological sequence, is essential, first, to defining the region, or slowly growing set of sub-regions, with which we are concerned. But second, and more important, a military and administrative survey serves not to answer but to pose in more acute form the question of the social and political struc-tures, the patterns of religious beliefs, and the communal identities and loyal-

38. *VC* III, 58, 1, trans. Richardson.
39. See 3.4 above and 8.4 below.

ties of the population, or populations, with which the Roman state found itself confronted.

Many questions about the Roman state itself are raised by such a survey. Why was it that this region was the object of steadily increasing military investment by the Roman state, and was to become by the end of the period the prime area where the long tradition of Roman imperialism was still active? The novelty of the Imperial period was not the mere fact of Roman campaigns here. As far as the northern part of it was concerned, Mesopotamia and the city of Nisibis had already been captured by Roman forces under Lucullus in 68 BC. But Cassius Dio, recording this in the first half of the third century AD, can reflect a development of a quite different order, the long-term Roman implantation there: 'this city . . . is now ours, and has the status of a *colonia* of ours'.[40] Equally, it was only four years later, in 64 BC, that the first Roman pro-magistrate, Aemilius Scaurus, had come into contact with a king Aretas of Nabataea; and after a further abortive campaign in 62, Scaurus was subsequently, in 58, to issue coins representing King Aretas, quite falsely, as kneeling in submission.[41] The significant fact was not mere military contact, but rather the period of more than a century which followed, when the Roman Near East remained essentially a mere bridgehead based on the two main areas of Hellenistic city-foundations, northern Syria and the Decapolis; and then, by contrast, the new phase of expansion which began in the later first century AD and led to the creation of Rome's 'desert frontier', from the Red Sea to the Tigris.

Rivalry with Parthia and then Sasanid Persia, and the memory of Alexander's conquests, will explain some aspects of this development. Dio's image of Trajan as the only Emperor ever to reach the shores of the Persian Gulf, longingly watching a ship setting off for India, remains one of the keys to Roman Imperial history. But quite different considerations must have determined the Roman military investment in what was to become Syria Phoenice, and in Judaea—later Syria Palaestina—and Arabia. Quite different, that is, *unless* we were to think of these regions as inhabited by an 'Oriental' population which might look to Parthia or Persia as readily as to Rome. Such a view would certainly be grossly misleading. But we cannot dismiss so easily the evidence that trade-routes did lead eastwards through virtually all the areas to which Roman military occupation was extended—down the Red Sea, and through the Hedjaz, perhaps through the Wadi Sirhan, the route via Palmyra to the Euphrates, the route across Mesopotamia to Nisibis and beyond. That there was regular human movement between the Roman Near East and the Parthian and then Persian Empire is beyond question. But whether those con-

40. Dio XXXVI, 6, 2.
41. For the coins, M. H. Crawford, *Roman Republican Coinage* I (1974), 446, no. 422.

tacts were significant for culture, attitudes or communal identities in the Roman area is quite another question, as is that of whether these trade-routes
were themselves a motive for Roman expansion.

That the Roman Near East could be looked at, in more than a purely
geographical sense, as part of Asia, or 'the Orient', cannot be denied. The
mere currency there of a group of related Semitic languages is sufficient evidence of that. But it was also an area of already long-standing Greek city-
foundation and settlement. To look at the culture of any one of the sub-
regions of the Near East is to see how profoundly the Greek language and
Greek culture were rooted in the civilisation of this region. Any notion of a
crude contrast between 'Greek' on the one hand and 'Oriental' or 'Semitic'
on the other must seem wholly inadequate. Too much time had passed since
Alexander's arrival in 332 BC. Yet the military history of the region itself
serves to suggest that this contrast is not completely meaningless. The Roman
forces here fought many successive campaigns, large and small, in contexts
other than rivalry with Parthia or Persia: repeatedly in Judaea but also in
Commagene, in Nabataea in 106, against Palmyra and finally, under Diocletian, against the 'Saracens'. But none of these operations was directed against
a community or political formation which we would be tempted to characterise as unambiguously Greek.

Nonetheless, any attempt to understand the culture or cultures of the region in terms of a simple contrast between 'Greek' and 'Oriental' would be
inevitably misleading. There is little or nothing to suggest that the supposed
'Orientals' shared any sense of common identity. On the contrary, everything
shows that Jewish identity, whose maintenance is beyond question, conflicted
rather than cohered with the identities of other groups using Semitic languages. Nor did these others show anything like the same capacity for survival. Whether anything distinctive remained of Commagene after the end of
the dynasty, of Nabataea after it was made into the province of Arabia, or of
Palmyra after Aurelian's reconquest is precisely one of the crucial questions
we need to answer.

Equally, perhaps even more, puzzling is what appears to be a growing
awareness, and a positive encouragement by Rome, of Phoenician identity.
The Phoenician cities represent the one case—the Jews apart—where affirmation of a pre-Greek identity and history is clearly visible in the Imperial
period. But was it this self-identification, shared even by inland cities like
Emesa, Damascus and perhaps Palmyra, as 'Phoenician' which led Septimius
Severus to resurrect 'Phoenice' as the name of a Roman province stretching
to the Euphrates? Or was the sequence the reverse: that it was this artificial
geographical division, with no historical roots, which provided a collective
identity which had previously been lacking? Some explanation is at any rate

required as to why Heliodorus, at the end of his novel *Aethiopica,* should have chosen to identify himself as 'a Phoenician Emesene'.

Yet the complexities of personal and communal identity do not end there. One of the most distinctive features of the period is the way in which many small places found themselves elevated, by Herodian kings or by Roman Emperors, into being Greek cities with Greek—or Latin-Greek—names. But this was above all a feature of Judaea/Syria Palaestina and Arabia: in each, for instance, there appeared under the Tetrarchy a new 'city' with the Latin-Greek name 'Maximianopolis'. But it was not a prominent feature of Phoenice: its major cities—Berytus, Sidon, Tyre, Ptolemais, Heliopolis, Emesa, Damascus and Palmyra—kept names which owed nothing to Rome. But then again, that is true only if we keep to the single geographical name used to locate them. For every one of these places in fact became in the course of the Empire a Roman *colonia,* and Heliopolis even owed its status as a city to Severus, as it did its full Roman name: 'Colonia Iulia Augusta Felix Heliopolis'. The impact of Roman measures, going far beyond the universal grant of Roman citizenship by Caracalla, is an important further influence on the curiously malleable identities of Near Eastern communities, and one whose significance has yet to be assessed. Above all, the military and political history of the third century, when looked at in detail, at least raises the question as to whether the 'empire of Palmyra', far from being an Arab uprising against Rome, is not to be explained as a movement led by a Roman senator from within a *colonia.*

Had it been *consciously* an 'Arab' movement, whatever that might have meant, it is hard to imagine that Vaballathus would have included in the list of victory-titles which he took as Emperor the name 'Arabicus'.[42] That would not of course mean that others in antiquity might not have seen the Palmyrenes themselves as 'Arabs', or even that we should not. How, and whether, we should use 'Arab' as a way of characterising the origins and true nature of any settled or urban groups in the Roman Near East is the most treacherous of all the questions which confront us. But what does seem clearly established is that ancient observers generally associated the term 'Arab' not with a language or culture but with an unsettled way of life, as they did even more clearly with the word 'Saracen'. Whatever else remains uncertain about the role of the Empire and its forces in the Near East, one thing is clear, that the long evolution of Roman military dispositions brought them everywhere into more and more direct contact with the 'Saracens' of the steppe. One indication of this is the changing geographical and military shape of Judaea/Syria Palaestina. Up to the second century the level of Roman forces there steadily

42. 4.3 above, text to n. 52.

increased; and it was there above all that the Roman army could be seen as an occupation force directed to the control of a civilian population. So it remained for perhaps a century and a half after the end of the great revolt under Bar Kochba in the 130s. But in the Tetrarchic period we find that the province has expanded to cover the southern part of Trajan's Via Nova; and the legion X Fretensis has left Jerusalem and moved to Aila. Most of the units, forts and walled cities which now constituted the Roman 'frontier' in the Near East were not now disposed so as to confront Persia, but along the steppe from the Euphrates to the Red Sea. That is not to say that we can simply characterise the army as it now was as a defence force positioned against external enemies. For Roman guard-posts lined the roads within the provinces also; and it is precisely in the fourth century that, from Sinai in the south to Mesopotamia in the north, vivid evidence shows that 'Saracens' were to be found within the provinces as well as outside. What looks on the map like a 'frontier' was also itself a police-system protecting roads. How we should see the tripartite relations of the Roman forces, the settled population and the 'Arabs' or 'Saracens' is precisely the most complex question raised by the military history of the Near East.

II

✦ ✦ ✦

REGIONS
AND
COMMUNITIES

CHAPTER

6

COMMUNAL AND CULTURAL IDENTITIES

A social and economic history of the Near East in the Roman period cannot be written. None of the conditions for such a history are present. Though good descriptions of the geology and (in very broad terms) the ecology of the region are available,[1] nothing is clearer than the fact that in this area above all we cannot speak of constant or enduring patterns of social and economic life. To take only the crudest and most obvious variables, the extent of cultivation along the margin of the steppe and the heights reached by regular settlement in the very large mountainous zones have both varied widely according to political and military circumstances. The most important factor of all has been simply the presence or absence of political stability and of effective policing. Even within the present century the area under cultivation and marked by regular settlement has expanded immensely within the modern states of Syria, Israel and Jordan. Conditions have thus changed dramatically within the period covered by modern archaeological and epigraphic researches; and precisely those books which are fundamental to the understanding of the region in antiquity may set their discoveries in a context which, while valid over half a century ago, bears no relation to the conditions prevailing now.

Take for instance the wonderful account of the antiquities of the Hauran contained in Maurice Dunand's book on the museum at Soueida, published in 1934—one of the most impressive presentations of the art and archaeology

1. See, e.g., J. M. Wagstaff, *The Evolution of Middle Eastern Landscapes: An Outline to AD 1840* (1985); E. Wirth, *Syrien: Eine geographische Landeskunde*[2] (1971); D. Baly, "The Geography of Palestine and the Levant in Relation to Its History", in W. D. Davies and L. Finkelstein (eds.), *Cambridge History of Judaism* I (1984), 1; and the still evocative and informative work of G. A. Smith, *A Historical Geography of the Holy Land* (1894).

of a sub-region from anywhere in the Empire.[2] Some things are of course unchangeable, for instance the black basalt of the region, which was perforce the medium in which a striking local variant of Graeco-Roman sculpture and architecture had to be expressed. But the situation described in Dunand's preface belongs in another world: a French company encamped in the Roman theatre of Bostra and then annihilated in the Druse uprising of 1925; the museum beginning life in that same year as an open-air enclosure outside Soueida. The photographs show the museum in a rolling, barren landscape, with a few one-storey houses beyond it. Nothing would prepare the reader for the substantial modern town of today (nor for the fact that the Jebel Hauran, entirely inhabited by Druse, is now officially called Jebel Arab).

Though archaeology, in the Hauran above all, has made immense strides since then, modern historical circumstances have meant that the detailed archaeology of (for instance) farming, animal husbandry, the means of human subsistence, the exchange of food and manufactured objects and of the products of longer-distance trade has not arrived at anywhere near the stage at which a strictly economic interpretation of the history of the region could be written. If standing remains can be surveyed and mapped, some sites excavated, and objects and inscriptions collected, that is as much as can yet be expected. Even in those respects many of the more mountainous regions remain unknown territory to historical research, as do many areas which lie too close to the boundaries of modern states.

This book can thus make no pretence whatsoever to present a social or economic history of the region. Desirable as such a work might be, it cannot begin from a coherent body of knowledge—or even any serious hypotheses about the economic history of the area—or locate within that the major social formations visible in our fragmentary evidence, the nature of their communal life, their role within the wider Greek-speaking world and their relation to the Roman Empire.

Instead the book presents a map of surface appearances, of communal and cultural identities as seen and expressed by both insiders and outsiders. That has at least the advantage of relying above all on explicit statements in words, preserved on inscriptions, in perishable documents and in literary works, which at a certain, and important, level cannot be falsified. If, as we have seen, the latest known document from Dura-Europos presents the place as 'Kolōneia of the Eurōpaioi of [Seleukos] Neikatōr, the sacred and inviolate and autonomous', that piece of self-representation remains a historical fact even if we could prove that the place had not been founded by Seleucus Nicator in the early Hellenistic period, or was not entitled to the status of *colonia*.[3]

2. M. Dunand, *Le musée de Soueida: Inscriptions et monuments figurés* (1934).
3. *P. Dura*, no. 32; cf. 4.3 above and 12.4 below, text to n.14.

Similarly, if Heliodorus, the author of the novel *Aethiopica,* finishes his work by identifying himself as an 'Emesene Phoenician', we may well want to discuss why he should have chosen to describe himself in this way; but we cannot argue away his own self-representation, or presume to prove that the people of Emesa were 'really' Arabs.

That is not to say that such self-identifications are not liable to be completely misunderstood in the modern world. Take the case of Tatian, the second-century author of a composite version of all four Gospels called in Greek *Diatessaron,* of which a fragment in Greek was found at Dura-Europos.[4] He also wrote an *Address to the Greeks* in which he describes himself as 'he who philosophises in the manner of barbarians, born in the land of the *Assyrioi,* educated first on your principles, secondly in what I now profess'.[5] Does he mean to say that he came in reality from 'Assyria', that is, from an area (Adiabene or Babylonia?) east of the Euphrates? Was he in origin therefore a Syriac- or Aramaic-speaking 'Oriental' from outside the Roman Empire? Not at all. 'Assyria' and 'Assyrioi' were common terms for Syria and its inhabitants;[6] which is why, like so many other people from that area, he had a name which is in origin Latin, with an extended ending, and transliterated into Greek. Another, closely comparable, 'Assyrian' of the second century was the satirist Lucian, that is, 'Loukianos' from Samosata in Commagene.[7] The education which Tatian, like Lucian, had received in Syria was Greek, and the 'barbarian philosophy' which he practised was Christianity.

These questions of personal and communal self-representation are crucial, if only because the relevant names and identities might change and evolve so profoundly. Tatian was at some point a pupil, perhaps at Rome, of another man from a Near Eastern province, with a transliterated Latin name, that is, Justin Martyr: or, as he presents himself in the *Apology* which he addressed to Antoninus Pius, 'Ioustinos, son of Priskos, son of Bakcheios, of those from Flavia Neapolis, belonging to Syria Palaistinē'.[8] Every element in his self-identification is a product of rapidly changing circumstances under the Empire: the Latin names of his father and himself, the name of his city, and the name of the province to which it belonged. The village of 'Mamortha' or 'Mabartha' in Samaria had become the city of 'Flavia Neapolis' in 72/73, and its Greek coinage had begun under Domitian. (Josephus had evidently been anticipating when he mentioned Vespasian, on campaign in 68, as passing

---

4. *P. Dura,* no. 10.

5. Tatian, *Oration ad Graecos* 42. For the misunderstanding about his origins see, e.g., the edition and translation by M. Whittaker (1982), p. ix. On Tatian see further 12.3 below.

6. See the classic and often neglected article of Th. Nöldeke, "ΑΣΣΥΡΙΟΣ, ΣΥΡΙΟΣ, ΣΥΡΟΣ", *Hermes* 5 (1871), 443.

7. 12.4 below.

8. Justin, I *Apol.* 1.

'the place called Neapolis, but Mabartha by the natives [*epichōrioi*]'.)[9] 'Syria Palaestina' had replaced 'Judaea' as the name of the province only after the Bar Kochba war of 132–135.

Such a transformation raises in particularly acute form the question of what such an instantly created Greek city really 'was'. Justin is in fact unusual among writers in Greek, whether pagan or Christian, originating from the Near East, in reflecting so much of the local history, culture and languages of his native region: the Bar Kochba war and the destruction of Jerusalem; the nefarious careers of two magicians originating from Samaritan villages; the original Hebrew meanings of words like 'Jesus' and 'Israel'; and 'the language of the *Suroi*', or what we would call Aramaic.[10] In converting to Christianity Justin had of course, like everyone else, simultaneously embraced a historical tradition enshrined in texts originally written in a Semitic language; and this would have been so irrespective of his local origins. Nonetheless, as a man of pagan origin, born perhaps about AD 100, from the recently formed Greek city of Flavia Neapolis, he is aware of three separate non-Greek groups present in his native region: Jews, Samaritans and 'Syrians'.

Justin and the city from which he came thus represent a special case. But even in the case of much longer established 'Greek cities', their names, constitutions and formal public identities as Greek cities, while important facts in themselves, must leave open the question of the cultural roots and personal identity of their individual citizens, and their relation to the surrounding world of villages.

Even for the modest first step of surveying the public nature of the communities we find in the various sub-regions of the Near East, the evidence is often simply non-existent. We know for instance that at the northern limit of the region, in the western part of Commagene and just below the Taurus Mountains, there was a city which the geographer Ptolemy calls Germanikeia (Germanicia), and whose coins, also of the second half of the second century, label its inhabitants as 'Kaisareis Germanikeis'. It is normally located at present-day Maraš in southern Turkey. Its Latin-Greek name had clearly been given to it to honour a member of the Imperial house, perhaps Germanicus during his visit in AD 18/19, when Commagene had been temporarily part of the province of Syria. But Gaius (37–41), Claudius (41–54) and Nero (54–68) each had 'Germanicus' as part of their full official names, and the city might equally have been a royal foundation, by the last king of Commagene, Anti-

9. Josephus, *BJ* VII, 8, 1 (449). See Pliny, *NH* V, 14/69: 'Neapolis, quae antea Mamortha dicebatur . . .'.

10. I *Apol.* 31; 47 (Bar Kochba); 26 (magician from Samaritan villages); 33 ('Jesus'); *Dial.* 125 ('Israel'); *Dial.* 103 ('Satanas' in 'the language of the *Suroi*'). On Neapolis and Justin see further 10.3 below.

ochus IV (AD 38–72).[11] If so, it was a parallel to the succession of royal foundations by the Herodian dynasty. In each case both the conception that what should be created was a 'Greek city' and the Imperial names used to denote the new community are significant features of the social and cultural map of the whole region. But the almost complete lack of local evidence (other than a few coins) and even of passing allusions in literary sources means that we cannot attach any real meaning to the creation of the city of Germanicia in its more immediate context.[12] We are hardly much the wiser in learning from brief later quotations that the third-century Roman historian Asinius Quadratus, who like Cassius Dio wrote in Greek, referred to 'Germanikeia' in his *Parthica,* as he did to places and peoples in Armenia, to a village called Tarsa down the Euphrates from Samosata and to 'Thelamouza', a fort on the river.[13] At least some of his 'Parthian History' narrated the war fought by Lucius Verus in the 160s. We might therefore, if the work had survived, have gained some extra insight into routes and geography in this little-known area. But it is not until the writings of Theodoret, bishop of Cyrrhus in the fifth century, that we can find even passing allusions to places in this region which come from someone closely involved in it. Even in his case his only allusion to 'Germanikeia' simply records that it was a city on the borders of Cilicia, Syria and Cappadocia, whose bishop managed under Constantine to get himself improperly translated to the see of Antioch.[14]

Much the same indeed applies to Cyrrhus itself, a substantial Greek city first attested in the Hellenistic period. Not only was it the focus of a large and fertile area, which has never been explored for ancient remains, but, lying on the river Afrin which runs down to the plain of Antioch, it was on the route from Antioch to the Euphrates at Zeugma, and the station of a Roman legion as early as the reign of Tiberius. The surviving remains—of walls, the acropolis, bridges, a temple and two churches, as well as a vast theatre, 115 m in diameter—make clear that it was a considerable urban centre. But until we come to the writings of Theodoret himself, we have virtually no evidence to illuminate the social history of the city or the very extensive area of villages attached to it.[15] For our whole period, therefore, we have to admit that there

---

11. See 2.3–4 above.

12. On Germanikeia probably the most detailed treatment is the article in *RE* Supp. IX (1962), cols. 70–72 (unfortunately marked by a succession of elementary errors).

13. *FGrH* 97, F. 10, 11, 13.

14. Theodoret, *HE* II, 20.

15. For Cyrrhus see E. Frézouls, "Recherches historiques et archéologiques sur la ville de Cyrrhus", *AAS* 4/5 (1954–55), 89; "L'exploration archéologique de Cyrrhus", in J. Balty (ed.), *Apamée de Syrie: Bilan des recherches archéologiques, 1965–1968* (1969), 81, with excellent photographs of the site and the remains; "Cyrrhus et la Cyrrhestique jusqu'à la fin du Haut-Empire", *ANRW* II.8 (1977), 164.

is no means of access to the life and culture of this northern part of the Syrian region. It is not even possible to say what language, if any, other than Greek, was spoken there.

It must be accepted that even on the most superficial level the evidence of all kinds is inadequate, discontinuous and very erratically distributed. If the works of Josephus provide a unique density of narrative information, not just for Judaea but for the surrounding area and even for places like Antioch— or even a brief glimpse of Palmyra—there is no comparable view from any contemporary living in the second, third or fourth century. The nearest parallel is provided by the works of Eusebius of Caesarea. Nor do we have any continuous history of any one city until we come to the *Chronicle* of John Malalas, written in the sixth century; in intention a Christian world chronicle, it nonetheless comes close to being a history of his native Antioch. Yet its account of this period, which certainly contains a mass of valuable information, is also riddled with misconceptions, above all about the relation of the city to the Roman state and the Emperor.

Any attempt to grasp the nature of culture and social formations in the region has to depend largely on representations by contemporaries, whether in literature (and if so whether by outside observers or by insiders), in formal public documents such as inscriptions and coins (the most deliberate of all symbols of public identity), in perishable documents (of which the number discovered is now rapidly increasing) or as embodied in buildings and artefacts. It is useless to complain of the obvious inadequacy of the evidence available. For it lies in the nature of our access to the past (as indeed to the present) that it is wholly dependent on the means of information which happen to be available.

Pessimism is in any case unjustified. For, first, the evidence, though grossly inadequate, is nonetheless very extensive in total volume. Second, a vast range of evidence securely located in space and time is available to us. It can thus be set, with all due caution, against the varied and impressive landscapes of the region. However dependent we are on the accidents of the 'epigraphic habit', on the interests of our literary sources and on the further hazards of modern discovery and excavation, it is still possible both to compare the various sub-regions with each other and to see how the visible and surviving manifestations of the culture of each change over time. Of course we cannot always distinguish between a change of interest in our sources and a real change in society and culture. For instance, biographical portraits of fourth-century Christian hermits immediately take us down to social levels, and to geographical contexts in the countryside and the steppe, which earlier literature hardly touches. We will not always be able to tell whether the social patterns revealed were new or are only now revealed to us. Had there, for instance, always been 'Saracens' in the Negev, and thus well within the 'frontier' of the Empire as it appears on the map? Or had the process of 'beduinisation', which Werner Caskel suggested took place during the Imperial period in Arabia proper, beyond the frontier,[16] been matched by a growth of nomadism within? We can say only that they are visibly present, in a way not paralleled before, in the pages of Jerome's *Life* of the hermit Hilarion.[17] At all events we cannot deny the significance of the ascetic movement itself, which began in the first few decades of the fourth century and represented a revolution in Christian values. The hermits, by the nature of the symbolic postures which they adopted, were to be found by the faithful out on the fringes of settled and cultivated land, on mountains or on the edge of the steppe.[18] Thus Theodoret, in describing the career of a hermit of the early fourth century named Julianus, begins by describing the geography of Osrhoene: 'in this province there are many large and heavily populated cities, and a countryside which is largely inhabited, but also largely uninhabited and desert'; Julianus chose the edge of the desert.[19]

It is often just such a narrative of the establishment of a hermit which itself reveals the existence of the large villages which were characteristic of the whole region, and in some cases the significance of the rural cult-centres located near them. For instance, further on in his account of the hermits of Syria, Theodoret describes how Asterius, a young man of good family, founded what was to become a monastery 'in the countryside round Gindarus—this is a very large village *(kōmē)* placed under the control of Antioch'.[20] The place, modern Genderesse, situated near the river Afrin, was probably in origin an early Hellenistic settlement; but its only earlier significant mention in our sources comes from Strabo, reflecting the unsettled condition of the first century BC: to him Gindarus was a *polis*, the acropolis of the district called Cyrrhestice and a natural stronghold for robbers.[21] The large settlement *(polis* or *kōmē?)* of Gindarus had thus always been there. The complete silence about it is broken only thanks to the literary record of the two great historic changes which mark the limits of the period studied here: the

16. See W. Caskel, "The Beduinization of Arabia", in W. E. von Grünebaum (ed.), *Studies in Islamic Cultural History* (1954), 36.

17. Jerome, *Vita Hilarionis* 16 (*Vite dei Santi,* ed. C. Mohrmann, IV, 1975). See 10.4 and 11.4 below.

18. On this see P. Brown, "The Rise and Function of the Holy Man in Late Antiquity", *JRS* 61 (1971), 80, and "Town, Village and Holy Man: The case of Syria", in D. M. Pippidi (ed.), *Assimilation et résistance à la culture gréco-romaine dans le monde ancien* (1976), both reprinted in *Society and the Holy in Late Antiquity* (1982), 103–165.

19. Theodoret, *Philotheos Historia* II, 1–2. The language used is quite precise: ταύτης ἐσχατιὰν τῆς ἐρήμου καταλαβών.

20. Theodoret II, 9.

21. Strabo, *Geog.* XVI, 2, 8 (751).

Roman imposition of order over a large part of the world as known to Strabo, and the beginnings of the monastic movement. It is only the latter which takes us close to the rural world of the Near East. Theodoret again provides what is perhaps our only picture of a rural sanctuary in the territory of the little town of Gabala, which lay on the coast some 30 km south of Laodicea. Some 7 km from the town was a shrine for the worship of 'demons', whom the country-people had to appease with constant sacrifices to avoid harm to themselves, their asses, mules, cattle, sheep and camels. A hermit named Thalelaios then took up his station exactly there, nullified the power of the demons and was later assisted in destroying the *temenos* and substituting for it a shrine to some Christian martyrs.[22]

However many isolated insights into the life of the region we may be able to accumulate, we will not necessarily be able to construct out of them any meaningful history. Moreover, it has already been conceded that a true social and economic history of the region is still wholly out of reach. But at a different level three lines of approach are feasible. One has already been exploited: to survey the progressive stages by which large parts of the Near East came under Roman direct rule, and to raise some initial questions about the nature of the Roman impact on them. Second, there is the question which the story of the imposition of Roman rule itself serves to raise: the nature of the different political formations and social groupings which the Romans encountered. For instance, the political map of the Near East under Augustus was dominated by kingdoms. But by the early second century all those west of the Euphrates had disappeared. What was the significance of that disappearance, and did the kingdoms leave no legacy behind them, in terms of monuments, of traditions or of group identities or loyalties which might be capable of reactivation? If, as seems clear, they left very little trace, why was that so, and what other forms of communal or personal identity were more significant?

Third, even our fragmentary and erratic evidence can yield some meaning, or potential meaning, when different sub-regions are compared. Take for instance the linguistic history, or rather histories, of the region, involving the complex interplay of Greek, Latin and a series of Semitic languages. As elsewhere, Greek words were readily transliterated and absorbed into Latin, and Latin into Greek. But in the Near East we can see how Latin words could pass through Greek to be absorbed by transliteration into Semitic languages. So *centurio* could become *kenturiōn* in Greek, as in the New Testament (for instance in Mk 15, 39), and then QṬRYN' or QṬRYWN' in Palmyrene and QNṬRYN' in Nabataean;[23] *colonia* could become *kolōneia* in Greek,

22. Theodoret XXVIII, 1–5.
23. Palmyrene: M. G. Bertinelli Angeli, *Nomenclatura pubblica e sacra di Roma nelle epigrafi semitiche* (1970), 106; Nabataean: *CIS* II.1, no. 217, cf. Bowersock, *Roman Arabia*, 57.

and QLNY' or QLWNY' in Hebrew, Jewish Aramaic, Palmyrene and Syriac.[24]

The interplay of languages can also be viewed from quite different perspectives. One major question is whether the oral use of at least one Semitic language was in fact characteristic of all the sub-regions of the Near East without exception. In most areas it is beyond doubt. But some question must persist as regards Commagene, from Germanicia in the west to the Euphrates in the east, and over the north-Syrian tetrapolis, with the major early Hellenistic foundations of Antioch, Seleucia, Laodicea and Apamea.

What is certain at least is that these two areas have not so far produced any examples of formal public inscriptions (for instance, communal decrees, statue-bases, dedications or epitaphs) in a Semitic language. This fact might be regarded as insignificant (a mere product of a conventional association of Greek with the epigraphic habit), if it were not for the presence of such inscriptions in all the other areas; notably in the territory of Palmyra, which directly bordered on that of Apamea. If we cannot draw a map of the distribution of spoken languages, we certainly can draw provisional maps of the distribution of languages as inscribed.

Any such map would be a complex one, for it would have to allow for the co-existence of inscriptions in different languages—for example, Greek and Latin, especially in Berytus and Heliopolis, or Greek and one or more Semitic languages (as for instance in the ossuary-inscriptions from Judaea). But it would also have to reflect a different phenomenon, systematic inscriptional bilingualism, especially in Palmyra, where a large proportion of the inscriptions are in both Greek and Palmyrene. A few Palmyrene inscriptions are even trilingual, in Greek, Palmyrene and Latin.

The small but growing number of archives preserved on perishable materials (papyrus or parchment) cannot of course yet yield results which can be plotted on a linguistic map. But they do show that Greek and Syriac could both be used within the same archive; that a single archive (that of Babatha, covering the years from the 90s to the 130s) could contain documents in Nabataean, Aramaic and Greek; and that witnesses to documents in Greek could add their names in Nabataean or Aramaic or Syriac.

In the case of Babatha we are at an important moment of transition, for the archive covers the last decades of the kingdom of Nabataea and the first three decades of the Roman province of Arabia. There is a clear progression, from Nabataean under the kingdom to Aramaic and then (for the main text of each document) Greek in the provincial period. Precisely one of the more important questions concerns progression in time: did Roman rule tend to depress (or in certain areas forbid?) the public or official use of Semitic lan-

24. Millar, "Roman *Coloniae*", passim.

guages? Or does that question itself embody anachronistic assumptions about the nature and ambitions of the state? But here again comparisons between regions and across time will be suggestive.

Any results of such a comparison must, however, be tentative. For, first, we must allow for the presence of oral bilingualism; that is, the use of different languages in different contexts and to different interlocutors. Such a pattern is perfectly exemplified in Acts, when Paul, after speaking to the Roman tribune in Greek, is represented as turning to address the crowd 'in the *Hebrais dialektos*'.[25] It is only unfortunate that we cannot be certain whether Luke means to represent him as speaking in Hebrew or in Aramaic (or even whether he was fully aware of the difference).

Second, and more important, it remains to ask whether the Semitic languages employed in the East were either a necessary or a sufficient condition for the transmission of local cultures or of distinctive, conscious ethnic identities. Language is only one aspect of culture. There are any other questions to be asked about social and political structures, about cities and villages and about gods and temples in the different regions of the Near East. But here again, if our scattered evidence can be made significant at all, it is only by comparison between areas.

Such a survey and comparison can hardly fail to emphasise differences. At the same time these differences have to be seen within the context of two unifying factors. One is the progressive imposition of Roman direct rule, military occupation and taxation. Hence the survey will take the different sub-regions in roughly the order in which they seem to have been absorbed into the provincial system. Second, however strong the imprint of any local culture may have been, the dominant factor is the absorption of the region within the wider Greek world. Persons educated in the common stock of Greek literature and tradition, and writing in Greek, might come from Petra and Bostra, from Emmaus/Nicopolis or Flavia Neapolis, from Damascus, Emesa, Tyre, Apamea, Antioch, Samosata, Carrhae or Nisibis. An actual map of the origins of known writers in Greek, whether pagan or Christian, would of course be an absurdity. But at the level of a wider popular culture a map really can be drawn of those places which were the location of the named recurrent *agones*—musical, theatrical and athletic contests—which were so important a feature of the communal life of Greek cities. Once again comparison is significant: they are attested as far south as Gaza and Bostra, but no further; at Damascus but not at Palmyra; and up to, but not across, the Euphrates. In that very respect, the status of the public contests put on by its cities, all of the Near East clearly enjoyed no more than a secondary rank within the wider Greek world. By contrast, however, as a perpetual military or frontier zone

25. Acts 21, 37–40.

within the Roman Empire, it was open to an exceptional degree of Romanising influence, from the widespread conferment of the rank of *colonia* to the popularity of gladiatorial and wild-beast shows.

The social and cultural history of the Near East in this period is no simple matter of a conflict between 'Classical' and 'Oriental'. The various local cultures could find expression in ways which were strikingly different one from another. The most vigorous impulse to urbanisation and the creation and adornment of Greek cities was that due to a king of Judaea, a Jew by religion, the son of an Idumaean father and a Nabataean mother, who was also a Roman citizen. Within a century, or at the most two centuries, of Herod's death both pagan Greek philosophical ideas and Christian theology were to find expression in Syriac. But whatever metaphor we use for the interplay of cultures in this region, every aspect of society and culture was influenced both by Greek civilisation and by the progressive extension of Roman rule. When we have examined the different sub-regions of the Near East in comparison with each other, it will be necessary to ask whether the region as a whole should be seen as part of the 'Orient' or as part of the wider Graeco-Roman world.

THE TETRAPOLIS AND
NORTHERN SYRIA

7.1. THE GEOGRAPHICAL CONTEXT

The Roman *provincia* of Syria, as it was under Augustus, consisted of three different regions, of which one was an enclave physically separate from the others. The first was northern Syria, stretching across from the Mediterranean coast, and the two ports of Laodicea and Seleucia, through Antioch to the Euphrates. The second was the Phoenician coast, which in its northern part backed into the mountain-chain now called the Jebel Ansariyeh and in the south onto Mount Lebanon and then the hills of Galilee. Provincial territory seems indeed to have extended south not only to Ptolemais-Akko but beyond Mount Carmel to the small town of Dora.

Then, isolated beyond Anti-Lebanon was the ancient city of Damascus, and further south at least some of the cities of the Decapolis. All these regions could be characterised in general terms as areas dominated by Greek cities. Being now under Roman direct rule, they strongly contrasted with the kingdoms of Commagene to the north and Emesa on the upper Orontes, various dynasties whose territories were located on and around Mount Lebanon and Anti-Lebanon, the kingdom of Herod and the Nabataean kingdom with its capital at Petra. Whether there were more profound contrasts between these different zones, in language, culture or ethnic identity, remains to be seen.

As the military evolution of the *provincia* shows, the single Roman governor of this early period was firmly based in Antioch, and his legions were all also grouped in northern Syria. The Roman presence was thus shaped by the major city-foundations of Seleucus Nicator at the end of the fourth century BC: Seleucia, where Seleucus was buried, Laodicea, Antioch and Apamea. Any appreciation of the impact of Seleucus on the map of this area, where under the Persian Empire there seem to have been no major cities, has to begin from a classic article by Henri Seyrig, published in 1970, on his city-foundations.[1] Beroea (Aleppo) is also recorded as a foundation of Seleucus, and the map of the region was by now heavily marked by places whose names were borrowed either from Macedonia and its environs or from the Seleucid dynasty: so for instance the 'very large village' of Gindarus in the territory of Antioch;[2] Cyrrhus in the north, on the borders of Commagene; Seleucia (Zeugma) on the Euphrates, with another small 'Apamea' opposite it; or along the Orontes southwards from the major city of Apamea, Larissa, Epiphania, Arethusa, and beyond Emesa the small city of Laodicea ad Libanum.

Time and geography are crucial to any consideration of the nature of these places as they were in the Roman period. First, there is hardly the slightest evidence to suggest that in any one of these cities there was conscious continuity with the populations which had lived there before the Macedonian conquest. Even in the case of the ancient city of Aleppo, with its striking natural acropolis, strategically situated where a river (the Chalos, or modern Qweiq) crosses a route from the coast to the Euphrates, no more than a minor settlement seems to have existed in the Assyrian and Persian periods. In terms of its urban character, Seleucus' settlement there, now called Beroea, seems to have been a new foundation; and the streets of its central area retain to this day the chequer-board plan imposed then.[3] Of all the cities in this region only one, Bambyce/Manbog, which had come in the Hellenistic period to be called Hierapolis, also retained a non-Greek name in common use, and an identity which was in no way a product of Macedonian settlement.[4]

The fact that the major cities of this region were nearly all early-Hellenistic foundations in origin had two opposite consequences. On the one hand, as Greek cities they could never compare in antiquity, prestige or historical associations with those of Greece and the Aegean, or western Asia Minor—or even, as we will see, with those of Phoenicia. On the other hand, Greek and Macedonian settlement there was, by Augustus' reign, already some three centuries in the past. The time which had elapsed was easily long enough both for the cities to have developed the institutions, communal ceremonials and urban frameworks characteristic of the standard 'Greek city' and

1. H. Seyrig, "Seleucus I et la fondation de la monarchie syrienne", *Syria* 47 (1970), 290. For a full study of all the Hellenistic foundations in this area see J. D. Grainger, *The Cities of Seleukid Syria* (1990).

2. Ch. 6 above.

3. See J. Sauvaget, *Alep: Essai sur le développement d'une grande ville syrienne des origines au milieu du XIXᵉ siècle* (1941), 22ff.; 40ff.

4. 7.2 below.

for the Greek language and customs to have become rooted also in the rural areas around them. But the question of whether either of these developments had in fact occurred remains to be answered.

The other essential factor is geography. For instance, the visitor to the site of Apamea can see at a single moment a whole series of different geographical zones. First, there is the city itself, laid out on its plateau overlooking the Orontes from the east, within its 11-km circuit of Hellenistic and Roman walls. Below it is the flat, heavily cultivated valley of the Orontes. Beyond that, to the west, is the mountain-chain of the Jebel Ansariyeh dividing the valley from the sea. To the north lie the southernmost outcrops of the lime-stone massif, which stretches north to beyond the route between Antioch and Beroea, and carries the remains of innumerable late-Roman villages, the best preserved from anywhere in the ancient world. To the east a flat, rolling plain extends out into the steppe proper.

It is perhaps this direction which offers the least-se e problems of inter-pretation. For in the eyes of the best observer we have for the Augustan pe-riod, Strabo, Apamea was a frontier-zone next to nomadic territory. As we saw earlier, Strabo records how Caecilius Bassus, when besieged in Apamea in the 40s BC, had been allied with Alchaedamnus, king of a nomadic people called the Rhambaeans; and he continues by describing the region east of Apamea as 'the Paropotamia of the Arab *phylarchoi*', and that to the south as belonging to *skēnitai* ('tent-dwellers'), whom he explicitly describes as being similar to those in Mesopotamia. So too, in the eyes of Diodorus, writing a few decades earlier, Chalcis (Qinnesrin), to the north-east of Apamea, was situated on the borders of 'Arabia', but prosperous enough to be capable of supporting an army. This little-known place lay south-west of Beroea on the same river Qweiq (the ancient Chalos, or possibly Belos) which further south peters out into marshland.[5] This too was a fertile zone, bordering on the de-sert, and the location of a small city with no history in our period except the record of having been the native city of Iamblichus, the most important Neo-Platonist philosopher of the first half of the fourth century.[6] When Jerome retired to near there in the 370s to live the life of a hermit, it was still on the margins of the territory of the 'Saraceni'; and any communication had to be in a 'barbarian speech'—by which he is presumed to mean Syriac.[7]

That places like Chalcis and Apamea were, in terms of economy and social

5. Strabo: 2.1 above; Diodorus XXXIII, 4a. Pliny, *NH* V, 23/82, speaks of 'Seleucias . . . duas, quae ad Euphraten et quae ad Belum vocantur'. For the suggestion that 'Belos' was the, or an, ancient name of the river, see J. Ch. Balty, "Le *Belus* de Chalcis et les fleuves de Ba'al de Syrie-Palestine", in *Archéologie au Levant: Recueil R. Saidah* (1982), 287.

6. For the remains of the city, never excavated, see P. Monceaux and L. Bossé, "Chalcis ad Belum: Notes sur l'histoire et les ruines de la ville", *Syria* 6 (1925), 339.

7. Jerome, *Ep.* 5, 1; 7, 1–2; 15, 2. See J. N. D. Kelly, *Jerome* (1975), 46ff.

structures, outposts on the margins of the steppe is an important fact about them. But, as modern surveys have shown, the steppe too, as it was (or became) in the Roman period, was a mixed zone; by no means a true, empty desert, but crossed by tracks and dotted by small settlements.[8] The date and character of much of what has been reported still remains uncertain. For instance, in the marginal zone north-east of Hama/Epiphania surveyed by Jean Lassus, the remains suggest a much denser population in the Christian fifth and sixth centuries than in the first three to four.[9] It is reasonable to suppose that sedentary occupation did increase in the Roman period, without ever coming near to excluding the 'Saracens'.

That therefore leaves entirely open the question of the real character of such cities. Did they remain bastions of Greek language, culture and customs? Or were they places within which, or within whose immediate territories, quite different cultures co-existed? Before an answer can be attempted, we have to look towards another far more mysterious geographical zone, also visible from Apamea, the Jebel Ansariyeh. It is important to recall that not only the cities and settlements of the Orontes Valley but those of the coast were dominated by this mountain-chain. So too was Antioch, where Mount Silpius, the northernmost point in the chain, rises dramatically just behind the city to the south. At its southern end, in the territory of Arados and around the great sanctuary of Zeus at Baetocaece, areas which were to form part of 'Syria Phoenice' and will be treated along with other Phoenician places, it is possible to gain some fragmentary evidence about culture and social structures.[10] For the area in between, however, the evidence of literary sources, inscriptions and archaeology combines to leave an almost complete blank.

Yet this northern section of the chain was settled and cultivated, just as was the area round Baetocaece, some 1000 m above sea-level. Strabo's description makes this quite clear, as it does also the relation to the mountain-chain of both Laodicea on the coast and Apamea in the Orontes Valley:

> Then one comes to Laodiceia, situated on the sea. It is a city most beautifully built, has a good harbour, and has territory which, besides its other good crops, abounds in wine. Now this city furnishes the most of the wine to the Alexandreians, since the whole mountain that lies above the city and is possessed by it is covered with vines almost as far as the summits. And while the summits are at a considerable distance from Laodiceia,

---

8. See R. Mouterde and A. Poidebard, *Le limes de Chalcis: Organisation de la steppe en Haute Syrie romaine* I–II (1945).

9. J. Lassus, *Inventaire archéologique de la région au nord-est de Hama* I–II (1936).

10. 8.3 below.

sloping up gently and gradually from it, they tower above Apameia, extending up to a perpendicular height.[11]

Strabo thus gives a very clear (and correct) impression of how the mountain-chain rises gradually from the coast, in fact over a distance of some 30 km, to a line of summits overlooking the Orontes Valley, into which it then drops much more sharply. Without any archaeological survey, it is impossible to confirm his view that vines could be and were cultivated up to or near the crest itself, which reaches a maximum of some 1400 m, sloping down at the southern end to where the river Eleutheros (Nahr el-Kebir) cuts across between it and the northern fringes of Mount Lebanon.

Strabo might be thought to suggest, but does not explicitly say, that the wine-producing area stretching up behind Laodicea all belonged to the territory of that city. In default of any precise evidence it would indeed be natural to assume that the division of city-territories followed the natural line of the watershed. If so, we should imagine an extensive area of wine-growing villages in the gradually rising territory behind Laodicea; a clear parallel is provided by the temple of Baetocaece and its associated villages, lying just below the crest further south, which certainly belonged to the territory of Arados, which occupied an island off the coast.[12]

But if Laodicea, as a major Hellenistic foundation, possessed an extensive territory with a rural population living in villages (which itself cannot be certain), it is much less clear whether the same was true of the three very minor places which lay along the coast between Laodicea and Arados, namely Gabala, Paltos and Balaneae. All three seem to have functioned as *poleis*, and minted coins at least occasionally in the Imperial period; and, as we will see, by an all too typical paradox, an inscription from Balaneae gives what is perhaps the fullest list of city-magistracies which we happen to have from this whole region.[13]

That leaves open the question of whether the entire territory of the mountain-chain was, even in principle, divided between city-territories; and even if it were, whether a degree of real independence was not in practice enjoyed by the population there. The same may well have applied on the east side of the chain, where it may be that the narrower and steeper mountain-sides belonged to the territories of cities in the Orontes Valley. It is perhaps here that we should look for the rural temple, situated on a hill-slope *(klima)* in the

11. Strabo, *Geog.* XVI, 2, 9 (751–752).

12. See further 8.3 below. For once I would not be tempted to subscribe to an idea put forward by Jean Balty, namely the suggestion in "L'Apamène antique et les limites de la Syria Secunda", *Géog. admin.*, 41 on pp. 65ff., that Baetocaece was the temple in the territory of Apamea where Bishop Marcellus was killed in the late fourth century.

13. 7.4 below.

territory of Apamea, which Bishop Marcellus of Apamea was trying to destroy when he was attacked and killed in the 390s.[14] The episode belongs in a quite different phase of the relations of town and country; but it is not likely to have been the first occasion on which authorities from a city met violent resistance in this mountainous area.

If this almost unknown area were not formally divided among city-territories, it is possible that this is where we should look for the 'tetrarchia' of the Nazerini which Pliny the Elder says was across the river Marsyas (the Orontes or a tributary of it?) from Apamea.[15] But if so, we have no conception of the social structure or culture of this people, mentioned only here. It is best to admit that the mountainous hinterland of the cities both of the coast and of the Orontes Valley remains still an unknown quantity in any map of social and cultural identities in northern Syria. Nonetheless, some at least of the more than forty villages in the territory of Apamea whose names are known may have lain on the mountain-chain. We will look at them more closely when we examine the more immediate social and geographical contexts of the Greek cities.

So far as our evidence goes, in almost all cases 'Greek cities' is a correct and adequate description both of the formal public status and constitutions and of the social character of the major urban centres of northern Syria in the Roman period. There is almost nothing to suggest that any of them were conceived of by contemporaries as having a historical identity which went back before Alexander's conquests; though, once again, Josephus' comment that the *epichōrioi* still used the name 'Hama' for Epiphania is a hint that this question may have been more complex than we realise.[16] Equally uncertain are the implications of the recently published bilingual Jewish ossuary-inscription from Jerusalem, naming someone as Aristōn in Greek and 'RSṬWN 'PMY—'the Apamean'—in Hebrew; he can hardly be unconnected with the 'RSṬWN who appears in the *Mishnah* as bringing first-fruits from Apamea (M'PMY'), identified as being 'in Syria' (BSWRY').[17] But whether we should imagine any other groups, in Apamea or its territory, as having spoken a Semitic language remains unclear. Contemporaries do not seem in general to have regarded citizens of these places as marked by any distinctively 'Syrian' characteristics or culture. We cannot find in our period comments comparable to what Socrates, the Church historian, says of Severianus, bishop of Gabala in the early fifth century: 'though thought to have had some education, he

14. Sozomenus, *HE* VII, 15, 11–15. See Balty in n.12 above.

15. Pliny, *NH* V, 19/81: 'Coele habet Apameam Marsya amne divisam a Nazerinorum tetrarchia'.

16. Ch. 1 above.

17. T. Ilan, "New Ossuary Inscriptions from Jerusalem", *SCI* 11 (1991–92), 149, no. 1.

did not speak Greek entirely clearly, but even when speaking Greek sounded Syrian'.[18] Whether this reference to a distinctive 'Syrian' accent in Greek is meant to imply that Severianus also spoke Syriac is not at all clear. In any case, by Severianus' time we are again in a different epoch. For perhaps the most clearly marked and distinctive fact about the linguistic history and linguistic map of the Near East in the Roman period is that, whatever languages or dialects may have been *spoken,* neither Syriac nor any other Semitic language was used on inscriptions in northern Syria until the late Roman period. As a language and script for public purposes, Syriac was already in use along the Euphrates and in Osrhoene. But it spread westwards only in the fourth century at the earliest, and more certainly in the fifth and sixth.[19] It cannot be stressed too clearly that from northern Syria, the core of the original Roman province and of the eventual 'Syria Coele', not a single document or coin using any Semitic language can be securely dated before the death of Constantine. Nothing could be more misleading than the idea that 'Syriac' is characteristic of the area which the Romans called 'Syria'. Or so it seems; like all negative generalisations, this one could be upset by a single counter-example.

7.2. LOCAL CULT-CENTRES: HIERAPOLIS AND DOLICHE

Even if, as we have seen, all the public documents of this region are in Greek (or Latin), that does not prove that every urban centre there was unambiguously a 'Greek city', or that questions do not remain open about the culture of each one of them. In one case in particular, Hierapolis, contemporaries conceived of a city as exhibiting a distinctively Syrian character: 'Bambyce which is (also) called by another name, Hierapolis, but by the *Syri* Mabog; there the monstrous goddess Atargatis is worshipped, but called Derceto by the Greeks'.[1]

As regards the identity of the place, the form 'Bambyce' is in fact not very common. But the Semitic name, in the form 'Mabog', 'Manbog' or 'Mambog', which is still in use (Manbij), is well attested in contemporary sources. 'Manbogaios' appears as a name in Greek, as does the adjective MNBGYT'

---

18. Socrates, *HE* VI, 11, 3.

19. Examples (not claimed to be exhaustive) of relatively early dated Syriac inscriptions from west of the Euphrates include *IGLS* II, no. 310 (trilingual with Greek and Arabic), from Zebed/Zabad, some 70 km south-east. of Aleppo, AD 511; no. 337, AD 508/509, from Mektebeh, some 45 km south-south-east. of Aleppo; Littman, *PAES* IV B (1934), 4, no. 4, AD 433–434; 7, no. 7, AD 473–474 (*IGLS* II, no. 553); 10, no. 11, AD 441–442; 39, no. 50, AD 491–496, all from the limestone massif. Littman, *AAES* IV. *Semitic Inscriptions* (1904), 47ff., argued that nos. 22–23, also from Zebed/Zabad, belong to the fourth century.

1. Pliny, *NH* V, 19/81.

in Nabataean;[2] and a remarkably frustrating Syriac text, *The Oration of Meliton the Philosopher,* a Christian apology perhaps written in the early third
century, briefly talks of the cult of Nebo and Hadaran at MBWG. Alas this
text, far from producing an authentic 'insider's' view of a native 'Syrian' cult,
offers only further confusion: the image of Nebo there, it says, was really that
of 'Orpheus, a Thracian magus' ('RPWS MGWŠ' TRQY'), while Hadaran's
was that of 'Zaradusht, a Persian magus' (ZR'DWŠT MGWŠ' PRSY').[3] The
passage may serve as a salutary warning as to the impossibility of arriving at
a 'true' definition of the nature of Near Eastern deities.

Almost nothing remains of the city of Mabog/Hierapolis, with its temple
of the 'Syrian Goddess', situated some 75 km north-east of Aleppo/Beroea,
and some 24 km from the Euphrates, which forms a wide arc round it. The
city was thus on one of the main routes from Antioch, via Beroea and Batnae,
to the Euphrates, and it was from there that the Emperor Julian wrote his last
known letter, on his march into Persian territory in 363. By then it was a
regular city with gates (and hence presumably walls), and porticoes lining the
streets.[4] Once again we should imagine it as an urban centre in a cultivated
and populated landscape, lying well within the Fertile Crescent. Julian says
nothing about the place; but he does describe the small stopping-place of Batnae, some 40 km to the west, as lying in a thickly wooded plain with groves
of young cypresses, and containing an official rest-house *(basileia)* in a rich
garden.[5] As with so many other regions, neither literary evidence nor survey
nor excavation enables us to gain any more precise impression of the area.

The few and fragmentary Greek inscriptions from Hierapolis are just
enough to confirm that in the Imperial period the place had the basic elements
of a city constitution, a council and an assembly (*boulē* and *dēmos*).[6] But even
the bronze coins which the city minted between the reigns of Trajan (98–117)
and Philip (244–249) gave a very special place to the goddess to whom the
community owed its identity. The coins were stamped on the obverse with
the name of the Emperor and on the reverse with 'Of (the) Syrian Goddess of
the Hieropolitans'; and some, though not all, show the goddess seated on
a throne, with a lion standing on either side.[7]

2. See G. Goossens, *Hiérapolis de Syrie* (1943), 8ff.: in Nabataean, e.g., *CIS* I, no. 422
(Petra); in Greek, e.g., Le Bas-W., no. 2554–2555 (Halbun, on Anti-Lebanon, north of
Damascus).

3. W. Cureton, *Spicilegium Syriacum* (1855), 22ff., in Syriac section. The passage relating
to Mabog is translated on pp. 44–45 of the English section. On this work see briefly 12.5 and
App. C below.

4. Ammianus XXIII, 2, 6.

5. Julian, *Ep.* 58 (Loeb); 98 (Bidez-Cumont).

6. See *IGLS* I, no. 231.

7. *BMC Syria*, 139ff.: ΘΕΑΣ ΣΥΡΙΑΣ ΙΕΡΟΠΟΛΙΤΩΝ. For the seated goddess, e.g., Pl.
XVII, 14.

That both the place and its (now) chief deity were represented in this way was the result of an evolution which (for once) can be traced over centuries. In essence the cult there took on many Greek aspects, while remaining, in the eyes of all observers, distinctively exotic and non-Greek; and a female deity, Atargatis, or 'the Syrian Goddess' in Graeco-Roman terms, came to be emphasised more and more at the expense of her male consort, Hadad.[8] Here, as elsewhere, it is futile to try to define exactly what the deity, or her cult, really 'was'. In attempting to do so modern observers have a painful tendency to show no more logical self-awareness than ancient ones, and to forget that ancient deities 'were' whatever different things observers or worshippers chose to regard them as. Take for instance Plutarch, recording the unfavourable omens which had attended Crassus' invasion of Parthian territory in 53 BC. One of Crassus' errors had been to rob this temple of its treasures: 'And the first warning sign came to him from this very goddess, whom some call Aphrodite and others Hera, while others still regard her as the natural cause which supplies from moisture the beginnings and seeds of everything, and points out to mankind the source of all blessings.'[9]

It is more to the point that the place had indeed existed as a cult-centre before the Macedonian conquest, and had acquired its Greek name ('Holy City') in the Hellenistic period. Coins from there of Alexander's time name Alexander in Aramaic ('LKSNDR) and show a priest in a conical hat and long tunic standing at an altar: he is named as Abdhadad ('servant of Hadad'), 'priest (at) Manbog' ('BDHDD KMR MNBG), '(who) resembles Hadaran his lord' (ZY YDMN BHDRNN B'LH). Strictly speaking, these coins represent the latest evidence from this place which is expressed in a Semitic language, though a papyrus of 156 BC from Egypt happens to record a slave who was 'by race a Syrian from Bambyke', and who was 'tattooed on the wrist with two barbarian letters', evidently Aramaic.[10]

By the second century BC inscriptions from Delos show that the place had acquired its Greek name, Hierapolis (or Hieropolis, which is also used), and that the cult was now thought of as that of a divine couple, Hadad and Atargatis.[11] It was in this Hellenised form that the cult gained a widespread currency, and Atargatis was often labelled, for Graeco-Roman worshippers, as 'the Syrian Goddess', even on coins of the city itself. As we have seen in the case of Plutarch, varying interpretations of her nature could be offered. Our

8. For this process, rapidly summarised here, see Goossens, op. cit. (n.2 above); H. J. W. Drijvers, *Cults and Beliefs at Edessa* (1980), 85ff.; Millar, "Hellenistic Syria", 126–127.

9. Plutarch, *Crassus* 17 (Loeb trans., keeping Greek names).

10. *P. Zenon*, no. 121; see G. Vaggi, "Siria e Siri nei documenti dell'Egitto greco-romano", *Aegyptus* 17 (1937), 29. For these early coins see H. Seyrig, "Le monnayage de Hiérapolis de Syrie à l'époque d'Alexandre", *RN* 13 (1971), 11.

11. Ph. Bruneau, *Recherches sur les cultes de Délos* (1970), 466ff.

entire evidence for the interpretation of the cult consists of retrospective analyses of something conceived of as exotic and distinctively local.[12] If we were to grasp more fully the nature of the cult as it was *in situ,* we would need far more archaeological and other evidence from Hierapolis itself than we actually have. But the one important item of such evidence does not relate explicitly to the worship of 'the Syrian Goddess' or of her consort. This is an extremely striking bas-relief sculpture in basalt, of which one of the two surviving parts was found at Manbij, and which represents a typically 'Syrian' priest, dressed in a long tunic falling to the ankles, and bound by a girdle; he is wearing a conical hat topped by a crescent and with a tiara tied round it. The figure is represented in the act of making a libation on a small altar, and a Greek inscription in verse identifies him as a High Priest *(archiereus):*

> Achaios has placed here (a portrait of) the incomparable High Priest Alexandros, noble in friendship, making a libation while he prays to the blessed gods that they may preserve his native city in good order *(eunomia).*[13]

The relief seems to date to the middle of the first century BC, and thus to be roughly contemporary both with the royal sculptures of Commagene to the north and with the first intrusion on this area by the Romans. The 'blessed gods' worshipped by a High Priest at Hierapolis will surely have been Hadad and Atargatis. If so, the relief is sufficient to show at least some elements of continuity between the cult as it was in the fourth century and what is portrayed in the famous account by Lucian of Samosata in *On the Syrian Goddess,* written in the middle of the second century AD. If nothing else, the priestly costume of a long tunic and conical hat had survived the centuries unchanged: 'They (the priests) all wear white clothing and have a pointed cap on their heads. A different *archiereus* is appointed each year, and he alone wears purple, and (his head) is bound with a gold tiara.'[14] This is only one of many concrete details of the temple, the cult and the priests which Lucian reveals; most cannot be explored here. At the same time we should not forget the ambiguities inherent in this text. On the one hand Lucian is producing a deliberate linguistic parody of Herodotus as a vehicle for this portrayal of an exotic cult for a wider Greek readership. On the other hand he explicitly identifies himself as an 'Assyrios'. The reader would not, however, know from that which Lucian's home-city was, or even from what region he came; it is

12. For the best account see M. Hörig, "Dea Syria-Atargatis", *ANRW* II.17.3 (1984), 1536. See also H. J. W. Drijvers *s.v.* "Dea Syria", *LIMC* III.1 (1986), 355.

13. See R. A. Stucky, "Prêtres syriens II: Hiérapolis", *Syria* 53 (1976), 127. The inscription is *SEG* XXVI, no. 1634.

14. Lucian, *de dea Syria* 42. See esp. R. A. Oden, *Studies in Lucian's De Syria Dea* (1977); C. P. Jones, *Culture and Society in Lucian* (1986), 41ff.

indeed only in his *How to Write History* that he concretely identifies Samosata as his native city. The question of what Lucian's origin meant belongs elsewhere;[15] but for the reader of *On the Syrian Goddess* what matters is that the author is simultaneously representing himself as an Oriental 'insider'; adopting the well-known pose of the amazed, naive traveller; and putting a distance between the cult described and both himself and the reader.

Only a few points from this portrait can be emphasised here. Lucian duly underlines the antiquity of the cult. But what he can offer by way of its legendary origins is a selection of alternative Greek myths: Deucalion and the flood; Semiramis of Babylon (a figure in *Greek* semi-historical writing about the Near East); Cybele and Attis; or Dionysus. As for the actual construction of the temple, he attributes it to Stratonice, 'the wife of the king of the Assyrians' (in fact Seleucus Nicator), of whom he relates a short historical novella. But the temple which he actually describes must have been built (or reconstructed) in the Roman period, for it is a Roman-style temple on a podium, reached by steps from the front.[16]

In setting the temple in context as something distinctively 'Syrian', it is striking that the parallel cases of ancient and exotic cults which Lucian gives are all in Phoenicia: Herakles (Melqart) at Tyre; Astarte (or perhaps rather Europa) at Sidon; an unidentified Phoenician (or Egyptian) cult at Heliopolis; Aphrodite and Adonis (or perhaps Osiris) at Byblos; and the temple of Aphrodite at the source of the river Adonis near Byblos—in fact the sanctuary at Aphaca whose closure was to be ordered by Constantine.[17] It is only a seeming paradox that it is in general those sites which had a long-established place, or image, in Greek culture which were to be most clearly associated in the Roman Empire with ancient cults which had a strongly local colouring. The truly distinctive architecture and iconography of Palmyra, Dura-Europos, the Hauran or Nabataea had no place in this mental map.

Lucian does twice stress from how many different regions or peoples, some outside the Empire, offerings came to the temple: from 'Arabia', the Phoenicians, the Babylonians, Cappadocia, the Cilicians and the 'Assyrioi'; and later Egyptians, Medes, Armenians and Babylonians.[18] As we have seen, the cults of 'Mabog' are in fact reflected in a work preserved in Syriac and probably written at Edessa;[19] and one of the most specific confirmations of the iconography of Hierapolis as reported by Lucian comes from Dura-Europos.[20] For a limestone relief found there represents an enthroned male

15. 12.3 below.
16. *de dea Syria* 24.
17. *de dea Syria* 3–9; 5.3 above.
18. *de dea Syria* 10; 32.
19. Text to n.3 above, and see further below.
20. See H. Seyrig, "Les dieux d'Hiérapolis", *Syria* 37 (1960), 233.

and an enthroned female deity seen from the front, with on either side of the former two small bulls, and of the latter two somewhat dispirited-looking lions. In between them is represented a pole topped by a crescent, with three disks fixed to its upper part, and above them a cross-bar, from each end of which two strips of cloth are hanging. The correspondence is too close for these not to be the cult images from the inner chamber *(thalamos)* of the temple at Hierapolis, as Lucian describes them: 'Zeus' seated on bulls and 'Hera' on lions, and in between them a cult-object *(xoanon)* bearing images of other deities.[21] The *Assyrioi*, Lucian says, themselves have no word for it, but call it *sēmeion*. Well they might, for what the object represented at Dura most closely resembles is in fact a Roman military standard, for which Greeks used the word *sēmeion*.

What Lucian says must imply that the *Assyrioi* of Hierapolis might have had a native word for this object, but in fact did not. Although there are no Semitic-language inscriptions or literature from Hierapolis in this period, we could reasonably take what Lucian says as a hint that Syriac or Aramaic was in use. The divine names 'Hadad' and 'Atargatis' must also have persisted, although Lucian speaks only of 'Zeus' and 'Hera'. But the iconography of the main cult-objects of the city now included a third element, the *sēmeion*, represented also on some coins of the city,[22] of a form which could only have been borrowed in the context of Roman military domination. Moreover, the Greek term used to describe it evidently passed as a loan-word into Syriac/Aramaic. What is more, it gave rise to a new myth there. For Lucian's *sēmeion* must be the origin of the female deity from Mabog, 'Simi the daughter of Hadad' (SYMY BRTH DHDD), mentioned in the Syriac *Oration of Meliton the Philosopher*, probably written in the early third century.[23] As was noted earlier, the fact of having been written in Syriac did not necessarily prevent Christian analyses of pagan cults in Syria from representing the same concatenation of confused and incompatible elements as Lucian himself reveals.

Nonetheless, the Greek name which the city had acquired in the Hellenistic period, like the iconography of its coins, expressed the fact that the identity of the place depended on that of the goddess who steadily became its best-known deity. It is perhaps Strabo, in describing the route from Syria to Babylonia, who (in spite of some geographical confusions) best expresses the identity of the place: 'Bambyke, which they also call . . . Hierapolis, in which they worship the Syrian Goddess, Atargatis'.[24]

21. *de dea Syria* 31–33.
22. See H. Seyrig, "Bas-relief des dieux d'Hiérapolis", *Syria* 49 (1972), 104.
23. See text to n.3 above and (briefly) 12.5 and App. C below.
24. Strabo, *Geog.* XVI, 1, 27 (748). In fact Strabo seems to be under the impression that Hierapolis was east of the Euphrates and was to be identified with Edessa. This hopeless confusion has been omitted from the quotation.

None of the other cities of northern Syria appeared in this light to contemporaries, if only, as we have seen, because they were known to have been Hellenistic foundations. But the point that continuity with a pre-Hellenistic past might most probably be represented by cult-places, and cult-practices, is relevant for them too. Thus for instance one of the very few reflections of the local culture of the area round Cyrrhus is a relief from Kilis representing a priest in this same costume—a conical hat and long tunic—making a sacrifice on an altar.[25] How we are to understand the partially surviving representation of an enormous bull standing before him is unclear. But at least the person and his deity are identified by a Greek inscription. As Cumont noted, the mixture of Latin, Greek and Semitic names here perfectly mirrors the social evolution characteristic of the Roman period: the deity concerned is the god Bel, the priest *(hiereus)* is 'Gaius', and he lists also his wife Emeous and his children Antiochos, Epigenēs, Dioklēs, Markos, Petrōnios, Gaios, Thēdion and Marthas. The relief and its inscription are a small sign of a world to which we might in principle gain more access if this large region (which lies along the Turkish-Syrian border) were to be thoroughly surveyed.

In the area to the north of that, in the region which in the earlier first century BC probably formed part of the kingdom of Commagene, there is just one cult-site where the iconography of the local deity shows an unmistakable derivation from the remote pre-Hellenistic past. This is Doliche, modern Dülük, a village a few kilometres north of Gaziantep. It lies almost due west of Zeugma, which, as we have seen, was almost certainly taken over by the Romans as part of the province immediately in 31 BC.[26] The region where Doliche lies may thus also have become provincial at the same time; its political and social history shares the complete uncertainty which characterises all of the westerly part of Commagene, stretching up to the Amanus and Taurus mountains. But it is at any rate certain that Doliche was provincial by the later 50s AD, when a Greek dedication there to 'Theos Dolichēnos' was dated by the fourth year of the rule of Nero. The roughly carved basalt altar on which the inscription is carved again shows a priest in a conical hat and long tunic; he is named as 'Ennaios son of Barnanaios'. This inscribed relief is enough also to show that Doliche was indeed the rural cult-centre from which (for reasons which seem wholly obscure) the worship of 'Theos Dolichēnos', or in Latin frequently 'Iuppiter Optimus Maximus Dolichenus', was to be spread, largely as it seems by soldiers, all over the Empire.[27]

As is always the case in such instances, the very fact that the deity was

25. F. Cumont, *Etudes Syriennes* (1916), 257ff.

26. 2.1 above.

27. See J. Wagner, "Neue Denkmäler aus Doliche", *Bonn. Jahrb.* 182 (1982), 133; M. Hörig and E. Schwertheim, *Corpus Cultus Iovis Dolicheni (CCID)* (1987), no. 2 and Taf. I.

transposed into so many different environments makes the already difficult question of his 'real' nature infinitely more complex. For, as in the other cases, his worshippers could literally make of him what they would. Thus one worshipper at Aquileia actually constructed a composite deity 'Iuppiter O(ptimus) M(aximus) D(olichenus) Heliopolit(anus)'.[28] In spite of all the caution which is essential, one feature of his iconography is undeniable: the characteristic representation of the 'Zeus' or 'Iuppiter' of Doliche as a bearded male figure, wearing a hat and girdled tunic, standing on the back of a bull and wielding an axe in his right hand, is found not only on objects of the Imperial period from the region of Dülük (though none is explicitly labelled), but also, with many variations, on representations of the deity (a number of which *are* explicitly labelled) throughout the Empire.[29] A particularly fine example is the relief-carving dedicated in AD 183 to 'Iuppiter Optimus Maximus Dolichenus' at the 'Dolichenum' on the Aventine in Rome by Aquila son of Barhadad.[30]

What is significant about this iconography is, however, the fact that it is an unmistakable borrowing from relief-carvings of a deity found in the region of Gaziantep and dating to the neo-Hittite period (1200–700 BC). Comparable representations of a deity standing on a bull are known from both Cappadocia and Mesopotamia, from an even earlier period, around the beginning of the second millennium.[31] It cannot be proved that there was an actual continuity of cult on the site of Doliche, or of beliefs about the nature of the deity (though equally neither can be disproved). The evidence, all from the first three centuries AD, would indeed be compatible with the idea that this form of divine representation was literally borrowed under the Empire from surviving Hittite reliefs which were still visible in the area. Beyond that, we cannot go, just as we know nothing of the shrine itself, or of Doliche, which in the second century briefly minted coins with the legend 'of the *Dolichaioi*', and hence must have counted as a *polis*.[32] The cultural and religious history of this region remains to be explored.

28. Hörig and Schwertheim, op. cit., 290, no. 447.

29. For local examples, see Hörig and Schwertheim, op. cit., nos. 5–6—but with two figures standing on bulls and a third wielding the axe; 8, 9, 10, 11, 18, 19, 21, 22, 28. For explicitly labelled examples from elsewhere see, e.g., no. 62 (Troesmis), 90 (Moesia Superior), 201 (Kömlöd, Hungary), 207, 217, 222, 242, etc.

30. Hörig and Schwertheim, no. 363, Taf. LXXV.

31. For the neo-Hittite reliefs from the region of Gaziantep see I. Temizsoy, *Gaziantep Museums* (1989), figs. 54–55 (where the deities have all the other characteristics mentioned, but are not standing on bulls). For the early parallels from a much wider area see Hörig and Schwertheim, op. cit. (n.27), on no. 5 (a votive triangle from Dülük). Whether we should think of a unitary concept of a 'weather-god' is another question. See H. W. Haussig, *Götter und Mythen im Vorderen Orient* (1965), 135ff.

32. *BMC Syria*, 114.

7.3. VILLAGES AND RURAL TEMPLES

As has been stressed many times, we can in fact assume, in general terms, that all the major cities which dominate any modern map of the Roman Near East were each individually no more than the focal point, and probably the largest single concentration of population, in an area filled with villages, which may often have been the main social units by which people identified themselves. So, for instance, far away in Aquincum (Budapest), a 'Syrian from the region of Doliche' records in the year 228 the name of his native village.[1] But there are, within northern Syria, only two overlapping regions where we may gain any impression of this world of villages: the territory of Apamea, and the limestone massif which lay at the heart of the region and included parts of the territories of Antioch, Apamea, Chalcis and Beroea. The boundaries between city territories are not always clear, and may not have been very important, given the size and relative independence of many villages. But we know for instance from the Emperor Julian's last letter that Litarbae (Terib), on the road between Antioch and Beroea, was 'a village of Chalcis', some 20 km away,[2] while Immae (Yenisehir) and Gindarus (Genderesse on the river Afrin) were in the territory of Antioch.[3]

If we look first at the territory of Apamea, three important items of evidence stand out.[4] First, the Roman census of the *civitas Apamenorum*, conducted around AD 6, already recorded 117,000 people.[5] Even if (as is not likely) this included every inhabitant, free or slave, of either sex and of any age, and had succeeded in reaching every centre of habitation in the territory, it still implies a very large population living in villages as well as those living within the walls of the city itself. In reality it must imply a total population of the territory of several hundred thousand. Second, it seems almost certain that the boundaries of Palmyrene territory which successive Roman governors marked out at Khirbet el-Bilaas were those bordering on Apamean territory;[6] if so, that territory stretched some 100 km into the steppe in a southeasterly direction. Third, a collection of the evidence from inscriptions and literary sources has yielded the names of over forty villages of the Roman Imperial period. Almost all of these names are Semitic; the considerable Graeco-Roman influence on the toponymy of the Near East made only a very

---

1. *CIL* III, no. 3490.

2. Julian, *Ep.* 58 (Loeb) = 98 (Bidez/Cumont).

3. 4.2 and ch. 6 above.

4. For the discussion of the territory of Apamea and the villages (but inexplicably with no map), see J. Balty and J.-C. Balty, "L'Apamène antique et les limites de la Syria Secunda", *Géog. admin.*, 41.

5. 2.2 above.

6. 2.2 above.

limited impact at village level. But whether we should conclude that the in-habitants of these villages continued to *speak* a Semitic language is quite an-other matter. The question must be left open. It may be significant that there are as yet no Semitic-language inscriptions from the region, while there are several hundred Greek (and some Latin) ones.[7]

As it happens, the known names of villages hardly depend on these local inscriptions but depend almost entirely either on inscriptions left by people from Apamean territory in other parts of the Roman Empire or (as so often) on later Christian narratives. These inscriptions put up in other provinces are, however, extremely significant, precisely because of their tendency to identify the person by his village. The best-known example is a Greek inscription from Trier which reads: 'Here lies Azizos son of Agrip(p)a, a Syrian of the village *(kōmē)* of the Kaprozabadaioi, in the territory of Apamea'.[8] 'Kaprozabadaioi' clearly incorporates both the root KPR ('village') and a name cognate with 'Zebedee'; the local name thus includes two different terms meaning 'village'. In most cases all that we can tell is that the person saw his village as his primary means of identification, even when in far distant parts. But occasion-ally we can come closer to a localisation: for instance Theodoret records that in the late fourth century one Markianos founded two monasteries in 'a very large and well-populated village' called Nikertas, which was situated only 4–5 km from Apamea. Only literary narratives, all of a later period, allow us even glimpses of the way of life or the social structures of these villages: one was that of the 'Maratocupreni' near Apamea, whom Ammianus describes as noted brigands in the 360s.[9] But nothing enables us to envisage the degree of self-government or the functioning of local cult-centres among the very large village populations which surrounded Apamea. It can only be reiterated that any conception of what such a city or community (the '*civitas* of the Apa-meni', in Roman terms) 'was' must take into account the population of the varied geographical zones, stretching far out into the steppe, by which it was surrounded.

The situation is very different with the villages of the limestone massif, sur-veyed in the great work of Georges Tchalenko.[10] The massif embraces a series of modest limestone ranges, with fertile interior valleys, stretching north-

7. For the known inscriptions see esp. *IGLS* IV (1955), nos. 1311–1997.

8. *IG* XIV, no. 2558 = N. Gauthier, *Recueil des inscriptions chrétiennes de la Gaule* I (1975), no. 10: Ἐνθάδε κῖται Ἄζιζος Ἀγρίπα Σύρος κώ(μης) Καπροζαβαδαίων, ὅρων Ἀπαμέων. The in-scription is probably of the fifth century.

9. Theodoret, *Hist. Relig.* IV, 5; *Ep.* 119. Ammianus XXVIII, 2, 11–14.

10. G. Tchalenko, *Villages antiques de la Syrie du Nord: Le massif du Bélus à l'époque romaine* I–III (1953–1958).

wards from near Apamea and rising up to the east of the Orontes and the plain of Antioch, to shade off imperceptibly eastwards into the steppe itself and the plains around Beroea. Unfortunately for present purposes, the immense significance of this region belongs chiefly to a later period: it lies above all in the still-standing remains of innumerable villages of the late Roman period, up to the Islamic conquest, and in its central importance in the history of monasticism, symbolised above all by the church of Qalaat Seman, built in the fifth century around the base of the pillar of the famous hermit Symeon Stylites.

The incomparable work of Tchalenko, carried out almost single-handedly, consisted of a survey, recording and analysis of the standing remains. It inevitably left essentially untouched the question of the evolution of settlement here, and its nature in the first three centuries AD. As for this area in the period before the death of Constantine, we have three means of access. The first is from the only excavation so far carried out at any of the villages, at Dehes on the Jebel Barisha, a range which lies at the heart of the massif, and just to the south of the Antioch–Beroea road.[11] These excavations suggested that there was some habitation already in the Hellenistic period, and modest construction in the first three centuries. But major expansion belonged to the third and fourth centuries and after. They also confirmed Tchalenko's view of the importance of olive-growing in this region (twenty-one presses were found around the village), while modifying it in showing that animal husbandry was also practised. On this evidence the villages visible today are likely to represent a more developed phase than those of the earlier period.

Such villages certainly existed, however. For our second means of access is the Greek inscriptions of the period, and above all those put up under the tetrarchy to mark the boundaries between villages.[12] Those which are known come from the Jebel Seman, in the north-east of the region.[13] They record, for instance, the village *(kōmē)* of the Kaprokēroi; that of the Kaproliaboi (the present-day Kafr Lab); the *ep(oikia?)*—estate—of Zaero (probably the modern Baziher); another where the full name is lost; and the *ep(oikia?)* of Kaperou[.]amis(?). The missing name might be that of Kaper Nabou (modern Kafr Nabo), mentioned on a building-inscription of 207/208. Here too we sometimes find that the Semitic root KPR has become absorbed in a group-name, and that the Greek word *kōmē* has then been added.

There is no need to accumulate more of the evidence from these and other

---

11. See the long report by J.-P. Sodini, G. Tate, B. Bavant, S. Bavant, J.-L. Biscop and D. Orssaud, "Déhès (Syrie du Nord), Campagnes I–III (1976–1978)", *Syria* 57 (1980), 1. For this region see also I. Peña, P. Castellano and R. Fernández, *Inventaire du Jébel Baricha* (1987).

12. See 5.2 above, and for full texts App. A.

13. See H. Seyrig, "Bornes cadastrales du Gebel Sim'ān", in Tchalenko, op. cit. III, 6ff. For Kaper Nabou, *IGLS* II, no. 359.

inscriptions, almost all in Greek, with occasional epitaphs in Latin. They are enough to show that a rural population was there, in this part of the massif at least, by the end of the third century, living in places typically known as 'village of the (group name)'. The alternative expression, 'estate of', clearly seems to suggest actual possession of an area by a landowner; and exactly this is attested later by Theodoret, in recounting how a city-councillor *(bouleutēs)* of Antioch came to a village of which he was the owner *(despotēs)* to collect the revenues due him.[14]

As for the culture of this rural area, the personal names used show the same mixture of Semitic, Greek and Latin elements as elsewhere. Again there are no Semitic inscriptions of this period. Here, as elsewhere in northern Syria, the known Syriac inscriptions are all Christian, and belong in the fifth century and after.[15] But the earliest known Christian inscription in Greek dates to 341/342 and comes from Sermada, a village at the south end of the plain of Dana: 'One is God and his Christos, year 390 (of Antioch)'.[16]

The importance of this proclamation need hardly be stressed. But it gains an extra significance precisely in this local context from the fact that in this small area inscriptions, archaeological remains and Christian narratives combine to show us the conflict of paganism and Christianity as vividly as anywhere in the Empire. The key elements are provided by a group of four hilltop temples of the second century which span an area at the heart of the limestone massif, and need to be considered together.[17] First, some 6 km to the west of Sermada, on a spur of the Jebel Barisha overlooking both the plain of Antioch and the interior plain of Dana, there is the well-preserved pagan temple at Burj Baqirha. A Greek inscription on the lintel of the gate identifies the deity worshipped there, and gives the date of construction:[18]

> To Zeus Bōmos, great, attentive, Apollonios and Apollophanes and Chalbion, the sons of Marion, erected the gate, from (the funds of the ?) *epoikion* of Merthos, year 209, (month) Gorpiaios (AD 161).

Below the temple, on the north slope of the hill, looking down to the plain of Antioch, there lies the late-Roman village of Baqirha, with two churches, of the fifth and sixth centuries. But for the religious conceptions dominant in our period, as we saw much earlier, the concept of a 'Zeus (the) Altar' may

14. Theodoret, *Hist. Relig.* XIV, 4.

15. See 7.1, n.19.

16. *IGLS* II, no. 518.

17. See O. Callot and J. Marcillet-Jaubert, "Hauts-lieux de Syrie du Nord", in G. Roux (ed.), *Temples et sanctuaires* (1984), 185.

18. *IGLS* II, no. 569. On a column of the temple itself there is another inscription, of AD 238; see H. Seyrig in Tchalenko, op. cit. III, 21, no. 20. For the late-Roman village see Peña et al., op. cit. (n.11), 72.

be of great significance.[19] In its local context it can be compared to the second
of the series, the ruined temple dedicated to 'Zeus Tourbarachos' at Srir on
another spur of the Jebel Barisha, to the east of Sermada; unpublished inscriptions show that this belongs to the first half of the second century. The name
of the deity clearly derives from the Semitic roots ṢWR ('rock') and BRK
('bless').[20] Then, 23 km to the north-east, at Kalota on the Jebel Seman, is a
temple dedicated to two or more 'ancestral gods'. The fragmentary inscription shows that one of their names ended in '-aitulos', and that the construction commemorated involved a temple and a golden cult-object *(xoanon)*.
What the deities were is probably made clear by an inscription of AD 224
from nearby Kafr Nabo, recording the dedication of an olive-press to 'Seimios
and Symbetylos and Leōn, the ancestral gods'. The second divine name must
recall, if in no very clear way, the 'Zeus Betylos, the ancestral god of those by
the Orontes', to whom a soldier made a dedication at Dura-Europos.[21]

    This temple was later reconstructed and converted into a church. But it is
in the history of the fourth temple that we see most clearly both the nature of
local pagan cults and the Christian challenge to them. Here we are concerned
with the only real mountain in the limestone massif, Jebel Sheikh Barakat,
some 870 m high and dominating the whole surrounding area.[22] A long series
of Greek inscriptions, of which not all have yet been published, record the
practice of a cult and the construction of a sanctuary there, on the very summit of the mountain, in the Imperial period. What we are concerned with here
is by no means just a small rural sanctuary, of a sort typical of the Near East,
but a major construction. The wall of the sanctuary formed a square of about
68 m, on a partially artificial esplanade, and lined with an inner portico. A
temple of perhaps 11 m by 20 m occupied the centre of the *temenos*. In scale
and design the whole sanctuary is thus comparable to the great temple of
Baetocaece in the hills behind Arados, at a similar height above sea-level.[23]

    The forty-seven reported inscriptions, published and unpublished, and all
in Greek, make it clear that the temple was constructed relatively early, beginning about AD 80 and being completed in the 140s. The deities worshipped
were 'Zeus Madbachos and Selamanes, the ancestral gods'. As has always
been recognised, the expression 'Zeus Madbachos' must mean the same as

    19. Ch. 1 above.
    20. See Callot and Marcillet-Jaubert, op. cit., 192–195.
    21. Callot and Marcillet-Jaubert, op. cit., 198–200. The inscriptions mentioned are *IGLS*
II, nos. 383 and 376. For 'Zeus Betylos' see ch. 1 above.
    22. For the most recent account see Callot and Marcillet-Jaubert, op. cit., 187–192 men-
tioning (p. 188, n.12) thirty-four unpublished inscriptions. The inscriptions so far published are
IGLS II, nos. 465–740, and J. Jarry, "Inscriptions arabes, syriaques et grecques du massif du
Bélus en Syrie du Nord", *Annales Islamologiques* 7 (1968), 139, nos. 41–43.
    23. See 8.3 below.

'Zeus Bōmos' at Burj Baqirha, 17 km away, namely 'Zeus (the) Altar'. For behind 'Madbachos' there must lie a Semitic root meaning 'sacrifice' (ZBK in Hebrew, DBK in Aramaic). From that derives MDBK' ('altar') in Aramaic (used for instance in Ezra 7, 17). 'Selamanes' was indeed a truly 'ancestral' divine name, for it is attested in the second millennium BC, and also appears (as ŠLMN) in a Sidonian inscription of the Hellenistic period.[24] The site is of exceptional interest, whether we attempt to look back to its earlier history or forward to the confrontation with Christian hermetism which took place there in the fourth century. Looking back, what is certain is only that the worshippers there regarded themselves as subscribing to 'ancestral' cults; that one of the divine names did have a long history; and that the other derived from a Semitic root whose meaning was evidently known (since 'Zeus [the] Altar' is attested in Greek not far away), and thereby presents itself as one of two related local examples of the identification of deity and altar. But what the actual prehistory of the cult in this prime example of a 'High Place' was we do not know. Continuity of cult over centuries is quite possible. Even if that must remain a mere hypothesis, our evidence from this rural area makes it certain that the Hellenistic cities did not wholly determine the nature of religious practices even at the heart of the most Hellenised part of the Near East. Yet the *expression* given to this cult in architectural form belongs, as always, to the Roman Empire.

As has never been doubted, we can also see this cult through Christian eyes. For Jebel Sheikh Barakat must be the mountain of which Theodoret gives so vivid a description:[25]

> Lying east of Antioch and west of Beroea, there is a high mountain that rises above the neighbouring mountains and imitates at its topmost summit the shape of a cone . . . On its very peak there is a precinct of demons much revered by those in the neighbourhood . . . At the very skirts of the mountain there is a large and well-populated village which in local speech *(enchōrios phōnē)* they call Teleda. Above the mountain-foot there is a dale, not very steep but sloping gently towards that plain and facing the south wind. Here one Ammianus built a philosophical retreat *(phrontistērion)*.

It will have been in the middle of the fourth century that Ammianus established himself in his hermit's cell on the side of the mountain. By the time when Theodoret wrote, a century later, there were monastic establishments

24. See the commentary to *IGLS* II, no. 465. The Sidonian inscription is G. A. Cooke, *A Text-Book of North Semitic Inscriptions* (1903), no. 7.

25. Theodoret, *Hist. Relig.* IV, 1 (and 13), trans. R. M. Price, *A History of the Monks of Syria by Theodoret of Cyrrhus* (1985).

circling the mountain, whose inhabitants, as he said, hymned their Maker 'some in Greek, others in the native language'. Once again, the geography of rural Christianity had been dictated by the need to offer a deliberate challenge to the pagan cult-centres; and it is again Christian evidence which gives us our best impression of the reverence which these centres evoked. It is this evidence too which perhaps suggests that though Greek was the only language to be inscribed in this area, Syriac or Aramaic had functioned in the earlier Roman Empire as a spoken language. The language and cursive script of those later Christian inscriptions from here which are in a Semitic language can be defined as Syriac. But without documents we cannot know how the (hypothetical) spoken Semitic language of the first few centuries (and Hellenistic period?) ought to be classified.

Fragmentary as our evidence is, it is sufficient to make clear how complex was the cultural and religious context within which the Greek cities of northern Syria lived. Even of the cities, one, Hierapolis, had a dual identity, both as the centre of the cult of Atargatis, 'the Syrian Goddess', and as a Greek city like others; and another, Doliche, seems to have grown out of a local cult-centre with some very ancient features.

7.4. THE MAJOR CITIES: APAMEA

As for what it in fact meant to be a Greek city like others, our fragmentary evidence hardly allows us, in the case of most of those of northern Syria, to catch more than glimpses; and nothing will be gained by laboriously compiling all those items of evidence which we happen to have. Even the broad criteria for what constituted a 'Greek city' are not entirely unambiguous: one of the central themes of this book is that the whole area was marked by large agglomerations of population which we do not always know whether to call 'cities' or not. But relevant criteria for defining a 'Greek city' would be, for instance, the exclusive use of Greek in public and communal life; the possession of a constitutional structure of local self-government, with an assembly, a council and annual magistrates; the capacity to mint coins bearing the name of the community; the possession of a territory in which there were villages (kōmai) which were in some sense dependent on the city; and no similar dependence on any other city. That was the point of the short-lived measure by which Septimius Severus is said to have punished Antioch for its support of Pescennius Niger in the civil war of 193/194: he is recorded by Herodian as having declared that Antioch would become a kōmē in the territory of Laodicea.[1]

---

1. Herodian III, 6, 9. Cf. 3.4 above. This degradation, if historical at all, can have lasted only a few years.

The most explicit symbols of a city's identity and status were its coins. But behind that statement lies a multitude of problems. What is certain is that until the second half of the third century the vast majority of the base-metal coinage in circulation in the Greek East was produced in the name of cities.[2] The coins usually, though not always, showed the portrait and title of the reigning Emperor; and they would typically list on the reverse the name of the community and display some symbol or symbols (often temples or deities) associated with it. What a 'mint' actually was, however, and whether we should speak of permanent entities called 'the mint of Antioch' or 'the mint of Laodicea', is quite uncertain. In Syria, as in Asia Minor, it is clear both that minting 'by' any one city could be episodic, and that the same workshops were producing coins for different cities.[3] The city of Chalcis, for instance, produced coins only between the reigns of Trajan and Antoninus Pius, with the bare legend 'Of the Flavian Chalcidians' on the reverse.[4] That may serve to remind us that although we speak of *places* in whose names coins were produced, the coins themselves almost invariably named collectivities of *persons:* 'the Chalcidians'. With that proviso, the list of communities named (sometimes only for very brief periods) on coins can serve as a map of 'the Greek cities' of northern Syria: Zeugma on the Euphrates, Doliche and Germanicia (all three at some point part of Commagene); Hierapolis, Beroea, Cyrrhus, Chalcis, Antioch, Apamea, Seleucia and Laodicea (which occasionally also produced silver coins); and the three small places on the coast, Gabala, Paltos and Balaneae. For reasons which are not entirely clear, all minting by Greek cities everywhere, the Near East included, came to an end soon after the middle of the third century, and with it both a distinctive art-form and a significant means of self-representation.

In general, the self-representations embodied in the coins might have been those of Greek cities anywhere. Hierapolis of course had a different image, and its coins might represent Zeus/Hadad and Hera/Atargatis, with the standard *(sēmeion)* placed between them.[5] More strikingly, given the origin of Seleucia as an early-Hellenistic foundation, some of its coins portrayed, as well as the thunderbolt which was supposed to have indicated the site to Seleucus I, a large stone placed within a four-pillared shrine and labelled 'Zeus

2. For the bare outline which follows I am dependent especially on C. J. Howgego, *Greek Imperial Countermarks: Studies in the Provincial Coinage of the Roman Empire* (1985), and K. W. Harl, *Civic Coins and Civic Politics in the Roman East, AD 180–275* (1987). But see now A. Burnett, M. Amandry and P. P. Rippollès, *Roman Provincial Coinage* I (1992), which will enable the entire subject to be renewed.

3. See K. Kraft, *Das system der kaiserzeitlichen Münzprägung in Kleinasien* (1972).

4. *BMC Syria,* 147–148.

5. 7.2 above.

Kasios'. It seems clear that there was a shrine of 'Zeus Kasios'—that is, the Zeus of Mount Kasios, which rises to the south of the mouth of the Orontes; the peak is clearly visible from the city, which rises up the hillside on the northern side of the plain. But whether this too should be seen as a pre-Greek 'High Place'; whether the stone represents the mountain itself or is a cult-object like that at Emesa; and if so whether we should conclude that in the sanctuary there was no representational cult-statue of this Zeus—all this is uncertain.[6] The evidence must suggest at least the possibility that the cults of even a major Hellenistic foundation such as this embodied elements derived from local customs.

The description of the cities of the Near East simply as 'Greek' has to be qualified in another way also. For one distinctive feature of the Near East as a whole was the transformation of many of these cities into Roman *coloniae*, especially from the reign of Severus onwards. But, given how extensive this process was, it is striking to what degree it was primarily a feature of the eventual 'Syria Phoenice', rather than of the tetrapolis and northern Syria. Was it a sign of their *relatively* well-grounded identity as Greek cities that in fact only two of them became *coloniae*, namely Antioch and Laodicea? Antioch was made a *colonia* by Caracalla in 211–217, with no remission of tribute. But the impact of the change seems to have been minimal. Almost the only visible signs of its new status are coins of the period 218–253, with legends, all in Greek, which read 'of the *mētropolis* (and) *kolōnia* of the Antiocheis'. There is nothing to show that Latin-speaking, even in public life, took root there; and it is noteworthy that Libanius, born in 314, begins his *Autobiography* by feeling it necessary to explain that the fact that his grandfather had once made a speech in Latin did not mean that he had been an immigrant.[7]

Rather clearer evidence for the transformation of identity involved comes from Laodicea, which took Severus' side in the civil war, and gained the title of *mētropolis* in 194 and of *colonia* in 198. From here there are several series of coins with legends in Latin, ending in the mid-third century with one reading 'of Colonia Laod(icea) metropolis'. Other coins of this period, equally with legends in Latin, show that the city now celebrated 'Capitoline' games imitated from those established at Rome by Domitian. But the new status also appears on an example of one of the most characteristic types of document from the Greek East under Roman rule, the record of his victories by a boxer (and pancratiast and athlete) who came from Laodicea, which was inscribed

6. See H. Seyrig, "A propos du culte de Zeus à Séleucie", *Syria* 20 (1939), 296, expressing more confidence than I could share. See now *RPC* I, 630–631.

7. See Millar, "Roman *Coloniae*", 41–42. See also 4.2 above for the petition posted in 245 in 'Antioch(eia) kol(ōnia) mētropolis', at the Hadrianic baths.

there in AD 221.[8] The man is described by the pseudo-Greek term *kolōn*—
'Laodicean *kolōn* (and) *mētropoleitēs*'. The full list of his victories would take
us almost all round the Greek world; but as regards the cities of northern
Syria, he records that in Laodicea, his native city, when the Pythian festival
was first introduced (under Caracalla), he won 'the oecumenical Antoninian
men's boxing contest'; he was also victorious in boxing and running at Leucas
(Balaneae), and in other contests at Hierapolis, Beroea, Zeugma, Apamea and
Chalcis. Other comparable lists of victories would add, for instance, the
'Pythian', 'Olympian', 'Hadrianic' and 'Commodean' games at Antioch (the
latter two named after the Emperors).[9] The fate of various recurrent cycles of
games there plays a large part in the sixth-century *Chronicle* of John Malalas
as it relates to this period. In that, as in the importance which it attaches to
building, it faithfully reflects the values of early-Imperial city life. But its evidence, often confused in detail, will not be used further here. It is, however,
impossible to exaggerate the significance of the athletic and other contests
which were so important a part of the collective life of Greek cities in this
period;[10] all else apart, by offering the possibility of prizes to the professional
athletes and actors who toured these contests, they literally served to make
the cities of Syria part of a wider Greek world, which embraced Asia Minor,
Greece proper and the games of Naples and of Rome itself. Yet in this respect,
as we have seen earlier, the steppe and the Euphrates seem to have constituted
a real frontier. Games were held in Chalcis, on the border with the steppe,
and in Zeugma looking over the Euphrates; but not, so far as we know, in
Palmyra or across the Euphrates in Mesopotamia.

As for the functioning of these communities as Greek cities, the lack of
narrative evidence and the relatively small number of public inscriptions (in
no way comparable to those of the major cities of western Asia Minor) mean
that what we happen to know is episodic and can hardly be made to make
sense except by understanding it as reflecting the standard institutions of the
Greek city. Almost nothing significant, for instance, is known of the public
life of Laodicea in the Imperial period. More serious still, the silting-up of the
site of Antioch during the intervening centuries means that we have hardly
any epigraphic record of the functioning of this major city as it was in the
first few centuries AD. As regards contemporary evidence, we are left with a
few passing allusions in narrative sources: Mucianus, the *legatus* of Syria in

8. 3.4 above; Millar, op. cit., 31–32. The inscription is *IGR* III, no. 1012 = *IGLS* IV, no.
1265 = Moretti, *IAG*, no. 85. For the 'Capitoline' games there see R. Ziegler, *Städtisches Prestige
und kaiserliche Politik* (1985), 147ff.

9. *IAG*, nos. 65; 68; 69; 81; 86.

10. See esp. L. Robert, "Deux concours grecs à Rome", *CRAI* (1970), 6; M. Wörrle, *Stadt
und Fest im kaiserzeitlichen Kleinasien* (1988); S. Mitchell, "Festivals, Games and Civic Life in
Roman Asia Minor", *JRS* 80 (1990), 183.

69, going to the theatre, 'where it is their custom to deliberate', to persuade the citizens to support Vespasian; or, from the same years, the episode when a renegade Jew also addressed the people in the theatre, urging them to compel the other Jews to follow pagan customs. A fire which then broke out destroyed a whole group of the public buildings characteristic of a Greek city: a four-sided agora, an official building for magistrates, a record-office and some basilicas. Subsequently Titus too, at the request of the *boulē* and *dēmos*, spoke in the theatre. It would be possible to collect further glimpses of Antioch as a city; but it is not until the middle of the fourth century that we can enter into its life.[11]

It is all the more paradoxical that almost the fullest record of the public offices of any one of these cities should come from the little place called Balaneae, situated on the coast, apparently recognised as a city independent of Aradus by Marcus Antonius in 37 BC, and acquiring the name 'Claudia Leucas' under Claudius—how or why is not known.[12] In any case its coins of the second century show its inhabitants again as 'Balaneōtai'. We can hardly pretend to gain much insight into what being a 'Balaneōtēs' meant. But the handful of inscriptions from the site show that the city did have a council and an assembly, which we find erecting statues of benefactors. Even more striking is a very fragmentary inscription which shows someone being honoured for almost the full range of functions which would have been expected of an office-holder in a major city: having been *stratēgos, agoranomos, dekaprōtos* and *archōn*, having been on an embassy to the Emperor, and having purchased corn at his own expense and distributed it; as a result he had been 'testified to' before the Emperor by his city. We should not underestimate the significance of this structure of self-government, even (or perhaps especially) as expressed by very small communal units; nor should we overlook the fact that one of its functions was to express the will of the community before governors and Emperors—the embassy from a city was one of the fundamental institutions of the Roman Empire.

If we can find these institutions at work in Balaneae, it will hardly be a surprise to find that under Hadrian the 'Seleucians at Zeugma' could despatch an ambassador to set up an honorific statue of a Roman senator at Pergamon; or to come across a certain Publius, a man of town-councillor rank at

---

11. See 2.4 above (Mucianus); Josephus, *BJ* VII, 3, 3–4 (43–62); 5, 2 (110–111). For what can be known of Antioch see G. Downey, *A History of Antioch in Syria from Seleucus to the Arab Conquest* (1961), chs. 8–12 (relying too much on Malalas). For fourth-century Antioch see, e.g., J. H. W. G. Liebeschuetz, *Antioch: City and Imperial Administration in the Later Roman Empire* (1972).

12. See H. Seyrig, *Syria* 27 (1950), 22–24; *IGLS* IV, 49; see also R. Fleischer, "Die Tychegruppe von Balanea-Leukas in Syrien", *Arch. Anz.* (1986), 707. The inscriptions mentioned are *IGLS* IV, nos. 1302–1303. For the coins of the first century see *RPC* I, 639–641.

Zeugma, who set up as a hermit in the second half of the fourth century.[13] But to gain any real impression of the now lost city life of this region, we can best turn to a remarkable set of inscriptions from Apamea, the only one of all these cities where large-scale excavation has been carried out.[14] On the one hand the city remained within the circuit of its Hellenistic walls, reinforced in the third century, and retained its original chequer-board street-pattern. But what is actually visible of the urban structure of the city belongs to the second century AD and after, and more specifically to extensive and elaborate re-building after the great earthquake of AD 115, which so profoundly affected Antioch.[15] It is from this phase that we happen to have some inscriptions, from the baths constructed near the Great Colonnade, which perfectly encapsulate the evolution of a Hellenistic-Roman city in Syria, and the values which informed city life.[16] They refer to the benefactions of a citizen of Apamea who was also a Roman citizen, and had a fully Roman name, L. Iulius Agrippa. Looking back over a century, one of the inscriptions records that Agrippa's great-grandfather, Dexandros, had been recorded on bronze tablets on the Capitol at Rome, at the instance of Augustus, as a friend of the Roman People. Whether or not Dexandros had actually been a local dynast operating outside the bounds of a city framework, as has been suggested, is not certain. But he had clearly fulfilled some important individual role in the troubled period before the province settled down under Imperial rule. The inscription also, concordantly with that, records that Dexandros had been the first High Priest *(archiereus)*, evidently of the province of Syria. This is in fact the first indication that a league *(koinon)* of the cities of Syria had come into existence already under Augustus, and had performed the quickly established role of conducting the worship of the Emperor. Nothing is known of the temple, or temples, of the cult; but the games of the *koinon* of Syria are attested in the first century, and took place at Antioch.[17]

The inscription says nothing specific of Agrippa's grandfather and father. But he himself is revealed as a perfect example of the city benefactor *(euergetēs)*, of a type which is familiar from the inscriptions from elsewhere, but otherwise not well attested in Syria. He had undertaken a long list of city

13. See Chr. Habicht, *Altertümer von Pergamon* VIII.3, *die Inschriften des Asklepieions* (1969), no. 21. Publius: Theodoret, *Hist. Relig.* V, 1.

14. For a portrayal of Apamea see J. Balty and J.-C. Balty, "Apamée de Syrie archéologie et histoire I: Des origines à la Tétrarchie", ANRW II.8 (1977), 103; J.-C. Balty, *Guide d'Apamée* (1981); idem, "Apamea in Syria in the Second and the Third Centuries AD", *JRS* 78 (1988), 91.

15. 3.3 above.

16. For these inscriptions see J.-P. Rey-Coquais, "Inscriptions grecques d'Apamée", *AAAS* 23 (1973), 39 = *AE* (1976), nos. 677–685 (L. Iulius Agrippa); 686 (Iulius Paris).

17. Moretti, *IAG*, nos. 62 and 67. For the very little that is known of this *koinon* see J. Deininger, *Die Provinziallandtage der römischen Kaiserzeit* (1965), 87–88.

offices and benefactions, including distributing grain and oil, and going on embassies to the Emperor and the governors. Moreover, he had constructed a considerable number of miles of an aqueduct, an item which gains in significance when it is realised that the traces of the city's aqueduct show that it started 75 km to the south-east, in the steppe to the east of the Orontes.[18] All this he had undertaken in spite of a grant of exemption from liturgies *(aleitourgēsia);* but most notably he had purchased the site and built the baths, along with a *basilica* and *stoa* in front of them, and adorned them lavishly. It is of particular interest that one of the inscriptions specifies which figures from Greek mythology were represented by the bronze statues set up in the baths: Theseus and the Minotaur; Apollo; Olympos (in legend one of the earliest flute-players); Skythes (a son of Herakles); and Marsyas (a satyr, also associated with flute-playing). Why precisely these figures were selected for a sculptural programme is not obvious, though some connection with the legendary origins of Greek music is clear. It remains significant that sculptures of this sort, along, for instance, with mosaics with mythological scenes, represent vehicles by which some of the content of Classical Greek culture could be transmitted to an environment between the Jebel Ansariyeh and the Orontes on the one side and the steppe on the other. What people coming in from the villages around Apamea will have made of such statues is not recorded; nor do we know if there was any alternative, non-Greek, mythical history which could be transmitted to them by some other means.

If such villagers did not necessarily enter the baths, it is more likely that they will sometimes have joined the audience in the vast theatre of Apamea (139 m in diameter, perhaps the largest from the whole ancient world), where again the content of the wider Graeco-Roman culture will have been transmitted in popular form. An honorific inscription put up at Apamea under Hadrian by the sacred *synodos* ('association') of the actors devoted to Dionysus celebrated Iulius Paris, a citizen of 'Claudia Apamea' (clearly a title now enjoyed by his native city), of Antioch and of other cities, and 'honoured with the *sexviratus* in the *kolōneia* Berytus' (the Latin title of this office in the *colonia* is given in transliteration). Iulius Paris was (literally) 'an actor of tragic movement *(kinēsis)*'; in other words he performed mimes or ballets, acting out scenes from Greek mythology.[19]

We could leave Apamea, and the cities of northern Syria, after seeing these reflections of how Greek culture was transmitted here at a popular level, if it were not for another Greek inscription from near the Great Colonnade, of which only the last few words survive:

18. See J.-C. Balty, "Problèmes de l'eau à Apamée de Syrie", in P. Louis, F. Métral and J. Métral (eds.), *L'homme et l'eau en Méditerranée et au Proche Orient* IV (1987), 9.

19. Rey-Coquais, op. cit., 63ff., no. 10; *AE* (1976), no. 686.

[. . .] on the orders of (the) Greatest God, Sacred Bēlos, Aur(ēlios) Bēlios Philippos, priest and successor *(diadochos)* in Apamea of the Epikoureioi.[20]

The important Neo-Platonic philosopher of the later second century, Numenius, came from Apamea, and the major Neo-Platonist of the early fourth century, Iamblichus, from Chalcis, also taught there. But there had been no previous evidence to suggest that an established Epicurean school existed there.[21] Here, however, an attachment to a characteristic element of Hellenistic culture is visibly combined with an apparently quite different one, the worship of Bel. One element in the man's composite Roman name, with Latin, Greek and Semitic elements, is obviously derived from the name of the god, Bel. Best attested as the name of a supreme god (or chief god of an individual city) in Babylonia, Bel was also the god of the major temple of Palmyra, whose territory bordered that of Apamea.[22] How and when this deity became established in Apamea is quite uncertain. Typically of our evidence, his role is attested there—as a deity who gave oracular responses (notably to Septimius Severus)—only in the later second and early third centuries.[23] Cassius Dio, in reporting the oracle given to Severus, explicitly equates 'Bēlos' with Zeus, long since represented on the coins of the city. The presumed site of the temple of Zeus, never excavated, occupies a large area of the city to the west of the Great Colonnade. The story of its eventual destruction by Bishop Marcellus in the 380s shows that it was a massive pillared construction of the standard type, surrounded on all four sides by a portico forming a *temenos*.[24] But how the deity worshipped there came, at least for a time, to be identified with Bel represents simply another question about non-Greek elements in the cults of the cities of northern Syria. These questions remain. But it is more significant that, Hierapolis apart, they retained more clearly than those of any other region of the Near East the imprint of early-Hellenistic colonialism.

20. Rey-Coquais, op. cit., 66ff.: [..]οιν[..] ἐπὶ [κελεύ]σεως θεοῦ μεγίστου ἁγίου Βήλου Αὐρ. Βήλιος Φίλιππος ἱερεὺς καὶ διάδοχος ἐν Ἀπαμείᾳ τῶν Ἐπικουρείων.

21. For the difficult question of the significance of the local origins of philosophers coming from Near Eastern cities, see 13.1 below.

22. 9.4 below. For Bel see *LIMC* III.1 (1986), 90 *s.v.* "Bel".

23. 3.4 above. See J.-C. Balty, "L'oracle d'Apamée", *Ant. Class.* 50 (1981), 5.

24. Theodoret, *HE* V, 21. See G. Fowden, "Bishops and Temples in the Eastern Roman Empire, AD 320–435", *JThSt* 29 (1978), 53.

THE PHOENICIAN COAST AND ITS HINTERLAND

8.1. HISTORY AND GEOGRAPHY

In two different ways, which may nonetheless be connected, the cities of Phoenicia played a quite different role within the Empire—and within Graeco-Roman culture—from that of the cities in other regions of the Near East. First, both in 'real' history and in legend the Phoenicians had had an integral part in Greek culture from the beginning. There was the legend of the foundation of Boeotian Thebes by Kadmos, the son of King Agenor, from Tyre or Sidon (which in the modern world has even been claimed as a historical reality, obscured by racial and cultural prejudice);[1] the associated story of his sister Europa, and her rape by Zeus; the repeated appearance of Phoenicians in the *Odyssey;* the acceptance, from Herodotus onwards, of the (valid) tradition of the derivation of the Greek alphabet from the Phoenician one;[2] Herodotus' identification of the chief god of Tyre as Herakles;[3] and above all the long-established Greek historical tradition recording the Phoenician colonisation of the western Mediterranean.[4]

1. See M. Bernal, *Black Athena: The Afroasiatic Roots of Greek Civilisation* I (1987).

2. Herodotus V, 58. The date and context of the borrowing have been much disputed, and in this context do not matter. See L. H. Jeffrey, *The Local Scripts of Archaic Greece,* rev. ed. by A. W. Johnston (1990), esp. 425ff. For a radical reappraisal of the chronology, see now P. James et al., *Centuries of Darkness* (1991).

3. Herodotus, II, 44. See now C. Bonnet, *Melqart: Cultes et mythes de l'Héracles tyrien en Méditerranée (Studia Phoenicia* VIII, 1988).

4. See F. Bunnens, *L'expansion phénicienne en Méditerranée, Essai d'interprétation fondé sur une analyse des traditions littéraires* (1979). See also M. Gras, P. Rouillard and J. Teixidor, *L'univers phénicien* (1989).

It is important to stress that these traditions continued to be given substance in commemoration and actual observances through the Hellenistic period. For instance, about 200 BC a man from Sidon won the chariot-race at Nemea in Greece. The inscription recording his victory ends as follows: 'You were the first of the citizens to bring back from Greece the glory of the chariot race to the house of the descendants of Agenor. The sacred town of Cadmeian Thebes also rejoices to see her mother-city made famous by her victories'.[5] In the second century we can find two brothers from Tyre making a bilingual dedication on Malta to a deity identified in Greek as 'Herakles *archēgetēs*' and in Phoenician as 'Melqart, lord of Tyre' (MLQRT B'L ṢR);[6] and at about the same time, to be precise in 162 BC, a Carthaginian ship was on its way to take first-fruits to its mother-city, Tyre.[7] Carthage was to be destroyed by the Romans only sixteen years later. Its recognition as the mother-city of Carthage, as of other cities in North Africa, was of course to give Tyre, at second hand, a place both in the real history of early Rome and ultimately, in Vergil's depiction of Aeneas and Dido, in its legendary origins.[8] The story of the foundation of Carthage by Elissa, or Dido, goes back at least to Timaeus in the early Hellenistic period; but her connection with Aeneas may be no earlier than Vergil himself.[9]

There is in fact nothing to show that this particular literary elaboration of the legend ever took root either in the historical traditions generally associated with the cities of Phoenicia or in their image of themselves. But all the other, and earlier, elements of the tradition clearly did, and above all the historic role of these cities in trade and colonisation. This is for instance how Strabo characterises Tyre and Sidon in his *Geography*:

> After Sidon one comes to Tyre, the largest and oldest city of the Phoenicians, which rivals Sidon, not only in size, but also in its fame and antiquity, as handed down to us in numerous myths. Now although the poets have referred more repeatedly to Sidon than to Tyre (Homer does not even mention Tyre), yet the colonies sent into Libya and Iberia, as far even as

5. See the illuminating article by E. Bickerman, "Sur une inscription grecque de Sidon", *Mélanges Dussaud* I (1939), 91; inscription trans. in M. M. Austin, *The Hellenistic World* (1981), no. 121. For this and what follows see F. Millar, "The Phoenician Cities: A Case-study of Hellenisation", *Proc. Camb. Philol. Soc.* 209 (1983), 55. See now also J. D. Grainger, *Hellenistic Phoenicia* (1991).

6. M. G. Guzzo Amadasi, *Le iscrizioni fenicie e puniche delle colonie in Occidente* (1967), 15, no. 1; H. Donner and W. Röllig, *Kanaanäische und aramäische Inschriften* (1962), no. 47 (henceforward Donner and Röllig, *KAI*).

7. Polybius XXXI, 12, 11–12.

8. For Dido see W. H. Roscher, *Griechische und römische Mythologie* I (1884), s.v. "Dido".

9. For Elissa/Dido as the founder of Carthage, Timaeus, *FGrH* 566, F.82, and more fully Justin XVIII, 4–6. See O. Skutsch, *The Annals of Ennius* (1985), 8.

outside the Pillars, hymn rather the praises of Tyre. At any rate, both cities have been famous and illustrious, both in early times and at the present time; as to which of the two one might call the metropolis of the Phoenicians, there is a dispute in both cities.[10]

He goes on to speak of the still-flourishing dye-industry of Tyre, the tradition of the Sidonian contribution to astronomy and arithmetic, and the current prominence in philosophy of men from both cities.

Pliny the Elder, writing some decades later, evokes the same historical associations of Tyre, if in more pessimistic terms:

> Next Tyre, once an island separated from the mainland by a very deep sea-channel 700 yards wide, but now joined to it by works constructed by Alexander when besieging the place, and formerly famous as the mother-city from which sprang the cities of Leptis, Utica and the great rival of Rome's empire in coveting world-sovereignty, Carth. ͜ , and also Cadiz, which she founded outside the confines of the world; but the entire renown of Tyre now consists in a shell-fish and a purple dye![11]

As we have already seen, when the Roman Emperor was a man from Leptis, married to a lady from Emesa, which contemporaries also thought of as a Phoenician city, these traditions would contribute to a profound change in the map of the Roman Near East. For it was he who made 'Phoenice' the name of a Roman province.[12]

The central area of Phoenicia could be defined as the line of ancient cities on the coast, backing onto Mount Lebanon: from south to north Tyre, Sidon, Berytus, Byblos and Tripolis. Phoenician influence and settlement had, however, at times extended much further north, even beyond Mount Amanus, and further south, to the Idumaean coast. Given this lack of definition, it will be simplest to use, in the north, the boundary of 'Syria Phoenice', as Septimius Severus established it, which ran just south of Balaneae.[13] There are in any case good reasons for treating Aradus, on its island off the coast, as part of Phoenicia, and with it the great temple of Baetocaece, high up below the crest of the southern end of the Jebel Ansariyeh. 'Phoenicia' as used here will also embrace Mount Lebanon, with its sequence of important shrines in remote and elevated sites, as well as the Bekaa Valley, with Heliopolis/Baalbek. In spite of the important effects of Roman colonial settlement there, Lucian

10. Strabo, *Geog.* XVI, 2, 22 (756), Loeb trans., with one correction.

11. Pliny, *NH* V, 12/76, Loeb trans.

12. 3.4 above.

13. *Itin. Burdig.* 582, 7–10: 'Civitas Balaneas, mil. XIII; finis Syriae Coelis et Foenicis; mutatio Maraccas, mil. X; mansio Antaradus, mil. XVI'. There are complications about this boundary, but this is the best evidence.

(writing before Severus made 'Phoenice' an official term) treated Heliopolis, along with Tyre, Sidon and Byblos, as a place where there was an exotic cult observed by 'Phoenicians'.[14] Further south along the coast, in terms both of how contemporaries spoke and of provincial boundaries, 'Phoenicia' stretched as far as the little town of Dor, or Dora, on the coast between Mount Carmel and Caesarea.

Our survey of Phoenicia will begin in this southern area, up to Ptolemais (for which rabbinic works still used its Semitic name, Aco—'KW), and will then look at the northern region, from Aradus to Berytus and Heliopolis, before reaching the two places which disputed the right to the title 'metropolis of Phoenicia', Tyre and Sidon.

8.2. PHOENICIA: THE SOUTHERN REGION

As we have seen earlier, Josephus' story of what happened in the early 40s, when some young pagans in Dora placed a statue of Claudius in the synagogue there, shows that the place, traditionally on the borders of Jewish territory, was within the then province of Syria. Agrippa I complained to the *legatus* of Syria, Publius Petronius; and he sent a centurion, to whom the magistrates of the city were ordered to hand over the perpetrators.[1] It is indeed a classic instance of how Roman force could be applied, if very episodically, in a distant southern corner of the province. A few years later its frontier situation gave it an equally contentious role: for Josephus, as commander of the Jewish forces in Galilee, found that Cestius Gallus had taken hostages from Sepphoris and placed them in Dora, 'a city of Phoenice';[2] again, this terminology was in current use long before Severus employed it as the official name of a province.

Nothing in the minimal evidence about Dora goes to prove that it still retained any distinctively Phoenician characteristics. Instead, in its official self-image it exuded all the self-importance of a Greek city: it minted coins between the reigns of Nero and Antoninus Pius and again under Elagabal; at their most expansive the legends call the city 'sacred', 'inviolate', 'autonomous' and 'mistress of a fleet *(nauarchis)*'.

If the public identity of the ancient city of Dor (D'R or DWR), which in the early fifth century Eshmunazar, the king of Sidon, had claimed as his own,[3] was now entirely Greek, this was all the more true of Aco, the only city

14. 7.2 above.

1. Josephus, *Ant.* XIX, 6, 3 (300–303). See 2.3 above. For the little that is known of Dora, see Schürer, *HJP* II, 118–120, and Y. Meshorer, "The Coinage of Dora", *INJ* 9 (1986–87), 59; E. Stern, "The Walls of Dor", *IEJ* 38 (1988), 6; see now *RPC* I, 660–661.

2. *Vita* 8/31.

3. Donner and Röllig, *KAI*, no. 14.

on the entire Phoenician coast to have acquired a Hellenistic dynastic name, Ptolemais. Yet in fact a Greek writer, whose name, 'Claudius Iolaos', shows that he cannot have been writing his *Phoenicica* earlier than the Imperial period, recorded the Phoenician foundation of both cities, and gave their original names, as 'Akē' and 'Dōr'.[4] The fact is significant, for the possession of ancient historical associations is precisely what distinguishes these cities from the Hellenistic foundations of northern Syria.

Very little is known of the social history or even the physical structure of Graeco-Roman Ptolemais.[5] Its coins of the early Roman period record it too as being 'sacred' and 'inviolate' in the classic manner of Greek cities. But, as we have seen earlier, it played an important role in the strategic structure of the Roman Near East in the first century, as the last major city on the route from the province of Syria to the troubled area of Judaea. Perhaps in consequence, its inhabitants found themselves in the early 50s with a new designation, 'the Germanikeis'—or 'Germanieis'—'i ̓tolemais', evidently borrowed from the Latin 'Germanicus', one of the names of Claudius. But within a year or two there came another and more radical transformation: the settlement of Latin-speaking veterans and the transformation of the place into a Roman *colonia,* with the title 'Colonia Claudia Stabilis Germanica Felix Ptolemais'.[6] It can be taken as certain that the original population, both Greek and (as was to appear shortly) Jewish, remained *in situ:* in 66 the pagan inhabitants killed two thousand Jews and imprisoned many others.[7]

The standard Graeco-Roman deities who appear on both the pre-colonial and the (relatively late) colonial coinage of Ptolemais reveal nothing distinctive about cults or temples there. But as a city on the borders of Galilee it did also function as a sort of frontier zone between the world of Jewish villages and that of the Graeco-Roman city. It is in this light that it appears in the first major compilation of rabbinic legal rulings and discussions, put together not long after AD 200, the *Mishnah.* Here we have the well-known episode of how Rabbi Gamaliel replied to a pagan critic there:

> Proklos the son of Philosophos [or 'the philosopher'?] asked Rabban Gamaliel in Acre ('KW) while he was bathing in the Bath of Aphrodite ('PRWDYṬY), and said to him, 'It is written in your Law, And there shall cleave nought of the devoted thing to thine hand. Why [then] dost thou bathe in the Bath of Aphrodite?' He answered, 'One may not make answer in the bath'. And when he came out he said, 'I came not within her limits:

4. Jacoby, *FGrH* 788, F.1–2.
5. See Schürer, *HJP* II, 121–125.
6. 2.3 above.
7. Josephus, *BJ* II, 18, 5 (477).

she came within mine! They do not say, "Let us make a bath for Aphrodite", but "Let us make an Aphrodite as an adornment for the bath"'.[8]

The episode, if we regard it as historical, should belong around the end of the first century, when Ptolemais had been a *colonia* for some decades. Typical of the linguistic interplay characterising the period, Gamaliel's questioner is identified via a Hebrew transliteration of a Greek version of a Latin name (Proclus or Proculus). The odds are strong that the conversation will have been conducted in Greek (the goddess is 'Aphrodite' not 'Venus'). As abundant evidence from the first century to the fifth shows, the surviving rabbinic writings, in Hebrew and Aramaic, represent only one side of a multilingual culture, in which Greek played an important part.[9] Whether Ptolemais, as a *colonia,* remained to any significant degree trilingual, with Latin in continuing use also, is quite uncertain. The fact that the colonial coins of the city are consistently in Latin until the end of the minting in the 260s is significant of its conscious public status, but is not evidence for what language was spoken in the streets.[10]

A few accidental items of evidence, all from the period of the war of 66–70, allow us to gain some impression of the hinterland of Ptolemais. For instance Cestius Gallus, setting out from Ptolemais in 66, advanced to a town (Josephus calls it a *polis*) called Chabulon on the borders between the city's territory and Galilee: he set it on fire 'although he admired its beauty, with its houses built in the style of those at Tyre, Sidon and Berytus'.[11] This description neatly catches both the fundamental feature of the social structure of the Near East—the lack of a clear distinction between 'city' and 'village'—and the fact that this southern area was in cultural terms within the orbit of the major Phoenician cities.

Another 'town' *(oppidum)* which our sources happen to reveal is that which lay on Mount Carmel between Ptolemais and Dora. It will have been to here that Vespasian came to sacrifice in 69 and receive a prophecy of his future success. Tacitus explains that 'Carmelus' was the name of both the god and the mountain; there was, he says, no cult-statue or temple, but only worship conducted on an altar.[12] We seem with this to gain a brief insight into

---

8. *Mishnah, Aboda Zara* 3, 4, trans. Danby.

9. See more fully 10.4 below.

10. For its coinage see L. Kadman, *The Coins of Akko Ptolemais* (1961), reviewed by H. Seyrig, "Le monnayage de Ptolemais en Phénicie", *RN* 4 (1962), 25. See now also Y. Meshorer, *The City Coins of Eretz-Israel and the Decapolis in the Roman Period* (1985), 11–15, and *RPC* I, 658–660.

11. Josephus, *BJ* II, 18, 9 (504), Loeb trans. See Avi-Yonah, *Gazetteer, s.v.* "Chabulon".

12. Pliny, *NH* V, 17/75: 'promunturium Carmelus, et in monte oppidum eodem nomine'; Tacitus, *Hist.* II, 78.

the functioning of a pagan 'Semitic High Place', perhaps showing a direct continuity with the Old Testament period, and the cult confronted by Elijah. Eusebius (a much better placed observer) offers a parallel case, reporting that Mount Hermon, 'which the *Phoinikes* call *Saniōr*', was said to be revered as sacred by the pagans.[13] But in fact exactly what most clearly characterises worship at locations high up on mountains, as it was practised in the Near East in the Roman period, was the erection of temples in Classical style. Moreover, archaeological evidence shows that on Mount Carmel itself cult-statues were not unknown, or at least had come into use by the end of the second century. For the foot—all that remains—of a colossal statue (twice life-size) found on the mountain bears the Greek inscription: 'to Heliopolitan Zeus, (god of?) Carmel, G. Ioul(ios) Eutychas, *kol(ōn) Kaisareus*'. The dedicator was a citizen of the *colonia* of Caesarea, of which more below. But what is significant is that the god (Zeus) of Carmel can be represented in sculpture, and that he is here (uniquely) identified with the famo⌐ ⌐eus of Heliopolis.[14] Once again it is futile to ask what an ancient deity 'really was': for he was whatever his worshipper said he was. But the choice made by this worshipper was to identify him with the (by now) best-known deity of the central Phoenician zone. Once again, therefore, this is an indication that we should see this coastal region as a border-zone of 'Phoenicia'—as well, of course, as an area of cities with Greek constitutions, a border-zone (as Tyre and Sidon were also) with the properly Jewish area, and the site of the second Roman *colonia* of the Near East.

Nowhere in this southern extension of 'Phoenicia', however, do we have any positive evidence from the Imperial period of the continued use of the Phoenician language. In that respect there is a contrast, though a very slight one, if we move to the northern coastline of what was to be 'Syria Phoenice'.

8.3. THE NORTHERN COASTLINE
AND ITS HINTERLAND

What had once been the most important place in the northern part of Phoenicia was the island city of Aradus, lying off the coast north of the Eleutherus River and of the passage inland through to Emesa and Palmyra. Once under its own kings, and a city which had minted its own silver and bronze coins through the Hellenistic period, using an era beginning in 259 BC, it seems from the very little that we know of it in the Imperial period to have been of

13. Eusebius, *Onom.* 20, 9–12.
14. See M. Avi-Yonah, "Mount Carmel and the God of Baalbek", *IEJ* 2 (1952), 118 = *AE* (1952), no. 206 = Y. Hajjar, *La triade d'Héliopolis-Baalbek* I (1977), no. 227 and Pl. lxxxvi.

minor importance.[1] The known inscriptions are enough to show that it had the normal structure of a Greek city, with a council *(boulē)* and an assembly; and like other cities it minted bronze coins, all with Greek legends, intermittently until the reign of Gordian. It is notable, however, that some are also marked with individual Phoenician letters.

The significance of Aradus lies in two aspects. First, it provides the only securely dated Phoenician-Greek bilingual inscription of the Imperial period. It dates to 25/24 BC, hence under Augustus, and is in fact the earliest known inscription from the city.[2] Fragmentary as the text is, it is enough to give the year (235), indicated in Greek letters in both halves of the text; to show that something was being dedicated by someone acting as gymnasiarch; and to give the names of the deities to whom the dedication was made: in Greek Hermes and Herakles, and in Phoenician Hermes (transliterated as 'RM[. . .]) and Melqart (MLQRT). It would be difficult to find a document which in a few fragmentary lines exhibits more precisely the fusion of Greek and Phoenician elements.

It does, however, serve to raise a question common to the whole Near East, but particularly problematic in Phoenicia. Does the subsequent absence, from the known evidence, of *inscribed* texts in Phoenician mean that the language was no longer written, or even no longer spoken? Clearly, it can *prove* no such thing. But even if it were certain that Phoenician did indeed die out in the early Empire, the issue would remain of how essential a local language was to the transmission of a local culture or of indigenous cults.

This question arises also in the case of the second significant feature of the city, the existence in the mainland territory controlled by it of the great temple of Baetocaece,[3] situated some 30 km inland, and just below the crest of the Jebel Ansariyeh. As in almost all cases, the physical structure which survives is a product of the Roman Empire. A Greek inscription records that an area beside the temple was paved, steps built and a bronze altar dedicated in AD 185/186 by a Roman centurion, T. Aurelius Decimus, a native of Oescus in Moesia Inferior; another dedication was made by a soldier who describes himself as 'highest (*summus*—transliterated in Greek as *soummos*) of the *eq-*

---

1. See J.-P. Rey-Coquais, *Arados et sa Pérée aux époques grecque, romaine et byzantine* (1974); idem, *IGLS* VII, *Arados et régions voisines* (1970). For the coins see *RPC* I, 641–643.

2. *IGLS* VII, no. 4001. For some reason it is not included in Donner and Röllig, *KAI*. For a photograph of the text and a discussion of the Phoenician text, given in Hebrew characters, see R. Savignac, "Une visite à l'île de Rouad", *RB* 13 (1916), 565 on pp. 576–579.

3. For the physical structure see D. Krencker and W. Zschietzschmann, *Römische Tempel in Syrien* I (1938), 65–101. For its history and inscriptions, H. Seyrig, "Arados et Baetocaecé", *Syria* 28 (1951), 191; *IGLS* III, nos. 4028–4041. Cf. A. Baroni, "I terreni e i privilegi del tempio di Zeus a Baitokaike (*IGLS* VII, 4028)", in B. Virgilio (ed.), *Studi Ellenistici* I (1984), 135.

uites singulares'. Once again the devotion of Roman soldiers to these Near Eastern shrines is worth noting.[4]

The altar stands beside a small Ionic temple within a vast walled precinct, of some 135 m by 85 m; an inscription records that part of it was constructed by devotees *(katochoi)* of the god in AD 223/224.[5] That shows only of course the familiar pattern by which it was in the Roman Empire that architectural expression was given to Near Eastern cults. But in this case we know, from the major inscription carved on the wall beside the main gate, that the sanctuary of Zeus of Baetocaece had been in existence at least since the third century BC.[6] For it records that King Antiochus (probably either I, 293–261 BC, or II, 261–246) had allocated the revenues of the village of Baetocaece for the support of the cult; had instituted a twice-monthly tax-free market there; and had declared that the village would be exempt from the exactions of official travellers.

The inscription also records that under Augustus, in circumstances which are not made clear, 'the city' (which must be Aradus) had sent to the Emperor a decree that market officials should permit without taxation the transit of goods and animals due for sale at the twice-monthly fair at Baetocaece. Whatever the nature of the exchanges which led to this decree and its despatch, it is one of the very few reflections of Imperial decision-making in this region in the first century of the Empire.

The dossier owed its existence as an inscription, however, to the fact that a petition was presented to Valerian (and nominally also to Gallienus and Saloninus) in 258/259, and a brief reply in Latin obtained, laying down that the governor of the province would see to it that the 'ancient *beneficia* of the kings' were to be preserved against the violence of an adversary. The dossier concludes with the record in Greek of the inscribing of the reply by the beneficiaries: 'The *katochoi* of Sacred Heavenly *(hagios ouranios)* Zeus put up the divine rescript, worshipped by all, (as the record) of the piety of the Emperors towards the god and of their (grant of) freedom to the place'. It is impossible to say exactly what is meant here by *katochoi* ('devotees'), except that they are clearly free people with control of their own funds, and not 'temple slaves'. Nor can we say whether the cult had been in existence before the Hellenistic period. The name of the place (variously transliterated as 'Baitokaikē', 'Betocheichei' and so forth) seems certainly to incorporate the Semitic root BYT ('house'). Beyond that all interpretations, including, somewhat improbably, 'house of the castor vine', are merely speculative.[7]

---

4. *IGLS* VII, nos. 4034 and 4037.

5. *IGLS* VII, no. 4031.

6. *IGLS* VII, no. 4028.

7. For this interpretation see F. Piejko, "A Bronze Plaque for the God of Baetocaece", *Berytus* 30 (1982), 97, on *IGLS* VII, no. 4041; see *SEG* XXXII, no. 1446.

This place-name, whatever its meaning or origin, represents the only specifically 'Semitic' element in the evidence for the cult. It is of course only to be expected that exchanges with rulers will have been conducted in Greek or Latin. But all the dedications from the site are also in Greek. Nothing whatever is known of the priesthood or of the form of the cult-object worshipped there.

If much thus remains unclear, what is certain is the continuity of the cult over (probably) some five centuries, its location in a village context, and the importance of the twice-monthly fair held there. The sheer scale of the construction, to which we must add a subsidiary sanctuary built some 50 m from the north-west corner of the *temenos*, must give some hint of the resources available in these cultivated lands which rise up gradually from the coast to the crest of the Jebel Ansariyeh (terracing is visible up to the very top of the mountain-chain). As such, it is much the largest of the rural sanctuaries whose remains can be found high in the hills of what the ancient world regarded as Phoenicia. A few other prominent examples, out of many, will be mentioned below. But whether we should characterise the god of Baetocaece and his cult as 'Phoenician' is a question which at the moment we have no means of answering.

Nothing significant is known of other small places lying along this coast, Carne, Antaradus, Marathus, Simyra, Orthosia, or even the city at the northern tip of Mount Lebanon, Arca or Caesarea Libani, notable only for having been the native city of a man with a Latin name, Gessius Marcianus, who married a niece of Iulia Domna from Emesa, and was thus to be the father of the Emperor Severus Alexander. As we have seen, this place became a *colonia* in the reign of Alexander's cousin, 'Elagabal'.[8] Even what had been an important Phoenician city, Tripolis, has hardly left any distinctive trace in the Imperial period. But, for instance, an inscription from Athens, of the reign of Hadrian, shows Tripolis with both the normal institutions of a Greek city and the array of grandiose Greek titles characteristic of the Phoenician cities of this period: 'the magistrates and council and people of (the city of the) Tripolitai of Phoineikē, the sacred and inviolate and autonomous and mistress of a fleet'.[9]

The history of the hinterland in this area, that is to say, the northern end of Mount Lebanon, between the coast and the upper Orontes Valley, is almost wholly obscure. From Strabo's account it seems to have been dominated by Ituraean mountain-peoples in the later Republic; and a Roman officer, Aemilius Secundus, was still operating against the Ituraeans of Mount Lebanon towards the end of Augustus' reign.[10] The area may have been the territory

8. See 3.4 and 4.2 above.
9. *OGIS*, no. 587.
10. 2.2 above. For the situation before Pompey's arrival, Strabo, *Geog.* XVI, 2, 18 (755).

of the 'Ituraean Arabs', as Dio describes them, given to one Soaemus by Gaius in 38, and then reincorporated into the Empire on his death in 49; but some of it at least seems to have belonged to Agrippa II.[11] The details are not worth pursuing. It is more important to note that here too we can find rural temples and shrines constructed in the Imperial period; if inscriptions are found in association with these temples, they are again always in Greek.[12] Once more the existence of these rural temples implies that here too there was a village population. But the economy, social structure and culture of this hinterland all remain very little known. We may note that both Strabo and Cassius Dio describe at least some of its inhabitants as 'Arab'; but what they meant by this remains obscure. Nor can we ever be certain whether rural temples built in Classical forms, whose known worshippers used Greek when they put up inscriptions, did or did not embody older local traditions and forms of belief. It must nonetheless be significant that such hypothetical older traditions could now be expressed in Greek forms.

8.4. THE MAJOR CITIES: BYBLOS AND BERYTUS

The area which above all did retain, in the eyes both of outsiders and of its own people, an identity which was distinctively 'Phoenician' was the line of coastal cities from Byblos south through Berytus to Sidon and Tyre, with their hinterland extending far inland (in the case of Berytus, covering the northern part of the Bekaa Valley). But even here we do not find any certain examples in the Roman period of inscriptions put up in the Phoenician language. The one possible exception is an inscription in Phoenician from Byblos, which may date to the first century AD. In it someone called Abdeshmoun ('BD'ŠMN) makes a dedication 'to our lord and to the image (or statue) of Baal (L'DNN WLSML B'L)'. It has even been suggested that 'our lord' here is a reference to the Emperor. Better evidence would be needed, and it is surprising that he is not named; but the possibility remains open.[1]

This is in any case an instance of a private dedication on a small altar. On

11. Schürer, *HJP* I, 569–570.

12. See, e.g., Krencker and Zschietzschmann, *Römische Tempel* I, 102–104 (Bet Djalluk, also known as Maqam er-Rab; for Greek inscriptions from there see H. Seyrig, "Némésis et le temple de Maqâm er-Rabb", *MUSJ* 37, [1960–61], 261); 20–34 (a group of three temples at Hosn Sfiri); 8–19 (Kasr Naus) and 4–7 (Bziza)—both in the foothills south of Tripolis and west of Botrys. For their locations see Krencker and Zschietzschmann II, Tafel I. For the inscriptions of this area see esp. J.-P. Rey-Coquais, "Une inscription du Liban Nord", *MUSJ* 47 (1972), 87 (on the construction in AD 184 of a rural sanctuary on the Nahr Abou Moussa, inland from Tripolis).

1. Donner and Röllig, *KAI*, no. 12; for the suggestion see R. Dussaud, "Inscription phénicienne de Byblos d'époque romaine", *Syria* 6 (1925), 269.

any view the Phoenician cities did not produce whole series of Semitic-language public inscriptions, to compare with those at Palmyra, or even with the early Imperial inscriptions (in Latin and Neo-Punic) from Tripolitania, especially Lepcis Magna.[2] There are, however, some indications that Phoenician was still used and understood; and there are a couple of examples of inscriptions from this area in Semitic languages other than Phoenician. From Sidon there is a bilingual dedication to Dusares, in Greek and Nabataean, dating to the fifth year of Aretas IV, so 4 BC.[3] Similarly, from Harbata in the northern Bekaa Valley, which must have been in the territory of Berytus and then of Heliopolis, there is a stray inscription in Palmyrene, on one of a cache of Palmyrene sculptures.[4] In general, however, even central Phoenicia, with the Bekaa Valley, belongs in the zone characterised, in both town and country, by inscriptions in Greek. It thus offers a clear contrast both with the Palmyrene zone and with its own southern hinterland, Galilee, where Greek, Hebrew and Aramaic co-existed as inscribed languages.

The two Phoenician cities where the 'amnesia' about the pre-Hellenistic past, which characterises the Roman Near East as a whole, most clearly did not prevail were Sidon and Tyre. It will be simplest to approach them through the contrasting identities of Byblos and Berytus as they present themselves in the Imperial period.

From Byblos, as we saw, there is a single Phoenician inscription which may date from the first century AD.[5] For what it is worth, this is matched by a couple of coin-types, probably of the late Republic rather than of Augustus' reign, which repeat the Phoenician legend sometimes used in the Hellenistic period: 'to (or of) GBL the holy' (LGBL QDŠT).[6] There is no doubt that the modern name of the place, Jbail, is inherited from the Phoenician name GBL, used for instance in a series of Phoenician royal inscriptions in which the chief goddess is identified as the 'mistress (B'LT) of GBL'. But the fluidity of divine identities in this area is clearly illustrated by the fact that the important inscription of King Yehawmilk of Byblos, of the fifth or fourth century BC, al-

2. See G. Levi della Vida and M. G. Guzzo Amadasi, *Iscrizioni puniche della Tripolitania (1927–1967)* (1987).

3. *CIS* II.1, no. 160.

4. S. Ronzevalle, "Notes et études d'archéologie orientale", *MUSJ* 21 (1937–38), 1, 73ff., no. 8; J. Starcky, "Inscriptions palmyréniennes conservées au Musée de Beyrouth", *BMB* 12 (1955), 29, on p. 41, no. 10. See M. A. R. Colledge, *The Art of Palmyra* (1970), 230.

5. Text to n.1 above.

6. *BMC Phoenicia*, 98–99, nos. 18–19 (dating these coins to Augustus' reign). The prevailing view is, however, that they are dated by a Pompeian era, and hence belong in the late Republic. See H. Seyrig, *Syria* 31 (1954), 73–76; H. R. Baldus, "Syria", in A. M. Burnett and M. H. Crawford (eds.), *The Coinage of the Roman World in the Late Republic* (1987), 121, on p. 134; *RPC* I, 647–648.

ready represents the 'mistress of GBL' in Egyptian dress and style.[7] Some continuity of cult in Byblos must be regarded as certain, for the temple-area on the acropolis of Byblos, where this *stele* was found, seems to have functioned as a sanctuary, or series of sanctuaries, continuously from the third millennium BC to the Roman period; a major new sanctuary, surrounded by a portico, was constructed there in the second century AD.[8]

But precise identification of the divinities worshipped in these temples is not possible for any period, and continuity of cult was plainly compatible with the emergence of new conceptions of the divinities concerned. In the Hellenistic period, and apparently not before, the cults which were held to characterise Byblos were those of Aphrodite and Adonis, strongly coloured by association with those of Isis and Osiris. Strabo identifies Byblos as 'sacred to Adonis';[9] and it is ceremonials connected with the worship of Aphrodite and Adonis here of which Lucian offers a highly coloured account, as one of a series of Phoenician parallels to the exotic cult at Hierapolis.[10] According to him, ceremonials to mourn the killing of Adonis by a boar took place in the temple of Aphrodite in Byblos, followed by a procession to mark his resurrection. Women were obliged, as a sign of mourning, either to shave their heads or to prostitute themselves, with their payment going to Aphrodite. Some Byblians, however, explicitly argued that the deity concerned was actually Osiris.

The name 'Adonis' was also attached, Lucian says, to a river in the territory of Byblos, which ran with blood each year to mark his murder; and he records that on Mount Lebanon above Byblos there was an ancient sanctuary of Aphrodite. Lucian's account is vague; but he must be speaking of the river now called Nahr Ibrahim at whose source lay the mountain-sanctuary of Aphaca; as we saw, the notoriety of the ritual prostitution conducted here was such that the sanctuary was destroyed on the orders of Constantine.[11] Lucian makes no clear connection between the myth of Adonis and this site. But the Syriac *Oration of Meliton the Philosopher* does, though substituting 'Balthi, queen of Cyprus', for Aphrodite and Tamuz for Adonis: at the end, the author says, 'Balthi remained in Gebal, and she died in the city of Aphaca, where Tamuz is buried'.[12] These varying accounts demonstrate painfully that

---

7. Donner and Röllig, *KAI*, nos. 4–7 and esp. 10 (the inscription of Yehawmilk). For the *stele* see, e.g., *CIS* I, Pl. I; J. B. Pritchard, *The Ancient Near East* I (1958), fig. 130.

8. See the survey by B. Soyez, *Byblos et la fête des Adonies* (1977), 4–5 and 16–28; this book is also essential for what follows.

9. *Geog.* XVI, 2, 18 (755).

10. Lucian, *de dea Syria*, 6–9.

11. 5.3 above.

12. See W. Cureton, *Spicilegium Syriacum* (1855), esp. 44 (English trans.), and 7.2 above, on Hierapolis. There is no subsequent text or commentary.

we cannot reach a 'true' account of what such ceremonials, or the deities worshipped in them, really 'were'. The temple of the 'mistress of GBL' surely was on the acropolis of Byblos, and the same temple may be that which Lucian ascribes to Aphrodite; both might be identified with the female deity, normally labelled 'Astarte', who appears on some coins with the legend 'of sacred Byblos', and is sometimes represented within the columns of a temple.

But all such identifications are speculative, as is any interpretation of the famous coin of Byblos from the reign of Macrinus (217/218), showing a tall conical object within a rectangular precinct, itself approached by separate flight of steps, leading to a small temple apparently attached to the outer side of one portico.[13] Is the tall cone an aniconic cult-object, or even what Philo of Byblos described as a 'betyl', a 'stone imbued with *psyche (empsychos)*'? Or does the pyramid-shape not suggest rather a tomb, of a type well attested in the Near East—and perhaps the tomb of Tamuz, or Adonis, at Aphaca?[14]

Such a very distinctive architectural representation must be intended to display something specific to the city. But if it is an allusion to a 'tomb of Adonis', it is not explicit, and would be the only such allusion on the coins of the city. As so often, we cannot press the evidence too far in trying to make it yield coherent conceptions. We are in some sense on firmer ground in concentrating on dedications offered in the territory of Byblos to local manifestations of Zeus: to 'Zeus in Resa' from the city itself; or to 'Zeus (the) heavenly, highest, *Saarnaios,* attentive' at Abdat, north-east of the city, where *Saarnaios* clearly indicates the name of the locality. But it is again speculation to see these Greek dedications as reflections of an ancient Semitic Ba'al, a god of storms and mountains.[15]

These fragmentary items of evidence, however enigmatic, are of crucial importance precisely because they are localisable expressions of personal or group observance. But they offer only modest assistance when we try to interpret the only known explicit attempt made in the Imperial period to interpret Phoenician cults and beliefs for a Greek audience, the *Phoenicica* of Philo of Byblos, apparently written at the beginning of the second century AD.[16] Only a bare statement of what this enigmatic work seems to amount to is possible

13. *BMC Phoenicia,* 102, no. 36; Pl. xii, 13. See M. J. Price and B. L. Trell, *Coins and Their Cities: Architecture on the Ancient Coins of Greece, Rome and Palestine* (1977), 151–152 and fig. 271.

14. So Soyez, op. cit., 41–43.

15. For the evidence and the interpretation, Soyez, op. cit. (n.8), 87.

16. The fragments, almost all from Eusebius' *Praeparatio Evangelica,* are collected in Jacoby, *FGrH* 290, whose text is used in the translations and commentaries by H. W. Attridge and R. A. Oden, *Philo of Byblos: The Phoenician History* (1981), and A. I. Baumgarten, *The Phoenician History of Philo of Byblos* (1981). See now also I. Schiffman, *Phönizisch-Punische Mythologie* (1986).

here. Written in Greek, it claims to be a translation of a work on the Phoenician gods by one Sanchuniathon of Berytus, dating from before the Trojan War. As such, this claim must be wholly misleading. The interpretation, in a way familiar from both Lucian and the Syriac *Oration of Meliton*, is a mélange of Greek and non-Greek elements, including in this case Egyptian ones (or rather Greek versions of Egyptian ones). Its main principle of interpretation, which is shared both by the *Oration of Meliton* and, significantly, by Josephus when speaking of the chief god of Damascus,[17] is to see deities as having been in origin earthly rulers or other outstanding individuals. The fact that this conception is associated with the early-Hellenistic philosopher Euhemerus would not of itself prove anything about the real date of origin of the conceptions appearing in Philo. But it is in fact inconceivable that what Philo wrote (or copied, or interpreted) could be earlier than the Hellenistic period; and it may well be original to himself.

That would give it, if anything, an added significance. For, however confused the mélange of traditions which he brings to the interpretation of Phoenician deities, his work does contain a series of specific, and largely reliable, interpretations of Phoenician names and concepts. Thus for instance he says that 'Beelsamēn' among the Phoenicians means 'lord of Heaven' (B'L ŠMN), and is 'Zeus' in Greek. Less clearly, he speaks of two deities called Misōr and Sydyk, terms which he says mean 'easily solved' and 'just'. Although MYŠR and ṢDQ in fact both mean 'just', evidence of the second millennium BC from Ras Shamra does reveal a god with the double name ṢDQ MŠR.[18] Significant in a different way is his statement that a single son is 'still even now' called by the Phoenicians 'Ieoud' (YḤYD).

The work cannot be taken as a factual report on established communal beliefs; instead it is an erratic, pseudo-scholarly attempt to combine myth, adventurous etymologies (often relating to Greek names) and aspects of local history. Thus for instance 'Kronos' is said to have founded the first city, Byblos, and (later) to have given it to the goddess 'Baaltis' (a name which must derive from B'LT GBL), while he gave Berytus to Poseidon (who is indeed prominent on the city's coins). What Philo wrote is first of all a reflection of the long-standing prominence of Phoenician deities in Greek culture. But it does reveal genuine connections between Phoenician cults of a much earlier period and those of the Roman Empire; and it does suggest that at least the meanings of individual words in Phoenician were still understood. It leaves open the question of whether Phoenician was still spoken, or written; or whether coherent works in Phoenician were preserved, and could be understood. As with Lucian, and indeed the *Oration of Meliton*, it is precisely when

17. See 9.3 below.
18. See Baumgarten, op. cit., 175.

a work written in this period appears to offer a window into the meaning and nature of 'Oriental' cults that it is at its most deceptive.

Berytus appears in the surviving fragments of Philo's *Phoenicica* as one Phoenician city among others (those mentioned by name are Byblos, Berytus, Sidon and Tyre); it lies in the nature of the work that the reader would find no allusion in it to the fact that Berytus had for over a century been a Roman *colonia*. The fact deserves emphasis, partly because this status was to be gained also, in the Severan period, by Tyre and Sidon. But in their case it was to be a mere question of status, and a reflection of the complex set of traditions which united Phoenicia to the Punic cities of North Africa and to Rome, and contributed to the invention of a Roman province called Syria Phoenice.

In the case of Berytus, however, the status reflected, as we have seen, the settlement in 15 BC of Latin-speaking legionaries, spread over a territory which included the northern Bekaa Valley on the other side of Mount Lebanon. It is necessary therefore, first, to sum up the profound and long-lasting consequences of the foundation of this unique island of Roman culture in the Near East; second, to ask what if anything remained of the Greek or Phoenician culture of the city and its territory; and third, in the light of these two issues, to look at Heliopolis and the cult, which was to be known throughout the Empire, of 'Iuppiter Optimus Maximus Heliopolitanus'.[19]

So far as its official, public image was concerned, the 'Colonia Iulia Augusta Felix Berytus' minted coins which are without exception in Latin until the cessation of coining in the 250s. The *ordo* (town-council) of the city can also be found dedicating a statue with a Latin inscription as late as AD 344. The city had the normal colonial constitution, with a town-council and magistrates, of whom the most important were the two annual *duumviri*. On the view taken here, that Heliopolis did not become a separate *colonia* until the reign of Septimius Severus,[20] the workings of this unambiguously colonial city constitution will be illustrated (for example) by the statue-base erected at Heliopolis under Hadrian in honour of one M. Licinnius Pompenna Potitus Urbanus: he had been a town-councillor *(decurio)*, and had held a series of local offices—*pontifex, agonothetes,* and *flamen munerarius;* he had also been priest *(sacerdos)* of Iuppiter Optimus Maximus Heliopolitanus, and had been granted the honour of the 'public horse' by Hadrian.[21]

In combining local with Imperial rank, this man was also very typical of

19. All these questions are discussed in detail in Millar, "Roman *Coloniae*", 10–23 and 32–34; the treatment there will merely be summarised here, and only occasional salient items of evidence will be cited. See also R. Mouterde, "Regards sur Beyrouth phénicienne, hellénistique et romaine", *MUSJ* 40 (1964), 145. For the initial settlement see 2.1 above. For the coins see now *RPC* I, 648–651.

20. 3.4 above.

21. *IGLS* VI, no. 2791.

the Latin-speaking 'colonial' population of the area. A long series of Latin inscriptions reflects the role in Imperial service of soldiers and centurions from Berytus. Sometimes too, men are found in the higher orders, as equestrian officers, or even as senators. One example is M. Sentius Proculus, a town-councillor and *duumvir* of the *colonia* in the second century, who also had an equestrian military career before entering the Roman Senate. The inscription set up to him in Berytus is a reflection of the conscious loyalism of this colonial community and of the continued use of Latin there.[22]

It was surely this consciously 'Roman' character of the place which meant that, at least from the earlier third century onwards, it was to there that young men from various parts of the Greek East tended to gravitate in order to study Roman law. We can find examples, for instance, from Neocaesarea in Pontus, from Cilicia and from the province of Arabia. We know nothing of the formal structure of teaching there, and are hardly entitled to speak of a 'Law School'. Rather it was the wider, 'Roman' cultural setting and the possibility of finding instruction in Roman law in different 'schools' *(auditoria)* which attracted them. The establishment of a tradition of Roman law teaching here was to be of great importance in the late Empire; but its significance for our purposes lies rather in the paradox that Berytus, as a 'Roman' or 'Latin' place, came to play a role in the wider culture of the Empire which could not be matched by any of the Greek cities of the Near Eastern region. Though of course Greek sophists and writers came *from* many different cities in the region, until the mid-fourth century none of these cities became a place *to* which students came from other provinces. In the map of the pagan Greek culture of the Imperial period, the Near East remained firmly in the second rank.

At least one of these Greek writers, Hermippos, who wrote on 'Slaves who distinguished themselves in *paideia*', came from Berytus itself, or rather from an inland village in its territory. The inscriptional record, scanty though it is, does indeed show that Greek as well as Latin remained in use. Since there is no reason to suppose that the original inhabitants of the city and its territory had been driven out, that is not surprising. What is striking is merely that the 'Roman', or colonial, character of the place also maintained itself, without there being, as in other *coloniae* in the Greek East, a steady reversion to general use of Greek.

Inscriptions from the city also reflect the worship there of a remarkable range of Roman deities: Liber Pater, Venus, Mercurius, Apollo, Diana, Mars, Proserpina, and perhaps Ceres, as well as the Fortuna and Genius of the *colonia*, and the Fata. The most surprising importation must be Mater Matuta, an ancient deity whose temple was to be found in the Forum Boarium at

22. R. Cagnat, "M. Sentius Proculus de Beyrouth", *Syria* 7 (1926), 67; *AE* (1929), no. 150; H. Devijver, *PME* II (1977), S.25.

Rome. But it is precisely the identity of the one known dedicator, and the place where the dedication was made, which begins to raise the question of what other elements might have been present in the social and religious culture of Berytus and its territory. For the Latin dedication to Mater Matuta was made, following an oracular response from Iuno, by a lady called Flavia Nicolais (also called) Saddane, who has a Greek-Semitic name, and must come from a local family which gained the Roman citizenship in the Flavian period. She has thus adopted an imported, and distinctively 'Roman', cult.[23] We will see shortly an even clearer example of such an importation, in the absorption of 'Mercurius Dominus' as a deity in a remote mountain village.[24]

The site where Flavia Nicolais made her dedication was not remote, but it was a hillside sanctuary, on the slopes of Mount Lebanon overlooking Berytus. This is a place called Der el-Kala, where there is a whole series of dedications, in both Greek and Latin, to a deity called 'Theos Balmarkōd', or 'Zeus Balmarkōd'; a Greek inscription addressing him as 'lord of dances' ('koirane kōmōn') makes it certain that the underlying Semitic appellation, B'L MRQD, had the same meaning; for the root RQD means 'dance'. As so often, therefore, we can see that the meaning of a divine name in a Semitic language was known, and the name could be reproduced in transliteration in Greek. But it is not accompanied by any inscribed texts in a Semitic language; so whether the language in question remained in use there is uncertain.

Though all our inscribed evidence from Der el-Kala, in Greek and Latin, comes from the Imperial period, as do the remains of the temple there (which may be of the first century AD),[25] it is very likely that the cult represents the observance by the Latin- and Greek-speaking population of the *colonia* of a long-established local cult. If so, it is of some importance that inscriptions quite frequently refer to the god as 'I(uppiter) O(ptimus) M(aximus) B(almarcod)', thus treating this local deity as in some way an equivalent of the most important Roman deity, Iuppiter Optimus Maximus, whose temple had stood on the Capitol in Rome since the late sixth century BC.

As is well known, the same appellation came into widespread use for the chief male deity of Heliopolis: 'Iuppiter Optimus Maximus Heliopolitanus'. It is a natural assumption that here too we have a local Ba'al, who has become either 'Iuppiter' or 'Zeus Hēliopolitēs'. He is often, though by no means always, associated in inscriptions with two other Roman deities, Venus and Mercurius. Hence there has been a temptation, which has even been incorporated into the title of the most important modern work on the gods of Heliopolis, to see this group of Roman deities as representing a 'Semitic triad',

---

23. *CIL* III, no. 6680.
24. Text to n.32 below.
25. Krencker and Zschietschmann, *Römische Tempel* I, 1–3.

and to assert that there is no doubt these names relate to 'Semitic' divine beings, Hadad, Atargatis and a minor male consort whose native name is unknown.[26]

But is there really no doubt? First, nowhere in the contemporary evidence is there any explicit identification of the Iuppiter of Heliopolis with Hadad, or of Venus with Atargatis. There might have been: for, as Philo of Byblos noted, 'the Phoenicians say that Astarte is Aphrodite'.[27] The divine names 'Hadaran' (if not precisely 'Hadad') and 'Atargatis', or 'the Syrian Goddess', do indeed appear in this region: not, however, at Heliopolis, but at another very interesting local settlement and cult-centre, Niha, on the eastern side of Mount Lebanon, and some 25 km south-west of Heliopolis.[28] Here we have what seems very clear evidence of Latin-speaking settlers subscribing to the cult of a deity whom they saw as both local and 'Syrian': for a Latin inscription shows a 'pagus Augustus' (a village, or association of settlers) making a dedication on behalf of the Emperor to the 'Dea Suria Nihathe(na)'; other inscriptions reveal Hochmaea, a virgin (priestess) of both the 'Deus Hadranis' and the 'Dea Syr(ia) Nihat(ena)', who is described in Greek as the 'thea Atargatis'. The impression that we are confronted with a cult which the population living there in the Imperial period consciously saw as 'Syrian' is reinforced by a relief showing a priest in a long tunic bound by a girdle, and wearing a tall conical hat—very similar in broad terms to the costume of a priest represented on a relief at Hierapolis.[29] This material, along with the remains of two substantial temples at another sanctuary (Hosn Niha) further up the valley, is certainly evidence of the observance of local cults, of the extraordinary architectural capacities of Near Eastern village communities in the Imperial period, and of a conception on the part of the worshippers that the cult was something distinctively regional. There is, however, nothing distinctively 'Phoenician' here; and no comparable allusions to Hadad (or Hadaran) or to Atargatis (or 'the Syrian Goddess') are known in relation to Heliopolis or its gods.

On the contrary, a bilingual inscription in Greek and Latin from Berytus

26. Y. Hajjar, *La triade d'Héliopolis/Baalbek* I–III (1977–1985). See vol. II, p. 511: 'Il ne fait aucun doute que ces dénominations recouvrent des entités sémitiques avec Hadad, Atargatis et un parédre mineur dont on ignore le nom indigène'. Since I take a quite different approach, it is only right to acknowledge the exceptional learning in this major work.

27. *FGrH* 790 F.10 (31).

28. For the temples see Krencker and Zschietschmann, *Römische Tempel* I, 105–137. For Niha see above all J.-P. Rey-Coquais, "Des montagnes au désert: Baetocécé, le pagus Augustus de Niha, la Ghouta à l'est de Damas", in E. Frézouls (ed.), *Sociétés urbaines, sociétes rurales dans l'Asie Mineure et la Syrie hellénistiques et romaines* (1987), 191, on pp. 198–207. The inscriptions of Niha and Hosn Niha are *IGLS* VI, nos. 2928–2948.

29. 7.2 above.

shows 'thea Atargatis' in Greek equated with 'Dea Syria' in Latin, while 'Venus Heliopolitana' is mentioned separately.[30] The explicit evidence thus counts clearly against an identification of this Venus with Atargatis. The much-canvassed notion of a triad is also dubious. When Heliopolis finally became a separate *colonia* under Septimius Severus, its coins, with legends almost all in Latin, duly name 'I.O.M.H' and represent his temple, with a flight of steps leading to it;[31] but they give no hint of any 'triad'.

The temple shown must be the famous major temple of Baalbek, with steps leading to a hexagonal forecourt, and behind it another vast rectangular forecourt with an altar, before the temple itself. Iuppiter also had his own *sacerdos,* as we saw above. The temple of Venus may well have been the other temple which lies parallel to the main one, on its southern side. But that of Mercurius is known to have been on a different site, a small hill over a kilometre to the south.

In the case of Mercurius it is of some interest that we see the opposite process to the adoption of 'native' cults by Roman settlers, that is, the absorption of an imported colonial cult into a remote village context. In the Latin inscriptions of the area, just as Venus is sometimes called 'Venus domina' ('mistress'), Mercurius can appear as 'Mercurius dominus'. This is how he is described, in Greek transliteration, in an inscription from the frieze of a small temple at Nebi Ham, which lies in a remote valley between the foothills of Anti-Lebanon and the main range, and some 15 km south of Baalbek.[32] The inscription reveals both that Nebi Ham, like so many other villages in the region, has kept its ancient name and that its Imperial forerunner possessed a complex political structure:

> To Merkourios Dōminos, (the god) of the village *(kōmē)* Chamōn, year 484 (AD 172/173), priest Titos son of Iauda, sacred treasurers Basas son of Saarita and Oubesos, the village built (the temple), and Bēliabos son of Saphara recorded (met?) the costs of the village. Phlakos (Flaccus?) (was) the *technitēs* (builder?).

The god for whom they built this temple under Marcus Aurelius can only have derived his name from the 'Mercurius (dominus)' of the major cult-centre of Heliopolis, which was still an outlying part of the colonial territory of Berytus; it too may have been in formal terms a *pagus*. The vast temples of Heliopolis were constructed—on whose initiative and at whose expense we do not know—in the course of the first two centuries, and certainly before

30. Hajjar, op. cit., no. 211.

31. *BMC Syria,* 290–295.

32. See Krencker and Zschietschmann, *Römische Tempel* I, 168–171; Hajjar, op. cit., no. 168.

the place became a separate *colonia*. Over the same period the cult of Iuppiter of Heliopolis (and sometimes of Venus and Mercurius) also spread to large parts of the Near East, and to many other regions of the Empire.

If the notion of a 'triad' is in reality without foundation, that is not to prove that the conception of this 'Iuppiter', or 'Zeus', did not owe much to an earlier 'Ba'al' worshipped on the same site. There certainly had been a cult of Zeus there in the Hellenistic period. But what we know of how the Iuppiter of Heliopolis was conceived of is in effect based only on his characteristic iconography: a god standing erect, wearing a high Egyptian-style hat *(ka-lathos)*, and dressed in a tight tunic which comes down to his feet and is divided into figured panels; his right arm is raised and brandishes a whip, while his left holds a bunch of ears of corn; and he is flanked on either side by a bull.

But here again there is a problem. Of all the figurines, reliefs or coins representing a deity of this (or approximately this) type, only two are actually labelled as 'Iuppiter Optimus Maximus Heliopolitanus'—and one of these is from Sukneh, east of Palmyra, for which a Palmyrene sculptor had been employed. The essential features of the iconography are retained, but the style is Palmyrene.[33] That apart, there is precisely one altar from Nemausus (Nîmes), dedicated, by a *primus pilus* (senior centurion) from Berytus, to 'I.O.M. Heliopolitan(o)', and with a bas-relief incorporating all the features mentioned.[34] That most iconographic representations of this type, which include some coins of cities other than Heliopolis, for instance Ptolemais (but *not* Heliopolis itself), come from southern Syria or Phoenicia is clear. Hence there is no reason to doubt that this was a distinctively regional form of cult-image. But it would also be compatible with the evidence to say that this regional form of cult-image was also used to represent the Iuppiter or Zeus of Heliopolis.

The pitfalls in attempting to characterise the cults of this region are thus all too obvious. It is not even clear whether anything more than its attachment to Berytus as the territory of Augustus' *colonia,* or its location within the later province of 'Syria Phoenice', would justify our thinking of Heliopolis and the Bekaa Valley as 'Phoenician' at all. Yet we have already noted that Eusebius saw the cult of 'Aphrodite' (Venus) at Heliopolis as one observed by 'Phoenicians', and that Constantine's measures were directed against ritual prostitution there.[35] In this Christian view, the *colonia,* Iuppiter and Mercurius have all vanished. Yet Eusebius was at least a contemporary, living in a neighbour-

33. Hajjar, op. cit., no. 186 and Pl. LXX. For this dedication by a Roman auxiliary officer see 4.1, text to n.1.

34. Hajjar, op. cit., no. 285.

35. 5.3 above.

ing city. But the one-sidedness of even his testimony should make us beware of basing interpretations of any of these cults on retrospective analyses written in the late Empire. The most dubious of all is perhaps that of Macrobius, writing in the fifth century, who manages to identify the god of Heliopolis as both Iuppiter and Apollo/Sol, and to go on to state that the 'Assyrii' identify the supreme god as Sol, call him Adad (meaning 'unus, unus'—hypothetically 'ḤD, 'ḤD) and give him a consort called Adargatis.[36] Whatever the starting-point of our approach to these cults, it should not be this. As was said at the beginning, the more explicit our evidence, the more it represents a construction by the observer. If we begin from the documentary evidence, the most important aspect of the colonial territory, divided into that of two *coloniae* by Septimius Severus, is precisely that which makes a contrast with all other regions of the Near East: the creation of a colonial world where Latin continued to be used and the main gods had names borrowed from the Roman pantheon.

It thus remains highly uncertain what, if anything, remained of the Phoenician culture of Berytus and its hinterland. No similar problem arises with the two chief (and rival) Phoenician cities, Tyre and Sidon, even though there are no Phoenician inscriptions from either in the Imperial period, and both became Roman *coloniae* under the Severan dynasty.

8.5 SIDON AND TYRE

Sidon and Tyre form a clearly defined pair, but also need to be treated separately, if only because so much less evidence is available for Sidon in the Imperial period.[1] There is a marked contrast with the Hellenistic age, when Phoenician inscriptions left by Sidonians abroad in the Greek world are well attested; and the prominence of the city is reflected in items of evidence from Shechem in Samaria, Iamnia on the coast of Palestine and Idumaean Marisa, all of which reveal communities who identified themselves as 'Sidonians'.[2] In the Roman period the most distinctive surviving trace of the public character of Sidon is provided by its coins.[3] For, first, until the 40s AD, the city minted coins under its own name (sometimes in the form 'of Sidon the sacred and

36. Macrobius, *Sat.* I, 23, 10–21; Hajjar, op. cit., no. 331.

1. For a general survey see N. Jidejian, *Sidon through the Ages* (1971). For the coins see now *RPC* I, 651–655.

2. See Millar, "Phoenician Cities", 60–61; 'Sidonians' in Shechem: Josephus, *Ant.* XII, 5, 5 (257–264); 'Sidonians' in Marisa: *OGIS*, no. 593; 'Sidonians' in Iamnia: B. Isaac, "A Seleucid Inscription from Jamnia-on-the Sea: Antiochus V Eupator and the Sidonians", *IEJ* 41 (1991), 132.

3. For the pre-colonial coinage, *BMC Phoenicia*, 158–181; for the colonial coinage, pp. 182–199.

inviolate' in Greek) which carry no reference to or representation of the reigning Emperor. For that reason they are labelled by moderns as 'pseudo-autonomous'. Second, there are bronze coins, also with no reflection of the Emperor, with the Phoenician legends 'of the Sidonians' (LṢDNM) or 'of Sidon' (LṢDN), which appear throughout the first century AD. A variant legend is 'of Sidon (the) goddess' in Greek, or 'of Sidon (the) goddess, sacred, inviolate and mistress of a fleet'. At the same time there are coins which do portray Emperors, though none are actually named until Trajan. These coins very commonly represent Europa seated on a bull, a motif which reappears also after the city became a *colonia* under Elagabal, with the typically mixed Graeco-Latin title 'Colonia Aurelia Pia Metropolis Sidon'.

Concrete evidence of the official public use of the Phoenician language thus dies out in the first century. But the rival tradition according to which in legend Kadmos and Europa had really belonged to Sidon rather than Tyre was maintained in the Roman period, as it had been in the Hellenistic: hence the beginning of Achilles Tatius' novel *Leucippe and Clitophon* (written in the Imperial period, probably in the second century), with its description of the city as 'the mother of the Phoenicians' and its people as 'father of the Thebans', and its report of a temple of Astarte there, and of a painting of Europa to be seen in the city. Lucian, in *On the Syrian Goddess,* as usual producing several alternative explanations, records that there was in Sidon a great temple of Astarte, or (as he thought) rather of Selene (the Moon); but one of the priests told him that it was really a temple of Europa; and he correctly records that Sidonian coins portrayed Europa sitting on a bull.[4]

As we have seen, while the fact that the legend of Kadmos and Europa formed a distinctive aspect of the public image of both Sidon and Tyre is significant, it is not possible to characterise this as a Phoenician legend rather than as a common Greek one which gave these Phoenician cities a particular mythical role. If there were indeed distinctively Sidonian traditions, beliefs or cults, we have virtually no access to them (the city plays no part in the surviving fragments of Philo of Byblos).

As with all other cities, however, our conception of what Sidon 'was' cannot rest only on its central institutions (which consisted of the magistrates, council and assembly characteristic of any Greek city) and main cults, but must if possible take into account its territory. We could presume in any case that this territory covered the stretch of Mount Lebanon behind Sidon. But in fact the surprising indication by Josephus that Sidon had a common border with Damascus makes it likely that Sidonian territory stretched across the Leontes (Litani) River and the southern end of the

4. Lucian, *Dea Syr.* 4.

Bekaa Valley, and perhaps as far as some point on Mount Hermon.[5] Nothing seems to be known of the immediate hinterland of Sidon; but on this view some at least of the quite large group of rural temples in the southern Bekaa and on the south-western slopes of Mount Hermon will have been in Sidonian territory.[6] Here again we find that these rural communities could construct high-quality temples in stone, worshipped deities often identified mainly by the name of the locality itself, had quite complex administrative structures—and expressed themselves only in Greek. So we find, for instance, someone dedicating a bronze model of a ship as an offering to the 'theos Zeus of Baithmarē';[7] or the 'sacred treasurers' *(hierotamiai)* of 'thea Leukothea (of) Rachla' constructing a temple at a place which still has the same name, Rahle, in 268/269.[8] We cannot pretend to understand at all fully the nature of these deities or the social structures of the communities which worshipped them. But both the temples themselves and the inscriptions serve as yet further hints of the vitality and independence of village life, here as elsewhere. Yet, though personal names might keep a Semitic form, there is nothing to show that the local culture of the extensive hinterland of Sidon had any means of expression other than in Greek.

If circumstances in the modern world were ever to allow it, it would be of more than usual interest for what remains of the culture of this area to be closely surveyed. For it was somewhere on the border between this hinterland and that of Tyre that Mark's Gospel (7, 26) represents Jesus as encountering 'a Greek woman, a Syro-Phoenician by birth'; whether the meeting is historical or not, the description happens to fit perfectly with the dominant use of Greek, and with the meeting of Phoenician and more generally 'Syrian' features in the culture of these villages. But, as always, there are ambiguities in the representation of such local identities: telling the same story, Matthew (15, 21–22) describes the woman as a 'Canaanite'.

Where exactly that border lay there is no need to ask. But the pairing of the two cities is more than a matter of mere geography; for Tyre, even more than Sidon, occupied a position of conspicuous independence, and enjoyed a distinctive historical identity, within the Roman Empire.

Both had achieved *autonomia* from the Seleucids in the late second century BC, and the continuing significance of that was shown when Marcus Antonius refused Cleopatra's request to transfer the two cities to her in the

---

5. Josephus, *Ant.* XVIII, 6, 3 (153). For this deduction see Jones, *CERP²*, 270 and 287.

6. See also A. Alt, "Die Zeitrechnung der Tempelinschriften des Hermongebiets", *ZDPV* 62 (1939), 209. For routes and sites in this hinterland of Sidon, see also M. Tallon, "Sanctuaires et itinéraires romains du Chouf et du Sud de la Beqa'", *MUSJ* 43 (1968), 231.

7. H. Seyrig, "Antiquités de Beth-Maré", *Syria* 28 (1951), 101 = *IGLS* VI, no. 2989.

8. L. Jalabert, "Inscriptions grecques et latines de Syrie", *MUSJ* 2 (1907), 265, on p. 273, no. 68.

30s BC, 'knowing that they were free from the time of their ancestors'.[9] As we will see, one of Tyre's most famous sons, the Roman jurist Ulpian, claimed that his city had also had a treaty *(foedus)* with Rome; and a stray inscription on a medallion from Sidon, also of the third century, calls it an 'ally of the Romans'.[10] Cassius Dio claims that Augustus 'enslaved' both cities because of internal strife;[11] but whatever he meant (neither seems to have been a 'free city' in the formal sense of being exempt from jurisdiction and visits in person on the part of the governor), no long-term effects are known. Tyre appears on formal documents of the second century as 'sacred, inviolate, autonomous, metropolis of Phoenice (once also, under Trajan, adding 'and of the cities of Coele Syria') and other cities, and mistress of a fleet'.[12] The title tends to blur the distinction between 'metropolis' as a rank claimed by a city (perhaps only one in each province before Hadrian) and 'metropolis' as meaning literally 'mother-city', and thus (as here) as a historical reminiscence of Phoenician colonisation.[13]

Both this and other aspects of the special status of Tyre in the Empire are displayed most clearly on its coins.[14] From the moment of its acquisition of *autonomia* in 126/125 BC until AD 58/59, the city minted silver shekels and half-shekels (tetradrachms and didrachms) marked in Greek 'of Tyre, sacred and inviolate'. Minting by cities in base metals was of course common in the Greek East—indeed it functions as one of the standard signs that a place was a recognised *polis*. But minting in silver was rare, and must represent an exceptional privilege. These coins are also 'pseudo-autonomous', and show no reflection of the arrival of Roman rule, or of the existence of Emperors. It was also these Tyrian shekels which remained to the end the standard currency in which dues to the Temple in Jerusalem were to be paid; the fact that they displayed a head of Melqart and an eagle was apparently no objection. Clearly marked as Tyrian, they nonetheless carried no Phoenician writing beyond a single letter.

---

9. Josephus, *Ant.* XV, 4, 1 (95).

10. Ulpian: text to nn.23ff. below. Inscription from Sidon: H. Seyrig, *Syria* 27 (1950), 249.

11. Dio LIV, 7, 6.

12. For example, *Ins. Didyma*, no. 151 (adding 'and of the cities of Coele Syria'); *OGIS*, no. 595 (from Puteoli, see below).

13. For the multiplication of *metropoleis* from Hadrian onwards see G. W. Bowersock, "Hadrian and Metropolis", *Bonner Historia-Augusta-Colloquium* 182–183 (1985), 75.

14. For the silver and bronze coinage of Tyre in the Roman period, see *BMC Phoenicia* cxxxiv–xlii; 233–353; 255–296; A. Ben-David, *Jerusalem und Tyros: Ein Beitrag zur palästinensischen Münz- und Wirtschaftsgeschichte 126 a.c.–57 p.c.* (1969). For a general account see N. Jidejian, *Tyre through the Ages* (1969), and for the best analysis, M. Chéhab, "Tyr à l'époque romaine", *MUSJ* 38 (1962), 11. See now *RPC T,* 655–658.

The minting of Tyrian silver stopped in AD 58/59; there is no historical evidence as to how or why. But there must be some connection with the fact that in AD 59/60 there began an issue of silver tetradrachms, apparently struck at Antioch, showing the head of the Emperor, but also taking over the 'eagle' type shown on the silver coins of Tyre. In some way, therefore, this 'provincial' mint, assumed to be under Roman control, took over the functions of Tyrian minting in silver.[15]

Whether or not some action by Rome actually prevented further minting in silver by Tyre (the longest series in silver issued in the name of any provincial city in the Imperial period), the bronze coins of Tyre continued to be resolutely 'Tyrian', and to offer no reflection whatsoever of the existence of Emperors. From the later second century BC until the moment in the 190s (probably 198) when Tyre became a *colonia*,[16] they displayed only local types (often Melqart), and very commonly used the Phoenician legend LSR, 'of Tyre'. By the 90s AD the Greek term 'mētropolis' appears as well. As we saw above, it is used also in an inscription of Trajan's reign. But an entry in a Byzantine lexicon would imply that the title was formally confirmed only under Hadrian: 'Paulus, a Tyrian, a rhetor . . . who by an embassy to Hadrian had made his city a mētropolis'.[17] There is no real contradiction: it would fit perfectly with the nature of inter-city competition if Tyre had first used this title, then had it challenged, and then secured it by an embassy to the Emperor. It was perhaps on this basis that Tyre secured the right to hold 'Actian' games (that is, equal in rank to those at Nicopolis held to commemorate the battle of Actium), in the name of the *koinon* of Phoenicia, as some second-century coins record.[18]

The importance of the Tyrian bronze coinage of the second century needs to be stressed. In this period, from within the bounds of the established Empire, there was only one other coinage which both used a Semitic language and did not portray or name the Emperor—the Jewish coinage of the Bar Kochba revolt.[19] The coinage of Tyre did not of course serve to symbolise revolt, or even any real freedom. But it did, in a wholly distinctive way, express the continued attachment of Tyre to its identity as a Phoenician city with a long and glorious history. It was precisely this which enabled another

15. For the nearest to a clear account of this process, see D. R. Walker, *The Metrology of the Roman Silver Coinage* I (1976), 67ff. Even this remarkable work is not free from the allusiveness and lack of logical clarity which distinguishes almost all numismatic writing. A clearer account is now available in *RPC* I, 655ff.

16. 3.4 above.

17. Suda, *s.v.* Παῦλος (ed. Adler IV, 69).

18. *BMC Phoenicia*, 268.

19. 10.3 below.

rhetor from Tyre, Adrianos, on arriving in Athens, to open his first oration with the words 'Once again letters have come from Phoenicia'.[20]

That of course was an allusion which would be instantly intelligible to an audience familiar with *Greek* literature. Our problem, if we look for elements in the culture of Tyre which were not simply part of the common inheritance of Greek culture, is that they are so fragmentary, limited and non-coherent. The three Phoenician letters LṢR which appear on the bronze coins of the city are certainly, as a deliberate symbol, very significant. But they are not positive evidence that Phoenician was spoken, or that continuous texts could be written in it. Nor is the appearance (as elsewhere) of names of Semitic origin (as well as Latin) in Greek inscriptions: for instance Nikolaos son of Balēdōos (from B'LYD'–-'Ba'al knows'?), putting up an inscription in AD 60 to honour an *agoranomos* with the Roman name Gaius Iulius Candidus; Zoilos son of Bodas, as a city ambassador under Trajan; or Diodoros son of Nithumbalos (presumably from NTN, 'give', and B'L), making a dedication in 187/188 to the 'sacred god Herakles'.[21]

That of course was one undeniable element of continuity (but also one already represented in the pages of Herodotus), namely the cult of Herakles/ Melqart, who was the deity most often represented on the city coins. But in its public functioning Tyre was simply a Greek city (almost) like any other, as can be seen in the famous Greek inscription of AD 174 from Puteoli, with a letter from the *statiōn* of the Tyrians established at Puteoli to the magistrates, council and assembly of the city, and their reply, as quoted from the *akta* of the proceedings of the *boulē*. The only non-Greek linguistic influence here is Latin, with the Latin word *acta* transliterated (as we find also at Petra) to describe the proceedings of the council; and the Latin words *statio* and *stationarii* also transliterated to describe the Tyrian club-house at Puteoli and the resident Tyrian traders who used it.[22]

The year 174 is likely to have followed rather than preceded the birth of one of the two most prominent intellectuals produced by Tyre, Domitius Ulpianus, the major Roman jurist of the Classical period.[23] It is important to stress, as one sign of the complex cultural influences of the period, that he will certainly have been born long before Tyre was made a Roman *colonia* by Severus, and therefore in the period when Tyre was a Phoenician-Greek city, and was still minting coins with the legend LṢR. The Roman name which Ulpian bore was one of the many adopted by Greek families which had ac-

20. Philostratus, *VS* II, 10.

21. M. Chéhab, *MUSJ* 26 (1944–1946), 60–63; idem, "Tyr à l'époque romaine", *MUSJ* 38 (1962), 11, on p. 17. See also C. Bonnet, *Melqart* (1988), 62ff.

22. *OGIS*, no. 595. For ἄκτα at Petra, 11.4 below.

23. See T. Honoré, *Ulpian* (1982).

quired the Roman citizenship in the course of the first two centuries. As everywhere else, these Latin names took root in an entirely Greek context. In the case of this family, the *Deipnosophistae* of Athenaeus, written at the end of the second century, portrays an 'Oulpianos' of Tyre as the main speaker. The odds are strong that this is a member of the same established family; for a century later Eusebius records that another 'Oulpianos' from Tyre died as a Christian martyr in the Great Persecution.[24]

The 'Oulpianos' who appears in the pages of Athenaeus is represented as a learned devotee of Greek literature and an expert in its vocabulary, objecting when someone uses the Latin word *decocta* (boiled-down wine); but he is also addressed jokingly as a fellow-citizen of the writers of *Phoenicica*, Sanchuniathon and Mochos, and is characterised as 'Phoenician' by the other speakers; or alternatively as introducing a native custom (not eating fish) from Syria, an allusion which leads to some far-fetched discussions of the etymology of the divine name 'Atargatis'.[25] It lies in the nature of the work that what unites the speakers is their common immersion in Greek literature; and it is within that context that his local identity as a 'Tyrian', 'Phoenician' or 'Syrian' has to be seen.

Whether the Ulpian, or 'Oulpianos', from Tyre, whose works, written in Latin, represent almost a third of surviving Roman juristic writing, as reproduced in the *Digest,* was actually born in Tyre is not known and is not significant. What is important is that his discussion of *coloniae* which enjoyed the *ius Italicum* (formal equivalence to Italian soil for the territory) opens with a resounding declaration of the antiquity of Tyre and the nature of its relations to Rome. As we have seen earlier, it is in fact quite certain that Tyre gained this status as a result of taking Severus' side in the civil war of 194, and Ulpian goes on to make this explicit in the case of two other Near Eastern cities (Heliopolis and Laodicea). But the elevation of Tyre demanded to be set in a wider and more creditable historical context:

> It needs to be understood that there are certain *coloniae* enjoying the *ius Italicum,* for example in Syria Phoenice the most distinguished *colonia* of the Tyrians, in which my own *origo* lies, in a noble setting, of the most remote antiquity, powerful in war, most tenacious of the treaty which it struck with Rome; for to it the Deified Severus and our Emperor granted the *ius Italicum,* on account of its outstanding loyalty to the *res publica* and to the *imperium Romanum.*[26]

24. Eusebius, *Mart. Pal.* 5, 1.
25. Athenaeus, *Deipn.* 121F *(decocta);* 126A (Sanchuniathon and Mochos); 175A–176A; 346C–E (fish and Atargatis) 1. For Oulpianos as a 'Syrian', e.g., 669B.
26. *Dig.* L, 15, 1 *pr.*

It is an accident, but an appropriate one, that the earliest inscription reflecting the new status should come from Lepcis Magna in Tripolitania, the native city of Septimius Severus. At some time in the second century, but before Tyre became a *colonia*, Lepcis had set up at Tyre a statue personifying the city, with an inscription in Latin and Greek honouring it as the mother-city of Lepcis.[27] Now, as we saw earlier, Tyre put up at Lepcis a statue of Severus' son Geta, and called itself on the inscription 'Septimia Tyros Colonia, Metropolis of Phoenice and other *civitates*'.[28]

In terms of its official public image, therefore, the grant of colonial status to Tyre functioned not to replace an existing historical identity but to re-emphasise certain elements in its legendary past. It is in fact in the mainly Latin, but also Greek, coinage of the colonial period, until minting ceased in the 250s, and far more clearly than in the Greek coinage of the preceding period, that the legends which were (or could be) associated with Tyre were most fully exploited. The themes include Dido supervising the building of Carthage (and labelled 'Deidōn' in Greek); Europa (also labelled in Greek); and, most strikingly of all, Kadmos offering a papyrus roll to three standing male figures. In case anyone might have missed the allusion to the Greek acquisition of the alphabet from Phoenicia, he is labelled in Greek, as are they, 'Hellē(nes)'.[29]

Like the references to the 'Actian Herculian' games and to the *koinon* of Phoenice which still appear on the colonial coinage, these historic allusions represent a public identity of third-century Tyre in which 'Phoenician', 'Greek' and 'Roman' elements are inextricably fused. But they now found expression only in Latin or Greek. In the colonial period, Phoenician coin-legends finally disappear.

That would not of itself, however, prove either that the cults and social structures characteristic of the territory of Tyre were also so clearly absorbed into a wider culture or that the Phoenician language had entirely passed out of use. As everywhere else, we have to think of the urban centre against the background of a world of villages, usually illuminated only by sporadic archaeological or epigraphic remains, or passing allusions in literary sources. Tyrian territory, for instance, stretched inland at least as far as a place which Josephus calls Kadasa or Kydasa, to the north of Gischala in Galilee: 'a strong inland village of the Tyrians, always at feud and strife with the Galileans, having its large population and stout defences as resources behind it in its

27. J.-P. Rey-Coquais, "Une double dédicace de Lepcis Magna à Tyr", in A. Mastino (ed.), *L'Africa Romana* IV (1986), 597.

28. *IRT*, no. 437; 3.4 above.

29. *BMC Phoenicia*, 277, no. 409 (Dido); 290, no. 468 (Europa); 293, no. 488 (Kadmos).

quarrel with the nation'. Jewish forces duly attacked 'Kadasa of the Tyrians' when the revolt broke out in 66.[30] Josephus' references alone would give a powerful impression of yet another heavily populated *kōmē.* But in fact the place can be confidently identified with the archaeological remains at Kedesh, just on the Israeli side of the border with Lebanon, and overlooking the Huleh Valley from the edge of the hills to its west. Here again there is a temple, entered through a pillared portico, and surrounded by a large *temenos,* of some 80 m by 55 m, perhaps built in the early second century. Greek inscriptions show that the deity worshipped there was 'Theos Hagios Ouranios', 'the Holy Sky God', perhaps to be identified as Baalshamin.[31] Tyrian territory must have covered at least a large part of the northern half of the Galilean hills between the sea, the Leontes (Litani) River in the north, and the Huleh Valley to the east. But there seems to have been no detailed study of this region as it was in the Imperial period (nor, still less, is one likely in the foreseeable future) since the surveys by Ernest Renan and others were made in the last century.[32] The hinterland of Tyre remains essentially unknown.

The odds are strong, however, that if the remains of local cult-centres happened to be known here as elsewhere, their inscriptions would be in Greek, even if the names of deities, or of deities named by relation to places, contained Semitic elements. The combined evidence of the coins from Phoenicia and of Philo of Byblos provides us with no more than individual words or phrases in Phoenician; not a single connected sentence is attested as having been generated in Phoenician after the one Phoenician inscription of the Augustan period from Aradus, and the one possibly Imperial one from Sidon.[33] As our evidence now stands, there is a marked contrast, both in terms of public inscriptions and in the composition of legal documents in Aramaic, Hebrew, Nabataean and Syriac, with other regions of the Near East.[34] It remains of course possible that Phoenician could have been used on perishable documents, and impossible to disprove that it was still spoken. Ulpian himself *may* be referring to Aramaic and Phoenician when he discusses whether an *obligatio* could be created by a verbal exchange conducted entirely in Greek (as opposed to Latin), or even in other languages, such as *Assyrius sermo* or

30. Josephus, *BJ* IV, 2, 3 (104–105), Loeb trans.; II, 18, 1 (459), attack in 66.

31. See M. Fischer, A. Ovadiah and I. Roll, "The Roman Temple at Kedesh, Upper Galilee: A Preliminary Study", *Tel Aviv* 11 (1984), 146; idem, "The Epigraphic Finds from the Roman Temple at Kedesh in the Upper Galilee", *Tel Aviv* 13–14 (1986–87), 60. Cf. J. Magness, "Some Observations on the Roman Temple at Kedesh", *IEJ* 40 (1990), 173 (speculative).

32. For instance, E. Renan, *Mission de Phénicie* (1864), 632ff. See also C. R. Conder and H. H. Kitchener, *The Survey of Western Palestine* I, *Galilee* (1881).

33. 8.3 and 8.4 above.

34. Cf. esp. 10.2–3, 11.2, 11.4 and 12.5 below.

Poenus sermo.[35] *Assyrius sermo* could be either the Syriac of Mesopotamia or Osrhoene (recently made into provinces) or the Aramaic of Syria or Palestine, or even Arabia; *Poenus sermo* might more reasonably be taken as the language of his native Phoenicia than as the Neo-Punic of Africa or Sardinia. The pairing of the two languages then reads quite naturally. There is at any rate nowhere else in the surviving corpus of Roman legal writing where this possibility is raised. But to take Ulpian's words specifically as a reference to two known languages in contemporary use in the Near East, we have to read into his words an awareness of (hypothetical) local conditions which may be entirely anachronistic.

We have to do the same (or, worse, make use of unexamined stereotypes about the 'Orient') to find anything 'Phoenician' in the other of the two famous intellectuals who came from Tyre, Porphyry the Neo-Platonist philosopher.[36] Born (it seems) in 234, when Tyre had been a *colonia* for over three decades, he wrote in Greek. There seems to be nothing in all his work to suggest that the official status of Tyre as a Latin-speaking *colonia* had any effect on his language, culture, range of knowledge or outlook. If any feature of his local origin was significant at all, it was the Phoenician aspect. He himself records that his actual name (for 'Porphyrios'—'purple'—was a nickname), that is, 'Basileus' ('king'), had as its equivalent 'in my native language' the name 'Malchos'.[37] But again we are confronted with only a very limited relationship to Phoenician, the explication of individual words.

In his *Against the Christians* and elsewhere he made use of Philo's *Phoenicica*. But the few remarks about Phoenician customs which he makes in other works are drawn from standard Greek sources, and take their place along with comparable remarks about Egyptians, Chaldeans, Arabians or Hebrews.[38] The fundamental fact is that the culture to which Porphyry's works attach themselves is the universal one of Hellenism, in which the facts of a man's local origins were of marginal significance, and reflections on the customs of non-Greek peoples were drawn normally not from observation but from the common stock of allusions in Greek literature. It remains a typical paradox that while Ulpian must already (it seems) have been far advanced in

---

35. *Dig.* XLV, 1, 1, 6. Cf. XXXII, 11 *pr.* (also from Ulpian) on the possibility of *fideicommissa* in any *lingua*, even 'Punica vel Gallicana'.

36. I know of no overall study of Porphyry since J. Bidez, *Vie de Porphyre, le philosophe néoplatonicien* (1913). See A. Smith, "Porphyrian Studies since 1913", ANRW II.36.2 (1987), 717.

37. Porphyry, *V. Plot.* 17.

38. For example, in the *Life of Pythagoras* (ed. E. des Places, 1982), 6 (Pythagoras learning mathematics from Egyptians, Chaldeans and Phoenicians); 11 (from Antonius Diogenes—learning the interpretation of dreams from the Egyptians, Arabs, Chaldeans and Hebrews); *On Abstinence from Living Things* I, 56 (Phoenician use of human sacrifice in crises—from Philo of Byblos); II, 11 (Egyptian and Phoenician abstinence from eating beef).

the study of Roman law at the moment when his Phoenician-Greek native city became a *colonia* in 198,[39] Porphyry, born more than three decades after that moment, represents himself entirely as one Greek intellectual among others.

Indeed, far from representing himself as embodying the possibility of mutual understanding and influence between Greek culture and contemporary 'Oriental' languages and cultures, Porphyry goes out of his way to deny that such an understanding is possible. For instance there is the passage in *On Abstinence from Living Things* where he speaks of the unintelligibility and repulsiveness of other languages, including that of the Syrians, in the view of Greeks:

> For neither do Greeks understand the language of Indians, nor those brought up in Attica that of Scythians or Thracians or Syrians. But the language of the one group sounds like the screeching of cranes to the other. Nonetheless, each of their languages can be incorporated in writing and articulated by those others, as ours can by us. But the language of the Syrians for example or the Persians cannot be articulated or put into writing, just as, for all men, the language of animals cannot be.[40]

Quite apart from the record of his conquests in the Roman provinces which Porphyry's contemporary Shapur I found it not in the least impossible to set down in parallel texts written in Parthian, Middle Persian and Greek,[41] Porphyry's words show a puzzling unawareness of the possibility of literature in Syriac; yet he himself refers to Bardesanes (as 'a Babylonian' of the generation before his own) in the next book of his *On Abstinence*.[42] Nor, as it seems, had he ever visited a city which was also part of his own province of 'Syria Phoenice', and where Greek and a dialect of 'the language of the Syrians' were inscribed everywhere in parallel texts: Palmyra.

39. The biography of Ulpian is very uncertain; but it is known that he was at some point the Imperial *a libellis* (*Dig.* XX, 5, 12, *pr.*), and Honoré, op. cit. (n.23), 22ff. and 191ff., argues that his tenure was from 202 to 209.

40. Porphyry, *On Abstinence* III, 3, 4.

41. 4.2–3 above.

42. *On Abstinence* IV, 17. On Bardesanes see 12.5 below.

EASTERN SYRIA PHOENICE:
MOUNTAIN, OASIS AND STEPPE

9.1. GEOGRAPHICAL CONNECTIONS

The coastal region of what was to become the province of Syria Phoenice consisted, as we have seen, of a line of cities characterised on the one hand by a common past as Phoenician communities—trading cities and independent naval powers—by a common language of which rather faint traces still remained in the Imperial period, and above all by a recognised identity within Graeco-Roman culture. But how far inland we should think of a 'Phoenician' identity as extending is an insoluble problem. The question can be asked as regards the mountainous hinterland of Aradus, with the temple of Baetocaece; the chain of Mount Lebanon, also marked by temples on remote, elevated locations; the Bekaa Valley and Heliopolis; and the border-zone between the areas of Jewish and non-Jewish settlement in the hills of northern Galilee and around Mount Carmel. But Severus' division of Syria in 194 boldly classified as part of 'Syria Phoenice' places which no one until then had ever thought of as 'Phoenician'. As regards Emesa on the Orontes, there are complex questions, to which we will return. But the new province labelled as 'Phoenice' now embraced also the whole of the great mountain-chain of Anti-Lebanon and Mount Hermon, whose inhabitants Strabo had thought of as 'Ituraeans and Arabs'; and with that it included the relatively new city of Caesarea Panias on the slopes of Mount Hermon, founded by the tetrarch Philip, and, much more significantly, the ancient city of Damascus. More strikingly still, the province included Palmyra, and with it a vast stretch of steppe extending to the lower-middle Euphrates, below Dura-Europos.

In one sense the division was simply a matter of military convenience: to divide Syria into two sections, one of which, Syria Phoenice, would have only a single legion—III Gallica stationed at Raphaneae on the Orontes—and (as it may have seemed) had no significant external frontier. For no major Roman forces ever seem to have passed directly through Palmyra to the Euphrates and Babylonia, and no Parthian forces, or Persian ones, ever took that route in the opposite direction. All major military movements followed the rivers— the Euphrates, or Euphrates and Chabur, or the Tigris.

But if 'Phoenice' had been intended to be a military backwater, while re- ducing the legions under the command of the *legatus* of Syria Coele to two, it did not turn out so. As we have seen, by the early fourth century a road- system and line of forts, explicitly identified as the 'Strata Diocletiana', linked the Euphrates to Palmyra, the outer edges of the oasis of Damascus and the eastern fringes of the Hauran. These military installations in 'Phoenice' thus formed the central part of a system which stretched from Mesopotamia to Aila on the Red Sea. However we *interpret* its purpose or effectiveness, a 'desert frontier' was now there.

It was there in part because Roman control now reached everywhere to the borders of the steppe zone; but this 'frontier' was also a road-system along which traffic moved between Damascus and Nabataea or Arabia to the south, and from the Euphrates via Palmyra to Damascus, as well as directly west- wards to Emesa. To speak of the movements of trade west or south-west from Palmyra, however, though it no doubt corresponds to the facts, is to go be- yond what our evidence directly tells us. For, as we will see, while we have a considerable range of information about Palmyrene trade eastward, to the Euphrates, Babylonia, the Persian Gulf and even 'Scythia' (north-west India), movements west (to Emesa) and south-west (to Damascus) are much less well attested.

Nonetheless it is certain that a route did run between Damascus and Pal- myra. Its course was determined by that of the quite high and rugged moun- tain-range (rising to a maximum of about 1400 m) which runs approximately parallel to Anti-Lebanon and projects north-eastwards into the steppe almost to Palmyra. The 'Strata Diocletiana' and the Roman forts ran along the south- ern side of this range. The existence of the oasis of Palmyra itself, however, was determined by the range of mountains, reaching heights of between 1000 and 1400 m, which ran almost directly eastwards from near Emesa to reach its highest point some 40 km north-east of Palmyra. One further outcrop, the Jebel al-Bishri, of some 950 m in height, rises half-way between the end of this range and the Euphrates. It is no accident that the most north-easterly evidence for a Palmyrene presence comes from a point where a route ran between these two mountains, to go northwards to meet the upper-middle Euphrates at Callinicum.

The place concerned is Tayibeh, ancient Oresa, from which there came a bilingual inscription, in Greek and Palmyrene, now in the British Museum. It is a dedication, dating to AD 134, on behalf of Hadrian, to a deity named as 'Zeus Megistos Keraunios' ('thunderer') in Greek, and as 'Ba'alshamin, lord of the world' (B'LŠMN MR' 'LM') in Palmyrene. In a way which perhaps rather too neatly symbolises the unity of the area under discussion, and its connecting routes, the dedicator names himself as 'Agathangelos ('GTGLS in Palmyrene), an Abilene of the Decapolis'. What he is dedicating is called a *kamara* in Greek, apparently a niche for a statue, with a bench *(klinē)* in front of it.[1] At Sukneh, further south on the same road, and some 20 km nearer to Palmyra, there was discovered the statue of 'Iuppiter Optimus Maximus Heliopolitanus', in entirely Palmyrene style, dedicated by a Roman auxiliary officer, probably in the second half of the second century.[2] Both finds seem to demonstrate (*unless* the objects were transported here at a later date) how the eastern extension of the Palmyrene presence served to bring this remote region within the orbit of the culture (or cultures) of the settled Near East as it was when under Roman rule.

That need not seem surprising. For we have already seen how a Palmyrene military presence is attested on the lower-middle Euphrates at Gamla, and at Ana or Anatha, while Palmyrene soldiers are found at Dura-Europos before it passed into Roman hands.[3] Perhaps more important, the quite extensive series of Palmyrene inscriptions from Dura begins with what is almost the earliest of all such inscriptions, recording how two Palmyrenes in 34/33 BC dedicated outside the city a temple to Bel and Yarhibol (HYKL' LBL WYRHBWL). The word used here for 'temple' (HYKL') is of some significance; for, as we will see, it appears in Greek transliteration, outside the properly Palmyrene zone, on the important temple at Dumayr on the road from Palmyra to Damascus.[4] It is another sign of interconnections along the route which bordered the desert that in AD 94, the twenty-fifth year of the last Nabataean king, Rabbel II, members of the household of some Nabataean officers (with the title *stratēgos*—'SRTG') dedicated a hexagonal pillar at Dumayr, with an inscription in Nabataean.[5] Unless these years (about the time of the death of Agrippa II) were much more disturbed than we imagine, this

1. *CIS* II.3, no. 3912; cf. *OGIS*, no. 631, and *IGR* III, no. 1057 (Greek text only). It is possible, as claimed by G. W. Bowersock, "A New Antonine Inscription from the Syrian Desert", *Chiron* 7 (1976), 349, on p. 354, that this inscription (by a slip given as 3970) is a stray brought from Palmyra. But in fact—see Kennedy and Riley, *RDF,* 137—there are traces of at least late-Roman military occupation on the site.

2. 4.1 and 8.4 above.

3. 3.4 above.

4. For the Palmyrene inscription see du Mesnil du Buisson, *Inventaire des inscriptions palmyréniennes de Doura-Europos (32 avant J.-C. à 256 après J.-C.),* no. 1. For Dumayr, 9.3 below.

5. *CIS* II.1, no. 161; J. Cantineau, *Le Nabatéen* II, 19, no. 8; see D. Homès-Fredericq (ed.), *Inoubliable Petra: Le royaume nabatéen aux confins du désert* (1980), 107–108.

was not a sign of actual Nabataean rule at this place, situated some 43 km north-west of Damascus, but of respect being paid at a major local cult-centre. In any case one Nabataean (NBṬY'), a cavalryman serving 'at Hirta and the camp at 'An'a', erected two altars in Palmyra itself in 132.[6]

If the zone where a Nabataean presence was visible extended to Palmyra itself, that of the Palmyrene script and art also stretched beyond the formal boundaries of Palmyrene territory. As we saw, Roman governors placed that boundary, on another road from Palmyra to Damascus, on the north side of the mountain-range, at the point now called Qasr el Hair el Garbi, some 60 km from Palmyra and 150 from Damascus.[7] But in fact we find that in AD 146 five Palmyrene brothers erected what seems to have been a portico at Nazala, some 35 km nearer to Damascus, with an inscription in Palmyrene 'to the great god of Nazala' (L'LH' RB' DNZLY).[8] Nazala is the modern Qaryatayn, and like Dumayr, further south and much closer to Damascus, it, too, evidently had an important local cult; a Greek inscription from there records that Zenobios son of Moschos, 'Nazalēnos', was the High Priest *(archiereus)*.[9]

This southern mountain-range thus allowed on either side the possibility of some settlement, and therefore of routes passing through the settlements. As was indicated earlier, it was along these lines of settlement that the small Roman military outposts of the late Empire were eventually stationed: Nazala was to be the emplacement of the 'Equites Promoti Indigenae' under the *dux* of Phoenice.[10]

The northern range had a similar effect, in allowing the existence of a scatter of small settlements occupied by a population using Palmyrene, which stretched a considerable distance to the north and north-west of the city. The famous study of this region by Daniel Schlumberger was instrumental in making clear that 'Palmyra' cannot be understood simply as an isolated oasis, but, like almost all other cities, as the most important point in a terrain of villages.[11] There is the further consequence that we can envisage a substantial overall Palmyrene population, from which the Palmyrene units which served in large parts of the Empire—and presumably its independent forces of the 260s and early 270s—were drawn. It is noteworthy that, although there are some Greek inscriptions from this area, the vast majority continue to be in Palmyrene; Greek never attained here the prominent place which it occupied in the city of Palmyra itself in the third century.[12] It should be stressed also

---

6. *CIS* II.3, no. 3973.

7. 2.1 above.

8. *CIS* II.3, no. 3911.

9. Le Bas-W., no. 2571.

10. *Not. Dign, Or.* XXXII, 23. Cf. 5.1 above.

11. D. Schlumberger, *La Palmyrène du Nord-Ouest* (1951).

12. Schlumberger, op. cit., 133.

that the villages of this area, though it must always have been very poor compared (for instance) with Galilee or the Hauran, could still produce monumental art and public inscriptions, often directed to the worship of deities
named (as so often) after the locality. So, to take only one instance, there is
the dedication made in 191 'to the spirits of the village of Beth-Ptsi'el, gods
(who are) good and beneficent' (LGNY' DY QRYT' DY BT PṢY'L, 'LHY'
ṬBY' WSKRY'). The finely carved relief above the inscription shows seven
male deities, of whom six carry shields and spears, and one female diety; all
are heavily clad in long tunics down to the ankles. In other words the language, art and form of representation of the divinities are those of Palmyra
itself.[13]

In this direction also, the zone of Palmyrene language and artistic forms
may have extended beyond the formal boundaries set by Rome. As we saw
earlier, the boundary was established as early as AD 11–17 by Creticus Silanus
as *legatus* of Syria;[14] at the one point where its precis   )cation is known, it
stood at Khirbet el Bilaas on the Jebel Bilaas, some 75 km north-west of Palmyra. Epiphania/Hama lies another 80 km or so to the north-west, and
Emesa some 80 km west-south-west. To the north-west there is only a flattish
steppe between these hills and the Orontes Valley, an area which seems to
have been settled and developed only in the late-Roman Christian period.[15]
Westwards, however, the hills continue until near Emesa; but no detailed epigraphic or archaeological studies seem to have been conducted here, and the
nature of settlement, language and culture in this area remains unknown.
Eastern Syria Phoenice, however problematic its eventual designation as
'Phoenician', did nonetheless exhibit some degree of coherence.

9.2. EMESA AND ELAGABAL

The discovery which above all others links the zone of Palmyrene culture with
the origins and nature of the distinctive identity of Emesa and its most famous
deity does not come (it seems) from the border-zone of the two territories
discussed above; instead it is reported to have come from the place mentioned
earlier, Nazala (Qaryatayn), on the more northerly of the two routes between
Palmyra and Damascus, and some 75 km south-east of Emesa.[1] If this is so,
it would fit with the presence of other Palmyrene elements there. What we
are concerned with is a small limestone relief showing on the viewer's left a
standing deity armed with a spear and sword and carrying a round shield,

13. For the site, Schlumberger, op. cit., 25; inscription, 156, no. 39; relief, Pl. XXIX.1.
14. 2.1 above.
15. 7.1 above.
1. J. Starcky, "Stèle d'Elahagabal", *MUSJ* 49 (1975–76), 501.

and on the right a rock or mountain with an eagle with outstretched wings perched upon it. We can be confident that both parts of the relief represent deities. For the standing figure is labelled in Palmyrene lettering 'Arsu' ('RṢW); we now know that there was a temple to this deity at Palmyra itself.[2]

Much more significant in this context is the other representation, for this too is labelled: 'LH'GBL. The first part of the expression means 'god', and the second has been taken to be an Aramaic term meaning the same as 'Jebel', namely 'mountain'. The two words would then be in apposition, like 'Zeus Bōmos' or 'Zeus Betylos', and the meaning would be 'God Mountain'.[3] But whether the grammar or meaning of the divine name has been correctly interpreted or not, it is beyond serious doubt that the word 'Elahagabal' must lie behind the distinctive name of the chief deity of Emesa, 'Elagabal', or in later sources 'Heliogabalos'; his cult-image was a large black stone, which itself is represented on the earliest coins of Emesa, with an eagle duly perched upon it.[4]

These coins date from the reign of Antoninus Pius (138–161), while the relief is perhaps a century earlier. We cannot of course deduce any simple chronological progression from that. Rather we need to look at the very slight, scattered and puzzling information we have for Emesa, which emerges as the base of a local dynasty only in the first century BC, and by the fourth century AD was regarded by Libanius as a city already in serious decline.[5] Seyrig saw that decline as a function of Emesa's dependence on Palmyra and its long-distance trade; and it is certainly true that the prominence of the two cities follows a very similar rhythm—they both emerged in the first century BC, and neither had any significant role after the third century AD. But it is worth recalling the glimpse which (as so often) Theodoret provides of a large village on Mount Lebanon inhabited by free peasants who lived by selling nuts, and for which Emesa was the nearest city.[6] In economic and social terms all these 'cities' have to be seen primarily as the focal points of a much wider world of villages. Where and when long-distance trade was ever sufficiently important to give a distinctive character to a city, or even dominate its history, is a complex question.

The political history of Emesa may nonetheless present significant points

2. For an inscription referring to the temple of Arsu, see C. Dunant, *Baalshamin* III, no. 45.

3. So Starcky, op. cit. Sebastian Brock suggests to me that GBL should be a verb rather than, as Starcky took it, a noun (like 'Jebel') meaning 'mountain'.

4. *BMC Syria*, 237; for large-scale reproductions of coins of Emesa (from the reign of Caracalla) representing the stone, see M. J. Price and B. L. Trell, *Coins and Their Cities* (1977), 167–170.

5. For the most perceptive analysis, emphasising its close connections (and perhaps economic dependence) on Palmyra, see H. Seyrig, "Caractères de l'histoire d'Émèse", *Syria* 36 (1959), 184.

6. Theodoret, *Hist. Relig.* XVII, 2–3.

of comparison with that of Palmyra. We have already encountered some of the scattered evidence for its dynasts, last heard of supplying troops for the suppression of Commagene in about 72.[7] They are first referred to in our surviving evidence in a letter of Cicero from 51 BC, when he records that 'Iamblichus, a *phylarchus* of the Arabs', was thought to be well disposed to Rome in the face of an expected Parthian invasion. It may be to the same Iamblichus (or more probably to his son and grandson) that Strabo refers in speaking of Arethusa on the Orontes as 'belonging to Sampsikeramos and Iamblichos his son, *phylarchoi* of the people *(ethnos)* of the Emisēnoi'. He seems to be referring to the 40s BC. There is no allusion here to a *city* called Emisa or Emesa (both spellings are used), but only to a people or tribe— whom Strabo seems a paragraph later to include among the *skēnitai* ('tent-dwellers') to the south of Apamea, who in terms of political organisation *(hēgemonia)* were closer to the Syrians—one example being the fact that Arethusa was under Sampsikeramos.[8]

It has to be admitted that we know nothing of the culture or social organisation of these 'Emisēnoi' in the first century AD, except that the small Greek city of Arethusa was in some way dominated by them, and that their rulers could provide armies of up to some four thousand men for Rome, and themselves gained the Roman citizenship and the title 'king'. On an inscription from Heliopolis, 'the great king' *(rex magnus)* C. Iulius Sohaemus, son of the great king Sampsigeramus (not a Roman citizen evidently), is honoured as *patronus* of the *colonia* (which must be Berytus) some time in the first century.[9] The father will surely be the Samsigeramus who appears on a Palmyrene inscription in which Germanicus (GRMNQS) is also named: the fragmentary text has '[Sham]ashgeram king [of Emesa?], high [king?]'—[ŠM]ŠGRM MLK [ḤMṢ? ML]K' RŠY'.[10]

If the Semitic name of the place did indeed appear in this text, it is the earliest attested use of it; it reappears in Greek in Josephus' later references to the kings. Taken together, this scatter of evidence gives the impression of the settlement of an Arab tribe under a chief whose descendants are recognised by Rome as kings, and gain the Roman citizenship. But we cannot pretend to know anything of the urban history of their 'capital' in the first century, or of the social structure or culture of their subjects. Since it has often been supposed that there is some provable connection between these kings and the family into which Septimius Severus was later to marry, it should be

---

7. 2.1 and 2.4 above.

8. Cicero, *Fam.* XV, 1, 2; Strabo, *Geog.* XV, 2, 10–11 (753).

9. *IGLS* VI, no. 2760.

10. J. Cantineau, "Textes palmyréniens du Temple de Bêl", *Syria* 12 (1931), 116, on p. 139, no. 18.

stressed that there is nothing to show either that they were simultaneously a dynasty of priests or even that the cult of 'Elagabal' was already observed there. What seems to be the only dated Greek inscription from Emesa of the first century is that from the pyramid-tomb of C. Iulius Samsigeramus, son of C. Iulius Alexio.[11] It was put up in 78/79, and has always been taken as that of a member of the ruling dynasty, erected after they had ceased to rule. But when Greek inscriptions begin in rather greater numbers in the second century,[12] they reveal nothing either of any certain descendants of the dynasty[13] or of the operations of a normal city-state. When Emesa developed those institutions is not known, though it could be assumed that it was before the minting of coins began there under Antoninus Pius. But some city-councillors *(bouleutai)* of Emesa do appear briefly in Dio's account of the coup d'état of 218.[14]

In other words it has to be admitted clearly that we have no conception of the urban development of Emesa as a city or of its culture or social structure, as a background into which to set the family into which Septimius Severus married. There is at any rate no known connection, either in descent or in local function, between them and the first-century dynasty.[15] Worse still, such information as we have on the earlier members of the family comes from very brief fourth-century sources, rather than from contemporary reports.

All that is clear is that, like the family of Iulius Agrippa in Apamea,[16] this family had gained the Roman citizenship by the early first century AD, as the name 'Iulius' shows. Since his two daughters were both called Iulia, the 'Bassianus' who was the maternal grandfather of Caracalla and the great-grandfather of 'Elagabal' and Severus Alexander will have been a 'Iulius Bassianus'. It is only a fourth-century Latin epitome which states that he 'had been a priest of the Sun: whom the *Phoenices,* whence he came, called Heliogabalus'.[17] At one level at least, we are plainly dealing with a prominent Greek-speaking local family, long since Roman citizens, of the class whose members would enter Roman Imperial service.

11. *IGLS* V, no. 2212. Cf. 3.1 above.

12. The inscriptions are collected in *IGLS* V, *Émésène* (1959), with M. Moussli, "Griechische Inschriften aus Emesa und Laodicea ad Libanum", *Philol.* 127 (1983), 254.

13. The fact that in the first century Polemo II of Pontus had a wife called Iulia Mamaea is not enough to establish that this lady belonged to the Emesene dynasty, or that the family of the later Iulia Mamaea were their descendants. See Birley, *Septimius Severus,* 222, no. 40.

14. Dio LXXIX, 31, 3.

15. For a good example of the assumptions and overtones which enter modern discussion of the background, see the note on Herodian V, 3, 4 in the Loeb text: 'the cult was administered by the priest-kings of the principality (descended from the Arab sheik, Samsiceramus) even after the absorption of the state into Syria by Domitian'.

16. 7.4 above.

17. *Epit. de Caes.* 23, 2.

Iulius Bassianus will hardly have been born later than the 130s. Of his two daughters, presumably born in the 160s, Iulia Domna, as we saw earlier, married Septimius Severus, a senator from Lepcis, in the 180s. Her sister, Iulia Maesa, had a husband whom Cassius Dio calls Avitus, surely C. Iulius Avitus Alexianus from Emesa, an equestrian officer and *procurator* later promoted to the Senate, apparently by Septimius Severus. It was while *legatus* of Raetia under Severus (and hence before the rise of the god 'Elagabal' to general notoriety) that he dedicated an altar to 'his ancestral god of the Sun, Elagabal'.[18]

Of the two daughters of this marriage, presumably born in the 180s, Iulia Sohaemias Bassiana married Sextius Varius Marcellus, an equestrian officer with a perfectly Roman name, who nonetheless came from Apamea, now in 'Syria Coele'; and Iulia Avita Mamaea was first married to a senator who reached the consulship, and then to Gessius Marcianus, an equestrian *procurator* from Arca (Caesarea ad Libanum) in Phoenice.[19]

Whether by the accidents of our evidence or not,   : picture revealed is that of an important local family with marriage-connections to families in other cities in the region, and occasionally outside it, and a strikingly high level of involvement in Roman service, to which it would not be easy to find any parallel from any other Near Eastern city. From one point of view what we see is not a local 'dynasty', but an exceptionally high level of integration into the wider Imperial system.

But, as Avitus' dedication in Raetia showed, they did give particular emphasis to a deity of markedly local character, the Sun god 'Elagabalus'. The form in which this dedication expresses the divine name is of considerable importance. For it preserves the verbal link with the Aramaic or Palmyrene inscription from Nazala, 'LH'GBL, while adding the concept that this was a Sun god ('Deus Sol'). It is very significant that we can now prove that this was how the deity was conceived of in Emesa itself (the coins give him no name). For a Greek dedication found on the tell of Homs (which may well therefore have been the site of the temple) shows an exactly parallel verbal combination: 'to Theos Hēlios Elagabalos, Maidoumas son of Golasos out of gratitude dedicated (this)'.[20] It is essential to stress that the form of the name by which the two elements were collapsed into one, producing 'Heliogabalus', is *not* found in contemporary documents, or even in the more or less contemporary literary accounts by Dio and Herodian, but only in fourth-century Latin narratives. Herodian even reflects the double vowel of the original Semitic name, calling the god 'Elaiagabalos'.

18. *AE* (1962), no. 229 (Augsburg): 'Deo p[atrio] Soli Ela[gabalo] C. Iul. Av[itus] Alexi[anus] . . .'. See Birley, op. cit. (n.13), 223, no. 45.

19. See 3.4 above, where the evidence on the family is also treated.

20. Moussli, op. cit. (n.12), no. 2: Θεῷ Ἡλίῳ Ἐλαγαβάλῳ Μαιδουμας Γολασου εὐχαριστίας ἀνέθηκεν.

There can be no doubt that this divine name was derived from the Semitic 'LH'GBL, attached, in the only known example of its use, to a large stone, or just possibly a mountain, with an eagle perched on it. Nor can there be any doubt that the iconography also was transferred to Emesa, for the earliest coins, of Antoninus Pius' reign, show just that. Later coins, of the colonial period, show the stone resting on a base within a six-columned temple.

A double shift has visibly occurred. First, all the known inscriptions of Emesa and its region are in Greek. In a way which is familiar, a single divine name derived from a Semitic language has been relocated in a Greek-using context, which for Emesene senators and also for soldiers serving abroad becomes also a Latin-using context.[21] Second, the cult-object, a large stone, has taken its place as the chief cult-object—selected to symbolise the place on its coins—of what was now a Greek city with a rather conspicuously Graeco-Roman governing class.

In the process, however, the stone with its eagle has changed meaning and—rather improbably—has come to be interpreted as a symbol of the Sun ('Helios'). It is very striking that in Herodian's classic description of the cult, the awkwardness of this is clearly felt. Herodian is giving the background of the coup d'état which in 218 brought to the throne the son of Iulia Sohaemias Bassiana, Varius Avitus Bassianus, then to be nicknamed 'Elagabalus':

> Both boys were dedicated to the service of the sun god whom the local inhabitants worship under its Phoenician name of Elagabalus. There was a huge temple built there, richly ornamented with gold and silver and valuable stones. The cult extended not just to the local inhabitants either. Satraps of all the adjacent territories and barbarian princes tried to outdo each other in sending costly dedications to the god every year. There was no actual man-made statue of the god, the sort Greeks and Romans put up; but there was an enormous stone, rounded at the base and coming to a point on the top, conical in shape and black. This stone is worshipped as though it were sent from heaven; on it there are some small projecting pieces and markings that are pointed out, *which the people would like to believe are a rough picture of the sun, because this how they see them.*[22]

Herodian is clearly correct in saying that it was the 'insiders' from Emesa itself who 'saw' the stone as a representation of the Sun. But insiders within what culture? Herodian also describes the grandmother of the new Emperor, Iulia Maesa, as 'a Phoenician by race', and takes the Semitic language from which 'the local inhabitants' *(epichōrioi)* drew the name of the god to be Phoenician. We might take this as an inaccurate and confused 'outsider's' im-

---

21. See esp. J. Fitz, *Les Syriens à Intercisa* (1972), esp. 178, 183, 193.
22. Herodian V, 3, 2–5, Loeb trans. (my italics); cf. ch. 1 above.

pression of which group was which in the Near East. But it is not. For the
author of the Greek novel *Aithiopica* (perhaps written in the second century)
ends by identifying himself as follows: 'the person who composed this was
a Phoenician man, an *Emisēnos,* by race belonging to those from the Sun,
Heliodoros the son of Theodosios'.

Emesa and its citizens simply could not have been 'Phoenician' in the same
sense that the ancient cities of the coast were, for at the time of the independent, or semi-independent, existence of those cities, there is nothing to show
that Emesa had even existed. Like Palmyra, it was a recent formation, which
had no early history, Phoenician or otherwise. The use of the Phoenician language might at some stage have spread inland—Emesa lay only some 70 km
from the coast in a direct line, through the Homs gap, and so some 90 km
from either Tripolis or Aradus. But there is absolutely nothing in our documentation to suggest that this was so. On the evidence at our disposal the
crucial feature of the linguistic map was not this, but the linguistic 'frontier' to
the east and south-east of Emesa, from beyond which 'LH'GBL had somehow
come, we do not know when or how. The Emesene soldiers stationed in Pannonia who worshipped him used Latin or Greek.[23] (By contrast Palmyrene
soldiers abroad might take not only their gods but their language with them,
something which distinguishes them from all other soldiers in the Imperial
army.)[24] We catch a curious glimpse of this 'frontier' in Dio's story of the
Iulius Alexander of Emesa whose execution was ordered by Commodus
(180–192). Having managed to kill not only those sent to execute him but all
his enemies among the Emesenes, he mounted a horse and set off to the *barbaroi,* and nearly escaped.[25] If Dio meant to imply, by using the word *barbaroi,* that Alexander could have crossed into an area where a Semitic language was still current, he will have been correct.

It is no use our asserting that the Emesenes, or their leading families,
'were' really 'Arabs' or 'Phoenicians' or 'Greeks'. All three descriptions are
possible. Only two aspects of this complex question of cultural identity are
certain. First, the documentary evidence so far available puts Emesa and its
region firmly in the large area where Semitic personal names were common,
but where Greek was used on inscriptions, while Semitic languages were
not.[26] Second, the cult of Elagabal, both as observed in its setting at Emesa
and as exported by the young Emperor to Rome, exhibited a whole range of

---

23. See Fitz, loc. cit. (n. 21).

24. 9.4 below.

25. Dio LXXII, 14, 1–3.

26. See, e.g., E. Nitta, "Antroponomici semitici nelle iscrizioni greche e latine della Emesene", *Civiltà classica e cristiana* 10 (1989), 283.

features which contemporaries took to be 'Phoenician', 'Syrian', 'Assyrian', or 'barbarian'. Herodian's description of the cult continues:

> Bassianus, the elder of the two boys, was a priest of this god (as the elder of the two he had been put in charge of the cult). He used to appear in public in barbarian clothes, wearing a long-sleeved 'chiton' that hung to his feet and was gold and purple. His legs from the waist down to the tips of his toes were completely covered similarly with garments ornamented with gold and purple. On his head he wore a crown of precious stones glowing with different colours.[27]

In general terms the description of his costume fits with that known, from both Lucian and a relief sculpture, at Hierapolis,[28] as well as at occasional other places including Niha on Mount Lebanon and (on wall-paintings) Dura-Europos. The distinctive conical hat, however, is not described. As regards the cult which 'Elagabal' deliberately displayed in Rome in 219–222, Dio records the Emperor as abstaining from pork; having himself circumcised, as being appropriate to the service of the god (an operation which had therefore not been carried out before); as wearing the 'barbaric' dress of Syrian priests (and hence being nicknamed 'the Assyrian'); and as singing barbarian chants *(ōdai)* to the gods, and making exotic sacrifices, including those of young boys, in secret.[29] The impression that what contemporaries now 'saw' (and perhaps were intended to see) was something indiscriminately 'Oriental' is reinforced by Herodian, who says that the costume which the Emperor affected was 'something between Phoenician garb and the luxurious Median raiment'. A picture representing him sacrificing to his native god was sent on in advance, and when he reached Rome he and some Phoenician women could be seen dancing before the god with cymbals and drums, while the Praetorian Prefects and other high officials had to don the full-length Phoenician tunic with long sleeves and a purple stripe; Herodian later also confirms the detail about abstention from pork.[30]

Modern analyses have tended (as always) to read far too much into the stereotyped categories which the adolescent Emperor's deliberately exhibitionist behaviour evoked in contemporary historians.[31] But coins minted in Rome in his reign do duly name him (occasionally) as 'priest *(sacerdos)* of

27. Herodian V, 3, 6, Loeb trans.
28. 7.2 above.
29. Dio LXXIX, 11, 1–2 (Boissevain III, p. 462); 11, 3 (464).
30. Herodian V, 5, 3–10; 6, 9.
31. See, e.g., R. Turcan, *Héliogabale et le sacre du Soleil* (1985); *Les cultes orientaux dans le monde romain* (1989), 179ff. As noted above, there is no contemporary attestation for the form 'Heliogabalus'.

Deus Sol Elagab(al)', and portray him sacrificing while wearing a long robe, as well as displaying (among many other traditional images) the black stone being carried in procession on a waggon.[32] Any discussion should take into account the clear evidence that the representation of the cult was accompanied by features which deliberately accentuated its 'Oriental', 'Syrian' or 'Phoenician' features—and the fact that even in Emesa itself it has already been given a meaning, in a Greek-speaking context, to which neither the god's Semitic name nor his embodiment in a black stone in any way corresponded. There *was* no single meaning of the cult to which research will allow us to penetrate.

By the time that the god Elagabal made his brief appearance at the heart of the Empire, his home-city had become a Roman *colonia,* through a grant of this status by Caracalla (211–217). By this time the status was so common in the Near East that a particular explanation is hardly needed; but it was of course the home-city of Caracalla's mother, Iulia Domna. It is a small sign of the way in which this status was becoming compatible with that of being a Greek city that the 'colonial' coins are all in Greek: 'Emisō(n) kolōnias', and then under the Emperor 'Elagabal' himself 'Mētrokolōnias Emisiōn'—the hybrid Greek-Latin title *mētrokolōnia* ('mother-colony') appears in the third century as an analogy to 'mētropolis' ('mother-city').[33] The conical stone, sometimes with the eagle, continued to be displayed on the coins; but after the fall of the Emperor no coins are known until those of the next 'Emperor' from Emesa, Uranius Antoninus.

We have already encountered the striking but little-understood episode of 252/253 when, in the face of Shapur's invasion, a variety of sources—Shapur's own *Res Gestae;* the coins of a pretender with the name Lucius Iulius Aurelius Sulpicius Uranius Severus Antoninus; a contemporary pseudo-oracle in Greek verse, the *XIII Sibylline Oracle;* and the *Chronicle* of Malalas—combine to suggest just how much we do not know of social structures and local patriotism here. We need not consider again the details of how a local force from Emesa won a victory against the Persians—or at least contributed to the certain fact that their forces advanced as far south along the Orontes as Arethusa, but no further.[34] But if it is correct, as it seems to be, that the *XIII Sibylline Oracle* was both written at Emesa and originally stopped with this victory, the four lines concerning it gain a special significance: 'Then there will be a rout of the Romans; but immediately thereafter a priest will come,

---

32. *BMC Roman Empire* V (1950), e.g., 560, no. 197, black stone carried on waggon; 562, no. 209 (Pl. 89), Emperor sacrificing; 564, no. 225, sacrificing: SACERD DEI SOLIS ELAGAB; 572, no. 273 (Pl. 91, 2), stone carried on waggon: SANCT DEO SOLI ELAGABAL.

33. Millar, "Roman *Coloniae*", 41.

34. 4.3 above.

the last of all, sent from the sun, appearing from Syria, and he will do every-thing by craft; the city of the sun will arise, and around her the Persians will endure the terrible threats of Phoenicians'.[35] The coinage of the pretender, with legends in both Greek and Latin, names the *colonia* of Emesa (and no other city), and above all some of it portrays again the black stone in its temple.[36] The conception that it represented the Sun, and the self-identification of the citizens as 'Phoenicians', still persisted. But the rest of what little we know of it shows the city over the next two decades within the orbit of Palmyra—and simply as one small city of Syria Phoenice among others.[37] It should not be claimed that the few dramatic moments of its history can be put into any intelligible context of social or cultural history.

We are left also with the acute problem of whether the eastern trade of Palmyra really was significant for the evolution of Emesa into a notable city. That evolution, so far as we can trace it, does follow the rise of Palmyra, and equally its brief period of relative prominence does not outlast the fall of Palmyra. As we will see, however, the particular nature of our evidence about the long-distance trade of Palmyra means that it highlights only movements eastward from there. If goods were indeed brought back in significant quanti-ties westwards through Palmyra, they must have passed (it would seem) either through Emesa or through Damascus. But, if through Emesa, where next? There is nothing in our evidence to support the notion of an established trade-route going down the Orontes Valley from Emesa to Antioch and Seleucia. Equally, there is very little to suggest that such a route passed through the gap formed by the Eleutheros River (the Nahr el Kebir) to reach the northern Phoenician coast in the area of Aradus or Tripolis. But there is just one item of evidence to show that products from India did reach the Phoenician coast overland. In the second half of the second century Galen, the famous medical writer, was on his way back from Syria Palaestina, when by good fortune he got hold of some Indian *lycium* (a shrub with medicinal uses, which we know was also imported by sea from north-west India).[38] In this case the consign-ment had recently been imported to Phoenicia, and Galen was persuaded that it was genuine partly because it had been brought by camels.[39] Our evidence remains wholly inadequate. But it may be that long-distance trade across the steppe had brought about significant economic and cultural links between Palmyra, Emesa and the ancient cities of the Phoenician coast.

35. *Sib. Or.* XII, ll. 150–154, trans. Potter, *Sibylline Oracle*. For the composition of the work see Potter, 141ff.

36. See Baldus, *Uranius Antoninus*, Pls. IV–V, XII.

37. 4.3 above.

38. Cf. L. Casson, *The Periplus Maris Erythraei* (1989), 16–67, etc.

39. Galen, *de simplicium medicamentorum temperamentis,* ed. Kühn XII, 215 = Stern, *GLAJJ* II, F.385.

9.3. DAMASCUS AND ITS REGION

If anything, even more complex problems attend the history of Damascus in the Roman period. Here too it is not impossible that a 'trade-route' passing within the line of the later 'Strata Diocletiana' was a significant factor. Goods brought through Palmyra may indeed have been traded there. There is also one, though only one, hint of a trade-route reaching Damascus from the south. Strabo records that Arabs and Ituraeans inhabiting the mountainous areas around Damascus had been attacking both the people of Damascus and merchants from Arabia Felix, until order was restored under Augustus.[1] But that is a mere hint. What is more important is Strabo's (admittedly confused) reference to the *barbaroi* who inhabited Anti-Lebanon and Mount Lebanon behind the city, and also the broken lava-field of Trachonitis to its south. If any worthwhile information were available for the social, economic and cultural relations of Damascus to the vast area of mountain behind, it would be of considerable importance. But, as it is, the complex and fragmentary history of the dynasties found in this area in the early Empire is not worth pursuing further.[2] All that is clear is that, as at all periods, there was an established route from Damascus across the saddle between Anti-Lebanon and Mount Hermon to the Bekaa Valley, and then over Mount Lebanon to Berytus. On this saddle lay the small city of Abila, and the interaction between the Empire and this mountain community is perfectly caught in a Latin inscription carved on a rock-face there: '(Marcus Aurelius and Lucius Verus) by cutting through the mountain restored the road broken by the force of the river, through Iulius Verus, *legatus pro praetore* of the province of Syria, at the expense of the Abileni'. The work was supervised by a centurion of the legion XVI Flavia Firma.[3]

The social history of the two mountain regions on either side of the road remains, like its archaeology, an almost complete blank. The Latin inscriptions left by Ituraean soldiers serving in various parts of the Empire in the first and second centuries do show the continued use of Semitic names: 'Bargathes son of Regebalus'; 'Thaemus son of Horatius'; 'Monimus son of Ierombalus'; 'Caeus(?) and Iamlichus, sons of Hanelus'.[4] But unlike Palmyrene soldiers they never use a Semitic language or script; and our sparse evidence on their homeland itself similarly reveals only Greek inscriptions, and (as elsewhere) occasional perfectly Greek temples in remote locations,

---

1. Strabo, *Geog.* XVI, 2, 20 (756). Cf. 2.1 above.
2. What little is known is summed up in Schürer, *HJP* I, App. I, "History of Chalcis, Ituraea and Abilene"; G. Schmitt, "Zum Königreich Chalkis", *ZDPV* 98 (1982), 110; W. Schottroff, "Die Ituräer", ibid., 125.
3. *ILS*, no. 5864/a.
4. Schottroff, op. cit. (n.2), 148ff.

high up on the mountain. Most of the known rural temples of this region lie on the west side of Mount Hermon, and probably belonged in the territory of Sidon. But, for instance, the temple known as Kasr Nimrud lies in a valley on the eastern slope of Anti-Lebanon, some 40 km due north of Damascus; just enough of a Greek inscription survives to show that the temple, or part of it, was dedicated by 'Iamblichos son of Baribaos'.[5] It is matched by the vast temple at Der el Ashair at the northern end of Mount Hermon, and just south of the saddle over which the road passes. Here another Greek inscription records that a bench *(diphros)* was installed 'in the year 242, under Beeliabos, also called Diodotos, son of Abedanos, high priest of the gods of Kiboreia'.[6] What era is being used is not certain; but the temple, like so many others, was certainly constructed in the Imperial period. Once again a population still using Semitic names would express itself, in words or stone, via the medium of Greek culture. The complexity of the wider Graeco-Roman influences which could be felt in this region is shown nowhere more clearly than in the dedicatory inscription in Greek on an altar found in the upper valley of the Baradas River, on the probable site of Abila: 'In the year 381 (AD 69/70), month Dios, to the Greatest Heliopolitan Zeus, Seleukos son of Abgaros, priest of the Goddess Roma and of the Deified Augustus Caesar, and priest of Zeus and Apis, dedicated this from the resources of himself and his brother Alexandros'.[7]

It might be that the priesthood of Roma and Augustus was in fact held not at Abila but at Damascus, some 25 km away down this major route. At any rate, while the social history of the whole mountain region remains to be written, the fundamental factor in the life of Damascus at all periods was (and is) the river Baradas, which runs off the saddle and provides the main source of water for the city and for the wide oasis which stretches beyond it into the steppe. More clearly even than Palmyra, Damascus owed its existence to the run-off of water from the mountain-chain behind it. The well-watered oasis, with a considerable area of marshland, stretches out in a radius of some 30 km before the dry steppe begins.[8]

Contemporaries were of course well aware that this was an ancient city, continuously inhabited, which owed its existence to the rich agricultural region which lay before it, and not to Hellenistic or Roman foundation. But in fact neither characterisations of Damascus as a city by outsiders nor expres-

5. Krencker and Zschietzschmann, *Römische Tempel* I, 178–181.

6. Ibid. I, 256–264.

7. Hajjar, *Triade* I, 179, no. 165.

8. For an excellent account, on which what follows depends, see J.-P. Rey-Coquais, "Des montagnes au désert: Baetocécé, le *pagus Augustus* de Niha, La Ghouta à l'est de Damas", in E. Frézouls (ed.), *Sociétés urbaines, sociétés rurales dans l'Asie Mineure et la Syrie hellénistiques et romaines* (1987), 191, on pp. 207ff.

sions of its identity by insiders, whether in literature or in inscriptions, are at all easy to find. By a typical paradox, the very conditions which have made it the oldest continuously inhabited city in the world have operated to obscure or destroy most of whatever inscriptional record Graeco-Roman Damascus left.

For some impression of the nature of Damascus as a prosperous oasis city we have to turn to a letter preserved with those of the Emperor Julian, but which in fact seems to have been written in the second decade of the fourth century. The writer is sending a present of figs from Damascus to a friend of senatorial rank called Serapion. Figs of this quality would come from nowhere else:

> For it was fitting, I think, that the city which in very truth belongs to Zeus and is the eye of the whole East—I mean sacred and most mighty Damascus—which in all other respects bears the palm, for instance, for the beauty of its shrines and the size of its temples and for its exquisitely tempered climate and the splendour of its fountains, the number of its rivers and the fertility of its soil—I say it is fitting that she alone should keep up her reputation by the possession of a plant of this excellence and thus excite an excess of admiration.[9]

As one of a quite long list of Classical references to the products of Damascene territory,[10] this letter is perhaps most significant for the emphasis which it later places on the widespread export of these figs—interestingly *comparing* it, but not associating it, with the objects of long-distance trade from India, Persia or Ethiopia. But it is also important—especially if written within a few years of Constantine's victory—for its stress on the cult of Zeus in the city. The temple of Zeus was indeed the focal element in the plan of the city in the Roman period. The few but invaluable inscriptions which reflect the successive stages of the construction of the enormous *temenos* within which the temple stood are sufficient, as re-dated by Seyrig, to show that building-work stretched over almost the whole of the first century AD.[11] That has two important consequences: first, construction belongs to the period when Damas-

---

9. [Julian], *Ep.* 80, Loeb trans.; *Ep.* 180 Bidez-Cumont. For the probable context see T. D. Barnes, "A Correspondent of Iamblichus", *GRBS* 19 (1978), 99.

10. See T. Weber,"ΔΑΜΑΣΚΗΝΑ: Landwirtschaftliche Produkte aus der Oase von Damaskus im Spiegel griechischer und lateinischer Schriftquellen", *ZDPV* 105 (1989), 151.

11. For the temple and the *temenos* see C. Watzinger and K. Wulzinger, *Damaskus: Die antike Stadt* (1921), 28ff. (dating the inscriptions by a supposed Pompeian era, and hence much later); R. Dussaud, "Le temple de Jupiter Damascénien et ses transformations aux époques chrétienne et musulmane", *Syria* 3 (1922), 219; H. Seyrig, "Sur les ères de quelques villes de Syrie: Damas", *Syria* 27 (1950), 34 (dating by the Seleucid era).

cus, though part of the province of Syria, was effectively isolated from the main block of provincial territory where the legions were stationed; and second, it makes it broadly contemporary, if a little later, with the equally grandiose sanctuaries represented by the Temple of Herod in Jerusalem (whose porticoes were not complete until the 60s) and the temple of Bel at Palmyra dedicated in 32 (and where again work on the porticoes continued into the second century). In very broad terms, all these sanctuaries show a similar plan: a central temple surrounded by a rectangular walled *temenos* with inner porticoes. That of Zeus at Damascus was in fact more complex, and its sheer scale deserves emphasis: beyond the porticoed inner *peribolos,* itself some 156 m by 97 m, there was an enormous outer *temenos,* also lined with porticoes, measuring some 380 m by 310 m. It was thus larger than that of the Temple, and considerably larger than that of the temple of Bel.

All remains of the temple itself have disappeared, and only traces of the outer *temenos* remain. But the inner *peribolos* was used for the construction of a Christian basilica under Theodosius I; and the basilica-form was retained in the great Ommayad mosque which replaced it on the same site in AD 705. The mosque itself occupies the southern half of the sanctuary, and its beautiful open courtyard the northern half. The scale of the whole construction and its centrality within the chequer-board pattern of the Graeco-Roman walled city can leave no doubt as to the importance of the cult in the first century AD.[12] But, as always in the Near East, we have to ask in what terms the worshippers of Zeus of Damascus understood their chief deity, and whether there was indeed any one unambiguous interpretation.

Although, as is universal, the sanctuary as known from archaeology was constructed in the Roman Empire, modern interpreters are unanimous in asserting that the Zeus of Damascus (who also appears occasionally on inscriptions from elsewhere as 'Iuppiter Optimus Maximus Damascenus') 'was' unambiguously the ancient 'Hadad' of Damascus. In reality no such identification could have been unambiguous then, or should be seen as such now. First, there have been found in Damascus and its territory no Semitic-language inscriptions from the Roman period. If 'Hadad' were to be used as the name of a god, it could (so it seems) only be in Greek or Latin transliteration; as it happens, the nearest example of a dedication in Greek to the 'theos Adados' comes from Trachonitis. Since Hadad, often along with Atargatis, appears as a divine name in other places, there is no reason to suppose that

---

12. For the place of the sanctuary within the urban framework of the city, see D. Sack, "Damaskus, die Stadt *intra muros*", *Dam. Mitt.* 2 (1985), 207, and plan on p. 210. Whether, and if so when, the ancient city was systematically rebuilt on Graeco-Roman lines is a matter of speculation.

the dedicator conceived of this particular 'Hadad' as being the Zeus of Damascus—who is indeed referred to as such in a dedication from Bostra.[13]

It is not merely that inscriptions from the temple, like the striking early-fourth-century letter quoted above, spoke simply of 'Zeus', or that people elsewhere might speak of Zeus, or Iuppiter, 'of Damascus', without making any explicit identification with Hadad. It is also, more profoundly, that the dominant culture and historical perspective of the city were by now Greek. This is particularly clear in the works of Nicolaus of Damascus, first of all in his account of his father, Antipater, presumably born early in the first century BC. Nicolaus says that he was a skilled orator, filled all the offices (archai) in the city and represented its interests before the various dynasts who held power in the region. Nothing could express more plainly the internal structure and values of a Greek city—or the diplomatic means of self-preservation open to it in the unsettled conditions of the region in the middle of the first century BC. Significantly, Antipater's sole deathbed advice to Nicolaus and his brother Ptolemaus had been to make a incense-offering to Zeus. Equally, Nicolaus' account of his own education reads almost like a parody of conventional Greek values: second to none of his contemporaries in the city in *grammatikē* and *poiētikē*, he went on to compose tragedies and comedies, and to master rhetoric, music and philosophy before becoming a follower of Aristotle.[14]

Although the vast universal history in 144 books which Nicolaus wrote followed Herodotus in including an account of the monarchies and empires of the Near East,[15] there is hardly anything in what remains of it which betrays local knowledge or a regional perspective. Only the last part of it is heavily biased so as to give a very full account of Herod the Great, on which Josephus was to draw. In that sense books XV–XVIII of Josephus' *Antiquities* do represent, at second hand, the only available contemporary view of the Augustan period from a specific provincial perspective. But it lay in the nature of Nicolaus' education and culture that his *History* might have been written by a Greek born anywhere. So far as the remains of Nicolaus' published works represent him, the determining factor was not his local origins but his participation in the wider culture of the Greek world. There is indeed one local tradition about Damascus which Nicolaus happens to preserve—that Abraham had ruled the city before moving on to Canaan, and that a village

13. D. Sourdel, *Les cultes du Hauran à l'époque romaine* (1952), 41 (Hadad); 44 ('Zeus Damaskēnos', Bostra, *IGLS* XIII.1, no. 9013).

14. *FGrH* 90 F.131 (Antipater); 132 (Nicolaus). For Nicolaus see B. Z. Wacholder, *Nicolaus of Damascus* (1963).

15. So, e.g., F.1 (Semiramis); 2 (Sardanapalos ruling the *Assyrioi*); 6 (Achaemenes as the son of Perseus—and named so because of his descent from Achaea); 44–47 (kings of Lydia); 66 (Medes); 67–68 (Cyrus).

was still pointed out as his dwelling-place.[16] But even this found a partial parallel in the universal history written in Latin by Nicolaus' contemporary Pompeius Trogus, who came from southern Gaul: 'The name of the city was given by King Damascus, in honour of whom the Syrians consecrated the sepulchre of his wife Arathis as a temple, and regard her since then as a goddess worthy of the most sacred worship. After Damascus, Azelus, and then Adores, Abraham and Israhel were their kings'.[17] Out of this morass of confusion it could be reasonable to extract the information that a goddess called Arathes was still worshipped in Damascus—and then to use Strabo's report that 'Athara' was another name for 'Atargatis'.[18] It is also significant that Pompeius Trogus uses the same principle of interpretation which we have met before: that gods or goddesses may be in origin human rulers worshipped after death.

Was there therefore an inherited cult of Hadad/Zeus, perhaps along with his consort Atargatis, in Damascus? Our best (and indeed only) evidence that the cult of Zeus at Damascus was indeed understood as an ancient cult of Hadad is also, as will be seen below, based on the 'euhemeristic' principle just mentioned, and in being so provides an extraordinary example of logical confusion. For in fact our only reason to suppose that Hadad was an important deity in Damascus early in the first millennium BC is derived from the name used by one or more of its kings: BRHDD on Aramaic inscriptions, or 'Ben Hadad' in II Kings 6–8 (BN HDD MLK 'RM); in the narrative of Kings he is succeeded by a king 'Hazael' (HZH'L, or in the Aramaic inscriptions HZ'L).[19]

To add further confusion to the tradition, the Septuagint, which Josephus used, gives the king's name as 'Ader' (the very close resemblance between the Hebrew letters Daleth and Resh may have contributed to this odd variant). At any rate Josephus takes it that the king had himself come after his death to be worshipped as a god:

> Then he (Azaēlos) took over the royal power himself, being a man of action and in great favour with the Syrians and the people of Damascus, by whom Adados and Azaēlos who ruled after him are to this day honoured as gods because of their benefactions and the building of temples with

16. F.19, quoted by Josephus, *Ant.* I, 7, 2 (163–164) = Stern, *GLAJJ* I, F.83 (noting that the reference to the village may be due to Josephus).

17. Pompeius Trogus (Justin, *Epitome*) XXXVI, 2, 2–3, trans. Stern, F.137.

18. Strabo, *Geog.* XVI, 4, 27 (785).

19. For the relevant Aramaic inscriptions of the ninth century, see J. C. L. Gibson, *Textbook of Syrian Semitic Inscriptions* II (1975), nos. 1–2 and 5. See also I. Eph'al and J. Naveh, "Hazael's Booty Inscriptions", *IEJ* 39 (1989), 192, and for the evidence on the kingdom of Damascus, or Aram, H. S. Sader, *Les états araméens de Syrie* (1987), ch. 6.

which they adorned the city of Damascus. And they have processions every day in honour of these kings and glory in their antiquity, not knowing that these kings are rather recent and lived less than eleven hundred years ago.[20]

'Azaēlos' as a god remains a mystery. But Josephus' interpretation of an important cult at Damascus manages to combine (again) typically euhemeristic notions with Graeco-Roman ideas about the centrality of euergetism, and a brief but vivid glimpse of popular religious ceremonials in a major city. For what it is worth, the evidence just set out *is* the evidence that the main cult of Damascus, that of Zeus, in the Imperial period was conceived of as being an ancient cult of Hadad. *A fortiori,* therefore, we cannot know if the 'heavenly ancestral god' *(theos ouranios patrōos)* to whom an altar was dedicated in Damascus 'was', in the dedicant's conception, Zeus/Hadad or not.[21]

Beyond that we can hardly go, for the evidence is too slight. The known inscriptions from Damascus and its oasis are in Greek, though, as everywhere, revealing personal names of Semitic origin: for instance the basalt *stele* found at Harran el-Awamid, on the edge of the oasis, recording the murder in 214, and the avenging, of 'Gosamos son of Machchabelos'; or the limestone sculpture, in strongly Palmyrene style, of a reclining deity, perhaps Adonis, dedicated in the same year by Maanōs son of Libanos.[22] Different spoken languages and different cultures surely intermingled in fact in Damascus, and the presence of the nomads of the desert, of the Nabataeans—who may even briefly have ruled it in the later 30s[23]—and of the Palmyrenes must have been felt. But our evidence reveals only the Greek-speaking population of a Greek city. Its coins represent indistinctive Classical deities (not including Zeus), and from the reign of Hadrian onwards claim the status of 'mētropolis'; when colonial status arrived, apparently under Philip (244–249), the coinage duly transfers to Latin, sometimes with 'COL(onia) DAMAS(cus) METR(opolis)', or mentioning the 'Olympian Sebasmian' games held in the city.[24] Since the holding of athletic and stage competitions was one of the central features of the communal life of Greek cities in the Imperial period, the contrast between Damascus, where they were held, and Palmyra, where so far as we know they were not, again marks a real 'frontier'.

But of course a map which (like most existing maps) identified only places which counted as 'cities'—and would thus record nothing between Damascus

---

20. Josephus, *Ant.* IX, 4, 6 (93–94), Loeb trans.

21. P. Mouterde, *Syria* 6 (1925), 354, no. 8.

22. H. Seyrig, *Syria* 27 (1950), 238, no. 4; and "Un ex-voto damascain", ibid., 229.

23. 2.3 above.

24. *BMC Syria,* 282ff. For the earlier coins see *RPC* I, 663–665. For the *Sebasmia* at Damascus see Moretti, *IAG,* no. 90 (Athens, mid-third century); *CIL* XIV, no. 474 (Ostia).

and Palmyra—would wholly obscure the reality of settlement-patterns along the two routes between these places. Out in the oasis of Damascus, for instance, the inscriptions, left mainly by the Tetrarchic officials, marking out boundaries between villages or other collectivities serve to reveal a whole series of settlements (even if their names are often very puzzling): the 'Ixoleloi' (or 'Toleloi') and 'Drasarmeloi' (or 'Odragarmeloi'); the *kōmē* of Beteomara and the *kōmē* of Enakasna(?); the *kōmē* of Mezze (modern Mizze) and the Pamoioi(?); the *kōmē* of (the?) Gindaroi(?).[25] The details do not matter; but the fact that it was between collectivities at this local level—some of whose names have persisted to this day—that the state conducted this very large-scale operation of boundary-division is a reminder of the importance of these units.

Of all the settlements along the routes between Damascus and Palmyra, the one which has left the most distinctive evidence is the place apparently called Thelsea, which occupied the site of present-day Dumayr (or Dmeir), some 45 km north-east of Damascus. As we have seen, some 5 km from here there was eventually a Roman fort; and it was here also that persons attached to two Nabataean *stratēgoi* put up an inscription in Nabataean in 94.[26] But the significance of the place lies in the rather unusual monumental building still standing in Dumayr, which seems to have been converted, probably in the second century, to serve as a temple of Zeus.[27] What we can understand about it is due to the extensive inscriptions in Greek and Latin put up on the temple. They reveal something closely comparable to what we saw at Baetocaece, and of which we can catch at least glimpses at many other more or less remote locations, where there were social structures of some importance apparently independent of any city. If Thelsea indeed lay in the territory of a city, it must have been Damascus. But there is nothing in the extensive documents from there to suggest a functional dependence.

By far the best known of the inscriptions is also the one which most clearly underlines the independence of the communities or groups involved. This is the record, with its protocol in Latin and actual proceedings in Greek, of the case about improper occupation of the priesthood of Zeus, heard by Caracalla in person at Antioch in 216. Fortunately for us, the advocate for the community explained in detail to the Emperor what was involved in the case:

> To the peasants, the case is over matters of piety, to you nothing is more important than piety. So now they have confidence in the present instance

25. *SEG* VII, nos. 246–248; *MUSJ* 1 (1906), 150, no. 4. More fully in App. A below, nos. 16–18. *SEG* VII, no. 246, of which the reading is very uncertain, and which contains no datable elements, has been omitted from the Appendix.

26. 4.1 and 9.1 above.

27. See E. Brümmer, "Der römische Tempel von Dmeir", *Dam. Mitt.* 2 (1985), 55.

in engaging in a case before a most pious king and judge. There is a famous temple of Zeus in their territory, which is visited by people from all the neighbouring regions. They go there, and arrange processions to it. Here is the first wrong committed by our adversary. He enjoys [immunity from taxation and] exemption from liturgies, wears a gold crown, enjoys [precedence], has taken the sceptre in his hand and has proclaimed himself the priest of Zeus.[28]

The peasants *(geōrgoi)* involved in the case seem to be described as 'Goharieni', perhaps meaning people from a place called Gohara or Goara. It is therefore not clear how they relate to those involved in the other major case whose record is inscribed on the podium of the temple. Here too the protocol is in Latin, while the exchanges are quoted in Greek.[29] Neither the date nor the identity of the persons hearing the case is preserved. What it concerns is the disappearance of some cult-images *(xoana)*, of which the temple-warden *(naokoros)* stubbornly disclaims all memory. The advocate then presses his questions as to whether this denial can be regarded as credible:

> It follows that when the *taboularios* and the storekeepers and you the leading men *(prōteuontes)* of the *mētrokōmē* of the Thelseēnoi, and you the *naokoroi*, both those who had demitted office and those in office, were present on the occasion of the movement *(keinēsis)* of the Highest Zeus, that the doors will have been seen open. What sort of *xoana* are they?

Whether the reference to 'movement' is simply to a formal procession, or (as at Hierapolis) to the carrying of cult-statues which were thought to impel their bearers by divine power in one direction or another, is not clear. A brief allusion such as this is enough to give a general impression of the power of the god (or gods) of the temple, but not to explain the rituals or their meaning for participants. It is sufficient, however, to reveal again a complex structure of offices associated with the temple *(naokoroi* holding office in turn, presumably each year, and a record-keeper with a borrowed Latin title, *taboularios)*; and above all another 'mother-village', that of the 'Thelseēnoi', whose *prōteuontes* were in ceremonial attendance at the *kēinēsis* of their Zeus Hypsistos.

Here, on the edge of the steppe, we are still in an environment where Greek is the language of public record and can also be spoken by the persons concerned. For Laberianus, the Roman official, conducting the enquiry, is able to cross-question the *naokoros,* who was called Dorotheos, in Greek.

---

28. First published by P. Roussel and F. De Visscher, "Les inscriptions du temple de Dmeir", *Syria* 22 (1942–43), 177; *AE* (1947), no. 182; *SEG* XVII, no. 759. Important supplements by N. Lewis, "Cognitio Caracallae de Goharienis", *TAPhA* 99 (1968), 255.

29. Roussel and de Visscher, op. cit., 194ff. This priceless text seems never to have been reprinted or discussed since.

There is nothing to indicate the date or circumstances of this trial. But one further inscription, put up in AD 245, indicates that some part of the structure was completed only then:[30] 'there was consecrated and completed the *naos aeichalas* under those associated with Markos Aurēlios Aneaos son of Gaōros and with Gaōros son of Oasaithos(?), councillor *(bouleutēs)*, the sacred treasurers'. As in the villages of the Hauran, a *bouleutēs* might be understood as someone from the city (here presumably Damascus). The Semitic names (clearly related to Arabic ones) of the sacred treasurers, however, probably indicate that they are officials of the local community. But what was it that was consecrated? Not, it seems, the temple *(naos)* of a deity called Aeichala. Instead, the word presented here must be related to the Aramaic word HYKL' (Hebrew HYKL), meaning 'temple'. The Greek word *naos* ('temple') and the Palmyrene HYKL' appear as equivalents in bilingual Palmyrene inscriptions.[31] It is possible that what is meant is something like 'the (inner) temple of the sanctuary'.

Whatever the precise explanation, this is another case where not only Semitic personal names but individual Semitic terms are used in a Greek context, where a local temple seems to function as the central institution of its locality and where a village, or 'mother-village', has institutions which rival in complexity those of a city. The evidence from Dumayr, 'the mother-village of the Thelseēnoi', rather than showing the persistence of indigenous social structures, might be taken to illustrate more clearly the power of the model provided by the Greek city, and its application on the edge of the steppe.

9.4. PALMYRA

To a very significant extent, what was said above of the 'mother-village of the Thelseēnoi'—that it shows the power of the model provided by the Greek city—is true also of Palmyra itself, for all that it was simultaneously the most striking example of the flourishing of a local culture and social structure in the Roman Near East. What follows cannot pretend to do justice to the individuality of Palmyra, or to the innumerable questions it raises: for instance the sedentarisation of nomads, the explicit syncretism of Greek and Semitic deities, the evolution of a very distinctive local art and architecture, the consistent bilingualism of its public and private monuments, the unique deployment of military force by a provincial city or the significance of long-distance

---

30. Le Bas-W., no. 2562g = *AAES* III (1908), 284, no. 357 = *IGR* III, no. 1093.

31. See C.-F. Jean and J. Hoftijzer, *Dictionnaire des inscriptions sémitiques de l'Ouest* (1965), *s.v.* HYKL. One example is *CIS* II.3, no. 3959 = Cantineau, *Inv.* I, no. 2 = Dunant, *Baalshamin* III, no. 44 (the inscription recording the visit of Hadrian, 3.3 above), where *naos* and HYKL' appear in the parallel texts.

trade.[1] Instead it will attempt merely to pick out some significant aspects of the history, development and culture of Palmyra, to bring out both parallels and contrasts between it and other places in the Near East.

Like Emesa, but entirely unlike Damascus, Palmyra as an urban centre was a new creation, which did not go back beyond the first century BC. The place had certainly existed and had been referred to centuries before. But there is nothing in the archaeological record to show that there was any settled occupation of the site through the Hellenistic period; a grave located a few metres behind the second-century-AD temple of Baalshamin, and dating to the second century BC, is the only known construction from that period. Suggestions of a phase of urban development in Palmyra before the disturbances of the late Hellenistic period can only be speculation.[2] Inscriptional evidence does, however, now suggest, by the reconstruction of a family-tree, that the foundation of the first temple of Allat went back to the earlier first century BC.[3] We cannot at any rate construct a picture of a Persian or early-Hellenistic Tadmor from the fact that the Chronicler took the city 'Tamar' which Solomon built to be 'Tadmor in the desert' (II Chron. 8, 4). It is only Josephus who expands on this brief allusion to give one of the best pictures of Palmyra—but as it was in the first century AD:

> He (Solomon) advanced into the desert of Upper Syria and, having taken possession of it, founded there a very great city at a distance of two days' journey from Upper Syria and one day's journey from the Euphrates, while from the great Babylon the distance was a journey of six days. Now the reason for founding the city so far from the inhabited parts of Syria was that further down there was no water anywhere in the land and that only in this place were springs and wells to be found. And so, when he had built this city and surrounded it with very strong walls, he named it Thadamora, as it is still called by the Syrians, while the Greeks call it Palmyra.[4]

Josephus considerably underestimates the journey-times to Palmyra from both west and east. But he catches accurately the dependence of the city on

1. The essential modern work on Palmyra is J. Starcky and M. Gawlikowski, *Palmyre*[2] (1985). Note also H. J. W. Drijvers, "Hatra, Palmyra und Edessa", *ANRW* II.8 (1977), 799, on pp. 837ff.; J. Teixidor, *Un port romain du désert: Palmyra* (1984); J. F. Matthews, "The Tax Law of Palmyra: Evidence for Economic History in a City of the Roman East", *JRS* 74 (1984), 157 (an important article on which what follows draws heavily); M. Ruprechtsberger (ed.), *Palmyra: Geschichte, Kunst und Kultur der syrischen Oasenstadt* (1987). For specific aspects note M. A. R. Colledge, *The Art of Palmyra* (1970); also now M. Gawlikowski, "Les dieux de Palmyre", *ANRW* II.18.4 (1990), 2605.

2. R. Fellmann, *Le sanctuaire de Baalshamin à Palmyre V, die Grabanlage* (1970), 131ff.

3. See M. Gawlikowski, "Le premier temple d'Allat", in P. Matthiae, M. van Loon and H. Weiss (eds.), *Resurrecting the Past: A Joint Tribute to Adnan Bounni* (1990), 101.

4. Josephus, *Ant.* VIII, 6, 1 (153–154), Loeb trans.

its oasis and the fact of its dual name, as given by Greeks and 'Syrians' (TDMWR or TDMR in Palmyrene). There is no reason to suppose that he ever went there or was aware of its distinctive art and architecture or of the fact that, alone of all the Semitic languages of the Near East, Palmyrene had for the past century come to be used, in a very Greek manner, for a long series of public monumental inscriptions.

The earlier stages of urbanisation on the site cannot be traced. As a place, it first comes within the view of Graeco-Roman narrative history when Antonius' forces raided it in 41 BC. Appian, writing two centuries later, describes how the Palmyrenes vacated the city and fled across the Euphrates, preparing to defend the bank with their expert bowmen (he seems to imagine the Euphrates as being much closer than it really is, some 200 km). His account implies nothing about whether Palmyra was already walled or not. Nor is it evidence as to whether Palmyrene long-distance trade had already begun in the first century BC. For when he speaks of this, it is a comment in the present tense: 'for being traders they buy Indian and Arabian goods from the (territory of) the Persians, and dispose of it in that of the Romans'.[5]

His implication that there was already a city *(polis)* of Palmyra is certainly correct. For the earliest known Palmyrene inscription dates from 44/43 BC and records the erection of a statue by the priests of Bel (KMRY DY BL), in the year 269 (of the Seleucid era, starting from October 312 BC, which was used throughout Palmyrene history).[6] It comes from the site of the great temple of Bel dedicated in AD 32, and it seems clear that an earlier temple already occupied the site. Moreover, as we saw, as early as 34/33 BC two Palmyrenes at Dura-Europos erected a temple to Bel and Iarhibol (HYKL' LBL WYRHBWL).[7] The divine names used at Palmyra are already in evidence ('Bel' being a borrowing from Babylonia), and the construction of temples is already a feature of society.

Though the great bulk of Palmyrene inscriptions belong later, there are sufficient from the century up to the 60s AD to suggest some distinctive features of Palmyrene civilisation at this period. The earliest of the long series of sepulchral inscriptions belongs to 12 BC and records the construction of a tomb (BT 'LM'—'house of eternity') by MLWK son of LŠMŠ.[8] Perhaps the most important documents of this period are three honorific inscriptions of the 20s AD found in the temple of Bel. One, dating to 21, survives only in

5. Appian, *BC* V, 9/37–38.

6. Cantineau, *Inv.* XI, no. 100; see H. Seyrig, R. Amy and E. Will, *Le temple de Bel à Palmyre* (1975), 227.

7. See 3.4 above; du Mesnil du Buisson, *Inventaire*, no. 1.

8. M. Gawlikowski, "Recueil d'inscriptions palmyréniennes provenant de fouilles syriennes et polonaises récentes à Palmyre", *Mém. prés. . . . à l'Académie des Inscriptions* 16 (1975), 263, no. 164.

Palmyrene and records the erection of a statue of ḤŠŠ son of NŠ', son of BWLḤ' (also called) ḤŠŠ, by two Palmyrene tribes, the 'sons of Komara' and the 'sons of Maththabol', 'because he made peace between them'.[9] Finding an equivalent for social groupings identified in Semitic languages is always problematic and is liable to involve unjustified presumptions. But in this case it at least has the justification that the second of this group, a bilingual inscription of 24 in honour of MLKW (Malichos), this man's brother, speaks of him as belonging to 'sons of Komara' (BNY KMR'), while using in Greek the term *phylē*, which we normally translate 'tribe': 'of the *phylē* of the Chomarēnoi'.[10] The reference in the earlier inscription to 'making peace between them' has naturally served to reinforce the idea that we might see Palmyra as a grouping of separate (Arab?) tribes, who only slowly coalesced into a unified group with a formal constitution. In fact, we find a whole series of group-names used with the expression BNY (literally 'sons of'), and we cannot be sure whether all of them should be labelled 'tribes'; moreover, it is in only the second century, when Palmyra had the formal constitution of a Greek city, that we find evidence of 'the four tribes of the city', each (as it seems) with its own special sanctuary.[11]

This group of honorific inscriptions of the 20s also provides the first documentary evidence for two very important aspects of the city: trade with Babylonia and the evolution of the Palmyrenes into a collectivity with a communal organisation. First, the Palmyrene text of the inscription of 24 records that the statue has been erected by 'all the merchants who are in the city of Babylon' (T[G]RY' KLHWN DY BMDYNT BBL). It is the earliest of a long series of inscriptions reflecting Palmyrene trade with places in the Parthian and then the Persian Empires. The information which these inscriptions provide is priceless. But it may be yet more important that they *are* honorific inscriptions on statue-bases, a borrowing from a central feature of the life of the Hellenistic and Imperial Greek city, namely the public expression of honour for a benefactor, or *euergetēs*.[12] Moreover, any discussion of Palmyrene long-distance trade has to be conducted with the awareness that the entire local evidence consists of documents of this very characteristic cultural form, the honorific inscription.

In the case of Malichos, the bilingual inscription seems to have been re-inscribed in the second century, and it is not impossible that two originally

9. Cantineau, *Inv.* IX, no. 13 = *CIS* II.3, no. 3915 (but the Greek inscription printed here belongs in fact with *Inv.* IX, no. 11, below).

10. Cantineau, *Inv.* IX, no. 11.

11. See the important article of D. Schlumberger, "Les quatres tribus de Palmyre", *Syria* 47 (1971), 121, with modifications by M. Gawlikowski, *Le temple palmyrénien* (1973), ch. 2.

12. For this fundamental theme see P. Veyne, *Le pain et le cirque* (1976), esp. ch. 2; Ph. Gauthier, *Les cités grecques et leurs bienfaiteurs* (1985).

separate inscriptions were combined. For the brief Greek text identifies a different dedicator, 'the people *(dēmos)* of the Palmyrenes'. If certainly contemporary, this would be the earliest formal evidence of the Palmyrenes as a collectivity. They reappear again in the third inscription also honouring Malichos, of 25; but this time there is a parallel Palmyrene text—GBL TDMRY'.[13] Unfortunately the etymology of GBL in this sense is unknown, and the meaning has to be derived from the parallel Greek term, *dēmos*. But nonetheless it marks a stage in the progressive evolution of Palmyra as a community with a constitution. This rapid evolution, always within Graeco-Roman models, is perhaps its most significant characteristic.

An important aspect of its evolution in the physical sense, and one which must have been much more conspicuous at the time, was the construction and dedication of the great temple of Bel which still stands today. The Palmyrene inscription of 24 records that MLKW (Malichos) had aided the merchants in Babylon 'in the construction of the temple of Bel' (BNYN' DY H[Y]KL' DY BL). Whether it was the influence of earlier Palmyrene merchants in Babylonia which had led to the existence of a temple of Bel (best known as a Babylonian deity) in Palmyra by the middle of the first century BC we can only guess. But here the connection is evident, and a Palmyrene inscription of AD 45 records that the temple had been dedicated on the sixth day of the month Nisan (April), AD 32. In fact, as the inscription states, it was formally the temple of a triad of male gods, Bel, Yarhibol and Aglibol. Nonetheless it must be significant that the sixth of Nisan was the day on which the Babylonian Akitu festival was celebrated, during which the legend of Bel was recited.[14]

What was dedicated in 32 was the central temple, or *cella*, of a design markedly different from the standard pattern of Graeco-Roman temples. Here the temple was entered by steps leading to a door placed asymmetrically on the long side; and once within the temple the worshipper saw, as the cult-objects, low-relief carvings placed in high recesses at either end. The use of low-relief carvings, with frontal representations of the deity or deities concerned, as opposed to a cult-statue in the round, was a characteristic feature of Palmyrene cult-practice, preserved also in the second-century temple of Baalshamin. The two 'chapels' at either end of the temple of Bel may each represent deliberate recreations of an original sanctuary (ḤMN'), a single oblong structure with relief-carvings, with an altar before it. In the case of the new temple of Bel, the altar was built outside the massive temple which now enclosed the two sanctuaries. But in detail what the Palmyrene inscription of AD 45 means by the temple having been dedicated 'with its sanctuaries'

13. Cantineau, *Inv.* IX, no. 12.

14. Cantineau, *Inv.* IX, no. 1. For this important point about the date, see H. J. W. Drijvers, "The Syrian Cult Relief", *Visible Religion* 7 (1989), 69, on p. 7.

(BQDŠWHY) is not known.[15] The vast porticoed *temenos* standing today, with sides of roughly 200 m and a monumental gateway, was constructed in the late first and second centuries.

It is significant that the dedication of the temple and the first documentary reflections of the formal structure of the community coincide in time, as we have seen, with the earliest evidence for a Roman presence and Roman influence.[16] Hence it is in this early period that we find one of the very few trilingual inscriptions from Palmyra, the sepulchral inscription, dating to 58, of L. Spedius Chrysanthus, in Latin, Greek and Palmyrene.[17] The Latin and Greek versions give him no title, but the Palmyrene calls him MKS' ('tax-gatherer'). The fact that he was a Roman citizen, and used Latin as well as Greek and Palmyrene, makes it possible (but *not* certain) that he was a Roman *publicanus* collecting Roman indirect taxes, rather than a local contractor for city taxes.

At any rate very shortly after this we see the first evidence for the crucial transformation which made Palmyra, in a certain sense, into a Greek city like others. That is the appearance of the double deliberative structure of a Greek city, not only an assembly *(dēmos)* but now, for the first time, a council *(boulē)*. The fact that this structure derives from that of standard Greek cities is signalled very clearly by the straight transliteration of the expression for 'council and assembly' into Palmyrene: BWL' WDMS. The word BWL' makes what seems to be its first appearance, very appropriately, in another trilingual inscription, of the year 74.[18] Here it is, uniquely, accompanied by an attempt at a Latin equivalent, where again the Greek 'boulē' is transliterated: 'bu[le et civi]tas Palmyrenorum'. The Palmyrene version appears again, this time along with the transliterated term for 'secretary' (*grammateus*—GRMTWS), in an inscription of 75/76.[19] Whether the Graeco-Roman influences so visible here were transmitted in the concrete form of Roman instructions, or permission, for the constitutional reform of the city is quite uncertain. A further transformation was to come, for we find that under Hadrian the city has been named after the Emperor 'Hadrianē Palmyra' (HDRYN' TDMR in Palmyrene). We may believe the Byzantine lexicographer Stephanus when he says that this took place when the city was 're-founded' by the Emperor. But

15. For the temple of Bel see Seyrig, Amy and Will, op. cit. (n.6). For the concept of the HMN' see H. J. W. Drijvers, "Aramaic HMN' and Hebrew HMN: Their Meaning and Root", *JSS* 33 (1988), 165. See also Gawlikowski, *Temple palmyrénien*, 81, who takes the phrase BQDŠWHY to mean rather 'during their festival'.

16. 2.1 above.

17. Cantineau, *Inv.* VIII, no. 57 (*IGR* III, no. 1539; *CIS* II.3, no. 4335).

18. J. Cantineau, "Tadmorea", *Syria* 14 (1933), 169, on p. 174, text B.

19. Cantineau, *Inv.* X, no. 39.

there is no basis for the modern notion that Palmyra now became a free city.[20] In the famous bilingual tax-law of 137, known from an inscription in the Agora, Palmyra appears with an extensive set of Greek city-offices, almost all expressed in Palmyrene in transliteration: *archontes* ('RKWNY'); a *grammateus,* as above; and *proedroi,* attested through the abstract noun for their office, PLHDRWT'. But the term *dekaprōtoi* (the 'first ten men'—liable for guaranteeing the city's tax-revenue) is translated as ŠRT', 'group of ten'.[21]

It is in the tax-law that the unique character of Palmyra/Tadmor, as a Greek city which, unlike all others, was bilingual in its public inscriptions, is most vividly expressed. The beginning of the heading which in the Palmyrene text serves to introduce the detailed provisions perfectly catches the way in which the language has been transformed by the adoption of Greek loan-words—NMWS' DY MKS' DY LMN' DY HDRYN' TDMR—literally 'the law of the tax-gatherer of the market of Hadrianē Tadmor'. The word for 'market' is an borrowing from the Greek *limēn,* 'harbour', while 'law' (NMWS') comes from the Greek *nomos,* just as in the Syriac title of Bardesanes' *Book of the Laws of Countries*—KTB' DNMWS' D'TRWT'.[22]

So far the discussion has tended, deliberately, to emphasise the way in which Palmyra, from the first moment that we can see it emerging as an urban centre, evolved step by step towards the structure of a 'normal' Greek city. That is an important aspect, which needs to be stressed; and it was accompanied by the adoption of loan-words and by the intrusion of Greek and Latin nomenclature alongside Palmyrene, as well as by the spread of the Roman citizenship among individual Palmyrenes. It was in the second century too that the Great Colonnade was built, matching that at the city of Apamea to the north-west. In the same period we can see the physical transformation of some temples, to make them conform to Graeco-Roman models. The prime example is the temple of Baalshamin, erected in the reign of Hadrian on a site already occupied by a series of courtyards whose successive construction went back to the beginning of the first century BC. The temple represents a classic example of Graeco-Roman architecture, with a *pronaos* fronted by six Corinthian columns. As its inscriptions, of which the great majority are in Palmyrene, show, throughout the period the site had served as a sanctuary in

20. Steph. Byz. *s.v.*Παʹλμυρα . . . οἱ δ᾽ αὑτοὶ Ἀδριανοπολῖται μετωνομάσθησαν ἐπικτισθείσης τῆς πόλεως ἐπὸ τοῦ αὐτοκράτορος. There is not much documentary reflection of this, apart from the tax-law, but see, e.g., Cantineau, *Inv.* X, no. 38: [᾽Αδ]ριανὸν Παλμυρηνόν. For the idea that Palmyra thereby became a free city, Gawlikowski, *Temple palmyrénien,* 47.

21. Not *decuria,* as suggested in Millar, "Roman *Coloniae*", 43, wrongly following Teixidor. The equivalence is quite clear in the preface of the tax-law, *CIS* II.3, 3913 (see below). So, correctly, Matthews, *JRS* 74 (1984), 174, n.5.

22. 12.5 below.

which Baalshamin was worshipped along with a series of distinctively local deities: so for instance in 63 someone belonging to the BNY M'ZYN, the 'tribe' most clearly associated with this sanctuary, dedicated an altar to Baal-shamin, to DWRḤLWN ('him [i.e., the god] of Rachle'?), to Rahim and to the God (Fortune) of Yedibel.[23] The interpretation of these and the long list of other deities named or represented at Palmyra is, to say the least, hazard-ous, and cannot be pursued here.[24] It is more important to note that a bilin-gual inscription of 130/131 records that the temple itself, of Zeus/Baal-shamin, was built by Male son of Yarhai, who was *grammateus* at the moment of the visit of the 'god Hadrian'.[25] This temple is the prime reflection at Palmyra of the classicising movement in the culture of the Greek East asso-ciated with this reign.

A somewhat comparable development can be seen in the case of the sanc-tuary of the goddess Allat, later enveloped in the 'camp of Diocletian', under the Tetrarchy. In the sanctuary, which had existed since the first century BC, a new temple was built in the second century—anomalously leaving within it an altar on the same spot as the original one, and thus breaking the normal rule that an altar stood outside. Allat could be identified in Palmyra either with Artemis or with Athena—as in other cases it is futile to ask what such a deity really 'was'. But one of the most characteristic features of Palmyrene art was that of representing deities fully dressed, and armed.[26] So, when a suit-ably classical representation of the goddess was sought for this sanctuary, the choice was made of a statue of Athena, holding a shield and lance—the beau-tiful Roman copy of a fifth-century original, which now stands in the museum of Palmyra.[27]

From one point of view the influence of Graeco-Roman models in the evolution of Palmyra is visible precisely because there was a vigorous local culture within which it could be received and expressed. So, just as Palmyra had been transformed (whether by official action or not) into a Greek city by the 70s, under (probably) Septimius Severus it underwent another transfor-mation and became a Roman *colonia*. This was a real transformation, even if the fact that all Palmyrenes now became Roman citizens did not as such, after the universal grant by Caracalla, distinguish them from other people. It is because, in the case of Palmyra, local pride expressed itself so much more

23. Dunant, *Baalshamin* III, no. 23.

24. For a masterly account of what can be known, or has been supposed, see M. Gawlikow-ski, "Les dieux de Palmyre", *ANRW* II.18.4 (1990), 2605.

25. *CIS* II.3, no. 3959 = Cantineau, *Inv.* I, no. 2 = Dunant, *Baalshamin* III, no. 44. For Hadrian's visit, 3.3 above.

26. See esp. H. Seyrig, "Les dieux armés et les Arabes en Syrie", *Syria* 47 (1978), 77.

27. See M. Gawlikowski, "Le temple d'Allat à Palmyre", *Rev. arch.* 1977, 253, and op. cit. in n.3 above. The full report on the excavations is awaited.

fully in inscriptions that we can see the individual Palmyrene so clearly as a Roman citizen, and his city as a *colonia*. As a *colonia*, it now had to have a pair of annual chief magistrates, called in Latin *duumviri*. But in Greek the equivalent term in common use was *stratēgoi*, literally 'generals'; so it is either this or its Palmyrene transliteration which we find in the third-century inscriptions of the city.[28] Contrary to what might have been expected, Latin, never very common, now disappears altogether from the inscriptions of the city. The 'colonial' character of Palmyra is expressed bilingually, in Greek and Palmyrene. As we have already seen, the public use of Palmyrene persisted through this period and into that of the rise of Septimius Odenathus in the 250s and 260s, and the brief Palmyrene 'empire' of Zenobia and Vaballathus in the late 260s and early 270s.[29] For the period before that it will suffice to give one example of how the institutions of Palmyra as a *colonia*, and its relations with the wider Roman Empire, could be accommodated and expressed in Palmyrene. What follows is a translation of the Palmyrene part of an honorific inscription put up in the Great Colonnade in 242/243:

> Statue of Iulius Aurelius Zabdilah . . . who (was) *stratēgos* of the *colonia* ('STRTG LQLNY') during the visit of the God Alexandros Kaisar (QSR), and who aided when he was here Crispinus, *hēgemōn* (HYGMWN'), and when he brought the legions (LGYNY') here on many occasions; who was in charge of the market (RB ŠWQ) . . . who was testified to by the god Yarhibol and by Iulius Priscus, the Praetorian Prefect ([RB'] DY SP'), and loved his city. The *boulē* and *dēmos* (BWL' WDMS) erected this statue . . .[30]

Once again it is the custom of the honorific inscription accompanying a statue to which we owe what little we can understand. But in this case it is important that both city-patriotism and the use of Palmyrene and of the borrowed Greek vocabulary for city institutions have survived the transformation of Palmyra into a *colonia*. There are many respects in which we can regard the Palmyrene/Greek/Roman city of the period from the 70s to the 270s as representing a coherent, and unique, example of a mixed city culture.

Three further features of Palmyra need to be stressed. The first is that the expression of the language, art and religious iconography of Palmyra was *not* simply a matter of official, communal action (as *may* have been the case with the Phoenician legends on the coins of second-century Tyre). The tombs and private sepulchral inscriptions of Palmyra (in which Palmyrene predominates,

---

28. Millar, "Roman *Coloniae*", 42ff.

29. 4.2–3 above.

30. *CIS* II.3, no. 3922 = Cantineau, *Inv.* III, no. 22 (*OGIS*, no. 640; *IGR* III, no. 1033, Greek only).

by contrast with official inscriptions) express it also, as do the remains of the villages in the mountainous region to the north-west of the city, and the evidence left by Palmyrenes in Dura-Europos. But by far the most significant evidence for the strength of Palmyrene local culture as a *popular* culture is the fact that its soldiers, alone of all 'nationalities' who contributed to the auxiliary forces of the Imperial army, might take their language and their art with them.[31] That Greek and Latin inscriptions set up by Palmyrenes abroad include dedications to Palmyrene gods—for instance Malachbel, and Aglibol and Yarhibol—is significant, though not unusual. But the fact that they are found using the Palmyrene language abroad is. Thus for instance there is the relief from Rome on which Aglibol and Malachbel are represented, one in conventional military dress and the other in Palmyrene costume. The Greek text identifies the dedicator as 'I(oulios) Aur(ēlios) Hēliodōros son of Antiochos, *Hadrianos Palmurēnos*'—although the date is 236, long after the formation of the *colonia*. But the Palmyrene text gives him as YRḤY son of ḤLYPY.[32] Or, at South Shields at the mouth of the river Tyne, some 4000 km from Palmyra, a Palmyrene, Barates, put up an epitaph for his Catuvellaunian freedwoman and wife, Regina. The Latin text is dominant, but a version is added in Palmyrene: RGYN' BT ḤRY ('daughter of freedom of') BR'Ṭ' ḤBL (alas!).[33] In a military context Palmyrene tended naturally enough to absorb Latin loan-words (or transliterations) rather than Greek ones. So a Palmyrene soldier in Dacia transliterates his rank *(optio)* as HPTYN, and one in Numidia his unit *(centuria)* as QṬRY'. He identifies himself as a 'Palmyrene archer' both in Latin and in Palmyrene: TDMWRY' QŠṬ'.[34]

The known Palmyrene inscriptions from outside the Near East are not numerous. But their importance lies in the fact that they reinforce the conclusion which is suggested by the epitaphs of Palmyra itself: that the written language was, or could be, at the disposal of people down to quite modest social levels. It does not of course follow that each soldier in a

---

31. The evidence is collected by J. Starcky and M. Gawlikowski, *Palmyre*², 41ff. For dedications by Palmyrenes abroad see most fully R. Turcan, *Les cultes orientaux dans le monde romain* (1989), 170ff.

32. *CIS* II.3, no. 3902 = Moretti, *IGUR* I, no. 119. See E. E. Schneider, "Il santuario di Bel e delle divinità di Palmira: Communità e tradizione religiose dei Palmireni a Roma", *Dial. di Arch.* 5.1 (1987), 69.

33. *CIS* II.3, no. 3901 = R. B. Collingwood and R. Wright, *Roman Inscriptions of Britain* I (1965), no. 1065.

34. Dacia (Temesvar): *CIL* III, no. 7999 = *CIS* II.3, no. 3906; Numidia (al Kantara): *CIL* VIII, no. 2515 = *CIS* II.3, no. 3908. See L. Bianchi, "I Palmireni in Dacia: Communità e tradizioni religiose", *Dial. di Arch.* 5.1 (1987), 87.

Palmyrene unit in Britain, Numidia or Dacia was literate in both Latin and Palmyrene. But it does follow that such soldiers could (at least) have access to persons who could compose brief texts in Palmyrene, and then have them inscribed.

So far, we have no evidence of documents on papyrus or parchment written in Palmyrene, as there are in Aramaic, Hebrew, Nabataean and Syriac. But the parallels with these other Semitic languages make it in fact extremely unlikely that legal documents were *not* drawn up in Palmyrene, or in Palmyrene and Greek. As so often, our knowledge is a function of the nature of our archaeological evidence.

If Palmyrene could be written, as it was, it follows that both it and Greek must have been taught in the city. But there our evidence stops. We do not know whether there was or was not any literature in Palmyrene, whether there were traditions transmitted orally, or whether the few sculptural reliefs (for instance from the temple of Bel) apparently representing events of religious significance reflect myths about the Palmyrene gods. Nor do we know what performances (if any), or in which language, were put on in the beautiful theatre of Palmyra, built in the Severan period and never completed. The quite extensive evidence for the places in which athletes or actors of various types had won victories never includes Palmyra.

It is essential to stress that in this sense we have no comprehension at all of the culture of Palmyra, or even of whether there was a Palmyrene culture in which an educated Palmyrene would have been brought up. All that is clear is that there was a distinctive artistic tradition, expressed above all in funerary portraits and the iconography of the gods, which was closely related to standard Greek provincial art, but at the same time was characteristic, with variations, of a zone stretching from Mesopotamia (above all Hatra) through Dura-Europos and Palmyra to the Hauran. There is general agreement that this art, with its emphasis on the details of the elaborate clothing of both deities and mortals and its frontal presentation of both to the beholder, is in some sense a forerunner of Byzantine art. But there is nonetheless serious doubt as to whether it should be labelled as 'Parthian', or indeed conceived of as having derived *from* any particular area. In the entire zone in question this distinctive regional art cannot be identified before the latter part of the first century BC, or beyond the end of the third century AD. There is thus no concrete evidence for the idea that it arose somewhere else, and was then brought to Palmyra. It is better to think of it as a parallel development, common to places both east and west of the Euphrates; explaining *why* such a distinctive regional art might have arisen is another matter. The characteristic use of low-relief carvings, rather than of cult-statues in the round, for the representation of deities offers a significant context for the deployment of 'frontality' in religious art, while leaving that custom itself in need of explanation.[35]

This problem, if posed in terms of hypothetical influences on Palmyra from within the Parthian Empire, Babylonia above all, is only made more complex both by the very limited and precise character of our evidence and by the fact that it is all a function of the evolution of the city itself, with its (lost) public statues and (surviving) honorific inscriptions. So for instance the centrality of the cult of Bel at Palmyra may well be due to Babylonian influence. But the cult was already established at least half a century (and probably longer) before we happen to have explicit evidence of trading contacts with Babylonia.

Our evidence for these contacts is both extremely evocative and striking, and very limited. For it is provided almost entirely by honorific inscriptions, which by their nature allude to services within a context which itself is taken for granted, and which thus provide only the merest ¨mpses of the wider system itself.[36]

So far as our evidence allows us to grasp it, this trade had no connection with any 'silk route' across central Asia. It was directed to the lower-middle Euphrates, where, as we have seen, Palmyra maintained outposts in the second century,[37] and then down the river to Vologaesias, and to Spasinou Charax in the region of Mesene, on the shores of the Gulf. Even Seleucia on the lower-middle Tigris is mentioned (at most) only once, on a very fragmentary inscription of AD 19, and Babylon (BBL) only on the inscription of 24 mentioned above.[38] From the head of the Persian Gulf, where Trajan wistfully observed a ship setting off for India, Palmyrene merchants sailed as far as 'Scythia', that is, north-west India. One of the many inscriptions of the mid-second century in honour of M. Ulpius Iaraios, or YRḤY, was put up by 'the merchants who have returned from Scythia in the ship of Onainos son of Addoudanos', because of the assistance which he had given them.[39] The fact that Palmyrene merchants went as far as 'Scythia' is of some significance,

35. The problem was posed by M. Rostovtzeff, "Dura and the Problem of Parthian Art", *YCS* 5 (1935), 157; for the latest of many subsequent discussions, see the valuable articles of M. Pietrzykowski, "The Origins of the Frontal Convention in the Arts of the Near East", *Berytus* 33 (1985), 55; G. Ploug, "East Syrian Art 1st Cent. BC–2nd Cent. AD", *Acta Hyperborea* 1 (1988), 129; and esp. (for the relevance of the use of low-relief carvings) Drijvers, op. cit. (n.14).

36. For Palmyrene trade with the East see esp. E. Will, "Marchands et chefs de caravannes à Palmyre", *Syria* 34 (1957), 262; the works of J. Teixidor and J. F. Matthews, n.1 above; and M. Gawlikowski, "Le commerce de Palmyre sur terre et sur eau", in J.-P. Salles (ed.), *L'Arabie et ses mers bordières: Itinéraires et voyages* (1988), 163.

37. 3.3 above.

38. *CIS* II.3, no. 3924 = Cantineau, *Inv.* IX, no. 6a (Seleucia); Babylon, text to n.14 above.

39. Cantineau, *Inv.* X, no. 96. For 'Scythia', see also *SEG* VII, no. 156.

because they will have encountered there other traders from the Graeco-Roman world, who had come by ship from the Red Sea and Egypt. What is more, the *Periplus of the Erythraean Sea,* an anonymous work of AD 40–70 which describes this trade, supplies what is totally lacking for Palmyrene commerce—some idea of the products which might have been brought back from India; most are precious stones, silk or cotton, or other luxury items such as spices or herbs. For what it is worth, one item, *lycium,* which is listed by the *Periplus,* was also, as we have seen, brought by camel to the Phoenician coast, certainly through Palmyra.[40] On the outward journey Palmyrene traders will surely have used boats to go down the Euphrates; and for the return (as M. Gawlikowski suggests) the river may have been navigable upstream as far as Hit. Hence the long road (approaching 500 km), of which long stretches are still visible from the air, between Hit and Palmyra may have been used by merchants disembarking at the highest point possible.[41]

Any crossing of the steppe to the Euphrates involved a journey of between 200 km (directly across to Dura-Europos) and nearly 500 km to Hit. So it is no surprise that the inscriptions referring to Palmyrene trade speak repeatedly of *synodiai,* 'caravans', formed for the journey. Ulpian, recording that Palmyra had become a *colonia,* speaks of it as 'located next to barbarian *gentes* and *nationes*'.[42] We have no more precise account than this of whatever nomads occupied the vast region to the south-east of Palmyra, but it is evident that the Palmyrenes, whom we tend to see as sedentarised 'Arabs' themselves, will have had complex diplomatic, economic and military relations with these other peoples. Relations between nomads and passing caravans did not necessarily involve simply attack and defence. A model of a different relationship is provided by Strabo's account of how the *skēnitai* of Mesopotamia exacted lower tolls from travellers than did those living along the Euphrates itself, and also provided watering-places.[43] It may therefore have been the case that the assistance for which the members of *synodiai* honoured the great magnates of Palmyra was sometimes of a financial or diplomatic nature, in ensuring the cooperation of the steppe peoples: for instance almost the latest known caravan-inscription, that of 257/258, honours Aurēlios Salamallathos

40. See the excellent edition, translation and commentary by L. Casson, *The Periplus Maris Erythraei* (1989). For 'Scythia', approximately the Indus plain, see paras. 38 and 41 and commentary. The products which are described as being brought from 'Scythia' to the Red Sea are (p. 16): costus, bdellium, *lycium,* nard, Indian myrrh (whose nature is problematic), indigo, turquoise, lapis lazuli, onyx, perhaps agate, ivory, cotton, cotton garments, silk, Chinese pelts and pepper. For camels bringing *lycium* to Phoenicia, see 9.2 above, text to nn.38–39.

41. For this area see esp. M. Gawlikowski, "Palmyre et l'Euphrate", *Syria* 60 (1973), 53, and the map on p. 54.

42. *Dig.* L, 15, 1, 5.

43. Strabo, *Geog.* XVI, 1, 27. See 12.1 below.

Malē, an *archemporos* (chief trader), for having 'brought back the *synodia* at no cost (to the participants), at his own expense'.[44] But on certain occasions it is quite clear that the protection of the caravans involved actual fighting: the clearest case so far published is the inscription honouring Ogēlos son of Makkaios in 199 'for his having given satisfaction through continual commands against the *nomades* and having provided safety for the merchants and the caravans in all his caravan-commands *(synodiarchiai)*'.[45] A similar situation is clearly implied by the inscription honouring Soados son of Bōliadēs in 132 for having 'saved the *synodia* which has recently arrived from Vologaesias from the great dangers which threatened it'; and in fact, an unpublished inscription from the temple of Allat is reported as recording that Soados fought bravely against a band of brigands who were threatening a caravan.[46]

This very distinctive, but by its nature limited, evidence is highly revealing, while inevitably raising many problems. It shows ɔth that groups of Palmyrenes were actually established in various places in the Parthian Empire, notably Babylon, Spasinou Charax and Vologaesias, and that diplomatic and political relations could be conducted with such places—one Palmyrene seems to have gone on an embassy to King Vorod (WRDW MLK') of Elymais, and another served as a satrap under Meerdates, king of Spasinou Charax (a region which enjoyed varying degrees of independence from Parthia).[47] But what our evidence does not allow us to grasp is what may have been the cultural significance of regular traffic between Babylonia, and the lower reaches of the Tigris-Euphrates, and Palmyra. We can be certain that a branch of Aramaic was spoken there by the gentile as well as by the Jewish population. But we know almost nothing of the social and cultural history of this region; and it is at least as likely that Palmyrene trade served to reinforce Graeco-Roman influences there, as that it transmitted elements of 'Oriental' culture to Syria. The (unanswerable) question of such mutual influences will recur later.[48]

What the references to *nomades* and 'brigands' do strongly suggest is that the Palmyrenes, as an urban society with a sedentary population attached to it, saw a marked contrast and opposition between themselves and the peoples

---

44. Cantineau, *Inv.* III, no. 13.

45. Cantineau, *Inv.* X, no. 44 = *SEG* VII, no. 139.

46. Dunant, *Baalshamin* III, no. 45; for the unpublished inscription, Gawlikowski, op. cit. (n.36), 168.

47. Cantineau, *Inv.* X, no. 114 (Vorod); 38 (satrap). See now the interesting paper by D. S. Potter, "The Inscription on the Bronze Herakles from Mesene: Vologeses IV's War with Rome and the Date of Tacitus' *Annales*", ZPE 88 (1991), 277, arguing that the kingdom of Mesene remained in alliance with Rome after Trajan's Parthian war.

48. 13.1 below.

of the steppe. We may wish to see them as 'Arabs', as an example, in the words of the title of R. Dussaud's major work, of the penetration of Arabs into Syria;[49] but our—admittedly very restricted—evidence nowhere suggests that either they or contemporary outsiders saw them in these terms. The Palmyrenes seem rather to have seen themselves in opposition to the *nomades*. If they did indeed identify themselves as 'Arabs', it was at least a curious oversight that 'Arabicus' appears among the victory-titles of Vaballathus as Emperor.[50]

But of course the social history of the whole marginal zone between the steppe and the cultivable land remains to be written, if it ever can be. It was, however, its location on this zone and on the limits of the Empire which gave Palmyra its particular role, unique among provincial cities, in the exercise of armed force. It is true that other Greek cities can be found from time to time exercising force against bandits. But what was unique to Palmyra was the deployment of force and (as we saw) the maintenance of posts, along major routes, up to a distance of several hundred kilometres from the city.[51] We cannot be certain that Roman forces, either those stationed at Palmyra or ones detached for the purpose, did not sometimes collaborate in the maintenance of order along the trade-routes: in 135 a *synodia*, after returning from Spasinou Charax, put up a statue of Iulius Maximus, centurion of a legion (QṬRYN' DY LGYWN' in the Palmyrene text).[52] But there is nothing to indicate that Roman forces regularly garrisoned or patrolled this vast area.

Unfortunately the few references to conflicts with the peoples of the steppe and occasional inscriptions of Palmyrene officers or soldiers stationed on or near the Euphrates give us no idea at all of the size or structure of Palmyrene forces. Unlike the dependent kings of the first century, the Palmyrenes are never recorded as sending their own forces to aid the Roman army. We have simply to admit ignorance, while noting that we have relatively good evidence for Palmyrene forces serving as part of the Roman army in the second century.[53] The earliest evidence is two discharge-diplomas of 120, one granted to a Palmyrene soldier called Hamasaeus son of Alapatha, and found at Porolissum in Dacia Superior; and another, concerned with a unit of Palmyrene ar-

49. R. Dussaud, *La pénétration des Arabes en Syrie avant l'Islam* (1955), ch. 4.

50. 4.3 above.

51. 3.4 and 4.1 above.

52. Cantineau, *Inv.* X, no. 81.

53. There is no satisfactory treatment of the scattered and confusing evidence for Palmyrene units, known from Egypt, Africa, Dacia and (the Cohors XX Palmyrenorum) from Dura. See *RE* XVII (1937), 2549–2552; F. Gilliam in *Dura Final Report* V.1 (1959), 26ff. = *Roman Army Papers* (1986), 207ff.; M. Speidel, "The Rise of Ethnic Units in the Roman Imperial Army", *ANRW* II.3 (1975), 202 = *Roman Army Studies* I (1984), 117; J. C. Mann, "The 'Palmyrene' Diplomas", in M. M. Roxan, *Roman Military Diplomas 1978–1984* (1985), 217.

chers in Dacia, and also found in Rumania.[54] As we saw, Palmyrene soldiers
and other Palmyrenes, when abroad, might continue to have their native language inscribed;[55] and it is significant that at some time in the second century
soldiers from the unit at Porolissum put up a bilingual inscription in the agora
of Palmyra to their commander—'*eparchos (praefectus)* of the archers stationed in Parolisson *(sic)* of Upper Dacia'.[56] The *praefectus* is likely to have
been a Palmyrene also, and the inscription is presumably the work of veterans
from the unit. Such evidence might perhaps serve to suggest that Palmyrene
units elsewhere in the Roman army retained both a sense of local identity and
active links with their native city.

A Palmyrene unit remained at Porolissum at least until the reign of Decius
(249–251).[57] The caravan trade, still presumably requiring the use of force,
or at least the exercise of police functions, continued until the same period.[58]
But neither of these two contrasted aspects of the military role of Palmyra
and its citizens provides anything like an explanation of the role of Septimius
Odenathus in fighting against Persia in the 260s, or of the 'empire' claimed,
for a few years in the late 260s and early 270s, by his widow Zenobia and
his son Vaballathus. It is in this context, for the first time, that we hear of
Palmyrene generals and a Palmyrene army. The documentary evidence comes
from two bilingual inscriptions placed on columns in the Great Colonnade in
271: one is addressed posthumously to Odenathus, 'King of Kings', and the
other to Zenobia, 'the most illustrious and pious Queen'—in Palmyrene
SPṬMY' BTZBY NHYRT' WZDQT' MLKT'. The two dedicants are Septimius Zabda, 'commander in chief', and Septimius Zabbai, 'commander of the
army in Tadmor'—SPṬMYW' ('Septimioi') ZBD' RB ḤYL' RB' WZBY RB
ḤYL' DY TDMWR.[59]

It may be that the brief claim to empire by a 'queen' and her son from
Palmyra did represent the abortive assertion of an 'Arab' or 'Syrian' nationalism, based on a city whose social and cultural history was unlike that of any
other provincial community in the Empire. But until we have better evidence,
an alternative hypothesis has to be entertained also: that Odenathus was the
governor (*consularis* or *hypatikos*) of his own province, Syria Phoenice, and
stepped into a vacuum created by Persian raids and Roman civil wars. And
that the coup d'état of his wife and son began—as Vaballathus' successive

54. *CIL* XVI, no. 68; M. M. Roxan, *Roman Military Diplomas 1954–1977* (1978), no. 17.
55. Text to nn.31–34 above.
56. Cantineau, *Inv.* X, no. 79 = *AE* (1947), no. 170. The Palmyrene text has remained
unpublished.
57. *AE* (1944), no. 56.
58. The latest person praised for 'bringing back' *synodiai* is Septimius Vorod, a major figure
of the 260s, Cantineau, *Inv.* III, no. 7. Cf. 4.3 above.
59. Cantineau, *Inv.* III, nos. 19–20.

titles clearly show—as a claim to joint rule with successive Emperors, Claudius and Aurelian, far away in Europe. The two routes which their soldiers took, to occupy Egypt and to advance across Asia Minor, were precisely those which Vespasian's forces had followed, exactly two centuries before. The movement came from a Roman *colonia* whose upper classes publicly emphasised their Roman ranks, as *equites* and senators. The facts suggest that it was not a *separatist* movement, designed to detach Syria, or the whole Near East, from Roman rule, but an abortive claim to the Empire.[60]

Nonetheless, it would be premature to conclude firmly that the brief Palmyrene 'empire' should be understood solely as a function of the senatorial status and Imperial ambitions of its leading family. For it seems that with its fall in 272 there disappeared also everything that went to make Palmyra distinctive: the Palmyrene language and art, and continued construction and architectural adornment in Palmyrene style. But even this conclusion is not quite certain.[61] As we have seen, the city was not in fact destroyed, even if part of it, including the temple of Allat (which was preserved, with some alteration of its *temenos*), was taken over for the *castra* of the Roman garrison.[62] The Great Colonnade and (at least) the temples of Bel, Baalshamin and Arsu still stood. It was at the temple of Baalshamin that a Roman *optio princeps* made a dedication in Greek, addressed to 'Zeus Hypsistos', in 302. Moreover, for at least a few years, Palmyrene continued to be used for inscriptions. One concerning the 'guardians' (MHDMRYN) of the temple of Bel dates to March 272, so just before the siege by Aurelian: it is worth noting that it is dated by the presidency of a banqueting association of Haddudan, a (Roman) senator (SNQLṬYQ', transliterated from the Greek *sunklētikos*). But a parallel Palmyrene inscription, also naming Hadudan as a senator, seems to refer back to his presidency in 272, and certainly names the month Ab (August). It also refers to Aurelian—['W]RLYNWS QSR. This inscription (whose date is missing) seems therefore to date to 273, and might in principle be later. In any case, fragmentary as it is, it shows that the officials of the cult of Bel were still functioning.[63]

That is not all. A Greek inscription from the Great Colonnade, clearly dated to the Seleucid year 591, AD 279/280, records (if restored by compari-

---

60. For the details of this sequence of events, as recoverable from contemporary evidence, see 4.3 above. It should be stressed that the reconstruction of the successive roles and statuses of Odenathus suggested here is hypothetical; for a different view see Potter, *Sibylline Oracle*, App. IV.

61. It *was* stated much too definitely in *JJS* 38 (1987), 156.

62. 5.1, text to nn.26–27, above.

63. See M. Gawlikowski, "Inscriptions de Palmyre", *Syria* 48 (1971), 407, 412–421; *Le temple palmyrénien* (1973), 76–80.

son with a parallel inscription) that the *phylē* of the Maththabōlioi had honoured someone because he had paid for the roofing of 'the great basilica of
Ares, the ancestral god'—that is, Arsu;[64] both inscriptions are accompanied
by very fragmentary Palmyrene texts. No later Palmyrene inscription is
known as yet, and Greek ones also become very rare. Even so, apart from
the construction of the Diocletianic baths, we find in 328 a *logistēs,* Flavius
Diogenes, carrying out restoration-work on the Great Colonnade, 'with its
decoration'.[65] The office of *logistēs* (or *curator*), originally an imperial nomination, was by now a city office. Palmyra now had a Roman garrison, and
was a modest provincial city among others; but as a *polis* (or *colonia,* as
Tetrarchic milestones call it), it was still functioning. Whatever led to the disappearance of Palmyrene as the language of public inscriptions, it does not
seem to have been the deliberate and immediate Roman repression of a distinctive ethnic identity.

64. K. As'ad and M. Gawlikowski, "New Honorific Inscriptions in the Great Colonnade of
Palmyra", *AAAS* 36–37 (1986–87), 164, nos. 7–8.
65. Cantineau, *Inv.* III, no. 278.

CHAPTER

10

FROM JUDAEA TO
SYRIA PALAESTINA

10.1. HISTORY, RELIGION AND GEOGRAPHY

In the case of Palmyra, in spite of the distinctiveness of its social structure and its urban character, and the public use of a Semitic language in parallel with Greek, the real connection between culture and political action remains enigmatic. It may be that we should see Palmyra during the 260s and early 270s not as leading an 'Arab' ethnic movement against Rome, but as a Roman *colonia* whose leading citizens were seeking an Imperial role for themselves.

No doubts of this type can be felt in the case of Judaea. The extensive evidence for the two great Jewish revolts, of AD 66 and 132, shows unambiguously that both gave rise to regimes which were clearly nationalist, and sought the fulfilment of national traditions in independence from Rome. After the defeat of the second revolt, in 135, the expression of Jewish identity never again, in the period up to 337, took the form of an armed uprising. Nor indeed was it able to depend on any visible political structure or on any distinctively Jewish urban or territorial institutions. The emergence of a dynasty of Jewish 'Patriarchs' becomes visible to external observers, and finds reflection in the documentary record, only in the third and fourth centuries; and in any case the real powers of this institution remain very uncertain. It in no way displaced the structure either of Roman provincial government or of the cities of the region.

The fact that there was a Jewish identity which was able to maintain itself through a series of very drastic changes of political structure—and even, as we will see, of geographical location and patterns of settlement—was a function of the existence of something to which none of the other ethnic groups in the Near East possessed any equivalent: the Bible.

[337]

It is a typical paradox that it should have been Josephus, writing in Rome in Greek as a protected favourite of the Flavian dynasty, who gave the most vigorous and defiant expression of the meaning of the Bible for Jews:

> Our books, those which are justly accredited, are but two and twenty, and contain the record of all time. Of these, five are the books of Moses, comprising the laws and the traditional history from the birth of man down to the death of the lawgiver. This period falls only a little short of three thousand years. From the death of Moses until Artaxerxes, who succeeded Xerxes as king of Persia, the prophets subsequent to Moses wrote the history of the events of their own times in thirteen books. The remaining four books contain hymns to God and precepts for the conduct of human life . . . From Artaxerxes to our own time the complete history has been written, but has not been deemed worthy of equal credit with the earlier records, because of the failure of the exact succession of the prophets . . . We have given practical proof of our reverence for our own Scriptures. For, although such long ages have now passed, no one has ventured either to add, or to remove, or to alter a syllable; and it is an instinct with every Jew, from the day of his birth, to regard them as decrees of God, to abide by them, and, if need be, cheerfully to die for them. Time and again ere now the sight has been witnessed of prisoners enduring tortures and death in every form in the theatres, rather than utter a single word against laws and the allied documents . . . What Greek would endure as much for the same cause? Even to save the entire collection of his nation's writings from destruction he would not face the smallest personal injury.[1]

Josephus thus makes quite explicit the position that the books of the Bible constituted not only the source of theological beliefs and the rules of moral and social conduct, but a national history. He is of course aware that this history was incomplete, breaking off in the Persian period; and he evidently did not count as part of this corpus of specially authoritative books the First Book of Maccabees, which he himself had used in re-telling the story of the revolt against the Seleucids in the 160s, and the wars down to 135 BC which had led to the foundation of an independent Jewish state.

Josephus had depended on the books of the Bible to compose a narrative from the Creation to the Persian period; had then put the First Book of Maccabees together with whatever other Hellenistic sources he could find; then used parts of Nicolaus of Damascus' *History;* and finally deployed his own knowledge of events from within a generation of his own birth (in AD 37/38).

---

1. Josephus, *C. Apion.* I, 38–44, Loeb trans.

That had enabled him to compose in his *Antiquities* a complete history of the Jewish people in Greek up to the outbreak of the revolt in AD 66:

> The present work contains the recorded history, from man's original creation up to the twelfth year of the reign of Nero, of the events that befell us Jews in Egypt, in Syria, and in Palestine. It also comprises all that we suffered at the hands of Assyrians and Babylonians, and the harsh treatment that we received from the Persians and Macedonians and after them the Romans.[2]

Of all the Jewish writing which survives from the Roman Imperial period, only Josephus' *Antiquities* embodies the conscious conception of Jewish history and experience as a continuity from the Creation to the present. As such, it remains isolated; if it ever became known and read in Judaea, there is no evidence for it. As is well known, it was to be Christian writers of the second century and onwards who adopted and deployed its view of the greater antiquity, and hence superiority, of Jewish tradition as against those of Greece and Rome. On the other side, manuscripts discovered in the last half-century reveal both many aspects of Jewish religious culture in the Hellenistic period which Josephus' political narrative inevitably passes over and the continued relevance of these in Josephus' lifetime. Texts of Biblical books, and commentaries on these, along with strictly sectarian works, written in Hebrew or Aramaic in the Hellenistic period, were still in use at Qumran in the time of Josephus.[3] Similarly, *The Wisdom of Ben Sira (Ecclesiasticus)*, written in Hebrew around 200 BC, was never to form part of the Hebrew Bible, and was to survive intact only in the Greek translation made two generations later. But we know now that it did circulate in Hebrew in the period of Josephus, for the Hebrew text of about five of the fifty chapters of the book was discovered on Masada.[4] Though too much should not be made of the accidents of discovery, it is still of great significance that the famous reflection on the main figures of Biblical history ('Let us now praise famous men . . .') could be, and was, read in Hebrew in Judaea in the years leading up to the revolt.

In general, so far as our limited knowledge goes, neither those literary works composed in Hebrew or Aramaic in the Hellenistic period nor the dramatic history of the Maccabean revolt and the Hasmonean state, which had lasted until the Roman conquest of the 60s BC, came to be central to Jewish

---

2. Josephus, *Ant.* XX, 12, 1 (259–260), Loeb trans.

3. For a survey see G. Vermes, *The Dead Sea Scrolls: Qumran in Perspective* (1977); the Hebrew texts are surveyed by E. Tov, "Hebrew Biblical Manuscripts from the Judaean Desert", *JJS* 39 (1988), 5, and the Aramaic Apocryphal texts and Biblical versions ('targums') are collected and translated in K. Beyer, *Die aramäischen Texte vom Toten Meer* (1986), 156ff. (henceforward Beyer, *AT*).

4. Y. Yadin, *The Ben Sira Scroll from Masada* (1965); Schürer, *HJP* III.1 (1986), 198–212.

consciousness in the Imperial period. As regards the former, the exception proving the rule is the book of Daniel, written in Hebrew with sections in Aramaic, which had reached its established form in the 160s. Daniel's vision of one 'like a son of man' (KBR 'NŠ) was to provide a central (if extraordinarily enigmatic) element in the presentation of Jesus in the Gospels.[5] But it seems quite certain that the work was not *read* as a product of the Hellenistic period or (in particular) of the Maccabean resistance-movement. It presents itself as a set of stories and visions set in the Babylonian and earlier Persian periods, and this was where Josephus duly placed it; but he also stressed his view that Daniel, as a prophet, had been able to speak not only of Antiochus Epiphanes (as he in fact had) but also of the capture of Jerusalem and the destruction of the Temple by the Romans.[6]

As regards the key moments in the history of the Hellenistic period, we know only that the festival of Hanukkah, marking the restoration of Temple worship in 164 BC, was celebrated in the Imperial period. It appears (as *ta enkainia*—the festival of renewal) in the Gospel of John (10, 22); and Josephus records that it was celebrated for eight days, and was called Light *(phōs)*.[7]

This festival also appears in the brief and enigmatic Aramaic text, preserved in various versions in medieval manuscripts, the *Megillat Taanit,* or 'Scroll of Fasting'.[8] Some version of it certainly goes back to the first century AD; listing the days on which celebration was due, and hence fasting or mourning was *not* in order, it also illuminates the way in which the record of past events could be embedded in the annual calendar: 'on the 25th (of the month Kislev) the Feast of Dedication (for) eight days' (HNKT' TMNY' YWMYN). Some of the other events celebrated had also certainly taken place in the Hellenistic period: for instance the day when 'Antiochus the king ('NṬYWKWS MLK') was removed from Jerusalem'.

Further details are not relevant in this context. It is enough that the sense of history having evolved in a significant way could be related to the post-Biblical Hellenistic period also. But beyond question it was the Biblical period itself which supplied the chief frame of reference within which current events

---

5. Daniel 7, 13. For the 'Son of Man' question see, e.g., G. Vermes, App. E in M. Black, *An Aramaic Approach to Gospels and Acts*[3] (1967). See now J. Ashton, *Understanding the Fourth Gospel* (1991), 337ff.

6. Daniel is presented in Josephus, *Ant.* X, 10–11 (186–281). See Schürer, *HJP* III.1 (1986), 245–250, and cf. now G. Vermes, "Josephus' Treatment of the Book of Daniel", *JJS* 42 (1991), 149.

7. *Ant.* XII, 7, 7 (323–326).

8. For a text see, e.g., J. A. Fitzmyer and D. J. Harrington, *A Manual of Palestinian Aramaic Texts* (1978), no. 150 (henceforward Fitzmyer, *PAT*); Beyer, *AT,* 354–358 (with very over-confident identifications of the events celebrated).

could be invested with meaning, or conflicting meanings. There were bound to be conflicting meanings, if only because there were two rival communities which laid claim to the inheritance of the Pentateuch: the Jews and the Samaritans.[9] The rival Samaritan Temple on Mount Gerizim had been constructed in the later fourth century BC, and had been destroyed by John Hyrcanus in the later second century. How Samaritans of that period saw themselves is expressed most vividly by two Greek inscriptions from Delos:[10] 'the Israelites ... who pay their tithes to sacred (holy) Argarizein'. The real history, size and settlement-patterns of the Samaritan community in Samaria itself are all extraordinarily little known. In evidence from this period we encounter them only from the outside, for instance in the description in Saint John's Gospel of how Jesus talked with a Samaritan woman at the Well of Jacob: 'Our fathers worshipped on this mountain; but you say that in Jerusalem is the place where one should worship' (Jn 4, 20). Not long after the dramatic date of this meeting Pontius Pilatus was to send a detachment of troops to massacre a crowd of Samaritans who had gathered at a village near Mount Gerizim, in the hope of being shown sacred vessels deposited there by Moses.[11] Three decades later, in the early stages of the Jewish revolt, a large number of Samaritans again gathered on their holy mountain, and in the summer of AD 67 over eleven thousand were slaughtered by forces sent by Vespasian.[12] Thereafter we hardly hear of them as a group taking communal action, until the repeated Samaritan revolts of the late Empire. But we have to recall that they were there, and that their presence both contributed another element to the communal conflicts which marked this region, and influenced the process of Greek city-formation taking place during the Empire, which was also distinctive of this area.

Even within the Jewish community proper, however, conflicting lessons could be drawn from the models provided by Biblical history. We have only to think of the debate which in 66 preceded the cessation of the sacrifices in the Temple on behalf of the Emperor, and thus symbolised the outbreak of the revolt:[13] was it or was it not legitimate, in terms of historical precedents, for sacrifices to be accepted from Gentiles? Or, again, Josephus was—subsequently at least—to compare his own role in trying to persuade the defenders of Jerusalem to surrender with Jeremiah's warnings against resistance to Babylon.[14]

9. For an invaluable up-to-date survey of what little can be known of the Samaritans, see A. D. Crown (ed.), *The Samaritans* (1989).

10. Ph. Bruneau, "Les Israélites de Délos et la juiverie délienne", *BCH* 106 (1982), 465.

11. Josephus, *Ant.* XVIII, 4, 1 (85–87).

12. Josephus, *BJ* III, 7, 32 (307–315).

13. Josephus, *BJ* II, 17, 1–4 (409–417).

14. See D. Daube, "Typology in Josephus", *JJS* 31 (1980), 18.

But of course the most profound testimony to the role of Biblical history in the shaping of popular religious consciousness is provided by the Gospels. For, although we cannot state when, where, by whom or for whom any one of them was written, it is beyond question that they emerged out of the same world, the Jewish life of Galilee, Judaea and Jerusalem itself, as do the works of Josephus. Indeed those works of Josephus, written far away in Rome between the 70s and the 90s, provide the essential starting-point for all discussion of the Gospels. For they are rooted in Josephus' experience of a world which had by then disappeared: that of the self-governing Jewish community of Jerusalem, the Temple and the High Priests, the high-priestly families, 'the Sanhedrin', and great crowds coming for the major festivals. But there was also another world which was still there, but from which he was now cut off: that of the villages and small towns of the Jewish region, Galilee and its neighbouring territories above all.

The world which the Gospels reflect is precisely the same as that which Josephus experienced, but as it was in the decade before his birth, when Galilee was still part of the tetrarchy of Herodes Antipas.[15] The fact that they do genuinely reflect this world with its social divisions and its religious disputes, as it was in the 20s and 30s, does not mean that they were written either there or then. But they remain authoritative testimony to the concerns, and the historical consciousness, of Jewish society, in Galilee and Jerusalem above all, before the fall of the Temple:

> It happened that on the Sabbath he was going through the corn-fields, and his disciples began, as they went along, to pluck the ears of corn; so the Pharisees said to him, 'Look, why are they doing what is not permitted on the Sabbath? He said to them, 'Have you never read what David did when he was in need and was hungry, both he and his followers? How he entered the House of God when Abiathas was High Priest and ate the Shewbread, which no one is allowed to eat except the Priests, and gave it to his companions?[16]

The Gospels provide an extremely vivid, and in geographical terms quite extensive, view of what the area of Jewish settlement was in Jesus' time: Judaea itself, that is, the hill-country round Jerusalem; Jericho and the Jordan Valley, where the Peraea, ruled by Herodes Antipas, perhaps stretched most of the way up the very steep opposite side of the valley, to the edge of the Jordanian plateau; some of the eastern side of the Dead Sea, as far south as Herodes' fortress at Machaerus, where John the Baptist was executed; and Galilee, separated from Judaea by the area of Samaritan settlement. The Gos-

15. See 2.2 above.
16. Mk 2, 23–26.

pels also faithfully reflect the fact that there was no clear boundary between Jewish and gentile settlement either eastwards, in Peraea and Gaulanitis, or in the territory of Caesarea Panias, founded by the tetrarch Philip; or north-westwards into the territory of Tyre and Sidon. But they make no mention of the established Greek city of Scythopolis, situated in the Plain of Jezreel south of Galilee, or of the newly founded gentile city of Sebaste, placed by Herod on the site of the ancient Israelite capital of Samaria; and even the mixed gentile and Jewish city of Tiberias, founded by Herodes Antipas on the shore of the Sea of Galilee, is only mentioned once, as a geographical point of reference (Jn 6, 23). Sepphoris, also with a mixed gentile and Jewish population, and situated only a few kilometres from Nazareth, finds no mention at all.[17]

As was demonstrated by popular reactions on both sides when the Jewish revolt broke out in 66, Jewish communities were also found in a wide penumbra of cities around Judaea, including those of Phoenicia, as well as Damascus and the Decapolis. So no precise limits of Jewish settlement can be drawn. Nonetheless it is important to stress the substantial Jewish presence in two areas which the Gospel narratives do not touch: the coastal plain from Ptolemais southwards through Herod's new city of Caesarea at least as far as Ascalon; and Idumaea (from which, however, followers come to hear Jesus, Mk 3, 8). Occasional outbreaks of conflict between Jews and gentiles, such as we have already seen at Dora (apparently the southernmost city in the province of Syria),[18] or even really major conflicts, such as that in Caesarea in the 60s AD,[19] were perfectly compatible with co-existence in normal circumstances, and with Jewish participation in the politics and office-holding characteristic of a 'Greek city'; there is no reason to suppose that Jews and gentiles represented separate communities in any formal or constitutional sense.[20] In some cities there might be a majority of Jews, with a gentile minority. Philo, a directly contemporary witness, records this for Iamnia, if in very prejudicial terms: 'Iamnia, one of the largest cities in Judaea, has a mixed population, the majority being Jews and the rest gentiles who have wormed their way in from neighbouring countries'. He goes on to relate how the gentiles there, hearing of the importance which the Emperor Gaius (37–41) attached to worship of himself, erected an altar (to the Emperor, as is implied), which the Jews then pulled down.[21] Philo has in fact almost certainly reversed the history of the balance of population there. Iamnia had probably had no significant Jew-

17. See 10.3 below.
18. 8.2 above.
19. 10.2 below.
20. I would not accept this presumption, which lies behind the valuable article of S. Applebaum, "The Status of Jaffa in the First Century of the Current Era", *SCI* 8–9 (1985–86), 138.
21. Philo, *Legatio* 30/200–202, trans. E. M. Smallwood.

ish population until the late Hellenistic period. But, as the place to which the famous rabbi Johanan ben Zakkai was recorded to have resorted during the great revolt, it was, under its long-established Semitic name of Iabneh (YBNH), to have a central place in the traditional story of the emergence of rabbinic Judaism.[22] Other places in the plain also seem to have been predominantly, or almost wholly, Jewish: in a telling detail, Josephus records that in the autumn of 66, Cestius Gallus was able to take the city *(polis)* of Lydda unopposed, because the whole population had gone up to Jerusalem for the feast of Tabernacles.[23]

But the territory whose population subscribed to Judaism and worshipped at the Temple of Jerusalem now stretched considerably farther south, not only in the area where the coastal plain shades off into the Negev, but down the full extent of the Judaean hills, to a line roughly between Beersheva and a point a few kilometres north of the south end of the Dead Sea. Again, precise boundaries cannot be established, and there were probably no substantial places in the entire region where the population was either wholly Jewish or wholly gentile. But it is of the greatest significance for the entire religious and cultural history of Judaea that there were now major Jewish centres in the hill-country south of Jerusalem: Herodion, where Herod created a palace, which would also serve as his monumental tomb; Engeddi, beside the Dead Sea; Masada, Herod's great fortress almost at the south end of the Dead Sea; and Hebron, where it was (as it seems) again Herod who built the monumental shrine which enclosed the traditional tombs of the Patriarchs in the Cave of Machpelah. Josephus lists both Herodion and Engeddi as places after which districts, or 'toparchies', were named; and he lists another 'toparchy' by the less specific name of Idumaea.[24] Its central point was perhaps Baitogabra (Beth Guvrin), which under Septimius Severus was to become the Greek city of Eleutheropolis.

The extension of a substantial Jewish presence into the coastal plain, where there seems to have been none in the time of the Maccabees in the second century BC, had been a product of the expansion of the Hasmonean state, and then of the rule of Herod the Great, and will have occurred by stages which cannot now be traced. But the existence of a large, essentially rural, population which subscribed to Judaism, and looked to Jerusalem, in both Idumaea and Galilee was a product of much more specific circumstances in the Hellenistic period. It is probable in the case of both areas that the extension of Judaism had occurred not by emigration (which no doubt took place also), but by the forcible conversion of the existing population. In the case of

22. See Schürer, *HJP* I, 525–526, and II, 109–110.
23. Josephus, *BJ* II, 19, 2 (515).
24. Josephus, *BJ* III, 3, 5 (54–55).

Galilee this seems to have been carried out by Aristobulus I in 104/103 BC, at the moment when he is explicitly described as applying the same procedure to the Ituraeans.[25] In the case of Idumaea, this had already been done by John Hyrcanus a few years earlier, when he is described as having captured the towns of Adora and Marisa, and as having compelled the Idumaeans either to undergo circumcision and accept the Jewish laws or to leave.[26] Naturally, we must allow for much more complex long-term processes, and for the continued presence of a mixed population in these areas, as elsewhere. What role was played by voluntary proselytism, over a longer period, it is impossible to say.

We should not fail to grasp the immense historical significance of that process of the Judaisation of these very large rural populations which is (at least) symbolised by these narrative allusions. Herod's father, Antipater, had been an Idumaean Jew (his mother came from Nabataea). In the great revolt of 66 'the Idumaeans', though distinguished by Josephus as a separate group among the various participants on the Jewish side, contributed a considerable proportion of the Jewish forces both in their own region and, from 68 onwards, in Jerusalem. According to Josephus, a force of twenty thousand men was collected in Idumaea and was brought to Jerusalem, playing a central role from then on, not least in the brutal internal conflicts which marked the resistance.[27] Later in the same year Vespasian marched into the heart of Idumaea, took two villages, 'Bētobris' (Beth Guvrin?) and 'Caphartoba', killed, so Josephus says, ten thousand of their inhabitants, imprisoned one thousand and expelled the rest, and left garrisons there.[28] Further details are not needed. It is enough to recall that the last fortress held by the resistance was Masada, in the south-east corner of Idumaea, in territory which two centuries earlier had been firmly pagan.

In the next great revolt, the war of 'Bar Kochba' in 132–135, a similar pattern is even clearer. From the little that our fragmentary evidence allows us to see (and it has to be remembered that most of our documents owe their survival to having been buried in caves in just this mountainous area west of the Dead Sea), the region in which the rebel state operated was the same one, between the Dead Sea on the east and Bether and Herodion to the north-west of Hebron. The known hoards of the coins struck by the rebel state tell the same story, and in fact cluster around Hebron.[29]

25. Schürer, *HJP* I, 217–218.

26. Schürer, 207. For a detailed discussion of this phase, attempting to disprove the element of coercion, see A. Kasher, *Jews, Idumaeans and Ancient Arabs* (1988), ch. 3.

27. Josephus, *BJ* IV, 4, 1–2 (231–235), and Kasher, op. cit., 224ff.

28. *BJ* IV, 7, 6 (446–448).

29. L. Mildenberg, *The Coinage of the Bar Kokhba War* (1984), 53 (map of coin hoards and finds); 83 (localities mentioned in the documents).

However drastic were the after-effects of the war, on which—as regards this area—we have no information, they were not sufficient to disrupt the continuity of Jewish rural, or village, settlement in Idumaea. Here too we owe a series of vivid if random snapshots of patterns of settlement to the *Onomasticon* of Eusebius, reflecting the situation at the end of the third century. For he happens to list a series of places here, each of which he describes as 'a very large village *(kōmē)* of Jews': Anaia, south of Hebron; Engeddi; and Eremmōn, Thala and Ietta, all located to the south of Eleutheropolis.[30]

The long-term significance of (apparently) forced Judaisation here in the late Hellenistic period can, however, in no way stand comparison with that in the case of Galilee. For it was in the (now) Jewish villages and small towns of Galilee, with their synagogues, that a new interpretation of Judaism and the meaning of Biblical prophecy was preached by Jesus of Nazareth.[31] The fact was evidently regarded by observers as paradoxical in more than one way—the first of which was that Galilee, with no significant Biblical associations, was entirely the wrong place for Jesus to come from:[32] 'And they said, "Surely the *Christos* does not come from Galilee? Has not Scripture said that it is from the seed of David, and from Bethlehem, the village where David was, that the *Christos* comes?"'

However complex were the different associations of the idea of anointment, and however varied the expectations of a coming 'anointed one', or Messiah (MŠY'), it is indisputable that the earliest Christians both related these expectations to Jesus and believed, as Paul did, that he came 'from the seed of David'.[33] Hence there arose the two contradictory birth-narratives which the Gospels offer, both designed to show how Jesus will nonetheless in fact have come from 'Bethlehem of Judaea'. One, that of Luke, is a historical impossibility, making use of the traumatic memory of the first Roman census of Judaea in AD 6.[34] The other, that of Matthew, makes more plausible use of the succession of rulers in Judaea and Galilee in the years concerned; and both provide genealogies (wholly different) linking Jesus to King David.[35] That the notion of anointment was central to the contemporary perception of Jesus is

30. *Onom.* 26, 9 (Anaia); 86, 29 (Engeddi); 88, 17 (Eremmōn); 98, 26 (Thala); 108, 8 (Ietta). See M. Avi-Yonah, *The Jews of Palestine* (1976), 16.

31. For synagogues, where preaching, usually following a reading of the Law, takes place on the Sabbath, see, e.g., Mk 1, 21 (Capernaum); 6, 2 (Nazareth).

32. Jn 7, 41–43.

33. *Romans* 1, 2. For the ancient evidence on the varieties of Messianic expectation, see Schürer, *HJP* III (1979), 488ff. See also J. Neusner, W. S. Green and E. Frerichs (eds.), *Judaisms and Their Messiahs at the Turn of the Christian Era* (1987).

34. 2.2 above.

35. For these points, F. Millar, "Reflections on the Trials of Jesus", in P. R. Davies and R. T. White (eds.), *A Tribute to Geza Vermes* (1990), 355.

also undeniable; for why else should his followers have applied to him a term meaning 'having been anointed with oil', which had no religious significance except in this context, and none at all for gentiles? Equally central was the notion of kingship. Both were to appear in Latin, Greek and Hebrew (or Aramaic?) on the Cross: 'Jesus Christos, King of the Jews'.

That such a claim could be made on behalf of a man from one of the many large Jewish villages of Galilee is one sign of the major shift in the religious geography of the region which had taken place since the beginning of the first century BC. Whether this shift had been the product primarily of emigration or of the conversion, forced or otherwise, of gentiles will never be known. But a Messiah might perhaps almost as easily have arisen in any one of the other, relatively marginal, Jewish zones from which Gospels describe people as coming to hear Jesus: not only from Jerusalem and Judaea but from Idumaea and across the Jordan and 'about Tyre and Sidon'; or, in a different formulation, 'from Galilee and (the) Decapolis and Jerusalem and Judaea and beyond the Jordan'.[36]

Galilee was, however, the most extensive and surely the most heavily populated of the various zones of large Jewish villages which surrounded Judaea itself. It is also by far the best known, partly from the very detailed accounts by Josephus of his own role as the Jewish commander in Galilee in 66 and 67.[37] Josephus claims that he enrolled in Galilee an army of over 100,000 young men, later modifying this to say that over 60,000 were actually ready for service.[38] It is not necessary to take these figures literally; but the impression of a dense population, in large villages and small towns, is not misleading.

Until the Temple was destroyed in 70, all these regions, Galilee included, remained in close contact with it, and enormous numbers made the journey up to Jerusalem for the three major festivals, Passover, the Feast of Weeks, and Tabernacles. Passover was the most important, and Josephus is able to claim that a calculation made (apparently) in 66 had produced a figure of 2,700,000 participants, assuming an average of 10 persons for each animal sacrificed.[39] We need not concern ourselves with the accuracy of the figures, which may well be grossly exaggerated. It is enough to assert the centrality of the Temple, to which large groups made their way regularly from Galilee, as from elsewhere.[40] It may even be that the normal quest for 'the historical

36. Mk 3, 8; Mtt 4, 25.

37. See, e.g., S. J. D. Cohen, *Josephus in Galilee and Rome* (1979), ch. 6; T. Rajak, *Josephus: The Historian and His Society* (1983), ch. 6.

38. Josephus, *BJ* II, 20, 6 (576); 20, 8 (583).

39. Josephus, *BJ* VI, 9, 3 (422-425).

40. For example, the Galilean pilgrims attacked by Samaritans in Josephus, *Ant.* XX, 6, 1 (118).

Jesus', by basing itself on the Synoptic Gospels, in which Jesus goes to Jerusalem only for the final Passover, has missed the centrality of the Temple in Galilean Judaism; for if we were to follow John's Gospel, the entire account is patterned around journeys up to the Temple for successive festivals, and much of Jesus' preaching takes place in and around Jerusalem.[41]

But if that view were accepted, it would only accentuate our conception of what must have been the devastating effects of the destruction of the Temple in 70, and the end of the High Priesthood, the sacrificial cult, and the major festivals as conducted at the Temple. We can assume that hopes of their restoration persisted; but equally nothing suggests that the Romans ever contemplated allowing it. Recognition of this profound change would also, however, make more urgent the enquiry as to how, and through what social institutions and means of transmission, Judaism in fact survived this catastrophe.

The full significance of the Judaisation of a large population living either in villages or in 'Greek' towns, which might have either a gentile or a Jewish majority, was to be seen only after the defeat of the second great revolt. After the first revolt, whatever the extent of devastation, or the effects of the presence of a Roman legion, it seems that some Jewish population persisted in Jerusalem and its neighbourhood. Direct evidence is almost totally lacking, but such a background is implied by the fact that after 70 the Christian community of Jerusalem is reported as having had a series of bishops of Jewish origin. The first gentile bishop is recorded only after the foundation of the *colonia* of Aelia Capitolina.[42]

It is perhaps not always sufficiently emphasised that it was this which was the decisive transformation in the religious demography of the Holy Land in the Imperial period. It was not merely a matter of enormous casualties: for what it is worth, Cassius Dio in his *Roman History* reports that 50 fortresses and 985 villages were destroyed, and 580,000 men killed in skirmishes and battles, as well as countless numbers by starvation, disease and fire.[43] What was to be significant was not that, but the wholesale replacement of a Jewish by a gentile population, not merely in the city of Jerusalem itself but in its surrounding territory. Christian writers were to emphasise, with profound satisfaction, that now Jews could not even look on Jerusalem from afar. It may not be accidental that the two known contemporary expressions of this view both come from Christian natives of Greek cities in the immediate region: Ariston of Pella, in a dialogue between a Christian and a Jew; and Flavius Iustinus (Justin Martyr) from Flavia Neapolis, in a similar work, his *Dia-*

41. So Millar, op. cit. (n.35 above).
42. Bishops of Jewish origin: Eusebius, *HE* IV, 5, 2–4; first gentile bishop: IV, 6, 4.
43. Dio LXXIX, 14, 1.

logue with Tryphon the Jew.[44] But, so far as our evidence goes, it was left to another Christian author from the region, Eusebius of Caesarea, writing in the early fourth century, to exploit to the full the rhetorical and doctrinal possibilities presented by this transformation:

> Therefore it says this, 'Zion shall be ploughed as a field, and Jerusalem shall be as a storehouse of fruit' (Mtt 27, 25), a prophecy which was only fulfilled after the impious treatment of our Saviour. From that time to this utter desolation has possessed the land; their once famous Mount Sion, instead of being as once it was, the centre of study and education based on the divine prophecies . . . is a Roman farm like the rest of the country, yea with my own eyes I have seen the bulls plowing there, and the sacred site sown with seed . . . So Aquila says (in his Greek translation of Micah), 'Therefore for your sake the land of Zion shall be ploughed, and Jerusalem shall be a quarry of stone', for being inhabited by men of foreign race it is even now like a quarry, all the inhabitants of the city choosing stones from its ruins . . . And it is sad for the eyes to see stones from the Temple itself, and from its ancient sanctuary and holy place, used for the building of idol temples and the theatres for the populace.[45]

There is no precise evidence for where the boundaries of the territory of Aelia Capitolina now lay, or for whether they coincided exactly with the zone within which Jews could no longer come. It is argued, however, that rabbinic evidence reveals, negatively, seventy-five places in Judaea which are no longer cited as being inhabited by Jews;[46] and Tertullian, writing at the end of the second century, assumed that the zone from which Jews were banned included Bethlehem.[47]

Even though we cannot trace exact boundaries, or be certain how completely the original expulsions were carried out, whether acceptance of paganism (or Christianity) might have enabled Jews to remain, or whether exclusion could ever have been rigorously enforced, the essential fact is that in the area round Jerusalem a gentile population had replaced a Jewish one. The area from which Jews were now in principle excluded represented the heart of the zone of Jewish settlement around Jerusalem, as it had been three centuries before, on the eve of the Maccabean revolt.[48]

The major consequences of this were two. First, rabbinic Judaism as formulated in the *Mishnah* was to be, like Christianity, a product of the Jewish

---

44. Ariston of Pella is cited by Eusebius, *HE* IV, 6; for his *Dialogue of Papiscus and Jason*, read by Celsus, see Origen, *C. Celsum* IV, 52. On Flavius Iustinus see ch. 6 above.

45. Eusebius, *Dem. Ev.* VIII, 3, 10–12, trans. W. J. Ferrar, *The Proof of the Gospel* (1920).

46. See M. Avi-Yonah, *The Jews of Palestine* (1976), 16, and map, p. 17.

47. Tertullian, *Adv. Jud.* 13, 3.

48. For that area see Schürer, *HJP* I, 140–142.

villages and small towns of Galilee—and, as we will see, of the very similar zone of villages on the Golan, on the other side of the valley. Why Galilee, so far as we know, had played no significant part in the Bar Kochba revolt, and why the Jewish villages of the former Idumaean zone play only a small role in rabbinic literature, it is not possible to say. But since, as has been repeatedly emphasised, villages represented the most important social formation throughout the Roman Near East, Galilee must have a special place in any consideration of what that might mean. For while the villages of Galilee and the Golan were never isolated, and remained in active contact with the gentile, or predominantly gentile, cities around them—Damascus, Caesarea Panias, Sidon, Tyre, Ptolemais, Caesarea, Scythopolis—it was essentially a village society, using Hebrew, Aramaic and Greek, within which the heritage of the Bible was transformed both into the earliest preaching of 'Christianity' and into the classical formulation of rabbinic Judaism.

The second consequence was that when Constantine conquered the eastern part of the Empire, and proclaimed there his mission as a Christian Emperor, almost all the major Christian monuments which he immediately built in Palestine—in Jerusalem itself, on the Mount of Olives and in Bethlehem—were constructed within what was now a pagan environment. But in sweeping aside the monuments of paganism, Constantine too might lay claim to be honouring the sacred sites not only of the New Testament but of the Old as well. For he himself records that he had learned that the oak at Mambre near Hebron, 'where Abraham had his dwelling', was defiled with idols and an altar. So a Christian basilica was to be built there, which the Bordeaux Pilgrim of 333 duly admired.[49] Though certainty is impossible, the pilgrim, in visiting it, had probably already left the territory of Aelia Capitolina; but it was evidently close enough to the area of pagan settlement for pagan cults to flourish there. A short distance further on, the pilgrim came to Hebron itself and was able to admire a purely Jewish monument, the rectangular tomb *(memoria)* made 'of stones of wonderful beauty, in which are laid Abraham, Isaac, Jacob, Sarah, Rebecca and Leah'. It was, rather fittingly, the last monument which he saw. He was probably unaware that it too represented a quite recent expression of religious imperialism. For although the Book of Genesis did indeed record that all these persons had been buried in the Cave of Machpelah at Hebron, the area itself had been regained only by Judas Maccabaeus in the 160s BC; and the rectangular enclosure of 60 m by 33 m, which still stands, had been built by Herod the Great no more than a century after the population of the area had themselves become Jewish.[50] No Christian construction was to take place here until the sixth century. For while pagan temples could

49. Constantine's order: Eusebius, *VC* III, 51–53; cf. *Itin. Burd.* 599. For the site and its remains see E. Mader, *Mambre* I–II (1957).

50. *Itin. Burd.* 599. See J. Jeremias, *Heiligengräber in Iesu Umwelt* (1958), 90–94.

be swept away without significant resistance, the resilience of a tradition based on a sacred text was another matter. Major wars had been fought before the Temple could be destroyed, or Jerusalem converted into Aelia Capitolina; but under Constantine the symbolic gestures made by the newly Christian state were confined to those areas which it itself, in an earlier phase, had made pagan.

Thus there were two different reasons, the power of tradition and the current facts of geography and settlement, why a Christian basilica was duly built at Bethlehem, where Jesus should have been born, and it was believed that he had been. But at Nazareth, the Jewish village where he really had lived, no Christian building appeared. In Galilee the converted Jew, Joseph of Tiberias, in spite of Imperial authorization, succeeded in constructing in his native city no more than a small chapel, in a bath-house which had once been a temple of Hadrian. Otherwise he effected no change in the existing situation, which was that no Christian churches had obtruded in this area: 'Because', as Epiphanius relates, 'of the fact that there are neither Hellenes nor Samaritans nor Christians among them; this state of affairs, that there should be no non-Jew among them, is maintained above all in Tiberias, in Diocaesarea which is also called Sepphoris, in Nazareth and in Capernaum'.[51]

Yet the names in this account themselves reflect the other distinctive feature of the history of Judaea, or 'Syria Palaestina'. On the one hand this region provides by far the most clearly defined example from the whole of the Roman Near East of the maintenance of a local tradition—a religion, culture and set of rules for personal observance. But it was also the one where first the Herodian kings and then the Roman Emperors intervened most drastically, from the beginning of the period to the end, to reshape social structures by the formation of new Graeco-Roman cities.

10.2. JUDAEA BEFORE THE FIRST REVOLT

The discussion which follows will make no attempt to re-tell the narrative history of the province; the broad lines, as seen from the standpoint of military history and the structure of provincial administration, have already been examined.[1] It will, however, take the successive periods separately, for, as has been seen above, the effects of the major crises in the history of the province

---

51. Epiphanius, *Panarion* 30, 4–12 (the story of Joseph of Tiberias); the quotation is from 30, 11.

1. Part I above, passim. The narrative history of Judaea to AD 135 is set out in Schürer, *HJP* I (1973). For the following period the nearest to a satisfactory account is M. Avi-Yonah, *The Jews of Palestine* (1976), reissued as *The Jews under Roman and Byzantine Rule* (1984). For an up-to-date survey of the archaeology see now H.-P. Kuhnen, *Palästina in griechisch-römischer Zeit* (*Handbuch der Archaeologie, Vorderasien* II.2, 1990). See also R. Hachlili, *Ancient Jewish Art and Archaeology in the Land of Israel* (1988).

were so drastic as to produce radical changes in the communal geography of the area. But in each period it will not be inappropriate to start from the model, or hypothesis, of a sharp contrast between Greek city (and later Roman *colonia*) on the one hand and Jewish community on the other. The tendency of recent scholarship has been to deny, or at least to limit, the significance of this contrast; to argue that the effects of Hellenism in Judaea, after three hundred years, were so profound, in language, culture, outlook, architecture and art, that the Judaism of Judaea should itself be seen as 'Hellenistic', and hardly less so than that of the Diaspora.[2] These arguments certainly contain very important truths: not merely the physical but also the cultural environment of Judaea was largely indistinguishable from that of any other part of the Greek world under the Empire. It is a fact of the greatest importance for the earliest history of Christianity that it developed in a city, Jerusalem, in which Greek was in current use alongside Hebrew and Aramaic.[3] It was not only a matter of Greek-speaking Jews from the Diaspora (like Simon from Cyrene or Paul from Tarsos) who were settled in Jerusalem. If the texts found at Qumran included, as they did, at least some of the books of the Septuagint, we can be confident that the Bible could be read in Greek translation elsewhere in Judaea also.[4] By contrast, an impression of a wholesale retreat from a Hellenised environment might be created by the massive Hebrew text of the *Mishnah*, compiled in the earlier third century. But it is belied by the inscriptions of Galilean synagogues and by those of the necropolis of Beth Shearim, where many rabbis of the third and early fourth centuries were buried; in both the synagogues and the epitaphs Greek is freely used along with Hebrew and Aramaic.[5]

The linguistic history of the area is thus highly complex, and one of the purposes of what follows is precisely to bring out from the mass of contemporary documentation now available how the use of one language or another might be a matter of mere choice, context or convenience. Nonetheless, to stress these very real elements of a common culture, of compromises and mutual influences in daily life, is to miss precisely what is significant in the history of this area. For the Jews, unlike all the other groups in the Near East which used a Semitic language, did have a national history and sacred text in that language. There were in fact irreducible areas of conflict: was it allowable to

2. See esp. M. Hengel, *The 'Hellenization' of Judaea in the First Century after Christ* (1989); but cf. L. H. Feldman, "How Much Hellenism in Jewish Palestine?", *HUCA* 57 (1986), 83.

3. For this important point see M. Hengel, *Between Jesus and Paul* (1983), esp. ch. 1.

4. For a survey of Biblical and Apocryphal texts in Greek from Qumran and the Judaean Desert, see J. A. Fitzmyer, *The Dead Sea Scrolls: Major Publications and Tools for Study* (1977), 11ff.; Schürer, *HJP* III.1 (1986), 487–488. See now E. Tov, *The Greek Minor Prophets Scroll from Nahal Hever* (DJD VIII, 1990).

5. See 10.4 below.

worship more than one deity or not, and were physical representations of such a deity permissible? And, finally, the history of the area was marked both by communal hostilities of a sort which cannot be paralleled elsewhere and by major conflicts with the Roman state to which there is also no other parallel. The fact that these conflicts broke out must colour any interpretation of the social history of the region. But 'Judaism and Hellenism' may be not quite the right label for the contrasts involved; at one level it was a conflict between Judaism and *paganism,* and at another between Empire and a claim to liberty.[6]

Although we will be concerned primarily with the period after the imposition of Roman direct rule in Judaea proper, in AD 6, two major features of the preceding seven decades need to be stressed. First, the initial period of Roman rule, in the 60s and 50s BC, had been marked by the programmatic restoration of a whole series of Greek cities which had previously been under Hasmonean rule. In Josephus' narrative this process takes the form first of the liberation of these cities from Hasmonean rule by Pompey, and then of their re-building by the proconsul Gabinius in 57–55. Since we have no precise archaeological or other evidence for their physical character either before or after this moment, and no documentary evidence for their operation as Greek cities in this period, it will be enough to list the various cities mentioned in these contexts: Raphia, Gaza, Anthedon, Azotos, Iamnia, Ioppe, Stratonos Purgos (the later Caesarea), Apollonia and Dora, which all lay on the coast; Samaria (a former Macedonian colony, the later Sebaste); and Hippos, Gadara, Dion and Pella, which belonged to the 'Decapolis' on the other side of the Jordan. However little we know about the immediate effects of these gestures, *as gestures* they were to be of great importance. Roman rule was thereby associated with the rights of Greek cities; and the cities themselves, by adopting eras, subsequently used on their coinage, which went back to this period, explicitly acknowledged that their identity as Greek cities was a function of the steps then taken.[7]

The question of the Greek cities was to be important also in the complex political relations of the period of Herod the Great (37–34 BC). As we saw earlier, some at least of the Greek cities which were incorporated in Herod's kingdom made strenuous efforts to get themselves excluded from it and

6. As will be obvious, a survey such as this, attempting to set the communal history of the region into the context of the Roman Empire, and to compare it to other regions of the Near East, cannot attempt any significant theological analysis of the Judaism of the period. Note for example P. Hayman, "Monotheism—a Misused Word in Jewish Studies", *JJS* 42 (1991), 1, and the important study by E. P. Sanders, *Judaism: Practice and Belief 63 BCE–66 CE* (1992), of which I have not been able to take full account.

7. Schürer, *HJP* I, 91–92. For the coinage of some these places in the first century of the Empire, see now *RPC* I, 666–677.

attached to the province of Syria. In 20 BC an appeal to Augustus by Gadara was unsuccessful. But on Herod's death Nicolaus of Damascus reports that 'the Greek cities' renewed that appeal; Gaza on the coast and Gadara and Hippos in the Decapolis were successful, and became part of the Roman province.[8]

These successful efforts, however, more clearly reflect a conflict between city independence and the claims of royal rule than between 'Hellenism' and 'Judaism' as such. For, first, at the same moment, the Jewish community itself was demanding liberation from royal rule and attachment to the Roman province, a demand which was satisfied, as regards Judaea, Samaria and Idumaea, in AD 6. But second, and more important, the creation of pagan Greek cities was itself an important aspect of the ideology of Herodian rule. We need to see the foundation of cities by Herod and his sons first in the context of his long list of benefactions to other Greek cities (and the one Roman *colonia*) in the Near East. For, given the silence of literary, documentary and archaeological evidence about the public or monumental character of 'the Greek city' in the Near East in the late Hellenistic period, the programmatic lists of public buildings given by Herod to the cities of the area must be taken as representing a major new phase. So far as our evidence goes, the history of the Near Eastern Greek city of the Imperial period, marked above all by its monumental public buildings, begins with Herod the Great:

> Thus, he provided gymnasia for Tripolis, Damascus and Ptolemais, a wall for Byblus, halls, porticoes, temples, and market-places for Berytus and Tyre, theatres for Sidon and Damascus, an aqueduct for Laodicea on the sea, baths, sumptuous fountains and colonnades, admirable alike for their architecture and their proportions, for Ascalon . . . And that broad street in Syrian Antioch, once shunned on account of the mud—was it not he who paved its twenty furlongs with polished marble, and, as a protection from the rain, adorned it with a colonnade of equal length?[9]

The same values were applied in the creation of a whole series of 'cities' within Herod's kingdom and the domains of his sons. In many cases we know no more than their names, and cannot reconstruct the physical character or political organisation of such a place in its early years: this is true for instance of Anthedon, re-named either 'Agrippias' or 'Agrippeion' in honour of Augustus' friend Marcus Agrippa; of Antipatris and Phasaelis; of Iulias, lying north-east of the Sea of Galilee; 'Livias' or 'Iulias', founded by Herodes Antipas across the Jordan from Jericho; or Esbous on the Jordanian plateau. In such cases we cannot even always be sure whether we should categorise them

8. 2.1 above.
9. Josephus, *BJ* I, 21, 11 (422–425).

as 'Greek cities' at all; it was not until the early third century that Antipatris and Anthedon briefly minted some city coins; and the others never did.[10]

It is more important to concentrate on the major foundations which un-ambiguously altered the social and religious geography of the region. Herod's two most important foundations were Caesarea on the coast, on the site of Stratonos Purgos, and Sebaste on the site of Samaria (and itself directly on the site of Israelite Samaria, destroyed by the Assyrians in the eighth century). It is not necessary to repeat the well-known details from Josephus' descrip-tions of both places, or the partial archaeological confirmation available for both.[11] It is more important to stress that these are the only examples from the entire Near East of Greek cities newly founded in the reign of Augustus, and named after the Emperor. No such steps were taken in the Roman provin-cial area, or in the kingdoms of Nabataea, Emesa and Commagene. They both involved the elaboration of the full physical structure of a Greek city; each was settled predominantly by a pagan population; and both contained temples of the Imperial cult. That at Caesarea was evidently dedicated jointly to Augustus and 'Roma', a personification of the city: 'It contained a colossal statue of the emperor, not inferior to the Olympian Zeus, which served for its model, and another of Rome, rivalling that of Hera at Argos'.[12]

The Imperial names of these two cities (as of 'Tiberias', founded in Galilee by Herodes Antipas, or 'Caesarea Panias' or 'Caesarea Philippi', founded by the tetrarch Philip) may serve as a hint that the drastic innovations made in this period meant something more complex than just the extension of 'the Greek city'; a newly founded, or re-founded, city of the Imperial period is better seen as Graeco-Roman. It is important also not to miss the implications of Josephus' account of the four-yearly festival which Herod instituted at Caesarea: 'For he announced a contest in music and athletic exercises, and had prepared a great number of gladiators and wild beasts and also horse races and the very lavish shows that are to be seen at Rome and in various other places.'[13] As Josephus explicitly indicates, the models for what was to constitute a festival were taken from Rome as well as from Greece. Gladiato-rial combats and wild-beast hunts represented some of the relatively few Ro-man imports into the popular culture of the Greek East. There is no certain example earlier than Herod's dedicatory festival of 10 BC of gladiatorial shows as being part of the repertoire of displays in a Greek city.[14]

Nonetheless the ambience which was being instantly created was predom-

10. For a recent general survey, incorporating some hazardous presumptions, see Y. Mesh-orer, *The City Coins of Eretz-Israel and the Decapolis* (1985).

11. See Schürer, *HJP* II, 115–118 (Caesarea); 160–164 (Sebaste).

12. Josephus, *BJ* I, 2, 7 (414), Loeb trans.

13. Josephus, *Ant.* XVI, 5, 1 (137), Loeb trans.

14. See still L. Robert, *Les gladiateurs dans l'Orient grec* (1937), 263ff.

inantly a Greek one. The theatres which Herod built at Caesarea, at Jericho, where it looks out along the hippodrome, and (allegedly) in Jerusalem itself, where nothing further is heard of it, were also the earliest ever known to have been constructed in the Palestinian area.[15] In geographical terms Caesarea was of course marginal to the area of Jewish settlement, and but for political considerations might have been not much more significant for tensions between Jews and pagans than the long list of Greek cities and their territories in which mutual communal violence took place on the outbreak of the revolt in 66. As Josephus lists them, they include Philadelphia, Esbous, Gerasa, Pella, Scythopolis, Gadara, Hippos and the Gaulanitis (Golan), Kadasa (the Tyrian village mentioned earlier),[16] Ptolemais, Gaba (in southern Galilee), Anthedon and Gaza. In all of these, Josephus claims, violence began on the Jewish side. When he comes to the pagan reaction, he mentions also places further away: Tyre, Sidon, Apamea and Antioch; later he records a massacre of 10,500 Jews in Damascus, prompted partly by the conversion of many gentile women there to Jewish observances.[17]

The much greater significance of Caesarea as the focus of pagan-Jewish tensions arose, first, from its role as the normal seat of government of the Roman *praefecti* of the first provincial period, then (to a lesser extent) that of Agrippa I in 41–44, and then that of the *procuratores* of AD 44–66. Hence, as the narratives of both Josephus and Acts show, representations by the Jewish authorities to the governors frequently had to take place there. Second, communal tensions were immeasurably worsened by the fact that units raised from the gentile populations of Caesarea and Sebaste formed an important part of Herod's army, then (it seems certain) of the army of the *praefecti*, then that of Agrippa I and finally that of the *procuratores*. Josephus does not make clear whether either the Roman auxiliary soldier who caused a riot and massacre in the Temple one Passover by exhibiting his private parts to the crowd or the one who was executed for tearing up a scroll of the Law which he found in a village in Judaea was a native of Caesarea or Sebaste.[18] But these incidents of about AD 50 deserve mention because they happen to illustrate both the importance of the Jewish festivals and the means for the transmission of Judaism in village contexts; they also serve to confirm the reality of the communal tensions which the co-existence of Judaism and paganism evoked. That both groups were to a large degree 'hellenised' was irrelevant.

Finally, such communal conflicts came in the early 60s to take on a particularly acute form in Caesarea:

15. See A. Segal, "Theatres in Ancient Palestine during the Roman-Byzantine Period", *SCI* 8–9 (1985–1988), 145.

16. 8.5 above.

17. Josephus, *BJ* II, 18, 1–5 (457–480); 20, 2 (559–561).

18. Josephus, *BJ* II, 12, 1–2 (228–231), and *Ant.* XX, 5, 3–4 (105–117).

Another disturbance occurred at Caesarea, where the Jewish portion of the population rose against the Syrian inhabitants. They claimed that the city was theirs on the ground that its founder, King Herod, was a Jew. Their opponents admitted the Jewish origin of its second founder, but maintained that the city itself belonged to the Greeks, since Herod would never have erected the statues and temples which he placed there had he destined it for Jews.[19]

This dispute led to large-scale street-fighting, to a hearing before Nero in person at which the Greek side gained the decision, and then to a renewed conflict in the city. The argument which arose from the construction of pagan temples there was very significant. But, as in so many cities of the Near East, these two religious systems had until then co-existed physically. In the case of Caesarea there was at least one synagogue, next to which was a plot whose Greek owner had long refused to sell it. Now he deliberately (according to Josephus) built workshops on it, leaving only a narrow entrance. An attempt to stop the building by violence was repressed by the *procurator*. Then on a Sabbath, when the Jews gathered at the synagogue, a Caesarean Greek constructed a makeshift altar beside the entrance and performed sacrifices on it. After further communal violence the Jews removed 'the Laws' (a Torah scroll presumably) and retired from the city.[20]

This incident, which immediately preceded the outbreak of the revolt in 66, again illustrates the fact that we are not dealing with a homogeneous society, but one in which there were profound differences in religious systems: the whole concept of 'the Laws' as written documents housed in transportable form in a religious building was wholly alien to paganism. Nor was it one in which these systems lived in assured mutual tolerance. Most of the time of course they did co-exist. Yet open conflict between the two communities might break out at any time.

But which two communities? It is noticeable that in the passage just quoted Josephus describes the pagan side once as 'Greeks' and once as 'Syrians'. There is no sense in which we can resolve this ambiguity by deciding that the pagan populations of the Palestinian region were 'really' the one or the other. It does raise the question, however, of whether Aramaic (or even Phoenician?) remained in use among the pagan population of the coastal cities, or whether there was any continuity of cult-practice or historical identity with the pre-Hellenistic period. That all these places now functioned publicly as Greek cities is certain. But Gaza ('ZH), Ascalon ('ŠQLWN) and Azotus

19. Josephus, *BJ* II, 13, 7 (266–270), Loeb trans. Cf. *Ant.* XX, 8, 7 (133–137).

20. Josephus, *BJ* II, 14, 4 (284–292). For the difficult problem of how Jews had come to regard as holy the actual scrolls on which Biblical texts were written, see M. Goodman, "Sacred Scripture and 'Defiling the Hands'", *JThSt* 41 (1990), 99.

(Ashdod—'ŠDWD) had all been major Philistine cities, and the cult of Mar-
nas at Gaza may represent an element of continuity; so, more certainly, will
that of Astarte (or Atargatis or Derceto) at Ascalon.[21] As everywhere in the
Near East, Semitic personal names, mingled inextricably with Greek and
Latin ones, continued in use among the gentile population: for instance there
is the soldier in the praetorian cohorts identified in a Greek inscription from
Rome as 'Iamour son of Asamos, an Ascalonite in Palaistinē, brother of
Antōninos'.[22] But it is surely more significant that, like the Phoenician-
Greek cities further north, both Gaza and Ascalon, in their public self-
representation, asserted their status as Greek cities and their privileged position within the Empire: Ascalon had the formal status of a free city, and Gaza
is described in an inscription of AD 239 as 'sacred, inviolate and autonomous'.
Both seem to have become *coloniae* in the third century;[23] and both belong in
the list of cities which held Greek athletic festivals.[24] But these places were
situated in any case in a very distinctive geographical zone, on the coast-road
from Palestine to Egypt and between the sea and the steppe, shading off into
the desert, of the Negev and Sinai. A trade-route reached Gaza from the Hedjaz; and it was a short step for someone from Gaza to go out into the desert
as a hermit.[25]

The culture and religious practices of whatever pagan population was
present in the cities and villages of inland Galilee, Samaria, Judaea and Idumaea remain almost invisible to us. As we will see, the treatise in the *Mishnah*
'On Pagan Worship' *(Abodah Zara)* does provide, for a later period, some
reflection of the rural and village paganism whose effects observant Jews had
to learn to circumvent.[26] But if there were rural pagan shrines and temples in
this wide region, our archaeological and documentary evidence does not reveal them. The pagan cults and the Greek, or Graeco-Roman, city institutions
which we can see are only those of the cities deliberately created within the
Imperial period.

In one case at least—that of Tiberias, founded by Herodes Antipas—a
new city, with a Greek constitution and named after the reigning Emperor,
seems not to have maintained itself as a pagan enclave. The site, it is true,
contained graves which produced ritual impurity for Jews, and the royal pal-

---

21. For a summary of the evidence on these cities see Schürer, *HJP* I, 98–109 (cities); 30–34
(cults). See also J. Teixidor, *The Pagan God* (1977), 94ff. I cannot find in *BMC Palestine*, 104ff.,
any consistent evidence for a deity in Ascalon called Phanebaal; so H. Seyrig, *Syria* 47 (1970),
96–97.

22. *IGR* I, no. 266 = *IGUR* II, no. 560.

23. Millar, "Roman *Coloniae*", 55.

24. Moretti, *IAG*, no. 72 (Gaza); 85 (Ascalon).

25. 10.4 below.

26. 10.4 below.

ace was adorned with 'images of animals, although the Law forbids us to create any such thing'—thus Josephus, reporting that in 67 he had been ordered to destroy these, but was anticipated by Galilean extremists, who also massacred all the Greek inhabitants of the city.[27] In this case the newly created Greek city, while retaining its Greek constitution, remained, or perhaps rather became, a predominantly Jewish town.[28] Its conventional Greek coinage with representations of deities and temples seems not to have been minted after the reign of Commodus.[29] The mosaic inscriptions of its synagogue, dating to the late third or early fourth century, in Greek, Hebrew and Aramaic, represent perhaps the best symbol of the fact that a mixed culture—but not a real compromise between paganism and Judaism—was possible.[30]

The distinctive feature of the first century and the first half of the second was the fact that conflicts of religion and communal identity had led not merely to outbreaks of inter-communal strife in areas of mixed population but to major Jewish revolts against the Roman state. The sheer scale of the war of 66–74, already examined, should be stressed again.[31] For it has very significant implications for the structure of the Roman Empire as a whole, and also in the contrast which it offers to the relatively easy suppression of dependent kingdoms (which in the case of Nabataea or Osrhoene seems to have involved no fighting at all), or even to the defeat of Palmyra by Aurelian.

This is not the place for any detailed re-examination of the background to the revolt of 66, recently the object of a powerful study by Martin Goodman.[32] But certain very broad features need to be sketched in. First, in spite of Herod's massive investment in the re-building of the Temple, neither he nor his son Archelaus (4 BC–AD 6) had won any general acceptance as leaders or representatives of the Jewish people; Archelaus had indeed been removed by Augustus at the joint request of Jews and Samaritans. A single testimony as to attitudes toward Herod from within the Jewish community survives (indirectly) from these years, a pseudo-prophecy written in Hebrew and known only in an early Greek translation:

> And an insolent king shall succeed them, who will not be of the race of
> the priests, a man bold and shameless, and he shall judge them as they

27. For the graves, Josephus, *Ant.* XVIII, 2, 3 (38); images of animals, and massacre, *Vita* 12/65–67.

28. See Schürer, *HJP* II, 178–182.

29. *BMC Palestine*, 5–10; but cf. Meshorer, *City Coins*, 34–35, claiming that Tiberias was made a *colonia* in the Severan period, and that there are colonial coins of the reign of Elagabal.

30. 10.4 below.

31. 2.4 above.

32. M. D. Goodman, *The Ruling Class of Judaea: The Origins of the Jewish Revolt against Rome, AD 66–70* (1987). The details of the political history of AD 6–66 are set out in Schürer, *HJP* I, 357–470, and a survey of what can be known of Jewish institutions in II, 184ff.

deserve. And he shall cut off their chief men with the sword, and shall destroy them in secret places, so that no one may know where their bodies are . . . And he shall execute judgements upon them as the Egyptian executed upon them, during thirty and four years, and he shall punish them.[33]

Although Herod's grandson Agrippa I (AD 41–44) was more successful in balancing his role as a dependent king with an ostentatious observance of the Law, there is nothing in the extensive evidence on the events of AD 6 to 74 to suggest that the movement, or movements, which culminated in revolt aimed at the restoration of a monarchy. Or rather there is one such hint, which Josephus brings in only retrospectively, in looking back at the omens and expectations which preceded the war:

> But what more than all else incited them to the war was an ambiguous oracle, likewise found in their sacred scriptures, to the effect that at that time one from their country would become ruler of the world. This they understood to mean someone of their own race, and many of their wise men went astray in their interpretation of it. The oracle, however, in reality signified the sovereignty of Vespasian, who was proclaimed Emperor on Jewish soil.[34]

Given the oddly casual nature of this allusion, and the ambiguity of our evidence, we cannot seize on this as the essential clue to the aims of the revolt. What is certain, however, is that the Herodian dynasty could never have fulfilled this role; for its current representative, Agrippa II, tried to prevent the revolt, and fought on the Roman side when it happened. Moreover, when an independent Jewish regime was established in 66, it did not give rise to a king, but to a communal government marked by incessant conflict between different groups.

What is certain also is that the collective leadership which had replaced the kings after AD 6 was also first caught up in and then swept aside by the revolt. Our greatest weakness in trying to analyse the history of the Jewish community in the decades leading up to 66 is that we cannot adequately define either the social composition of the ruling group (which, as seen 'from below', is described in strikingly variable terms in the Gospels and Acts) or its formal structure. What was the membership of 'the Sanhedrin', and how were they appointed? Was there indeed 'a' Sanhedrin, with a fixed membership at all, or does our evidence relate to a council of advisers summoned at

---

33. The *Assumption of Moses*, 6, 2–6, trans. in R. H. Charles, *Apocrypha and Pseudepigrapha of the Old Testament* II (1913), 407ff. See Schürer, *HJP* III.1 (1986), 278–288.

34. Josephus, *BJ* VI, 5, 4 (312–313), Loeb trans. For the varieties of messianic expression as attested, see Schürer, *HJP* II, 488ff.

will by the High Priest?[35] If it was a regular council with a fixed membership, how closely did it resemble the *boulē* of a Greek city, and should we indeed think of Jerusalem itself as having been a sort of Greek *polis?*[36] None of these questions can be answered with any certainty. What we can be certain of is the centrality of the very distinctive office of High Priest, which has no known parallel in any other community ruled by Rome. It is no accident that Josephus was to conclude the twenty books of his *Antiquities* with a survey of the succession of High Priests since Aaron, and the varying means by which they had been appointed. The last twenty-eight High Priests, since the beginning of Herod's rule, 107 years before the Temple was destroyed, had been appointed successively by Herod himself, Archelaus and the Romans. Josephus oddly omits here the crucial fact that the High Priests of the last period had been appointed (and deposed) by Agrippa I, then by his brother Herod of Chalcis and then by Agrippa II. But his summary of the phase since AD 6 is perfectly apt: 'After the death of these kings, the constitution became an aristocracy, and the High Priests were entrusted with the leadership of the nation'.[37]

There is no doubt that being a *cohen,* a notional descendent of Aaron, was an essential qualification for being High Priest. But all attempts to define the 'aristocracy', or 'ruling class', of first-century Judaea are defeated by the fact that the only group which we can actually perceive is the small number of families from whom in practice the High Priests of this period were chosen: of the eighteen High Priests successively appointed and dismissed between AD 6 and 66, all but two came from four families.[38] We can see from Acts (4, 6) that some people could be perceived as belonging to the category of 'such as were of high-priestly family'; and John's Gospel also gives the clearest impression of the fact that former holders continued to retain the appellation 'High Priest' *(archiereus):* for in his account of the examinations of Jesus he both describes Annas as 'High Priest' and identifies him as 'father-in-law of Caiaphas who was High Priest in that year' (4, 12–24). Caiaphas was in fact High Priest for the period from about AD 18 to 36; Annas or Ananus had been High Priest from AD 6 to about 15, and was to have five sons who held the same office. One of these, appointed in 37, had a Greek name, Theophilos. One of the very few documentary references to High Priests comes from the Hebrew inscription on the ossuary of Theophilos' granddaughter: 'Yehohanah daughter of Yehohanan son of Theophilos the High Priest' (BR TPLWS

---

35. See Goodman, *Ruling Class,* 112ff.

36. See V. A. Tcherikover, "Was Jerusalem a 'Polis'?", *IEJ* 14 (1964), 61.

37. Josephus, *Ant.* XX, 10, 1–4 (224–251), Loeb trans.

38. For discussions of the definition of this group see, e.g., E. M. Smallwood, "High Priests and Politics in Roman Palestine", *JThSt* 13 (1962), 14; J. Jeremias, *Jerusalem in the Time of Jesus* (1969), 147ff., 377–378; Schürer, *HJP* II, 227ff.

HKHN HGDL).[39] Another text, written in ink on a sherd from Masada, *may* name the Ananias who appears as High Priest in Acts 23–24, and certainly gives the Aramaic version of the title: Ḥ[NNY]H(?) KHN' RB'.[40]

Our problem, in trying to understand this central institution of the Jewish community, is that the group of holders can be defined only in a way which is circular, by the fact of their having been appointed by the political authority of the time, whether Roman or Herodian. No formal basis for the *de facto* limitation to very few families from within the wider class of *cohanim* can be discerned. That being so, and it also being the case that we see them only in this context and cannot trace back their ancestry to earlier periods, it is not clear whether we ought to talk of a 'priestly aristocracy' or a 'ruling class'; still more awkward is the fact that we have even less conception of how any hypothetical wider ruling class of *cohanim*—and others—will have been made up. The salient point is the anomalous combination of dependence on political patronage on the one hand with centrality   the Temple cult on the other.

Nonetheless we can be certain that the connection between wealth and social class on the one hand and the occupation of the High Priesthood on the other was an issue in contemporary society. Josephus himself describes how Ananias' servants, imitated by (other) High Priests, used force to take from the threshing-floors the tithes due to the wider class of *cohanim*.[41] More significant still is the episode in Jerusalem in the winter of 67/68 which marks the first appearance of the group whom Josephus calls Zealots *(zēlōtai)*; the notion, widespread in modern books, that such a group was active in Jesus' time, or was involved in the occupation of Masada, is wholly misleading. Their attested role was in Jerusalem during the war, and their most important symbolic act was to reject the principle of birth and appoint a High Priest by lot, the last ever to hold office.[42]

Whatever the explanation of the outbreak of the revolt in 66, it cannot lie in any profound level of popular support on which the 'High Priests' could draw. They did not inspire the revolt, but on the contrary were engulfed by a

---

39. D. Barag and D. Flusser, "The Ossuary of Yehoḥanah Granddaughter of the High Priest Theophilus", *IEJ* 36 (1986), 39. Cf. 2.2 above.

40. Y. Yadin and J. Naveh, *Masada I, The Aramaic and Hebrew Ostraca and Jar Inscriptions* (1989), no. 461. It is this Aramaic version of the title which is transliterated by Josephus, *Ant.* III, 7, 1 (151): τῷ ἀρχιερεῖ, ὃν ἀναραβάχην προσαγορεύουσι (the textual transmission is clearly confused).

41. Josephus, *Ant.* XX, 9, 2 (206–207).

42. See Josephus, *BJ* IV, 3, 6–8 (147–161); *Ant.* XX, 10, 1 (227). For the necessary definitions, removing a mass of confusions, see the late M. Stern, "Sicarii and Zealots", *World History of the Jewish People* VIII (1977), *Society and Religion in the Second Temple Period*, ed. M. Avi-Yonah and Z. Baras, 263.

popular movement. The history of the period—a series of major disturbances after the death of Herod, taking place both in Jerusalem and also in Galilee and Peraea; the rise of the *sicarii*, first in resistance to the census in AD 6; and a succession of minor prophetic leaders in the 50s, coinciding with renewed terrorism by the *sicarii*—makes clear that large sections of the population could be roused to violence, often directed internally as much as against the Romans. Since we depend for our conception of all this entirely on Josephus, we cannot hope to write anything resembling a social or ideological history of these movements. The significant fact is simply that there were such movements.

What is possible is first to define the geographical areas from which a Jewish army in revolt could recruit manpower. We see it precisely set out in Josephus' account of the first measures taken in 66 to organise resistance to Rome:[43] the areas for which generals *(stratēgoi)* were appointed were Jerusalem itself, from which Cestius Gallus had just been driven in defeat; Idumaea; Jericho; Peraea (so there were different military commands on either side of the Jordan); Thamna, that is, the north-western section of the Judaean hills, with the addition of Lydda, Emmaus and Ioppe, thus an area extending across the plain to the coast; Gophnitikē and Akrabattēnē, north of Jerusalem; and the two Galilees (Upper and Lower) under Josephus himself.

Of all these areas, there are only two of which we can gain any real impression. First, obviously enough, is Jerusalem, dominated by the vast esplanade of the Temple Mount as reconstructed by Herod, but also with fortifications, royal palaces, rich private houses now revealed by excavations, and a large population regularly swelled by enormous numbers coming for the major festivals.[44] Then there is Galilee, with its dense network of large fortified villages, more or less indistinguishable from towns or cities, portrayed in the Gospels as it was when under Herodes Antipas, and as it was in 67 between the lines of Josephus' account in the *War* and the *Life* of the operations which he conducted there.[45]

What we lack for this period is anything more than passing allusions to the Jewish villages and small towns of Idumaea, Peraea and Judaea proper. There is, however, every reason to suppose that these will have contained synagogues housing scrolls of the Law, just as we see them in Galilee; that

---

43. Josephus, *BJ* II, 20, 4 (566–568).

44. The account by J. Jeremias, *Jerusalem in the Time of Jesus* (1969), remains essential. The results of excavations over the last few decades, both around the Temple Mount and in the Upper City, are available only in general, semi-popular accounts: see, e.g., B. Mazar, *The Mountain of the Lord* (1975); N. Avigad, *Discovering Jerusalem* (1980). For the Temple see now also E. P. Sanders, *Judaism: Practice and Belief, 63 BCE–66 CE* (1992), 47ff.

45. For Galilee see, e.g., S. Freyne, *Galilee from Alexander the Great to Hadrian: A Study of Second Temple Judaism* (1980); idem, *Galilee, Jesus and the Gospels* (1988).

people from these areas will have attended the major festivals in Jerusalem, as did those of Galilee or (as we saw) almost the whole population of Lydda at Tabernacles in 66; and that the main language of daily speech here will have been Aramaic.

When contemporary documentation is so rare (we have no rural synagogue-inscriptions from this period to match those known from later), we must use what we can. Not enough has been made of the fact that one Aramaic document found among others from the Bar Kochba period in the Wadi Muraba'at in fact dates to a decade before the revolt.[46] Fragmentary as it is, the document is of great significance for several reasons. First, it is securely dated to 55/56, 'the second year of Nero Caesar': [ŠN]T TRTYN LNRWN QSR. Second, it is a purely civil document, an acknowledgment of a debt: the vast majority of the manuscript evidence, whether texts and documents from the Judaean Desert or the inscriptions from before the fall of the Temple, which is written in Aramaic by Jews belongs in som 'egree in a religious context—for instance inscriptions on ossuaries. But here the parties are composing and witnessing a civil document in Aramaic. Yet, but for the name of the Emperor, we would not know that we were in the Roman Empire at all. The three witnesses, Joseph, Jonathan and another Joseph, are all Jewish, as are the creditor and debtor: 'Absalom, son of Hanin from Siwaya (or Sina), has declared in my presence that there is on account with me, Zechariah son of Yehohhanan, living at KSLWN, the sum of twenty zuzin (ZWZYN)'. Settlement will be made even if it is a sabbatical year—'year of release' (ŠNT ŠMṬH). The mention of the creditor's place of residence is also significant, for this will be the 'very large village' of Chasalōn, 17 km west of Jerusalem, near the edge of the Judaean hills; but when Eusebius later referred to it in these terms it was 'in the territory of Aelia'.[47] The document thus constitutes one of the very few glimpses which we can gain into the Aramaic-speaking (and Aramaic-writing) world of the Jewish villages of Judaea proper, as it was while the Temple still stood.

It was also, as it seems, written shortly before a Diaspora Jew, Paulos from Tarsos, returned from his third missionary journey, and was advised by the Christian elders to demonstrate his observance of the Law and his respect for the Temple. The gesture backfired, for Paul was then accused by other Diaspora Jews, from the province of Asia, of polluting the Temple by introducing a gentile Greek. The story, as it unfolds, perfectly illustrates the bilingualism of a city which was a place of pilgrimage for Jews from all over the Greek-speaking world. Paul speaks to the Roman tribune in Greek, and reveals his origin in Tarsos. But then he turns to the crowd and addresses them 'in He-

46. *DJD* II, no. 18 = Fitzmyer, *PAT*, no. 39 = Beyer, *AT*, p. 306.
47. Eusebius, *Onom.* 172, 16.

brew dialect'—by which, if he understood the distinction at all, the author of Acts ought to have meant Aramaic.[48]

That the famous inscription on the boundary of the Court of Israel in the Temple, which threatened with death any gentile who entered, should have been in Greek was only natural.[49] Equally, the bilingualism of Paul himself is matched on the ossuary from Jerusalem which contained the bones of Nicanor from Alexandria, who (perfectly in the style of a Hellenistic *euergetēs*) 'made the gates'—surely 'Nicanor's Gate' in the Temple. The Aramaic text merely identifies him and his origin: NKNR 'LKS'.[50]

The single document which most clearly expresses the way in which the Jerusalem of the period before the destruction of the Temple was, and had to be, outward-looking to the Greek-speaking Diaspora is the famous Greek inscription recording the construction of a synagogue. It too illustrates the importation of Hellenistic euergetism, but deployed for distinctively Jewish purposes; and it is also very important evidence for the role of the synagogue in the deliberate transmission of a 'religion of the book', even when the Temple still stood:

> Theodotos son of Vettēnos, priest (that is, *cohen*) and *archisynagōgos*, son of an *archisynagōgos*, grandson of an *archisynagōgos*, built the *synagōgē* for the reading of the Law and the teaching of the commandments, and the guest-house and the rooms and the equipment(?) for water, for the reception of those who require it from abroad . . .[51]

It is thus possible to see, in very broad terms, some of the characteristics of Jewish identity and some of the conditions which made possible a national uprising of a sort which the Roman Empire never encountered elsewhere. There was a large rural population living in villages and small towns which also had synagogues 'for the reading of the Law and the teaching of the commandments', just as Jesus encountered them in Galilee. There was a single main city which acted as a centre of pilgrimage for all the regions of large-scale Jewish rural settlement, as well as from overseas. There was a leading group in Jerusalem, from within which a mere handful of families provided the High Priests. The relatively recent emergence of this in-group and its dependence on political patronage (the nomination and dismissal of High Priests by Herodian kings or Roman *praefecti* and *procuratores*) may well, as Martin Goodman has suggested, have meant that it had no real roots in popu-

48. Acts 21, 17–22, 1: τῇ Ἑβραΐδι διαλέκτῳ. For the fullest survey of the interplay of languages, and the confusion in contemporary references to Hebrew/Aramaic, see Schürer, *HJP* II, 20–28; 60–80.

49. *CIJ* II, no. 1400.

50. *CIJ* II, no. 1256.

51. *CIJ* II, no. 1404.

lar sentiment.[52] But it is important to stress that, as both the Gospel narratives and the military dispositions at the beginning of the revolt show, the high-priestly families and 'Sanhedrin' represented not just city officials and a city council but (at least in aspiration) a national leadership.

This ruling group had until 66 consistently co-operated with the Romans in the suppression of popular leaders, Jesus among them. But what Josephus' narrative leaves wholly unclear is how it suddenly came about in 66 that some of the ruling group came out on the side of a full-scale independence movement. Once the defeat of Cestius Gallus in the autumn of 66 had taken place, the rest of the ruling group followed, including Josephus himself.

10.3. FROM THE FIRST JEWISH REVOLT TO THE SECOND

Josephus' subsequent narrative of the revolt, in the *W* ·· and his *Life*, notoriously reflects the ambiguity of his own position: his ultimate role as a protégé of the Flavian dynasty; his profound conviction that, as so often before, the foreign victor was the instrument of God's intention to punish the Jewish people for their sins; and the fact that a national movement for independence had led not to unity but to brutal internal factional strife, which continued even during the siege of Jerusalem by Titus in 70.

The course of civil conflict within the independent area, and above all within Jerusalem itself, along of course with Roman military movements, provides the main content of Josephus' account of the war. But even his narrative makes clear that Judaea proper, north and south of Jerusalem, was not re-captured by Rome until 69; and that even then Roman forces penetrated no farther into Idumaea than Hebron. The fortresses of Herodion and Masada, along with Machaerus on the other side of the Dead Sea, and with them presumably large parts of the hill-country of southern Judaea and of Idumaea, remained in rebel hands for several years. Herodion and Machaerus were retaken in the early 70s, in what year is not clear, and Masada not until 73, or more probably 74. Jerusalem itself was thus outside of Roman control for four years, and the area to its south-east for longer.

By its nature, Josephus' narrative is not designed either to explain the public ideals and objectives of this short-lived independent state or to analyse the workings of society and the degree to which normal routines might have been maintained under it. But he does note that the daily sacrifice in the Temple continued until the seventeenth of the month Panemos (Tammuz) in 70, that is, until about the beginning of July. The same moment was to be recorded in the *Mishnah*: 'on 17 Tammuz the daily offering (TMYD) ceased'.[1]

---

52. Goodman, *Ruling Class*, esp. Pt. I.
1. Josephus, *BJ* VI, 2, 1 (94); *Mishnah, Taanit* 4, 6.

Although we can thus see that an independent Jewish community, even an abortive state, must have existed in Jerusalem until 70, and in southern Judaea and Idumaea for a few years longer, we could perhaps hardly expect to have access to any documentary reflections of its existence. Yet, as it seems, we have. First, the seven hundred or so Hebrew and Aramaic inscriptions on pottery found on Masada probably all date to the period of occupation by the resistance in 66 to 73/74. If that is so, it is noteworthy that some of these inscriptions are concerned with designating produce for the tithes due to *cohanim*: M'ŠR KHN, 'priest's tithe'; LQWDŠ', 'for hallowed things'; or KŠRYN LTHRT MQDŠ, 'fit for the purity of hallowed things'.[2] More significant still, however, is a deed of divorce written in Aramaic and found with other documents in the Wadi Muraba'at. In it one Joseph son of Naqsan, resident at Masada, repudiates his wife Mariam, daughter of Jonathan, also living there. It is dated 'on the first of Marheshwan, year six, at Masada' (B'[H]D LMRHŠ[WN] ŠNT ŠT BMṢD'). Masada never formed part of the 'new province of Arabia', established in 106. So in spite of the close interconnections between Jewish families living around the Dead Sea on either side of the provincial 'frontier', as we will see shortly, this cannot be the era used here. It is a hypothesis, but an entirely reasonable one, that we have here a unique glimpse of ordinary life going on within the independent Jewish 'state'. The date will then be October 71, more than a year after the fall of the Temple.[3]

The fact that the Jewish state did have its own era is known from the coins which it issued, in silver and bronze, dated by Years One to Five (if a Year Six was in use, the deed of divorce is the only evidence for it). More important are the emphatically nationalist legends, in Palaeo-Hebrew script, which the coins display: 'Shekel of Israel' and 'Jerusalem is holy' (YRWŠLM QDŠH); 'Freedom of Zion' (ḤRWT ṢYWN); 'For the Redemption of Zion' (LG'LT ṢYWN). If the calendar of the Jewish state began in the spring, with the month Nisan, then coining may have ended in Year Five when Jerusalem was captured.[4] The fact that hundreds of these coins were found at Masada is the best evidence for a short-lived state and society of which Josephus' narrative (which for all its ambivalence is by far the most important contemporary account of any event in the history of the Roman Empire) reflects only the most traumatic moments.

As regards the immediate aftermath of the revolt, Jewish evidence falls

2. Y. Yadin and J. Naveh, *Masada I, The Aramaic and Hebrew Ostraca and Jar Inscriptions* (1989), 32ff.

3. *DJD* II, no. 19 = Fitzmyer, *PAT*, no. 40 = Beyer, *AT*, p. 307. See Yadin and Naveh, op. cit., 9–11.

4. For an equally brief summary see Schürer, *HJP* I, 605–606. More fully in Y. Meshorer, *Ancient Jewish Coins* II (1982), 96–131, and idem ap. Yadin and Naveh, op. cit., 101–119.

silent. We have already seen, however, how Titus celebrated the fall of Jerusalem by using captives for gladiatorial displays in a series of Greek cities in the
region.[5] Caesarea was rewarded for its role as a base, and as the place where
Vespasian was first hailed as Emperor in person, by becoming a Roman *colonia,* apparently without the arrival of new settlers.[6] The legion X Fretensis
was established at Jerusalem, where some habitation evidently continued.
Apart from territory used for the legionary camp, and the settlement of eight
hundred veterans near Jerusalem, other confiscated land in Judaea was sold.[7]
The concrete after-effects were thus profound—above all in the evident ending of the role of Jerusalem as a place of resort for the major festivals—but
still far less drastic than the wholesale transformation of patterns of settlement which took place in the 130s.

Nonetheless the topography of the region did show some significant
changes, part of that process of transformation of communal identities which
went on here throughout the period, at a level which ´ferentiates this area
from all other parts of the Near East. The fact that Ioppe now (as it seems)
became 'Flavia Ioppe' was probably no more than the acquisition of an honorific title (and in any case this title is known only from coins of 218–222);
the city had a mixed Jewish and gentile population in the second century and
after.[8] But if we knew more about it, the foundation under Vespasian of a
'new city', Neapolis, on the site of the Samaritan village of Mabartha or Mamortha, might well seem very much more significant than other changes in
this period.[9] For it lay very close to the main Samaritan centre of Shechem,
and the foundation must suggest that the Samaritan revolt put down in 67
had been of some importance. The coins of the city begin under Domitian,
and show that it had been founded as early as 72/73, and also had the title
'Flavia'.[10] What we cannot tell, given a complete lack of evidence, is whether
the appearance of this new Greek city meant the creation of a new social
and cultural formation for an existing population, or the introduction of new
settlers, or a combination of both. In an honorific inscription of AD 123/124,
set up at Ephesos, the city presents itself as 'the council and people (*boulē* and
dēmos) of the Flavian Neapolitan Samarians'. The two ambassadors (to the
then proconsul of Asia, and former *legatus* of Judaea) are called Phlaouios

5. 2.4 above.

6. 2.4 above.

7. See B. Isaac, "Judaea after AD 70", *JJS* 35 (1984); idem, *Limits,* 348.

8. 10.1 above.

9. Ch. 6 above, in connection with Flavius Iustinus. See Josephus, *BJ* IV, 8, 1 (449), and
Pliny, *NH* V 13/69, both written in the 70s, and calling the place simply 'Neapolis.'

10. *BMC Palestine,* 45ff.; Y. Meshorer, *City Coins of Eretz-Israel and the Decapolis*
(1985), 48–49.

Iounkos and Oulpios Proklos—Hellenised Latin names very comparable to that of their famous Christian contemporary Flavius Iustinus.[11] He, as we saw, seems to identify himself as a gentile convert to Christianity, and to distinguish Samaritans (by religion) as a separate group.[12] Equally significant, well-known coins of Flavia Neapolis, minted under Antoninus Pius and later, show a temple on a mountain peak, with a long flight of steps leading to it; this has been interpreted as the pagan temple of Zeus Hypsistos, said to have been constructed by Hadrian, and built (it seemed from excavations) on the actual site of the destroyed Samaritan temple. But in fact what is portrayed seems to be the lower peak of Mount Gerizim, Tell er-Ras, where the temple of the Imperial period had recently been built. The Samaritan centre, as new excavations are reported to have demonstrated, had lain on the higher peak.[13] How we should envisage the relations of the formally Greek city, which was to become a *colonia* in 244–249, with its theatre, hippodrome and (later?) amphitheatre, with the continuing Samaritan population of the area is still wholly obscure.

It is not impossible that within the context of what was in formal terms a Greek city different religious communities could have co-existed successfully. A parallel case is offered by Sepphoris in Galilee, which had been adorned by Herodes Antipas and which in 67 seems to have been predominantly Jewish, but nonetheless took the Roman side. In 68 it issued some programmatic coins giving itself the title 'Eirenopolis ('city of peace') Neronias Sepphor(is)'. In the reign of Trajan it was again issuing coins as a Greek city, and by the reign of Antoninus Pius had not only acquired a pagan Roman-Greek name, 'Diokaisareia' ('Caesarea of Zeus'), but was describing itself on its coins as 'sacred, inviolate and autonomous', in a way characteristic of the long-established cities on the coast. By the early third century the coins even speak of friendship and alliance with the Roman People, a claim to parallel that which Ulpian made at the same moment for Tyre—but surely with no concrete historical justification.[14] Renewed excavations have also revealed strongly pagan features there in the second and third centuries: a theatre which may date back to the first century, and a monumental building, apparently of the third century, containing a beautiful mosaic with scenes from the

11. *I.K. Ephesos,* no. 713.

12. Ch. 6 above.

13. For the coins see M. J. Price and B. L. Trell, *Coins and Their Cities* (1977), 172–175. For a report of recent excavations see R. Pummer, "Samaritan Material Remains and Archaeology", in A. D. Crown (ed.), *The Samaritans* (1989), 135, on pp. 165ff.

14. *BMC Palestine,* 1ff.; Y. Meshorer, "Sepphoris and Rome", in O. Morkholm and N. M. Waggoner (eds.), *Greek Numismatics and Archaeology* (1979), 159, with very speculative readings and interpretations. See also *RPC* I, 671.

myth of Dionysos, in which the episodes are labelled in Greek.[15] But another mosaic inscription, probably of the earlier fourth century, is in Aramaic and names Rabbi Iudan.[16] We could safely assume that pagan and Jewish communities co-existed here. If Epiphanius is right in saying that under Constantine the Jews followed a principle of excluding gentiles from Diocaesarea/Sepphoris (which is far from certain), this predominance may have been very recent.[17] For the preceding two centuries it is better to suppose that the central role of Sepphoris (ṢYPWRYN, with variations, in rabbinic texts) in the history of rabbinic Judaism was played out in the context of a small city which not only contained gentiles as well as Jews, but had a Greek constitution and issued Greek coins.[18]

In spite of many attempts, a social and religious history based on the vast mass of rabbinic literature cannot yet be written, for the works themselves have not been studied in a way which would produce securely established texts, let alone a clear conception of the processes and dates of their composition, or of the handling of traditions within each work.[19] Instead, we should use as a starting-point the quite extensive evidence we have from sources which are unquestionably contemporary, inscriptions and perishable documents above all, as well as the side-lights on the region available from Christian contemporaries, such as Justin, Origen and Eusebius. Any serious historical study must go *from* there to confront the complex mass of rabbinic material.

Thus, rather than re-examine later stories about Rabbi Akiba and his contemporaries, if we want some secure way, however limited, of approaching the second great revolt, under Bar Kochba, we should ask what documentary evidence we have for Jewish life before the war in the relevant region. From there we could go on to the quite extensive documentation emanating from the second independent Jewish state itself. The region mainly concerned was, as we saw, the hill-country of southern Judaea and of the former Idumaea, and the area around the Dead Sea, from Jericho south to Masada. We will look later at the experience of a Jewish family living across the notional frontier, at Maoza in the kingdom of Nabataea, and then the 'new province of

15. See E. M. Meyers, E. Netzer and C. L. Meyers, "Sepphoris—Ornament of All Galilee", *BA* 49.1 (1986), 4; "Artistry in Stone: The Mosaics of Ancient Sepphoris", *BA* 50.4 (1987), 197.

16. F. Hüttenmeister and G. Reeg, *Die antiken Synagogen in Israel* I (1977), 400ff.

17. Epiphanius, *Panarion* 30, 11, 10.

18. See, e.g., L. I. Levine, *The Rabbinic Class of Roman Palestine in Late Antiquity* (1989), passim.

19. See now the admirably clear guide by H. L. Strack and G. Stemberger, *Introduction to the Talmud and Midrash*, trans. M. Bockmuehl (1991), which makes clear how fundamental the problems of the nature and date of all these texts are.

Arabia' which succeeded it in 106.[20] But this same 'archive of Babatha' happens to contain a number of documents relating to Engeddi, a fertile spot on the western shore of the Dead Sea, and situated in the province of Judaea—and about as remote from the presence of anything we would call a 'Greek city' as it would be possible to get. Yet they illustrate again the fact that the Jewish inhabitants of this world of villages could not merely deploy written documents for a variety of practical purposes, but could do so in different languages. As it happens, the main text of every one of the documents of the earlier second century relating to Engeddi is in Greek.[21] Engeddi indeed had become an Imperial property: in a document drawn up in 124 'in Engeddi a village of the Lord Caesar', Ioudas son of Elazar acknowledges a debt due to a Roman centurion there. Perhaps not surprisingly, the entire document is in Greek. But in the marriage-contract of 128, also in Greek, drawn up at Maoza, the bridegroom, who originated from Engeddi, wrote his acknowledgment of the dowry of 500 *denarii* with his own hand in Aramaic. The deed of gift in which a few days later the father of the bride named her as heir to all his property in Engeddi gives a vivid impression of how 'urban' even such a small place might be, with an agora and perhaps a synagogue; again the father makes an attestation in Aramaic, as do most of the witnesses (except for one in Greek). Finally, on August 7, 131, the year before the revolt broke out, a contract was drawn up in Greek by which a Jewish woman living in Maoza was taken in marriage by Jesus son of Menachem from the village of Sophphathe 'near(?) the city of Livias of the P[eraea?]'. The area to which this network of families belonged thus stretched from the south end of the Dead Sea to Engeddi, and to the Jordan Valley to the north.

If we did not know that a great revolt was to erupt in the year after the last of them was drawn up, these documents would give the impression of a settled Jewish society spread through a series of villages, in which complex documents were drawn up to cover normal family and business relationships. Greek was the standard language, with Aramaic generally, though not always, used for personal attestations. One might suppose that a peaceful accommodation had been reached, within which the norms of Jewish life could be expressed in the dominant language of culture, public life and business.

The same impression might be conveyed even more strongly by a closely comparable document which comes from the central area of Judaea proper.[22]

---

20. See 11.2 and 11.4 below.

21. *P. Yadin* 11 (AD 124), see 3.3 above; 18 (AD 128), see ch. 1 above; 19 (deed of gift, AD 128); for the same properties, also 20; 37 (marriage contract, AD 131).

22. *DJD* II, no. 115. See E. Koffmahn, *Die Doppelurkunden aus der Wüste Juda* (1968), 126ff., with the map on p. 132.

This is a re-marriage contract, written in Greek and dated by the consuls of
124, and found in the Wadi Muraba'at. It was drawn up in 'Baitobaissaia . . .
of the *toparchia* of Herodion'—the place still called Beit Bassa, 3 km north-
west of Herod's fortress-palace. The bridegroom is described as 'of those from
the village of Galoda of the district around Akrabatta', a district in the northern part of Judaea proper, bordering on Samaria. But he was actually resident
in 'the village of Baitoarda of the district around Gophna', thus some 20 km
north of Jerusalem. It was presumably the bride, Salome, daughter of Ioanos
Galgoula, who was resident near Herodion. By a stroke of fortune this single
Greek document reflects the life of a circle of Jewish country districts round
Jerusalem, a few years before the second revolt broke out. Both Herodion
and Gophna fell within the area from which Jews were soon to be excluded;
and Salome must have been a relative of the Yeshua son of Galgoula (YŠW'
BN GLGLH) who was soon to find himself receiving peremptory letters in
Hebrew from the leader of the revolt, ŠM'WN BN KWSBH, more generally
known as Bar Kochba.

Only the most general points as regards the war and the quite extensive
documentation which survives from it need be made here. First, as we saw
earlier, the arrival of a second legion in Judaea preceded rather than followed
the outbreak of the revolt.[23] Second, it now seems probable that, as Cassius
Dio's account implies, Hadrian's plan for a *colonia* called Aelia Capitolina
also preceded rather than was prompted by the revolt. For some of the coins
of the revived independent Jewish state have been found in hoards along with
coins of the *colonia*. A general ban on circumcision was also promulgated,
and must be relevant.[24]

No narrative of the war is possible, or required. It is more important to
stress that its meaning for the participants was again deliberately symbolised
by coins with legends in Palaeo-Hebrew script of Years One and Two, along
with others which are undated. The series begins with silver tetradrachms
showing the Temple on the obverse, along with the word YRWŠLM; and on
the reverse a palm-branch and citrus-fruit with the words 'Year One of the
Redemption of Israel': ŠNT 'ḤT LG'LT YŠR'L. The role of the person named
on other coins of Year One as 'Elazar the priest' is a mystery. But the leader
of the revolt is named unambiguously as the head of an independent state,
'Simeon, prince of Israel': ŠM'WN NŠY' YŠR'L. We need not list all the various types and legends, except to note that in Year Two, and also on undated
coins, there appear the words 'for the freedom (LḤRWT) of Israel' or 'of
Jerusalem'.

23. 3.3 above.
24. For what is still the most detailed survey of the evidence, Schürer, *HJP* I, 534ff. See also
P. Schaefer, *Der Bar Kochba-Aufstand* (1981). For the coins of the revolt see in great detail

The numerous documents now known from within the independent state, not all of them yet fully published, tell a similar but of course more complex story.[25] First, they provide dates from Year One to Year Four. Taken as a series, they confirm that the war will have lasted some three and a half years, from the spring of 132 to the autumn of 135. The formulae vary: in Years One and Two it is 'for the redemption of Israel' (LG'LT YŠR'L); but in Year Three it is 'of ŠM'WN BN KWSB' NŠY' YŠR'L', or alternatively 'of the freedom of Israel', or 'of Jerusalem', with once 'in the days of Simeon ben Kosba' added. The only dated document of Year Four returns to 'of the redemption of Israel'. The ideology of the state is unambiguous.

Of some thirty surviving documents, three are in Greek and the rest divide more or less equally between Hebrew and Aramaic. It is not surprising that in a nationalist revolt Greek was used less readily than it clearly had been among the Jewish population of the same region beforehand. One very significant letter actually offers an explanation of why it is written in Greek (the two addressees, Ionathas and Masabala, appear in other letters, and this one was found with others in the 'Cave of Letters' in the Nahal Hever). Unfortunately, because of a gap in the text, the precise nature of the explanation is uncertain: 'It has been written in Greek because the impulse *([hor]man)*—or [Her]mas (a person)?—has not been found to write *Hebraesti*'.[26] This word probably does in this context mean 'Hebrew', not 'Aramaic'. For the fact that a whole series of documents, of various types, are written in Hebrew is perhaps the most important novelty of this evidence: they include two deeds of sale of land, contracts for leases of land, and letters both by Bar Kochba himself and by others. Comparison with earlier documents does suggest that the use now made of Hebrew in mundane practical contexts was a deliberate choice. But the fact that it could be so used is the decisive disproof of the long-held notion that Hebrew had by now become a dead language, not spoken or written, and used only in religious contexts. The background of the Hebrew used for the hundreds of pages of the *Mishnah*, compiled in the earlier third century, and the thousands of pages of the *Tosephta* ('Addition'), probably of the late third or fourth century, is immediately revealed.[27]

L. Mildenberg, *The Coinage of the Bar Kochba War* (1984), 99–101, or more briefly, L. Meshorer, *Ancient Jewish Coinage* II (1982), 264ff.

25. So far as I can discover, no provisional handlist of such documents has been published. One is therefore provided, on very summary lines, in App. B.

26. App. B, no. 19.

27. See now M. Bar-Asher, "L'Hebreu mishnique: Esquisse d'une description", *CRAI* (1990), 199. The immense complexities of dating the Tosefta, or its individual tractates, are discussed in H. L. Strack and G. Stemberger, *Introduction to the Talmud and Midrash* (1991), 167ff., concluding (p. 176) that final redaction took place in the late third or fourth century.

Both in these works and in the Bar Kochba documents Hebrew was of course deployed in close conjunction with Greek, with much use of loan-words. On the back of one of the Hebrew deeds of sale the seller, Kleopos son of Eutroapelos, signs with his own hand in Greek; his name appears in the body of the document as QLBWS BR 'WTRPLWS (using the Aramaic form of 'son of').[28] Similarly, an Aramaic letter from Bar Kochba uses the transliterated Greek word *asphaleia:* B'SPLY' ('with assurance').[29]

Amid the processes of administration of an independent territory, two features characteristic of a religiously inspired national rebellion stand out: the threatening tone required to compel obedience, and the repeated references to observance of the Sabbath and the festivals, Tabernacles in particular. No real light is cast on the course of the war itself, and none on the claim made by Justin Martyr (Flavius Iustinus from Flavia Neapolis) that Bar Kochba had persecuted Christians during it.[30] There is, however, nothing improbable in the idea that there were already Christians living in the area temporarily under Bar Kochba's control. Any such revolt will certainly have led to internal divisions among the civilian population. Behind the brief narrative sources, and the multilingual scatter of documents from within the area held by the rebels, there lie not only a major military history but a social and religious crisis which we can as yet only dimly perceive.

10.4. SYRIA PALAESTINA

The revolt was crushed, with great civilian casualties; 'Judaea' became 'Syria Palaestina' under a consular *legatus;* a second Roman legion became a permanent feature; and Jerusalem and its territory duly became the *colonia* of Aelia Capitolina, containing temples of pagan deities, including Venus and Capitoline Iuppiter. Very little is known of the life of this officially Latin-speaking community, up to the point when Constantine intervened to build churches in and near it.[1] Almost all that remains of the *colonia* is its unremarkable coinage with Latin legends, which continued with intervals until the 250s. On the one side it names and represents the Emperor or Emperors, and on the other it names the *colonia* and normally represents a deity (or the she-wolf with Romulus and Remus).[2] The very colourlessness of the types might itself be taken as a sign of how effectively Hadrian had imposed an alien presence on the site of Jerusalem.

28. App. B, no. 5.

29. App. B, no. 17.

30. Justin, I *Apol.*, 31.

1. For Aelia Capitolina see Millar, "Roman *Coloniae*", 28–30. For Constantine's intervention, 5.3 above.

2. See Y. Meshorer, *The Coins of Aelia Capitolina* (1989).

The foundation of the *colonia,* accompanied as it was by the exclusion of Jews from the surrounding territory, must be seen as decidedly the most far-reaching intervention by the Empire in the social structure of the region. It was not, however, the last. As we saw, Sepphoris had become 'Diocaesarea' by the reign of Antoninus Pius, while under Septimius Severus, in 200, both Lydda (Lod) and 'Baitogabra' (Beth Guvrin) emerge with grandiloquent Graeco-Roman titles connecting them to the Severan dynasty: 'Diospolis' and 'Eleutheropolis', both entitled 'Loukia Septimia Seouēria'. Both also minted coins with Greek legends and pagan types. There seems to be no way of assessing the context or the consequences of these changes; except that Severus may have travelled through Syria Palaestina, from Egypt to Syria Coele, in 200/201, and that it was he too who made Sebaste into a *colonia,* which duly minted coins with Latin legends.[3] Whether the amphitheatre seating some five thousand persons, excavated at Eleutheropolis, was built at this precise moment is not known.[4] But its existence is another hint that, like so many other places in the Near East, this city should be thought of as Graeco-Roman, a product of the Imperial period, rather than as 'Greek'.

One way in which an existing community might gain the status of a city or a *colonia* was simply to ask for it. This was the case for instance with Emmaus, situated where the Judaean hills meet the plain. Eusebius, followed by Jerome, records that under Elagabal, the Christian chronographer Iulius Africanus acted as ambassador for Emmaus, and obtained for it the status of a city with the name 'Nicopolis'.[5] It is of some interest for the culture of Palaestina in this period that this man, born perhaps in the 180s, the author of a variety of learned works in Greek, and later a correspondent of Origen, seems to have been a native of Aelia Capitolina. So he seems to say himself in a fragment of his *Kestoi,* preserved on papyrus: for he refers to 'the archive of (our?) ancient native city Colonia Aelia Capitolina in Palaestina'.[6] We should not underestimate the significance of such a change of identity: to Eusebius in the *Onomasticon* 'Emmaus . . . is now Nicopolis of Palestine, a distinguished city', and Gezer counted as one of its villages.[7] The coins which it now issued show that it had an extensive Imperial title: 'M(arkia) Au(rēlia)

3. Millar, "Roman *Coloniae*", 38 (Sebaste). Severus' journey is not precisely dated, and may have been by sea, cf. Halfmann, *Itinera,* 220–221. For the coins see *BMC Palestine,* xxiii–xxiv (Diospolis), and lxv–lxvi (Eleutheropolis).

4. A. Kloner, "The Roman Amphitheatre at Beth Guvrin: Preliminary Report", *IEJ* 38 (1988), 15.

5. Eusebius, *Chron.* ed. Schoene, II, 220–221.

6. See J.-R. Viellefond, *Les 'Cestes' de Julius Africanus* (1970), 289–291: ἔν τε τοῖς ἀρχείοις τῆς ἀρχαίας π[α]τρίδος Κολων[ία]ς [Α]ἰλίας Καπιτωλίνης.

7. Eusebius, *Onom.* 90, 16; 66, 21 (Gezer).

Antōnin(iana) Nikopolis'.[8] Three new cities with Greek names had been created in the area between Aelia and the coast in the early third century, and
for a brief period all issued coins showing pagan deities.

That is of course not to say that such foundations meant radical social
and cultural changes comparable to the establishment of Aelia. But they did,
as Eusebius shows, literally change the map of Palestine, and they must have
meant changes in the structure and nomenclature of local government and
office-holding.

One effect seems to have been, as we have seen, that villages might be
defined as belonging 'in the territory' of a newly founded city. An example of
this is Ziph in Idumaea, defined by Eusebius as follows: 'of the tribe of Judah.
It is now a kōmē in the Daromas in the territory of Eleutheropolis, near Hebron, eight (Roman) miles to the south. Where David hid'.[9] This definition
happens to be of particular importance, for it is from this place that we have
what seems to be the only bilingual inscription reflecting (if in a highly puzzling way) the political structure of the region as it was in the third century.[10]
The Greek inscription, on an ossuary, is straightforward: 'Kunōros son of
Diodo[to]s, prōtopoleitēs' ('leading citizen'). The Aramaic parallel text
roughly transliterates his name—QNRWS BR DYṬWS—but then describes
him as RŠ [M]RWM or [M]RYM. It seems quite uncertain whether the second word is intended to signify a group of people ('citizens') or a region ('the
high land', 'Daromas', of the Hebron area). But RŠ clearly means 'head [of]'
and refers to his status as a 'leading citizen'; on any construction it has some
bearing on exaggerated interpretations of what might have been meant by RŠ
TDMR in contemporary Palmyra.[11] The most likely context here is that the
man concerned was a local landowner who was a member of the leading
group (sometimes described as prōteuontes) in the boulē of Eleutheropolis.
All discussions seem to assume that he was Jewish, which is of course possible. But there is nothing to rule out the possibility that this is a gentile notable being envisaged through the medium both of Greek and of the Aramaic
of the gentile population of the area; some, but only some, of the villages in
this region were wholly Jewish.[12]

There were still Jewish communities in this area, but they existed in a
context which was ever more dominated by cities with Graeco-Roman names.

8. *BMC Palestine*, 159–161; Y. Meshorer, *City-Coins of Eretz Israel and the Decapolis in the Roman Period* (1985), 56. By implication I remain unconvinced that there can have been minting by Nicopolis under Marcus Aurelius.

9. Eusebius, *Onom.* 92, 15.

10. L. Y. Rahmani, "A Bilingual Ossuary-Inscription from Khirbet Zif", *IEJ* 22 (1972), 113; *SEG* XXVI, no. 1688 (Greek only); Fitzmyer, *PAT*, pp. 272 (A53); Beyer, *AT*, p. 368.

11. 4.3 above.

12. 10.1 above.

One trace of an Aramaic-speaking Jewish community here comes from Esh-temona, south of Hebron, one of the places described by Josephus as 'a very large *kōmē* of *Ioudaioi*': an Aramaic inscription was put up in the fourth century to the memory of a *cohen* called E(?)lazar and his sons, who had given part of a synagogue (DKYR LṬB L'ZR KHN['] WBNWY . . .).[13]

So far as our evidence goes, however, it was not primarily here but in the northern zone, above all in Galilee and the Golan, that 'rabbinic' Judaism developed. This area too was encircled by Greek cities like Ptolemais, Caes-area, Ioppe, Scythopolis/Beth Shean, Gadara and Hippos; and Galilee con-tained Greek cities within it, Tiberias and Diocaesarea/Sepphoris, where it is probable that Jewish influence gradually came to predominate. Here too we find one further example of the emergence of a Graeco-Roman city. Much of the history of the region is encapsulated in the fact that the village of Capar-cotna (spelled in various ways), in the valley of Jezreel, first came to be known as 'Legio' ('Legeōn' in Greek) after the legion VI Ferrata was established there under Hadrian, and then in the fourth century appears as 'Maximianopolis', a Graeco-Roman name evidently derived from the full name of the tetrarch Galerius (C. Galerius Valerius Maximianus). We know nothing of how this came about (and in fact it was the Latin term which was to pass into Arabic as the place-name 'Lejjun'). But the map had changed all the same, as we see in the report of the indirect route by which the Bordeaux Pilgrim of 333 approached Jerusalem: from Caesarea, where there was the bath of Cornelius the centurion; to the 'civitas Maximianopolis'; to the 'civitas Stradela' (Esdraela/Jezreel), where Elijah had prophesied and David had killed Goliath; and then to Scythopolis.[14]

As Martin Goodman's important study has shown, we have to see the Judaism of personal observances which was taught by the rabbis as emerging, and slowly winning a precarious authority, in a world of villages which were largely but not wholly Jewish, and were encircled by Graeco-Roman cities where Jews were in a minority.[15] For the cultural and religious history of Syria Palaestina, the most significant of these cities was of course Caesarea, now a Roman *colonia* and the normal residence of the *legatus,* and a place where, as we saw earlier, even a Tetrarch might reside and put on wild-beast shows in Roman style. But it was also a Greek city, and developed into a major centre of Christian scholarship in Greek: Origen taught there from the 230s to his death in the early 250s; Pamphilus established his library there; and his

13. See F. Hüttenmeister and G. Reeg, *Die antiken Synagogen in Israel* I (1977), 117–121; Beyer, *AT*, p. 365.

14. *Itin. Burd.* 585–586. See, however, A. Zertal, "The Roman Road Caesarea-Ginae and the Location of Capercotani", *PEQ* 122 (1990, pub. 1992), 21, giving a different view of the topography.

15. M. D. Goodman, *State and Subject in Roman Galilee, AD 132–212* (1983).

pupil Eusebius was bishop from about 313 until 339. But there was also an important Jewish community, with which Origen had regular contact, and the city thus represented one of the essential points of reference on the map of the bilingual, or trilingual, world of developing rabbinic Judaism. No reflection of that is more vivid than the anecdote in the Jerusalem Talmud of how Rabbi Levi went to Caesarea (QYSRYN) and heard them reading the Shemaʿ ('Hear, O Israel . . .') in Greek ('LYNSTYN). He was indignant and wanted to stop them. But the more general view was that it could be read in any language.[16]

Less significant compromises had to be made all the time. By its gentile inhabitants Scythopolis, for instance, was publicly proclaimed as '(one) of the Greek cities of Coele Syria'. To Jews who wished to obey the Law, it represented a partly foreign world, and it might be difficult to know whether or when business could be done with the gentiles there or not. In any case, for the compilers of the *Mishnah* the name of the place was not 'Scythopolis', but, as it always had been, 'Beth Shean' (BYT Š'N or BYŠ'N): 'If there was an idolatrous festival in a city ('YR) and some shops therein were adorned and others not adorned—such a case happened in Beth Shean and the Sages said: Those that are adorned are forbidden and those that are not adorned are permitted'.[17] Scythopolis/Beth Shean was clearly a gentile, pagan city, though there were Jews who were resident there.[18] Elsewhere it might be uncertain whether Jews or gentiles were in the majority: 'If both Israelites and gentiles dwelt in a city and in it was a bath-house which was open and heated for bathing on the Sabbath, if most (of the people in the city) were gentiles (an Israelite) may bathe there at once (after the close of the Sabbath); but if most of them were Israelites, he must wait time enough for the water to be heated'.[19]

The *Mishnah* itself belongs explicitly to precisely the same bilingual or trilingual world which the documents of the period up to Bar Kochba reveal; for instance it accepts that a valid bill of divorce (GṬ) might be written in

16. For shows at Caesarea, ch. 1, and 5.2 above. See, e.g., L. I. Levine, *Caesarea under Roman Rule* (1975); J. Ringel, *Césarée de Palestine: Étude historique et archéologique* (1975); N. R. M. de Lange, *Origen and the Jews* (1976); T. D. Barnes, *Constantine and Eusebius* (1981), 81ff.; L. I. Levine, *The Rabbinic Class of Roman Palestine in Late Antiquity* (1989). The passage from the Jerusalem Talmud is *Sota* 7, 1 (21b).

17. *Mishnah, Aboda Zarah* 1, 4 (trans. Danby). For Scythopolis as 'one of the Greek cities', ch. 1 above.

18. 10.2 above. For ossuaries of Jews from Scythopolis in Jerusalem see, e.g., Frey, *CIJ* II, nos. 1372–1374, all bilingual in Greek and Hebrew (e.g., Παπίας/PPYS HBŠNY). See G. Fuks, "The Jews of Hellenistic and Roman Scythopolis", *JJS* 33 (1982), 407.

19. *Mishnah, Makshirin* 2, 5, trans. Danby.

Hebrew and witnessed in Greek, or vice versa.[20] Moreover, many of the forms of reasoning employed here and in later rabbinic texts have close parallels in Greek thought and Greek methods of interpretation of texts.[21] But these considerations do nothing significant to diminish the profound originality and distinctiveness of this vast work and its successors—as embodying an exposition of the required rules of conduct in a Jewish context; as a literary composition in a Semitic language, apparently reaching written form in the third century; and, in the tractate 'Sayings of the Fathers', as the conscious expression of a chain of tradition going back to Moses.

Whether and in what way a history of the Jewish community could or should be written by using the vast mass of rabbinic literature is a question which will not even be attempted here. Instead, a different question will be asked: what trace has the unique religious and social development of the Jewish community in this period left either in the archaeological or documentary record or in accounts or references by outside observers? For instance, any series of maps of place-names in this area in chronological sequence would show a continuing spread of cities with mixed Graeco-Latin names, at the expense of a surrounding network of villages with Semitic names. Similarly, by their nature, the quite long series of inscriptions left in the Huleh Valley and the Golan by the *kēnsitores* at work under the Tetrarchy reflects just the same mixture of village and communal names as we find in the limestone massif of northern Syria or in the Hauran.[22] We could not tell from them that *this* world of villages was Jewish at all.

If it were the case that the rabbinic Judaism of this period had left no trace in our evidence outside its own massive texts, a serious historical problem would arise. For if we had to treat this as an example of a local culture, whose reality is beyond doubt, but which is invisible in the external record, a major question would confront us as regards all the other regions of the Near East. Might a pagan 'Syriac', 'Arab' or 'Oriental' culture and tradition also have been transmitted there without leaving any physical trace?

In fact this problem does not arise. On the negative side, the rural temples of the Imperial period, which are so frequent on Mount Hermon, around the Bekaa Valley and on Mount Lebanon, are not to be found in the neighbouring hill-country of Galilee. In that sense the temple at Kadesh (Kydasa or Kadasa), which Josephus saw as a Tyrian outpost confronting the Jewish area,

20. *Mishnah, Gittin* 9, 8.

21. See P. S. Alexander, "Quid Athenis et Hierosolymis? Rabbinic Midrash and Hermeneutics in the Graeco-Roman World", in P. R. Davies and R. T. White (eds.), *A Tribute to Geza Vermes: Essays on Jewish and Christian Literature and History* (1990), 101.

22. See App. A.

does mark a real 'frontier'.[23] Second, the emergence of 'rabbi' as a title is very well documented in the inscriptional record. RB meaning 'master' or 'lord' is attested in other Semitic languages of the period; for instance we have encountered in Palmyra RB ŠWK for 'controller of the market' or RB ḤYL' for 'commander of the army'.[24] But it was only in Hebrew and Jewish Aramaic that the form of address in the first person, RBY ('my master'), became (like 'monsieur' or 'monsignore') a title which could be used in the third person and attached to someone's name. Once that usage was established, it came immediately into use in Greek, and later Latin, transliteration.

Thus even an epigraphist who was wholly unaware of rabbinic Judaism would be confronted with this distinctive title attached to names, but not usually accompanied by the indication of any other office or function. The problem would often remain, however, of trying to date this usage. For instance it appears on tomb-inscriptions in Hebrew, Greek and Aramaic from Ioppe (Jaffa); but no precise date can be attached to any of these.[25] It is best attested in the inscriptions from the well-known necropolis of Beth She'arim, dating to the third and earlier fourth centuries, which represents the most significant archaeological and documentary side-light on the rabbinic period.[26] Two aspects of the necropolis are of particular importance. One is its location, on the southern, or south-western, edge of the Galilean hills, facing out over the north-western corner of the Plain of Jezreel; the other is that the predominant language of the inscriptions is Greek. 'Rabbi' (RBY in Hebrew) appears in a variety of transliterations in Greek: 'rabbi', 'rabi', 'rib', 'ribbi' or contracted as 'r'. Here too, Hebrew, Aramaic and Greek (and occasionally, in transliteration, Latin) functioned in close conjunction. In Catacomb 20, for instance, we can find Hebrew inscriptions relating to an extended rabbinic family ('this is the sarcophagus of the three sons of Rabbi Judan, the son of Rabbi Miasha'—RBY YWDN BNW ŠLRBY MY'ŠH), while in Catacomb 1 a Greek inscription incorporates two transliterated Latin words (*mēmorion*— 'tomb'—and *palatinos*), as well as using 'Ribbi' as a title attributed to a man with a Greek name, Paregorios.[27] Here, as everywhere in the Near East, Greek

23. 8.5 above.

24. 9.4 above. See C. F. Jean and J.-J. Hoftijzer, *Dictionnaire des inscriptions sémitiques de l'Ouest* 1965), *s.v.* RB.

25. See, e.g., Frey, *CIJ* II, no. 892 (Aramaic); 900 (Greek/Hebrew bilingual).

26. The inscriptions have not all been assembled in coherent form, and it is unfortunate that even where they have been collected, the purely Semitic-language inscriptions have been separated from the Greek and bilingual ones. But see B. Mazar, *Beth She'arim* I, *Catacombs* 1–4 (1973), ch. 5, Hebrew and Palmyrene inscriptions; M. Schwabe and B. Lifshitz, *Beth She'arim* II, *The Greek Inscriptions* (1974); N. Avigad, *Beth She'arim* III, *Catacombs* 12–23 (1976), ch. 4, Hebrew and Aramaic inscriptions.

27. Catacomb 20: III, p. 247, no. 22; Catacomb 1: II, p. 40, no. 61.

and Semitic personal names mingle; what is distinctive is the continued use of both Hebrew and Aramaic, and the repeated presence of a unique personal title. Its meaning is nowhere explicitly indicated; but its presence is nonetheless testimony to the important role of rabbis, as the *Mishnah,* followed by subsequent Jewish literature, displays it.

Synagogues, as places 'for reading of the Law and the teaching of the commandments', are of course firmly attested by documentary evidence from before the fall of the Temple, by Josephus and by the New Testament; and buildings which may well have been synagogues of that period are known from Herodion, Masada and Gamla, though none is explicitly identified in words as such. By that test, it would have to be admitted that there is very little unambiguous documentary proof of the existence of synagogues in Galilee and the Golan even in the rabbinic period. Even the three *archisynagōgoi* attested at Beth She'arim are all identified as having come from elsewhere: Berytus, Pamphylia and Sidon.[28] Yet there are a number of public buildings of this period from Galilee which are certainly not temples and do not have altars or pagan inscriptions, and are identified as Jewish by the presence of Jewish symbols—and also, more significantly, by inscriptions in stone or mosaic, which may again be Hebrew, Greek or Aramaic, and which usually refer to the giving or construction of some part of the building in question. Most are thus local off-shoots, in a multilingual context, of the Hellenistic *euergesia*-inscription. Hardly any of the buildings incorporate inscriptions giving a precise date, and none is formally labelled as a synagogue (*prosēuchē,* or more commonly in this period *synagōge,* in Greek; BT HKNŠT in Hebrew).

The exceptional case is a Greek dedication from Qasyon north of Zefat which was put up 'for the safety' of Septimius Severus and his family. The fragmentary text identifies the dedicants as *Ioudaioi,* but leaves it unclear whether there is a reference to their 'prayer' *(euchē)* or to a synagogue *([pros]euchē).* The inscription comes from a public building, but the presence of an exterior portico makes it uncertain whether it should be classified as a synagogue.[29] Much more certain is the building at Chorazain, 4 km north of Capernaum, which has the expected form of a synagogue, being an oblong structure of some 23 m by 17 m, divided by two lines of pillars and with benches around the walls. It is thought to have been built in the third century, and contains a stone chair, perhaps to be identified as a 'seat of Moses' (Mtt 23, 2). On the seat there is an Aramaic inscription: 'remembered (be) for good Iudan bar Ishmael who made this stoa (STWH) from his property. May he have a share with the righteous'.[30] The borrowing both of the conception of

28. *Beth She'arim* II, nos. 164, 203, 221.

29. *CIJ* II, no. 972, Hüttenmeister, *Synagogen,* p. 359.

30. For the synagogue, *EAEHL* I, *s.v.* "Chorazain". For the inscription, Beyer, *AT,* p. 382. See L. Y. Rahmani, "Stone Synagogue Chairs: Their Identification, Use and Significance", *IEJ* 40

building as a benefaction and of vocabulary is also very clear in the Aramaic inscription on mosaic from the village of Kafr Kanna (Cana) near Nazareth, which probably comes from the floor of a synagogue: here one Iose and his sons are recorded, probably in the fourth century, as having made a panel (ṬBLH—*tabula*) of the mosaic: 'may there be blessing (BRKTH) on them, amen!'[31]

It is not necessary to list further examples, for there is sufficient evidence that monumental communal buildings for Jewish religious use were being constructed in Galilee in the third and fourth centuries, even if in fact none is formally identified, in any language, as a synagogue.

Such a formal identification can in fact only be found on the other side of the Sea of Galilee, in the Golan, a closely comparable area of village settlement, with a mixed population of Jews and gentiles.[32] The most striking remains from this region come from Dabbura, an ancient village some 17 km north of the northern tip of the Sea of Galilee, and situated on the plateau above the Huleh Valley. On architectural fragments here were discovered one bilingual Greek and Aramaic building-inscription, three other brief Aramaic inscriptions and a Hebrew inscription of the greatest importance. Carved on a lintel from a building which itself does not survive, it reads 'Eliezer ha Qappar. This is the Bet-Midrash which (belongs) to the Rabbi': ʼLYʽZR HQPR. ZH BYT MDRŠW ŠHLRBY.[33] Its significance can hardly be exaggerated. For this ought be the ʼLʽZR HQPR who is quoted in the *Mishnah* (and subsequently in later rabbinic sources), and belonged to the last generation of rabbis to be cited there.[34] It gives a geographical and social context—a village in the Golan—for at least one stage of his career; and it demonstrates for the first time that the school, or 'bet-midrash', in which such a rabbi taught could, even in so modest a social context, be a monumental building publicly identified as a school. Very little is really known of the successive stages of education in a Jewish context; but it is evident that a 'bet-midrash' should have represented secondary education rather than primary training in literacy, and will have been devoted to the explication of texts. At all events we

(1990), 192. For the varieties of synagogue architecture see, e.g., E. M. Meyers and J. F. Strange, *Archaeology, the Rabbis and Early Christianity* (1981), 140ff.

31. Beyer, *AT,* p. 389.

32. See, e.g., D. Urman, *The Golan: A Profile of a Region during the Roman and Byzantine Periods* (1985); cf. C. M. Dauphin, "Jewish and Gentile Communities in the Roman and Byzantine *Gaulanitis*", *PEQ* 1982–83, 129; C. M. Dauphin and J. J. Schonfield, "Settlements of the Roman and Byzantine Periods on the Golan Heights", *IEJ* 33 (1983), 189.

33. D. Urman, "Jewish Inscriptions from Dabbura in the Golan", *IEJ* 32 (1972), 16; Hüttenmeister, *Synagogen,* 91–95; Beyer, *AT,* p. 396.

34. *Mishnah, Avot,* 21–22.

have here a brief glimpse of the structures through which the understanding of the Bible was transmitted to this world of villages; and, beyond that, this brief inscription seems to enjoy the distinction of being the only documentary reference to any form of educational institution from the entire Roman Near East.

The world of the *Mishnah* does appear here in concrete form. This essential text also contains one, but only one, allusion to the central figure of rabbinic Judaism, not just as 'Rabbi' or 'R. Judah' but as 'Rabbi Judah the Prince'. For the treatise *Avot*, which may possibly be later than the rest of the *Mishnah*, speaks once of 'Rabbi Gamliel, the son of Rabbi Judah the Prince' (RBY GMLY'L BNW ŠL RBY YHWDH HNŠY').[35] That the title which had been adopted by Bar Kochba came back into use for the members of what became a sort of rabbinic dynasty is of great significance. But how far back can we properly extend the later rabbinic picture, largely confirmed in the later fourth century by Roman legal evidence, of a Jewish NŠY' or *Patriarcha* wielding real authority, even outside Palestine, acting as a judge, and surrounded by an almost royal court?[36] The *Mishnah* itself gives no impression of any such official status in the second or early third century.[37] But Origen, writing in Caesarea in the period after 230, does clearly confirm that what he calls the *Ethnarchēs* did have real power, and could even order executions, which the Romans did not formally permit, but did not act to prevent.[38] As always, however, there are problems of definition. It is probably right to see the well-attested role of the Jewish *Patriarcha* in the fourth century as continuous with the position which Origen here calls that of *Ethnarchēs*. But is it then the same position to which Origen refers when he mentions raising a question about Psalms with 'Ioullos (Hillel?) the *Patriarchēs*, and one of those regarded among the Jews as *sophoi* ('wise'—HKMYM?)?[39]

There can be no clear answer, and we do not reach any consistent outsider's description of a *Patriarchēs* exercising power until we come to Epiphanius' account of the activities of the converted Jew Joseph of Tiberias, late

35. *Avot* 2, 2.

36. See for the evidence, e.g., J. Juster, *Les Juifs dans l'Empire romain* I (1914), 391ff.; L. I. Levine, "The Jewish Patriarch (Nasi) in Third Century Palestine", *ANRW* II.19.2 (1979), 649; idem, *The Rabbinic Class of Roman Palestine* (1989), ch. 4; M. D. Goodman, "The Roman State and the Jewish Patriarch in the Third Century", in L. I. Levine (ed.), *Galilee in Late Antiquity* (1992), 127.

37. See M. D. Goodman, *State and Subject in Roman Galilee* (1983), 111ff.

38. Origen, *Epistula ad Africanum* 20 (14); see M. Harl and N. R. M. de Lange, *SC* 302 (1983), 469ff.

39. *Selecta in Psalmos* 18 (*PG* XII, 1056 B). Origen refers to the rule of the *ethnarchēs* also in *de Princ.* IV, 1, 3—but Rufinus' Latin tradition substitutes 'patriarcha'. For the context of these references see N. R. M. de Lange, *Origen and the Jews* (1976), 23–24, 33–34.

in the reign of Constantine and under Constantius II.[40] In this narrative the *Patriarchēs* of the time was called Hillel, who was regarded as a descendant of the Gamaliel of the time of Christ, and was succeeded by his own son, apparently called Judah. The powers of the *Patriarchēs* by now extended even outside Palestine, and *apostoloi* could be sent to Cilicia to collect tithes.

Again we need not pursue the details of this story, inserted in Epiphanius' account of the Ebionites, and perhaps less confused and fantastic than most of the content of his collection of heresies. Its significance lies perhaps more in the fact that there is some documentary and archaeological confirmation of the conception of the role of the *Patriarchai* which it presents. For it finds an extraordinarily vivid reflection in the floor-mosaics, with inscriptions in Hebrew, Aramaic and Greek, of the fourth-century synagogue from the hot springs near Tiberias, Hammath Tiberias.[41]

Perhaps no other product of the period more fully exhibits the confident expression of Jewish tradition and identity within a multilingual context, or combines that with so many elements of Graeco-Roman artistic decoration. The mosaic occupying the central aisle of the synagogue is divided into three panels. The first is a representation of a Torah shrine flanked by two menorahs with burning candles. Then, remarkably, there is a circular representation of the twelve signs of the zodiac, centering on a picture of the chariot of the sun with Helios personified: each sign is named in Hebrew, for instance 'RYH, the lion, or DGYM ('fishes') for *Pisces*. They are grouped into four seasons, for which the Hebrew term TQWPH is used, and they are represented as young women, also identified in Hebrew by using the Hebrew names of four months: Nisan, Tammuz, Tishri, Teveth.

The third panel contains, between representations of two lions, a series of brief inscriptions in Greek giving the names of benefactors: Maximos, Aboudemos, Zōilos, Ioullos, Kallinikos, Eiortasis. The name of a further benefactor, Seuēros (Severus), can be restored from another, parallel, Greek inscription, this time accompanied by a blessing in Aramaic. The Aramaic reads: 'Let there be peace (ŠLMH) on anyone who has carried out a commandment (MṢWTH) in relation to this holy place, or will carry one out. Let there be blessings on him. Amen, amen, sela. And for me, amen'. The notion of the synagogue as a 'holy place' ('TRH QDYŠH in Aramaic) recurs in yet another Greek inscription in which a donor, also with a transliterated Latin name, 'Prophotouros' ('Profuturus'), is described as having made 'this *stoa* of the *hagios topos*'.

40. Epiphanius, *Panarion* XXX, 4–12.

41. See M. Dothan, *Hammath Tiberias: Early Synagogues and the Hellenistic and Roman Remains* (1983), esp. ch. 5. The Aramaic inscription is in Beyer, *AT*, p. 385, and the Greek ones are discussed in B. Lifshitz, "L'ancienne synagogue de Tibériade, sa mosaique, et ses inscriptions", *JSJ* 4 (1973), 43.

The benefactor concerned, Severus, is identified in the two Greek inscriptions as a '*threptos* (a person brought up in the household) of the *lamprotatoi* (most distinguished) *Patriarchai*'. If used correctly, the term should mean that the Patriarchs now enjoyed senatorial rank. At any rate the conception of them as persons of high public status, and as a dynasty with a household conferring some reflected glory on its members, is clearly expressed. So of course is the centrality of the synagogue as a 'holy place'. If this synagogue has been correctly attributed to the first part of the fourth century, it provides invaluable confirmation that an important local dynasty of Jewish *Patriarchai* was now a reality.

It needs to be stressed again how profound a series of changes had taken place in the social and religious geography of Syria Palaestina. In the same period the Roman *colonia* of Aelia Capitolina was taking on the appearance of a Christian city. Pilgrims, like the one who came from Bordeaux in 333, could of course seek out, and be shown, sites whose associations were with the Old Testament as well as the New: the remains of the palaces of David or Solomon, or the place where Jacob wrestled with the angel. But where the Temple had been there was nothing to be seen except two statues of Hadrian, and near them a stone with a hole in it, 'to which Jews come each year and lament with groans and tear their clothes and retire'.[42]

But it was not only between Judaism, paganism and Christianity that complex contrasts and forms of accommodation could be observed in this period. A wholly new element had suddenly entered Christianity itself, and is best displayed in the Latin *Life* of Hilarion of Gaza, composed by Jerome soon after his arrival in Bethlehem in 386.[43] That this vivid biographical sketch should have been written in Latin was, as it happened, quite appropriate. For Gaza, an ancient Philistine city long since Hellenised, had become in the third century yet another example of a place which enjoyed the status of a Roman *colonia*. Its constitution ought now therefore to have been that of a *colonia*, with an annual pair of *duumviri*, and Latin ought to have been the language of its public life.[44]

Gaza was nonetheless still a Graeco-Roman rather than a fully Roman place, and in the first decade of the fourth century the young Hilarion, born perhaps about 291, had been sent by his pagan parents to study in Alexandria with a *grammaticus*. But there, instead, he heard of the famous Christian hermit Saint Antony, and returned to set up as a hermit himself, moving out into the robber-infested desert outside Gaza. A wholly new model of the perfect life, marked by an ever-increasing level of self-deprivation, had presented it-

---

42. *Itin. Burd.* 591.
43. Text, trans. and comm. in Chr. Mohrmann (ed.), *Vite dei Santi* IV (1975), 69ff.
44. Millar, "Roman *Coloniae*", 55–56.

self to the population of the region; Christians are described as coming to seek his aid from all the cities of Palestine, such as Eleutheropolis and Jerusalem, from Syria, and from Egypt itself. His influence was also felt in Gaza, where, as a 'Roman city', the custom was now observed of chariot-races in honour of the god Consus, to commemorate the rape of the Sabine women. A Christian, so Jerome relates, was due to enter a *quadriga* to race against one owned by a pagan magistrate *(Gazensis duumvir)*, and persuaded Hilarion to provide holy water to ward off spells. As a result, the Christian chariot overtook its rival so rapidly that the pagan driver could hardly see the backs of the horses as they flew past: 'Marnas has been conquered by Christ!'[45]

Quite different cultures and traditions thus mingled, or collided, in a Graeco-Roman city in Palestine such as Gaza. Others would become visible as soon as a member of the upper class of such a city stepped outside the ambit of the Graeco-Roman literary culture for which his formal education had destined him. We cannot tell whether such a person, in the preceding centuries, would have been able to do as Hilarion did, and expel a demon from a Bactrian camel by speaking to it in Aramaic *(sermo Syrus)*.[46] It may be that, but for his choice of an ascetic life in the desert, Hilarion would never have encountered or used this language at all. Jerome's vivid and journalistic narrative represents nonetheless the first explicit testimony that a Semitic language was the normal speech of the gentile population living in and around this coastal city in the south-west corner of Syria Palaestina.

But that was not all. In Jerome's description Hilarion was later to penetrate further into the desert, to the city of Elusa, once part of the kingdom of Nabataea, and now populated by people whom Jerome calls *Saraceni*.[47] How we should understand the intermingling of cultures and ethnic groups in the area which the Romans called Arabia presents us with rather different and no less complex problems.

45. Jerome, *Vita Hilarionis* 20.
46. *Vita* 23; for *sermo Syrus* see also 22.
47. *Vita* 25.

ARABIA

11.1. REGIONS AND CULTURES

The large area which in the second and third centuries made up the Roman province of 'Arabia' was composed of several different zones with different histories. What united them was above all the presence of a steppe, which in the south became a barren mountain zone (the northern part of the Hedjaz, stretching down the east coast of the Red Sea). The southern part of the area had indeed two distinctive characteristics. First, like the whole of the eventual Roman 'frontier', from the Red Sea to Mesopotamia, it bordered on a steppe whose inhabitants were not under Rome's military or political control; but here there was also the important factor of an inner 'frontier', with a similarly unsettled population, the desert and mountains of Sinai. Second, the existence of Nabataean and then Roman ports on the Red Sea meant that there were important cultural and trading contacts with Egypt, with Arabia Felix (the Yemen) and with the Indian Ocean.

It is tempting to try to write a history of the rise and fall of the Red Sea trade passing through the kingdom of Nabataea and the subsequent province of Arabia, as if the accidents of narrative references could allow any such thing. All that needs to be stressed now is that this trade never disappeared altogether. Eusebius, in his priceless series of snapshots of Palestine and Arabia as they were in about AD 300, refers to Aila (Aqaba/Elath) as 'on the borders (of Palestine, as it now was), lying next to the southern desert and to the Red Sea which is beside it, sailed by those voyaging from Egypt and those from India. The tenth Roman legion is stationed there'.[1]

---

1. Eusebius, *Onom.* 6, 17. For the legion and the transfer of this part of 'Arabia' to 'Syria Palaestina' see 5.1 and 2 above.

The fact that Sinai was also an inner frontier zone inhabited by 'Saracens' is also reflected in Eusebius. The term 'Sarakēnoi' had, however, been used for the first time, in the sources available to us, by Ptolemy in his *Geography*, written in the mid-second century. There he identifies 'Sarakēnoi', 'Skēnitai' and 'Thamudēnoi' (as well as 'Thanouitai' and 'Thamuditai') as different peoples living in Arabia proper. But he also uses 'Sarakēnē' of part of Sinai.[2] But to Eusebius of course Sinai had profound historical associations: 'Pharan: it is a city on the far side of Arabia, lying next to the Sarakēnoi of the desert through which the children of Israel journeyed on leaving Sinai. It lies on the other side of Arabia toward the north; three days' journey to the east lies Aila, where, so Scripture says, there dwelt Ishmael, from whom the Ishmaelites descend'. We have already seen much earlier the significance of the identification of contemporary 'Arabs' as the descendants of Hagar and Ishmael.[3] It is thus noteworthy that Jerome, in his Latin version of the *Onomasticon,* duly adds an explanation at this point: 'from whom the Ishmaelites descend, who are now *Saraceni*'.[4] And in fact, before he wrote this, the first major threat to this area from 'Saracens' had already arisen, in the revolt under 'Queen Mavia' in 378; but it had come, in the first instance, not from beyond the line of Roman forts, but from within Sinai.[5]

There had been a real Nabataean presence in southern Sinai, as the discovery of thousands of Nabataean graffiti there attests. We can even find here too, in the Wadi Mukateb—'Wadi of Inscriptions'—a reflection of the imposition of Roman rule in 106: graffiti dated by year 45 and year 85 'of the province' (LHPRKY')—AD 149 and 191—and a reference to 'three Caesars' (TLTT QYSRYN), apparently Severus, Caracalla and Geta.[6] But, beyond that, the nature of settlement and social structures, and the relation to successive ruling powers, the Nabataean kingdom and then Rome, can hardly be determined for Sinai.

To envisage the area of the kingdom and the province realistically, we have to take into account the following elements. First, there was a band of settled territory stretching across the northern Negev almost to the Mediterranean, bordering on the southern part of Judaea/Syria Palaestina, and incorporating towns such as Elusa, Nessana, Mampsis and Oboda (Avdat).

Then, to go to another extreme, there was the barren and mountainous

---

2. Ptolemy, *Geog.* VI, 7, 21 ('Skēnitai', 'Thamudēnoi' and 'Sarakēnoi'); VI, 7, 23 ('Thanouitai'); VI, 7, 4 ('Thamuditai'); V, 17, 3 ('Sarakēnē'). See G. W. Bowersock, "Arabs and Saracens in the Historia Augusta", *Bonner Historia-Augusta Colloquium 1984/1985* (1987), 71.

3. Ch. 1 above.

4. Eusebius, *Onom.* 166, 12 (Eusebius); 167, 12 (Jerome).

5. See most recently Z. Rubin, "Sinai in the Itinerarium Egeriae", *Atti del Convegno Internazionale sulla Peregrinatio Egeriae, 1987* (1990), 177.

6. *CIS* II.1, nos. 963 (three Caesars), 964, 1325.

zone of the northern Hedjaz. But here too there were substantial settlements, above all at Hegra (Medain Saleh), marked by a large number of fine rock-cut tombs of the first century AD, many with long inscriptions in Nabataean.[7] On the coast there was also the harbour of 'Leuke Kome', 'through which', as the *Periplus of the Erythraean Sea* reports, 'there is a way inland up to Petra, to Malichus, king of the Nabataeans'. Because of the trade coming up from Arabia (Felix), there was also a customs-officer, to collect a 25 percent duty, and a 'commander of 100 men' *(ekatontarchēs)* with soldiers.[8] The king will be Malichus II, AD 40–70, and the commander will not have been a Roman centurion, but a Nabataean officer. At Hegra the equivalent rank is even given the title *centurio,* transliterated into Nabataean (QNṬRYN').[9] Leuke Kome itself will be the Nabataean settlement of Aynuna, just east of the mouth of the Gulf of Aqaba.

Very little has been found of any settlement on the presumed land-route up the east side of the Gulf of Aqaba.[10] But from Aila northwards up the east side of the Wadi Arabah, and especially north of the escarpment which rises up from the barren plain (the Hisma) stretching down to Aila, traces of settlement are increasingly dense. The 'King's Highway', soon to be marked out as the Via Nova Traiana 'from the borders of Syria to the Red Sea', indicates the approximate eastern limit of such settlement as there was. But Petra, which lies just beyond the zone of 200-mm annual rainfall, which covers the fertile high plateau of Moab, in fact comes—very significantly—just within the tip of a narrower zone, between the Wadi Arabah and the steppe, in which some trees will grow.[11] The question of the relation of the steppe and its peoples to the culture of this whole area is fundamental. Petra itself, however, is not a desert settlement, but a city carved out in a hollow among dramatic sandstone outcrops, with springs, and within a zone where there is vegetation.

Whatever contribution was made by long-distance trade to the extraordinary urban development of Petra in the first centuries BC and AD, it owed its role as a royal city to the combination of inaccessibility and defensibility, on the one hand, and on the other to its location at the limits of a zone where agriculture and settlement were possible. The main area of Nabataean settle-

7. 11.2 below.

8. *Periplus* 19, translated by L. Casson, *The Periplus Maris Erythraei* (1989), with excellent introduction and commentary.

9. *CIS* II.1, no. 217.

10. For an invaluable survey on which these remarks, and all others on the whole Nabataean zone, depend, see R. Wenning, *Die Nabatäer—Denkmäler und Geschichte: Eine Bestandaufnahme des archäologischen Befundes* (1987), 107ff. ('Region P: Midian'). I owe a great deal throughout also to G. W. Bowersock, *Roman Arabia* (1983).

11. See I. Künne and M. Wanke, "Petra: Landschaft und Pflanzenwelt", in M. Lindner, *Petra und das Königreich der Nabatäer5* (1989), 233ff., and map on p. 240.

ment, and the core of the Roman province, thus lay to its north, in the fertile plains of Moab, bisected by great wadis running down to the Wadi Arabah and, further north, to the Dead Sea. From around Petra northwards we are again entering a world of villages and small towns. Two of the villages near Petra appear in Eusebius' *Onomasticon:* Thaima, fifteen Roman miles from Petra, where a garrison was stationed, and Mabsara, 'a very large village' in the region called Gebalene, in the territory of Petra.[12] In this area it may well be that settlement increased in density or extent with the security provided by Roman forts. But further north the high plateau of Moab provides a steadily widening zone of cultivable land, beginning south of the southern end of the Dead Sea and stretching up to Madaba. For instance, above the Wadi Hesa which opens into the Wadi Arabah just south of the Dead Sea, there was the major Nabataean cult-centre of Khirbet et-Tannur, established in the first century BC, and undergoing successive developments until the second century AD. Its elaborate sculptures include rich bas-reliefs of deities thought to be Hadad and Atargatis; but a Nabataean inscription shows that the (or a) deity worshipped there was the Idumaean god Qos.[13] A few kilometres to the south, at ed-Dharih on a tributary of the Wadi Hesa, lie the remains of a Nabataean village, now under excavation, with houses, a cemetery, an oil-press (thus calling into question Strabo's view that the Nabataeans did not produce olive-oil) and a temple, probably of the first century AD, on a remarkably large platform, of some 115 m by 45 m.[14] Alternatively, to follow the Wadi Hesa down to the Wadi Arabah would be to come to the region of Zoara, just to the south of the Dead Sea, and the village of Maoza, where a Jewish family was living under the last Nabataean king, Rabbel II (AD 70–106), and in the early years of the province of Arabia. It is the archive which they later hid in a cave in the Nahal Hever which tells us more than any other source about the village life of the Nabataean area.[15]

To people living in this remote corner Petra was 'the metropolis of Arabia'; but the nearest *polis* was Rabbathmoba or Rabbathmoaba, up on the plain of Moab. Later, under Septimius Severus, it was to issue coins as the Greek city of 'Arsapolis' (also called 'Areopolis'); other places from within the former Nabataean kingdom which did likewise, apart from Petra, were Charachmoba (Kerak), Madaba, Esbous (Hesban—if it had

12. Eusebius, *Onom.* 96, 18; 124, 20.

13. For an evocation of the site, with a chronology which has since been questioned, N. Glueck, *Deities and Dolphins: The Story of the Nabataeans* (1966), 73ff. For brief accounts, *EAEHL* IV (1978), 1152ff.; Wenning, *Nabatäer,* 76ff.

14. See F. Villeneuve, "Fouilles à Khirbet Edh-Dharih (Jordanie) 1984–1987", *CRAI* (1988), 453.

15. See 3.2 and 3.3 above, and more fully 11.4 below.

been within the kingdom) and, far to the north-east, in the southern Hauran, Bostra.[16]

The purpose of emphasising these geographical patterns is to make clear that the central zone of the Nabataean kingdom which the Romans took over in 106 was the fertile plateau stretching south from Madaba, affording the possibility of settled habitation about as far south as Petra itself. As for the plateau of Moab proper, it hardly needs to be stressed that the small places which eventually counted as *poleis* belonged within a wider zone of villages: for instance 'Agalleim', eight Roman miles south of Areopolis (Arsapolis), or 'Dannea', eight miles to its north, or 'Loueitha', between Areopolis and Zoara.[17] Further north Eusebius records a village called Karaiatha, ten Roman miles west of Madaba, inhabited entirely by Christians.[18]

There was no geographical barrier or contrast between the northern part of what was until 106 the kingdom of Nabataea and the area of Greek cities, the so-called Decapolis, beyond it. To the west the Jordan Valley, on both sides of the river, belonged to the Herodian kingdom, as did the eastern shore of the Dead Sea as far south as the fortress of Machaerus; all this then passed to the province of Judaea or Syria Palaestina. We have already seen how in the 40s a violent conflict broke out between the Jewish villages of Peraea (the area 'across the river') and the inhabitants of a village, 'full of warlike men', called Zia or Mia in the territory of Philadelphia.[19] Philadelphia, like the other Greek cities which clustered in this fertile area, formed in the first century an enclave which belonged to the province of Syria, but was physically separated from it: the others were Gerasa, Pella, Dium and perhaps Capitolias (which seems to have acquired this Latino-Greek name, and to have come into existence as a city only in 98/99); Hippos and Gadara, detached from the Herodian kingdom in 4 BC; and Abila and Adraa (Deraa, on the present border of Jordan and Syria). That these places owed their special status in relation to the Roman province to their claims to be Greek cities of the Hellenistic period is certain. What is much less clear is first the nature of their relations to the Nabataean area before 106, and second the sort of contrast we should see between this area and the surrounding zones after they had all become provincial territory. Should we see these cities too as representing the flowering of a regional culture under Roman protection? Or as conscious bastions of Hellenism in an 'Arab' world?

16. For the coinage of all these places see A. Spijkerman, *The Coins of the Decapolis and Provincia Arabia* (1978).

17. Eusebius, *Onom.* 36, 19 (Agalleim); 17, 10 (Dannea); 122, 28 (Loueitha).

18. *Onom.* 112, 15.

19. 2.3 above.

The form taken by Nabataean settlement or control in the marginal zone on the edge of the steppe to the east of the Decapolis, that is, between the area of Madaba and that of Bostra, is quite uncertain. The known Nabataean evidence is very sporadic: there is a Nabataean tomb-inscription from Qasr-al-Hallabat out in the steppe, where there was later a Roman fort;[20] and more important, a scatter of Nabataean pottery and inscriptions along the Wadi Sirhan, culminating in substantial evidence of a Nabataean presence at Jawf (Dumatha) some 450 km south-east of Bostra.[21] We have already seen the significance which this remote place eventually attained in the structure of the Roman frontier.[22] That a Nabataean presence there had preceded a Roman one is certain: the most substantial item of evidence, among coins, inscriptions and pottery, is an inscription of AD 44 recording the construction of a sanctuary to 'Dusares the god of Gaia who is at [Duma]t' (LDWŠR' 'LH GY' ' DY [BDWM]T).[23] Whether it can really be shown that there was a major trade-route leading through here either to southern Mesopotamia or to the Persian Gulf is another question. What is significant in the first instance is that Jawf can hardly have been reached except from the oasis of Azraq, that is, from the steppe zone east of Philadelphia.

We must assume, even in the absence of direct evidence, that this marginal area was in some way Nabataean territory, for it can only have been through there that the Nabataeans could have reached the well-attested northern Nabataean area which occupied the southern part of the plain of the Hauran, and of the hill-country to its east (the Jebel Hauran, Jebel Druse or now Jebel Arab). The alternative would be to take it that the zone along the edge of the steppe was unsettled and 'belonged' neither to the kingdom nor to the Decapolis, as an enclave of the Roman province. As for the southern Hauran itself, however, it is certain that it was Nabataean territory. This area was densely settled, mainly in the form of villages, but with one city, Bostra. A series of Nabataean inscriptions dated by kings from Aretas III of the first century BC onwards makes clear that this fertile area was established royal territory. One example will suffice in this context, an inscription from Salhad, east of Bostra, recording the building of a temple in AD 57: 'This is the temple (BYT') which Ruhu, son of Maliku, son of Aklabu, son of Ruhu erected to Allat their goddess who is in Salhad (L'LT 'LHTHM DY BSLḤD) . . . in the month of Ab, year 17 of Maliku, king of the Nabataeans (MLK NBṬW), son of Haretat, king of the Nabataeans, who loves his people'.[24]

20. Cantineau, RES, no. 2035; Kennedy, Explorations, 37, no. 1. See 4.1 above.

21. Wenning, Nabatäer, 114–115.

22. 5.1 above.

23. R. Savignac and J. Starcky, "Une inscription nabatéenne provenant du Djôf", RB 64 (1957), 196.

24. CIS II.1, no. 182.

Again, there was no natural frontier between this area and the northern half of the flat Hauran plain (the Nuqra) or of the Jebel Hauran to its east. But, as we saw earlier, a real political and military frontier did exist here in the first century AD. For, in the Imperial period, the northern area, after a few years (30–23 BC) under Nabataean control, was continuously under successive Herodian kings, until the death of Agrippa II, except for a brief spell in the middle of the century. Thus ten years before Ruhu built his temple to Allat, a different dating-system was in use at Hebran, only some 14 km to the north: 'In the month Tišri, year seven of Claudius Caesar (LQLDYS QYSR). This is the gate which Maliku son of Qas[iu?], priest of Allat (KMR 'LT) made'.[25]

It was just an accident of political history that Claudius happened to be the ruler who needed to be named at this moment. The succession of Herodian kings who are named on Greek and Semitic inscriptions from the major cult-site at Sia' near Kanatha (Qanawat) represents the established rulers of this region in the first century: Herod the Great himself; his son the tetrarch Philip (year 33 of 'our lord Philippos'—LMRN' PLPS); and his great-grandson Agrippa II.[26] After Agrippa's death, this area must briefly have been part of the province of Syria. But in 106 it was absorbed into the new province of 'Arabia', of which Petra and Bostra were to be the two chief cities.

That we must see a considerable degree of distinction between the determinedly 'Greek' cities of the Decapolis and the Nabataean zone to their south and east is certain; if we doubted the significance of this distinction in the eyes of contemporaries, the inscriptions and coins of these cities make it unambiguous.[27] It is much less clear what contrast, in terms of culture, language or social history, we should think of as between the Nabataean area and that which had been under the Herodian kings. It is certainly significant that Nabataean inscriptions tended to name their kings not merely for dating purposes but in loyalist, even nationalist, terms. Haretat (Aretas) 'king of the Nabataeans, who loves his people', was to be followed later by Rabbel II (AD 70–106), the last of the dynasty, sometimes described as he 'who has brought life and salvation to his people' (DY 'ḤYY WŠYZB 'MH).[28] There is of course no way of knowing whether these terms were sincere, merely conventional, or forced. What is significant is simply the public proclamation of a beneficent relationship of a king to 'his' people, 'the Nabataeans' (NBṬW). However little else may have changed with the extension of provincial rule, this rela-

25. *CIS* II.1, no. 170. See 2.3 above, text to n. 18.
26. Herod: *IGR* III, no. 1243. Philip: *RES*, no. 2117. Agrippa II: *IGR* III, no. 1244; *RES*, no. 1091 (HGRP' MLK'; see J. Starcky, in Dentzer, *Hauran*, p. 175).
27. 11.4 below.
28. See, e.g., A. Negev, *IEJ* 13 (1963), 113, no. 10 (from Avdat).

tionship, and with it the explicit conception of the NBṬW as a people, would be at an end. Whether any attachment to the dynasty lingered on in the Roman province is a question to which we will return.[29]

Their close geographical relationship therefore masked a real difference between the southern and northern halves of the Hauran in the first century. Given the arbitrary nature of political boundaries, and their vulnerability to circumstance, it might be that we should nonetheless see the wider culture of the two areas as effectively identical. And indeed there are a number of Semitic-language inscriptions from the northern zone, from Kanatha, the sanctuary of Siaʿ, Suweida (the later Dionysias) and Hebran, which have always, until recently, been classified as 'Nabataean'.[30] But the late Jean Starcky argued that the letter-forms of these texts are different from those of Petra, and that they should be regarded simply as 'Aramaic' rather than 'Nabataean'.[31] That view would cohere with the wider conception of seeing the culture of the northern Hauran in the 'pre-provincial' period as an indigenous local phenomenon, of which the most conspicuous feature is the cult-centre of Baalshamin at Siaʿ near Kanatha.[32]

It is significant that here, as in the Nabataean zone, the earliest monumental constructions so far attested belong in the first century BC. But, by comparison with Nabataea, the inscriptions which accompany them, and on occasion serve to date them precisely, are sometimes, from the beginning, bilingual in Greek and (as we may call it) Aramaic. What may be the earliest known monument from the region is the pyramid-tomb (now destroyed) at Suweida, erected by a man named Odainathos son of Annēlos for his wife Hamretē. He records the fact in both Greek and Aramaic, in which the text reads 'tomb of Hamrat which her husband Odenat built for her': NPŠH DY ḤMRT DY BNH LH 'DYNT BʿLH. The date is variously estimated as either early or late in the first century BC.[33]

Much more striking and important are the bilingual building-inscriptions from the major cult-centre at Siaʿ near Kanatha. The main buildings, including at least two temples, were built on a series of artificial terraces on the spur of a hill on the western slopes of the Jebel Hauran. Construction seems to have taken place in phases from the late 30s BC to the last quarter of the first

---

29. 11.4 below.

30. For example, in CIS II.1, no. 162 (Suweida); 163–168 (Siaʿ); 170–172 (Hebran), or Cantineau, Le Nabatéen II, pp. 11–16.

31. J. Starcky, "Pétra et la Nabatène", SDB VII (1966), cols. 930–931, and his important article "Les inscriptions nabatéennes et l'histoire de la Syrie du Sud et du Nord de la Jordanie", in Dentzer, Hauran, 167. I am very grateful to M. C. A. MacDonald for help with these questions.

32. For this view J.-M. Dentzer, "Développement et culture de la Syrie du Sud dans la période préprovinciale (1er s. avant J.-C.–1er s. après J.-C.", in Dentzer, Hauran, 387.

33. CIS II.1, no. 162.

century AD, with some elements being added in the second century.[34] Even if they cannot easily be related to particular surviving architectural elements, the building-inscriptions remain of exceptional importance.[35] The earliest firmly dated inscription from the site, and indeed from the whole region, records construction continuing from the Seleucid year 280 to 311, that is, from 33/32 to 2/1 BC. The inscription is reconstructed from fragments, and not all the details are certain. But the builder is firmly identified as 'Malikat, son of Auso, son of Moaiero', and the deity as Baalshamin (B'[L]ŠMYN); one element of the construction is called a TYṬR' *(theatron?)*. Moreover, a long-known Greek inscription, also very fragmentary, names the same man, and was put up by 'the community *(koinon)* of the Seeiēnoi'.[36] Considerably more significant is the bilingual inscription recording further building by a member of the same family, called in Greek 'Maleichathos son of Moaieros', and in Aramaic MLYKT BR M'YRW. For it explicitly identifies the group which erected a statue to him: 'the tribe Obaishat' ('L 'BYŠT) in Aramaic, and 'the *dēmos* of the Obaisēnoi' in Greek. Assuming that this inscription too belongs in the Augustan period, this is the earliest documentary reference we have to any of a long series of 'tribes' (or, to be more cautious, groupings which seem to be defined by relationships rather than, like the 'Seeiēnoi', by locality) attested in the Hauran and in the steppe region to its east. A grouping, or tribe, identified as the Obeishat ('L 'BŠT) also appears a couple of times among the thousands of graffiti in the Semitic language called by moderns Safaitic (after the volcanic region called the Safa, east of the Hauran).[37]

We will need to return later to the problem posed by the existence, beyond the 'frontier', of a steppe population which, quite remarkably, was in some sense literate.[38] For the moment what is significant is that the cult-centre of Sia', although Herodian rulers were honoured there, does not seem to have been in any sense a royal creation; on the contrary, it was the product of local communal structures, in which groups from the steppe to the east in some way shared. Whether we should see the Obaishat, or other 'tribes', as having been 'dimorphic'—partly nomadic and partly settled—is at the moment an unanswerable question.

These local communities evidently both possessed the wealth to create a monumental cult-centre and participated sufficiently in late-Hellenistic culture to use Greek architectural forms and to erect statues. That representing

34. For the fullest recent survey see J.-M. Dentzer, "Six campagnes de fouilles à Sia': Développement et culture indigène en Syrie méridionale", *Dam. Mitt.* 2 (1985), 65.

35. Cantineau, *Le Nabatéen* II, pp. 11–15.

36. Le Bas-W., no. 2367.

37. See A. G. Grushevoi, "The Tribe 'Ubaishat in Safaitic, Nabataean and Greek Inscriptions", *Berytus* 33 (1985), 51.

38. 11.5 below.

King Herod—which alas does not survive—put up 'at my own expense' by 'Obaisatos, son of Saodos', was not the only one;[39] there was also the image (ṢLM'—the same word as in Palmyrene and Syriac) of Malikat, and a personified representation of the place Sia' itself (or herself). As regards the statue, only a foot and the lower draperies of a female figure survive, but a bilingual inscription makes the identification certain. In Aramaic it reads simply: 'this is the image of Seeia' (D' ṢLMT' DY Š'Y'W). In Greek the meaning of the location of the cult-centre is expressed more vividly: 'Seeia established over against (the) land (of) Auraneitis'.[40] On its terraced spur of the hillside, Sia' does indeed look out over the flat plain of the Hauran.

At Kanatha itself, the nearest town, and at various points on the plain, including the lava-field of Trachonitis in the north, there are a few other Semitic inscriptions, which ought now provisionally to be classified as 'Aramaic' rather than as 'Nabataean'.[41] One result of that classification is that these inscriptions, mostly fragmentary, can be brought into ⌐lation with the important Aramaic inscription of the Seleucid year 305 (8/7 BC) from el-Mal. For this inscription comes from yet another area covered by a network of substantial ancient villages, namely the region east of the Golan Heights which the Israeli archaeologists who were able to survey it in November 1973 delicately called Northern Bashan.[42] El-Mal in fact lies quite close to the lava-field of Trachonitis (the Lejja) and only some 16 km north-east of Sanamein, the find-spot of the most north-easterly of the known 'Nabataean' inscriptions. This region was indeed the Classical Batanaea, and formed part of the domain of the Herodian family. In terms of settlement, we can suppose with confidence that there was a network of villages stretching from the Golan (Gaulanitis) across Batanaea and Trachonitis to Auranitis, a zone which was under Herodian rule through most of the first century, and will have had a mixed Jewish and gentile population in its north-eastern part.

The Aramaic inscription of el-Mal is categorically pagan: '[In the month . . .], year 305, YQYM BR ḤMLT BR NṢRMLK built a "house of god" (BYT 'LH)'.[43] The basalt block on which the inscription is cut appears clearly to be part of a building; the BYT 'LH was therefore a temple or shrine, and not a

---

39. Cf. 2.1 above for Herod's rule here.

40. *RES*, no. 1092; Cantineau, *Le Nabatéen* II, 14: Σεεῖα κατὰ γῆν Αὐρανεῖτην ἑστηκυῖα. On this inscription see J. Dentzer, "A propos du temple dit de 'Dusarès' à Sî'", *Syria* 56 (1979), 325.

41. Again I rely on the invaluable survey by Wenning, *Nabatäer*, regions C and E, and on the article by J. Starcky in Dentzer, *Hauran*, 16 (n.31 above).

42. G. Barkay, Z. Ilan, A. Kloner, A. Mazar and D. Urman, "Archaeological Survey in the Northern Bashan", *IEJ* 24 (1974), 173, with sketch-map on p. 174.

43. J. Naveh, "An Aramaic Inscription from El-Mal—a Survival of 'Seleucid Aramaic' Script", *IEJ* 25 (1975), 116, Pl. 13A; Fitzmyer, *PAT*, no. 149.

'betyl', a stone functioning as a cult-object.[44] It is a testimony to the life of the Aramaic- and Greek-speaking pagan population of Batanaea which lived almost continuously under the rule of the Herodian family until the death of Agrippa II, apparently in the 90s, and which then (it seems) came under the province of Syria, being joined to 'Arabia' only under the Tetrarchy.[45]

Provincial boundaries in this north-western area, east of the Jordan and the Sea of Galilee, were arbitrary and liable to change. It does not greatly matter, therefore, that in the case of several of the Greek cities of the Decapolis—for instance Hippos, Gadara, Abila, Capitolias and Pella—we cannot tell for certain whether in the second century they were part of Syria or of Judaea/Syria Palaestina. What is clear is that the new province of Arabia took in Philadelphia (Amman), Gerasa and (almost certainly) Adraa. But although the claim to the status of Greek city by all these places in the Decapolis was strongly emphasised in contemporary coin-legends and inscriptions, that does not mean that the Decapolis had previously been sealed off against Nabataean presence or influences.[46]

On the contrary, there are clear traces of such influences from the period when the Nabataean kingdom still existed, both in some of the Greek cities which did not become part of the new province of Arabia and in those which were to be incorporated into it. The traces are of various kinds: a Greek dedication to the most typical Nabataean god, Dusares, at Hippos, or a fragmentary Nabataean tomb-inscription from the little-known site of Capitolias (Beit Ras).[47] It is only in relation to the two major cities which were to be incorporated into the province, Philadelphia and Gerasa, that the evidence is a little more substantial. At Philadelphia there have been finds of Nabataean pottery and of coins of Aretas IV and Rabbel II—hardly surprising given how close it lay to the border with Nabataea: Madaba, some 25 km to the south-south-west, was in Nabataean territory. For what it is worth, a fragmentary bilingual inscription, in Nabataean and Greek, found at Zizia, east of Madaba, seems to describe the dedicant's father as 'from Amman' (or 'an Ammo-

44. Ch. 1 above.

45. For the complex and largely insoluble problems of provincial boundaries in this area, see E. Kettenhofen, "Zur Nordgrenze der Provincia Arabiae *(sic)* im 3. Jahrhundert n. Chr.", *ZDPV* 97 (1981), 62, with map on p. 63.

46. For these questions see D. F. Graf, "The Nabataeans and the Decapolis", in Freeman and Kennedy, *DRBE* II (1986), 785; P.-L. Gatier, "Philadelphie et Gerasa du royaume nabatéen à la province d'Arabie", in P. L. Gatier, B. Helly and J.-P. Rey-Coquais (eds.), *Géographie historique au Proche-Orient* (1988), 159.

47. A. Ovadiah, "Was the Cult of the God Dushara-Dusares Practised in Hippos-Susita?", *PEQ* 113 (1981), 101; *CIS* II.1, no. 194 (Beit Ras). For what little is known of the site see C. J. Lenzen and E. A. Knauf, "Beit Ras/Capitolias: A Preliminary Evaluation of the Archaeological and Textual Evidence", *Syria* 64 (1987), 21.

nite'?)—'MNY; the son had constructed a shrine to a local Zeus—'Zeus in Beelpheg[ō]r'.[48] It is not surprising either that coins of Nabataean kings are found at Gerasa. But in relation to this city there is rather more significant evidence. A Nabataean inscription from the Siq at Petra (the dramatic canyon leading into the city) happens to give the Semitic name both of Petra itself (RQMW—'Reqem') and of Gerasa, where the man commemorated had died—GRŠW.[49] The border between a dependent kingdom and the nearest Roman province will never have been in any sense a closed frontier; and, as the subsequent course of the Via Nova Traiana was to show, the natural route from the main Nabataean zone to Damascus led through the Decapolis (though east of Gerasa itself). From Gerasa there is one damaged bilingual Nabataean-Greek inscription, apparently dated by 'year 11 of Rabbel the king', that is, AD 81. There seems to be a reference to a statue (DNH ṢLM'), and the text seems to relate to the establishment of a sacred area.[50] Beyond that, the epigraphy of the Decapolis shows a mixture ˙ Semitic, Greek and Latin personal names similar to that found everywhere else in the Near East. As it is not peculiar to the Decapolis, it will not serve as a clue to any distinctive local culture; and in any case the conscious significance, if any, of personal names remains uncertain, as does the relation of nomenclature to the language, or languages, of ordinary life, or to wider cultural issues.

The area which was to become the Roman province of 'Arabia' thus presents exceptional complexities. First, it was made up of a number of strikingly different geographical and cultural zones: the northern Hedjaz and the Red Sea coast; Sinai; the semi-desert Negev bordering on southern Judaea; the arid plain (the Hisma) north of the port of Aila; the (as it seems) thinly settled marginal zone south of Petra; the central area of settled habitation, the plateau of Moab, of which Petra itself should be seen as the southernmost extension; the northern part at least of the Wadi Arabah, running south from the Dead Sea; the Decapolis; and the Hauran plain and the Jebel Hauran. A Nabataean and then Roman presence was also to be found far down the Wadi Sirhan. But even without that it is patent that the entire settled, or semi-settled, zone has to be seen in relation to the steppe and its peoples.

This complex geographical and social pattern would alone make very difficult any confident characterisation of the culture of the region. But the question of its evolution over time adds a much more difficult further dimension. What was the history of the Nabataean language and culture after the sup-

48. *IGLS* XXI.2, no. 154, see *RES*, no. 1284.

49. J. Starcky, "Nouvelle épitaphe nabatéenne donnant le nom sémitique de Pétra", *RB* 72 (1965), 95.

50. C. B. Welles, in C. H. Kraeling (ed.), *Gerasa*, 371, no. 1, with revisions by J. T. Milik, quoted by G. W. Bowersock, "Syria under Vespasian", *JRS* 63 (1973), 133, n.54.

pression of the kingdom? Along with the sudden appearance of both Bostra and Petra as Greek cities ('Nea Traianē Bostra' and 'Hadrianē Petra') and later as Roman *coloniae*, should we see the history of the united province as that of the advance of Graeco-Roman culture and of Graeco-Roman city life? By the mid-third century there were some fourteen cities, including Philip's new foundation of Philippolis, which minted (or had at some moment minted) coins in Greek and Latin. As we will see, it was perhaps even more significant that the villages of the Hauran area in the second to fourth centuries produced a mass of inscriptions, written in a Greek whose very incorrectness shows that it was a language of current use, and which reveal communal structures closely modelled on those of Greek cities.[51] Similarly, Aila on the Gulf of Aqaba never seems to have been categorised as a 'city', and never minted coins. But when Jerome describes Hilarion encountering someone from there in the first half of the fourth century, he identifies him as 'a leading man, and very rich, of the city *(urbs)* of Aila, which is by the Red Sea'. Jerome seems to have envisaged Aila as a city like any other.[52]

On the other hand, when his hero Hilarion reaches Elusa, he describes the place as an 'oppidum semibarbarum', and speaks of crowds of *Saraceni* coming to worship at the temple of Venus there, and greeting Hilarion in a Semitic language ('barech!').[53] That might suggest a model of precisely the opposite development: that is, the Imperial period as one when Graeco-Roman urban culture was on the retreat in the face of the infiltration of *Saraceni* either from the inner unsettled zone of Sinai or, more important, from beyond the 'desert frontier'. It will be recalled that the first Imperial campaign recorded to have been conducted against *Saraceni* took place about 290; and, more significantly, that the facts of the developing Roman military dispositions in the Near East show that by the fourth century the majority of the Roman forces were committed not against Persia, but along the edge of the steppe, from the Euphrates to the Red Sea.[54]

These stark alternatives do not of course represent the only possible models; as Glen Bowersock has recently argued, one of the functions of Graeco-Roman culture in this region may precisely have been to offer a vehicle for the expression of an indigenous local culture.[55] We could hardly ask for a more perfect amalgam of Greek, Roman and local elements than the games held at Bostra, and recorded on the city's colonial coinage in Latin

51. 11.4 below.

52. Jerome, *V. Hilar.* 10, 5: 'vir primarius et ditissimus urbis Ailae, quae mari rubro imminet'.

53. *V. Hilar.* 25; cf. 10.4 above.

54. 5.1 above.

55. G. W. Bowersock, *Hellenism in Late Antiquity* (1990), esp. ch. 3.

in the third century as the 'Actia Dusaria of the colonia metropolis of the Bostreni'.[56]

But we know of these games only from the coins, which soon ceased, as did those of all other cities in the Greek East. In the mid-third century Bostra already had a Christian bishop, Beryllos, whom Eusebius describes as '*episkopos* of the Arabs at Bostra', and who held heretical views (essentially a denial of the pre-existence of Christ), over which Origen and others met in a synod to debate with him, evidently in Greek.[57] Further questions are thus raised. What would remain of the communal character of the cities of this region in the Christian period? And did Christianity here owe anything significant to its local environment? How soon, if at all, was it preached here in any language other than Greek, and in particular had it yet reached the *Saraceni* of Sinai or the steppe? In this context as in all others, we need to recall that it is much more likely that the *Saraceni* were influenced by the dominant elements of the culture of the settled zone than the otȷ way round. But the problem remains that the question of what, in this region, those elements actually were is itself of particular complexity.

In fact, the available evidence—archaeological remains, inscriptions and perishable documents in Greek, Latin, Nabataean and Aramaic, and an erratic scatter of pagan and Christian literary evidence—will not serve, highly suggestive as it is, to answer the most important questions. All that can be done is to offer a few pointers to possible answers, and (even more) to suggest further questions which need to be asked.

11.2. THE KINGDOM OF NABATAEA

An even broader approach will be needed in regard to the culture of Nabataea as a kingdom, before it was absorbed as a province. Some essentials can, however, be clearly established. First, the geographical limits of the Nabataean zone have already been outlined. Second, in the latter part of the first century BC, Diodorus and Strabo were unanimous in characterising the Nabataeans as 'Arabs', and also described them as inhabiting a mainly desert and partly cultivable area, and as exploiting the Red Sea both for piracy and for trade. Diodorus, perhaps because he depends on early-Hellenistic sources, emphasises their nomadic and pastoral way of life, with the use of Petra as a place of refuge; but Strabo, more explicitly using contemporary information, speaks of the royal dynasty, of Petra as a real city and of the conduct of legal affairs among the Petraeans.[1] Neither would leave the reader with any impression of

56. See, e.g., A. Kindler, *The Coinage of Bostra* (1983), 158–159.

57. Eusebius, *HE* VI, 20, 2; 33, 1–3.

1. Diodorus II, 48; III, 43, 4–5; XIX, 94–100; Strabo, *Geog.* XVI, 4, 18 (777) and 21 (779). On the question of 'Arab' origins, see now J. F. Healey, "Were the Nabataeans Arabs?", *Aram*

the architecture of Petra or of the existence of an extensive zone of Nabataean settlement in Moab and the Negev.

The fact that there was a long-lasting royal dynasty is of great importance. From external allusions, coins and inscriptions we can trace what seems to be a single royal line, of kings called typically Aretas (ḤRTT), Obodas ('BDT), Malichus (MLKW) and finally Rabbel (RB'L), for a period of over two centuries, from the second century BC to AD 106. It must be significant that their coins begin in the late Hellenistic period by using Greek and emphasising attachment to Greek culture—'of king Aretas, *philhellēn*'; but then throughout the Roman period, from the late 60s BC onwards, they use only Nabataean. They thus represent the longest and most consistent series of coins with purely Semitic-language legends from any area; they also, like the inscriptions mentioned earlier, emphasise the character of the Nabataeans as a people, calling all the kings 'king of the Nabataeans' (MLK NBṬW), and under Aretas IV (*circa* 9 BC–AD 40) adding programmatic elements: 'who loves his people' (RḤM 'MH).[2]

Like other dependent kingdoms, Nabataea maintained an army of at least several thousand. Conveniently, even our very slight scatter of evidence happens to reveal Nabataean military officials stationed at a number of points on the outer reaches of the kingdom: at Medain Saleh (Hegra) in the Hedjaz; at Leuke Kome on the Red Sea; at Jawf (Dumatha), far down the Wadi Sirhan; and at Madaba close to the border with the Decapolis. Here, in AD 37, Abdobodas ('slave of Obodas') the *stratēgos* ('BD'BDT 'SRTG') put up a sepulchral inscription to his father, also a *stratēgos*, and to another man who was 'commander of the camp at Lahito' (RB MŠRYT' DY BLḤYTW), a place near Madaba. Between them the father and son had served thirty-six years under Aretas, 'who loves his people'.[3]

The evidence we have is of course nothing like sufficient for a history of the Nabataean army, or still less of the government and administration of the kingdom. But we can perceive that there was a standing army, part of which at least was stationed on the borders. It is also clear that there was a tax-collector at Leuke Kome, as the *Periplus* reports. But while it would be valuable to be able to visualise what changes in style of government were brought about when the area became provincial, it is more important to stress that we do have just enough evidence to glimpse the workings of a legal and religious system, which operated in Nabataean, a branch of Aramaic. It is often ar-

---

1.1 (1989), 38, unfortunately based on the presumption that the question is capable of a factual answer. See also D. Graf, "The Origin of the Nabataeans", *Aram* 2.1–2 (1990), 45 (speculative).

2. See Y. Meshorer, *Nabataean Coins* (1975). See now also K. Schmitt-Körte, "Nabataean Coinage I", *NC* 149 (1989), 33; "II", 150 (1990), 105; "III" (forthcoming).

3. *CIS* II.1, no. 196 = *RES*, no. 674 = Cantineau, *Le Nabatéen* II, p. 44.

gued, not to say asserted, that this was merely an official language, used only for written documents, while the population, being 'Arabs', actually spoke a variety of Arabic. The proposition seems strange in several ways, not least in defining a hypothetical spoken language of the first century AD in terms of a language of which we have no more than scattered items of evidence before the late seventh century. Moreover, the existence of literally thousands of graffiti in Nabataean from Sinai (in quantity, the substantial majority of Nabataean inscriptions) rules out any notion that the language was deployed only in official, public contexts.[4] Though the relatively extended documents in Nabataean to which we will come shortly, written both on stone and on perishable documents, are all of an official or legal character (so far we have, for instance, no private letters in Nabataean), the idea that the language was not simultaneously spoken seems perverse and is very difficult to prove. It is certain that the related dialect of Aramaic, (using of course the same alphabet but rather different letter-forms) which was employed by Jews was a spoken language; and it is highly improbable that the Aramaic used by gentiles in Palestine and the Hauran was not also spoken. Any attempt to define the language spoken by the Nabataeans in terms of classical Arabic must thus be hazardous. Far more significant is the important new step taken by Avrahm Negev in bringing together, from the point of view of onomastics, the Nabataean inscriptions and graffiti with the thousands of 'Safaitic' graffiti known from both the steppe and the settled zones. If the question of how far different scripts and languages represent different ethnic groups remains open, for the first time the way has been cleared for the joint study of a vast mass of contemporary documentary material.[5]

Nonetheless there is now one striking and extremely important bit of evidence to show that Nabataean and Arabic did co-exist in the period of the kingdom, or the early years of the province. This is a rock-cut inscription in Nabataean lettering found near the city of Oboda (Avdat) in the Negev.[6] The inscription is notable first of all as another in a series of documents of the cult of a deified king Obodas—'Obodas the god': 'BDT 'LH; it is to him that the dedicant, Garm'alahi son of Taym'alahi, records setting up a statue, ṢLM('?). But it is at this point that he gives an explanation in Arabic of why he had made the dedication. Any interpretation of these two lines must be highly

---

4. For the graffiti see *CIS* II, nos. 490–3233; Wenning, *Nabatäer*, 188ff.

5. A. Negev, *Personal Names in the Nabataean Realm* (Qedem 32, 1991). This major work will require detailed study. I would, however, stress that even if Nabataean *inscriptions* are confined to the religious sphere (pp. 209ff.), this was not true of Nabataean *writing*, which is used for legal documents in the Babatha archive.

6. Published by A. Negev, "Obodas the God", *IEJ* 36 (1986), 56; re-examined by J. A. Bellamy, "Arabic Verses from the First/Second Century: The Inscription of 'En 'Avdat", *JSS* 35 (1990), 73, whose translation of ll. 4–5 is used here.

speculative, not least because they are not in standard Arabic script. But the latest study takes them to be in verse, and to read as follows:

> For (Obodas) works without rewards or favour, and he, when death tried to claim us, did not let it claim (us), for when a wound (of ours) festered he did not let us perish.

The linguistic and cultural history of the region is very far from being fully understood. But it is important to stress that there are enough complex, if relatively brief, documents in Nabataean to show that the language and script could be, and were, deployed in ordinary life, and were certainly not the preserve of some scribal class.

Only a few examples need be given. One category is the series of substantial inscriptions of the first century AD from the fine rock-cut tombs of Medain Saleh (Hegra) in the Hedjaz. Like comparable Greek texts, they tend to list the intended and legitimate occupants of the tomb, and then to pronounce a curse, and lay down a penalty, on anyone who usurps or disturbs it. For example one of AD 11 ends:

> Whoever acts otherwise than is written above, let him be liable, in view of the sanctity of what is (written above), to pay a total sum of 1000 *sl'in* of Aretas to Dusares the god (LDWŠR' 'LH') and to our lord Aretas the king (ḤRTT MLK') similarly. In the month Shebat, year 13 of Aretas king of the Nabataeans who loves his people.[7]

More complex, and less formulaic, inscriptions from religious contexts are not common. But one from the temple of Atargatis or Al-'Uzza at Petra seems, though unfortunately fragmentary, to contain rules for offerings (to a deity?) and to priests: 'Whatever comes to him of silver or gold or offerings (KSP WDHB WQRBWN) . . . and to the priests, the other portion (WLKMRY' PLG' 'ḤRN') . . .'. This too is dated to the reign of Aretas.[8]

But, obviously enough, we come closer to the active use of the written language in daily life when we have access to perishable documents. As yet, these are very few; and the most important group, discovered in 1961, has still not been published in full. The earliest (found in the early 50s somewhere in the Judaean Desert, along with other fragmentary documents in Nabataean which seem never to have been published) is a contract dated to year 4 of Malchus, so AD 43.[9] It is thus a few years earlier than the equally significant

---

7. *CIS* II.1, no. 199 = Cantineau, *Le Nabatéen* II, p. 28.

8. P. C. Hammond, D. J. Johnson and R. N. Jones, "A Religio-legal Nabataean Inscription from the Atargatis/Al-'Uzza Temple at Petra", *BASOR* 263 (1986), 77. See also R. N. Jones, "A New Reading of the Petra Temple Inscription", *BASOR* 275 (1989), 41.

9. J. Starcky, "Un contrat nabatéen sur papyrus", *RB* 61 (1954), 161.

acknowledgment of debt in Aramaic from Judaea.[10] The contract concerns the division of property, including gardens and 'two shops and the rooms which they contain . . . in the souk (at) Mahoz 'Agaltain' (TRTY' ḤNWT' WTWNY' DY GW' MNHM . . . BŠWQ MḤWZ 'GLTYN). The parties have Nabataean names, though one is called Eleazar (and so seems to be Jewish) and his father is called Nikarchos (NYQRKS); and another Jewish participant is the witness, Joseph bar Yehuda, whose name appears on the back of one of the fragments.

Subsequent exploration of a cave in the Nahal Hever, a wadi running down to the Dead Sea south of Engeddi, showed this was in fact where the Nabataean document of AD 43 had been found; two further fragments of it were discovered in the same cave.[11] It may thus be related to the most important find in the cave, the 'archive of Babatha', documents in Nabataean, Aramaic and Greek embodying the complex affairs of a Jewish family from Maoza near Zoara, at the south end of the Dead Sea, between AD 94 and 132, after which they were evidently concealed during the Bar Kochba war. Various documents from this archive have already been mentioned, including the census-return of 127, one of the most vivid reflections of what the imposition of Roman provincial rule meant.[12] But, potentially, the greatest novelty of the archive is the series of documents in Nabataean, written in the last years of the kingdom, under Rabbel II: one of AD 94 and three of 99.[13]

Since these have not yet been published in full, we must rely on partial reports. It is important nonetheless to stress that these are extensive and detailed legal documents relating to property transactions. The earliest, running to fifty-two lines, concerns the giving of a dowry and the consequent pledging of property: a private document such as this, as it turns out, would also be dated by 'Rabbel the king, king of the Nabataeans who has given life and deliverance to his people' (RB'L MLK' MLK NBṬW DY 'ḤYY WŠYZB 'MH).

The next document, of 99, is a bill of sale relating to a palm-grove at

10. 10.2 above.

11. See N. Lewis, *The Documents from the Bar Kochba Period in the Cave of Letters: Greek Papyri* (1989), 3. Documents cited as *P. Yadin*. It is more than regrettable that those responsible for the Semitic-language documents in this remarkable trilingual archive were not able to match Naphtali Lewis in control of the material; the Semitic-language documents, in Nabataean and Aramaic, await publication in a second volume, in which the document of AD 43 will appear as no. 36.

12. See ch. 1, and 3.2, 3.3, 10.3.

13. See Y. Yadin, "Expedition to the Judaean Desert, 1961: Expedition D—the Cave of the Letters", *IEJ* 12 (1962), 227, on pp. 238–241; and, slightly more fully, idem, "The Nabataean Kingdom, Provincia Arabia, Petra and En-Geddi in the Documents from Nahal Hever", *Phoenix: Jaarbericht ex Oriente Lux* 16–19 (1965–66), 227, on pp. 229–232.

Mahoz 'Agaltain (Maoza), the same place as in the document of AD 43, and the same palm-grove as later recorded by Babatha in her census-declaration of 127. At this point it is being sold by one Ibna'un to a man with a Greek name, Archelaos. Though the documents, as reported so far, do not reveal anything of the royal administration, the royal presence is very evident in them. The palm-grove is bordered by one owned by 'our lord Rabbel the king', and the document ends with a penalty for non-compliance payable to the king: 'and to our lord Rabbel the king likewise' (LMRN' RB'L MLK' KWT). Then, in the same year, the palm-grove was sold to Simeon, the father of Babatha, hence its appearance among her property. It is again defined by reference to neighbouring properties, of the king and of individual Nabataeans, and the days and hours of water-rights are also specified. Nothing has been reported of the fourth document except that it too is a deed of sale.

Much more will of course be revealed when these documents are finally published, but three points may need to be stressed now. First, these complex and extensive documents must cast further doubt on the notion that Nabataean was not the, or at least a, language in current use among the people (that they also spoke a language closely related to classical Arabic of course remains possible). It is true that the first document was written by a scribe, who also signs as a witness ('RQBW BR 'WTY SPR' KTBH). But both before and after 106, witnesses are found writing their attestations in Nabataean or Aramaic. Like Palmyrene, these were therefore languages in which at least a portion of the population were to some degree literate.

Second, we see that this corner of the Nabataean kingdom, inhabited by both Nabataeans and Jews, was an area of settled cultivation, with established property rights and conventional rules about access to water for irrigation. The documents owe their survival to the accident of their concealment during the Bar Kochba war. But there is no obvious reason to think that the world which they reveal would not have been paralleled on the plateau of Moab as far south as Petra, and in the areas of Nabataean settlement around Bostra and in the Negev. That would not mean that society and culture in these settled areas were not influenced profoundly by the nearby steppe and its peoples.

Third, the presence of the king, and the use of loyalist expressions to refer to him (and his family), is as evident here as it is in public inscriptions. Penalties for non-compliance, payable to the king, appear here just as they do on the tomb-inscriptions of Medain Saleh.[14]

Although we can be certain that in Nabataea as elsewhere the predominant form of settlement will have been the village, with drastically varying densities of population, it is significant that cities, or at least towns, had

14. Text to n.7 above.

emerged also. At Mampsis in the eastern Negev, a substantial Nabataean settlement underlies the remains of the town of the provincial period; but the
clearest example from this region is the city of Avdat (Oboda or Eboda) in
the south-central Negev, where terracing, with a temple built on it, seems
from associated inscriptions to have been built during the reign of Aretas IV
(*circa* 9 BC–AD 40). Whether or not (and if so, when) there were phases of
destruction in the history of the town, a city continued here into the Byzantine
period, as the remains of its churches attest. Very significantly, a number of
Nabataean inscriptions from the last years of the kingdom, found in the area,
attest the construction of dams. This is also, as we will see, one place where
inscriptional evidence immediately reflects the arrival of the provincial
regime.[15]

But of course the prime example of Nabataean architecture and urbanism
remains Petra itself. It is important to stress that the city as revealed by its
rock-cut tombs and the results of relatively limited excavations (mostly never
published in full) is a product of the kingdom. Only a very few elements, and
none of the major features, seem to date to the provincial period. Inscriptions
serving to date either rock-cut features or buildings are rare, but an invaluable
source of dated material for stylistic comparison is provided by the inscribed
rock-cut tombs of Medain Saleh, which range from AD 1 to 76.[16] The main
phase of evolution at Petra, so far as yet known, clearly belongs to the end of
the first century BC, and the first century AD. A single rock-cut banqueting
chamber *(triclinium)* is firmly dated earlier than this, in the 90s BC. Otherwise
the dedication of a statue to Aretas IV (*circa* 9 BC–AD 40) shows from its
location that the central sanctuary area with the one standing temple, the so-
called Qasr el Bint, was already laid out. The famous rock-cut facade at the
end of the Siq, the Khasneh, also belongs to this period, while the main theatre
was cut out of the rock in the first century AD.[17] A further catalogue is not
needed. The archaeological, epigraphic and stylistic evidence makes it certain
that Petra, as a city with a refined architecture and rock-carvings, has to be
seen, like the tombs of Medain Saleh, as a local off-shoot of late-Hellenistic

---

15. For the city see *EAEHL s.v.* "Eboda"; Wenning, *Nabatäer,* 159ff. For the inscriptions
see A. Negev, "Nabataean Inscriptions from 'Avdat (Oboda)", *IEJ* 11 (1961), 127; 13 (1963),
113 Much remains uncertain, and it is impossible to be more specific about the history of the
town in this period. See now, however, A. Negev, "The Temple of Obodas: Excavations at Oboda
in July 1989", *IEJ* 41 (1991), 62.

16. For the urban evolution of Petra, I depend entirely on the magnificent study by Judith
Mackenzie, *The Architecture of Petra* (1990), which is also an exceptional repertoire of photographs. See also P. C. Hammond, "Nabataean Settlement Patterns inside Petra", *Anc. Hist. Bull.*
5 (1991), 36.

17. See Mackenzie, op. cit., 33–34.

art; the authoritative recent study by Judith Mackenzie argues that the models for this architecture were drawn from Alexandria.

It should be stressed, first, that the evidence so far available relates mainly to rock-cut elements, and to the sanctuary area and the central colonnaded street (which may be early or late in the first century AD). Very little is as yet known of Petra as a town—for instance, of its side-streets or private houses. Second, nearly all the inscriptions which date from the kingdom are, like the coins of the period between the 60s BC and AD 106, in Nabataean. Greek or bilingual inscriptions are very rare. One exception comes from the gorge leading to the Siq proper (the 'Gate of the Siq', Bab el Siq), where a Nabataean inscription records that one 'BDMNKW son of 'KYS (Achaios) son of SLY (Syllaios) son of 'TYH(W) has made the tomb for himself and his descendants under the rule of MNKW. A poorly preserved Greek inscription repeats the message: 'Abdmanchos son of Achaios made this *mnēmeion* for himself and his sons'. The ruler referred to may be either Malichus I of the mid-first century BC or Malichus II of the mid-first century AD. The reference may be to the 'Obelisk Tomb' and *triclinium* which are to be found opposite, on the other side of the gorge.[18]

Unfortunately we are in no position to know whether Greek inscriptions were a common feature of the city of Petra in the royal period, or indeed to be certain whether the question of language was significant at all. But the monolingualism of the royal coins is suggestive; so also, as we will see, is the quite abrupt shift away from Nabataean in the 'archive of Babatha', as soon as the provincial regime was imposed. But as regards the use or significance of Greek in the kingdom, our evidence simply fails us. There was for instance a formal Greek inscription on the facade of the theatre; but its fragmentary remains do not allow us to say whether it was put up before or after 106.[19]

What is now certain, however, is that Petra, as a city with monumental architecture and rock-cut facades, belongs in that period in the history of the Near East when Roman domination was assured, but Roman direct rule was either absent or still relatively lightly imposed. The royal monuments of Commagene belong in this period, if in the earliest phase of it; but so also do the temple of Bel at Palmyra, Herod's Temple in Jerusalem (as well as his other major monuments), the temple of Baalshamin at Sia' and, as will be seen, the temple of Zeus at Gerasa. The major constructions of this period were sometimes royal creations, as in Commagene or Judaea; but the others were the expression of the culture of local communities, as in Palmyra, Sia' or Ger-

---

18. See J. T. Milik, "Une inscription bilingue nabatéenne et grecque à Pétra", *ADAJ* 21 (1976), 143; Mackenzie, op. cit., 34.

19. See P. C. Hammond, *The Excavation of the Main Theatre at Petra* (1965), 72.

asa. Thus, though it is surely certain that Petra owed its sudden burst of spectacular architectural activity to its having been a royal capital, we cannot be certain whether we should see this solely as the expression of the royal will or of the self-assertion of a community, or of both.

It may be significant that nothing at Petra can be unambiguously dated to the reign of the last king, Rabbel II (AD 70–106). For there are slight indications that it was Bostra rather than Petra which he treated as his main city. The evidence is suggestive, if hardly unambiguous. First, Nabataean inscriptions mentioning Rabbel II tend to concentrate in the Nabataean zone in the southern Hauran rather than elsewhere. Second, a series of inscriptions refers to 'Dushara, god of Rabbel our lord, who is at Bostra'. It can be only a hypothesis that behind these allusions lies a shift either to dependence on the agriculture of this region or to trade through the Wadi Sirhan, as opposed to that through the Red Sea.[20]

Nabataean Bostra, unlike Petra, is overlaid both by the remains of the Roman town and by a modern settlement. There is nonetheless sufficient evidence to show that it had had some monumental urban features. The eastern quarter of the town is planned on a different alignment from the larger western part, which surely represents the main area of the city in the Roman period. But it remains unclear whether the 'Nabataean Arch', standing at a point where the two zones meet, belongs to a westward expansion of the city in the late royal period or to the provincial period.[21]

There is no doubt that Nabataea as a kingdom contained urban centres with monumental buildings which represented a local variant of Hellenistic architecture. But whether these places should be seen as cities in the other sense, as communities with a formal structure of self-governing institutions and annual magistrates, is quite unknown. No such institutions are reflected in Nabataean inscriptions; and the only coins minted during the royal period were those with legends in Nabataean, issued by the kings themselves. The sudden emergence of both Petra (as reflected in the 'archive of Babatha') and Bostra as 'Greek cities' is thus one of the most marked changes which followed the imposition of provincial rule.

11.3. THE DECAPOLIS IN THE FIRST CENTURY

One major effect of the imposition of Roman rule in AD 106 was, as we have seen, to bring a concrete Roman presence, in the shape of both a governor

20. See J. T. Milik, "Nouvelles inscriptions nabatéennes", *Syria* 35 (1958), 227; M. Sartre, *Bostra des origines à l'Islam* (1985), 54ff.; cf. A. Segal, *Town Planning and Architecture in Provincia Arabia* (1988), esp. 59ff.

21. J.-M. Dentzer, "Les sondages de l'arc nabatéen et l'urbanisme de Bostra", *CRAI* (1986), 62.

(who might be found at Bostra, at Petra or elsewhere) and a legion, to the region south of Damascus, where there had been (so far as we can tell) effectively none before.[1] But the provincial territory here will already have paid tribute to Rome. Josephus' narrative happens to reveal that the Hauran and the other neighbouring districts had paid tribute to Rome both in the brief interval after the tetrarch Philip's death in AD 34 and again after the death of Agrippa II in the 90s. So we ought to presume that the Greek cities of the Decapolis had done likewise, even though, through most of the first century, they represented a physically separate enclave belonging to the province of Syria. For what it is worth, the slight inscriptional evidence from the Decapolis in the first century seems to contain no reflection of the existence of the *legatus* of Syria until a building-inscription from Gerasa which refers to L. Ceionius Commodus, *legatus* in AD 79–81.[2] Nor do we find any building-inscriptions invoking the name of the Emperor until one recording the dedication of the theatre at Gerasa to Domitian in AD 90. As we saw earlier, the fact that the inscription records that the dedication was 'in accordance with' a decree of the *legatus Augusti pro praetore,* Lappius Maximus, also represents the earliest record of a decision by a governor of Syria in this region.[3] If the change which came about in 106 had been slightly foreshadowed in the preceding decades, it must still have greatly altered the relationship of these cities to the Empire.

The effect may have been more profound in the case of those cities, Philadelphia, Gerasa and almost certainly Adraa, which now found themselves grouped—as geography would in any case have suggested—with the former Nabataean territories to their south, and perhaps to their east (if there had indeed been Nabataean occupation there at all) and north-east, as part of the new province of 'Arabia'. The very complex question of mutual influences, and contrasting communal and personal identities, over the whole area which after 106 was to be classified as 'Arabia' will be touched on later. It is not of course to be expected that our evidence will allow more than the most tentative of answers. But before that we need to ask whether any real content can be given to the description of the cities of the Decapolis, especially Philadelphia, Gerasa and Adraa, as 'Greek cities' in the period before 106.

Very little is known of the actual circumstances of the 'foundation' of any of these places as Greek cities in the Hellenistic period, if indeed an actual

1. 3.2 above.
2. C. B. Welles, in C. H. Kraeling (ed.), *Gerasa: City of the Decapolis* (1938), ins. no. 50; for the problems and suggested emendations of this very fragmentary text, see G. W. Bowersock, "Syria under Vespasian", *JRS* 63 (1973), 133 or 138.
3. *SEG* XXVII, no. 1009, cf. 1010–1011. Cf. 3.2 above.

moment of foundation occurred; nor is there much archaeological, and even less inscriptional, evidence for them in the Hellenistic period; consequently the interpretation of the relatively extensive archaeological and inscriptional evidence of the Imperial period leaves room for conjecture about the true nature of the local culture.[4] For our purposes it is necessary only to recall that all those places which had Greek names will have gained them in the Hellenistic period, and that some—Gadara, Hippos, Dium, Scythopolis and Pella— are listed as having been re-built, or liberated from Hasmonaean rule, in the early years of the Roman conquest, under Pompey and Gabinius. Hippos and Gadara later owed their detachment from the Herodian kingdom, and their attachment to the province of Syria, to their status as Greek cities.[5] Unfortunately, nothing is said by Josephus about Philadelphia, Gerasa or Adraa in the context of the early restorations; but it is certain that after 4 BC (the death of Herod) all these cities belonged to the province of Syria. A confused list of the cities of the Decapolis provided by Pliny the Elder seems to group together Damascus, Philadelphia, Rhaphana(?), Scythopolis, Gadara, Hippos, Dium, Pella, 'Galasa' (presumably Gerasa) and Canatha.[6]

Of the places in this group which were to become part of 'Arabia', nothing is known of Adraa in the first century, and all the (very slight) evidence for it as a city belongs to the second and third centuries. The two major places were Philadelphia and Gerasa. In the case of Philadelphia our best evidence for its self-representation as a Greek city in the first century comes from its coins, some of which are, like those of Tyre, 'pseudo-autonomous'—that is to say, they do not name or portray the Emperor. But in fact the earliest of these coins to carry dates, of AD 80/81, are contemporary with others which do name and represent Titus as Emperor and Domitian as 'Caesar'. Thereafter all the coins of the city, which start again under Hadrian, acknowledge the Emperor in the usual way. But the earliest coins are significant in various respects: in portraying a conventional set of Greek deities (Demeter, Pallas Athene, Nike, Herakles, and the Tyche-Fortune of the city), and (in one case) in identifying the coin as being 'of the Phil(adelpheis) of Koilē Syria'.[7] This form of description, which neither then nor later corresponded to any official

4. For a survey of the data then available see Schürer, *HJP* II, 130–160; for new archaeological evidence see R. H. Smith, "The Southern Levant in the Hellenistic Period", *Levant* 22 (1990), 123. For an interpretation of the evidence from the Imperial period see J. M. C. Bowsher, "Architecture and Religion in the Decapolis: A Numismatic Survey", *PEQ* 119 (1987), 62.

5. 2.1 above.

6. Pliny, *NH* V, 16/74. Pliny admits that different accounts of the Decapolis listed different cities. Since there is no reason to think either that there was a fixed list or that its members constituted some sort of league, the problems are not worth pursuing further.

7. A. Spijkerman, *The Coins of the Decapolis and Provincia Arabia* (1978), 242ff.

Roman geographical usage, was to receive further emphasis in the second century.

The Greek inscriptions of Philadelphia are very few, and unfortunately no date is attached to a potentially revealing one which shows the *boulē* and *dēmos* of the city honouring a man who was a *gymnasiarchos* and *bouleutēs* and (apparently) responsible for the construction of a temple of Herakles.[8] It may well date to the first century, and we need not seriously doubt that Philadelphia then possessed the normal constitutional structure of a Greek city. How far its urban framework had developed is more difficult to say; all the impressive remains of monumental buildings, of which the theatre is the most notable, seem to belong to the second and third centuries.[9]

Thanks to extensive excavations and a quite rich series of Greek inscriptions, a much better conception can be gained of the urban development of Gerasa in the early Empire.[10] But once again the self-portrayal of the city on its coins is of great significance. Coinage was issued briefly in AD 67/68, and here again 'pseudo-autonomous' coins and others representing Nero appeared simultaneously. The Emperor is named in the most minimal way, simply as NER(ōn), in strong contrast to the full titles of the later period. Artemis is portrayed, but not named, along with Zeus and Tyche. Here too, coinage did not re-start until the reign of Hadrian; then and afterwards the Emperor was honoured in the usual way.[11] More important, a combination of excavation and dated inscriptions makes it possible to see how some elements in the urban make-up of Gerasa changed significantly between the early and the later first century AD. As elsewhere, we can as yet have little notion of the urban character of the Hellenistic city. But in the case of the first temple of Olympian Zeus, though soundings indicate occupation of the hill on which it stands in the Hellenistic period, a brief, recently published inscription reveals that the original courtyard, built on terracing, was constructed in the reign of Tiberius: 'Year 90 (AD 27/28). Diodoros son of Zebsaos (Zebedas?), Gerasene, was the architect'.[12] The vaulted entrance-way concerned could not have been constructed without its retaining walls; so we have a clear reflection of a major project which might perhaps have been begun in the previous

8. P.-L. Gatier, *IGLS* XXI.2. *Inscriptions de la Jordanie: Région centrale* (1986), no. 29; the inscriptions of Amman are nos. 10–47.

9. See A. Segal, *Town Planning and Architecture in Provincia Arabia* (1988), 5ff. Not in *RPC* I.

10. All consideration of the city must start from the major work of C. H. Kraeling (n.2 above).

11. Spijkerman, *Coins of the Decapolis*, 156ff.; *RPC* I, 669.

12. J. Seigne, "Le sanctuaire de Zeus à Jerash: Éléments de chronologie", *Syria* 62 (1985), 287.

reign, under Augustus. What is more, we also have longer-known inscriptions which reveal both the operation of euergetism here in this early period and an equally early functioning of the Imperial cult in the city. One reads as follows:

> To Good Fortune. To Olympian Zeus for the safety of the *Sebastoi* (that is, *Augusti*) and the harmony of the *dēmos*, Zabdion son of Aristomachos, having been priest of Tiberius Caesar in year 85 (AD 22/23), gave from his own property for the construction of the temple 1000 *drachmai* out of piety.

In the 40s two further gifts are recorded, explicitly 'for the building of the temple of Olympian Zeus', made by two persons who are each described as having been gymnasiarch. They too allude to the 'harmony of the people'.[13] These inscriptions have a very considerable significance. They show the workings of typical Greek city institutions in a way which is very rare for this period anywhere in the Near East. They show beyond doubt that the temple was a local project, designed and paid for by local people. They show an institutionalised symbolic link to the Emperors (the two *Augusti* who had so far reigned, Augustus and Tiberius). But, perhaps most significantly, they show that the community explicitly chose to characterise 'their' Zeus as 'Olympian', a colourless term which could have been employed anywhere in the Greek world. As in so many other cases, we cannot be certain that a cult of a specifically local Zeus, or even 'Hadad' or Baalshamin ('Lord of the Heavens'), had not preceded this cult on the same site. But we can only *know* how people chose to identify this cult, at this time.

This is not the place for a detailed account of the evolution of the city: the construction of the earlier temple of Artemis, for which gifts were being made by AD 79/80; the south theatre, next to the temple of Zeus, from the same period; or the whole new city lay-out, implied by the construction of the north-west gate, associated with a new city wall (the gate is dated, as we have seen, by Ceionius Commodus as *legatus* of Syria in 79/80). The famous oval 'forum' (agora?) also seems to belong to this period. Thus, even if the most spectacular monuments, especially the later temple of Artemis in its vast *temenos* rising up to the west of the colonnaded main street, belong (as is typical) to the second century, there is ample evidence that monumental public building began early in the first century, and continued through it. If we needed any confirmation that first-century Gerasa had the normal institutions of a Greek city, it is provided by an inscription of AD 66/67 mentioning a *proedros*, a *dekaprōtos* for life, *archontes* and a *grammateus* (secretary).[14]

There is thus no reason to doubt that the public character of the two main

13. Welles, *Gerasa*, ins. nos. 2–4.
14. Welles, *Gerasa*, ins. no. 45.

cities which after 106 ceased to be part of the province of Syria and were joined to Arabia was unambiguously Greek. But before this attachment could take place, complex changes were required in the Hauran to the north. First (as it seems), after the death of Agrippa II in the 90s his territories must all have become temporarily part of Syria, briefly creating a single province from Commagene to the Decapolis. We have noted earlier Josephus' reference to the increased Roman taxation which now afflicted the Jewish settlement at Bathyra in Batanaea;[15] the same weight was presumably felt throughout the former royal domains. But a more profound shift also seems to have been taking place. This whole region had been a bilingual zone in which a distinctive local culture had been expressed, most notably at the cult-centre of Siaʻ, in both Greek and Aramaic. But in the second century and after, though Greek inscriptions emanating from local village communities are remarkably frequent and informative, Semitic-language inscriptions seem to die out (there are at any rate none from this area which are clearly dated to the second century or after).

We might take as a symbol of that shift the inscription on a basalt stele, of unknown provenance, in the museum at Suweida, dated by the sixteenth year of Domitian (AD 96). It is as clear an example as any of how a local group whose personal names were all purely Semitic could come to use Greek for communal purposes:

> Zaamanēs son of Thaimos, Nachaphos son of Zaamanēs, Nachaphos, Thaimos, Samethos, A[m]aiēlos, sons of Zobaidos, Samethos son of Thaimos, Zaamanēs, Nazaphos, Zobaidos sons of Azbodos, all twelve built the tomb on an equal basis, and (in order that) no one else should have a right to it except the associates listed above. Year 16 of Domitianus Caesar.[16]

It is only by implication that this inscription signals the disappearance of Agrippa II (and with that the end of the Herodian dynasty), and the arrival of provincial status, reflected in the mention of the Emperor. 'Provincial status' meant still, of course, being part of Syria, as it may have done when Cornelius Palma, the *legatus* of Syria who was responsible for the 'acquisition' of Arabia, was credited with the forethought *(pronoia)* which led to the building of an aqueduct in the Hauran.[17] That being so, it is probably also he who is referred to as governor in an inscription from Suweida in which the 'city' *(polis)* records the dedication of a *temenos* and *nymphaion* (fountain-

15. 2.2 above.

16. M. Dunand, *Le Musée de Soueida* (1934), no. 75. See 3.2 above.

17. Dunand, op. cit., no. 101 = *SEG* VII, no. 969 = *AE* (1936), no. 146; Le Bas-W., nos. 2296ff.

house), following the construction of an aqueduct under Trajan. That in itself is a sign of the sudden appearance of city-institutions and urban facilities in this period; as so often, we cannot clearly distinguish the fact from the development of the medium (Greek inscriptions) which represented it, both to contemporaries and to ourselves. All that is clear in this case is that the modern place-name reflects an ancient communal name, 'Soadēnoi' or 'Soadeēneis', and that it is not until the Tetrarchic period that we have firm evidence that the *polis* had acquired the name 'Dionysias'.[18] But long before that, this and other places had been absorbed into the province of 'Arabia', originally formed in 106 by the 'acquisition' of the kingdom of Nabataea.

11.4. THE NEW PROVINCE OF ARABIA

As we saw earlier, absolutely nothing is known of the campaign of 106, or of whether there was any resistance, either official or popular.[1] The apparently noiseless disappearance of the kingdom, after nearly three centuries, deserves emphasis. For both inscribed and perishable documents produced under it had emphasised the nature of the NBṬW as a 'people' ('M) and the beneficence of their kings towards them. In reality, the arrival of Roman rule might in principle have been seen as a liberation, as it was by some in Judaea in AD 6, or have been viewed by the people with indifference, as Josephus reports of Commagene in the early 70s. But whatever the truth, which we cannot know, we cannot take as insignificant the immediate disappearance of the ethnic identity of the NBṬW; so far as we can determine from dated documents, the term seems not to have remained in regular use. A single fragmentary inscription from En-Nemara, in the steppe east of the Jebel Hauran, records a cavalryman of the legion III Cyrenaica who was 'by race a *Nabas*'.[2]

What we find instead is a quite widespread and immediate use of a dating-system using the years of the province: at Oboda in the Negev already in the year 2; at Madaba in Moab in year 3. The former inscription is in Nabataean, and transliterates the standard Greek term for province, *eparcheia*: ŠNT TRTYN LHPRKY'. That from Madaba is bilingual, and speaks in Nabataean of 'year 3 of the province of Bostra' ŠNT TLT LHPRK(Y') BṢRH and in Greek of 'the third year of the *eparcheia*'.[3] As public documents, it is not to be expected that such inscriptions, brief as they were, would carry any sign of regret for the vanished kingdom. On the other hand they constitute evi-

18. Le Bas-W., no. 2305 = *IGR* III, no. 1273 (aqueduct); Le Bas-W., no. 2370 = *SEG* VII, no. 1233 ('Soadēnoi'); *IGR* III, no. 1275: [Σ]οαδεη[ν]εῖς, AD 149; *IGR* III, no 1278: ὅροι Διον[υσιά]δ[ος?], Tetrarchic; App. A, no. 37.

1. 3.2 above.

2. Le Bas-W., no. 2271 = *IGR* III, no. 1257: ἱππεὺς Κυρ. γένο[ς] Νάβας.

3. 3.2 above.

dence that the use of Nabataean itself continued; it did not in any case lie within the ambitions of ancient states to impose, or to bar, the use of particular languages.

Nonetheless, on the very limited evidence available to us, there are clear indications both that Nabataean did in fact tend to go out of use and that Greek, and the city institutions associated with it, came into much more regular currency, and did so within a few years of the establishment of the province. This progression is visible (or, still, partially visible) above all in the 'archive of Babatha', where the context is further complicated by the fact that the family concerned is Jewish. So, after the Nabataean property-documents of 94 and then of 99, under Rabbel II, we come immediately to a badly damaged deed of deposit in Greek of 110: 'In the consulship of Marcus Salvidienus Orfitus and Quintus Peducaeus Priscinus, and of the foundation of the province year the fifth, in Maoza of the Zoara district, I Joseph son of Joseph surnamed Zaboudos, inhabitant of Maoza acknowledge . . .'.[4] The transaction is a private one, between uncle and nephew. Yet the consuls holding office in Rome can be named, a penalty payable 'to Caesar' (not to the king) is specified, and Greek has imposed itself—except that some fragmentary letters at the beginning may indicate that this is a translation, [*he*]*rmē*[*neia*]. If so, we cannot be sure whether the translation will have been from Nabataean or Aramaic. For there then follows a series of documents dating between 119 and the early 120s which are written in Aramaic. That brings them into relationship with the Aramaic documents from Judaea of before and during the first revolt, discussed above; and of course also with the Aramaic and Hebrew documents of the Bar Kochba period, all of which come from the Judaean Desert, and some from the same cave in the Nahal Hever in which the archive of Babatha was deposited after some or all of the family had fled there.[5]

At this time, however, the persons concerned were still living at Maoza in what had been Nabataean territory and was now part of 'Arabia'. For them Nabataean must indeed have been an official language, and they reverted for a period to Aramaic. However, as these documents, like the Nabataean ones, have not been fully published, only a few partial reflections can be given here.[6] One at any rate is an extensive deed of gift of AD 120, in which Babatha's father grants all his property to his wife Miriam. As in other documents from the archive, the properties concerned are plots of agricultural land at Maoza, or Maoz 'Agaltain, defined by reference to neighbouring properties and with water-rights carefully specified (according to Yadin, it is here that the word

4. *P. Yadin* 5, trans. N. Lewis.
5. 10.2–3 above.
6. These documents are reported by Yadin in *IEJ* 12 (1962), 241–246, and in *Phoenix: Ex Oriente Lux* 6 (1959–1966), 232–234.

'wadi' makes its first recorded appearance). Here too a complex dating-system involving the consuls in Rome, the Emperor (Hadrian) and the era (year 15) of the province is employed. As so often in Semitic documents, it is the Greek equivalent of the Latin term which is transliterated, in this case *hypatoi,* 'consuls' (or *hypateia,* 'consulship'?): 'in the consulship of Lucius Catilius Severus for the second time and of Marcus Aurelius Antoninus' ('L HPṬWT LYQYS QṬWLYS SWRS TNYNWT' WMRQS 'WRLYS 'NṬWNYNS).

For social history, even this document will be surpassed in importance by the 'marriage-contract' of Babatha (in fact, like other such *ketubot,* a unilateral written declaration by the bridegroom), dated sometime in the early 120s. Only a few phrases from it have been published; but one, using wording almost identical to that attributed to this period in the *Mishnah,* graphically illustrates the consciousness of lives conducted under a particular ancestral law: 'You will be as a wife to me according to the law of Moses and the Jews' ([KDY]N MWŠH WYHWD'Y).[7]

Even in these documents, which in language and form might have been written in a wholly Jewish context in Judaea, the formal recognition both of the Empire and its institutions and of the province of Arabia is very prominent. But in the mid-120s another transformation, of a multidimensional kind, takes place. Above all, from 124 to the latest item, dated August 19, 132, the whole archive is in Greek, with some personal attestations and signatures of witnesses in Aramaic. In part this is because the transactions involved necessitated an interaction with the administration of the Roman province. We have seen already the importance of the census-return made by Babatha in 127, which ends by translating into Greek both Babatha's attestation (from Aramaic) and the *subscriptio* of the *praefectus equitum* (from Latin). We have also looked at those documents which concern places in Judaea, including a loan from a Roman centurion stationed at En-gedi.[8] But two further aspects of the archive deserve emphasis. One is that Greek is now used even to record private transactions which, at least at the moment concerned, involve no recourse to the governor of Arabia or his officials. Thus for instance in 128 Greek is used for an acknowledgment of a deposit; what is more, the document ends by recording that the strictly Roman procedure of question and answer (a *stipulatio*) had been used to confirm the transaction.[9] Equally significant is the 'marriage-contract' of the same year. This one is, however, of a quite different form from the previous one, for it records transactions be-

7. On Jewish marriage-contracts of this period see L. Archer, *Her Price Is Beyond Rubies: The Jewish Woman in Graeco-Roman Palestine* (1990), ch. 2 and App. 1.

8. 3.2 and 10.3 above.

9. *P. Yadin,* no. 17.

tween the father of the bride and the bridegroom. One change is explicitly described as being 'in accordance with the Greek custom'; the terms of the agreement are in fact such that it can be seen as a Greek, not Jewish, document. But like other documents, it also shows very clearly how we are confronted with the employment of Greek as an official language. For both the father and the bridegroom then add attestations in Aramaic in their own hands, after which the words 'I, Theënas, son of Simon, *librarios,* have written it' follow in Greek, with finally the names of six witnesses in Aramaic (and perhaps one in Greek).[10]

From the point of view of the overall evolution from 'Nabataea' to 'Arabia', however, the most striking revelation of the archive is the sudden appearance of Petra in the guise of a Greek city with a council. As the archive shows, Greek becomes relevant not only in relation to Roman officials but because transactions involving the orphaned son of Babatha are handled by this council. This body is first mentioned in 124: 'Verified exact copy of one item of guardianship from the minutes *(akta)* of the council *(boulē)* of Petra the metropolis, minutes displayed in the temple of Aphrodite in Petra.'[11] Petra later appears, more explicitly, as 'metropolis of Arabia'. Which of its temples was now identified officially as that of Aphrodite is not known; Yadin's suggestion that it was the Qasr el Bint itself is not impossible. In fact the title 'metropolis' had been granted immediately, and appears in a Greek inscription of 114 from the triumphal arch there.[12] The relevance of the Babatha archive is to illustrate, if tangentially, the fact that this transformation was no mere matter of form. There was now a *boulē,* which conducted its business in Greek. Hence there must also have been the normal annual magistrates. (Even so, it is noticeable that this copy is witnessed by four persons writing their names in Nabataean, and one in Greek). Later proceedings were similarly in Greek; but again the parties attest in Aramaic or Nabataean, including one of the two people appointed by the *boulē* as guardians for Babatha's son.[13]

Like earlier evidence, these attestations and signatures of witnesses are enough to dispose conclusively of any general notion that Nabataean was not a language in normal use among the population. If a form of Arabic was also spoken, there is no evidence that it was the *exclusive* language of daily speech. But into this context there has suddenly intruded a whole complex apparatus

---

10. *P. Yadin,* no. 18, see also N. Lewis, R. Katzoff and J. C. Greenfield in *IEJ* 37 (1987), 229. For the view that this is in its nature a Greek contract, see A. Wasserstein, "A Marriage Contract from the Province of Arabia Nova: Notes on Papyrus Yadin 18", *JQR* 80 (1989), 93. Cf. ch. 1 above.

11. *P. Yadin,* no. 12.

12. See Bowersock, *Roman Arabia,* 84–85.

13. *P. Yadin,* no. 15.

of Greek city-government, Roman officialdom and Greek law, with elements of Roman law. The role of interpreters, and of scribes who could write long documents in Greek, has become crucial.

At the very least the change from kingdom to province completely altered not merely the actual wider framework of power within which ordinary people lived, but the forms of allusion to that power used in daily life—and this irrespective of the language employed. But it is also significant that a clear progression from Nabataean—and initially, in the case of a Jewish family, from Aramaic—to Greek is clearly visible within an archive of documents of a similar type.

What also *seems* to be clear is that the arrival of provincial rule meant that at least some urban communities were re-classified as Greek cities almost immediately after the conquest, or acquisition, of the new provincial areas. For this process is visible both in the former Nabataean kingdom and in the former domains of Agrippa II. Petra had become 'Petra mētropolis' by 114, and 'Hadrianē Petra' by 131, when the term appears (paralleling the same appellation for Palmyra) in the Babatha archive.[14] Similarly, Bostra became 'Nea Traianē Bostra', therefore already in Trajan's reign; and, as we will see, Kanatha, previously in Agrippa's domains, is described as a *polis* in the same period. In this case, however, there are sporadic issues of coins (with the legends 'Kanata' or 'Kanatēnōn') in the first century, which imply that it was already regarded as a city: in 124 we find a Greek dedication there for the safety of the Emperor, made by five men with Semitic names, during the term as *agoranomos* of someone with a transliterated Roman name, 'M. Oulpios Philippikos'.[15] Equally, Rabbathmoba or 'Rabbathmoaba', the later 'Arsapolis' or 'Areopolis', is described as a *polis* in the Babatha archive, and evidently possessed at least one public building, a basilica. Since it was a place where the *legatus* of Arabia could be expected to give jurisdiction, we should probably assume that the Romans did indeed regard it as a *polis*. By contrast Charachmoba (Kerak), which was considerably nearer, does not appear in the archive. But under Elagabal it too issued coins, as in the same period did Rabbathmoba.[16]

Not all the scattered evidence on this process is needed here; but it is relevant that a Greek inscription from the Siq at Petra was put up by a man who describes himself as '*panegyriarchēs* (president of a festival) of (the) *Adraēnoi*'.[17] Adraa too minted coins from the reign of Antoninus Pius to that of

14. *P. Yadin*, no. 25, l. 11.

15. *IGR* III, no. 1224. For the few coins, *RPC* I, 668–669.

16. *P. Yadin*, nos. 16 and 25 (jurisdiction); Spijkerman, *Coins of the Decapolis*, 108–109; 262–263.

17. F. Zayadine and Z. T. Fiema, "Roman Inscriptions from the Siq at Petra", *ADAJ* 30 (1986), 199 = *SEG* XXXVI, no. 1388.

Gallienus—when, as we saw, its walls were being built with Imperial help.[18] But there are more complex issues here. For both the dedication at Petra and some of the coins represent a 'betyl', a rounded, aniconic stone evidently portrayed as an object of worship. As we will see, this feature is known elsewhere in the area; such coin-types, deliberately chosen, must be indicative of conscious communal identities. Other perspectives were of course open to third parties: to Eusebius, Adraa, 'a famous city *(polis)* of Arabia', was also the place 'where Og the giant king of Bashan was killed, and all his followers'.[19]

We must presume that all these places now had annual magistrates, and city-councils. Occasionally there is clear confirmation, as in the inscription mentioning a town-councillor from Madaba—*bouleutēs Madabēnōn*.[20] Perhaps more significant are the two inscriptions which show people who give themselves a dual identity—from Canatha as their 'city' and from the village, or smaller settlement, from which they came. One is the Sithros son of Rabbēlos, who evidently came from Sia' and calls himself a 'Sēnos Kanōthēnos', a 'Seēnian Kanothian'.[21] But much the most remarkable expression of the dual (or in some sense triple) identities thus created is the famous third-century inscription in Greek and Latin from Trévoux in France.[22] It is the epitaph of a trader who died there, and who is described first as an 'Atheilēnos' or as coming from the *vicus Athelanus*. This must be the present-day village of 'Atil, a little over 3 km west of Qanawat. But the deceased, Thaimos also called Iulianos, son of Saados, is also described as a citizen and town-councillor of the *Kanōthaioi*, or in Latin 'decurio Septimiano(rum) Canotha(norum)'. We can take it that both Sia' and Atheila were villages in the territory of Canatha: as almost everywhere, a 'city' represented merely one agglomeration more prestigious than others. Like Sia', Atheila could in fact boast its own temples, built in the second and third centuries.

But in Greek, though not in Latin, Thaimos' native city is described as being 'in Syria'. Given the distant location of the inscription, this might be mere vagueness. It was still a choice, however. As will be seen in a moment, self-ascription to 'Syria' clearly could have real significance for cities in this region. Alternatively, a quite different identity could be represented. Thus when someone else from the same town was putting up an epitaph on the island of Thasos to his son, who had died there, also in the third century, he

18. Spijkerman, *Coins of the Decapolis*, 58ff.; cf. 4.3 above.

19. Eusebius, *Onom.* 84, 7.

20. *IGLS* XXI.2, no. 64: ἐγὼ Ζαιδαλλας Πετριγένους βουλευτοῦ.. Μηδαβ[ηνῶν].

21. *SEG* VII, no. 989. For the complex issues of the extent of the city's territory, see M. Sartre, "Le territoire de Canatha", *Syria* 58 (1981), 343.

22. *IGR* I, no. 25 = *IG* XIV, no. 2532 = *CIL* XIII, no. 2448 = *ILS*, no. 7529. For 'Atil and its temples see D. Sourdel, *Les cultes du Hauran* (1952), esp. 100. For a photograph of one, Dentzer, *Hauran*, 291.

described himself as an 'Arab of the city of Septimia Kanōtha'.[23] This description is perhaps more curious than might appear. The Nabataeans, so far as our evidence tells us, had never identified themselves explicitly as 'Arabs', even though others had. And in any case Canotha or Canatha had not been part of the kingdom at any time after 23 BC. Moreover, it seems to have been only under Septimius Severus, whose name was now attached to that of the city, that the northern Hauran ceased to be part of 'Syria Phoenice' and become part of 'Arabia'.[24] How people in this region now identified themselves is thus a highly complex question.

The predominant factor in the construction of personal and communal identities must be seen as the spread of city-statuses after the formation of the province. Apart from the cases singled out immediately above, coins in Greek were issued at some point in the second or third century also by the following cities: Abila, Capitolias, Dium, Esbous, Gadara, Hippos and Pella. In the early third century Petra and Bostra underwent a further transformation, into Roman *coloniae,* and were followed in the 240s by Philippopolis, newly founded by Philip 'the Arab'. There remained only the transformation of Sakkaia into 'Maximianopolis' in the Tetrarchic period.[25]

At one level it is possible to see the progress of 'urbanisation' (too all-embracing a term) as one which very significantly reduced the previously stark contrasts between the three politically separate regions of the first century: the Decapolis, the Herodian domains east of the Jordan Valley, and Nabataea. All were now studded with cities which it would be better to describe as 'Graeco-Roman' than simply as 'Greek'.

This process, however, was not entirely uniform in all areas. Those places in the Negev which were in physical terms towns—Elusa, Oboda (Avdat) and Mampsis—did not produce coins and are very little known. Inscriptions from Oboda do, however, cast some partial light on the culture of this region in the third century, showing, as we would expect (and just as in the Hauran), that Greek was now a natural medium of public expression for the local population.[26] So for instance there is the epitaph of a woman called 'Aurēlia Moulchē, daughter of Abdomanchos, also called Amlaiphos', who was born in 160 and died in 241. Or, more strikingly, there are several references to 'Zeus Obodas', of which the most revealing is dated to AD 293/294:

23. *IGR* I, no. 839; see L. Robert, "L'épitaphe d'un Arabe à Thasos", *Hellenica* II (1946), 47: Ἄραψ πόλεως Σεπτιμίας Κάνωθα.

24. See E. Kettenhofen, "Zur Nordgrenze der *provincia Arabiae* im 3. Jahrhundert n. Chr.", *ZDPV* 97 (1981), 62.

25. Millar, "Roman *Coloniae*", 51–55. Cf. 4.2 above.

26. See A. Negev, *The Greek Inscriptions from the Negev* (1981), no. 10 (Aurēlia Moulchē); no. 13 (and cf. nos. 1d, 3, 4 and 6), with A. Negev, *IEJ* 36 (1986), 59–60 (Zeus Obodas); '193/4 C.E.' here is a slip for 293/294.

To Good Fortune. O Zeus Obodas, help Eirēnaios, building the tower with good omens in the year 188, through Ouaelos the builder, a Petrean, and Eutychēs.

The reference might be simply to a local Zeus of (the city of) Oboda. But in fact the evidence for the cult of 'Obodas the god', continuing from the royal to the provincial period, is quite consistent. Whether we should take this as something more than the observation of a long-established local cult is another question; but it *could* be seen as a very rare, almost unique, indication of retrospective loyalty to a national dynasty. It is at least very suggestive that in his *Arabica*, which seems to date to the fourth century AD, a little-known writer named Ouranios identified the place Oboda as 'where Obodēs, the king, whom they worship as a god, is buried'.[27]

As will appear later, the Nabataean language itself remained in use at least until the fourth century, though the evidence is very clearly limited to the outer fringes of the former Nabataean zone. In Oboda itself there is so far no example later than 125. The formerly Nabataean Negev certainly remained an area of established settlement, and seems if anything to have developed further, like the marginal steppe zone east of the Orontes, in the Christian period. But in terms of Graeco-Roman, pagan urbanism, it is probably correct to see it, in this period, as a backwater.

The same seems in general to be true of the whole southern region from Petra south to the Red Sea, in spite of the developing Roman military presence. On our evidence Petra, too, hardly developed as a city after the end of the monarchy. If the relatively plain rock-cut tomb used for the Roman *legatus* of Arabia, Sextius Florentinus, in the 120s was actually cut in that period rather than earlier (which is not quite certain), it would count as one of the very few datable monuments of Graeco-Roman Petra.[28] The city seems to have lived on as a smallish provincial town like any other, with little development and hence very little trace of the usual building-inscriptions. But, for instance, one of a number of Greek inscriptions on statue-bases from the *temenos* of the Qasr el Bint shows the city, described as a *mētropolis* and *mētrokolōnia*, honouring a *procurator* of two Emperors through the two *stratēgoi* (that is, in Latin, the *duumviri* of the *colonia*).[29]

Though Petra thus retained an honoured status, it is perhaps not misleading to take it that the major evolution of urban life (and urban-style life conducted in villages) took place in the more fertile zone which stretched

27. *FGrH* 675, F.24; for the date see J. M. I. West, *HSCP* 78 (1974), 282–284. The thesis summarised here seems unfortunately to have remained unpublished.

28. For the very slight evidence of construction in the Roman period see J. Mackenzie, *The Architecture of Petra* (1990), 38–56.

29. Millar, "Roman *Coloniae*", 51.

north from the Wadi Hesa (or from roughly opposite the south end of the Dead Sea) through Moabitis, Auranitis, Batanaea (an ill-defined zone), Gaulanitis, the lava-field of Trachonitis to Damascus itself. In the zone immediately south of Damascus, it is true, there were, even in the third century, strikingly few places which counted as cities: none indeed between Caesarea Panias and Damascus, both lying at the foot of Mount Hermon, and the cities which lay on a line stretching roughly from the Sea of Galilee eastwards to the northern and north-western slopes of the Jebel Hauran: Hippos, Adraa, Souedias, Canatha, and eventually Philippopolis and Maximianopolis. But, as we saw in connection with Judaea/Syria Palaestina, Gaulanitis (the Golan) was marked by the same network of substantial stone-built villages as Batanaea, Trachonitis (especially round the fringes of the lava-field) and the Hauran.[30] It is perhaps the area between Trachonitis and Damascus which has for some reason been the least explored. But here too we can catch glimpses of a complex cultural and religious history, conducted in village contexts. Take the village which Eusebius calls Chōba, in the territory of Damascus, 'in which are those Jews who believe in Christ and are called Ebiōnaioi';[31] or the Jewish 'city' *(polis)* of Nineuē, which Eusebius locates 'at the corner of Arabia'—that is, Nawa in Batanaea, west of Trachonitis;[32] or the *kōmē* of Lebaba (the modern Deir Ali, between the lava-field and Damascus), where in 318/319 a *sunagōgē* (church?) was erected by followers of the Marcionite heresy.[33] Other villages in this period were still firmly pagan. At the site of the modern village of Deir el Leben, on the southern edge of the lava-field, a temple was erected in AD 320 to 'the lord and unconquered Sun God Aumos' by two men whose self-description perhaps illustrates more vividly than any other document the social and cultural complexity of this region: 'Kassi(o)s Malichathos of the *kōmē* of Reimea (and the) tribe *(phylē)* of (the) Chasētēnoi, and Paulos Maximinos of the *kōmē* Merdocha (and the) tribe *(phylē)* of (the) Audēnoi'.[34]

This scatter of roughly contemporary evidence from the northern zone will be enough to illustrate the facts both that a network of villages existed here as elsewhere and that the varied currents of competing religious systems were felt here as they were in cities. But we should not pass over, as being almost too obvious, the fact that the activities of this network of villages were now given publicity in Greek inscriptions. In the entire area from the southern

30. For the Golan, 10.4 and 11.1 above.

31. Eusebius, *Onom.* 172, 1. It is not worth pursuing here the confusing Christian references to 'Ebionites' or to Choba/Kochba.

32. Eusebius, *Onom.* 136, 1: περὶ τὴν γωνίαν τῆς Ἀραβίας. See Dentzer, *Hauran*, 415.

33. Le Bas-W., no. 2558.

34. Le Bas-W., no. 2393 (= OGIS, no. 619), cf. 2394–2395. See D. Sourdel, *Les cultes du Hauran à l'époque romaine* (1952), 54ff.

part of the territory of Damascus to the northern Hauran, not a single inscription is known from the Hellenistic period. The earliest known inscriptions are the Greek-Aramaic(?) bilinguals of the first century BC from Sia' and Suweida. But by the early fourth century the public use of Semitic languages had effectively disappeared. Greek was now the common language of public expression used by these village populations.

The same is true of the central area, from the northern Hauran south to Moab, where this same dense network of villages was also marked, in varying degrees, by places with the status of *polis*. Five issues need to be touched on here, but no more than sketched, for this is one of the most intensively and successfully studied regions of the ancient world: the way in which many of these cities, in their coins and inscriptions, seem explicitly to have disassociated themselves from their 'Arabian' environment; the opposite tendency, by which some of them deliberately displayed on their coinage an attachment to aniconic (Arab?) cults; the role here of Greek-style games and festivals; the relation of city and village, or rather the apparent independence of villages; and finally, as a major question which needs to be treated separately, the interplay between the settled population and the tribal groups which inhabited the steppe to the east.

As regards the first issue, we saw much earlier how Scythopolis, situated across the Jordan in the Plain of Jezreel, might describe itself programmatically as 'one of the Greek cites of Koilē Syria'.[35] This very vague geographical term had indeed had no very precise application (except that it was always used of the southern area around Mount Lebanon and Anti-Lebanon) until Septimius Severus, with remarkable perversity, chose it as the official name of the *northern* half of Syria as a separate province.[36] The cities of the Decapolis, however, showed a very determined attachment to this expression.[37] Thus an inscription from Philadelphia of AD 189/190 describes it as 'the city of the Philadelpheis in Koilē Syria'.[38] The same term is used on the coins of Philadelphia from the first century AD through to the last known coins of the city, issued under 'Elagabal' (218–222)—thus after the creation of Severus' new province, far to the north. It is also used on the coins of Abila, from Marcus Aurelius to Elagabal, on the short-lived coinage of Dium under Elagabal, on some of those of Gadara from Marcus Aurelius to Elagabal, and on those of Pella under Caracalla and Elagabal.[39] To whatever Roman *provincia* these

35. Ch. 1 above.

36. 3.4 above.

37. The point is merely sketched here; it will be the subject of a detailed study by Alla Stein of Tel-Aviv University.

38. *IGLS* XXI.2, no. 23.

39. Spijkerman, *Coins of the Decapolis*, 242ff. (Philadelphia); 48ff. (Abila); 116ff. (Dium); 126ff. (Gadara); 210ff. (Pella).

cities (other than Philadelphia) belonged at successive stages, which is not always clear, it was of course certainly not Severus' 'Koilē Syria'. In all cases the use of this term must imply some conscious assertion of an identity which preceded the rearrangement of 106. It is surely significant that no such claim is made by places which had been under either the Nabataean kings or the later Herods.

By contrast, there are elements in the city-coinage of the region which reflect certain strands from within Nabataean religious iconography.[40] Nabataean art had certainly not rejected systematically all use of representational motifs; a counter-example is provided, for instance, by the statuary which adorned the facade of the Khasneh. But its iconographical repertoire had included low-relief carvings of non-representational *stelai,* which in Nabataean inscriptions are labelled MSB (Hebrew MSBH), NSB or NSBH; or similarly low-relief portrayals of the rounded or oblong objects conventionally called 'betyls'. As we have seen, Classical writers were aware of the use of aniconic cult-objects in this region; it was specifically reported that at Petra 'Theos Ares' (Dusares) was worshipped in the form of a square black stone.[41] Moreover, as was also noted earlier, the Greek inscription of a *panegyriarchēs* from Adraa, set up in the Siq at Petra, is accompanied by a low-relief carving of a rounded (not oblong) cult-object. What seems to be just the same cult-object appears on some coins of Adraa, explicitly identified as 'Dousarēs, god of the Adraēnoi'.[42] Comparable, though not identical, representations appear on coins of Bostra, Charachmoba and Madaba (all of course formerly within the Nabataean kingdom). But in all cases these coin-series also use standard Graeco-Roman anthropomorphic portrayals of deities—and, paradoxically, the coinage of Petra uses these consistently. In other words, in a manner comparable to the representation of 'Elagabal' as a black stone at Emesa, this was one strand in the religious and artistic culture of the region, and one which it proved possible to combine with the more conventional divine images which the cities also used on their coinage. What is more, whatever outside observers might suppose about the objects worshipped by 'Arabs', the coinage of Bostra under Commodus could use a representational bust of Dusares, labelled 'Dousarēs of the Bostrēnoi'.[43] The use of aniconic images was certainly a distinctive and significant element in the public art of the cities of this region; but it was not adhered to rigidly.

Whatever the significance of this regional form of cult-object, it is clear

40. For what follows see the very suggestive study by J. Patrich, *The Formation of Nabataean Art: Prohibition of a Graven Image among the Nabataeans* (1990).

41. Ch. 1 above.

42. Patrich, op. cit., 70ff.

43. Spijkerman, *Coins of the Decapolis,* 74–75.

that it co-existed with the holding of Greek games in many of the cities. As mentioned before, it is one sign of the combination of very distinctive local elements with a remarkable malleability of communal identities that it is (only) the legends on the third-century coins of Bostra as a *colonia* which tell us that the city now held games entitled 'Actia Dusaria'. But we hardly need in any case to rely on such tangential evidence. Aerial photographs of Bostra show with perfect clarity the hippodrome laid out to the south of the city; and its theatre, of the second century, used as a fortress in the medieval period, remains the best preserved from the entire Roman Empire.[44]

Similar athletic and theatrical festivals were certainly held at Gerasa, where there were two theatres and a hippodrome; a much-quoted Greek inscription of the world-wide association of actors reflects the establishment there of an annual festival *(agōn)* for the safety of the Emperor Trajan. Athletic festivals took place also at Scythopolis and Philadelphia; but not, so far as we know, at Petra or anywhere else except (eventually) Bostra from within the former kingdom.[45] However, that may be merely a sign of our ignorance: as with the theatre at Palmyra, what use was made of the two theatres at Petra in the second and third centuries remains a mystery.

Poor as our evidence is, it is perhaps not wrong to suppose that at the level of city life some tension continued to be felt between standard Graeco-Roman customs and others, whether we label them 'Arab' or not. If we were to follow the late-fourth-century account of Epiphanius (one of the most unreliable and fantastic of writers), the cult of a goddess conceived of as a virgin was conducted in the 'Arab dialect' at both Petra and Elusa, and embraced her son 'Dousarēs', 'that is, the only son of the lord'.[46] But, as is obvious, he is seeking alleged pagan models for the birth of Jesus. We do not know whether 'Arab' elements had in fact become predominant in fourth-century Petra. In Elusa, in spite of Jerome's report of how Hilarion encountered there *Saraceni* speaking a Semitic language, there is quite clear evidence that Greek culture persisted in the late Empire.[47]

Paradoxically, it was at the level of village life that the 'Hellenisation' brought about by Roman rule had the most profound effects. 'Hellenisation' is, however, not quite the right word, although it does fit the exclusive use of Greek in local documents of the second century and onwards, and

44. For the aerial photograph see Segal, *Town Planning*, fig. 109, and Kennedy and Riley, *RDF,* 124; for the theatre see H. Finsen, *Le levé du théâtre romain à Bostra, Syrie* (1972).

45. Welles, in *Gerasa*, ins. no. 192. For the other cities Moretti, *IAG*, nos. 72, 85.

46. Epiphanius, *Pan.* 51, 22, 9–11.

47. 10.4 above. See Ph. Mayerson, "The City of Elusa in the Literary Sources of the Fourth–Sixth Centuries", *IEJ* 33 (1983), 247. As a Greek inscription records, there was a theatre there in the fifth century. See A. Negev, *Greek Inscriptions from the Negev* (1981), no. 25, and J. Bingen, "Sur une dédicace protobyzantine d'Elusa (Negev)", *ZPE* 53 (1983), 123.

the construction of quite elaborate and richly decorated public buildings and temples in and by villages. But the prevalence of Latin personal names and the extensive reflection in the inscriptions of the presence of locals who were veterans of the Roman army means that 'Graeco-Roman', if there were an appropriate abstract noun for the process, would be a better description.

The villages of the Hauran and the neighbouring areas have been intensively studied, largely through their inscriptions, and only a few general points need be made here.[48] First, it is the hill-country of the Jebel Hauran and the fringes of the lava-field of Trachonitis which have provided the greatest density of inscriptions. Relatively little is known of village life in the plain (the Nuqra) between Bostra and Adraa. Second, town-councillors (bouleutai) of the cities of the region do appear in the inscriptions. But they do so as individuals, performing local functions. It would be virtually impossible to guess from the inscribed records of building projects and other activities undertaken by village communities that they were sub   to any control by cities; and though some must in fact (like Sia' and Atheila mentioned above) have lain in the city territories, it is by no means certain that they all did. Some of the villages of the lava-field laid claim to the superior title of mētrokōmia, 'mother-village', though this does not necessarily imply any recognised formal status. But we have seen earlier how Iulius Saturninus, as legatus of Syria in the 180s, addressed to the 'Phaenēsioi, mētrokōmia of Trachōn' a letter about exactions by official travellers, which was then inscribed on an elaborate public building there, now destroyed.[49]

Out of the large crop of those distinctively regional documents, it may be sufficient to quote a couple of examples of inscriptions reflecting the communal functioning of these villages. One, from Kefr-Laha, illustrates how conscious villagers in these remote localities might be of the wider framework of the Empire. It was put up 'for the safety' of Maximinus (235–238) and his son, and mentions the legatus of the province and even the consuls of 236. It records that the villagers (kōmētai) established something (evidently a public building) out of their own funds, for the public benefit, and (also) by the

48. See, e.g., G. M. Harper, "Village Administration in the Roman Province of Syria", YCS 1 (1928), 105; F. Villeneuve, "L'économie rurale et la vie des campagnes dans le Hauran antique (Iᵉʳ siècle av. J.-C.–VIIᵉ siècle ap. J.-C.): Une approche", in Dentzer, Hauran, 63; M. Sartre, "Le peuplement et le développement du Hauran antique à la lumière des inscriptions", ibid., 189; H. I. MacAdam, "Epigraphy and Village Life in Southern Syria during the Roman and Early Byzantine Periods", Berytus 31 (1983), 103; idem, Studies in the History of the Roman Province of Arabia: The Northern Sector (1986); M. Sartre, "Villes et villages du Hauran (Syrie) du Iᵉʳ au VIᵉ siècle", in Frézouls (ed.), Sociétés urbaines, 239 (on which what follows mostly depends). See now also D. F. Graf, "The Syrian Hauran", JRA 5 (1992), 450.

49. 3.3 above.

generosity of several people with transliterated Latin names, each described as *ouetranos*. The project was carried out in the *stratēgeia,* evidently a local office, of another man with a Latin name, Oulpios Skaurianos.[50]

Construction continued in these villages into the fourth century. At the site of the modern Druse village of Orman near Salhad, and some 27 km east of Bostra, a basilica and gate were erected in AD 330 by a group of 'supervisors' *(pronoētai)* whose names perfectly illustrate the way in which projects like this were the work of local groups exposed to wider influences: Boēthos son of Proklos, Nestor son of Saddathos, Azizos son of Oulpianos and Thiemos son of Asmathos.[51]

It seems beyond doubt that the network of substantial villages, built in the very distinctive local black basalt, which came to characterise the lava-field and the Jebel Hauran as the Imperial period progressed, represented their attraction to a Graeco-Roman urban, or sub-urban, style of life and communal organisation. Whatever the spoken language, or languages, of these villages may have been, their public written language was Greek.

This phenomenon raises a difficult question: had Aramaic and Nabataean in fact died out in this area? We have noted earlier the only known perishable documents in Nabataean, and there is no evidence to suggest that there was ever a Nabataean literature, any more than there was a Palmyrene one. But a scatter of Nabataean inscriptions from the second, third and fourth centuries, mainly from the outer fringes of the former Nabataean area (Sinai and the Hedjaz), is enough to demonstrate that the language was still known, and could be written.[52] The significance of that fact for the culture of the region as a whole remains quite unclear. Except for the Jewish Aramaic inscriptions from neighbouring Gaulanitis, there is nothing to show that the local Aramaic was still written in the northern region. In other words the exceptionally complex linguistic history of the various areas which became part of Roman Arabia, the Hauran above all, leaves many important questions unanswered.[53]

50. Le Bas-W., no. 2399.

51. Le Bas-W., no. 2044 = *PAES* III, no. 701.

52. For the second century, e.g., *CIS* II.1, no. 1325 (year 45 of the province, AD 150/151); 164 (year 85, 190/191), both from Sinai; for the third century see A. Negev, *IEJ* 17 (1967), 250ff. (Sinai); for the fourth century see, e.g., *CIS* II.1, no. 333 (year 200), and A. Jaussen and R. Savignac, *Mission archéologique en Arabie* II (1914), no. 386 (year 201), both from el-'Ela in the Hedjaz, AD 305/306 and 306/307; R. Stiehl, "A New Nabataean Inscription", in R. Stiehl and H. E. Stier (eds.), *Beiträge zur Alten Geschichte und deren Nachleben* II (1970), 87 (year 251, AD 356/357), apparently from Hegra (Medain Saleh); two persons are referred to as RYŠ ḤGR' and RYŠ TYM' respectively.

53. For an exploration of this complex question see R. Contini, "Il Hawrān preislamico: Ipotesi di storia linguistica", *Felix Ravenna,* ser. 4, 1–2 (1987), 25.

But the fact of the continued use of Nabataean on the outer limits of the provincial area raises specific problems about the connections between the settled zone and the steppe.

11.5. THE NOMADIC PRESENCE

Two features of the epigraphy of the Hauran area in the provincial period are of particular importance. Both bear on the same fundamental question, the nature of the connection between the settled population and the peoples of the steppe to the east. It should be stressed that, as always, our knowledge is wholly dependent on the structure of our evidence: in this case the fact that building in extremely durable basalt did take place in this area and was accompanied by the importation of the 'epigraphic habit'. The same question arises in principle along the whole of the 'desert frontier', from Aila to the Tigris. But elsewhere we have h   ly any comparable evidence.

The first feature of these inscriptions is that some of them show two different forms of communal identity, by locality (village) and by group, often explicitly described as 'tribe' *(phylē)*. As we saw earlier, 'tribal' groupings are present from the very beginning of the inscribed record, in the form of the tribe Obaishat ('L 'BYŠT) connected with the building of a temple at Siaʻ; it is significant that this grouping is also named in some Safaitic graffiti from the steppe to the east.[1] Although, for the reasons given, almost all our evidence on 'tribal' groupings present in both the provincial area and the steppe comes from the Hauran, one relevant document comes from Madaba, the bilingual inscription dated by year 3 of the province.[2] The person recorded here as constructing a tomb for his son is identified in the Nabataean text as 'Abgar who is called Eision son of Mnʻt from the tribe 'Amrat' ('BGR DY MTQR' 'YŠYWN BR MNʻT DY MN 'L 'MRT). This affiliation, which is passed over in silence in the Greek text, is, however, found also in the same form ('L 'MRT) in Safaitic graffiti from Qasr Burqu, just over 100 km east of the Hauran, at a point in the rocky basalt steppe where water collects,[3] as well as at other sites. Two further graffiti come from the area of the Roman fort at Deir el Kahf on the Roman frontier road leading south from the eastern fringe of the Hauran.[4] Given the identity of the terms used, we have to assume that the documents refer to the same group. Furthermore, as J. T. Milik has

1. 11.1 above.

2. Published by J. T. Milik, *Syria* 35 (1958), 243, no. 6 (*IGLS* XXI.2, no. 118); for the Safaitic material see J. T. Milik, "La tribu des Bani 'Amrat en Jordanie de l'époque grecque et romaine", *ADAJ* 24 (1980), 41.

3. See Kennedy and Riley, *RDF,* 71–73.

4. See 5.1 above, text to n.44.

suggested, this may perhaps be the same group as 'the sons of Iambri from Madaba' with whom Jonathan Maccabaeus had come into conflict in the second century BC.[5]

If we find that persons from the steppe and others at Madaba identified themselves as belonging to the same tribal grouping, it does not follow that we have to think of a nomadic people passing in and out of the area of settled agriculture. It may be that this is an example of the well-attested phenomenon of 'dimorphism', whereby both styles of life were followed by people who nonetheless saw themselves as sharing a common 'tribal' identity.[6] Both possibilities, which are not mutually exclusive, have to be borne in mind in considering the extensive reflection of 'tribal' or group attachments from the Hauran.[7]

Two further examples may suffice to illustrate the role of 'tribes' in this area (we have already encountered a man from Deir el-Leben, identified both by his village and by his tribe, 'the *phyl[ē]* of the Audēnoi').[8] One is a brief Greek inscription from a temple at Hebran: '(The) *phy(lē)* of (the) Mozaiedē-noi (honours) Aur. Antōnios Sabeinos, *ouetranos*, the *patrōn*, out of gratitude, year 109' (AD 215/216).[9] The inscription is noteworthy not only for illustrating the role of Roman veterans in local society, but for bringing together two transliterated Latin terms with a Semitic 'tribal' name, all transposed into Greek. Nothing else is known of this tribe, unless it is to be identified with the 'L MŠ'YDW referred to in a Nabataean inscription from Bostra. In many other cases we cannot tell whether a Semitic group-name which appears without the term *phylē* is intended to refer to a 'tribe' or to a community defined by its village. This is the case, for instance, with a brief Greek inscription from the village of Rama: 'To Odainathos son of Saouados, formerly *stratēgos* of (the) Aouidēnoi, and formerly *phylarchos*, Thomalechē his wife and Saoudos *(sic)* his father set up (this)'.[10] Is the first post, as *stratēgos*, that of another village official who had held an annual office, or that of the chief of the 'tribe' of 'Aouidēnoi? And if so, how does it relate to the second post,

5. I *Macc.* 9, 36: οἱ υἱοὶ Ιαμβρι οἱ ἐκ Μηδαβα.

6. See, e.g., F. M. Donner, *The Early Islamic Conquests* (1981), ch. 1.

7. For recent studies of this evidence see, e.g., M. Sartre, "Tribus et clans dans le Hauran antique", *Syria* 59 (1982), 77; H. I. MacAdam, *Studies in the History of the Roman Province of Arabia* (1986), 101ff.; also D. Graf, "Rome and the Saracens", in T. Fahd (ed.), *L'Arabie préislamique et son environnement historique et culturel* (1989), on pp. 358ff.

8. 11.4, text to n.34. For the Audēnoi, MacAdam, op. cit. (n.7), 121, and Graf, op. cit. (n.7), 361–363, who identifies them with the tribe 'Awidh, known from Safaitic graffiti.

9. Le Bas-W., no. 2287, also for the Nabataean inscription.

10. Le Bas-W., no. 2236; MacAdam, 132. For the reading φυλαρχήσαντι, which is hypothetical but convincing, see Ch. Clermont-Ganneau, *RAO* 5 (1903), 147–148. Graf, loc. cit. (n.8), takes this as a further reference to the 'Awidh.

'phylarchos'? The conventions of the Graeco-Roman honorific inscription tend to mean that for us the entire background remains obscure.

On either interpretation this document has to be seen as closely related to a brief series of inscriptions, all in Greek, honouring individuals as '*stratēgos* of the *nomades*', or 'of the camps of the *nomades*'; another is called '*syndikos* (advocate) of the *nomades*'. All come, significantly, from the eastern slopes of the Jebel Hauran. One at least is early, for it dates to the reign of Agrippa II. Another should be of the second century, for the epitaph is that of 'Adrianos also called Soaidos (son of ?) Malechos, *ethnarchos, stratēgos nomadōn*'.[11] It is quite clear from the names of the individuals, where they survive, that they are local men. But the inscriptions will not tell us whether these are royal or provincial officials appointed from outside to control the *nomades,* or whether these titles are Greek ways of expressing the position of a tribal 'chief'. All that is certain, in either case, is that the inscriptions reflect an area of contact and interchange between the Graeco-Roma   ulture of the settled region and the communal structures of the nomads. Both in the reference to a *syndikos* and in another inscription in which 'the *nomades* of the province *(ethnos)*' honour a Roman *legatus,* a diplomatic relationship is clearly implied.[12] There is nothing in *these* documents, however, to suggest any parallel to the formal alliances of the late Empire with major 'Saracen' tribal groupings. The context is a local one.

Whatever the real nature of these contacts, they must have owed their wider context to the simultaneous extension eastwards of settled habitation and of Roman forts, linked by a road running down the east side of the Jebel Hauran. An example of both processes is the ancient village on a site now called Diyatheh on the eastern flank of the Jebel, where in the third and fourth centuries, as it seems, there grew up a settlement of over 100 houses, immediately next to a Roman *castellum,* and with access to a wadi for the water needed for cultivation. It may be that here, as perhaps elsewhere, the extension of cultivation and settlement functioned rather to exclude the *nomades* than to produce an economic or social 'symbiosis'.[13]

It would be absurd to pretend that our limited evidence allows confident answers to these wider questions. But the extension of the area of settled habitation, and the growth of individual settlements, is an undeniable fact, no-

11. Le Bas-W., no. 2112 (Agrippa II); 2196 (Adrianos); *PAES* III, no. 752 (camps of *nomades*); *AAES* III, no. 383 *(syndikos).* See esp. M. Sartre, *Trois études sur l'Arabie romaine* (1982), 121ff.: "Les nomades et l'Empire en Arabie". See now also Ph. Mayerson, "The Use of the Term *Phylarchos* in the Roman-Byzantine East", *ZPE* 88 (1991), 291.

12. Le Bas-W., no. 2203: οἱ ἀπὸ ἔθνους νομάδων *(sic).*

13. So F. Villeneuve, "Citadins, villageois, nomades: Le cas de la *provincia Arabia* (II^c–IV^c s. après J.-C.)", *DHA* 15 (1989), 119.

where better exemplified than at the remarkable site of Umm el-Jimal, whose black basalt houses of the late Roman period still stand in the plain 25 km south-south-west of Bostra, and a short distance east of the Via Nova Traiana between Bostra and Philadelphia.[14] It thus lies on a dry but cultivable plain, roughly at the limit of the 200-mm-rainfall zone, and well within the eventual network of Roman forts, along the roads to Azraq oasis.

There had been some Nabataean settlement here, though (as it seems) on a site slightly to the east; the known Nabataean inscriptions of this area lie within the marginal zone which in some sense connected the central Nabataean area with the southern Hauran around Bostra. For at Umm al Quttain (el Qottein), some 25 km to the east of Umm el-Jimal, there is a considerable series of inscriptions: nine Nabataean, one Nabataean-Greek bilingual, twenty-three Greek and six Latin (explained by the presence of the Roman fort). One of the Nabataean inscriptions is dated to year 23 of Rabbel (II). Here, too, Greek came to be adopted for public use by a population with purely Semitic names, closely related to later Arabic ones. For instance building was undertaken there in AD 265/266 by 'Abdala (son) of Abdos (and) Saeios (son) of Sadallos'.[15]

At Umm el-Jimal there seems to have been a Roman fort in the second century, and subsequently a larger *castellum,* probably of the Tetrarchic period, around which the subsequent settlement may well have grown up. But the fact that it was not on the margin of the occupied zone but well within it gives all the greater significance to the most famous inscription from the site, the bilingual epitaph of the tutor of an Arab king.[16]

The Greek text reads: 'This is the grave-monument *(stēlē)* of Pheros (son) of Solleos, tutor *(tropheus)* of Gadimathos, king of (the) Thanouēnoi'. The parallel text is written in Nabataean, but in a more cursive form than standard Nabataean, that is to say, one in which more of the letters are joined. It reads: 'This is the tomb (NPŠW) of PHRW BR ŠLY, master (RBW) of Gadimat, king of Tanukh (GDYMT MLK TNWḤ)'.

Neither version of the text is dated. Nor, strictly speaking, does it indicate where Gadimat had been ruling when (at some time in the past?) Pheros had been his *tropheus,* or RB. All that it makes clear is that Pheros was buried here. It thus more clearly suggests the extension of Graeco-Roman culture to an Arab court than it does the activity of a people called Tanukh within the

14. See esp. B. De Vries, "Umm el-Jimal in the First Three Centuries AD", in Freeman and Kennedy, *DRBE,* 227; Wenning, *Nabatäer,* 48–51; Kennedy and Riley, *RDF,* 183–184.

15. H. I. MacAdam and D. F. Graf, "Inscriptions from the Southern Haran Survey", *ADAJ* 33 (1989), 17ᵛ, no. 7. Nabataean inscriptions listed by Wenning, *Nabatäer,* 51.

16. *PAES* III, no. 238; *PAES* IVA, no. 41 (the fullest discussion, by E. Littmann). See also Bowersock, *Roman Arabia,* 132ff.

provincial zone, or even near it.[17] But do we know who the Tanukh were, or what role was played by Gadimat and when? The 'Thanouēnoi' of the Greek text might be identifiable with the 'Thanouitai' whom Ptolemy, in the second century, places somewhere in central Arabia. But that hardly helps.[18]

If we can claim to know any more than this, it can only be on the basis of the *History of Prophets and Kings,* a universal history written in Arabic by al-Tabari (AD 839–923) and using some earlier Arabic historians of the eighth and ninth centuries.[19] This vast work begins with Biblical history, covers the interval between that and the rise of Islam as best it can, bringing in also the history of Iran, and then goes in great detail over the life of Muhammad and the subsequent history of Islam, terminating in AD 915.

Such a work, now being translated in its entirety for the first time, cannot fail to be of the greatest interest in itself. Above all else, as regards the pre-Islamic period (which occupies less than a twentieth of the whole), it illustrates how the self-perception of Islam was rooted in　　Bible, a fact of unlimited significance which had its distant origin in our period, when Josephus identified contemporary Arabs as the descendants of Ishmael and Hagar.[20] But the notion that we have here a reliable *history* of the Near East in the Imperial period, to act as a foil to Classical accounts, or to the *Res Gestae* of Shapur I, will not stand up to a moment's inspection of the text. A confused compilation of diverse elements from earlier history, heavily embroidered with legend, the work has to be considered in the light of contemporary documents, where available, rather than being used as a framework for their interpretation. It is a sign of the characteristic allusiveness which marks the historical study of the Near East (and is equally true of the treatment of the Syriac sources discussed below) that no discussion of the relation of Arab peoples to the Empire begins with any attempt to set out what the available Arabic narratives are, or what is known of their authors' sources, methods or historical outlook.

17. For the Hellenistic overtones to this inscription see M. Sartre, "Le tropheus de Gahhimat, roi de Tanukh: Une survivance en Arabie d'une institution hellénistique", *SBFLA* 29 (1979), 253.

18. Ptolemy, *Geog.* VI, 7, 23, ed. Nobbe.

19. For a partial translation and commentary for the sections relating to this period, see the classic study of Th. Nöldeke, *Geschichte der Perser und Araber zur Zeit der Sassaniden* (1879). For an invaluable English translation now in progress, see the annotated version being produced by F. Rosenthal and others, published by State University of New York Press since 1985. The first part of the period with which we are concerned is covered by *The History of al-Tabarl* IV, *The Ancient Kingdoms* (1987), trans. M. Perlmann. The next volume is still awaited. No clear account of al-Tabari and his *History* emerges from F. Rosenthal, *A History of Muslim Historiography*[2] (1968). A brief and factual account is given in F. Sezgin, *Geschichte des arabischen Schrifttums* I (1967), 323ff. For al-Tabari's most relevant source, Hisham al Kalbi, see Sezgin, op. cit., 286ff.

20. Ch. 1 above and 13.1 below.

Such a treatment cannot be supplied here. It will be enough to note that al-Tabari, in the relevant part of his *History,* supplies first a legendary account of the Jews, and then an account of the Persians and (with extreme vagueness) the Parthians, before stories about Mary and Jesus, and a brief tabulation of the Roman Emperors. After that he comes to the history of a group of Arab tribes settled in north-east Arabia (broadly south-western Iraq), who 'became allies known as al-Tanukh, which means "abode"'. They were joined, some-time (it seems to be implied) in the long period between Alexander and the rise of the Sasanids, by one Jadhimah and his followers. Jadhimah became a major ruler, still in Iraq. One of his feats is recorded as a successful campaign against 'Amr b. Zarib, 'the ruler of the Arabs in the Jazirah and the fringes of Syria', after whose death the latter's daughter al-Zabba reigned in his place. She had a fortress on the western bank of the Euphrates (evidently the Byzantine fortress called Zenobia, of which there are extensive remains),[21] and would also go to Tadmor (Palmyra). In short, this figure clearly derives from the historical Zenobia, seen in a historical vacuum without either her husband Septimius Odenathus or her son Vaballathus, not to speak of the Roman and Sasanid Empires. After long exchanges al-Zabba is said to have been killed by Jadhimah's nephew, 'Amr ibn 'Adi, whose most remote named ancestor was 'Lakhm' (hence the appellation 'Lakhmid' for his dynasty, which ruled from al-Hira in Iraq), and who is claimed to have died at the age of 120.

It is surely best to confess that we lack the means to decide whether any of this can be given a real historical framework. The presumption that the inscription from Umm el-Jimal can be dated on the basis that this Jadhimah/ GDYMT/Gadimathos was a contemporary of Zenobia must in itself be baseless. Nonetheless, from Strabo onwards, to Ammianus' account of Julian's Persian expedition, it is clear that there always were 'Arab' tribal groups in the steppe and desert zone on either side of the Euphrates. But for the moment we must be content to know only what the inscription tells us: that there was indeed *a* king of a people called Thanouēnoi or Tanukh, who was called Gadimat, and who had a teacher with the Greek title *tropheus*. Moreover, the developed form of the Nabataean script (and perhaps the relatively late evolution of the town itself) might in fact suggest that the third century is the right context. But whether the eventual burial of Pheros at Umm el-Jimal implies that the Tanukh as a group had moved from the lower Euphrates area, either occasionally or permanently, to operate on the borders of Roman 'Arabia' is quite uncertain. If there is any evidence that the Arabs of the steppe

21. For the site and its geographical context see J. Lauffray, *Halabiyya-Zenobia: Place forte du limes oriental et la Haute-Mésopotamie au VIᵉ siècle* I (1983). There seems to be no evidence for the name until Procopius, *Aed.* II, 8, 15–19, 1, which is also the only evidence that anything was built here by Zenobia. Her Palmyrene name was BTZBY, 9.4 above.

zone were by now a significant *strategic* threat, it is the campaign against 'Saracens' of about 290.[22] Rather than add to speculation on the legendary history of the confederation called Tanukh, it might be better to note the continued possibility of using Nabataean here, in parallel with Greek, just as—in another border-area of the Nabataean zone—in the second-century inscription of the Thamud at Ruwwafa in the Hedjaz.[23]

Nonetheless, even a sceptical approach such as this has to acknowledge the significance of the famous document with which the inscription of Pheros has always been paired, the epitaph of another Arab king, who died in the reign of Constantine.[24] Here again the exact place is important, as is the date, which in this case is given explicitly: year 223 (of the province of Arabia), on the seventh of the month Kislev, therefore AD 328/329. The place is en-Nemara, a small site in the steppe some 30 km east of the edge of the Jebel Hauran, where there are traces of a Roman outpost and a scatter of fragmentary Roman military inscriptions. There is no evidence to show that the site was in military occupation under Constantine. But it lay not far outside the area covered by the extension of the Strata Diocletiana southwards from the Damascus-Palmyra route, to reach Azraq.[25]

This place thus belonged on the outer fringes of the provincial area, though much more marginally so than Umm el-Jimal. The script of the inscription is also significant: basically Nabataean, but in a more cursive form, tending towards classical Arabic script, than in the inscription of Gadimat. The *language,* it is universally agreed, is Arabic. But there the problems begin. There is no agreement even on what the correct transcription of the individual letters is, let alone on the *meaning* of the whole text. The normal view is that the text begins 'This is the tomb of Imru'l-qais son of 'Amru, King of all the Arabs' (TY NPŠ MR 'LQYŠ BR 'MRW MLK 'L 'RB KLH). But KLH, meaning 'all', has been questioned in the latest reading. As for the rest of the text, virtually nothing is certain except that an extensive area of rule is claimed for this king, apparently extending to the southern Hedjaz (Najran), and that there is a reference to the Romans.

This text too gains a greatly increased potential significance from its possible confirmation of some elements in al-Tabari's narrative. In the *History* the nephew of Jadhima, 'Amr ibn 'Adi, is succeeded by his son, Imru'l-qais, who was a Sasanid vassal and converted to Christianity. Al-Tabari cites His-

22. 5.2 above.

23. 4.1 above.

24. *RES,* no. 483; Cantineau, *Le nabatéen* II, 49. See Bowersock, *Roman Arabia,* 138ff. For drastically different readings of the text see, e.g., A. F. L. Beeston, "Nemara and Faw", *BSOAS* 42 (1979), 1, and J. A. Bellamy, "A New Reading of the Namārah Inscription", *JAOS* 105 (1985), 31.

25. 5.2 above.

ham al-Kalbi (died AD 819) as his authority for the statement that he ruled for 114 years, under a succession of Persian kings, from Shapur I (240–272) to Varahran (perhaps II, 276–293).[26] A succession of two rulers, father and son, with the names 'MRW and MR 'LQYS is indeed confirmed by the inscription. But the dates simply do not fit with the evidence of the inscription from en-Nemara; and neither of the two inscriptions would of itself suggest any role for either king within the geographical area ruled by Persia. Moreover, later Arabic tradition itself reveals an apparent interregnum in the fourth century, before the Lakhmid kings ruling from al-Hira come fully into the light of history in the fifth century.[27] No reliable reconstruction is thus possible. But these two inscriptions make it feasible to suppose that if there had been a real 'pre-history' of the Lakhmids, they may have begun as a minor dynasty in the steppe zone on the edge of Roman Arabia, probably in a condition of some dependence on Rome, and only later, in the course of the fourth century, moved across into the border-land of Sasanid territory. If Amru, or 'Amr ibn 'Adi, ever really confronted Zenobia, which may be pure fantasy, it must have been almost sixty years before his son's death; and (if it happened at all) it will as probably have been when Vaballathus' forces marched through Arabia on the way to Egypt as in a raid conducted, from the opposite direction, from the Euphrates. But since in any case he did *not* kill Zenobia (who died in Rome), the whole story is legend.

It is better here to admit our ignorance. On any construction our evidence, taken collectively, suggests the possibility of movement between the steppe east of the Jebel Hauran and the marginal zone south of the middle Euphrates, where al-Hira lay. Whether such movements will have passed by the Wadi Sirhan and the distant Nabatacan and Roman outpost of Jawf, we cannot tell. Nor do we know whether, alternatively, movement was possible, or normal, for nomadic groups travelling further northeastwards, outside the line of the Roman frontier zone, from Roman Arabia to the Euphrates. The social history of the steppe, or desert, remains to be written.

What is certain is that this 'desert frontier', in the sense of roads and a chain of forts, now existed; and also that the inhabitants of the Empire had come, by the third and fourth centuries, to use the word 'Saracen' for any groups in the steppe who led an unsettled life and might be regarded as a local threat. This confrontation, which contemporaries do not seem to have perceived as 'symbiotic', was the product of a long step-by-step advance of the Roman military presence and of a settled population into the edge of the steppe. Not only a long history of progressive military advance but a social

---

26. See Nöldeke, *Geschichte* (n.19 above), 46–47, on the first Imru'l-qais. Later bearers of the same name appear in the narrative on pp. 78–79.

27. See I. Shahid in *Enc. Islam*[2] V (1986), 632, *s.v.* "Lakhmids".

and cultural history is encapsulated in the Latin inscription of AD 334, found half-way between Bostra and the oasis of Azraq, which records how a *protector* built a reservoir so that the peasants, while collecting water, would not be exposed to ambush by the *Saraceni*.[28] The same term was by now used for any unsettled peoples, from Sinai to the Negev, to the Syrian steppe, the Euphrates and Roman Mesopotamia.

28. 5.1 above.

THE EUPHRATES AND MESOPOTAMIA

12.1. GEOGRAPHY, CULTURE AND LANGUAGE

From the beginning of the Imperial period the Roman presence in the Near East extended as far as Seleucia on the Euphrates, more often called Zeugma, 'the bridge', where the river now marked the border between the Roman and the Parthian Empires.[1] It was only by successive stages that that presence was greatly extended. First it came to reach further along the river, both north and then south. To the north, the conquest of Commagene in the early 70s meant that Rome now occupied directly all of the cultivable area of northern Syria up to the Taurus Mountains. As far as the hinterland, stretching west to the borders of Cilicia and the meeting-point of the Taurus and Mount Amanus, is concerned, so little is known that nothing more need, or can, be said. But the capital of the kingdom, Samosata, lay directly on the Euphrates. In one direction, from the tell, or acropolis, of Samosata one could look northwards across the fertile plain where a succession of royal monuments were erected in the first century BC, to the mountainous skyline where the artificial royal tumulus on the summit of Nemrud Dag, at a height of over 2000 m, was visible 60 km away. In the other direction, one could look across the river to the rolling, and also fertile, plain of Osrhoene, a small kingdom which until the mid-second century was part of the Parthian Empire. It is not entirely surprising that the last king of Commagene, Antiochus IV, could be accused of dubious loyalty to Rome.[2]

Southwards, or south-eastwards, down the Euphrates, Roman control

1. 2.1 above.
2. 3.1 above.

may have extended in the later first century to the confluence with the river Balikh (Bilēcha), which ran south from the Mesopotamian shelf, in the area where lay the cities of Edessa, the capital of Osrhoene, and Carrhae. But it was only in the 160s that Roman occupation was carried a long distance further south, past the confluence with the Chabur (Abouras), to include the small Macedonian settlement of Dura-Europos, which for the best part of three centuries had been a Parthian outpost.[3] Excavations there between the First and Second World Wars have produced a mass of evidence, still far from fully digested, which from the perspective of the Roman Empire has given it almost too great an importance. For it lasted as a 'Roman' place for less than a century, until its complete destruction by the Persians in the 250s. When Julian's army marched past it in 363, it was a 'deserted town in Persian territory'.[4] Roman territory now stopped at the confluence of the Chabur and Euphrates, where Diocletian had built the fortress of Circesium.

Long before that, however, Roman control had extended across the Euphrates, to cover the whole of the shelf which lies between the Taurus Mountains and the Mesopotamian plain proper, finally to reach the Tigris. South of the shelf, or of the Jebel Sinjar which marks its southern edge in the east, it was only for a brief period in the third century that Roman forces found themselves stationed at the city of Hatra, the capital of a small kingdom which had formed part of the Parthian Empire. So far as we know, Hatra was never to be Roman again after its capture by Shapur I in about 240.[5] As regards the eastern part of the shelf, lying south of Mons Masius, an outlying spur of the Taurus (the Tur Abdin, later to be the heartland of Syriac monasticism), and including the city of Nisibis, Roman dominance was to be enshrined in the treaty with Persia in 298 or 299, only to be surrendered forever after the defeat and death of Julian in 363. Thereafter, the zone where Syriac Christianity flourished was to be divided, west of Nisibis, by the frontier between the two empires. Between the two treaties, of 298/299 and 363, however, the Roman military presence had also extended north of Mons Masius to take in an even less known area: the plain between the mountain and the Tigris, along the stretch where the river, on leaving the main Taurus range, turns almost due east, before swinging south round the end of Mons Masius past the eventual Roman fort of Bezabde to enter the north-east corner of the Mesopotamian plain. It was on this stretch of the Tigris, just before it turns east, that in the 330s Constantius, as 'Caesar' under his father Constantine, was to fortify the city of Amida (Diyarbakir).[6] Virtually nothing is known, as

3. 3.4 above.
4. Ammianus XXIII, 5, 8.
5. 4.2 above.
6. Ammianus XVIII, 9, 1–2. Cf. 5.3 above.

regards this period, of the culture, language or social history of this plain on the right bank of the Tigris, looking across the river to what was then the kingdom of 'Armenia', with its capital at Tigranocerta.[7] It was in a monastery near here that in the late eighth century an unknown monk composed a world chronicle in Syriac which, among much else, provides the fullest record of the royal dynasty which ruled in Edessa from the second century BC to the third century AD.[8]

Three different features serve to define the area with which this chapter is concerned. One is of course geography: the region is shaped to the north by the Taurus and its spurs, to the east and west by the Tigris and Euphrates, and (equally important) by the two major tributaries which run off the north Mesopotamian shelf to join the Euphrates, that is, the Balikh and the Chabur. The area of northern Mesopotamia which became Roman under Septimius Severus in the 190s is roughly defined by the edge of the shelf, or by the limits of 200-mm annual rainfall. The major cities of Roman Mesopotamia lie along the borders of the shelf and cluster round the upper reaches of the streams which feed into the two major tributaries: Edessa and Carrhae belong in the area of the scattered headwaters of the Balikh, and Constantina (if it was situated at modern Viransehir), Reshaina, Nisibis and also Singara, lying on the southern side of the Jebel Sinjar, in those of the Chabur.

As we have seen in looking at the military evolution of this area, these rivers have to be understood not as frontiers marking off blocks of territory, but first as providing strips of cultivable land, and second as offering routes through the uncultivable steppe on either side. In consequence the issue of relations between the settled population and the peoples of the steppe presented itself here in just the same terms as it did elsewhere. 'The same terms' in this context is meant literally: the same shifting vocabulary—'Arabes', 'skēnitai' ('tent-dwellers') and 'Saracens'—is used here as elsewhere.

The presence of these peoples is reflected in literary sources and documents from within both the Roman and the Parthian and then the Persian Empires, from Strabo's *Geography* to Ammianus' vivid account of Julian's dealings with the chiefs of the *Saraceni*, or Jerome's perhaps too vivid report of Saracen bandits infesting the road between Beroea in Syria and Edessa in Mesopotamia.[9] Unfortunately the account which Strabo, at the beginning of

---

7. That Tigranocerta lay in this region, north of this stretch of the Tigris (and not in what was to be Roman Mesopotamia), is certain. See R. Syme, "Tigranocerta: A Problem Misconceived", in S. Mitchell (ed.), *Armies and Frontiers in Roman and Byzantine Anatolia* (1983), 61 = R. Syme, *Roman Papers* IV (1988), 245. For discussion of the precise location of the site, which clearly lay in this area, see T. A. Sinclair, *Eastern Turkey: An Architectural and Archaeological Survey* III (1989), 357ff.

8. See further 12.3 and App. C below.

9. 12.6 below.

our period, gives of the route then taken by traders between northern Syria and Babylonia is filled with errors. But it is at least clear that he means to say that they did not follow the whole course of the Euphrates, but crossed over it, and only then travelled southwards, leaving the river a considerable distance to their right. The reason he gives, rightly or wrongly, is that the *skēnitai* living further east were less exploitative and more helpful than those along the Euphrates:

> The Scenitae are peaceful, and moderate towards travellers in the exaction of tribute, and on this account merchants avoid the land along the river and risk a journey through the desert, leaving the river on the right for approximately a three days' journey. For the chieftains who live along the river on both sides occupy country which, though not rich in resources, is less resourceless than that of others, and are each invested with their own particular domains and exact a tribute of no moderate amount.[10]

The crucial factor which Strabo failed to make clear is revealed by his probable contemporary Isidorus of Charax, whose *Parthian Stations* traces the same route in more detail.[11] The rationale for this route was that travellers would cross over from Zeugma to the headwaters of the Balikh, and then travel down it to where it joined the Euphrates. A comparable route, though starting further south, from Hierapolis, was to be followed by Julian's army in 363. Either route was actually shorter than following the bend of the Euphrates.

Isidorus' account, brief as it is, serves to introduce the second significant feature of the social history of this region: like most other parts of the Near East, it had been profoundly affected by Hellenistic settlement, which in Isidorus' view had begun with Alexander himself. Thus in Isidorus' itinerary we find the following places listed, which either have Greek names or are explicitly designated as Greek foundations: Apamea, just across the river from Zeugma; Charax Sidou, '(called) Anthemousia by the Greeks'; Ichnai, a Greek city, a foundation of the Macedonians, on the river Balikh; Nikēphorion, by the Euphrates, a Greek city, a foundation of King Alexander; and then 'Doura, a city of Nicanor (properly Nicator), a foundation of the Macedonians; by the Greeks it is called Eurōpos'.

There is no need to pursue the scanty evidence on the actual historical circumstances of the foundation of these cities, or of other little-known places with Greek names scattered further up the Euphrates. It may, however, be

---

10. Strabo, *Geog.* XVI, 1, 27 (340).

11. Text in C. Müller, *Geographi Graeci Minores* I (1855), 244–254; *FGrH*, no. 781; M.-L. Chaumont, "La route royale des Parthes de Zeugma à Séleucie du Tigre d'après l'itinéraire d'Isidore de Charax", *Syria* 61 (1984), 63. See esp. M. Gawlikowski, "La route de l'Euphrate d'Isidore à Julien", in *Géog. Hist.*, 77.

relevant to note that the creation of places with Greek or Macedonian local names, or dynastic names, had been a tradition which persisted through the whole Hellenistic period. As it happens, perhaps the most perfect expression of that ideal comes from one of the immense royal inscriptions of Commagene, put up in the mid-first century BC. In the inscription which he ordered to be put up at Arsameia on the Nymphaios—a river which joins the Euphrates above Samosata—Antiochus I (*circa* 69–36 BC) recalled how his ancestor Arsames had exploited the potentialities of the site, a saddle between two peaks:

> This Arsameia which in the hollow between two breasts gives forth the spring Nymphaios of eternal waters, my ancestor Arsames founded as a city. As it lay by nature on two rocky hills, and as he perceived a god-given flow of nourishing water pouring forth into a deep cleft, he took advantage of the site, walled the double summit on either side, established a city around them, and called it Arsameia after himself. By increasing the impregnability of the fortifications by his own care and provision he created an unassailable base for his native land.[12]

Behind the flowery and poetic diction Antiochus manages to express rather accurately the military character of early-Hellenistic city-foundations, and of Hellenistic monarchy in general. He later claims to have added to the fortifications himself, as well as (a new motif) adorning the city. The monuments of the cult of his royal ancestors, most notably the great series of statues around the summit of Nemrud Dag, were also his work.

A city such as this, or another 'Arsameia' which lay directly on the Euphrates, at Gerger in the north-east corner of the kingdom, was—like the cities later founded by the Herodian dynasty—a tribute to the idea of the Greek city. It was surely not, as the earliest Hellenistic foundations under Alexander and Seleucus I had been, a colonial implantation of a Greek-speaking population in a 'barbarian' landscape. Seleucia/Zeugma, which in the middle of the first century had been controlled by the kings of Commagene, until the Romans took it over,[13] had, however, once been such a settlement. So, as Isidorus believed, had other places on the route to Babylonia, including 'Doura which the Greeks call Eurōpos'. To the very end, as we will see, the foundation of Dura by Seleucus I Nicator was to be formally recalled there.[14]

---

12. F. K. Dörner and Th. Goell, *Arsameia am Nymphaios* (1963), 36 (text and German translation), ll. 13ff. Here, as in all references to Commagene, I owe everything to the classic article of J. Wagner, "Dynastie und Herrscherkult in Kommagene: Forschungsgeschichte und neuere Funde", *Ist. Mitt.* 33 (1983), 177.

13. 2.1 above.

14. 12.4 below.

By that time, as it seems, Dura also enjoyed the status of a Roman *colonia*. In quite a significant sense the Roman military occupation, organisation and (in formal terms) 'colonising' of this region was to be a re-enactment of the early-Hellenistic occupation. For our understanding of what this Roman occupation meant for the region, it would therefore in principle be important to have some conception of how profound the impact of Greek settlement had been, and how far any of the cities on the Euphrates or in Mesopotamia still functioned, and still saw themselves, as Greek cities. Isidorus' *Parthian Stations,* written while the area was still part of the Parthian Empire, gives a strong impression of identifiably 'Greek' cities interspersed among other places with non-Greek names; very significantly, in view of what we have seen of settlement patterns elsewhere in the Near East, he gives several of these other places the label 'kōmopolis', 'village-city'.

In fact it has to be admitted that we have almost no significant evidence on the character of any of the 'Greek' cities of the region as they were in the couple of centuries before the definitive Roman occupation. The one exception is Dura, the only place from which there is archaeological and documentary evidence from both before and after the Roman conquest. Elsewhere, a major Hellenistic settlement on the Euphrates at Jebel Khalid is in the course of excavation; but it seems to have been entirely abandoned before the Roman period.[15] From the rest of the area there are only a scatter of documentary items of evidence from before the mid-second century—though, as we will see, of immense significance—and only later Syriac chronicles to offer some conception of internal history, of Edessa at least. There is no literary evidence in Greek from within this whole region until the provincial period. The one item that we have is again in Syriac. It is all too typical of the bias of our evidence that the few snapshots we have of the cities here derive from Greek narratives written in the Imperial period and describing the campaigns fought by the Romans here in the late Republic. These, moreover, have a notable tendency to emphasise the self-identification of the Greek cities of the Parthian Empire as 'Greek', and their consequent welcome and assistance for Roman armies.

The real history and the remarkably flexible and confused nomenclature, both Greek and non-Greek, of these places are matters of great complexity, and are not worth pursuing here.[16] The complications involved can be illus-

---

15. For an interim summary see G. W. Clarke, "Australian Classical Studies and Mediterranean Archaeology", in R. Sinclair (ed.), *Past, Present and Future: Ancient World Studies in Australia* (1990), 1; or P. Connor, "A Fortified Macedonian Military Settlement at Jebel Khalid, North Syria, Excavations 1986–1987", in A. M. Tamis (ed.), *Macedonian Hellenism* (1990), 11.

16. See, as always, Jones, *CERP*², ch. 9, "Mesopotamia and Armenia".

trated from a Byzantine dictionary of place-names: the third of ten different places called Antiochia was that 'of Mesopotamia, called "Mygdonia", which is called by the natives "Nasibis", whence there came Apollophanes the Stoic philosopher, a "Nasibēnos", and Pharnouchos who wrote a *Persian History;* which is also called "Nesibis" and "Nisibis"'.[17] But to Strabo 'Nisibis' was also called 'Antiocheia *in* Mygdonia', that is, it lay in the territory of a people whom the Macedonians had labelled 'Mygdones'.[18] To save even further confusion, it will be called 'Nisibis' here; but both its coins and one of the newly discovered Greek papyri of the mid-third century in fact call it 'Nesibis'.

The Greek names of such places were usually either dynastic, like 'Antiochia', or borrowed from place-names in Macedonia itself. The place which continued to be called in Syriac 'Orhai' had both types of Greek name, 'Edessa' and 'Antiochia (on the) Callirhoe'. But for the question of what this identity as a Greek or Macedonian settlement might have meant in the Parthian period we are dependent, as mentioned, on narratives written under the Roman Empire. Thus it is claimed by Cassius Dio that in 65 BC the *legatus* of Pompey, Afranius, marching back to Syria through Mesopotamia, would have been totally lost if 'the Karraioi, being settlers of the Macedonians and living there', had not rescued him. There had indeed been an early-Macedonian settlement there; yet Carrhae, the ancient city of Harran, with its famous temple of the Moon-goddess, was precisely one of the places where the question of cultural and ethnic identity arises most acutely.[19] Later Dio reports more programmatically that when Crassus invaded Parthian territory in 54 BC, he quickly captured various Greek cities, including Nikephorion: 'for many settlers, (descendants) of the Macedonians and the other Greeks who had campaigned with them, held down by force and having high hopes of the Romans as being philhellenes, changed sides not unwillingly'.[20] A similar set of attitudes is implied when Plutarch describes how in 53 BC, when Crassus was defeated and killed near Carrhae, help was offered to his son by 'two Greeks from among those who lived nearby in Carrhae, Hieronymos and Nikomachos'; they urged him to flee to Ichnai, a *polis* which had taken the Roman side.[21] It would be a mistake, however, to build too much on the overtones of passing references in these later Greek narratives. Nisibis, as we saw, had also been a Macedonian settlement, as 'Antiochia in Mygdonia'. But when Dio describes how Lucullus besieged and took it in 68, he characterises

17. Stephanus Byzantinus, *Ethnica, s.v.* Ἀντιόχεια.

18. Strabo, *Geog.* XVI, 1, 23 (747); cf. XI, 14, 3 (527), and Plutarch, *Lucullus* 32.

19. Dio XXXVII, 5, 5; Diodorus XIX, 91 (Macedonian settlers already there in 312 BC). See W. Cramer, *RAC* XIII (1986), cols. 634–650.

20. Dio XL, 13, 1.

21. Plutarch, *Crassus* 25.

its inhabitants as *barbaroi;* so when he adds that 'it is now (in the third century) ours and is classified as a colony of ours', he misses the significant truth that this was in fact a second western 'colonisation'.[22]

None of this evidence therefore tells us anything in detail about the communal structures or about the culture (or cultures) of these cities under Parthian rule. But the way in which Isidorus in his *Parthian Stations* chooses to characterise each place on the itinerary is clear evidence that the question of being a 'Greek city' or not was a significant one to contemporaries—or at least to other Greeks. It is surely relevant that Isidorus himself came from another small Greek city under Parthian rule, Spasinou Charax in Mesene on the shores of the Persian Gulf.[23] Any of these places might have continued to conduct themselves publicly as Greek cities, and to be treated as such by the Parthian kings. That this possibility was a real one is made certain by the letter in Greek written in AD 21 by Artabanus III of Parthia, and found on an inscription from Susa.[24] Perhaps surprisingly, the king, in addressing this Greek city in present-day Iran, does not use its formal title, 'Seleucia on the Eulaeus'; instead he writes to 'Antiochus and Phraates, being the *archontes,* and the *polis'*. But the body of the letter leaves no doubt that this is a Greek city with fixed rules governing the holding of magistracies, whose holders were expected to contribute out of their own pockets, and would receive appropriate honours in return. When the need arose, the city would send an embassy *(presbeia),* presumably to the king. It is somewhat paradoxical that this place, the ancient Persian capital of Susa, lying below the southern Zagros Mountains and some 1200 km from the Mediterranean, should present a more clearly defined image as a 'Greek city' than any of those on the Euphrates or in northern Mesopotamia which were to become part of the Roman Empire.

In any case, a 'Greek city' within the Parthian Empire might have a population which was clearly divided along ethnic, cultural or linguistic lines, as has been common in the Near East in more recent periods—but is *not* clearly visible in the cities west of the Euphrates, except in Judaea and its surrounding region. But precisely there, as we have seen, Josephus sometimes hesitates between describing the gentile population as 'Greeks' or as 'Syrians'. In the case of the other major city called Seleucia and lying within the Parthian Empire, however—that is, Seleucia on the Tigris—he has no such hesitation: 'At Seleucia life is marked by general strife and discord between the Greeks and the Syrians, in which the Greeks have the upper hand. Now when the

22. Dio XXXVI, 6, 2.

23. See S. A. Nodelman, "A Preliminary History of Mesene", *Berytus* 13 (1960), 83, wrongly arguing, however, for a later first-century date for Isidorus.

24. C. B. Welles, *Royal Correspondence in the Hellenistic Period* (1934), no. 75.

Jews came to live in the city there was continuing strife, and the Syrians got the upper hand by coming to terms with the Jews'.[25] It is of some significance that, just as 'Assyrian' can be used of people living in Roman Syria, 'Syrian' can be used of the non-Greek inhabitants of Parthian Babylonia. We have to assume, for lack of any other indication, that the most probable principle of division was linguistic: that the opponents of the (generally) dominant Greeks of Seleucia on the Tigris were speakers of a dialect of Aramaic. Similar divisions *may* therefore have existed also in those cities which did eventually come to form part of the Roman Empire.

Whether or not language in fact functioned, in the area which progressively fell under Roman control, as the basis of internal communal divisions—and even perhaps of wider political loyalties—it is the appearance of a new written language, Syriac, which provides the last of the three features which define the area concerned. Literary and documentary evidence, some very recent and still in the course of publication, shows that the emergence of this dialect of Aramaic, with its distinctive script, was something common not only to Edessa but to the whole Mesopotamian shelf up to and across the Tigris—and also, as was not known so clearly before, to the middle Euphrates as far south as Dura-Europos. For many reasons it will be at Dura that our investigation of the culture of the region begins.

12.2. DURA-EUROPOS IN THE PARTHIAN PERIOD

As was mentioned above, it is only at Dura-Europos that we have access to contemporary evidence to test any hypothesis about the life of Greek settlements under Parthian rule. But even here the difficulties are acute, perhaps more so than is generally admitted. For the excavations of the 1920s and 1930s were followed all too rapidly by publications offering very detailed, often bold, reconstructions of various aspects of the history, physical structure, religion and culture of the city, then by some but not all of the intended *Final Reports,* of which some are of the highest quality, on particular buildings and bodies of material. These have included a classic volume on the parchments and papyri (in Greek, Latin, Aramaic, Hebrew and Middle Persian), but none on the large number of inscriptions and graffiti, in a striking variety of languages: to be precise, Greek, Latin, Aramaic, Syriac, Palmyrene, Middle Persian and Safaitic.[1] Without a full study of these, the particular questions which are raised in this book concerning communal and personal identity, or 'ethnicity', can only be sketched. It is an equally serious problem,

25. Josephus, *Ant.* XVIII, 9, 9 (374), Loeb trans.
1. The best sketch of this profusion of languages remains G. D. Kilpatrick, "Dura-Europos: The Parchments and Papyri", *GRBS* 5 (1964), 215.

however, that the entire range of identifications of buildings, reconstructions of building-histories and interpretations of the evolution of the city as a whole really need to be critically reviewed, rather than taken as the basis for the few general portrayals of the city which have so far been published.[2]

In very broad lines there is no reason to doubt that this settlement, situated on cliffs overlooking the Euphrates from the west, was established by Seleucus I, and will have involved the distribution of lots *(klēroi)* of land to individual Macedonian and Greek settlers, most probably discharged soldiers. Such *klēroi* are mentioned in the only significant document surviving from pre-Parthian Dura, a deed of sale of the second century BC; and a Greek parchment written in Greek in the last decades of the city's existence still contains a copy of provisions about succession, and the ultimate possibility of property reverting to being 'royal'.[3] From beginning to end Dura retained essentially its original gridded lay-out within an irregular polygon of walls whose longest side did not exceed 1000 m. There was an *agora,* but no theatre or any other building for public entertainment. The period of Parthian domination, from the end of the second century BC onwards, seems to have seen the construction of a number of temples, dedicated to deities with both Greek and non-Greek names (Atargatis, Bel, Adonis, Aphlad, Zeus Theos, Azzanathkona, Zeus Megistos); the characteristic plan is of a distinctive local type, a modest central temple in a courtyard lined with small rooms which sometimes functioned as subsidiary shrines. The absence of colonnades and of Greek-style masonry, and the concealment of the shrines within their courtyards, has led the excavators to see the origin of this type of sanctuary in Babylonia.

There is no reason to question this view, which obviously fits with the role of Dura for over two and a half centuries as a frontier town in the Parthian Empire. It was not, however, in any real sense a 'Parthian' town. There is nothing whatever to suggest that there was any introduction of Parthian settlers, or any large-scale immigration from other parts of the Parthian Empire (any such point has to be made with deliberate vagueness, for even less is understood of the ethnic or linguistic composition of the Parthian world than of the Roman Near East). While our evidence is wholly inadequate, what we have is compatible with the gradual and partial adjustment of a Hellenistic settlement to its local environment, and to the influence of traders and others from both east and west. Our conceptions of any social or cultural *evolution*

2. See above all M. I. Rostovtzeff, *Dura-Europos and Its Art* (1938); A. Perkins, *The Art of Dura-Europos* (1973); C. Hopkins, *The Discovery of Dura-Europos* (1979). For the beginnings of a critical review of the excavations and the results to be deduced from them, see the papers in *Syria* 63 (1986), 1ff, and 65 (1988), 259 ff.

3. *P. Dura,* nos. 15 (second century) and 12.

of Dura is complicated by the fact, for which there seems no obvious explanation, that inscriptions, including those serving to date buildings, began on a significant scale exactly in the same period, the later first century BC, as in the Roman provincial area. So for instance the Palmyrene inscription dated to the Seleucid year 279 (34/33 BC), and recording the dedication of a temple (HYKL') to Bel and Iarhibol, is simultaneously one of the earliest Palmyrene texts and one of the earliest inscriptions from Dura in any language.[4]

Both the inscriptions and the very important series of legal documents drawn up in the Parthian period show that Greek continued to be both the standard language of the population and the official language not only of the city government but of the Parthian royal administration. Officials with the Greek titles *stratēgos* ('general') and *epistatēs* ('overseer'), or in full form '*stratēgos* and *epistatēs* of the *polis*', are attested (perhaps) in the later first century BC, throughout the first and second centuries AD, and even into the early Roman period, although the function of *epistatēs* is very rare in the Empire.[5] The workings of the Greek administration of Parthian Dura are reflected, for instance, in a long Greek deed of gift of AD 87 and a mutual distribution of 85–89.[6] But almost everything about the wider framework, both of government and of society, within which the city then lived is expressed in a Greek loan-contract of AD 121. The text begins:

> In the reign of the King of kings Arsakes, benefactor *(euergetēs)*, just, manifest *(epiphanēs)* and philhellene, year 368 as the king of kings reckons (the Parthian era), but by the former (Seleucid) reckoning [432], on the 26th of the month Daisios, in the village *(kōmē)* Paliga of the district around Iarda, in the term of office of Mētolbaissas ... garrison-commander(?) and one of the First and Most Honoured Friends and of the Bodyguards (of the king), the eunuch Phraates, *arkapatēs,* one of the household of Manēsos son of Phraates ... tax-collector, *stratēgos* of Mesopotamia and Parapotamia ('the district along the river') and *Arabarchēs,* made a loan to Barlaas son of Thathaios son of Ablaios, one of those from ... village *(kōmē)* ...[7]

The titles of the king and of his local commander perfectly express one aspect of the Parthian regime, as one late-Hellenistic monarchy among others. But, except for the Iranian word *arkapatēs* (the same term which appears as *argapet* in Palmyra),[8] and some Iranian personal names, we are in a social land-

---

4. 9.4 above.

5. See R. N. Frye, J. F. Gilliam, H. Ingholt and C. B. Welles, "Inscriptions from Dura-Europos", YCS 14 (1955), 127, on pp. 140–141.

6. *P. Dura*, nos. 18–19.

7. *P. Dura*, no. 20.

8. 4.3 above.

scape very similar to that which we encountered in Roman Arabia. Here, however, the *polis* in question is not so much surrounded by villages as situated at a central point in a line of villages stretching along the Euphrates. The village called Paliga, where this Greek document was drawn up, is surely the *kōmē* called Phaliga by Isidorus, lying some 70 km up the river, just above its confluence with the Chabur. Beyond the zone of villages, as in Roman Arabia, lay the steppe. Even the office of *Arabarchēs,* 'ruler of the Arabs' (or perhaps 'of the 'Arab', the steppe), seems closely similar to the '*stratēgos* of the *nomades*' attested in the Hauran; and a similar office appears in Syriac at Edessa in the Parthian period.[9] The awareness of being on the edge of the steppe is indeed curiously reflected in a Greek loan-agreement of 134, described as having been drawn up 'in Europos by Arabia'.[10]

Insofar as inscriptions and graffiti are any guide, Greek remained the normal language of daily use in Dura throughout the Parthian period. The question is of course complicated both by the systematic uncertainty as to whether people may not have spoken one language and used another for public, written documents, and further by the fact that the vast majority of the inscriptions, as well as parchments and papyri, date to the Roman period. What does seem certain, however, is that there was no consistent use of Aramaic in public documents to rival the role of Palmyrene at Palmyra; indeed the exception proving the rule of the public dominance of Greek is that those inscriptions and graffiti from Dura which are in a Semitic language are mostly in Palmyrene, put up by Palmyrene visitors or soldiers; like those from Palmyra itself, they are quite often bilingual with Greek.[11]

On the other hand the presence of long series of graffiti in Greek, for instance in the 'Temple of Bel' (formerly labelled the 'Temple of the Palmyrene Gods'), is supporting evidence for the view that Greek remained throughout a spoken language, and possibly the main one in use in the city.[12] It will be no surprise to find that Greek could be used both by people with Greek names and by those with Semitic names: for instance in the group of inscriptions from the 'Temple of Artemis' dating to the years before and after the turn of the eras, and giving the names of women: '(of) I[m]aboua daughter of Salamnēs, the daughter of Bēloobassaros and (of) [M?]ēkatnanaia daughter of P(?)apios the wife of Zebidadados, year 306 (7/6 BC)'—one of the earliest known inscriptions from Dura.[13]

As elsewhere, it is also highly significant that Greek could be used in

9. 12.5 below.

10. *P. Dura,* no. 22: ἐν Εὐρωπῷ τῇ πρὸς Ἀραβίᾳ.

11. See du Mesnil du Buisson, *Inventaire des inscriptions palmyréniennes de Doura-Europos (32 avant J.-C. à 256 après J.-C.)* (1939).

12. See F. Cumont, *Fouilles de Doura-Europos* (1926), 369ff.

13. Cumont, op. cit., 412, no. 57 (cf. nos. 58–68).

inscriptions recording the worship of deities of a strictly local character, by people with Semitic names. Two well-known examples from the first and second centuries AD will suffice. The first is inscribed on a sculpted panel representing a priest in a conical hat and long tunic down to his calves, who is making a sacrifice to a bearded deity in full armour, who is standing on two griffins and carrying a staff in his left hand. The Greek inscription leaves no doubt about the identification:

> This foundation of the sanctuary of Aphlad, called god of the village *(kōmē)* of Anath on the Euphrates, Adadiabos, the son of Zabdibōlos the son of Sillos, erected as his vow on behalf of the safety of himself, his children and all his house.[14]

Fortunately we are also left in no doubt as to the date. For an accompanying inscribed block gives the Seleucid year 365, AD 53/54, and names a group of men who dedicated an *andrōn* (whatever that might be in this context) to the god 'Apalados'. Their names are Baribagnaios son of Rachipnaios; Nabousapdos son of Abemmēs; Sabdisamsos son of Zabdibōlos; Naboudaraos son of Phalazzacheis; Abouis son of Zabidadados; Salamis son of Phalazzacheis; Roumēs son of Ochanou(-os?); Nabouazzanēs son of Rachipnaios; Theogenēs (the only Greek name) son of Zabidadados; Adadiadbos son of Zabdibōlos (the dedicator of the carved relief); and Addaios son of Phalazacheis.

Again, we see Dura as a focal point in a long line of villages stretching along the Euphrates; for 'Anath' is the place called Ana or Anatha, 80 km down the river, discussed earlier in connection with Palmyrene and Roman military outposts.[15] It is not certain whether the group of dedicants all came from there. But what is significant is that they could and did put up a visual representation of their local deity, with an accompanying Greek identification, within a Greek city. As with the document drawn up in Greek in the village of P(h)aliga, 70 km on the other side of Dura, it is probable that Greek was also used, at least as an official language, at Anath(a) itself.

A different form of expression of a local cult is provided by a Greek inscription from the temple of the goddess 'Azzanathkona'. Here at least the identification of the deity worshipped in the temple seems secure, for this divine name already appears on a Greek inscription from this building dating to the Seleucid year 345 (AD 32/33). In the middle of the second century, just before the final Roman acquisition of Dura, the cult was still being practised, but the deity had acquired a Greek divine name as well:

14. *Dura Report* V (1934), 112, no. 416, trans. C. Hopkins. The accompanying inscription is no. 418.

15. 4.1 above.

In the year 473 (AD 161/162), in the month Dios, Barnabous son of Zabid-konos the son of Raeibēlos erected a room *(oikos)* in the (temple?) to the goddess Artemis, called Azzanathkona, by his own expenditure, for the safety of himself and his children.[16]

Speculation on the etymology of the name 'Azzanathkona' is futile, and in any case would not necessarily tell us how the deity was understood by her local worshippers in the first and second centuries. If there is a clue, it is the relief sculpture from the temple showing a heavily robed goddess seated be-tween two bulls, in a manner not unlike the Atargatis of Hierapolis. But, unlike Aphlad, the deity on this relief is not explicitly labelled.[17]

The temple architecture, the iconography of deities, the names of deities and the Semitic-Greek nomenclature of the population of both the city and the villages which stretched up and down the Euphrates on either side of it all indicate how a Greek-speaking Macedonian colony, originally settled more than four and a half centuries before the final Roman conquest, could give expression to the culture of its local environment. So far as we can deter-mine, the culture of Dura in the Parthian period is best seen as that of the focal point of a settled zone along the Euphrates. There must also have been contacts with the *nomades* of the steppe, against whom the Palmyrenes fought to protect their caravans; but the only concrete trace of these is a small scatter of 'Safaitic' graffiti.[18]

What is clear throughout is that the public character of the city continued to be determined by its origins as a Macedonian colony. The religious iconog-raphy of both 'Parthian' and 'Roman' Dura showed indeed very clear resem-blances to that of Hatra, in the Mesopotamian steppe 200 km to the north-east, and of Palmyra. But there was to be no parallel whatsoever to the long series of Aramaic inscriptions from second-century Hatra,[19] or even to the public bilingualism of Palmyra, which persisted even after it became a Roman *colonia*.[20] Nor do we find any parallel to the Syriac epitaphs of Edessa and its region, though it too had, as we have seen, a Hellenistic name (or rather two alternative Hellenistic names). But the geographical spread of the writing of Syriac and its relevance to the culture of Dura is a topic which has yet to be discussed.

16. *Dura Report* V, 177, no. 504 (inscription of AD 32/33); 142, no. 453 (AD 161/162).

17. *Dura Report* V, 172–176, and Pl. XIV, for the representation of Atargatis of Hierapolis, 7.2 above.

18. For Safaitic inscriptions from Dura see *Dura Report* II, 172–177.

19. See H. J. W. Drijvers, "Hatra, Palmyra und Edessa: Die Städte der syrisch-mesopotamischen Wüste in politischer, kulturgeschichtlicher und relionsgeschichtlicher Bedeu-tung", *ANRW* II.8 (1977), 799; F. Vattioni, *Le iscrizioni di Hatra* (1981).

20. 9.4 above.

Since, as will be seen, there are Semitic-language documents of various types from Roman Dura, it is important to stress that, the few Safaitic graffiti apart, the *only* common Semitic-language inscriptions or graffiti from Parthian Dura are Palmyrene ones, beginning with that of 34/33 BC, and in fact continuing into the Roman period. A particularly notable group of three Palmyrene inscriptions belongs to the latest period of Parthian Dura, when—in a context which is not entirely clear—Palmyrene archers were stationed in the city.[21] These inscriptions serve to identify the three figures represented on a deeply carved relief from the 'Temple of the Gadde'. On the viewer's left is the Palmyrene donor, labelled 'image (ṢLM) of Hairan son of Maliku son of Nṣor', making an offering on a small altar. On the right is a standing figure in armour, holding a staff in his left hand, and placing a crown on the central figure with his right. He is duly identified as the founder of Dura, Seleucus Nicator (SLWQWS NYQṬR). In the centre is the bearded figure, seated on a throne, of the Fortune (Tyche, or Gad) of Dura (GD' DY DWR'), made by Hairan in the year 470 (AD 158/159).[22]

An iconographic style comparable to that in use at Palmyra (not to say examples of Palmyrene art as such) was thus available at Dura. But if a comparable local dialect of Aramaic was in use, it was not deployed in public. Nor, equally, was 'Parthian' Dura in any real sense Parthian. The visible Iranian influences are minimal, and the Parthian dynasty expressed itself there as a late-Hellenistic kingdom. Nonetheless, as we have seen, the dominance of the Parthian Empire was clearly expressed there. So even if, as it seems, after the Roman conquest the 'Roman' garrison continued at first to be a Palmyrene one, the fact of incorporation into a new, much wider and quite different political structure must have been as evident in daily life in Dura as it had been in Arabia. But that recognition could be combined with a reassertion of the identity of Dura as a Hellenistic foundation, as is apparent in a Greek deed of sale belonging to the spring of AD 180:

> In the consulship of Bruttius Praesens for the second time and of Julius Verus for the second time, in the twentieth year of the principate of Imperator Caesar Marcus Aurelius Antoninus and the fourth of his son Imperator Caesar Lucius Aurelius Commodos, Augusti, and 491 of the former reckoning (the Seleucid era), on the fourth of the month Peritius, in Europos toward Arabia. In the year when Lysanias, son of Zenodotus and grandson of Heliodorus, was priest of Zeus; Theodorus, son of Athenodotus and grandson of Artemidorus, was priest of Apollo; Heliodorus, son

21. 3.3 above.
22. *Dura Report* VII–VIII, 258–260 and Pl. XXXIII (the relief); 277, no. 907 (the inscriptions). Other related reliefs and inscriptions accompany this one. See du Mesnil du Buisson, *Inventaire*, nos. 28–32.

of Diocles and grandson of Heliodorus, was priest of the Ancestors; and Danymus, son of Seleucus and grandson of Danymus, was priest of King Seleucus Nicator. There has been sold by Lysias, son of Lysias, grandson of Heliodorus the great-grandson of Aristonicus, a citizen of Europos but resident in the village of Nabagath of the hyparchy around Gabalein, his slave named Achabus, about twenty years old, and there has been sold similarly the half-share belonging to him of the vineyard which is in the 'epiphyteutic' lands around the same Nabagath . . .[23]

We cannot in fact be certain whether these city cults represent elements of continuity which happen not all to be attested in Parthian Dura, or whether Roman rule was accompanied by the institution, or re-institution, of priest-hoods serving to recall the Hellenistic past. But other forms of continuity are very evident. It is also striking that a citizen of Europos ('Eurōpaios') could be resident in a village *(kōmē)* which was so distant. For Isidorus tells us where Nabagath was: it was a 'village-city' *(kōmopolis)* near P(h)aliga, but apparently on the left bank of the Euphrates, for 'the river Abouras (Chabur) flows past it, which joins the Euphrates'. It will thus have been some 60 km from Dura; we encountered earlier another deed of sale from Dura which reveals vineyards and orchards beside the Chabur.[24] But before we look more closely at the newly 'Roman' area of the Euphrates, the Chabur and northern Mesopotamia created by the absorption of Commagene by Vespasian and then by the conquests of Septimius Severus, we need to look at other aspects of its history before it was absorbed by Rome.

12.3. THE MIDDLE EUPHRATES AND THE COMING OF ROME

In some parts of the Euphrates region, such as Commagene, nothing approaching an answer to questions about local culture is possible. It is true that the very distinctive evidence presented by the long Greek inscriptions, and by the sculptures and reliefs of the royal dynastic cult, consciously identifies the dynasty as embodying both Greek and Persian traditions.[1] But this material is exclusively royal, and in any case none of it postdates the third quarter of the first century BC. The sole indication we have that the dynasty of the first century AD had any roots in popular loyalty is Josephus' report that in AD 17, when Antiochus III died, the 'powerful' wanted the kingdom to be made provincial, but the mass of people preferred 'to be ruled by kings according to their ancestral custom'. Yet when Roman forces marched in in

23. *P. Dura*, no. 25.
24. *P. Dura*, no. 26 (AD 227); 4.1 above.
1. See the major paper by Wagner, 12.2, n.12, above.

the early 70s, though the royal army resisted quite effectively, the population remained passive.[2]

Since we have hardly any local evidence from either before or after the Roman acquisition of Commagene, *a fortiori* we have no way of assessing what the change from royal to Imperial rule will have meant. Moreover, the one place in the interior of Commagene from which we do have some very distinctive local evidence, Doliche, on the southern edge of the region, seems to have been incorporated into the province of Syria by the middle of the first century; perhaps indeed already from 31 BC, at the same time as Zeugma, which lies some 40 km to its east-south-east.[3] Under Antiochus I (*circa* 69–36 BC), it had certainly belonged to the kingdom, as a fragmentary inscription of his cult-regulations shows.[4]

Elsewhere, apart from the great monuments and inscriptions of the royal ancestral cult, the archaeological and epigraphic record of Commagene is almost a blank. Perhaps our sole significant reflection of the social history of this period is a newly published Greek tomb-inscription from the heart of the kingdom, a village now called Sofraz Koy, some 45 km west-north-west of Samosata.[5] The builder of the tomb, a man with a Latin name, 'Markellos', records seven generations of his family: his great-great-grandfather Antiochos; his great-grandfather Mithridates, a royal official *(monokritēs),* and his wife Laodikē; his grandfather, apparently called Takitos (Tacitus), and the latter's wife Apsebis, the daughter of Antas; his father Sakerdōs, and his wife, another Laodikē; then his own generation, including his sisters Laodikē and Apsebis, and his wife Markellē; his own son, another 'Sakerdōs', and his granddaughter, another 'Markellē'. The genealogy seems to cover roughly the period from the earlier first century BC to the later first century AD—though whether the inscription itself belongs before or after the conquest is uncertain. On any dating it demonstrates a remarkable combination of typical Hellenistic dynastic names with an early introduction of Latin personal names. It may not be mere speculation to see this in relation to the preparedness of the 'powerful' in AD 17 to accept provincial rule.

That apart, we have only the most slight and superficial indications of the communal structures which marked the provincial period. Under the Flavians—and probably under Vespasian himself—Samosata, the royal capital, became 'Flavia Samosata', and from Hadrian's reign onwards issued coins inscribed 'of the Flavian Samosateans, mētropolis of Commagene'.[6] No other

2. Josephus, *Ant.* XVIII, 2, 5 (53); *BJ* VII, 7, 1–3 (219–243).

3. 7.2 above.

4. See J. Wagner, "Neue Denkmäler aus Doliche", *Bonn. Jahrb.* 82 (1982), 3, on pp. 161ff.

5. G. Schmitz, S. Sahin and J. Wagner, "Ein Grabaltar mit einer genealogischen Inschrift aus Kommagene", *Epig. Anat.* 11 (1988), 81.

6. *BMC Syria,* 117–123.

city from within the final borders of the kingdom did so. It is thus not certain which (apart from Samosata) were the 'four *civitates* of Commagene' which honoured Septimius Severus on a Latin inscription put up on the columns erected on the still perfectly preserved Roman bridge over the river Chabinas.[7]

This rich and beautiful region occupies the angle between the Euphrates and the Taurus Mountains, where the tumulus on the summit of Nemrud Dag is clearly visible on the horizon from Samosata. Whether the population as a whole regretted the royal dynasty, we cannot know. But since the great monuments on Nemrud Dag and elsewhere are still to be seen today, they must have been features of the landscape then too. Equally, though we have hardly a trace here of the epigraphic, documentary or archaeological evidence for village life which is so abundant in other areas, this too must have been a world of villages; if anything, they should have been more prosperous than elsewhere. Perhaps our sole epigraphic trace of such a village community is the fragmentary Tetrarchic inscription recording the boundary between a village, or village-community, called Ardoula or Ardouloi and some other community whose name cannot be read.[8]

But between them these two facts—the still visible reminders of a royal dynasty, and the unquestionable existence of a large village population—combine with a third to raise real questions about the culture of this region as part of the Roman Empire. The third fact is simply that the whole area looked directly across the Euphrates to Osrhoene. It was perhaps less significant (except to the final Roman suspicions of Antiochus IV) that Osrhoene was part of the Parthian Empire until the 160s, as that before and after that date it was the birthplace of the Syriac language, script and literature. That being so, *can* it have been the case that some dialect of Aramaic was not spoken also in Commagene?

The question presents itself with particular urgency, of course, because of what is said of himself and his background by Lucian (Loukianos) of Samosata.[9] As we have seen, he introduces his famous account—a parody of Herodotus—of the 'Syrian Goddess' at Hierapolis both by identifying her as 'the Assyrian Hera' and by saying of himself, 'I write being an Assyrian'.[10] Elsewhere, writing of himself in the third person, he describes himself as 'still barbarous in speech and almost wearing a jacket *(kandys)* in the Assyrian style'. He might at the same point have written 'Syrian'—and indeed does so in the same dialogue, and elsewhere; the one term was simply a more affected

---

7. *IGLS* I, nos. 42–44.

8. *IGLS* I, no. 59. From Atyntas-qale, some 40 km north-west of the confluence of the river Marsyas and the Euphrates. See App. A, no. 1, below.

9. For the best account see C. P. Jones, *Culture and Society in Lucian* (1986).

10. Lucian, *de dea Syr.* 1. Cf. 7.2. above.

version of the other.[11] None of these brief allusions would give us any idea of exactly where he came from. One other remark takes us further, when he calls himself 'a Syrian, one of those from the banks of the Euphrates'.[12] But it is only in one single place that he names his native city. The context is significant, for it is his satirical account, entitled *How to Write History,* of the absurdly inaccurate and overblown works written to record and celebrate the Parthian war fought by Lucius Verus in 162–166.[13] Some of these writers had not the remotest notion of the geography of the area:

> One man, for example, who had never met a Syrian nor even heard as they say 'barber-shop gossip' about such things, assembled his facts so carelessly that when speaking of Europus he said: 'Europus is situated in Mesopotamia, two days' journey from the Euphrates; it was colonised by men of Edessa'. Even this was not enough for him: my own birthplace, Samosata, this fine writer in the same book lifted, acropolis, walls and all, and transplanted to Mesopotamia, so as to surround it by both rivers, which passed close to it on either side and almost touched the walls.[14]

The acropolis (in fact an ancient tell) and walls of Samosata are visible still, or will be until the Euphrates dam drowns them forever. This is not quite Lucian's only allusion to his city; but his essay 'Praise of One's Patris' is wholly general, and might have related to any city.

We cannot in fact expect that a sophisticated Greek writer of the second century AD would ever offer us an analysis of the local culture of his home region. For precisely the nature (and, in a sense, the purpose) of the Greek culture of this period was that it was not regional; the style, vocabulary, literary forms and conventions of allusion (to the common stock of mythology, to Archaic and Classical literature and to Classical history) which defined it made it a common, supra-regional culture. The reader of the vast majority of Lucian's works would be wholly unable to tell from what part of the Greek world he came.

Even in *On the Syrian Goddess,* where he begins by claiming to be 'Assyrian' like the goddess herself, he actually adopts the literary standpoint of the bemused stranger, witnessing an exotic cult from the outside. It is thus only when local knowledge becomes relevant to Roman campaigns that he makes a specific point of his origin in Samosata. The other, oblique, allusions to his being a 'Syrian' or an 'Assyrian' contain by implication a concealed apologia. For they stress the distance, literal and figurative, which he had needed to

11. *Bis accus.* 27 ('Assyrian'); 14; 25–34; *Ind.* 19.
12. *Pisc.* 19: Σύρος . . . τῶν Ἐπευφρατιδίων.
13. Cf. 3.4 above.
14. *Hist.* 24, Loeb trans.

travel in attaining the *paideia* which made him an accomplished writer.

The unfortunate effect of these allusive and defensive references, as regards our knowledge of his background, is that we cannot tell, either from remarks about being 'Assyrian' or 'Syrian' or from the one reflection of his having been 'barbarous in speech', whether he is referring to a still unpolished style of Greek or to his having, in youth, spoken a dialect of Aramaic. Attractive as it might be to think of the Greek of the most accomplished of second-century writers as a second language, laboriously acquired, the first possibility is more likely. We still do not *know* whether Lucian, or anyone else in Samosata, or in Commagene generally, spoke a dialect of Aramaic.

That possibility must, however, remain open, for even without the documentary evidence now available we could be sure that some Semitic language, and perhaps more than one, was spoken on the other side of the Euphrates. As we saw earlier, Strabo, in part depending on Posidonius, speaks of the affinity of customs and language between the 'Armenioi', 'Syrians' (or 'Arimaioi' or 'Arammaioi') and 'Arabes', and notes that it was in Mesopotamia that they lived in the closest conjunction.[15] Pliny the Elder also gives a clear impression of the area, emphasising both its 'Arab' character and the presence in it of cities with Greek names. The Euphrates, he says, once it has broken through the Taurus, forms the boundary between Commagene on the right bank and 'Arabia' on the left, namely the district called 'that of the Orroei' (transliterating a Greek genitive plural which comes close to the Syriac name of Edessa, Orhai—'WRHY). He then continues:

> The 'Arabia' mentioned above contains the *oppida* Edessa, which was once said to be 'Antiochia', called 'Callirhoe' from its spring, (and) Carrhae, famous for the disaster of Crassus. Next comes the *praefectura* of Mesopotamia which owes its origin to the 'Assyrii', in which are the *oppida* Anthemusia and Nicephorium. Then the 'Arabes' who are called 'Praetavi'; their capital is Singara.[16]

As will be seen, Pliny here covers some of the same ground as Isidorus, though not in the more precise form of an itinerary with distances, or with any awareness of the rivers, the Euphrates apart. We would gain from him a clear, and for what follows quite significant, impression of the variety not only of peoples but of political units (all, though he does not say so, under Parthian suzerainty). We would not, however, gain any impression that at Edessa, in the 'Arabia' of the 'Orroei', there was a stable dynasty of 'phylarchs' or kings, often with the name 'Abgar(os)' or 'Mannos', whom later Syriac sources re-

15. Ch. 1 above.
16. Pliny, *NH* V 20/85; 21/86.

cord, and who appear from time to time in Graeco-Roman narratives of the conflicts between Rome and Parthia.[17] But none of these narratives gives any clear indication of how far the territory of these kings extended. Pliny's impression of a number of separate territories seems indeed to be correct. For when Trajan advanced into Mesopotamia, Cassius Dio reports that he encountered not only 'Augaros' (earlier called the 'Orroēnos') at Edessa, but also envoys from 'Mannos, the ruler of the neighbouring part of Arabia'; none, however, were sent by Sporakes, the *phylarchos* of Anthemousia.[18]

This is no need to go in vain pursuit of the question of exactly what these various political regimes amounted to; they will in any case no doubt have been fluid and changeable. But it is important to stress that we have no reason to think that the rule of the kings of Edessa, the place with which the birth of Syriac literature is most closely associated, extended over all of north-western Mesopotamia, or to the entire left bank of the Euphrates between Zeugma and the mouth of the Balikh. This uncertainty has to be borne in mind when we look at the tiny scatter of evidence which attests the use of the Syriac language and script in the first century AD.

The earliest known text, by a considerable margin, is an inscription from a very significant location, the modern Birecik on the left bank of the Euphrates, lying a few kilometres south of Zeugma, and where the modern road to Urfa (Edessa) crosses the river. It is defined as 'Syriac' by its use of the rounded semi-cursive script known as 'Estrangela' (from the Greek 'strongylos', 'rounded'), which bears some resemblance to the script of Palmyrene inscriptions.[19] (As we will see, these two scripts were to meet at Dura.) Estrangela was the script in which all the earlier Syriac manuscripts were to be written, from the earliest known literary manuscript, copied at Edessa in AD 411, until the eighth century. After that it was gradually replaced as the most common script by that called 'Serta', more cursive and closer to Arabic.[20] It is somewhat typical of the many barriers which present themselves in any attempt to grasp the evidence for the earlier stages of Syriac culture that the standard edition of the first Syriac parchment of the third century to be published—itself written in a cursive script which more closely resembles Estrangela—presents the text in Serta, thus obscuring the fact that there is some relationship between its script and that of contemporary Syriac (and Palmyrene) monumental in-

17. For example, Plutarch, *Crassus* 21–22 (φύλαρχος Ἀράβων, Ἀριάμνης ὄνομα), apparently the same as the Αὔγαρος ὁ Ὀρροηνός of Dio XL, 20, 1, the betrayer of Crassus in 53 BC; Tacitus, *Ann.* XII, 12 ('rexque Arabum Acbarus', AD 49).

18. Dio LXVIII, 18 (Augaros the 'Orroēnos'); 21, 1–22, 1.

19. See J. Pirenne, "Aux origines de la graphie syriaque", *Syria* 40 (1963), 101, with much comparative material, and rather wide-ranging speculations.

20. See W. H. P. Hatch, *An Album of Dated Syriac Manuscripts* (1946).

scriptions.[21] In view of the allusiveness and lack of up-to-date aids which characterise early Syriac studies, a basic guide to the material and its bibliography is offered at the end of this volume.[22]

Given its historic significance, as the first evidence for a script, or family of scripts, and language which persist to this day, the earliest of the known Syriac inscriptions deserves translation:

> In the month of Adar of the year 317 I, ZRBYN BR 'B[GR?], ruler of Birtha (ŠLYṬ' DBYRT'), tutor (foster-father?) of 'WYDNT [BR] M'NW BR M'NW, made this tomb (BYT QBW[R']) for myself and for ḤWY', mistress of my house, and for my children . . . every man (KL 'NŠ) who will enter . . . and shall see and give praise . . . HŠY sculptor (GLP') and SLW[K?] (Seleukos?) . . .[23]

The inscription thus records that a tomb for himself and his family was erected in AD 6; as at Palmyra, in Mesopotamia dating by the Seleucid era of autumn 312 was standard. The person concerned was an important local figure who is in command of Birtha (literally 'fortress'), that is, presumably, of the place on the site of Birecik. Though he has also been tutor (MRBYN') of someone whose father and grandfather were both called Ma'nu (Mannos), a common name in the royal dynasty of Edessa, there is no explicit reference to any current king. It remains very probable, nonetheless, that this is not an independent local ruler, but an official of the kingdom. We saw earlier how in AD 49, according to Tacitus, 'the king of the Arabs, Acbarus', met the Parthian pretender Meherdates at Zeugma and took him to enjoy the delights of Edessa.[24]

If, as is not quite certain, the earliest Syriac document already reflects the political structure of the kingdom of Edessa, this is less clear in the case of the next in time, which dates to the Seleucid year 385, AD 73/74.[25] This comes from a fine stone-built tower-tomb situated at a place called Serrin, approximately opposite the ancient Hierapolis, on the other side of the Euphrates,

21. *P. Dura*, no. 28, and Pls. LXIX and LXXI. First edited (also in Serta) by Ch. C. Torrey, "A Syriac Parchment from Edessa of the Year 243", *Zeitschr. f. Semitistik* 10 (1935), 33. It is printed in Estrangela in H. J. W. Drijvers, *Old-Syriac (Edessean) Inscriptions* (1972), 54–57.

22. App. C.

23. Drijvers, *Inscriptions*, no. 1; translation from J. B. Segal, *Edessa, 'the Blessed City'* (1970), 23, n.3. A photograph of a squeeze of the text in A. Maricq, "La plus ancienne inscription syriaque: Celle de Birecik", *Syria* 39 (1962), 88, Pl. III (and of that from Serrin, discussed below, Pl. IV).

24. Tacitus, *Ann.* XII, 12, 4; 2.3 above.

25. Drijvers, *Inscriptions*, no. 2; translated in Segal, *Edessa*, 23, n.4. A photograph of the tomb in Pirenne, op. cit., *Syria* 40 (1963), 110.

and thus some 70 km to the south of Birecik. From the discussion above of the various minor political structures attested in western Mesopotamia, this area is more likely than not to have been outside the kingdom of Edessa. But, although Edessa is the place most closely associated with the early stages of Syriac literature, there is no obvious or necessary connection between political boundaries (which in any case were all those of local dynasts under Parthian suzerainty) and the areas where particular dialects or scripts were in use. The inscription is again of a common type, recording the construction of a tomb (NPŠ') by someone for himself and his sons, and cursing anyone who disturbs it. This man also has a characteristic Edessan name, Ma'nu son of Ma'nu, and is described as QŠYŠ' (priest?) and BDR DNḤY, whose meaning is unknown.

When all allowances are made for the accidents of discovery (in a region between the Euphrates and the Balikh which has been very little explored), it is surely not entirely accidental that these two first-century Syriac inscriptions belong within the same period as the other earlier series of inscriptions in Semitic languages, from Palmyra and Petra, and happen to match almost exactly the time-spread of the dated Nabataean tomb-inscriptions of Medain Saleh. They are, in other words, a function of building activity, all conducted in sub-Hellenistic style. But the fact that Syriac had a future as a literary language, which Palmyrene and Nabataean did not, cannot but give these two isolated inscriptions some extra significance. They also serve, however, to raise other questions. When did literary composition in Syriac begin, and was it in fact associated with Edessa in particular?

Nearly all the earlier Syriac literature, like the coins of the Edessene kings, and the vast majority of the dated inscriptions, belongs to the period after Edessa had passed into Roman domination in the 160s, and then under direct provincial rule in 212/213. Since it was also in the 160s that Dura became 'Roman', this represents a different phase in the history of the region, within which both places will be treated in parallel. But do we have evidence for the literature or history of the region east of the Euphrates before it came under Rome? The question has to be approached in two quite different ways. First, again, is there any literature which itself derives from this area in this period? And second, is any real evidence about it to be derived from later narratives, whether in Syriac or in Greek?

There is no known literature in Greek from within this region before the 160s, any more than there is from Palmyra or Nabataea/Arabia. There might have been. Isidorus of Charax, as we saw, came from a Greek city in Mesene on the shores of the Persian Gulf. Greek sculpture was also to be seen there. An already famous, newly published bilingual inscription of Vologaeses IV of Parthia, in Greek and Parthian, on a statue of Herakles records how he brought this statue as booty when he reconquered Mesene in the mid-second century.[26] Greek writing might well have emanated from Dura, Nikephorion, Anthemousia, Carrhae, Nisibis or Edessa. Indeed, as we saw earlier, it has often been believed that the major Christian Greek writer of the mid-second century, Tatianos, actually came from within the Parthian Empire. But the evidence is simply that at the end of his *Address to the Greeks,* he describes himself as (now) 'philosophising in the style of *barbaroi* (that is, Christians), born in the land of the *Assyrioi,* but first educated in your (that is, the pagan) manner'. In reality he no more came from 'Assyria' (Adiabene on the Tigris, or Babylonia?) than did that other 'Assyrian' with a Latin name, Loukianos from Samosata. The point is of some significance, for two reasons. First, the harmony of the Four Gospels which Tatian composed, the *Diatessaron,* was much used and commented on later, in a Syriac version, by Syriac Christian writers; Ephrem, born in Nisibis in the early fourth century, wrote a commentary on it.[27] But the Greek title of the work suggests that he wrote it, or composed it, in Greek. The deduction is surely made more probable by the fact that a fragment of it in Greek was discovered at Dura; it is thus one of the very few ancient literary texts which date to within a century of the time of composition.[28] Second, as will be seen, the early history of Syriac-speaking Christianity at Edessa is immersed in legend.

Nonetheless, there is no reason in principle why we should not have testimony in Greek from east of the Euphrates, written before the last part of the second century, even if Tatianos' *Address* is not in fact an example of it. There seems, however, to be none available. But there is a brief text in Syriac, of exceptional interest, which may possibly derive from this place and time. This is the *Letter of Mara bar Serapion* ('GRT' DMR' BR SRPYWN) addressed 'to my son Serapion' (LSRPYWN BRY ŠLM). It is known from a single manuscript, which also contains the *Book of the Laws of Countries,* the *Oration of Meliton the Philosopher* and other texts, and was written in the seventh century

---

26. For the statue see W. I. Al-Salihi, "The Weary Hercules of Mesene", *Mesopotamia* 22 (1987), 159, and for the inscription F. A. Pennachietti, "L'iscrizione bilingue greco-partica dell' Eracle di Seleucia", ibid., 169.

27. On Tatianos, see briefly ch. 6 above. To his near-contemporary Clement of Alexandria, Tatian was a Σύρος, which of course leaves the question of his geographical origins open, *Strom.* III, 12, 81. It is only the unreliable and fanciful Epiphanius, *Panar.* XLVI (and cf. *Anaceph.* 3, 46), in the late fourth century, who deduces from what Tatian says of himself that he came from Mesopotamia. For the currency of the *Diatessaron* in Syriac see I. Ortiz de Urbina, *Patrologia Syriaca*[2] (1965), 35ff. and 61–63 (Ephrem's commentary). For a full discussion see W. L. Petersen, *The Diatessaron and Ephrem Syrus as Sources of Romanos the Melodist* (1985), ch. 2.

28. *P. Dura,* no. 10. Note, however, that W. L. Petersen, "New Evidence for the Question of the Original Language of the Diatessaron", in W. Schrage (ed.), *Studien zum Text und Ethik des Neuen Testaments: Festschrift H. Greven* (1986), 325, argues strongly for a Syriac original.

in Estrangela; the *Letter* has been published only once, in 1855, in Serta.[29]

No precise date or place of origin of the *Letter* can be determined. Nor can it be quite certain that a literary composition such as this, cast in the form of a letter of consolation, actually did arise from a concrete situation. The only context which is *presented* in the document is that at some point friends of the father and son had been driven out of Samosata (ŠMYŠT), had been unable to return and had been on their way to Seleucia (SLWQY'), where the writer had gone to meet them. The reference might be to Seleucia/Zeugma, but more probably to Seleucia in Babylonia. Later it turns out that it is the Romans who had acted so as to bar people (who now seem to include the writer) from their country; but it is still to be hoped that they will act justly.

Searching in incomplete narrative sources for suitable contexts for enigmatic items of evidence is a notoriously treacherous process. Nonetheless it is obvious that if there is an appropriate context, it is the early 70s, when Rome first gained control of Samosata, and the sons of Antiochus IV of Commagene fled to Vologaeses of Parthia, only to be brought back in honourable style by a Roman military mission.[30] But even so it has to be admitted that the letter contains no reference to a conquest by armed force. Otherwise any number of relevant episodes may have occurred without ever being recorded in surviving narratives. It does, however, seem improbable that the episode could have belonged after the mid-160s, when Osrhoene became a Roman dependent kingdom, or certainly after the 190s, when Mesopotamia was a heavily garrisoned province.[31]

If by any chance this text does reflect a real situation, specifically the absorption of Commagene in about 72, we still have no explicit indication of where the writer was, except that he refers to his having gone to meet the exiles between Samosata and Seleucia. This specific context might, however, also give extra significance to one of the writer's reflections: 'For what advantage did the Athenians gain by the murder of Socrates, the recompense of which they received in famine and pestilence? Or the people of Samos by the burning of Pythagoras, because in one hour their whole country was entirely covered with sand? Or the Jews by the death of their wise king, because from that same time their kingdom was taken away?'. Could this be the earliest

---

29. W. Cureton, *Spicilegium Syriacum* (1855), pp. 43–48 (text); 70–76 (English translation). The MS is B.M. Add. 14.658, see W. Wright, *Catalogue of the Syriac MSS in the British Museum* III (1872), 1154ff. The only systematic re-examination is by F. Schulthess, "Der Brief des Mara bar Sarapion", *ZDMG* 51 (1897), 365, with discussion and German translation, to which the treatment in this discussion owes much. See now K. E. McVey, "A Fresh Look at the Letter of Mara bar Serapion to His Son", *V Symposium Syriacum* (Or. Chr. Anal. 236, 1990), 257, who regards it as a later Christian composition taking up the stance of a pagan observer.

30. 3.1 above.

31. 3.4 and 4.1 above.

Christian expression of the idea that the crushing of the Jewish revolt and the destruction of the Temple in 70 should be seen as divine punishment for the Crucifixion? It seems probably not; for the writer goes on to say that 'the wise king still lives in reality because of the laws which he promulgated'.

The reference might perhaps be to Solomon and to the subsequent fall of the northern kingdom. But if so, the apparent implication that the Jews were responsible for his death is puzzling. It remains possible that, rather than being an expression of early Syriac Christianity, the *Letter* is a prime example of how the historical perspective of educated people in the Near East was determined by Greek tradition, to which eventually Biblical history was added. The text does not name Christ, but, apart from the passage quoted, it refers elsewhere to Darius, Polycrates, Achilles, Agamemnon, Priam, Archimedes, Socrates, Pythagoras and Palamedes. In other words it shows the absorption of commonplace Greek learning and moralising, of a Stoic colouring, within a Syriac-speaking environment. Or rather, the environment concerned will surely have been bilingual. The concrete illustrations of this before the Roman period are almost non-existent. But, for what it is worth, there is one example of a bilingual tomb inscription, which may date to the early second century, from Mar Yakoub near Edessa.[32] This too comes from a tower-tomb, and records simply the name of the deceased, Amassamsēs the wife of Saredos son of Mannos, which appears in Syriac in two forms: 'MŠMŠ 'TTH or 'NTT DŠRDW BR M'NW. Both the tower, which seems to be of the later first century AD, and the script, which may be early second, show signs of relationship to what would be found at Palmyra at these dates. There is of course nothing surprising in the idea that western Mesopotamia was a bilingual, and bicultural, zone, like the territory of Palmyra, or that the language and script which were to be established as Syriac had not yet fully attained their classical forms.

The *Letter of Mara bar Serapion* does seem (possibly) to date to the 70s and, whatever its date, illustrates the fundamental importance of Greek thought in the evolution of Syriac literature. It is probably not, however, evidence for early Syriac Christianity. Is there such evidence? Or, to put it in other terms, did Christianity function as another element in the culture of this region which was imported from further west? The question is doubly important, for it involves the issue of whether there is any historical content in certain later Greek and Syriac traditions about pre-Roman Osrhoene.[33]

32. H. Pognon, *Inscriptions sémitiques de la Syrie, de la Mésopotamie et de la région de Mossoul* (1897), 104, nos. 57–58. For consideration of the date of the tower and the inscription see Pirenne, op. cit. (n.23), 109–115 (with a photograph of the tower on p. 110).

33. For all the discussion which follows I am dependent on the paper by S. Brock, "Eusebius and Syriac Christianity", in H. W. Attridge and G. Hata (eds.), *Eusebius, Christianity and Judaism* (1992), 212.

It should be made clear, first, that what is at stake is the question of a Christianity transmitted and, in communal terms, organised via the use of a Semitic language: in other words, of an early Syriac church. Second, here as elsewhere, it is virtually impossible to prove a negative; it is hardly conceivable that we could *prove* that there was no Syriac church east of the Euphrates in the first century or the early second. Third, by the time we arrive at the major Syriac work, *The Book of the Laws of the Countries,* 'of' Bardesanes (that is, in which he appears as the main speaker in the dialogue), written in the early third century, the spread of Christianity, east of the Euphrates as elsewhere, can simply be assumed as the conclusive item of evidence for the variability of human customs: 'What shall we say of the new people of us Christians (KRSTYN'), that the Messiah has caused to arise in every place . . . Those who live in Media do not flee away from their dead . . . those who live in Edessa ('WRHY) do not kill their wives or sisters who have committed adultery . . . and those who live in Hatra do not stone thieves'.[34] Whether we can trace the early evolution of an 'eastern' Christianity is too complex a question for now. But what is certain is that by the end of the third century it was claimed that the king Abgar who had been ruling in Osrhoene at the time of Christ had been a convert. For Eusebius in his *Ecclesiastical History* was able to quote extensive documents, translated from 'the language of the Suroi', and preserved in the archives at Edessa: a letter of Abgar to Jesus, with Jesus' reply; and a longer narrative, also translated from Syriac, of how, after the Crucifixion, Judas Thomas sent the apostle Thaddaios to Abgar, and of how he healed Abgar and preached the gospel.[35]

Later, probably in the early fifth century, the story was much more fully embroidered and took the form of a wonderful Christian historical novel, the *Teaching of Addai* (that is, 'Thaddaios'), preserved in a Syriac manuscript of about AD 500.[36] As evidence for the invention of tradition, and (something of considerable importance) the continued relevance of the memory of the kings of Edessa long after the dynasty had ceased, both texts are of great significance. As to the latter aspect, there is also independent confirmation. When the western pilgrim 'Egeria' visited Edessa in the 380s, she was shown Abgar's palace, with the king's portrait and that of his son 'Magnus', and was given a copy of Abgar's letter and Jesus' reply.[37]

But neither text can tell us anything of first-century Edessa, and both leave entirely open the question of when Christianity was first preached there. The

---

34. Trans. H. J. W. Drijvers, *The Book of the Laws of Countries: Dialogue on Fate of Bardaisan of Edessa* (1965), 59–61.

35. Eusebius, *HE* I, 13.

36. For a text and facing translation of this splendid and highly readable work, see G. Howard, *The Teaching of Addai* (1981).

37. Egeria, *Itin.* 18–19; see J. Wilkinson, *Egeria's Travels to the Holy Land*[2] (1981), 113ff.

dynasty unquestionably remained pagan throughout the pre-Roman period, and almost certainly during it also. Similar problems attend the two entirely spurious Syriac martyr-acts, of Sharbil and of the bishop Barsamya, which will also, probably, have been written in the early fifth century. They owe their form to the (relatively) authentic martyr-acts of the Tetrarchic period, discussed below, but otherwise also belong to the category of the evocative historical novel. But nonetheless they too attest to a sense of history in Christian Edessa. The *Acts of Sharbil* begins:

> In year 15 of Autokrator Traianos Kaisar, and in year 3 of the kingship of King Abgar the Seventh, and in year 416 of the kingship of Alexandros, king of the Greeks (MLK' DYWNY') and in the priesthood (KWMRWTH) of Sharbil and Barsamya, Traianos Kaisar gave orders to the governors (HGMWN'—from the Greek *hēgemōn*) of the countries of his dominions, that sacrifices and libations should be increased in all the cities of their administration . . .[38]

The context is quite unhistorical: Trajan gave no general order for sacrifice, and in any case neither in AD 104/105 (by the Seleucid year) nor in 112/113 (by his regnal year) was he in control of what the text calls 'Edessa of the Parthians' ('DS' DPRTWY'). But the vocabulary does reflect that of pagan Edessa, and it may be that the document could properly be used (as it has been) in reconstructing what the pagan city had been like, and what gods were worshipped there.

What is certain is that the historical consciousness of Christian Edessa, centuries after the dynasty had disappeared, continued to give that dynasty a central place. In this way the kings were to enjoy an after-life which makes an extraordinary contrast with the complete disappearance, as regards local traditions, of their counterparts in Commagene or Nabataea or Judaea (a few passing Talmudic references to the Hasmonaeans and Herodians hardly constitute an exception). That prominence was maintained when Christian Syriac writers came to compose historical works. Three out of a number of Syriac chronicles of the Byzantine and medieval periods deserve a brief mention here, precisely because they provide a picture of the dynasty of before the 160s.[39] The first is the *Chronicle of Edessa*, written in about AD 540, which begins, out of chronological order, with a vivid account of a flood in the Seleucid year 513 (AD 201/202), to which we will come, and then continues with the following set of entries. To avoid unnecessary division, the quota-

38. W. Cureton, *Ancient Syriac Documents* (1864), 41ff.

39. For a survey see (as always) S. Brock, "Syriac Historical Writing: A Survey of the Main Sources", *Journal of the Iraqi Academy (Syriac Corporation)* 5 (1979–80), 1, repr. in Brock, *Studies in Syriac Christianity* (1992).

tion will include all those down to the 340s AD. As remained the general rule in Syriac literature as well as documents, the text uses the Seleucid era beginning in October 312 BC:

> In the year 180 (133/132 BC) the kings began to reign in Orhai.
>
> In the year 266 (47/46 BC) Caesar Augustus reigned.
>
> In the year 309 (4/3 BC) our Lord was born.
>
> In the year 400 (AD 88/89) King Abgar built a funerary tower (NPŠ') in honour of his death.
>
> In the year 449 (AD 137/138) Marcion left the catholic church.
>
> [. . .] Caesar Lucius (LWQYS QSR), however, in collaboration with his brother subjected the Parthians to the Romans in the fifth year of his rule (AD 165/166?).
>
> On Tammuz 11 in the year 465 (July 11, 154) Bardesanes (BRDYṢN) was born.
>
> In the year 517 (AD 205/206) Abgar built the palaces (BYRT') in his city.
>
> In the year 551 (AD 239/240) Mani was born.
>
> In the year 614 (AD 302/303) the walls of Orhai collapsed for the second time in the days of King Diocletian (DYQLYṬYNWS MLK').
>
> In the year 624 (AD 312/313) Bishop Qona laid the foundation of the church of Orhai. His successor Ša'd built and completed it.
>
> In the year 635 (AD 323/324) the *koimētērion* of Orhai was built, in the days of the bishop Aitallaha, a year before the great synod in Nicaea.
>
> In the year 636 (AD 324/325) Aitallaha became bishop of Orhai. He built the *koimētērion* and the east side of the church.
>
> In the next year there gathered at Nicaea the synod of 318 bishops.
>
> In the year 639 (AD 327/328) building and additions took place in the church of Orhai.
>
> In the year 649 (AD 337/338) there died Mar Yaqob, bishop of Nisibis (NṢYBYN).
>
> In the year 657 (AD 344/345) Abraham became bishop in Orhai. He built the chapel of the confessors.
>
> In the year 660 (AD 347/348) Constantius the son of Constantine built the city of Amida ('MD MDYNT').
>
> In the year 661 (AD 348/349) Constantius also built the city of TL' (Tella?), which was previously called Antipolis ('NTYPWLYS, Antoninopolis?).[40]

As will be seen, the emphasis is heavily Christian (and the chronicler has confused the year of Mani's birth with that of his first preaching). Two of the

---

40. Full references in App. C. The translation offered here owes much to the German translation of L. Hallier (1892).

kings appear in it, both in quite appropriate terms. One king Abgar builds a funerary tower (NPŠ') in the general period in which these began also in Palmyra; and the most famous of the kings, Abgar the contemporary of Severus, builds a palace (BYRT'). But although the beginning of the dynasty is recorded, nothing is said of its end. For that we have to turn to the major Syriac world-chronicle of about AD 775, probably written at Zuqnin near Amida, often unhelpfully described as being the work of 'Ps-Dionysius of Tell-Mahre', and never fully translated into any European language; to save, or at least limit, confusion, it will be referred to here as the *Chronicle of Zuqnin*.[41] Here the entries detailing what is evidently intended to be a complete list of the kings are scattered among other material. It will suffice to note that the author claims that the dynasty began in the 'year of Abraham' 1880 or the 161st Olympiad (136–133 BC), and ended in the 249th Olympiad (AD 217–220). As will be seen later, some sense can be made of the entries from the 160s onwards, by correlating them with contemporary evidence. As for the earlier entries, often full of circumstantial detail, all that need be noted is that the anonymous author both believed that he had a complete account of the kings to hand and felt that the individual reigns deserved a place in his universal chronicle.

Finally, the continuity of historical tradition in a Syriac context, and the lasting centrality within it of the dynasty of Edessa, is shown nowhere better than in the fact that the most coherent account of the kings is given in a single paragraph by the *Chronicle* of Michael the Syrian (AD 1126–1199). He agrees with the *Chronicle of Edessa* in dating the beginning of the dynasty to the Seleucid year 180 (133/132 BC); but he also offers a historical explanation, namely its having derived from the decline of the Greek and the rise of the 'Aramaean' element there. On his view the kings ruled for 386 years, falling under Roman control in the Seleucid year 477 (AD 165/166), and ending in the fifth year of the Emperor Philip, year 560 (AD 248/249).[42] As we will see later, unless there was a second restoration of the dynasty in the mid-third century, this must be wrong, as the contemporary parchments show. It remains striking that Michael speaks of the area as BYT NHRYN, literally 'between the rivers', exactly the expression used in the newly published Syriac parchment of AD 240.[43] In any case, whatever minor errors or displacements may be found in their narratives, all three writers preserve clear reflections

41. For details see App. C. I am extremely grateful to Sebastian Brock for providing a translation of the relevant sections of this and other Syriac chronicles, including the extract from Michael the Syrian.

42. Text and French translation in J.-B. Chabot, *Chronique de Michel le Syrien* I–V (1901–1924). The relevant extract is V, 5.

43. 12.5 below.

of the moment in the 160s when Edessa/Orhai passed under Roman domination.

12.4. ROMAN DURA-EUROPOS

As already indicated, it was in the 160s, with the Parthian war of Lucius Verus, that contemporary evidence for Edessa becomes relatively fuller. But this was also the moment when Dura passed under Roman rule, and the evidence from there, though it includes no more than fragments of literary works, is considerably more detailed, and much more varied in character and in language, than that from Mesopotamia. Partly for that reason, partly because the life of Dura ended abruptly in the 250s and partly because the evidence now available shows that Syriac documents were known also at Dura, and elsewhere on the middle Euphrates, we will turn back to 'Roman' Dura first, before moving again to Osrhoene.

As we saw earlier, Dura continued to be garrisoned by Palmyrene archers, apparently not yet as part of the regular Roman auxiliary forces, until the 180s or 190s, from which time onwards both other Roman auxiliary units and legionary detachments *(vexillationes)* are attested; from 208 onwards the vast bulk of the extensive surviving military archives in Latin concern the (now regular) Twentieth Cohort of Palmyrenes. The presence of a substantial Roman force, with other detachments stationed up and down the river, is the first and most obvious of the new circumstances which made Dura 'Roman'. From 194 onwards Dura, and the outposts dependent on it, formed an outlying part of Severus' new province of 'Syria Coele'.[1]

The second very general impression (it can hardly be more than that) left by the evidence which we happen to have is of a much more marked intermingling of different elements, in language, personal nomenclature, art and religion, than is apparent from the relatively scanty remains of Parthian Dura.[2]

As regards language, while Greek remains standard, Latin of course now appears in large quantities, not only in military archives proper but, for instance, in an inscribed dedication to the 'Genius of Dura' and 'for the safety of Commodus Augustus', put up by two *decuriones* of the Cohors II Ulpia Paphlagonum Equitata.[3] Palmyrene also continued in public use, as in a Greek/Palmyrene bilingual inscription of AD 228/229 to the goddess Nemesis

---

1. 3.4 and 4.1 above.

2. The best study remains C. B. Welles, "The Population of Roman Dura", in P. R. Coleman-Norton (ed.), *Studies in Roman Economic and Social History in Honor of A. C. Johnson* (1965), 279.

3. *Dura Report* I, 42, no. 1.

(LNMSYS in Palmyrene).[4] More significant is the fact that Aramaic appears for the first time. The extremely important Aramaic inscriptions of the third-century synagogue will be mentioned below. But there is also an enigmatic fragment in Aramaic of what appears to be a letter, also of the early third century; this too may, however, be Jewish.[5] More significant, there is a Greek deed of sale of the same period in which the seller acknowledges receipt in Aramaic: 'Zebida, and [I have received?] the price, *denarii* 5[. . .?]'.[6] So far, it has been only in Judaea and Arabia that we have encountered contexts in which documents were drawn up in Greek, but in which personal attestations could be entered in Semitic languages.

More significant still, there is evidence that Syriac was in use. The famous Syriac deed of sale of 243 had in fact been drawn up in Edessa, and full consideration of it belongs in that context. But it is still noteworthy that it had been in the possession of someone in Dura when the city was destroyed in the next decade; similar considerations apply to the two newly discovered Syriac documents from further up the Euphrates. The deed of sale is not, however, the only trace of Syriac at Dura. Two such items are inscriptions on portable objects, a silver vase and a fragment of pottery.[7] But one is a public document, a votive *stele* from the 'Temple of Hadad and Atargatis'.[8] The text may date to the end of the second century. The dedicator seems to be called 'Vologaeses son of Seleukos' (WLGŠ BR SLQ) and to describe himself as 'pupil of Rama' (TLMD' DRM'); he ends '(may he be) remembered before god' (DKYR QDM 'LH'). Given the public context in a pagan temple, the temptation to see this as a Christian text has to be resisted.

Roman Dura did, however, exhibit an extraordinary variety of different cults, co-existing in close conjunction, including the only known Christian house-church of before AD 312. Apart from the unique evidence provided by the altar which a soldier of IV Scythica chose to dedicate to 'Zeus Betylos of those who dwell by the Orontes',[9] it is conspicuous that local deities from elsewhere in the Roman Near East were widely worshipped there, and that (as it seems) their importation was due to the army. For example, a tribune makes a dedication to the Palmyrene god, Iarhibol; a *legatus* (and others) to Atargatis; and the freedman of a centurion in charge of *vexillationes* to 'I(up-

4. *Dura Report* I, 48 and 62; du Mesnil du Buisson, *Inventaire*, no. 12.

5. *P. Dura*, no. 151; see J. T. Milik, "Parchemin judéo-araméen de Doura-Europos, an 200 ap. J.-C.", *Syria* 45 (1968), 97 (speculative).

6. *P. Dura*, no. 22, fr. *d*., l. 3: [. . .]ZBYD' W[QB]L(?)T(?) [D]MWH DNR' HMŠ[. . .].

7. *Dura Report* IV, 178–191; Drijvers, *Inscriptions*, pp. 50–51.

8. *Dura Report* III, 68–71; Drijvers, *Inscriptions*, no. 63. I am very grateful to Sebastian Brock for comments on this text.

9. Ch. 1 above.

piter) O(ptimus) M(aximus) D(olichenus)' in AD 211.[10] Just before that, the temple of 'Deus Sol Invictus Mithras' had been restored, as a Latin inscription records, by *vexillationes* of the legions IV Scythica and XVI Flavia Firma. But the shrine of Mithras seems to have begun its existence, in a private house, in the 160s; and the earliest record of it is a bilingual inscription put up by a Palmyrene officer in AD 168/169.[11]

Of all the reflections of a complex set of cults, and of a highly distinctive artistic repertoire, which the Roman army left at Dura, the most striking must be the famous painting from the 'Temple of Bel' showing Iulius Terentius, whom we encountered earlier as tribunus of the Cohors XX of Palmyrenes, and who may have died during a Persian raid in 239.[12] This much-reproduced fresco shows Terentius, with a large group of soldiers behind him, and accompanied by a standard-bearer, making a sacrifice on a small altar. He is named in Latin, as 'Iul. Terentius trib.', and one of the soldiers, in Greek, as 'Themēs son of Mokimos, priest'. Five deities are symbolically represented. Three statues of male gods, or possibly deified Emperors, in armour and placed on pedestals, are not identified; but the two statues of seated female deities placed in front of them are: they are the Tychē (Fortune) of Dura and that of Palmyra, both here labelled in Greek.[13] It is striking that this fresco, one of the prime examples of partial frontality in Duran art, is in intention the representation of a Roman military unit celebrating jointly, in Latin and Greek, the 'Fortunes' of the two cities, of which one, Palmyra, was certainly a Roman *colonia* and the other almost certainly was.

For, as we have seen, the Hellenistic past of Dura was heavily emphasised in the early years of the Roman occupation, and continued to be so in the last years, when the city unquestionably was a *colonia*: in the Greek divorce-deed of a Roman soldier drawn up in 254 the city appears as the '*Kolōneia* of the Eurōpaioi of Seleukos Nikatōr, the sacred, inviolate and autonomous'.[14]

It cannot be stressed too strongly that, for all its distinctive regional architecture and art-forms—partially paralleled in both Palmyra and Osrhoene— as a community Dura always remained a Greek, or in the end a Graeco-

10. *Dura Report* II, 90, no. 3 (Iarhibol); III, 43, no. 145 (Atargatis); IX, 107, no. 970 = M. Hörig and E. Schwertheim, *Corpus Cultus Iovis Dolicheni* (1987), no. 32 (cf. no. 33, AD 250/251). For Zeus of Doliche see 7.2 above.

11. *Dura Report* VII–VIII, 83ff.; du Mesnil du Buisson, *Inventaire*, no. 19.

12. 4.1 above.

13. For the scene, in what was previously labelled the 'Temple of the Palmyrene Gods', see F. Cumont, *Fouilles de Doura-Europos*, 89ff. A. Perkins, *Art of Dura-Europos*, 42ff. The fresco is now in the Yale University Art Gallery. A small monochrome reproduction in S. B. Matheson, *Dura-Europos: The Ancient City and the Yale Collection* (1982), 23.

14. 12.2 (early years) and 4.3 (divorce deed).

Roman, city. The traces of the use there of Semitic languages (Palmyrene above all) and—in tiny scraps—of Iranian languages do not serve to refute this proposition. On our evidence, Palmyra, which was a recent growth and was not a Hellenistic foundation, was the only publicly bilingual city in the Roman Near East. But this aspect of the public life of Dura throws into sharper relief the remarkable evidence relating to the Jewish community there, as it was in the third century;[15] and it will also serve to raise questions about the Christian community.

The significance of the remains of the Jewish community lies first of all in the well-known series of frescoes depicting Biblical scenes from the synagogue. Even though the deity is himself of course not portrayed directly, the use of figurative art in this context naturally raises major questions about the religious conventions of this community. In the wider context of the Roman Near East, however, their greatest significance is quite different: not religious but historical. For, apart from scenes from Greek mythology (and frescoes from the church-house at Dura, mentioned below), these Biblical frescoes are the only visual representations from the entire region which explicitly portray events which occurred before the Hellenistic period: the Exodus and the Crossing of the Red Sea; Elijah on Mount Carmel; Samuel anointing David; or Solomon receiving the Queen of Sheba (he is identified in Greek as *Slēmōn*, strikingly reflecting a Syriac vocalisation of the name). The 'amnesia' which so strongly marked the outlook of those who lived in this region was not shared by this remote Jewish community.

What is more, the historical lessons to be imparted by the paintings were reinforced by labelling some of the key figures, either in Greek or in Aramaic, and sometimes by stating what it is that they were portrayed as doing: for example 'Moses, when he went out from Egypt and parted the waters' (MŠH KD NPQ MN [MN] MṢRYM WBZ' L'MH).

It is equally significant, in the absence of public inscriptions in Aramaic put up in Dura by gentiles, that the completion of the final version of the synagogue—created by the internal conversion of a private house—was recorded in a formal inscription in Aramaic, painted on two ceiling-tiles. This was not a public inscription, in the sense of having been visible to passers-by. But it was an official document, in the main place of communal resort:

> This house was built in the year 556, this corresponding to the second year of Philippos [. . .] Kaisar, in the eldership (BQṢYṢWTH) of Samuel, priest (KHNH), son of Yeda'ya the *archon* ('RKWN) . . .

---

15. See A. R. Bellinger, F. E. Brown, A. Perkins and C. B. Welles (eds.), *Dura Final Report* VIII.1, *The Synagogue*[2] (1979); for a brief summary see Schürer, *HJP* III.1 (1986), 10–12. Not all the details are mentioned here.

The year is thus AD 244/245, little more than a decade before the destruction of the city. One of the painted Greek inscriptions from inside the synagogue repeats the information relating to Samuel: 'Samouēl son of Eiddeos, *presbyteros* of the Jews, founded (it)'.

These and other texts, including a number of graffiti in either Greek or Aramaic, suggest that the community, both as a group and as individuals, was bilingual (or even trilingual, since there are a few brief Iranian texts). It seems, however, that Hebrew was retained for liturgical purposes: a Hebrew prayer for use after meals is preserved on scraps of parchment found near the synagogue.[16] That must give extra significance to the communal use of Aramaic and Greek by the Jews in other contexts. There is a close parallel to what we know of Jewish communities of the same general period in Palestine, for instance at Tiberias.[17] But no other fully bilingual Jewish community is known from anywhere else, outside Palestine, within the Roman Empire.

On a much more modest scale than the synagogue, another private house was converted for use as a Christian church.[18] Two features are of particular relevance. One is again the use of narrative art, this time to represent scenes both from the New Testament, for instance the healing of the paralytic, and Christ walking on the water, and from the Old, for instance David and Goliath. The second is the presence of brief painted or scratched inscriptions, nearly all in Greek. Here too, for instance, two Old Testament figures are labelled in Greek, 'Daouid' and 'Goliod' (reflecting the spelling found in Syriac bibles). Several inscriptions invoke the name of Christos, and one proclaims 'One God in Heaven'. One also supplies a date, the Seleucid year 544, AD 232/233.

Slight as the evidence is, it combines with the discovery of a fragment of Tatian's *Diatessaron* in Greek to suggest strongly that this was a Christian community which, like others, read the Old and New Testaments in Greek. If there was an Aramaic-using Christian community (as opposed to a community which might provide an oral translation into Aramaic of a liturgy in Greek, as in Palestine in the early fourth century),[19] there is no contemporary evidence for it at Dura, or anywhere else. The question remains open. But one graffito from the courtyard of the Christian building reveals another possibility: it is unmistakably a Syriac alphabet, written in Estrangela, and from right to left.[20] It is enough to suggest that, in a Christian context as in others, third-century Dura was a meeting-point of Greek and Syriac.

16. *P. Dura*, no. 10.

17. 10.4 above.

18. C. H. Kraeling, *Dura Final Report* VIII.2, *The Christian Building* (1967). The inscriptions are on pp. 87ff.

19. Cf. 5.2. above, text to n. 29.

20. Kraeling, op. cit., 91, no. 3.

12.5. EDESSA AS A KINGDOM AND ROMAN COLONY
UNTIL THE MIDDLE OF THE THIRD CENTURY

The intermingling of Greek and Syriac was also characteristic, as we can now dimly begin to perceive, of the Euphrates zone as a whole. For instance, at a place called El Mas'udiye, on the east bank of the Euphrates opposite Hierapolis and somewhat to the south of Serrin (the site of the Syriac inscription of AD 73/74), there was discovered a mosaic with an inscription in Greek and Syriac, which seems to be dated to the Seleucid year 539, AD 228/229.[1] The mosaic represents a bearded male figure wearing a crown of roses, seated between two female figures thought to represent 'Syria' and 'Mesopotamia'. The identification of the male figure at any rate is not in doubt, for it is the 'king' river Euphrates: 'Basileus Potamos Euphratēs' in Greek, with PRT MLK' written vertically in Syriac below. It is by no means certain that the domains of the dynasty of Osrhoene had ever stretched so far south-west as this; but at this moment, at any rate, the kingdom was no longer in existence, and the whole area was provincial territory. The use of Syriac was a regional phenomenon, which was not a function of any particular political structure. As the evidence from Dura, attached to Syria Coele and situated on the west bank of the river, shows, people living along the middle Euphrates were in connection with Palmyra, across the steppe to the west; with northern Syria, where the governor of the province was normally to be found; and with Mesopotamia, which they will have reached either by going up the Chabur past the site of the later fortress of Circesium, or up the Balikh, which joined the Euphrates at Nicephorium. The same connections are vividly illustrated, as we will see later, in the new archive of documents in Greek and Syriac, dating between the 220s and the 250s, which come from the area around the confluence of the Chabur and the Euphrates. But first we need to look at what we know of the last decades of the dynasty of Osrhoene, from the Parthian war of Lucius Verus in the 160s to the deposition of King Abgar in 212/213 by Caracalla, and the conferment on Edessa of the status of a Roman *colonia*. For, in spite of the caution expressed above, it is above all to Edessa that the evidence for a culture expressed in Syriac relates. It was not, however, a 'native' culture, but a new phenomenon of the Imperial period; to adapt Daniel Schlumberger's phrase about the art of western and central Asia, it was 'a non-Mediterranean descendant of Greek culture'.[2]

Contemporary documents relating to Osrhoene now allow a hypothetical

---

1. For recent treatments of the mosaic (now lost) see J. Balty, "La mosaique au Proche-Orient I", *ANRW* II.12.2 (1981), 347, on pp. 369–370, and Pl. XII.1; K. Parlasca, "Das Mosaik von Mas'udiye aus dem Jahre 228/229 n. Chr.", *Dam. Mitt.* 1 (1983), 263.

2. D. Schlumberger, "Descendants non-Méditerranéens de l'art grec", *Syria* 37 (1960), 131.

reconstruction of the succession of kings who ruled as allies and dependents of Rome; while the details need not be argued here (and hardly matter), it is now clear that the Syriac *Chronicle of Zuqnin* of the eighth century preserves real information, but has placed each king of this later period some twenty-six years too early.[3]

Hypothetically, therefore, it will have been in 162/163–164/165 that Wael son of Sahru 'reigned over Orhai for two years', as the *Chronicle* records. He duly appears on coins as W'L MLK', with Vologaeses IV of Parthia portrayed on the obverse. After him King Ma'nu 'returned from Roman territory, and ruled for twelve more years' (after twenty-four previously). This second period will be 164/165–176/177, and it will be he who is named on coins as either M'NW MLK' or in Greek as 'Basileus Mannos Philorōmaios'; Marcus Aurelius, Lucius Verus and Commodus are also duly represented on his coins. Then came the best-known king of Osrhoene, Abgar son of Ma'nu, who, as the *Chronicle* records, ruled for thirty-five years, so perhaps 176/177–211/212. He appears on coins along with Commodus as 'BGR MLK' or 'Abgaros Basileus', and along with Septimius Severus, in Greek only, with various versions of a Roman name: 'Bas(ileus) L(oukios) Ail(ios) Sep(timios) Abgaros'. Then, according to the *Chronicle,* 'Abgar Severus' ruled for one year and seven months. This seems to fit with the report that Caracalla deposed a king Abgar for cruelty to his subjects, and also with the fact that 212/213 was to be counted as the first year of the 'liberation' of Edessa. His rule was therefore in 211/212 to 212/213.[4]

It was thus the long-lasting (Septimius) Abgar son of Ma'nu, sometimes called Abgar the Great, whose kingdom had its boundaries defined under Severus in 195, and who made a notoriously grand display when visiting Severus in Rome.[5] Seen from within, it was he who was ruling 'in the year 513 in the reign of Severus and the reign of King Abgar son of Ma'nu', thus AD 201/202, when the river Daisan overflowed its banks and a great flood ensued. The detailed account of this which forms the first, and much the longest, entry in the sixth-century *Chronicle of Edessa* has all the style of an eyewitness narrative, and claims to be the work of contemporary scribes. 'Our lord King Abgar' (MRN 'BGR MLK') took steps to counteract the effects of the flood, later re-built his palaces and granted a five-year remission of taxes. His nobles also built themselves new residences in the neighbourhood of the palace.

In a more literal sense of 'seen', it is surely this King Abgar whose portrait occupies the centre of a splendid new funerary mosaic from Edessa, first published in 1981. The four corners of the mosaic are occupied by portraits of

3. For further details see App. C.
4. Cf. 4.2 above.
5. 3.4 above; Dio LXXIX, 16, 2.

the dedicator, BRSMY' BR 'ŠDW, and of other members of his family, each named. The central figure, the bust of a bearded man in a heavy cloak and flat cap, is duly identified as 'BGR BR M'NW; and a text of the dedication is set out below the portrait:

> I, BRSMY' BR 'SDW, made for myself this house of eternity (BYT 'LM'), and for my children and my brother, for the life of 'BGR, my lord and benefactor (MRY W'BD ṬBTY).[6]

In spite of some doubts (since the term 'king' is not used), this should be accepted as a contemporary portrait of Abgar; the dedicator will be a noble of the type mentioned in the narrative of the flood.

If this narrative is indeed essentially contemporary, as seems to be the case, there are two important consequences. One is that one of the buildings destroyed by the flood is described as the 'temple of the church of the Christians' (HYKL' D'DT' DKRSṬYN'). If this is not a later insertion (as is possible), the reference *should* be to a house-church of the type known at Dura; as we saw earlier, the sixth-century *Chronicle of Edessa* itself attributes the laying of the foundations of 'the' church at Edessa to 312/313, exactly when we would expect it.[7] Provisionally, then, this account is evidence of the existence of a Christian community at Edessa to parallel that at Dura.

Second, the narrative of the flood is itself a powerful and vivid piece of writing. As such, it belongs with a contemporary work, the most important product of early Syriac literature, the *Book of the Laws of Countries* (KTB' DNMWS' D'TRWT'). In fact the word translated as 'laws', transliterated from the Greek *nomos,* would be better translated as 'customs'. In structure also the work is a pure borrowing from the Greek dialogue ('A few days ago we went to visit our brother Shamashgeram, when Bardaisan [BRDYṢN] came and found us there . . .'), and it takes the form of a discussion in which Bardaisan demonstrates by reference to the variety of human customs in each area (and the maintenance of the same customs in different areas, as by the Jews) that human conduct is not and cannot be determined by the stars. It is thus that he arrives finally at the proof of this offered by 'the new people of us Christians', in a passage quoted earlier.[8]

We know that Bardaisan, or in Greek Bardēsanēs, belonged in the time of King Abgar, for the Christian scholar Iulius Africanus, a native of Palestine,

6. See H. J. W. Drijvers, "Ein neuentdecktes edessenisches Grabmosaik", *Antike Welt* 12.3 (1981), 17; more fully in "A Tomb for the Life of the King: A Recently-discovered Edessene Mosaic with a Portrait of King Abgar the Great", *Le Muséon* 95.1–2 (1982), 167. Some doubts in J. B. Segal, "A Note on a Mosaic from Edessa", *Syria* 60 (1983), 107.

7. 5.3 above.

8. 12.3 above. Ed. and trans. H. J. W. Drijvers, *The Book of the Laws of Countries: Dialogue on Fate of Bardaiṣan of Edessa* (1965).

encountered 'Bardēsanēs the Parthian' at the court of King Abgaros and his son Mannos.[9] By the early fourth century Bardesanes, 'a Syrian by birth, but who attained to the summit of Chaldaean (astrological) learning', is named as the author of the dialogue by Eusebius, who quotes a large stretch of it in Greek, without, however, saying explicitly that this is a translation. Yet in his *Ecclesiastical History* Eusebius had stated that Bardesanes' many works had been written in 'the language of the *Suroi*', and then been translated into Greek by his followers.[10]

There is no doubt that Bardesanes, whether literally the author of the dialogue or not, was a known personality at Edessa. Much of the thought in the work can be paralleled elsewhere; but in terms of the examples of different customs which it quotes, it is a unique view of the world as seen from the eastern fringes of the Empire. We have already encountered his observation about Christians in Media, Edessa ('WRHY) and Hatra, who did not follow the prevailing customs there, which he had earlier listed, and which were therefore not determined by the stars. Though not all of his examples belong in the Near East, some which do are particularly pointed: 'Recently the Romans have conquered Arabia and done away with all the customs there used to be, particularly circumcision'.[11] As noted earlier, by 'Arabia' ('RB) Bardesanes might have meant anywhere from the Red Sea to Mesopotamia itself. A series of Syriac tomb-inscriptions from Osrhoene, of which two date to AD 164/165, shows local officials, presumably under the kings, with the title 'ruler of Arab' (ŠLYṬ' D'RB). As in the Hauran, these were probably military officials whose role was to control the nomads on the fringe of the settled zone.[12]

Bardesanes' most-quoted local reference, however, is one on which too much has been built: 'In Syria and Edessa (BSWRY WB'WRHY) there was a custom of self-emasculation in honour of TR'T' (Atargatis), but when King Abgar HYMN he ordered that every man who emasculated himself have his hand chopped off. And from that day to this no one emasculates himself in the territory of Edessa (B'TR' D'WRHY)'.[13] The word HYMN, which means 'believed', has often been taken as evidence that Abgar converted to Christianity; and this conversion has then been interpreted as the origin of the legend that the earlier Abgar, the contemporary of Jesus, had been the first royal

9. Africanus, *Kestoi* I, 20; cf. 10.4 above.

10. Eusebius, *Praep. Ev.* VI, 9, 32 to 10, 48. For other sources see H. J. W. Drijvers, *Bardaisan of Edessa* (1966).

11. Trans. Drijvers, op. cit., 57.

12. Drijvers, *Inscriptions*, nos. 5, 7, 9, 10? (undated); 16, 23 (164/165). For the Hauran see 11.5 above.

13. Based on Drijvers' trans., op. cit. (n.8), 59. See Brock, op. cit., 12.3, n.33, for the correct interpretation.

convert. But in fact Bardesanes takes Christianity as a separate and unconnected source of changing customs; and above all Eusebius, in quoting this passage in Greek translation, sees no allusion to Christianity, but simply writes,
'at a single moment King Abgar ordered . . .'.[14] There is thus no good evidence
that the kings of Edessa were ever Christian. If we need a context for the
order which Abgar gave, it can be supplied by Dio's report that Caracalla's
reason, or pretext, for deposing a king Abgar was that he had been mistreating his subjects in the effort to make them conform to Roman customs.[15]

That Abgar, if we follow the eighth-century *Chronicle of Zuqnin*, will
have been Abgar Severus, the son of Abgar 'the Great'; and on the reconstruction given above the date will have been 212/213. But the process of forced
Romanisation might well have started under the father. The question of which
King Abgar is referred to by Bardesanes need not be decided. What is certain
is that 212/213 was to be counted later as year 1 'of the liberation'
(DḤRWR') of Edessa, and presumably therefore of its new status as a *colonia*.[16] For, as we now know from contemporary Syriac documents, the Seleucid year 553 (AD 241/242) counted as year 30 of the liberation, and year
554 (AD 242/243) as year 31. Year 1 was therefore the Seleucid year 524 (212/
213). We will come in a moment to the documents of the early 240s which
embody these dates, and which give the full titles of the city, as a *colonia*, in
that period. For the moment it need merely be noted that colonial status (as
well as 'liberation') did go back at least to the reign of Elagabal (AD 218–222);
for coins of Edessa as a *colonia* start then (or possibly under Caracalla), and
continue to that of Gordian.

But then a striking and unique change follows: coins appear representing
and naming the Emperor Gordian along with a king Abgar, 'Abgaros Basileus'. Moreover, a newly published Syriac document of the Seleucid year 552
(AD 240/241) shows that this year counted as year 2 of this king, whose full
name, in Latin form, was 'Aelius Septimius Abgarus' ('LYWS SPṬMYWS
'BGR MLK'). His year 1 had therefore been 239/240.[17]

We will come back later to the question of what Edessa/'Orhai was like
under its restored dynasty. But the other revelation of the new document is in
some ways even more significant. For it shows that the father of the restored
king Abgar had been a Ma'nu with the title PṢGRYB', 'crown prince'. The
word is used in this sense in yet another wonderful Christian historical novel
written in Syriac, the *Acts of Thomas;* but it also appears on a Syriac inscrip-

---

14. Eusebius, *Praep. Ev.* VI, 44: μιᾷ ῥοπῇ ὁ βασιλεὺς Ἄβγαρος ἐκέλευσε . . .

15. Dio LXXVII, 12, 1ᵃ–1².

16. For this and what follows see Millar, "Roman *Coloniae*", 46–50 (where the first year is
given, incorrectly, as 213/214).

17. See below, text to n.22.

tion from the citadel of Edessa naming 'Šalmath, the queen, daughter of Ma'nu the crown prince' (ŠLMT MLKT' BRT M'NW PṢGRYB');[18] the inscription is thus a reflection of the continued importance of the royal family in 'colonial' Edessa. For the new Syriac document shows also that Ma'nu the 'crown prince' had been the son of 'Abgar the king'. He was therefore (it seems) either the son or perhaps the brother of the Abgar (Severus) deposed in 212/213.

These details would hardly matter if, first, they did not happen to confirm that the *Chronicle of Zuqnin* was, up to a point, right in saying that after 'Abgar Severus' there had been a twenty-six-year reign of 'Ma'nu son of Abgar'. Placing the reign too early, the author in fact associated its end, very reasonably, with fighting in Mesopotamia under Caracalla ('Antoninos') and Macrinus (AD 217/218). But in fact, as is now clear, the twenty-six years will have been 212/213–238/239.

What role was played in Edessa in this period by Ma'nu as 'king-in-waiting' we cannot tell—indeed we do not know whether he was allowed to live there at all: two sons of *a* 'former king Abgaros' are known to have lived in Rome, where one died.[19] But it is to this first 'colonial' period of Edessa that two of the most striking of the mosaics of Edessa are dated. Both show in an extraordinarily explicit way the representation of Greek culture in a Syriac-speaking environment. The first is the mosaic on the floor of a tomb, constructed in the Seleucid year 539 (AD 227/228), which represents Orpheus seated under a tree and playing his lyre to birds and animals around him. In case the identification might be in doubt, a label is attached in Syriac: 'RPWS. The second dates to the year 547 (AD 235/236), and shows a large bird standing on a tomb in a grove of trees. Again it is identified: PNKS (phoenix). A number of other mosaics, none, however, precisely dated, represent the richly robed members of what seem to be Edessene leading families.[20] Though the use of pagan motifs, for instance a funerary couch or a tripod, would not prove that the persons concerned were pagan, there is nothing at all to show the influence of Christianity. But even in what was officially a *colonia*, minting Greek coins, very distinctive local art, dress and language flourished. It seems certain that Edessa remained predominantly a pagan city throughout our period. But Christianity was already established there, as we have seen; and a Christian apology preserved only in the same Syriac manuscript as the Bardesanes dialogue, the *Oration of Meliton the Philosopher* (M'MR'

18. Drijvers, *Inscriptions*, no. 27.

19. *IGR* I, no. 179 = Moretti, *IGUR*, no. 1142.

20. Orpheus: Segal, *Edessa*, Pl. 44; Drijvers, *Inscriptions*, no. 50; Phoenix: Segal, Pl. 43; Drijvers, no. 49. See J. Leroy, "Mosaiques funéraires d'Èdesse", *Syria* 34 (1957), 306; J. Balty, *ANRW* II.12.2 (1981), 387–390.

DMYLYṬWN PYLSWP'), *may* have been written originally in Syriac, and
may emanate from Edessa (or even from Hierapolis, to which it also refers);
if so, the 'Antoninos Kaisar' to whom the heading says that it was addressed
may have been either Marcus Aurelius or Caracalla (both 'M. Aurelius Antoninus') during his campaigns in 216 and 217. But if it really was so addressed, then it must of course have been in a Greek version. However, until
this neglected work, published twice in 1855, has been analysed more carefully, it must be left aside.[21]

The recent publication of authentic documentary evidence means in any
case that we can concentrate on that. The first revelation of the newly published Syriac document from the period of the restored monarchy, already
referred to above, is that not only the political framework but the nature and
even the name of the city have changed. It also gives a glimpse of other places
in the area:

> In the month Kanun of the former year 552, in the year 3 of Autokrator
> Kaisar Markos Antoninos Gordianos, Fortunate and Victorious, in year 2
> of 'LWS SPṬMYWS 'BGR MLK' BR M'NW PṢGRYB' BR 'BGR MLK'
> who is honoured with the HPṬY' (*hypateia*—a 'consular' rank) in 'RHY
> (sic), the fortress city, mother of all the cities of Mesopotamia (DBYT
> NHRYN—literally 'of between the rivers'), this document was written in
> HYKL' KRK' ḤDT' DṢYD' of Abgar the king . . .[22]

One of the parties is called Bageshu son of Abgar son of Shamishu, from the
village (QRYT') of Mihru; his attestation is written for him because he can
neither read nor write. The other is Worod son of Nisharyahab, resident at
Karka, but a native of a place called BYT PWRYN. It is this fact which explains why this contract was found in the new archive of mainly Greek documents which largely relate to places on the Euphrates. For, as we have seen
briefly earlier, 'Beth Phouraia' (spelled in its Greek form in a variety of ways)
was a village on the Euphrates above Dura, not far from its confluence with
the Chabur.[23] A hint of how these places were linked in practice is provided

21. Text (in Serta) in Cureton, *Spicilegium Syriacum* (1855), 22ff. (at end); translation, 41ff.
Text and Latin translation also in J. B. Pitra, *Spicilegium Solesmense* II (1855), xxxiiiff.
J.-M. Vermander, "La parution de l'ouvrage de Celse et la datation de quelques apologies", *Re-
vue des études Augustiniennes* 18 (1972), 27, on pp. 33–36, argues that the addressee
('NṬWNYWS QSR) is Marcus Aurelius, and the date 169. It is very briefly discussed in H. J. W.
Drijvers, *Cults and Beliefs at Edessa* (1980), 35–36. See 7.2 and 8.4 above for what it reports of
cults in Hierapolis and in Byblos.

22. A preliminary publication of the heading in J. Teixidor, "Les derniers rois d'Édesse d'a-
près deux nouveaux documents syriaques", *ZPE* 76 (1989), 219; full text in J. Teixidor, "Deux
documents syriaques du IIIe siècle provenant du moyen Euphrate", *CRAI* (1990), 144, document
A. Photograph on p. 145.

23. 4.1 above. The Greek documents, of which only no. 1 has been fully published (with
admirable speed) so far, will be referred to below as in the list in D. Feissel and J. Gascou,

by the fact that KRK' ḤDT' DṢYD', 'the new Karka of Ṣayda', must be the place which Isidorus refers to as lying on the route between the Euphrates at Zeugma and the headwaters of the Balikh: 'Charaka Sidou, (called) by the Greeks Anthemousia'. The place was 'new', presumably, because Syriac speakers could now revert to using its Semitic name. If it was really within the domains of the restored monarchy, these must have been extended west since Severus' reign.[24]

These Syriac speakers were also Syriac writers. For although the whole document was written by a scribe, five witnesses added their names on the back in Syriac. The use of the language, however, was to survive the abrupt ending of the kingdom and the restoration of colonial status to what was now called, even in Syriac, Edessa: this must have occurred between December of AD 240 and the date of the next Syriac document, also from the new archive, September 242.[25] It is dated by year 5 of Gordian, by the consuls of 242 and (as mentioned above) by year 30 of the liberation of 'the illustrious Antonina Edessa colonia metropolis Aurelia Alexandria' ('NTWNYN' 'DYS' NṢYḤT' QLWNY' MṬRPWLS 'WRLY' 'LKSNDRY'). This document too, however, was not written at Edessa, but at a place called Marcopolis Thera (?)—MRQPWLS TR'—which turns out to have its own local officials: 'in the priesthood (KMRWT') of Markos Aurelios 'NṬ'HYWRWS son of Aggai, and in the archonship ('RKWNWT') of Markos Aurelios Alexandros son of SWBS and of BR'T' BR ŠLMSYN'. Once again Worod from Beth Phouraia on the Euphrates is involved, leasing some land to a native of Marcopolis. 'Marcopolis', it seems, was in fact yet another name for Charaka Sidou/Anthemousia, and may have come into use before the brief royal restoration. But now at any rate a Greek/Syriac *polis* with a Latin/Greek name is functioning there; in this region city-formation continued to the end of the period.

The same context—the restored colonial status of Edessa under Roman rule—is also revealed in the famous Syriac bill of sale of 243, found at Dura but written, in this case, in Edessa itself.[26] One copy was to be entered in the archives (B'RKYWN—*archeion*) of the city. Various features of this document are worth emphasis. First, there is in this case no internal evidence to suggest why it will subsequently have been taken, in the course of the next

---

"Documents d'archives romains inédits du Moyen-Euphrate (IIIᵉ siècle après J.-C.)", *CRAI* (1989), 535.

24. Cf. 3.4 above.

25. The first nine lines of this difficult text are published by Teixidor as document B in *CRAI* (1990), 154ff. In l.4 Teixidor reads B'MRWT', 'in the residency', surely wrongly, as Sebastian Brock kindly confirms. For this was originally read in *P. Dura*, no. 28, l.4, but corrected to BKMRWT', 'in the priesthood', by J. Goldstein in *JNES* 25 (1966), 1. Teixidor unfortunately pursues the idea of a Roman 'resident' official being posted to the town.

26. *P. Dura*, no. 28; J. Goldstein, *JNES* 25 (1966), 1; Drijvers, *Inscriptions*, pp. 54–57. Cf. 4.2 above.

decade, to Dura. Second, the character of Edessa as a *colonia* is shown not only in its title but in the use of the transliterated Greek term *stratēgia* (B'STRTGWT')—the normal equivalent for *duumviratus*—for its two annual magistrates, thus exactly as at Palmyra in the same period. As at Palmyra, one of these is a Roman *eques,* a rank signified by transliterating the Greek words *hippeus,* 'horseman' (HPWS), and *rōmaios* (RHMWS). Third, one of the witnesses signs in Greek, and another, on the back, in both languages. He in fact is one of the two *stratēgoi,* Marcus Aurelius Abgar, and signs as 'WRLS 'BGR STRTG ŠHD (witness) in Syriac, and as 'Abgaros' in Greek. Formal proof of basic literacy in both scripts is rare. The other witnesses sign their names in Syriac. But the seller in the contract (for the purchase of a female slave) does not, because she is illiterate. Her husband therefore writes her attestation for her. Like everyone concerned, he is a Roman citizen with the *nomen* 'Aurelius': 'I, 'WRLS HPSY BR ŠMŠYHB, Edessene ('DYSY') of the twelfth tribe (PYLYS—from the Greek *phylēs*), declare that I have written on behalf of 'WRLY' MTR'T', my wife, in the subscription because she has not the capacity to write'.

Like the other Syriac documents, however, this one also takes us outside Edessa itself. For the purchaser comes from Carrhae/Harran—now, as we saw earlier, another Roman *colonia*—and duly has a full Roman name: LWQS 'WRLS TYRW BR BRB'ŠMN HRNY'—'Lucius Aurelius Tiro . . . Harranian'. Slight as it is, this glimpse of someone from this ancient city represents almost our only evidence for it in the Imperial period, between the first century BC, when its people are reported to have regarded themselves still as Macedonian settlers, and the late Empire, when the famous temple of the Moon-goddess (which Caracalla had been on his way to visit when murdered in 217) was still open, and the population was still firmly pagan.[27] But here as elsewhere in Roman Mesopotamia of the third century, brief snapshots are also available (or soon will be) from the new archive from the middle Euphrates. The fact that this is so is itself an indication of the links between the two areas.[28]

So, for instance, one of the new documents is a Greek contract of sale drawn up at Carrhae ('Aurelia Carrhae colonia, metropolis of Mesopotamia') in AD 250. The seller, Aurēlios Barbesumēs from Carrhae, belonging to the tribe 'Antōnianē', makes his attestation in Syriac, as do the witnesses. The purchaser of the mare in question comes from Beth Phouraia on the Euphrates.

27. See W. Cramer, "Harran", *RAC* XIII (1986), 634; for the site, with its circuit of walls, see S. Lloyd and W. Brice, "Harran", *Anat. Stud.* 1 (1951), 77.

28. As noted above, I depend on the list given by Feissel and Gascou, *CRAI* (1989), 557ff. In the order as mentioned below: no. 10 (Carrhae); nos. 8–9 (Nisibis); 6–7 (Marcopolis); 12 (Beth Phouraia); 3–4 (petition of *bouleutēs* of Neapolis).

The economic contacts made in daily life there prove to have stretched even as far as Nisibis. A contract for the sale of a slave at Beth Phouraia in 251 refers back to a previous contract, drawn up in the *colonia* of Nisibis in 250, for the sale of the same slave to a man named Absalmas son of Abdrodakos; he comes from the village of Bēathagaē in the territory of 'Theganaba', in an area called Abourēnē. This must mean the area round the Chabur River, probably its upper reaches. A similar slave-sale of the next year shows a native of another village in Abourēnē, resident at Beth Phouraia, re-selling a slave whom he had bought at Nisibis from the wife of a centurion. Here, for the first time, we come across a subscription in Syriac written at Beth Phouraia, west of the Euphrates.

Similarly, from the western part of Mesopotamia there are two copies of another contract for the sale of a slave drawn up in 249 at the place now called Marcopolis. Again, while the document is in Greek, the subscriptions are in Syriac, including a declaration by Aurelius Kozas on behalf of his sister Matthabeinē, who is illiterate. Finally, it is striking that some Greek documents drawn up at Beth Phouraia, and with no apparent involvement of people from Mesopotamia, also contain subscriptions in Syriac. One of these is a document of a different sort, a petition addressed to a Roman *praefectus*. The writer is Aurelius Abdsautas son of Abidierdos, a *bouleutēs* of Neapolis (as it seems, literally a 'new city' created out of the town of Appadana on the Euphrates north of Dura), but resident in Beth Phouraia. Even he, whose new rank might seem a prime example of the still active influence of Graeco-Roman models of urban life, and who is addressing a Roman official, nonetheless makes his subscription in Syriac. Even this one archive of the mid-third century must mean that the earlier history of the diffusion and use of Syriac has to be entirely re-considered.

In political terms, as we saw earlier, the new archive, with its dated documents, provides conclusive evidence that in the middle of the third century all of Mesopotamia, from Marcopolis eastwards to Carrhae and Nisibis, was in Roman hands. Like Palmyra, the whole region from the Euphrates to the Tigris was now 'Roman', 'Greek' and 'Syrian' at the same time.

12.6. SOCIAL AND RELIGIOUS CURRENTS IN THE FOURTH CENTURY

After the middle of the third century our evidence for the whole area shaped by the Euphrates, by the two rivers running into it from the Mesopotamian shelf, the Balikh and the Chabur, and by the Tigris, of which a long stretch became 'Roman' under the treaty of 298/299, is virtually non-existent for some decades.

Even taking a longer view, we know very little indeed either of the eastern part of what became Roman Mesopotamia, of the earlier social history of the Tur Abdin (Mons Masius) or of the plain to the north of it around Amida, which was to be fortified by Constantius in the 330s.[1] This latter area was to be the heartland of Syriac monasticism, whose last remnants still persist there.[2] Even of Nisibis, which was clearly the central place in the eastern part of the Mesopotamian shelf, we have only scraps of external information from the Parthian and earlier Roman periods.[3]

The effect of our ignorance is above all that we can supply no significant context or background against which to set the writings of the greatest figure in early Syriac Christianity, Ephrem, born at Nisibis in the early years of the fourth century.[4] We can take it as certain, however, that both as a Graeco-Roman city, a *colonia,* with a city-council as normal, and as a Christian community, Nisibis continued to be a bilingual, not to say trilingual, place. The earliest surviving Christian monument of the region is a baptistry at Nisibis dated by the Greek building-inscription of the bishop Vologaeses and the presbyter Akepsumas to AD 359.[5]

The social structure, the languages and the art and architecture of the whole region, of which part, the middle Euphrates, had been under Roman rule from the 160s and the rest from the 190s, all remain mysterious, to be glimpsed only in scattered items of internal and external evidence. The villages which certainly lined the rivers and covered the fertile area of the north-Mesopotamian shelf are as yet in most cases not even names. But the new archive is sufficient to show, what we could not have presumed, that daily life there involved the use of legal documents written in both Greek and Syriac—and the latter on the western bank of the Euphrates, as well as in Mesopotamia. Even the cities remain hardly more than names, at least until we encounter Ammianus' eye-witness narrative of events in the mid-fourth century. But again the new archive shows how real were the changes of identity brought

1. For the final stages of the Roman advance into this area, 5.3 above.

2. For an extremely interesting account, unfortunately accompanied by a quite remarkably unintelligible map (pp. xxi–xxii), see A. Palmer, *Monk and Mason on the Tigris Frontier: The Early History of Tur 'Abdin* (1990).

3. See, e.g., N. Pigulevskaya, *Les villes de l'état iranien aux époques parthe et sassanide* (1963), ch. 4, "Nisibe, ville frontière".

4. On Ephrem, whom I merely mention, not being in a position to say more, see, e.g., R. Murray, *Symbols of Church and Kingdom: A Study in Early Syriac Tradition* (1975), 29ff.; K. E. McVey and J. Meyerdorff, *Ephrem the Syrian: Hymns* (1989), introd. and trans. Cf. also S. Brock, *The Luminous Eye: The Spiritual World Vision of St. Ephrem* (1985).

5. For the 'ordo et populus' there, Ammianus XXV, 9, 2. For the baptistery of Mar Yakoup see, e.g., M. M. Mango, "The Continuity of the Classical Tradition in the Art and Architecture of Northern Mesopotamia", in N. Garsoian, T. F. Matthews and R. W. Thomson (eds.), *East of Byzantium: Syria and Armenia in the Formative Period* (1982), 115; C. S. Lightfoot, "Facts and Fiction—the Third Siege of Nisibis", *Historia* 32 (1988), 105, on pp. 109–110.

about by the conferment of the title *colonia,* as well as illustrating both the police-functions of the army and the economic exchanges between soldier and civilian.[6]

Yet a further—and still more mysterious—element in an already complex social and cultural pattern will have been created by trade passing through this part of the Fertile Crescent. Our earlier sources, Strabo and Isidorus, speak of trade going across the Euphrates and then down the Balikh and downstream along the Euphrates to Babylonia. Another of the documents in the new archive shows Worod of Beth Phouraia advising his son Nisraios about hiring pack-camels for the transport of goods from Beroea (Aleppo) to Zeugma.[7] They might perhaps have then gone on to the middle Euphrates, where Beth Phouraia lay. But it *may* be that later the main direction of long-distance trade changed: not down the Euphrates but across the Fertile Crescent and then down the Tigris. Ammianus records that when Julian reached Carrhae, two roads to Persia lay open—eastward by Adiabene and the Tigris, or south via the Euphrates.[8] But it is possible that a trade-route now led not down the Tigris to Babylonia and the Gulf but directly eastwards to central Asia. Any such conclusion would, however, be too much to build on a scatter of literary references, though these are certainly suggestive. There is, first, the role of Nisibis as a centre for commercial exchanges, as laid down in the treaty of 298/299. Then there is the description in the *Expositio totius mundi,* written in the mid-fourth century, of the wealth which Nisibis and Edessa (or Amida?) gained from trade with Persia, and from the re-sale of goods to the rest of the Roman world.[9] But above all there is Ammianus' account of Batnae, a town situated near the headwaters of the Balikh, in the area which Isidorus had called Batanē:

> The town of Batne, founded in Anthemusia in early times by a band of Macedonians, is separated by a short space from the river Euphrates; it is filled with wealthy traders when, at the yearly festival, near the beginning of the month of September, a great crowd of every condition gathers for the fair, to traffic in the wares sent from India and China, and in other articles that are regularly brought there in great abundance by land and sea.[10]

Whether there was really a profound change in the direction of trade remains uncertain, for this district had always, as we have seen, been on the

6. 4.1 and 12.5 above.

7. *CRAI* (1989), 560, no. 16.

8. Ammianus XXIII, 3, 1. For Ammianus' account of the Mesopotamian region, see above all J. Matthews, *The Roman World of Ammianus* (1989), esp. chs. 4 and 8.

9. Treaty: 5.1 above; *Expositio totius mundi et gentium* 22, ed. J. Rougé (*SC* no. 124, 1966).

10. Ammianus XIV, 3, 3, Loeb trans.

favoured road which led via the Balikh down the Euphrates. Ammianus' typically vivid narrative at this point is perhaps more significant in revealing how
all these places lay close to barren steppe, and were exposed to the raids of
the *Saraceni* who lived there. For in this year (AD 354) a daring Persian raid
along the southern edge of Roman Mesopotamia had been directed through
the steppe ('per solitudines') and had crossed the narrow fertile strip on either
side of the Chabur ('Aboraeque amnis herbidas ripas'); the Persian forces
were then joined by the *Saraceni,* of whom Ammianus gives a highly coloured,
if conventional, account. In his view all the unsettled peoples, practising no
agriculture, and using horses and camels, from the Nile to 'Assyria' had the
same customs.[11] He later returns to their dangerous and unstable diplomatic
and military relations with the Empire several times, in the course of narrating
Julian's march into Persia—first when the *reguli* of the *Saracenae gentes* came
to greet the Emperor at Callinicum, where the Balikh flows into the Euphrates.[12] Not much had changed since Strabo's time except that Roman forces
were now present on this 'desert frontier'; and now, for the first time, we see
these *gentes* playing that military role in relation to Rome which was to be so
important in later centuries.

There is no contradiction between describing the line of Roman forts and
roads along the edge of the steppe as a 'frontier' and admitting that *Saraceni*
were to be found inside that line as well as outside it. Those who came to
greet Julian at Callinicum may have come either from the east or from the
west of the Euphrates, that is, from the large space between Palmyra and its
territory to the south, and Chalcis, Beroea and Hierapolis to the north. Ordinary travellers in this area never ceased to be in danger of their attacks. This
fact provides the context for the brilliantly evocative *Life* of the hermit Malchus by Jerome, written in the early 390s and set in the first half of the fourth
century. Its hero, whose story is narrated by himself in the first person, as
allegedly told to Jerome many years before, came from a family of farmers at
Nisibis. Determining to be a monk, but unable to go east 'because of the
Persians and the Roman frontier' (the story is set before 363), he instead went
west to the desert of Chalcis. But then, wanting to see his parents, he began
to travel east again:

> Lying near the public highway from Beroea to Edessa, there is a desert
> through which nomad Saracens are always wandering back and forth. For
> this reason, travellers along the way group together and, by mutual aid,

11. Ammianus XIV, 4. See esp. B. Shaw, "Eaters of Flesh, Drinkers of Milk: The Ancient
Mediterranean Ideology of the Pastoral Nomad", *Ancient Society* 13–14 (1982–83), 5.

12. Ammianus XXIII, 3, 8; cf., e.g., XXIV, 1, 10; 2, 4: 'Malechus Podosacis nomine, phylarchus Saracenorum Assanitarum', perhaps the earliest reference to the Ghassanids; see Matthews, op. cit. (n.8), 352.

decrease the danger of surprise attack. There were in my company men, women, old men, young people, children, numbering in all about seventy. Suddenly, Ishmaelites, riding upon horses and camels, descended upon us in a startling attack, with their long hair flying from under their head-bands. They wore cloaks over their half-naked bodies, and broad boots. Quivers hung from their shoulders; their unstrung bows dangled at their sides; they carried long spears, for they had not come for battle but for plunder.[13]

The rest of the tale, his captivity and eventual escape, need not concern us. What matters is the vivid portrait of the *Saraceni*. Jerome does not trouble to indicate precise dates and places, and it is not even clear whether this dramatic episode is supposed to have occurred west or east of the Euphrates. It does not matter, for the whole route was similarly exposed. For all its stereotypical and over-dramatised elements, the story is a genuine reflection of social con-trasts and conflicts along the edge of the steppe.

Nonetheless, although this factor remained constant, very profound changes had occurred in the four centuries since Crassus had met his famous disaster outside Carrhae in 53 BC. There was the definite extension of Roman rule, even if in the mid-third century it withdrew again from Dura and the middle Euphrates below the Chabur, and in the mid-fourth from Nisibis and eastern Mesopotamia; the presence of Roman governors and soldiers, acting under the orders of distant Emperors; the re-enactment of the earlier Hellenis-tic process of city-formation, not only creating new Greek cities, like Marco-polis, Neapolis or Antininopolis (later Constantia), but making Roman *co-loniae* of Dura, Carrhae, Rheshaina, Singara, Nisibis and Edessa; the spread of Christianity; and the emergence of Syriac as a literary language.

Why this emergence should have coincided quite closely with the spread of Roman rule, it is impossible to say; no such development took place in the case of either Nabataean or Palmyrene. But Syriac was in any case not con-fined to the area ruled by Rome. The twenty-three surviving homilies of Aphrahat, dating to AD 336/337 and 343/344, were written outside the Em-pire, under Sasanid rule.[14] The emergence both of a Syriac-speaking church and of Syriac as a language in which Christian theology could be expressed was therefore a phenomenon which was not dependent on the existence of the Empire; nor on the other hand did the influence of this Graeco-Roman empire serve to suppress it. The contrast with Nabataean and Palmyrene re-mains to be explained.

---

13. Jerome, *V. Malchi* (PL XXIII, cols. 55–62), 4. Trans. M. L. Ewald in R. J. Deferrari (ed.), *Early Christian Biographies* (1952), 281ff. See J. N. D. Kelly, *Jerome* (1975), 71–72.

14. I. Parisot, *Aphraatis Sapientis Persae Demonstrationes, Patrologia Syriaca* I.1–2 (1904–1907); see A. Vööbus, "Aphrahat", *Jahrb. f. Ant. u. Chr.* 3 (1960), 152; I. Ortiz de Urbina,

The fact that Syriac was a living language in which not only theological disquisitions but real-life narratives could be written does, however, mean that we can see the Roman Empire of the early fourth century, and the city of Edessa, not only through Greek and Latin sources, but through the medium of two brilliant Christian historical narratives composed in Syriac, the martyr-acts of Shmona and Guria and of Habib the deacon, set in the Great Persecution.[15]

These texts, each known only from a single late manuscript, are certainly not documentary records of events; hence they were not used earlier in the description of the effects of the Great Persecution in the Near East.[16] But they are, on the other hand, not pure historical fictions like the Syriac martyr-acts of Sharbil and Barsamya, set under Trajan.[17] The three martyrs are named as such by Ephrem, and are also listed in a calendar of martyrs at Edessa which is contained in the earliest Syriac literary manuscript, of AD 411.[18] There can be no certainty that the surviving manuscripts of these martyr-acts themselves accurately represent what was originally written. But it does seem that what we have goes back to narratives, with strongly marked novelistic and didactic elements, which were written in Edessa in the fourth century, and do genuinely reflect the historical circumstances of the Great Persecution, the life of the city, the country-districts (QWRY') around it, or an individual village (QRYT'), and even the institutions of Edessa as a *colonia*.

Thus the *Martyrdom of Shmona and Guria* begins: 'In the year 618 of the kingdom of Alexander, the Macedonian king (MLK' M'QDWNY') . . . in the magistracy ('SṬRṬYGWT', as in the Syriac contracts) of Aba and of Abgar son of Z'ora, in the days of Qona bishop of Edessa ('PSQWP' D'WRHY), the wicked Diocletian had made a persecution'. The Seleucid year 618 was AD 306/307, when Diocletian had already abdicated. But the sequence of persecutions had been initiated by him in 303, and general orders for sacrifice were being enforced in the Near East in these years.[19] The writer's perception of exactly which Emperor had been in power when is vague, just as it is in the account (presented as being by the same hand) of the martyrdom of Habib. Here the year given is 620, 308/309, but the persecuting Emperor is named (wrongly) as Licinius (LYQNS MLK'), while rumours are spreading that Con-

---

*Patrologia Syriaca*² (1965), 46–51; T. D. Barnes, "Constantine and the Christians of Persia", *JRS* 75 (1985), 126.

15. See for texts and translations F. C. Burkitt, *Euphemia and the Goth, with the Acts of Martyrdom of the Confessors of Edessa* (1913).

16. 5.2 above.

17. 12.3 above.

18. See Brock, op. cit. in 12.3, n.33.

19. 5.2 above.

stantine, in the west, is not persecuting, and is about to march against him. The wider circumstances are hopelessly confused, reflecting (if anything) the relations of Constantine, Maxentius and Licinius in 312/313. But here too the office of the two chief magistrates of the city is correctly called 'SṬRGṬYGWT' (the *stratēgia* or *duumviratus* of a *colonia*); and the governor (HGMWN'—*hēgemōn*, the normal Greek for *praeses*) is portrayed exercising power in the city attended by his staff (ṬKS'—*taxis*) or *officiales* ('WPYQYN). It is indeed precisely the fact that the narrative is shot through with Greek and Latin loan-words that shows that this is the language of everyday life in a city under Roman rule: the governor's court of justice (BYT DYN') may also be called a DYQSṬRYN *(dikastērion)*; there he sits on his B'M *(bēma*—tribunal) in the BSLYQ' near the baths (BL'NY—*balaneia*). We thus see, in narrative form, something of the integration of two—and up to a point three—languages which is also visible in the public inscriptions of Palmyra.

The *purpose* of the narrative, however, is to display not accommodation and integration but the unyielding opposition of Christian principles and Christian tradition to the demands of the pagan state. Perhaps surprisingly, neither martyr-act has anything much to say of the pagan cults of the city. For an evocation of those we have to turn, unfortunately, to the fictional martyr acts of Sharbil and Barsamya, set under Trajan:

> The whole city was assembled together near the great altar which is in the middle of the city opposite the office of records, all the gods having been brought together, and then been decorated, and set up in honour, both Nebu and Bel together with their companions. And all the high-priests were offering sweet incense and libations, and the odour of the sacrifices was diffusing itself, and sheep and oxen were being slaughtered, and the voice of the harp and the tabor was heard in the whole of the city.[20]

But whether a valid reconstruction of the paganism of Edessa can be based on this and other later Syriac sources is a question which must be left aside here.[21] It is more important to stress that in the relatively authentic martyr-acts of the Great Persecution a ringing appeal is made to the historical inheritance of the Bible. Shmona, suspended head down by his torturers, invokes the God of Abraham, Joseph, Moses, Jephthah, David, Daniel, Simon, Paul and Stephen. Yet it is precisely this which serves to recall the paradox presented by the historical culture of the Near East in this period. The martyr

20. For the Acts of Sharbil and Barsamya see 12.3 above. Trans. W. Cureton, *Ancient Syriac Documents* (1864), 41.

21. See the extremely interesting book of H. J. W. Drijvers, *Cults and Beliefs at Edessa* (1980), which nonetheless seems to depend to a hazardous degree on later Syriac Christian works.

makes an appeal, in Syriac, to the central figures in a national tradition first set out in another Semitic language, Hebrew. But what he says could have been said, and was, just as well by contemporaries speaking in Greek, or in Latin. What, if anything, the historical perspective of Syriac-speaking Christians the Roman Empire was to owe to traditions from outside Greek culture is still mysterious. But it would not at any rate be any sense of the history of the period before Alexander other than that derived from the Bible.

Nor was the communal reaction of Christians in Edessa to the restitution ordered by Constantine and Licinius visibly different from that anywhere else: as the sixth-century *Chronicle of Edessa* records, from AD 312/313 onwards they built a church, a cemetery and a chapel to the memory of the confessors.[22] But by now the story of Abraham as told in Genesis could be exploited to give Carrhae a place in religious history to which Edessa could lay no claim. When the western pilgrim Egeria visited Carrhae in the 380s, she was shown a church outside the city which stood on the site of Abraham's house, and the well from which Rebecca had drawn water. The well where Jacob had watered the animals fed by Rachel lay further outside the city, but could be visited, whereas Ur of the Chaldees lay ten days' journey away, beyond Nisibis and the Persian frontier.[23] Most of the population of Carrhae itself was still pagan; for the Christians, however, the place had now acquired a special role in the earliest history of their faith. In a very similar way, as we have seen, some of the *Saraceni* whom Christians had long been accustomed to label 'Ishmaelites' would themselves begin to acknowledge their descent from Hagar and Abraham.[24]

22. 12.3 above.

23. *Itinerarium Egeriae* 20–21; cf. P. Maraval (ed.), *Égérie, journal de voyage* (SC 296, 1982), 21ff.; J. Wilkinson, *Egeria's Travels*[2] (1981), 117ff.

24. Ch. 1 above and 13.1 below.

CHAPTER 13

EPILOGUE:
EAST AND WEST

13.1. EAST?

If anything is clear about the social history of the Near East, it is the importance for it of the step-by-step advance of the Roman army; and few reflections of that are more vivid and illuminating than what is said of himself by the author of a Greek novel written in the middle of the second century. To be precise, what we know of this self-description comes from the summary of the novel, entitled *Babyloniaca*, which Photius included in his compendium of Greek literature, the *Bibliotheca* ('Library'), in the ninth century.[1] From the summary it seems that it was in an aside or parenthesis in the middle of the novel that the author, Iamblichus, went into some detail about himself and the historical circumstances under which he was writing. The occasion seems to have arisen from his account of different types of magic, including the employment of a ventriloquist 'whom the Greeks call "Eurycles" while the Babylonians use the term "Sakchoura"'. It was at that point that the author identified himself:

> The writer (Photius writes) says that he himself is a Babylonian, has studied magic and also Hellenic *paideia,* and is flourishing in the time of Soaimos the Achaemenid and Arsacid, who is a king and descendant of kings, but is also a member of the Senate in Rome, and consul, and then again king of Greater Armenia. It is in his time that he says that he himself

1. Photius, *Bib.* 94, ed. R. Henry II (1960), 34ff.; for the complete fragments of the *Babyloniaca* see the Teubner ed. by R. Hercher, *Iamblichi Babyloniacorum Reliquiae* (1960). It is translated with an introduction in B. P. Reardon (ed.), *Collected Ancient Greek Novels* (1989), 783ff. See T. Hägg, *The Novel in Antiquity* (1983), esp. 32–34.

is flourishing. He states that Antoninus is ruling the Romans, and when Antoninus, he says, sent Verus, his fellow-Emperor, brother and son-in-law, to fight against Vologaeses the Parthian, he himself predicted the war, both that it would take place and how it would end. Also that Vologaeses fled beyond the Euphrates and Tigris, while the land of the Parthians became subject to the Romans.

These words must thus have been written after the end of the Parthian war fought by Lucius Verus in 162–166, and perhaps after Verus' death in 169, since Marcus Aurelius seems to have been represented as the sole current Emperor. Taken literally, Iamblichus' picture of the effects of the Roman victory gives a more definite conception of the subjugation even of Mesopotamia, let alone of the rest of the Parthian Empire, than other evidence would suggest. But this was at any rate certainly the moment when Dura came under Roman occupation, when the kingdom of Osrhoene acknowledged Roman sovereignty and perhaps when Roman forces came to be stationed in Nisibis.[2]

As we saw also, this was the moment when Roman forces advanced, for a time, far beyond the upper Euphrates. A pro-Roman king, Sohaemus, was indeed installed in Armenia in 164, only to be driven out again in 172, and restored by Roman forces.[3] But who this Sohaemus was, and where he came from, is a mystery. The mere coincidence of the name is certainly not enough to prove that he was a member of the dynasty which had ceased to rule in Emesa in the 70s.[4]

What matters about this passage is the vividness and detail of its reflection of military history and successive political regimes in the Near East. But although the author who is here portraying himself is not a character in the novel (which is told in the third person), we should be careful before assuming that it is literally a report about a 'real' Iamblichus. It is perfectly possible that whoever wrote the work has constructed this authorial *persona*. That would not matter for historical purposes; it would be equally significant if a real historical setting—as this is—had been deployed in order to give substance to a fictional narrator.

In any case Photius' brief summary of the novel, originally of considerable length, may well have been too brief here, and have amalgamated two per-

2. See 3.4 above.

3. Dio LXXI, 2, 3. See 3.4 above, and M.-L. Chaumont, "L'Arménie entre Rome et l'Iran I", *ANRW* II.9.1 (1976), 71, on pp. 149ff.

4. His origin in Emesa is, however, assumed by G. W. Bowersock, "Roman Senators from the Near East: Syria, Judaea, Arabia, Mesopotamia", in S. Panciera (ed.), *Epigraphia e ordine senatorio* II (1982), 651, on p. 665, suggesting that the reference to his having been an 'Achaemenid and Arsacid' is a gloss.

sons, whether real or fictional. For a note inserted in the margin by the scribe who wrote the oldest manuscript of the *Bibliotheca,* of the early tenth century, claims that Iamblichus had not been by origin a Babylonian himself, but was a Syrian who had absorbed Babylonian learning. The unknown author of the marginal note must implicitly be claiming to have read the relevant passage more carefully than Photius had. If he had indeed done so, what 'Iamblichus' had written of himself had not only made even more extensive use of the military history of the second century than Photius reveals, but had made claims of far-reaching significance about the culture of the Near East in this period. What the marginal note contains needs to be set out in full:

> This Iamblichus was a Syrian by race on both his father's and his mother's side, a Syrian not in the sense of the Greeks who have settled in Syria, but of the native ones, familiar with the Syrian language and living by their customs. Until, as he says, a Babylonian tutor *(tropheus)* took charge of him, and taught him the Babylonian language and customs and stories, of which (he says) one is the tale which he is now writing down. The Babylonian had been taken prisoner at the time when Trajan invaded Babylon, and was sold to the Syrian by the dealers in spoils. He was skilled in barbarian learning, to the extent of having been one of the royal secretaries while in his native land. As for Iamblichus himself, who knew his native Syrian language, and subsequently learned also the Babylonian language, he says that he afterwards, by application and use, acquired Greek also, to the extent of becoming a skilled rhetor.[5]

This note could indeed derive from a closer and less hurried reading of the original novel than Photius' summary did. For the historical framework which it presents is, in broad terms, perfectly appropriate: a Babylonian sold as a captive after Trajan's campaign of 116, and then entering the service of a family in Syria; and his pupil using what he had learned of Babylonia to write a novel in Greek in the aftermath of Verus' Parthian war of 162–166. But again we have to be careful about taking all this too literally. For a start, the novel itself, as the summary shows, is in no way derived from any recognisably Babylonian, or Akkadian, tradition, but is a typical Greek romance set in exotic foreign parts and involving a beautiful young married couple called Rhodanes and Sinonis, a lustful king of Babylon called Garmos and a priestess of Aphrodite with three daughters called Euphrates, Tigris and Mesopotamia.

Since the claim that the novel is 'a Babylonian tale', acquired from a native, is itself fictional, it is perfectly possible that the alleged informant is also

---

5. I am very grateful to Nigel Wilson for guidance on this manuscript, and for supplying me with a photostat of the relevant page.

a construct. But this does not necessarily remove the significance of the claim for our understanding of the culture of the Roman Near East. For, as the evidence for long-distance trade through Palmyra and Mesopotamia shows, movement around the Fertile Crescent was constant. At a number of different levels the question thus arises of how important the contacts and exchanges thus created will have been. Should we, that is to say, see the area of the Near East which came to be ruled by Rome as having been more truly a part of the 'Orient' than of the Graeco-Roman world?

As will quickly become clear, our evidence allows no more than the construction of broad frameworks and the detection of a few hints at complex social and cultural connections. As for the broad framework, it is important to stress first that travel round the Fertile Crescent proper will normally have passed through the Tetrapolis and northern Syria, which, with the notable exception of Hierapolis/Manbog, was the most Hellenised part of the Roman Near East. It is worth recalling that Lucian, in his account of the 'Syrian Goddess' at Hierapolis, says that offerings came to the temple from the Babylonians, as well as from Arabia, and the Phoenicians, Cappadocians, Cilicians and 'Assyrians'.[6] Whether the social and cultural character of the emphatically Greek places further west, like Beroea, Antioch, Seleucia or Laodicea, owed anything to travellers or settlers from east of the Euphrates is much more difficult to say. We are reduced to slight and ambiguous items of evidence, such as Plutarch's report that when Antonius during his campaign in Parthia in the 30s BC needed someone who could speak *Parthisti* or *Suristi,* the person who came forward was Alexander, a citizen of Antioch.[7]

If we are to make even the most rudimentary sense of the possible significance of contacts beyond the Euphrates, a number of distinctions of place and time need to be made. First, there is the central part of the Fertile Crescent, the Mesopotamian shelf, from which a number of tributaries run into the rivers Balikh and Chabur, which themselves join the Euphrates. This was the area of previous Macedonian settlement where Syriac emerged as a written language, and as a vehicle for literature, in the course of the first three centuries. Ruled by a number of minor dynasties under Parthian sovereignty, it was this region which fell under Roman dominance (as Iamblichus records) in the 160s, to become the province of 'Mesopotamia' in the 190s. Though all such generalisations are rash, it seems from our evidence that we should see both the pagan and the Christian culture of this area, as expressed in Syriac, as derivatives of Greek culture, and not as a source of influence on the culture

6. Lucian, *dea Syr.* 10. See 7.2 above.
7. Plutarch, *Ant.* 46, 2.

of Syria proper. Above all, the notion that there was a 'Syrian' culture, embracing equally the zone of Syriac literature and Roman Syria, goes beyond our evidence.[8]

To the east of this area, sometimes invaded by Roman forces but never actually made into a province, lay the kingdom of Adiabene.[9] Although the main territory of the kingdom lay on the east side of the Tigris, in the ancient region of Assyria, in the course of the first century its kings had been granted by the Parthians control of Nisibis and Singara, and may have ruled Hatra as well. The kingdom was subjugated by Trajan; and if (as is very improbable) he did briefly create a province of 'Assyria', it might perhaps have been here.[10] But it is noteworthy that in the 190s the Adiabenians tried to retake Nisibis and were defeated by Septimius Severus, whose victory-titles included 'Arabicus', 'Adiabenicus' and 'Parthicus Maximus'.[11] The relevance of this kingdom is twofold; first, at least some of the territory which it acquired west of the Tigris was to form part of the heavily garrisoned Roman province of Mesopotamia; and second, this too was an area where Aramaic, and in the Christian period Syriac, was spoken.

The concrete evidence for whatever Semitic language was spoken here in the period before the establishment of Christianity is admittedly minimal. There appear to be no local documents, and the only (perhaps) relevant item is the inscription on the sarcophagus from the 'Tombs of the Kings' in Jerusalem with the name of a queen (given in two forms, as ṢDN MLKT' and as ṢDH MLKT').[12] She has frequently been taken to be the queen Helena of Adiabene who was buried there in about AD 60 after she and her son Izates had converted to Judaism. According to the well-known story told by Josephus in the *Antiquities*, Izates had first been converted by a Jewish merchant while staying at the court of another dynast under Parthian sovereignty, the king of Spasinou Charax (Mesene on the Persian Gulf).

After that evidence, such as it is, we encounter no further products of the language or culture of this region until we come to the *Homilies* of Aphraat,

---

8. See chs. 7 and 12 above. I cannot share the presumptions about a common 'Syrian' culture expressed for instance in H. Drijvers, "Syrian Christianity and Judaism", in J. Lieu, J. North and T. Rajak (eds.), *The Jews among the Pagans and Christians in the Roman Empire* (1992), 124.

9. See the suggestive paper, with very speculative elements, by J. Teixidor, "The Kingdom of Adiabene and Hatra", *Berytus* 17 (1967–68), 1.

10. 3.3 above, based, however, on C. S. Lightfoot in *JRS* 80 (1990), 115, who rejects this identification (as also, correctly, the historicity of the province).

11. See Dio LXXV, 1, 1–3; 3, 2.

12. The inscription is *CIS* II.1, no. 156 = Frey, *CIJ* II, nos. 1388 = Fitzmyer, *PAT*, no. 132; see J. Pirenne, "Aux origines de la graphie syriaque", *Syria* 40 (1967), 101. The story of Helena and Izates is told in *Ant.* XX, 2, 1–4, 3 (17–96).

written in Syriac at the very end of our period.[13] From our perspective it is worth recording also that the Syriac-speaking Christian inhabitants of what had been ancient Assyria apparently did not suffer from the historical 'amnesia' to which reference has been made several times. For the Syriac *Chronicle* of Karka de bet Selok (present-day Kirkuk), written in about the sixth or seventh century, begins with the foundation of the city by an Assyrian king, mentions further building by Seleucus and goes on to speak of martyrdoms under the Sasanids.[14] As for the Near East of the Roman Imperial period, there is nothing to suggest that Adiabene had as yet acquired any significance within the varied currents of cultural influences. Graeco-Roman writers might, however, recall that Nineveh had once been here; or, more vividly, that in this area there lay Gaugamela, where Alexander had defeated Darius of Persia.[15]

As we have seen, Hatra, lying in Mesopotamia across the Tigris from Adiabene, attracted more attention from Graeco-Roman writers. If it had been under Adiabene in the first century, it seems certainly to have been a separate sub-Parthian 'state', with its own kings, in the second. Both Trajan and Septimius Severus besieged and failed to take it; Roman troops were briefly stationed there in the 230s; and in about 240 Shapur I captured it, apparently bringing its existence to an end.[16] Its relevance to the questions being pursued here is threefold. First, it offers yet another example, like Hierapolis or Carrhae/Harran, of a city best known for its temple, that of the Sun ('Deus Sol', to the Roman soldiers stationed there). Second, as already mentioned, it has produced over three hundred Aramaic inscriptions, all apparently of the second century AD; at least this far round the Fertile Crescent, therefore, we find, if not a uniform linguistic zone, at any rate one marked by one of a family of closely related languages and scripts. To say that is of course to leave open the question of whether these related languages were in fact mutually intelligible, either when written (in the same alphabet of twenty-two letters, and in a variety of different but related scripts) or when spoken; and, more important, whether, even if they were mutually intelligible, this fact had any

13. See 12.6 above. According to J. Neusner, *Aphrahat and Judaism* (1971), 4, Aphrahat composed his *Homilies* near present-day Mosul; if so, in a region just to the north of Adiabene proper.

14. For this *Chronicle* see N. Pigulevskaya, *Les villes de l'état iranien aux époques parthe et sassanide* (1963), ch. 3; J. M. Fiey, "Vers la réhabilitation de l'histoire de Karka Bét Slôh", *Anal. Boll.* 82 (1964), 189, and briefly S. Brock, "Syriac Historical Writing", *Journal of the Iraqi Academy (Syriac Corporation)* 5 (1979–80), 1, on pp. 43–60, reprinted in Brock, *Studies in Syriac Christianity* (1991).

15. See, e.g., Strabo, *Geog.* XVI, 1, 2–3 (737).

16. See 3.3, 4.1 and 4.2 above.

significance for cultural exchanges, political attitudes or perceived identities.

Third, Hatra too, like many places lying along the Fertile Crescent, was thought of as being situated either in or next to 'Arabia'. Hence the kings who ruled there might take the title 'King of 'Arab' (MLK' DY 'RB) or 'King of the Arabs' (MLK' D'RBY').[17] Unfortunately, this leaves open a crucial ambiguity in how we should understand the term. Does the title present the king as ruling a territory (and a people?) which itself is identified as 'Arab'? Or is the implication that a king ruling from a city in the midst of the steppe has the power to control a hostile neighbouring territory characterised as being 'Arab'? The parallels from Dura and from Edessa, where there were officials called 'ruler of Arab' (ŠLYṬ' D'RB), would tend to support the second interpretation.[18] But the use of the expression 'King of the Arabs' more readily suggests the first. If so, this seems to be the earliest documentary evidence for a ruler who identifies himself as an 'Arab'.

Our evidence for culture and language in the central part of the Fertile Crescent, the area which was to become the Roman province of Mesopotamia, is also very poor, until we come to the earliest Syriac literature. But that lends all the more significance to the recent publication of the brief bilingual inscription mentioned earlier, which comes from the north-east corner of the region, at the point where the Tigris turns south, to flow past the eastern end of the Tur Abdin (Mons Masius). Probably belonging to the earlier third century, it is a dedication by a Roman *ouetranos* to Zeus Olympios, perhaps reproduced as LMRLH', 'to the lord of the gods', in Aramaic.[19] It is a sign of what remains to be discovered about a remote corner of the Empire, very little explored in modern times, and very little noticed in antiquity.

If northern Mesopotamia and the middle Tigris region had no very clearly defined cultural identity in the eyes of outsiders, the same was not true of Babylonia proper. But it is precisely here that we encounter the most profound difficulties of all. For the 'Babylonia' which presented itself to the minds of observers writing in Greek or Latin (and, as we will see, in Syriac) was the timeless, abstract world of astronomical and astrological learning, of 'Chaldaeans' skilled in discerning the decrees of fate. As such they belonged with other mysterious groups or castes possessed of some form of 'Oriental' learning, like the Brahmins or Egyptians. We can see this, for instance, in the Syriac

17. See H. J. W. Drijvers, "Hatra, Palmyra und Edessa", *ANRW* II.8 (1977), 799, pp. 820ff. For MLK' DY 'RB see F. Vattioni, *Le iscrizioni de Hatra* (1981), nos. 193, 195–199, 231 (MLK' D'RB). For MLK' D'RBY', no. 287.

18. See 4.2 above.

19. See C. S. Lightfoot and J. F. Healey, "A Roman Veteran on the Tigris", *Epig. Anat.* 17 (1991), 1, and 4.1 above. For the site, C. S. Lightfoot, "Tilli—a Late Roman *Equites* Fort on the Tigris", in Freeman and Kennedy, *DRBE,* 509, with sketch-map on p. 510.

Book of the Laws of Countries, discussed earlier. In Osrhoene, if anywhere, there ought to have been actual contact with a living culture and set of beliefs in Babylonia. But it was not so:

> Bardaisan said then: 'Have you read the books of the Babylonian Chaldaeans (KTB' DKLDY' DBBBL—'the Chaldaeans who [are] in Babylon'), in which it is described what influence the stars in their constellations exercise upon the horoscopes of men? And the books of the Egyptians, in which all the different things that may befall people are described?' Awida replied: 'I have read books on the Chaldaean doctrine, but I do not know which are Babylonian and which are Egyptian'.[20]

To Porphyry, writing a generation or two later, Bardesanes himself has become 'a Babylonian man', whether because he came from east of the Euphrates or was credited with a knowledge of astrology, or both.[21] Porphyry's own *Life of Pythagoras* is the classic representation of a Greek intellectual (of the remote past) gathering wisdom from a variety of Oriental sources.[22] Similarly, 'Chaldaean' oracles (written in Greek) were to play a large part in the Neo-Platonic philosophy of the better-known Iamblichus, the philosopher from Chalcis, of the first half of the fourth century. But they were—or were said to be—the work of two persons called Ioulianos, a father and son who lived in Rome in the second century.[23]

It is of course impossible to prove that the culture of the Graeco-Roman world in the Imperial period did not derive anything from active contact with a living culture, or cultures, in Babylonia; indeed two linked examples of such a borrowing are mentioned below. But several points need to be made. First recent studies have tended ever more clearly to see the 'Oriental' cults of the Roman Empire, for instance Mithraism, as internal constructs which cannot be shown to have owed anything to supposed origins in the East.[24] Second, the (perhaps fictional) representation of personal contact with a learned Baby-

---

20. Trans. H. J. W. Drijvers, *The Book of the Laws of Countries* (1965), 39–41.

21. Porphyry, *de abst.* IV, 17: ἀνὴρ Βαβυλώνιος.

22. See E. des Places (ed.), *Porphyre, Vie de Pythagore* (1982); see, e.g., sect. 6, or 11 (from Antonius Diogenes).

23. See H. Levy, *Chaldaean Oracles and Theurgy: Mysticism, Magic and Platonism in the Later Roman Empire* (1956). R. Majercik, *The Chaldaean Oracles: Text, Translation and Commentary* (1989), with the valuable review by David Potter in *JRS* 81 (1991), 225, expressing scepticism as to the alleged date and origin.

24. See esp. D. Ulansey, *The Origins of the Mithraic Mysteries* (1989). But note, e.g., the critical review by N. M. Swerdlow, *Class. Philol.* 86 (1991), 48. For a survey of the evolution of attitudes toward 'Oriental religions', see J. M. Paillier, "Les religions orientales, troisième époque", *Pallas* 35 (1989), 95.

lonian offered by the novelist Iamblichus seems to be the *only* such narrative account which we have from this period. In the story as reported by the marginal note to Photius' *Bibliotheca* (though not in Photius' own summary of the novel), the writer has actually learned 'the Babylonian language' and Babylonian stories. By implication, if both versions are taken together, he also acquired a knowledge of Babylonian magic.

But what, in the second century AD, was 'the Babylonian language'? And what if anything is known of the social and cultural history of this region, which had been under Parthian rule since the middle of the second century BC, and before that had been under the Seleucids? As we saw earlier, one component of the social structure of the area was the continuing presence of Greek cities, notably Seleucia, where Josephus claims that there was systematic conflict between the 'Greeks' and the 'Syrians', in which the Jews took the Syrian side.[25] The city was sacked by the forces of Lucius Verus in the 160s, perhaps in spite of having welcomed them as friends. Ammianus at any rate confirms that a statue of Apollo 'Comaeus' was taken from there and placed in the temple of Apollo on the Palatine.[26] But even if we could understand more of the survival of Greek culture here, or the conflicts of ethnic groups, Seleucia lay in the northern part of Babylonia proper, where the two great rivers converge most closely. It was in this northern sector also that there grew up the new Parthian foundations, Ctesiphon, in the middle of the first century AD, and Vologaesias, somewhere on the Euphrates, towards the end of the century. But what of Babylon itself, situated on the Euphrates to the south of Seleucia, or of the whole plain stretching down towards the Gulf?

The painful answer seems to be that for the first three centuries AD almost nothing at all is known of this area. Take for instance the question of language. The author of the marginal note to Photius (and hence probably Iamblichus himself) clearly distinguishes between the 'Syrian' and the 'Babylonian' languages. His account of learning the latter can hardly be meant as a reference to the acquisition of another branch of Aramaic, presumably written in the same alphabet (as the various branches were), but in a somewhat different script. He must surely intend to imply that what was learned was what moderns call Akkadian, also a Semitic language, but written in cuneiform. There is perfectly clear, and increasing, evidence for the continuing production of cuneiform tablets through the Hellenistic period, and indeed into the first century AD.[27] But if it is a historical reality (and not a piece of fiction,

25. See 12.1 above.

26. SHA, *v. Veri* 8, 1–4; Ammianus XXIII, 6, 23–24.

27. See, e.g., B. Funck, *Uruk zur Seleukidenzeit* (1984), or S. Sherwin-White, "Seleucid Babylonia: A Case Study for the Installation and Development of Greek Rule", in A. Kuhrt and S.

as it may be) that a captive taken by Trajan's army could still be learned in Akkadian, all presumptions about the culture of the area will need to be revised.

The question of the survival of Akkadian in Babylonia, and—if it did survive—of its role and significance, thus remains entirely open. As for other languages which one would presume were current there, there seems to be almost no documentary evidence at all from Babylonia itself. The obvious candidates are Parthian (an Iranian language written in Aramaic script), Greek and some branch of Aramaic. Greek is of course attested, as we have seen, for Seleucia itself; for the other Seleucia, the ancient Susa on the river Eulaeus, to the east; and for Mesene (Spasinou Charax).[28] Both Greek and Parthian, functioning as Imperial languages, were used on the inscription on the statue of Herakles which Vologaeses IV captured from Mesene in the middle of the second century and brought to Seleucia.[29] The normal assumption, which is no doubt correct, is that the prevailing language was a branch of Aramaic. But of this too there is almost no documentary evidence from the period before the death of Constantine. The sole exception is provided by the regal coinage of Characene, where from the late first century BC onwards Aramaic countermarks supplement the Greek legends with the names of the kings; and then from the early second century AD onwards each king (MLK') is named in Aramaic.[30]

We have thus simply to take it that the 'Syrians' in Seleucia of whom Josephus speaks were defined as such by their use of Aramaic. Beyond that it has to be admitted that all our other evidence for the region is indirect and transmitted by Jewish sources, first Josephus himself, and then the Babylonian Talmud, whose compilation may not have been complete until the sixth century AD.[31] Josephus' narrative of the fortunes of the Jews in Babylonia in the middle of the first century AD shows that the later Talmudic centre of Nehardea, on the Euphrates due west of Seleucia, was already a favoured location of Jewish settlement; and also that large numbers of Jews would regularly make the pilgrimage from there to Jerusalem (via the Euphrates, Palmyra and

---

Sherwin-White, *Hellenism in the East* (1987), 1. The latest dated cuneiform tablet comes from AD 74/5. See J. Oelsner, *Materialien zur babylonischen Gesellschaft und Kultur in hellenistischer Zeit* (1986), 54.

28. 12.1 above.

29. 12.3 above, text to n.26.

30. See *BMC Arabia,* pp. cxcivff. and 289ff.; see S. A. Nodelman, "A Preliminary History of Characene", *Berytus* 13 (1960), 83. Cf. Oeliner, op. cit., 245ff.

31. For an orientation on what can be known of the compilation of this important, if highly enigmatic, work, see H. L. Strack and G. Stemberger, *Introduction to the Talmud and Midrash* (1991), 208ff.

Damascus?), as well as sending offerings to the Temple. But the close connections which always existed between the Jewish communities of Babylonia and
those of Judaea are well known, and the evidence does not need be rehearsed
in detail here. There was certainly continual movement between the two, as
well as cases of migration from one area to the other.[32] A notable new item
of evidence for this movement is provided by the Aramaic inscription from
Jerusalem of a cohen (KHN') from there who went into exile in Babylonia
(GL' LBBL), and later returned; why this funerary inscription, probably of
the late first century BC or first century AD, should have been written in Paleo-
Hebrew script is a matter of speculation.[33]

Only a few points need be made in this connection. The first is that the
Jewish community in Babylonia must have read the Bible in Hebrew; but as
to how much more widely they could or did use Hebrew, there is no evidence
to parallel the now extensive evidence from Judaea, which proves conclusively that there it was not a 'dead language'.[34] By the time of the evolution of
the Babylonian Talmud, however, rabbinic discussion was conducted almost
entirely in Aramaic, even though it related, section by section, to the text of
the *Mishnah,* which itself is in Hebrew. Aramaic versions of the Bible, the
Targums, were also in regular use. It is thus highly probable—and seems always to have been assumed—that the first version of Josephus' *Jewish War*
had been in Aramaic rather than in Hebrew. His brief report of it at the beginning of his surviving *Jewish War* in Greek is itself not explicit on this point—
he proposed now to offer his account of the war to those under Roman rule,
'translating into the Greek language what I had previously sent to the *barbaroi* (non-Greek-speakers) of the interior, having composed it in my native
language'. What Josephus says is unambiguous, however, in making clear that
his intended original audience had been people living beyond the bounds of
the Roman Empire. He might have meant to indicate only Jews living there,
and indeed goes on to say that when the revolt broke out, those involved had
hoped that Jews living beyond the Euphrates would join in. But in fact what
he subsequently says about the Greek version makes it quite certain that this
Aramaic work had been intended both for Jews and for gentiles:

> I thought it monstrous, therefore, to allow the truth in affairs of such mo-
> ment to go astray, and that while Parthians and Babylonians and the most

32. Josephus' narrative is *Ant.* XVIII, 9, 1–9 (310–379). See J. Neusner, *A History of the
Jews in Babylonia* I–V (1965–1970); and above all, for the Talmudic period, A. Oppenheimer,
Babylonia Judaica in the Talmudic Period (1983). See also D. Goodblatt, "Josephus on Parthian
Babylonia", *JAOS* 107 (1987), 305.

33. See E. S. Rosenthal, "The Giv'at ha Mivtar Inscription", *IEJ* 23 (1973), 72 and Pl. 19;
J. Naveh, "An Aramaic Tomb Inscription Written in Paleo-Hebrew Script", *ibid.,* 82; Fitzmyer,
PAT, no. 68.

34. Ch. 10 above.

remote tribes of Arabia with our countrymen beyond the Euphrates and the inhabitants of Adiabene were, through my assiduity, accurately acquainted with the origin of the war, the various phases of calamity through which it passed and its conclusion, the Greeks and such Romans as were not engaged in the contest should remain in ignorance of these matters.[35]

The first version of the work must therefore have been written in an Aramaic which was intelligible to both the Jewish and the non-Jewish inhabitants of the area beyond the Euphrates. How we should understand this in relation to north-western Mesopotamia, where the earliest known literary composition in Syriac *may* perhaps date to exactly the same period, the 70s AD, is quite unclear. Some conception of what Josephus' *Jewish War* in Aramaic was like would be invaluable. As it is, this lost work represents the only known secular composition in Aramaic, from either side of the Euphrates, in the first three centuries. Aramaic-speaking Babylonia has left no documents and no literature which might allow it to 'speak' to us for itself. There is a striking contrast not only with Judaea but with Nabataea and Palmyra, as well as with Osrhoene and its neighbouring areas. Nonetheless, the implication of what Josephus says is that there was a potentially unified Aramaic-reading public on either side of the Euphrates.

It should be stressed, however, that if the Aramaic version of the *Jewish War* ever did get into circulation beyond the borders of the Empire, it will have been an example of information and conceptions of the meaning of events being transmitted from the Roman Near East to the region under Parthian, and later Persian, control. Is there evidence of significant influences travelling the other way? The available instances are few, and inevitably ambiguous.

One such case is the spread of the Judaising sect of the 'Elchasaites', included by Hippolytus in his *Refutation of All Heresies*, written in Rome in the early third century.[36] Christian accounts of heresies are notoriously confused and difficult to relate to any determinable time, place or social context, and it would hardly be worth noting this example if it were not for its relevance to the major religious movement which really did begin in Babylonia, and which spread rapidly to the Empire: Manichaeism. According to Hippolytus, a man from Apamea in Syria named Alcibiades had arrived in Rome bearing a book obtained from 'the Seres of Parthia' and containing a revelation originally made in the third year of Trajan to someone called Elchasai. The text, vouchsafed by an enormous angel, prescribed baptism for the remission of sins, while also enjoining reverence for Jerusalem, the practice of cir-

35. Josephus, *BJ* I, 1, 3–6 (1–2), Loeb trans.
36. Hippolytus, *Ref.* IX, 13.

cumcision and the observance of the Sabbath. The story clearly suggests a transmission of the beliefs of a Judaising sect from the Parthian domains to Syria and then to Rome. But it would not be worth our attention if the miniature Greek codex of the fifth century with materials about Mani (and extracts from his own preaching) did not report that Mani's own father had belonged to this same sect.[37] According to a tenth-century Arabic account, Mani was born in southern Babylonia in 216, just after his father had joined a baptising sect. The new codex shows that this was in fact the very sect which regarded 'Alchasaios' as its founder, which followed a relatively self-denying (though not rigorously ascetic) pattern of life, and seems to have observed the Jewish Sabbath. The codex further records that it was in 240, the first year of Shapur I, and the same year in which the Persians captured Hatra, that Mani had his own revelation, broke with the Elchasaites and moved with his followers to Ctesiphon.

Whether there ever was a historical person called Elchasai or Alchasaios must remain uncertain. All that is clear is that Mani was brought up in a context in southern Babylonia in which both Jewish and Christian beliefs and works were familiar. In that sense the Elchasaite movement, as practised there, also represented the effect of influences spreading from within the Roman Empire. But in what language did the sect function? By the time that the 'Book of Elchasai' arrived in Rome, brought by someone from Apamea, it will certainly have been in Greek. Equally, when Eusebius reports that the heretical doctrines of the 'barbarian' whose followers were called 'Manichaioi', were spreading from the Persian Empire to the Roman area in the 280s, he must be implying that transmission had taken place in Greek.[38]

It seems, however, to be universally agreed among modern scholars that the original language of Mani's preaching will have been an eastern dialect of Aramaic.[39] In this context, where it would be absurd to claim either to summarise the original dualistic and ascetic message or to retrace the steps by which it came to be preached in the Roman Empire, it can only be stressed that we have absolutely no direct evidence about this original preaching: there are no documents emanating from Mani's lifetime and originally written in Aramaic within the Persian Empire. If we have any hint of how Manichaeism

37. For the evidence, very roughly summarised here, see S. N. C. Lieu, *Manichaeism in the Later Roman Empire and Medieval China*[2] (1992), 33ff. (on both the Elchasaites and the biography of Mani). On the Cologne Mani Codex see 4.2 above. The best introduction to the issues and the context remains A. Henrichs, "The Cologne Mani Codex Reconsidered", *HSCPh* 83 (1979), 339.

38. Eusebius, *HE* IV, 31.

39. See esp. M. Lidzbarski, "Warum schrieb Mani aramäisch?", in G. Widengren (ed.), *Der Manichäismus* (1977), 249, and F. Rosenthal, "Die Sprache Manis", ibid., 255.

actually reached Roman territory, it is the allusion in the Mani Codex to a letter which Mani sent to Edessa.[40] As we have seen, it is beyond question that a Syriac-speaking Christianity already existed there; but how close, in language or script, the Aramaic dialect used by Mani was to the Syriac of Edessa is a matter of pure speculation. The earliest body of Babylonian Aramaic which we can encounter is the Jewish Aramaic of the Babylonian Talmud. It is of course of considerable significance that Manichaeism was one of the heresies which are most prominent in the works of Ephrem, written in Syriac in the fourth century.[41] But that does not tell us anything about language or modes of communication in the third century. For by the fourth century, and indeed by the end of the third, Manichaeism had spread throughout the Greek-speaking parts of the Empire, and even into Latin-speaking Roman Africa.

It would be satisfying if we could use Epiphanius' claim in his work on heresies, the *Panarion,* that Manichaeism was first brought west of the Euphrates by a veteran returning from Mesopotamia to near Eleutheropolis. Or still more if we could rely on his complex and detailed narrative of the social background of Mani's life, which seems to bear no relation to most of the other evidence, and involves movements between Roman Arabia, 'Sarakēnia', the Red Sea, Egypt and the trade-routes from Babylonia to India. Unfortunately this version of events was derived by Ephiphanius from a work which was itself a historical fiction, written in Greek probably towards the middle of the fourth century, the *Acta Archelai.* From our point of view it is a pity that it is not veridical, for it also records a long (and fictional) disputation between Mani in person and Archelaus, the bishop of a city called Carchai (Carrhae?) in Roman Mesopotamia.[42] The cold reality is that we cannot reconstruct any of the actual steps by which Mani's doctrines came to be current in Roman territory.

All that can be stressed here are two essential points. First, as Peter Brown argued before the Mani Codex was known, Manichaeism was not, as Diocletian and Maximian were to call it, 'Persian', but was in social and cultural terms a product of the Aramaic-speaking Fertile Crescent.[43] To say that is not of course to claim that Mani's doctrine of Light and Darkness was not

---

40. *Cologne Mani Codex* 64, 2–7.

41. See, e.g., Lieu, op. cit. (n.37), 133ff.

42. Epiphanius, *Panarion,* 66. See Hegemonius, *Acta Archelai* 62–64 (GCS XVI, 1906); the work is preserved in a Latin translation.

43. P. Brown, "The Diffusion of Manichaeism in the Roman Empire", *JRS* 59 (1969), 92 = *Religion and Society in the Age of St. Augustine* (1972), 94. See also Lieu, op. cit. (n.37), 70ff. Both use the evidence more confidently than I would be inclined to do. The same is true of L. Koenen, "Manichäische Mission und Klöster in Ägypten", in G. Grimm, H. Heinen and E. Winter (eds.), *Das römisch-byzantinische Ägypten* (1983), 93.

profoundly influenced by what we label as Iranian 'dualism'. Second, like the doctrines of 'Elchasai'—and later Islam—Manichaeism was an adaptation of Jewish and Christian beliefs and traditions: Mani proclaimed himself as 'the apostle of Jesus Christ'.[44] At a certain level its evolution and spread is thus testimony to the cultural unity of the Fertile Crescent. At another, however, the very rapidity of its spread elsewhere illustrates, just as had the early history of Christianity itself, the fact that religious ideas and systems are not to be fully explained in terms of social and cultural contexts.

Manichaeism thus exhibits both how Judaeo-Christian influences spread east into Babylonia, and how a version of them could be transmitted back in the reverse direction. But in speaking of a degree of cultural unity marking the Fertile Crescent, we may be going beyond the evidence, and have also not yet considered the full implications of what we are told about the 'author' of the *Babyloniaca*. For the anonymous marginal note is not only the one text which claims an active process of contact with Babylonian learning on the part of someone living in the Roman Empire. It is also the only text which claims that in the Roman Near East of the second century there was a whole class of persons who were distinguished by language and culture from Greeks living in Syria, and who could be described as 'Syrians'.

The implications of this claim, if it is taken literally, are very considerable. It does not seem that the early-tenth-century writer has been influenced by the fact, obviously long since well known, that there had been a long series of Christian writers in Syriac from the third century onwards. He does seem to be intending to convey what he found in the second-century text of Iamblichus' novel. Nor does it matter if what had been represented there had itself been a historical fiction. For the section of the novel where the writer turns aside to speak about himself carries the same implication, whether this is a literal report or a fiction related to current circumstances. That is to say, 'Iamblichus', a person of Syrian descent on both sides, acquired his Babylonian *tropheus* soon after Trajan's Parthian war, in a period when Rome was not in established control of any territories east of the Euphrates. The writer therefore represents himself as living west of the Euphrates.

We are thus presented with a difficult choice. For the studies of the different regions of the Roman Near East contained in this book have revealed a fairly clear, and certainly significant, linguistic 'frontier'. Aramaic, or versions of it (including Syriac), can be shown to have been in use in various areas: along the middle Euphrates, including Dura (but this zone also was not yet in Roman hands in the 120s); in Palmyra; in Judaea/Syria Palaestina (but much more clearly among Jews than among non-Jews); and in the province of Arabia (but only rather tenuously and in marginal areas at any time later

44. For this important point see Lieu, op. cit. (n.37), 51ff.

than the initial few years after the conquest of Nabataea). In any case the clearly stated contrast between the 'Greeks who have settled in Syria' and real Syrians, defined by descent, culture and language, most naturally points to northern Syria. It would be possible to think also of the Decapolis, where the borders between Roman 'Arabia' and 'Syria' moved progressively northwards, and the cities showed a very clear tendency to emphasise officially either that they were Greek or that they belonged to Syria (rather than to Arabia or Syria Palaestina), or both.[45] Ethnic and cultural labels were always used very loosely, and it may be significant that Eusebius was later to say that Petra 'is (still?) called "Rekem" among the Assyrians'.[46] But is he reflecting current usage, or just rephrasing a similar point made earlier by Josephus?[47]

Unless we reject the evidence of the *Babyloniaca* altogether, we have to accept that it potentially exposes a dimension of the culture of the Roman Near East of which our other evidence gives no hint. Given the detailed way in which the historical framework of the author's life and writing is set out, he can hardly mean to refer, in speaking of an inherited 'Syrian' culture, to Nabataea and its very recent transformation into 'Arabia'. He therefore must be implying that he came from within the established area of Roman rule, and most probably from the still unified Roman province of Syria. But in that area there was only one place where a Semitic language was used regularly in public in parallel with Greek, namely Palmyra. We have therefore to conclude either that Iamblichus is referring to the 'Syrian' culture of Palmyra, and thus to a tradition and pattern of education there to which otherwise we have no access at all, or that some or all of those cities where the documentary evidence is entirely in Greek nonetheless, in reality, exhibited a dual culture. That would have rather different implications in the case of an ancient, continuously settled city like Damascus (where admittedly the documentary evidence, all in Greek, is very slight);[48] of a place which evolved as a 'Greek' city only in the Roman period, like Emesa; but above all, if it were true, of the major Hellenistic foundations, whether in northern Syria or in the Decapolis. In the case of all those areas it is important to stress that the documentary evidence carries quite the opposite implication: that the visible, communal life not only of actual cities but also of villages was conducted consistently in Greek. Deities, places and individuals might all bear Semitic names. But the language of communal life, as expressed in written form, down to village level, was Greek.

What is more, there is nothing whatsoever to imply the existence of alter-

---

45. See 11.4 above.
46. Eusebius, *Onom.*, ed. Klostermann, 142.
47. Josephus, *Ant.* IV, 7, 1 (161).
48. 9.3 above.

native 'native' structures which maintained themselves either within cities which were predominantly Greek or in rural contexts. We might be tempted to suppose that a 'Syrian' identity will best have been preserved in the context of 'native' temples and cults, perhaps attended by a traditional or hereditary priesthood. But no dynasties of 'Syrian' priests are traceable at all; and in the most remote of rural, or mountain-top, locations the temples which we can find are built in Graeco-Roman style and are marked by Greek inscriptions.[49] In the Near East only Palmyra provides a (very partial) parallel to the persistence of Egyptian temples, with distinctive forms of priesthood, and which in the Imperial period were still constructed in Egyptian style, and still used the Egyptian language, written in hieroglyphics.[50]

The only priesthood known from the Near East under Roman rule which represented both an actual and a conscious inheritance from a distant, pre-Hellenistic past was the Jewish High Priesthood in Jerusalem, which was also a form of communal political leadership. But, as we have seen, its holders in the first century were nominated and dismissed either by Roman governors or by kings who were members of the Herodian dynasty;[51] and in any case the office disappeared forever with the destruction of the Temple in 70.

There was certainly some real continuity of cult, of historical tradition and possibly of language in the main cities of Phoenicia; but here the elements of Phoenician culture and tradition were interpreted within the institutions of what were by now Greek cities, of which the majority also became Roman *coloniae*. There is nothing in the evidence from any of them to suggest that separate, identifiably 'Phoenician' institutions persisted within them. In any case self-identification as 'Phoenician' (by people using Greek) is a clearly marked phenomenon; we can be confident that 'Iamblichus', in speaking of himself as a 'Syrian', did not mean to say that he came from one of the Phoenician cities or that his native language was Phoenician.

He might have come from Commagene, where the description of his own intellectual progress by Lucian of Samosata *could* be read as meaning that he had begun not with a relatively unsophisticated level of Greek, but with Aramaic as his first language.[52] Alternatively, we can see very clear elements of continuity of cult both at Doliche and at Hierapolis. Again, in both cases, the traditional cults were interpreted within the functioning of what became

49. See, e.g., 7.3; 8.3–5; 9.3 above.

50. See esp. A. K. Bowman, *Egypt after the Pharaohs, 732 BC–AD 642: From Alexander to the Arab Conquest* (1986), ch. 6. So far as I am aware, there has been no detailed recent study of the functioning of the Egyptian temples as they were in the Roman period. The standard work, W. Otto, *Priester und Tempel im hellenistischen Ägypten* (1905), relies in any case solely on Greek documentation.

51. 10.2 above.

52. 12.3 above.

Greek cities, and were reflected locally in inscriptions written in Greek.[53] Is it then possible that an educated class, which was consciously 'Syrian' in language and culture, nonetheless persisted within the (as it seems) profoundly Hellenised world of Syria proper or the Decapolis, without leaving any trace in the form either of social or political institutions, of documents on stone or perishable materials, or of a literature? The possible model for such a survival, the evolution of 'rabbinic' Judaism after the destruction of the Temple at the end of the High Priesthood, will not work. For although this development took place in the context of an ever denser network of 'Greek cities' (and Roman *coloniae*), which seem to dominate the map of Syria Palaestina, it has left very clear traces: not only its own literature, beginning with the *Mishnah,* but reports and reactions by outside observers, archaeological remains, and inscriptions in Hebrew, Aramaic and Greek.[54]

The possibility of a pagan 'Syrian' culture of this period, persisting within an apparently Hellenised world, cannot be dismissed; but it remains profoundly enigmatic. An alternative hypothesis might perhaps be found in the facts of geography. Might such a culture have survived in the more mountainous zones? In certain areas the implications of the evidence would go against this. What we know of the limestone massif of northern Syria (hardly a mountainous zone in any case), of Baetocaece high up at the southern end of the Jebel Ansariyeh, of Mount Lebanon and the fringes of Anti-Lebanon and Mount Hermon all suggests a profound penetration of the Greek language and of Greek (or rather Romano-Greek) architecture. But there do remain very large mountainous zones of which effectively nothing at all is known: all the northern part of the Jebel Ansariyeh, and the main areas of the Anti-Lebanon and Hermon ranges. There is every reason to suppose that the vast majority of the Jebel Ansariyeh was cultivated and inhabited. How high up on Anti-Lebanon and Hermon habitation reached is as yet unknown; but surveys of its southern fringes show that even olive-presses can be found at up to 1500 m.[55] That possibility would bring us back to the Ituraeans—or rather, in Strabo's terms, 'Ituraeans and Arabs'—against whom the Romans were still mounting expeditions under Augustus, and who later provided a substantial number of cohorts for the Roman army.[56] No more can be said, except

53. 7.2 above. There is a possible hint of the use of Aramaic at Hierapolis in what Lucian says (*dea Syria* 33) of the non-representational *xoanon* there: καλέεται δὲ σημήιον καὶ ὑπ' αὐτῶν Ἀσσυρίων, οὐδέ τι οὔνομα ἴδιον αὐτῷ ἔθεντο. But the reference *may* be to the absence not of an appropriate noun in Aramaic, but of a proper name in Greek.

54. 10.4 above.

55. Ch. 1, text to n.49. See now S. Dar and N. Kokkinos, "The Greek Inscriptions from Senaim on Mount Hermon", *PEQ* 124 (1992), 9. Senaim lies at a height of 1140m.

56. See 2.1, text to n.29, and 8.3 above. Strabo's description is in *Geog.* XVI, 2, 18 and 20 (755–756). The latest catalogue of the cohorts is E. Dabrowa, "Cohortes Ituraeorum", *ZPE* 63 (1986), 221.

that the 'internal frontier' represented by these two great mountain-ranges, between them occupying a considerable proportion of the land-mass of the Roman Near East, remains a complete mystery. We can certainly not assert confidently that a 'Syrian' society did not persist in either of these two zones.

The only place where we know that a bilingual pagan culture flourished throughout the first three centuries was Palmyra. It is not impossible that we should imagine 'Iamblichus' as coming from there. It is hardly significant that this Greek name happens not to be attested there; a number of others are.[57] What would be more interesting, if (hypothetically) true of Palmyra, is Iamblichus' picture of an inherited 'Syrian' culture, in relation to which Greek culture might, for an individual, be a subsequent acquisition. For the persistent (though not universal) binguality of the inscriptions from Palmyra, in which the Greek text often seems primary, necessarily gives the impression of a unified culture. The inscriptions might tend to suggest that, if there ever had been a literature written in Palmyra, it would have been, like most Syriac literature, both pagan (the *Letter of Mara bar Serapion*) and Christian, a derivative of Greek literature. But in fact there is no evidence either of a Palmyrene literature or of any Greek literature written by anyone who came from Palmyra.

One further possibility remains, though this too is a pure hypothesis, and one which presents many problems. But it is also a hypothesis which takes us back to the most important of all questions in the cultural history of the Near East. A 'Syrian' who represented himself as brought up in the Syrian language and customs might have come from the vast area of marginal land between the settled zone and the steppe. Palmyra was, it is true, the only place which, in its evolution from the first century BC to the third century AD, presents a fully tangible Graeco-Syrian or Graeco-Aramaic culture. It may be necessary to recall here that what we call 'Aramaic' was in Greek 'the language of the *Suroi*'; and that the Greek for 'in Aramaic' is *Suristi*: thus when Josephus speaks of the Greek and the Semitic names of this city, he says, 'it is still called thus ('Thadamora') among the *Suroi*, while the Greeks call it Palmyra'. Similarly, he says of the kingdom of Agrippa II, 'a mixed population of *Ioudaioi* and *Suroi* inhabit it'.[58]

By analogy, therefore, other groups living on the margins of the steppe might have identified their own language and culture as 'Syrian'. What other term would have been used in Greek by the tribe of Thamud to describe the Nabataean language, which they used, in parallel with Greek, to record their establishment of a temple at Ruwwafa in the northern Hedjaz, in the second

---

57. See J. K. Stark, *Personal Names in the Palmyrene Inscriptions* (1971), 131.

58. On Palmyra, Josephus, *Ant.* VII, 6, 1 (154), cf. 9.4 above. For Agrippa II's kingdom, *BJ* III, 3, 5 (57). Note that Josephus, *Ant.* X, 1, 2 (8), following the LXX, reproduces the 'RMYT of II Kings 18, 26, as συριστί.

half of the second century?[59] Nabataean and Greek were similarly the two languages used, probably a century later, to record the burial at Umm el Jimal of the *tropheus,* or RB, of the Arab king Gadimat.[60]

Although Nabataean too has left no literature, complex legal texts could be written in it, and it is not in the least impossible that it functioned for nomadic groups on the fringes of Roman 'Arabia' as a primary language of culture, with Greek being something which one might acquire subsequently from a *tropheus.* But these examples are recalled only as models for a pattern of linguistic and cultural relationships which might have been found any-where along the edge of the steppe. It remains far more likely that the geo-graphical context evoked by Iamblichus' self-reference is northern Syria, which in any case would be the area under Roman rule first reached by Ro-man forces, and slave-traders, returning from Trajan's Parthian war. We may recall the slave-boy named Abba, and described as 'from across the river (Eu-phrates)', who was sold at Seleucia Pieria in 166, at the end of another Par-thian war.[61] But of course slaves could be re-sold and then taken to different regions: one example is the 'Balsamea, by race an Osrhoenian Mesopota-mian', sold at 'Aurelia Tripolis of Phoenice' in the early 250s and re-sold the next year at Oxyrhynchus in Egypt.[62]

But if Iamblichus, as a 'Syrian' by descent and culture, did come from northern Syria, it is quite possible that his origin lay in the area of steppe bounded by the Orontes Valley in the west, with Apamea, Hama/Epiphania and Emesa; by the mountain-chain leading to Palmyra in the south; by the Euphrates in the east; and by the Fertile Crescent, with Chalcis, Beroea and Hierapolis, in the north. It was here that in the first century BC, as we saw earlier, Alchaidamnos, 'the king of the *nomades* on this side of the Euphrates', operated, at one point helping Bassus when besieged in Apamea, after earlier thinking himself wronged by the (Roman) governors and retiring into Meso-potamia.[63] In the second century this large area was ceasing to be an open frontier zone: in the 70s a Roman road already stretched east of Palmyra, presumably to reach the Euphrates either at its confluence with the Chabur or more probably at that, further upstream, with the Balikh; and, whatever uncertainties there are about the previous period, in the 160s Roman control came to extend all the way down the river to Dura.[64] The Roman posts along the river would certainly not have prevented all movement by nomads across it; but nonetheless we could properly regard the north-Syrian steppe as an

---

59. 4.1, text to n.59.

60. 11.5 above.

61. 3.4 above. R. Cavenaile, *Corpus Papyrorum Latinarum* (1958), no. 120: 'puerum, nati-one transfluminianum, nomine Abban . . .'.

62. *P. Oxy.,* no. 3035.

63. Strabo, *Geog.* XVI, 2, 10 (753); cf. ch. 1 above.

64. 3.4 above.

area which was steadily becoming another 'inner' frontier zone, inhabited but perhaps mostly not settled, surrounded by Roman forces but not (it seems) directly occupied by them. To say that, however, is to contradict the views of the authors of the main (and indeed only) historical study of this region in the Roman period, Mouterde and Poidebard, who believed that this area was fortified by the Romans in the course of the second and third centuries.[65] Yet there seems to be no clear archaeological or (more important) documentary evidence to confirm military occupation in this period, in clear contrast to the Euphrates itself and to the Strata Diocletiana leading from Sura to Palmyra, Damascus and beyond. It is not until the *Notitia Dignitatum* of the early fifth century that we have a clear picture of military posts dotted across the heart of this area.[66] Still, we should not underestimate the possibilities of habitation, and even cultivation, at least in the western part of this region: the limits of 200-mm annual precipitation stretch some 130 km to the east of Apamea and over 100 km to the east of Emesa.[67]

There is no question that there was regular habitation over much of this zone by the late-Roman Christian period. It is only necessary to mention, by way of example, the major Christian sites of Qasr Ibn Wardan and Sergiopolis/Resafa.[68] Moreover, if we look back to the period before 337, there are occasional dated inscriptions, even from the very heart of the zone, which seem to show that there was already settled habitation at some places—but they are all in Greek.[69] Perhaps the most striking evidence is provided by a group of Greek inscriptions from et-Touba, situated on a hill rising above an extensive area of salt marshes, and lying some 60 km south-east of Beroea. They date to between the Seleucid years 638 and 665, AD 326/327 and 352/353, and record the construction of a grain-store (transliterating the Latin *horreum*) and courtyard by a local dignitary with a Latin name, 'Aurelios Bellichos son of Liouianos'. But these inscriptions also invoke the Christian God.[70] Two separate developments at the end of our period were giving rise to a new phase in the history of Syria.

---

65. So R. Mouterde and A. Poidebard, *Le limes de Chalcis: Organisation de la steppe en Haute Syrie romaine* I (1945), esp. 236.

66. See *Not. Dign.*, *Or.* XXXIII, *Dux Syriae*, with the main map in Mouterde and Poidebard, op. cit.

67. See Mouterde and Poidebard, op. cit., map II (opposite p. 15).

68. See J. Lassus, *Sanctuaires chrétiens de la Syrie* (1947).

69. See, e.g., Mouterde and Poidebard, op. cit., p. 184 (Sabboura, some 80 km south-east of Apamea, an epitaph of the Seleucid year 521, AD 209/210); p. 187 (El-Bab, 41 km south-east of Beroea, year 535, AD 223/224); p. 216 (Seyh Hillal, 100 km east-south-east of Apamea, the lintel of a building dedicated in the year 541, AD 229/230, by three men with Latin names, 'Maternos', 'Pappos' and 'Markos').

70. The inscriptions are *IGLS* II, nos. 304–306, relocated (from Zebed) by Mouterde and Poidebard, op. cit., pp. 199–201.

In other words this large and mysterious zone, which might have revealed 'Syrians' clinging to an inherited culture, while either choosing or not choosing to acquire a Greek education also, does not do so. There are no pagan documents from here in Semitic languages, except the Palmyrene ones of the zone north-west of the city; it should, however, be noted that from this area there are also a few examples of the 'Safaitic' graffiti of which far larger numbers are known from the zone east of the Hauran.[71] We should not forget that it would never have been expected, until the new archive showed it, that Greek documents drawn up on the middle Euphrates around its confluence with the Chabur, in the third century, would have subscriptions written in Syriac.[72] But even these documents represent a bilingual world in which the dominant element for official purposes is Greek. We could nonetheless assume that when someone, as Jerome was to do, ventured into the marginal zone near Chalcis to try the life of a hermit, communicating in a 'barbarous' language would become necessary.[73] But that is by no means the same as the claimed 'Syrian' culture of someone whose family could buy a Babylonian *tropheus,* and who could later acquire a Greek literary education. Where, if anywhere, in the landscape and social structure of second-century Syria we should locate an apparently upper-class, and consciously 'Syrian', family remains wholly uncertain. But it is surely significant that while in Edessa and Nisibis a society which was already literate in Syriac immediately gave rise to a Christian Syriac literature, no such development is found in this period anywhere west of the Euphrates.

The tentative conclusion must be that while the whole Fertile Crescent, both 'Roman' and non-Roman, did in some sense exhibit a common culture, to which the use of related dialects of Aramaic contributed, as did the presence of 'Greek cities', the significance of this for Syria proper remains very problematic. For precisely here, where the cultural influence of contact with the East, created by movement round the Fertile Crescent, should have been most visible, we find the most firmly 'Greek' part of the Near East. If the Fertile Crescent was a heavily frequented route for traffic in both directions, there was also a sense in which the Euphrates remained a real frontier, even after the Roman conquest of Mesopotamia. Moreover, in terms of influences, pagan, Jewish and Christian, there are clearer indications that Mesopotamia and Babylonia were affected by various currents and changes in the Roman Near East than the other way round.

All such conclusions must in any case be hesitant. Before we look further

71. See 9.4 above, based on D. Schlumberger, *La Palmyrène du Nord-Ouest* (1951); the ten known Safaitic graffiti are listed on pp. 133–134. For 'Safaitic' see below, text to nn.88–89.

72. 12.5 above.

73. 7.1 above.

at the culture of the Roman Near East itself, there is another possible external factor to take into account: the peoples of the steppe zone, or rather zones. There are various sides to this question, often confused by unexamined presuppositions. The first is the military aspect. As has been shown in great detail, the gradual evolution of Roman military dispositions over more than three centuries led progressively to a situation where the majority of the Roman forces in the Near East were deployed not on a frontier with Persia but along the edge of the steppe. Apart from the loss of Nisibis and the 'Transtigritane provinces' in 363, the pattern shown in the *Notitia Dignitatum* closely mirrors that already arrived at in the period of the Tetrarchy and Constantine. If we count in terms of legions, and from south to north, we find the following: X Fretensis at Aila; IV Martia at Betthorum (almost certainly Lejjun); III Cyrenaica at Bostra; III Gallica at Danaba; I Illyricorum at Palmyra; IV Scythica at Oresa; XVI Flavia Firma at Sura; then the first legion on the frontier with Persia, IV Parthica at Circesium (with possibly another missing from the text); and finally two in Mesopotamia, I Parthica 'Nisibena', now at Constantia (almost certainly Viransehir), and II Parthica at 'Cefa'.

The 'desert frontier' was therefore, as the facts show beyond all doubt, at least as important a factor in the developed military structure of the Roman Near East as rivalry with Persia. Moreover, the *Notitia Dignitatum* also gives a vivid impression of the integration into the Roman army of forces drawn from the steppe peoples: leaving aside units of 'Equites Promoti Indigenae' or 'Equites Sagittarii Indigenae', whose ethnic composition is unclear, there are 'Equites Saraceni', for instance at Thelsea (Dumayr between Damascus and Palmyra), or 'Equites Thamudeni Illyriciani' in Palaestina.

As we have seen, fourth-century evidence in particular, both literary and documentary, is unanimous in regarding the 'Saraceni' as a threat to order, which might equally affect cultivators in the area south of the Hauran or travellers on the road from Beroea to Edessa.[74] But to say that the 'desert frontier' was a real one, to which very considerable resources of manpower and physical construction were devoted, is not to say that anyone could have anticipated, or had any reason to anticipate, large-scale invasions from beyond that frontier. How that in fact came about in the seventh century remains very difficult to explain.[75]

Was the relation between the Empire and its settled subjects, on the one hand, and the nomads of the steppe, on the other, simply an adversarial one, involving the more or less successful imposition of policing and order? Or, on the contrary, was the 'Arab' element fundamental to the nature of society in

74. 11.5 and 12.6 above.
75. For the best account see F. M. Donner, *The Early Islamic Conquests* (1981).

the whole region? If there were no major invasions which in any way fore-shadowed the Islamic conquests, was there nonetheless a steady penetration of groups who should be identified as 'Arab' into the settled zone? The sig-nificance of this question for modern conceptions of the area as it was in the Roman period can hardly be overestimated. For the notion that Roman Syria as a whole was essentially 'Arab' has even been incorporated into the title of a recent book.[76] Equally, the notion of a consistent penetration of 'Arabs' into the settled zone 'before Islam' is of course the topic of a major study by René Dussaud.[77] But the very title already reveals the presuppositions being deployed.

The problems of logic and evidence in these views are very considerable. First, 'before Islam' the criteria for identifying 'Arabs' are even more uncer-tain than after. They certainly *cannot* depend, for most of the period in ques-tion, on any attested self-definition by the groups concerned. As we have seen, local documentary references, from the Hauran, Dura, Osrhoene or Hatra, to people occupying positions of authority in relation to *Arabes,* or 'RB, gen-erally seem to imply relations of control of a hostile element or area, rather than statements of identity with the group in question.[78] Nothing in the ex-tensive epigraphic evidence from Palmyra or Nabataea suggests that either 'people' identified itself as 'Arab'; Nabataean documents for the period of the kingdom do stress the beneficence of the king towards 'his people' ('MH)—but the ethnic identity claimed is consistently NBTW. When we do come across someone identifying himself (in Greek) as an 'Araps', it is a century after the end of the kingdom, and the person concerned comes from Kanatha, which had not been part of it for the last century before provincial rule was imposed.[79]

These questions of nomenclature may seem trivial; but they are not. For it was, and could only be, in words that ethnic identities, whether claimed by insiders or attributed by outsiders, were expressed. Pagan writers, in Greek or Latin, had a variety of expressions for the peoples of the steppe: *no-mades* (also used in a Greek inscription from Palmyra to describe the attackers of a caravan);[80] *skēnitai* ('tent-dwellers'); 'Arabes'; and from the second century onwards *Sarakēnoi* or *Saraceni.* When they used the term 'Arab', as Greek writers had from the fifth century BC onwards, it was a loose term related either to the equally loose geographical term 'Arabia' or

76. R. Farioli Campanati (ed.), *La Siria araba da Roma a Bisanzio* (1989).

77. R. Dussaud, *La pénétration des Arabes en Syrie avant l'Islam* (1955).

78. See above, text to nn.17–18.

79. 11.4 above.

80. 9.4, text to n.45.

to a characteristic way of life.[81] Nabataeans, the inhabitants of Trachonitis, Ituraeans, as well as Osrhoenians or other inhabitants of Mesopotamia, and also the people of Hatra might on occasion be described by other people as 'Arabs'; so might the unsettled inhabitants of the eastern desert of Egypt, between the Nile and the Red Sea, an area which could also be called Arabia. The use of this or other terms was a matter of choice, or of shifting fashion.

We can see just such a shift, parallel to that occurring in the Near East, in a report by Dionysius, bishop of Alexandria: in the persecution under Decius in 250/251 many Egyptian Christians, he says, had fled to 'the Arabian mountain' and were enslaved by 'the barbarian Sarakēnoi'.[82] There was no reason, however, for Greek or Roman observers to go further, or to attempt to attribute to all the different groups whom one might call Arabs a real ethnic unity, or descent from a common ancestor. This idea was to be supplied by Josephus, the first person to identify contemporary Arabs unambiguously as the descendants of Hagar and Ishmael. From then on the notion was to be adopted by Christian observers; and, as we have seen, it was to form a crucial element in Christian conceptions of 'Ishmaelite' readiness to convert to Christianity, as the true inheritance of Abraham.[83] Nomad raiders on the road between Beroea and Edessa in the fourth century could then also be seen by Jerome as 'Ishmaelites'.[84] But, more important, Theodoret's account of the recruitment of ascetics in Syria in the fourth and fifth centuries makes perfectly clear that he saw Greek-speakers, 'Syrians' and the *barbaroi* of the desert who claimed to descend from Ishmael, as three distinct groups. We may note particularly Theodoret's description of a convert called Abba, 'who descended from the Ishmaelite stock, but was not expelled from the house of Abraham like his ancestor, but rather shared with Isaac in his ancestral inheritance'.[85]

The notion of a common genealogy of the peoples of the steppe was thus itself an attribution by outsiders, and one whose historical significance it would be hard to exaggerate. But it was also one which was necessarily foreign to Greek and Roman pagan observers, and which could only arise from an interpretation of Genesis, whether Jewish or Christian. As for the peoples

81. See the typically masterly and economical article of T. Nöldeke, "Arabia, Arabians", *Enc. Biblica* I (1899), 272.

82. Eusebius, *HE* VI, 42, 4.

83. Ch. 1 above. These propositions are explored more fully in F. Millar, "Hagar, Ishmael, Josephus and the Origins of Islam", *JJS* 44 (1993), 23.

84. 12.6 above, text to n.13.

85. Syriac (Aramaic?) speakers as opposed to Greek: Theodoret, *Hist. Relig.* V, 6; XIV, 2. Descendants of Ishmael: VI, 4; XXVI, 13; and esp. IV, 12 (Abba).

of the steppe themselves, there is no clear indication even that they identified themselves collectively as 'Arabs'. The earliest unambiguous expression of this idea 'from within' seems to be the Arabic epitaph of Imru 'l-qais at en-Nemara in 328, where he is described as 'king of all the Arabs': MLK 'L 'RB KLH.[86]

If the evolution of a conscious 'Arab' identity was something which took place only gradually, under the influence of both Graeco-Roman and Jewish-Christian conceptions, that is not of course to deny the real importance of the peoples of the steppe, or the fact that one of the Semitic languages used by them, even at this time, was closely related to the classical Arabic of the Islamic period; an even earlier attestation, as we have seen, is offered by two lines of a Nabataean inscription from Oboda in the Negev, perhaps of about AD 100.[87] But that is how the status of 'Arabic' in this period has to be expressed. Other Semitic languages are far better attested on the margins of the steppe: Nabataean itself (especially in the form of thousands of graffiti from Sinai); Aramaic in the Auranitis, Trachonitis and Batanaea; Palmyrene; Syriac; and the Aramaic of the inscriptions of Hatra. More significant still, thousands of graffiti in yet another Semitic language, labelled by moderns 'Safaitic' from the volcanic area called the Safa, east of the Jebel Hauran, attest that there was a population out in the steppe which was to some degree literate. It also seems, as noted earlier, that they might share 'tribal' identities with people living in the settled zone of Auranitis and Moabitis.[88] This language too is related to Arabic proper, but is not to be identified with it. How we are to understand the remarkable fact of literacy in this zone, or the social patterns dimly revealed in these brief and allusive texts, is a problem which will not be attempted here.[89]

Moreover, over the whole Arabian peninsula, far beyond the area of Roman control, a number of other Semitic languages, more or less closely related

---

86. See 11.5 above. As is implied, the recent re-reading which would remove the word 'all' (KLH) seems to run counter to the extravagant claims made in the text, and is therefore ignored here.

87. Ch. 1 and 11.1 above.

88. 11.1 and 11.5 above.

89. For Safaitic see E. Littmann, *Thamūd und Safā* (1940); *CIS* V (1950), and cf., e.g., R. Schmitt, "Die Ostgrenze von Armenien über Mesopotamien, Syrien, bis Arabien", in G. Neumann and J. Untermann (eds.), *Die Sprachen im römischen Reich* (1980), 187, esp. 198 (very incomplete); see also M. C. A. Macdonald, *s.v.* "Safaitic (Inscriptions)", in the *Anchor Bible Dictionary* III (1992), 418. I am very grateful to Mr. Macdonald for his assistance. The most comprehensive survey of linguistic relations in the Hauran and neighbouring areas is now the invaluable article of R. Contini, "Il Ḥawrān preislamico: Ipotesi di storia linguistica", *Felix Ravenna*, ser. 4, 1/2 (1987), 24.

to classical Arabic, are also attested on inscriptions.[90] By what stages Arabic proper came to be the dominant language of the Near East, and the only sacred language of Islam, is a question which belongs in quite a different context. The fact that there are a couple of attestations of it already in our period is certainly very significant; but it would be an anachronistic distortion to give it too prominent a place in our conceptions of the earlier Imperial period.

Two final questions need to be raised about the steppe peoples and the 'desert frontier'. First, to what extent were there trade-routes across the steppe (and the true desert) in the vast zone south of Palmyra? If there were any, they would represent further links between the Roman Near East and Babylonia and the Persian Gulf, and ones which were independent of the Fertile Crescent. The clear evidence for both a Nabataean and then a Roman military presence far down the Wadi Sirhan must strongly suggest that this was a frequented trade route.[91] Dumatha (Jawf), the furthest point which we know Nabataean and Roman forces to have reached, seems indeed to be mentioned in a passage of Pliny's *Natural History,* which speaks of travel between Gaza, Petra and Characene at the head of the Persian Gulf; however, Pliny's ideas of distances and locations here are completely confused; but by much interpretation a route via Dumatha to the Gulf can (perhaps) also be discerned in another passage of Pliny.[92] This route would have involved a passage of some 500 km from Philadelphia or Bostra via Azraq Oasis (Basiensis?) to Dumatha, and then nearly another 500 km to the nearest point on the Euphrates, before the descent to the Gulf. It is hardly possible to imagine that it can have borne constant traffic. But, as always, firm negative conclusions cannot be justified. One reason for caution is that Pliny the Elder gives a much clearer description of a route from Thomna in Arabia Felix (the Yemen) to Gaza in Judaea, covered by camels in sixty-five stages; Pliny's figure for the distance is unclear, but even as the crow flies it would have been very much longer than the route through Dumatha to the Euphrates, in fact well over 2000 km.[93] This route, it is true, will have led through the mountainous and (by comparison) well-watered region of the Hedjaz, passing the area of the later cities of Mecca and Medinah, as well as, further north, the Nabataean

90. For these languages see the survey by J. Ryckmans, "Alphabets, Scripts and Languages in Pre-Islamic Arabian Epigraphical Evidence", in A. A. T. al-Ansary (ed.), *Studies in the History of Arabia* II, *Pre-Islamic Arabia* (1984), 73.

91. See 5.1 and 11.1 above.

92. Pliny, *NH* VI, 32/144–146; VI, 32/157–159, on which see D. Potts, "Trans-Arabian Routes of the Pre-Islamic Period", in J. F. Salles (ed.), *L'Arabie et ses mers bordières* I, *Itinéraires et voyages* (1988), 127.

93. Pliny, *NH* XII, 32/64–65.

and then Roman outpost of Medain Saleh.[94] But its existence must mean that we cannot altogether discount the feasibility of a regular trade-route through the Wadi Sirhan and Dumatha to the Gulf.

One further channel of possible mutual influences, cutting across the arc of the Fertile Crescent, thus has to be taken into account in any assessment of the culture of the Roman Near East. As should by now be obvious, however, such an overall assessment would be premature. The evidence simply does not allow confident generalisations, and least of all negative conclusions.

Nonetheless a few general propositions may be offered, which may at least have the merit of raising doubts about the assumptions relating to 'the Orient' which inform many modern approaches—above all, paradoxically, approaches to both pagan and Christian authors writing in Greek and living in what is often, in modern books, called 'Syria', without regard either to Roman provincial names or to the diversity of the regional cultures of the Roman Near East.

Take for instance the proposition that the 'Chaldaean Oracles' composed in the second century AD were by their nature likely to attract Iamblichus— not the novelist, but the major Neo-Platonist philosopher of the first half of the fourth century.[95] For they were 'half-Oriental and half-Hellenic'; and he was a citizen of Chalcis, the Greek city on the border of the steppe in northern Syria. But, as we have seen above, the 'Chaldaean Oracles' were not a product of contemporary Babylonia; on the contrary, they were written in Greek, and perhaps in Rome. Their 'Chaldaean' character is a projection onto an imaginary 'Orient' generated from within Greek, or Graeco-Roman, culture. The 'Babylonian' world created by the other Iamblichus, the novelist, is another such projection. That is not to deny what is certain, that there was indeed constant traffic, via the Euphrates and Tigris, between the Roman Near East and Parthian and then Persian Babylonia. But if we think of contemporary, real-life contacts, there is far clearer evidence for influences emanating from within the area progressively occupied by Rome than in the reverse direction. This is true whether we think of the continuing effects of Hellenistic colonisation, of the remarkable impact in Mesopotamia of Roman (nominal) 'colonisation', of Greek influences on early Syriac literature, of the importance of Jerusalem and the Temple for the major Jewish community of Babylonia, of the spread of Judaising sects or of the preaching of Christianity. Even Manichaeism, which Diocletian and Maximian were to denounce as 'Persian', was itself in large measure a product of these influences.[96]

94. See 5.1 and 11.2 above.

95. So E. des Places, *Jamblique, les Mystères d'Egypte* (1966), 15: 'Mi-oriental, mi-hellénique, ce genre d'écrits devait séduire Jamblique'.

96. See above, text to nn.37–44.

To make these general points is not of course to assert that we *know* that contact with the non-Roman 'Orient' had no significant influence in the Roman Near East. It is simply to ask what precisely such influences will have been, how they were transmitted and in what language. One precise example (even if we cannot trace the process of transmission) would be the centrality at Palmyra of the cult of a Babylonian god, Bel, with the further dimension that the Zeus worshipped in the neighbouring Greek city of Apamea came to be conceived of as 'Zeus Bēlios'.[97]

So should we take that as a hint that the culture of the apparently 'Greek' cities of the Roman provinces was itself 'half-Oriental', and therefore, among other things, systematically open to the attraction of Chaldaean, or supposedly Chaldaean, writings? Just what is implied in such a claim has to be set out fully. For it presumes that there was a 'non-Greek' mentality, common to both the Roman and the non-Roman parts of the Fertile Crescent, and that this presumed cultural framework was sufficiently powerful to exert a profound influence also on the nature of the thought embodied in works written in Greek by people from this region.

It needs to be recalled that the search for a 'Syrian' tradition and education, prompted by what seems to have been said of himself by Iamblichus, the second-century novelist, has lead nowhere—except perhaps to Palmyra. If we think of a 'culture' in the full sense, as a tradition, an educational system, a set of customs and above all a collective understanding of the past, then we can find in the Roman Near East only two established cultures: Greek and Jewish. Christianity, as expressed in works written in Greek, was of course able to deploy systems of allusion and comparison to both traditions. In doing so Christian writers were of course above all making the Old Testament central to the historical consciousness of non-Jews. But they were also in practice paying tribute to the great works of Josephus, written in Greek in Rome: the *Antiquities* and the *Against Apion*. But this was (and is) true of Christianity as a whole, without regard to region. It is surely an accident, rather than a significant feature of a 'regional' Christian culture and outlook, that the earliest known Christian work to take over, for the benefit of Christianity, Josephus' demonstration of the superior antiquity of Jewish tradition should have been written by a second-century bishop of Antioch, Theophilus: 'It is obvious how *our* sacred writings are proved to be more ancient and more true than the writings of Greeks and Egyptians or any other historiographers'.[98]

The fact that these were two radically different historical cultures and systems of belief is not affected by the fact that the Old Testament itself had long

97. 9.4 and 7.4 above.

98. See Theophilus, *Ad Autolycum*, ed. and trans. R. M. Grant (1970); quotation from III, 26.

been available in Greek, or that Judaism, even as practised in the Holy Land, was a bilingual or even trilingual affair, in which Greek was very readily used, even for the epitaphs of Galilean rabbis.[99] It cannot therefore properly be claimed that, because Numenius, a Neo-Platonist of the later second century from Apamea, refers to Moses and the Exodus, he had some acquaintance with a Semitic literature—or properly implied that this might have wider implications for his knowledge or understanding of other 'Oriental' traditions.[100] Unfortunately, for this view, Numenius' appeal to the 'peoples of good reputation' was too all-embracing: after Plato and Pythagoras one should look to the Brahmins, the Jews, the Magi and the Egyptians.[101] These traditional sources of enlightenment, all of them 'Oriental', again represented inherited images within Greek culture. It is surely not to be supposed that Numenius is claiming actual direct acquaintance with writings in all four of the quite distinct languages which might theoretically have been concerned. In any case what is conspicuously lacking is an allusion to wisdom embodied in a non-Jewish Semitic literature, current or previously current, in the Near East. So far as our knowledge goes, there was only one such literature, though it is just possible that in Numenius' lifetime Phoenician was still used more widely than on the coins of Tyre.[102] The one clear exception was Syriac: but so far as we know, it was not, until later, current west of the Euphrates; and it too evolved as a 'non-Mediterranean descendant of Greek culture'.

There are therefore profound conceptual problems, to give only one instance, in the claim that the origin of Numenius' doctrine of two distinct souls *(psychai)* was 'Oriental'.[103] To which 'Orient' is reference being made? Precisely comparable problems arise with the Christian theological literature of the Near East. Here again, only some very general propositions can be established. First, while we need not doubt that Christianity was in fact preached in the Parthian Empire, in particular in Babylonia, our evidence for this in the first two centuries remains indirect, for instance the reactions to Christianity of the 'Elchasaite' sect mentioned above. As we saw earlier, Tatian, for all that he describes himself as an 'Assyrian', did not come from the Parthian Empire,[104] and there is indeed no surviving Christian literature written outside the area of Roman domination before the fourth century. Before that time the only 'eastern Christianity' which we can actually encounter is that of Osrhoene, beginning with Bardesanes, who also confirms that Christianity had

99. See ch. 10 above.
100. So E. des Places, *Numénius, Fragments* (1973), 21: 'une certaine connaissance des Écritures, donc d'une littérature sémitique'.
101. Des Places, fr. 1a.
102. 8.4–5 above.
103. So Des Places, op. cit., 22.
104. Ch. 6 above.

now spread to Hatra, Media and Parthia.[105] But the idea that the kings of Orhai ever converted to Christianity—whether the Abgar who was a contemporary of Jesus or Abgar 'the Great' who was a contemporary of Septimius Severus—is a myth, ancient or modern.[106] If the kingdom, and the subsequent *colonia,* remained pagan, the evolution of a Christian literature in Syriac is of immense significance. But it was a phenomenon which belonged east of the Euphrates, and we cannot read back from what we see in *Syriac* writings to what will have been the case in *Syria.* Take for instance an extremely important work preserved in Syriac, the church-order known as the *Didascalia.* The Syriac text seems to have been translated in the fourth century, from a Greek original written in the third, or at any rate in a period when paganism was still dominant and persecution was still possible. But there are no grounds whatsoever for the universal assumption that the Greek original must have reflected the workings of the Church in *Syria,* or in some subregion of it.[107]

Such an assumption rests on quite unsound foundations. Should we suppose that there was a 'Syrian' Christianity, or conceive of the theological presuppositions or doctrines of Christian writers in Greek who originated from Syria (Coele or Phoenice), from Judaea/Syria Palaestina (like Justin Martyr, Iulius Africanus or Eusebius) or from Roman Arabia either as showing a common, 'regional' character or as exhibiting contrasting, 'sub-regional' mentalities? And in either case are we entitled to relate these characteristics to the wider, necessarily pagan, belief-systems of the region or sub-region in question? Was there, to give a precise example, something 'Arabian' (or even 'Nabataean'?) in the doctrine propagated by the bishop Beryllus of Bostra in the mid-third century which denied both the pre-existence of Christ before his earthly life and his independent divinity? Or in the other heresy then current in Arabia, that the soul perished with the body, to be revived only at the Resurrection?[108] Any such claim would seem to presuppose a far more profound understanding of the culture and social history of the Roman province of Arabia than we actually possess. It would also run counter to the obvious fact that the infinite varieties of early Christian belief and practice knew no regional boundaries. Two examples will suffice. The earliest set of theological propositions emanating unquestionably from a bishop in Syria

105. 12.3 above.

106. 12.3 and 12.5 above.

107. For a translation of the Syriac text, with a very clear and helpful introduction, see R. H. Connolly, *Didascalia Apostolorum* (1929). The place and date of the Greek original are discussed on pp. lxxxviiff. Note p. lxxxix: 'I . . . would locate the *Didascalia,* roughly speaking, between Antioch and Edessa: yet without excluding the possibility of lower Syria(?), or even Palestine'.

108. Eusebius, *HE* VI, 33 and 37.

which we can encounter are contained in the letters of Ignatius of Antioch in the early second century.[109] Are they evidence (for instance) for Judaising tendencies in the Antiochene church? Perhaps so; but they are actually addressed to five churches in the Roman province of Asia, and to the church in Rome. Conversely, some decades later one of the most influential of Christian heresies was preached in Rome by Marcion, who came from Sinope in Pontus. His views were to receive much attention in the works of Ephrem; and we saw earlier how a church of Marcionites is attested by an inscription of the early fourth century from a village between Damascus and the Hauran.[110]

If we are not careful, what are simply westernising prejudices may enter modern interpretations of the evolution of Christianity in the Roman Near East: 'The further east, the less susceptible would theological thinking have been to Hellenising influence, and it is probable that primitive Syrian thinking spread as far west as the Syrian-speaking environs of Antioch itself'.[111] In fact the reference here is to the ascetic movement of the fourth and fifth centuries. Did this too, in the form it took in northern Syria and Mesopotamia, owe some profound debt to indigenous traditions?[112] What connection, for instance, is to be seen between Lucian's description in *On the Syrian Goddess* of the two pillars in the temple at Hierapolis on which a man would remain for seven days, offering prayers, and the most dramatic of all displays of self-deprivation, by the famous ascetic Simeon Stylites, who remained on his column for seven whole years? Our detailed conception of the ascetics who functioned both east and west of the Euphrates is a function of the existence of a local account, the *Religious History* of Theodoret, bishop of Cyrrhus, written towards the middle of the fifth century. Time is also significant—the movement described by Theodoret had begun about the beginning of the fourth century, with Iakobos of Nisibis; but the particular form of demonstrative piety devised by Simeon belongs more than a whole century later, in AD 422–429. Moreover, if we may believe Jerome, asceticism in the Near East also had an independent (but almost simultaneous) origin in the model provided by Saint Antony in Egypt and imported by Hilarion of Gaza in the first decade of the century.[113] Thus, though the relation of hermits to their local context, and specifically to rural pagan sanctuaries, is often brought out very vividly

109. They are most easily accessible in the Loeb *Apostolic Fathers* I, 165ff.

110. 11.4 above.

111. So D. S. Wallace-Hadrill, *Christian Antioch: A Study of Early Christian Thought in the East* (1982), 91 (in fact a scholarly and stimulating work from which there is much to be learned, however questionable some of its presuppositions).

112. See also S. P. Brock, "Early Syrian Asceticism", *Numen* 20 (1973), 1 = *Syriac Perspectives on Late Antiquity* (1984), no. 1.

113. 10.4 above.

in our sources,[114] whether we should understand the spiritual origins of this extremely important, indeed revolutionary, movement in terms of a regional culture (and if so which) is a quite different question.

To go 'in search of the Orient', in comparing social and political structures and the currency of different languages and scripts in the various sub-regions of the Roman Near East of the first few centuries of the Christian era, is certainly to bring out many features which distinguish this large area from other parts of the Classical world. Above all, Syriac was the only language which emerged for the first time in this period, developed as a vehicle for literature, both pagan and Christian, and has remained a Christian language to this day. But it is surely significant that this development began while Mesopotamia was not yet ruled by Rome, and was to persist on both sides of the eventual frontier between Rome and Persia.

Elsewhere, the effects of Roman rule were of a curiously ambiguous character. On the one hand, the early period, when Roman dominance was assured, but Roman direct rule was relatively limited, saw a remarkable flowering of local architecture and forms of monumental display, from the royal monuments of Commagene, to Palmyra, Damascus, the kingdom of Herod, the Hauran and Nabataea. Subsequently all these very distinctive architectural forms either came to a halt, as in Commagene, Petra or Palmyra, or suffered actual destruction, like the Temple in Jerusalem. Commagene, Petra and Palmyra were all areas where force was used by Rome to suppress political formations which were in different ways expressions of some independent identity. Over the centuries concerned, the effect of Roman rule was to produce a steadily more uniform world of Graeco-Roman cities. The history of language is closely comparable (not of course by pure accident, since much of our evidence for the expression of local identities comes from inscriptions, including building-inscriptions). By the moment of the conversion of Constantine in 312, there was almost no place west of the Euphrates where texts were being publicly inscribed in any language other than Greek or Latin. One isolated, if extremely significant, exception is provided by the Arabic inscription of an Arab king from En-Nemara; another is a few Nabataean texts from the outer fringes of Arabia; and the third is the continued use of both Hebrew and Aramaic in the epitaphs, mosaics and building-inscriptions from the Jewish areas of Syria Palaestina.

This last exception is of course the major one, the only historical and religious culture native to this region which, in spite of the violent repression of two great revolts, was to survive as a religion of the book. Based on texts of which most had been composed before Alexander's conquests, were written in a Semitic language, and expressed conceptions of a single deity which were

114. See esp. ch. 6 above.

wholly at variance with the anthropomorphic cults of Greek paganism, Judaism cannot but be seen in sharp contrast to Graeco-Roman culture. But whether 'Oriental' is an appropriate label for a belief-system which evolved in the first range of hills to the east of the Mediterranean is again an open question.

It would, however, be carrying scepticism too far to deny all connection between the aniconic sacrificial cult of the Temple in Jerusalem and the clear literary, epigraphic and iconographic evidence for non-representational objects of worship at a number of places in Roman Syria and Arabia.[115] We can allow also for the distinctive role of bas-relief carvings of deities (as opposed to statues in the round) functioning as objects of worship, above all at Palmyra; and the prevalence, never complete, of frontality in this context may be seen as an important clue to the distinctiveness of the art of Palmyra, and of Dura.[116] By contrast, hardly anything in the extensive evidence for the identity of local deities as understood by their worshippers, or for the iconography of deities or the decoration of temples, gives any support to the idea that the worship of the Sun was, as Tacitus supposed, characteristic of 'Syrians'; still less would it show, as moderns have supposed, that there was a tendency to syncretise other deities with Helios, or Sol, or even that there was a general 'solar theology'. The best-attested cult of the Sun, at Hatra, is irrelevant in the context of Syria proper in the first century AD. As for Syria proper, if 'LH'GBL had already, by the later first century, been interpreted as 'Helios' by the Greek-speaking inhabitants of Emesa, that might explain Tacitus' generalisation. But the idea of a general 'native' cult of the Sun in Syria is not supported by the evidence.[117]

Nonetheless, the vast variety of divine names and forms of devotion revealed by dedications in Greek will also serve to remind us of how dangerous any generalisations about the mentality of the population of the Roman Near East would be. What, for instance, do we make of a Greek dedication from the southern Hauran: 'Ausos (and) Obaidos his son, the two made this gift to Ilaalgēs and his *angelos* Idarouma'?[118] Once again we have here a local, or rather regional, divine name; for 'Ilaalgēs' is a transliteration of the Nabataean 'LHGY", the god of the place near Petra known in Greek as 'Gaia'. The original Nabataean version is also attested far away from there, at the distant

115. Ch. 1 and 7.3, 8.4, 9.2, 11.4 above.

116. 9.4 and 12.4 above.

117. Tacitus, *Hist.* III, 24–25; see 2.4 above. Given the very ambiguous status of the cult of 'Elagabal' at Emesa, I would be even more sceptical than H. Seyrig in his masterly survey "Le culte du Soleil en Syrie à l'époque romaine", *Syria* 48 (1971), 337.

118. J. T. Milik, *Dédicaces faites par des dieux (Palmyra, Hatra, Tyr) et les thiases sémitiques à l'époque romaine* (1972), 428 and Pl. XV.1; G. W. Bowersock, *Hellenism in Late Antiquity* (1990), 30.

outpost of Dumatha.[119] The secondary divine name is also Semitic in origin, incorporating the roots 'hand' (YD) and 'rise' or 'be raised' (RMH). But what will have been meant by saying that the one supernatural being was the *angelos* of the other? As regards the personal beliefs of the population of the Near East, questions are more appropriate than premature answers.

13.2. WEST?

To pursue the questions raised by the inscribed dedications put up by private persons in the Near East, though salutary in showing how enigmatic they are, is to run the risk of missing the most significant point about them: that they are inscriptions, and that they are nearly all in Greek. One specific example is the dedication from the southern Hauran discussed above. Cut in the black basalt of the area in the second or third century, and hence a local expression of the 'epigraphic habit', it too is in Greek. If there is a single conclusion which emerges from the mass of enigmatic items of evidence from the region, it is that the Greek language, Greek social structures and Greek frameworks for the construction and worship of deities penetrated to the most remote of rural contexts. Greek might thereby, as in the example just quoted, come to provide the means of expression of a cult originally conducted in a Semitic language. But it could of course also serve to transmit to this region a whole historical culture and mythology which had originally been foreign to it. Few examples of the transmission of the standard elements of Greek mythology into a local environment are more perfect than the carved lintel, also in black basalt, preserved in the museum at Suweida: it represents the judgment of Paris, and the figures portrayed are duly labelled in Greek—Paris, Hermes, Aphrodite, Athena, Hera and Zeus.[1] The same process of transmission could be illustrated from the long series of mosaics with mythological scenes known from the Near Eastern provinces; the best known are those of Antioch, but perhaps greater significance attaches to those from Philippopolis, the new foundation by Philip 'the Arab' (244–249), where the mosaics make a striking impression, surrounded as they are by the black basalt walls of the buildings put up in the new city of the mid-third century and afterwards. One may note above all the supremely elegant portrayal of Artemis bathing, surprised by Actaeon.[2]

At the level of mass popular culture, the most important influence from the wider Greek world may have been exercised by the festivals or competitions *(agōnes)* involving both athletics and stage-performances (and hence

119. See 11.1, text to n.23.
1. M. Dunand, *Le musée de Soueida* (1934), no. 1.
2. See the survey by J. Balty, "La mosaique au Proche-Orient I", *ANRW* II.12.2 (1981), 347.

representations of Greek myths) and attested almost—but not quite—all over the region: for example at Antioch, Zeugma, Damascus, Berytus, Tyre, Neapolis, Caesarea, Gerasa, Philadelphia, Bostra and Gaza. But, as noted earlier, they seem not to have taken root in the outer reaches of the Roman Near East—across the Euphrates, at Palmyra or at Petra.

It is easy to appreciate the still visible evidence of Greek mass entertainment—the vast theatres of Cyrrhus or Apamea, the still-standing theatre of Bostra, or its circus, clearly visible from the air. But it is much harder to grasp the more private process which must have been fundamental to the culture of the region, the teaching of written Greek to children. As everywhere, we begin to catch glimpses of the educational process only in its upper reaches, as in Eusebius' passing allusion to someone called Malchion who in the later third century was in charge of sophistic education in the Greek schools *(paideutēria)* at Antioch.[3] Even such an allusion hardly makes clear what age-group, or what level of education, was concerned. In most cases either we see the local products of what must have been a very widespread process of the diffusion of Greek, as represented in thousands of local inscriptions and some perishable documents, or we encounter the individual sophists or writers who contributed to the universal literary and rhetorical culture of the wider Greek world. A catalogue of these would serve no purpose, for it was precisely one of the defining features of the wider Greek culture that a man who made a name for himself within it might come 'from' anywhere. But one significant example is the Heliodorus whom Philostratus calls simply 'the Arabian', and who therefore came from the Roman province of Arabia.[4] Sent to Gaul to appear before the Emperor (Caracalla, evidently in 213), he not only gained rewards from him, but seized the opportunity to invite the Emperor to assign him a theme for an impromptu oration. The topic given was 'Demosthenes, having lost the thread of his oration before Philip, and accused of cowardice'. It could be assumed by both parties that this episode from fourth-century Greek history was familiar.

Five hundred years earlier, when Seleucus I had been spreading Greek colonies over much of the Fertile Crescent, it is very likely that there had been a large-scale immigration by Greek-speakers from Greece itself, the Aegean and Macedonia, as surely happened in Egypt also. There may even have been some immigration during the Hellenistic period, for instance when the Greek cities of the Decapolis, most of which were eventually to form part of Roman Arabia, came into existence. But, paradoxically, while the full expression of Greek city culture in the Near East was a feature not of the Hellenistic but of the Roman period, there is nothing whatsoever to suggest that this was

3. Eusebius, *HE* VII, 29, 2.
4. Philostratus, *Vit. Soph.* II, 32.

achieved by further immigration or settlement from the rest of the Greek world. It was not that, but the adoption of the norms of Greek city-culture by both dependent kings and local communities which progressively transformed not only cities, old and new, but a vast network of villages into urban, or sub-urban, communities using Greek. The effect was to be most striking in two areas close to the steppe, Palmyra and the Hauran. In the case of Palmyra it is very likely that the ancestors of those who created this wholly new city, from the first century BC onwards, would have been labelled by Graeco-Roman observers as 'Arabs'; indeed we surely meet just these ancestors in the ten thousand 'Arabs and some of those neighbouring on them', commanded by one 'Zabdibēlos', whom Polybius describes as fighting under Antiochus III at the battle of Raphia in 217 BC. This name was to be quite common in Palmyrene inscriptions.[5] But the Palmyrenes of the Imperial period never seem to have identified themselves as 'Arabs'; the significant fact about them is not that, but their progressive approximation to Graeco-Roman models, first as a 'Greek city' and then as a Roman *colonia*, statuses uniquely combined with the continued public use of their dialect of Aramaic.

Similarly, the long development which produced an 'Arab' who could exploit before a Roman Emperor the well-known theme of Demosthenes' failure of nerve before Philip was brought about neither by Greek immigration into the zone between the Jordan Valley and the steppe nor by the 'penetration' of Arabs into this area. It was a process of acculturation by a settled population, which is symbolised by the urbanisation of Petra, and simultaneously by the creation of a monumental cult-centre at Siaʿ and the bilingual inscriptions, in Greek and Aramaic, which accompanied it. By the early third century, when Heliodorus appeared before Caracalla, the now unified zone of Roman Arabia was a network of Greek cities, whose status was indicated by their minting coins with Greek legends, and which were embedded in a dense network of villages, stretching from Damascus southwards to around Petra. The most significant development lay in fact at the village level: that throughout this area almost the only written language in public use was now Greek.

But among the rustic Greek inscriptions of the Hauran area we find a considerable number in which individuals are designated by transliterated Latin terms, *ouetranos* ('veteran') or *ouetranikos* ('of veteran status'). Coming from a rural environment near the margins of the steppe, these inscriptions may serve to remind us that in searching, as we must, for the various forms of local languages, beliefs, cult-forms, iconography, perhaps even local literature and historical traditions, we are in danger of overlooking the obvious. For by far the most profound and all-pervasive of all external cultural influences in the Near East in the first few centuries was the Roman Empire itself.

5. Polybius V, 79, 8. For the name, in various forms, Stark, op. cit., 13.1, n.57, 16ff.

In the earliest phase of development its influence was, it is true, at best indirect. In a way which is by no means easy to explain, most of the major royal monuments of Commagene, put up under Antiochus I (*circa* 69–36 BC); the earliest known public inscription from Palmyra (and the earliest Palmyrene inscription from Dura, recording the building of a temple); as well as the earliest known phase of the sanctuary at Sia' in the Hauran, all date to shortly before rather than after the moment when a secure Roman domination, no longer marked by internal conflicts, had been achieved by the battle of Actium. But the existence of the established Roman monarchy must have been relevant to the phase of extravagant urban construction and monumental building which then took place in both the Herodian and the Nabataean kingdoms; it was paralleled, where we can trace it, by large-scale projects in Greek cities, such as Damascus and Gerasa. As noted earlier, Josephus' list of the buildings donated by Herod to cities outside his kingdom can be taken to mark the first phase in the evolution of the monumental 'Greek city' in the Near East: Tripolis, Damascus, Ptolemais, Byblos, Berytus, Tyre, Sidon, Laodicea, Ascalon, Antioch. What Josephus was to write later, in the *Antiquities,* of Herod's gift to Antioch perfectly expresses the ideal: 'And for the Antiochenes, who inhabit the greatest city in Syria, which has a street running through it lengthwise, he adorned this street with colonnades on either side, and paved the open part of the road with polished stone, thereby contributing greatly to the appearance of the city and to the convenience of its inhabitants.'[6] It is not incorrect to describe these places—the *colonia* of Berytus apart—as 'Greek cities'. But as physical structures, with monumental buildings including 'Roman' theatres, baths, basilicas and occasionally amphitheatres, and with the use of Roman techniques of construction, they would be better described as 'Graeco-Roman'.[7] The Imperial period marked a new phase in urbanism, in which Greek and Roman elements were fused. The influence of the Empire went far beyond the direct effects of taxation and military occupation.

It was only very gradually, step by step over several centuries, that the Roman military presence ceased to represent essentially a potential application of force, which could be deployed from northern Syria in emergencies, and evolved into a general policing function, which extended in very visible form to the whole 'desert frontier', from Aila to the Tigris. By the moment of the treaty which Diocletian made with the Persian king in 298 or 299, the population of the whole area directly ruled by Rome, between the Taurus

6. Josephus, *BJ* I, 21, 11 (422–425), cf. 10.2, text to n.9, above; Loeb trans. from *Ant.* XVI, 5, 3 (148).

7. For a valuable survey see H. Dodge, "The Architectural Impact of Rome in the East", in M. Henig (ed.), *Architecture and Architectural Sculpture in the Roman Empire* (1990), 108.

Mountains and the Red Sea, must have numbered at least several millions.[8] But even in relation to so large a population, the scale of the Roman military presence was significant. By the third century, if we assume that the number of auxiliaries was roughly equal to that of legionaries, there will have been something approaching 100,000 soldiers in the Near Eastern provinces; perhaps therefore approximately one for every hundred civilians.

In sheer scale, and in the fact that the deployment of the army was a process whose effects were continually renewed, by the movement of units, by recruitment and by discharge, the Roman army must represent by far the most substantial of all non-local influences on the Near East. Moreover, along with the importation of legionaries and auxiliary troops from other parts of the Roman world, we have to take into account local recruitment into the army, followed by the discharge, and re-settlement within local society, of the *ouetranoi* whom we can encounter from the Tigris to the Hauran. Here again, if we think of possible 'Romanisation', as opposed to 'Hellenisation', there is nothing to suggest that incorporation into the Roman Empire was accompanied by any significant immigration by Latin-speaking civilians. The only long-standing 'island' of Romanism in the Near East was the *colonia* of Berytus, created by the settlement of veterans under Augustus; its inland territory stretched over into the Bekaa Valley, later to be split off as the *colonia* of Heliopolis. These two linked areas were the only ones where Latin remained in general use, and even here always in combination with Greek. Outside these zones, individual Latin words, from official or military contexts, entered the Greek of everyday life and passed into Hebrew, Nabataean, Palmyrene and Syriac; royal and Imperial foundations spread Latin-derived city names across the map; and Latin personal names passed into very common use in Greek, whether or not the individuals concerned had gained the Roman citizenship.[9] But there is nothing to suggest that outside Berytus and Heliopolis Latin ever became *a,* let alone *the,* normal language of daily speech. Nor did it ever supplant Greek as the literary language of the Near East. The *Res Gestae* of Ammianus Marcellinus, a native of Antioch born about AD 330, seems to represent the earliest known literary work written in Latin by someone from the Near East. But the very substantial literary evidence for the fourth-century Antioch of Libanius and John Chrysostom serves to show just how surprising and exceptional this will have been.

There are, however, two linked exceptions to the general absence of any profound Romanisation. First, it is clear, as already noted, that Berytus remained consciously a place of Latin and Roman culture. It was thus there

---

8. For some observations see F. Cumont, "The Population of Syria", *JRS* 24 (1934), 187.

9. See J.-P. Rey-Coquais, "Onomastique et histoire de la Syrie gréco-romaine", in D. M. Pippidi (ed.), *Actes du VIIᵉ Congrès int. d'épigr. gr. et lat.* (1979), 171.

that Valerius Probus, the major Latin grammarian of the first century AD, was able to read older Latin works which had fallen out of favour in Rome.[10] Second, there was Roman jurisprudence, taught above all in Berytus itself. Access to Roman jurisdiction, however erratic or dilatory, became a crucial issue in the practical affairs of ordinary people within a Roman province, even those living in remote rural locations; we have seen the process of going to seek justice from Roman officials vividly reflected in both of the two new archives, that of Babatha's family from the south end of the Dead Sea, and that of the third century from the middle Euphrates.[11] How far the principles of Roman law, as opposed to the jurisdiction of Roman courts, or the forms of Roman procedure, came to affect the lives of individuals is a problem which arises throughout the Empire, and is too complex to embark on here.[12] But the 'archive of Babatha' shows that even within a few years of the creation of the province of Arabia the specifically Roman procedure of verbal question-and-answer (stipulatio) had come into use, even among non-citizens.[13] Even more remarkably, the archive contains three texts of a Greek translation of verbal formulae known from the praetor's edict.[14] Neither this nor any other evidence, however, can make it seem any the less surprising that the major exponent of classical Roman jurisprudence should have been Domitius Ulpianus, who came from a known family of Greek-speaking 'Oulpianoi' in the ancient Phoenician-Greek city of Tyre. He was certainly born long before his native city became a Roman colonia, probably in 198.[15]

Roman law could certainly become, as a rival to Greek rhetoric, a skill to which young men could aspire. The tension between the obligations of Greek city life and the attractions of Roman law as the key to a future career is visible in the rescript which Diocletian and Maximian addressed to 'Severinus and other scholastici Arabii': 'Since you affirm that you are devoting yourselves to liberalia studia, especially with regard to the professio iuris, by residing in the civitas Berytorum of the province of Phoenice, we have decided that it is in the interest both of the public benefit and of your future advancement that each of you should not, up to your 25th year, be called away from your studies'.[16]

The population of the Near East had long since been integrated within the

10. Suetonius, De gram. 24; see Millar, "Roman Coloniae", 16.

11. See 3.2–3; 4.2 above.

12. See H. Galsterer, "Roman Law in the Provinces: Some Problems of Transmission", in M. H. Crawford (ed.), L'Impero Romano e le strutture economiche e sociali delle province (1986), 13.

13. 11.4, text to n.9, above.

14. P. Yadin, nos. 28–30.

15. 3.4 and 8.5 above.

16. CJ X, 50, 1.

wider Imperial system, in which individuals might enter the Roman army as common soldiers, or people of more prominent birth enlist directly as centurions; and in which the Roman citizenship, beginning with kings and dynasts in the late Republic and Augustan period, slowly spread, to be capped by Caracalla's 'divine gift' of the universal citizenship in the second decade of the third century. In that period too, under the Severan dynasty and after, there came that remarkable tide of Imperial grants of the status of *colonia*, which was no mere matter of nomenclature or formal status and embraced a large proportion of precisely those places which exhibited the most strongly marked regional or local character: for instance Emesa, Sidon, Tyre, Petra, Bostra, Damascus, Palmyra and the cities of the newly conquered area across the Euphrates, Edessa, Carrhae, Reshaina, Nisibis and Singara. Thus it was that the formal, public reflection of Roman imperialism, and its capacity to offer citizenship and status to subject populations, is visible nowhere more vividly than in the documents of the Syriac-speaking area. When a deed of sale was drawn up in the *colonia* of Edessa in 243, the holder of the priesthood (KMRWT') was a man with a classically Romano-Greek name, 'Markos Aurēlios Antiochos' (MRQWS 'WRLYWS 'NṬYWKS), who was also a Roman *eques*. But to indicate this it was necessary to transliterate two Greek words into Syriac: HPWS RHMWS (*hippeus rōmaios*).[17]

Marcus Aurelius Antiochus was one of a quite small number of Roman *equites* who are known to have come from the Near Eastern provinces; when the careers of such men are known, it is very often as a product of honorific inscriptions from their home towns, a feature of Imperial urban life which was relatively little developed in this region.[18] But among such inscriptions those from Berytus and Heliopolis stand out, as do those from Palmyra—as a direct reflection of the unique bilingual version of the 'epigraphic habit' which prevailed there; so Greek terms for Roman ranks appear there too in Semitic transliteration (with *kratistos epitropos doukēnarios* appearing as QRṬSṬWS 'PṬRP' DQNR'). Some other men from the Near East, but surely fewer, rose into the Roman Senate itself, the earliest known dating to the later first century. Here again our view of them is sometimes owed to city-inscriptions of the type familiar from many parts of the Empire.[19] Our most consistent evidence, however, again comes from Palmyra, and relates to Septimius Odenathus, the husband of Zenobia, and his son, Septimius Airanes. Here too, therefore, in the 250s, we are able to see their Roman rank as ex-

17. *P. Dura*, no. 28; 12.5 above.

18. See H. Devijver, "Equestrian Officers from the East", in Freeman and Kennedy, *DRBE* I, 109, on pp. 179ff.; *equites* in third-century Palmyra, 4.3 above.

19. See G. W. Bowersock, "Roman Senators from the Near East: Syria, Judaea, Arabia, Mesopotamia", in S. Panciera (ed.), *Epigrafia e ordine senatorio* II (1982), 651.

pressed in Greek terms, and in Greek either transliterated or translated into Palmyrene: *vir clarissimus* (senator) has become *lamprotatos synklētikos* or SNQLṬYQ' NHYR'.[20]

Senators from cities in the Near East come most clearly into our view when they appear in narrative sources as making claims to the rank of Emperor. That in its turn, however, was an effect of the centrality of the Near East, northern Syria above all, in the military structure of the Empire. This was the case with Avidius Cassius, from Cyrrhus, whose attempted coup took place, perhaps by a misunderstanding, when he was the consular *legatus* of Syria in 175. Later coups d'état involving men from this region arose from a further consequence of the growing centrality of the Near East. After almost one and a half centuries when no ruling Emperor ever came there, from Trajan onwards the Near East became one of the primary fields for campaigns led by Emperors in person. Imperial campaigns were of course only an intermittent, and in a sense superficial, aspect of a much wider process of mutual contact, integration and conflict between the apparatus of the state and the communal structures of the region. We should certainly attach more importance to the gradual expansion of direct military occupation by the army, its diffusion in the form of the small police-posts along roads, so vividly reflected in Eusebius' catalogue of places mentioned in the Bible, and the extension of military occupation to the margins of the steppe. In that context a vast, long-term process of change is symbolised by the Latin inscription of AD 334 from the steppe south of the Hauran, in which a *protector* named Vincentius records his construction of a cistern, designed to reduce the danger to peasants seeking water from raids by the *Saraceni*.[21]

But these Imperial campaigns did reflect a fundamental shift in the strategic shape of the Empire; and for our purposes they also on occasion led to consequences which throw into sharp relief the profound nature of the problems which confront us in assessing ethnic or cultural identities, or the relation of these to political action.

In 244, for instance, Gordian III was killed during a campaign on the Euphrates, and was supplanted as Emperor by his Praetorian Prefect, M. Iulius Philippus, or Philip 'the Arab'. Narrative sources of the fourth century and later do indeed call him an Arab, or Trachonite Arab, a reflection of the fact that he came from an area at the northern tip of the Jebel Hauran, just south of the edge of the lava-field known as 'Trachonitis'. But the source which is by far the closest in time, the *Thirteenth Sibylline Oracle*, describes him as 'appearing from Syria'.[22] This area had not been part of the kingdom

---

20. Cantineau, *Inv.* III, no. 19; 4.3 above.

21. 11.5 above.

22. For the sources see *PIR*[2] I, 461. 'Arabs': SHA, *v. Gord.* 29; 'Arabs Trachonites': Aurelius Victor, *Caes.* 28, 1; 'Appearing from Syria': *Sib. Or.* XIII, 22, see Potter, *Sybilline Oracle, ad loc.*

of Nabataea; the documents from this region in the first century had indeed included some inscriptions in Aramaic, and Josephus had characterised its pagan inhabitants as *Suroi*.[23] In the second century and after, however, all the inscriptions from the settled zone are in Greek. When Iulius Philippus and his brother Iulius Priscus were born, perhaps around AD 200, their native district may (but it is not certain) have ceased to be part of 'Syria Phoenice', and been joined to 'Arabia'.[24] To sketch that background is to stress that we must leave entirely open the question of what ethnic description we ought to give to the two Greek-speaking (and surely also Latin-speaking) sons of a local Roman citizen, Iulius Marinus, who both now entered the Imperial service. It is clearly, in any case, more significant that both will have risen though equestrian military and civilian careers—and that Philippus' most notable monument was to be the foundation at his presumed birthplace of a new Greek-city-cum-Roman-*colonia*, named after himself, Philippopolis. It was mere chance which allowed him to rise from Praetorian Prefect to Emperor; and the city which he founded remains the most complete expression of the export to the edge of the steppe of the Graeco-Roman ideal of a city.

But, with an indeterminacy typical of our sources, the author of the *Oracle* written a decade later did then choose to refer to Philippopolis and Bostra as 'cities of the Arabs': 'Now be adorned, cities of the Arabs, with temples and *stadia* and *agoras* and paved streets . . . Bostra and Philippopolis'.[25]

By contrast, there had been significant purely regional elements in the coup which in 218 had made an Emperor of the adolescent Varius Avitus Bassianus; for its success partly depended on the prestige of the deity in Emesa whose priest he was, Elagabal. But his mother came from a local family which must have enjoyed the Roman citizenship since the first century, and which had made a marriage-connection with the Severi from Lepcis in Tripolitania, while his father was a Roman *eques* from the Greek city of Apamea. The cult of Elagabal, whose 'Oriental' features he was to flaunt so deliberately in Rome, was understood, even in Emesa itself, to be a cult of the Sun; that itself, however, reflected not a general 'Syrian' worship of the Sun, but a Greek interpretation of a Semitic term, 'LH'GBL, the first half of which sounded somewhat like 'Helios'. Far from being authentically 'Syrian', the cult which the juvenile Emperor displayed in Rome was a typically Greek construction of a genuinely local cult whose real origins were unknown and of no interest.[26]

The brief military domination of Palmyra, too, might be better understood

23. 11.1 and 13.1, text to n.58, above.

24. For different reconstructions of the stages of the northward movement of the border of Arabia, see E. Kettenhofen, *ZDPV* 97 (1981), 62, and Bowersock, *Roman Arabia*, 113ff.

25. *Sib. Or.* XIII, 64–66.

26. 9.2 above.

in terms not of presumed 'Arab' origins, but of the Greek and Roman models towards which it steadily progressed over three centuries, taking the form of a Greek city with the normal institutions, then of a Greek city named (as so often) after the Emperor, 'Hadrianē Palmyra', and then of a Roman *colonia*. In consequence, the forces which 'Vaballathus Augustus', precisely like Flavius Vespasianus two centuries before, sent into Egypt and across Asia Minor might better be seen as symbolising a claim to the Empire as a whole, rather than as a rejection of it, or as reflecting a separatist movement based on ethnic or regional loyalties.

In other words, if we seek to know who the inhabitants of the Roman Near East in these centuries really 'were', and what identity cities and communities there attributed to themselves, we must be content after all with ambiguous answers. This study began with the dedication which a Roman soldier at Dura-Europos made in Greek to 'the ancestral god, Zeus Betylos, of those by the Orontes', and with the multiple ambiguities which sprang from this characterisation of a regional deity. So it is only appropriate that it should end with the equally complex issues raised by Byzantine summaries of a Greek novel written in the second century, the *Babyloniaca* of Iamblichus. Was there still a living Babylonian culture, from which learning in the magical arts could be derived? Should we see the whole Fertile Crescent, from Babylonia to the Mediterranean, as the home of a unified 'Semitic', 'Syrian' or 'Aramaic' culture? Was there a whole class of persons in Roman Syria who defined themselves as 'Syrian' by descent and culture, and viewed Greek culture as something which they might or might not acquire? Was the 'Soaimos' who according to Iamblichus was a Roman senator and consul, and certainly became king of Armenia, really a descendant of the earlier local dynasty at Emesa? The only unambiguous feature of the two surviving summaries of what Iamblichus had said about himself is that they both reflect the author's awareness of the continued claims of Roman imperialism: the Parthian war fought by Trajan, and that of the 160s under Lucius Verus, when 'the land of the Parthians became subject to the Romans'. Iamblichus was of course exaggerating. But this was in fact the moment when Dura became Roman, and when Osrhoene, the birthplace of Syriac literature, became a Roman dependency. He had thus caught the crucial moment in the evolution of the Roman Empire in the Near East.

APPENDICES

MAPS

INDICES

THE INSCRIPTIONS OF THE
TETRARCHIC LAND-SURVEYORS

The inscriptions of the Tetrarchic land-surveyors have never been collected in full, and represent important evidence both for the working of the Tetrarchic state at the most local level and for local toponomy, communal nomenclature and forms of land-ownership. They divide into three main groups: (1) from the limestone massif of northern Syria; (2) from the Huleh Valley (the upper part of the Jordan valley) and the Golan Heights (Gaulanitis); and (3) the plain to the east of Gaulanitis, ancient Batanaea. There is also one important one (no. 35), and possibly a second (no. 36), from the Hauran (Auranitis).

In broad terms of function and character, they represent a single group, though with marked variations in the verbal formulae employed. As indicated above (5.2), the erection of these inscriptions clearly reflects the Tetrarchic taxation-reform of AD 297, and several of them are explicitly dated to this year. The attempt by W. Goffart, *Caput and Colonate* (1974), 44 and 129–130, to deny any connection between this process and the reform of taxation is not convincing. But it must certainly be admitted that the precise connection between these inscriptions marking out boundaries, on the one hand, and the forms of taxation on the other, is obscure.

The inscriptions will be presented in the order indicated above, which in Roman terms means taking in sequence the *provinciae* of Syria Coele, Syria Phoenice, Syria Palaestina (probably) and Arabia. Whether any come from Syria Palaestina remains uncertain, because all of the known markers come from the east side of the Huleh Valley (or actually on the Golan Heights), and none from Galilee proper or Judaea. In any case we do not know exactly where the 'borders' between Syria Phoenice, Arabia and Syria Palaestina lay in the Tetrarchic period. Discussion of the provincial boundaries has been greatly confused by the use of a seventh-century manuscript, the so-called *Laterculus Veronensis,* with a list of the provinces believed to go back to the Tetrarchic period. But, as noted above, there is no contemporary evidence for a province called either 'Arabia Augusta Libanensis' (so W. Seston, *Dioclétien et la Tétrarchie* I, 1948, 374ff.) or 'Augusta Libanensis.' For a properly cautious discussion of the latter, also questioning whether in principle the operations of *censitores* coincided with provincial boundaries, see A. Alt, "Augusta Libanensis", *ZDPV* 71 (1955), 173. All that is clear is that the same *censitor,* Aelius Statutus, is attested at work in the area around Damascus (nos. 16, 17, 18), in Gaulanitis (nos. 19, 24, 29) and in the Huleh Valley (no. 22).

It should probably be assumed that a similar operation was conducted everywhere in the Near East, and perhaps throughout the Empire. The texts of the inscriptions appear to suggest that they themselves were put up by the *censitores.* If that is so, the erratic survival of documents of this sort is due to subsequent conditions, rather than (as is often the case with inscriptions) to choices made at the time by interested parties.

The fullest discussion of these inscriptions to date is A. Deléage, *La capitation du Bas-Empire* (1945), 152ff.; note also especially H. Seyrig, "Bornes cadastrales du Ğebel Sim'ān", in G. Tchalenko, *Villages antiques de la Syrie du Nord* III (1958), 6ff.

It has not seemed worthwhile to reproduce all the texts, often fragmentary, from the printed editions, especially in the absence of direct work on the stones themselves. So most will merely be listed, with salient details noted. But a few more complete texts will be given as illustrations.

COMMAGENE, NEAR DOLICHE

1(?). *IGR* III, no. 1002 = *IGLS* I, no. 59. AD 293/305.
       Side 1. Dating by Tetrarchs of AD 293/305, followed by Ἀρδούλων
       εα(?) τοὺς ὅρους.
       Side 2. Same text, more worn, with ΕΛΛΑΚΑ[. .] in l. 8.

THE LIMESTONE MASSIF

Note the map of the locations of these inscriptions in Tchalenko, *Villages Antiques* III, p. 51, fig. 1. All the known ones from the limestone massif come from an area south of Brad in the Jebel Seman, and some 30 km north-west of Aleppo (see the fold-out maps in the same volume).

2.   Seyrig in Tchalenko, op. cit., p. 7, no. 8 = *SEG* XX, no. 335; cf. *BE* (1959), no. 459.

Burq Heidar. AD 297.

Erected ὑπὲρ σωτηρ(ί)ας καὶ [δια]μονῆς of the Tetrarchs. Establishment of ὅρ[οι] κώμης Καπροκηρων, ἐπὶ Ἰου(λίου) Σαβίνου τοῦ λαμπροτάτου κηνσείτορ[ος]. The dating, year 345 of the era of Antioch, in the month Panemos, can be restored by the parallel with nos. 3–6 and 9 below.

3. Seyrig, p. 8, no. 8a = *SEG* XX, no. 336.

    Kafr Lab. AD 297.

    Names of Tetrarchs missing; ὅροι [κωμῆς Καπρ]ολιαβων, under Iulius Sabinus, *kēnsitōr*. Dating as ἔτους εμτ´ (345), Πανήμου ή.

4. Seyrig, p. 8, no. 8b = *SEG* XX, no. 337, noting two further texts, not published.

    Kafr Lab. AD 297.

    This relatively complete text is worth giving in full as an example of the nature and lay-out of this visible expression of the Tetrarchic state in a rural locality.

    ὑπὲρ σωτηρίας
    καὶ νείκης
    τῶν κυρίων ἡμῶν
    Διοκλητιανοῦ καὶ
    Μαξιμιανοῦ τῶν
    Σεβαστῶν κ(αὶ) Κων-
    σταντ[ίου]
    κ(αὶ) Μαξιμιανοῦ ἐπιφ[αν]-
    εστάτων Κεσάρων.
    ὅροι ἀνεστάθησαν
    κωμῆς Καπρολιαβων
    ἐπὶ Ἰουλίου Σαβίνου
    [το]ῦ λαμπροτάτου
    κηνσίτορος
    ἔτους εμτ´, Πανήμου
    η´.

5. Seyrig, p. 9, no. 8c = *SEG* XX, no. 338.

    Kafr Lab. AD 297.

    Same text as above, more damaged.

6. Seyrig, p. 9, no. 8 = *SEG* XX, no. 339.

    Baziher, AD 297.

    Tetrarchs, as above. Establishment of ὅροι ἐπ(οικίας) Ζαερους, ἔτους εμτ´ (345), Δεσίου εί, δ(ιὰ) Σαβίνου λαμπρο[τάτου] κινσίτορος.

Note that the modern name of the village derives from the substitu-
tion of the term *beth* ('house') for ἐποίκιον or ἐποικία, attached to
Ζαερους

7. Seyrig, p. 10, no. 8e = *SEG* XX, no. 340.
    Between Kafr Nabo and Brad. AD 293/305.
    Fragmentary reference to Tetrarchs, as above. ἀ[νεστά]θησα[ν ὅροι
    . . . . κα]προ[. . .].
    The names of both of the modern villages are attested on local in-
    scriptions. *IGLS* II, no. 359 (Brad) has ἐν Καπερναβου, and no.
    530 has Καπροβαραδ.
8. Seyrig, p. 10, no. 8f = *SEG* XX, no. 341.
    Near Kafr Nabo. AD 293/305.
    Fragmentary formula for victory of Tetrarchs.
9. Seyrig, p. 11, no. 9 = *SEG* XX, no. 342.
    Ferkan. AD 297.
    Tetrarchs. ὅροι ἐπ(οικίου) καπερου[.]αμεως.
    Name of Sabinus(?) as κηνσίτορος missing. Year 345, month Lōos.
10. J. Jarry, "Inscriptions arabes, syriaques et grecques du Massif du Bé-
    lus en Syrie du Nord", *Annales Islamologiques* 7 (1967), 139,
    p. 158, no. 33 and Pl. XLII = *AE* (1968), no. 514.
    Near Kbesin, in the area of Kafr Lab.
    Tetrarchs. Establishment of ὅροι [κώμης] Καπροκηνων by Iulius Sa-
    binus. Year 345, Panemos.
11. Jarry, p. 159, no. 34 and Pl. XLII = *AE* (1968), no. 515.
    Near Kbesin. AD 297.
    Tetrarchs. Establishment of [ὅροι κ]ώμ[ης Καπρο]χερκεων by Iulius
    Sabinus. Year 345, Panemos.
12. Jarry, p. 160, no. 35 = *AE* (1968), no. 516.
    Burj Abdalou, on the route between Deir Seman and river Afrin. AD
    293/305.
    Tetrarchs. ὅροι KPONEA, rest illegible. Date uncertain.

NEAR JISHR ES SHOGHUR, IN THE
NORTHERN ORONTES VALLEY

13. M. Adunolfi, "Una iscrizione greca inedita e la 'capitatio' di Dioclezi-
    ano", *Oriens Antiquus* 4 (1965), 71.
    Near the Nahr el-Abyad, a tributary of the Orontes. AD 293/305.
    ὑπὲρ σωτηρίας κὲ νίκης of the Tetrarchs. ἀνεστάθησαν ὅ[ρ]οι ε.π[. . .].
14. Jarry, p. 160, no. 36 = *AE* (1968), no. 517.
    Mesmesan, near Jishr es Shoghur. AD 293/305.
    Tetrarchs. ὅροι Καπ[ρο]μεταλ[. . .].

TERRITORY OF EMESA

15(?). *IGLS* V, no. 2560 = *AE* (1947), no. 146.
   Zaidal, 5 km east of Emesa/Homs. AD 293/305(?).
   [ὑπὲρ σωτηρ]ίας καὶ νί(κ)ης τῶν κυρίων ἡμῶν Ἀυτοκράτορων Καίσ-
   αρων ὅρο[ι] Σαχαμῶ<ν?> <ἐξ?> ἄρκτο<υ>.

REGION OF DAMASCUS

For a sketch-map with the location of the then known boundary-markers in
this area, as well as the Golan Heights, the Huleh Valley and the Hauran,
see *'Atiqot* 1 (1955), 113.
16.   R. Mouterde, *MUSJ* 16 (1932), 234–235 = *SEG* VII, no. 248 = *AE*
       (1933), no. 145.
   Daraya, *circa* 8 km south-west of Damascus. AD 293/305.
   As the formula used in this province was different, the full text and
       lay-out of this relatively well-preserved example is given:

   Διοκλητειανὸς
   καὶ Μαξειμιανὸς Σεβ.
   καὶ Κωνστάντις
   καὶ Μαξειμιανὸς Καίσαρες
   λ[ίθ]ον διορίζοντα ἀγροὺς
   κώμης Μέζζης καὶ
   ΠΑΜΟΙΩΝ στηριχθῆναι
   ἐκέλευσαν φρυντίδι
   Αἰλίου Στατούτου
   τοῦ διασημοτάτου.

   The modern village of Mezze is situated 3–4 km to the north-east of
       the find-spot of the boundary-marker.
17.   Mouterde, p. 235 = *SEG* VII, no. 247 = *AE* (1933), no. 144.
   Between Jisrin and Saqba in the oasis of Damascus, some 8 km east
       of the city. AD 293/305.
   Same formula and reference to Aelius Statutus (named on seven
       markers; see *PLRE* I "Statutus": nos. 16, 17, 18, 19, 22, 24, 29).
   λίθον διορίζοντα ἀγροὺς κώμης ΒΕΤΟΣ(or E)ΜΑΡΑΣ κὲ κώμης ΕΝ-
   ΑΑΣΟ (or ΕΝΑΚΑΕΝΑΣ).
18.   L. Jalabert, "Aelius Statutus, governeur de Phénicie (*ca.* 293–305)",
       MUSJ 3 (1908–9), 313, p. 317; cf. 4 (1910), 223; *AE* (1908), no.
       195.
   Jermana, south-east of Damascus. AD 293/305.

Tetrarchs. [λίθο]ν διο<ρ>ίζ(ι)οντα ἀπ[ὸ κώμης?] Γι[ν]δαρων(?). Establishment by Aelius Statutus.

SEG VII, no. 246, is too uncertain to include in the list.

GAULANITIS AND THE HULEH VALLEY

19. G. Dalman, "Inschriften aus dem Ostjordanland", *ZDPV* 36 (1913), 249, no. 1.

    Near Kuneitra. AD 293/305.

    Tetrarchs. λίθον διορίζοντα κωμ(ῶν?) Σαρισῶν καὶ Βερνίκης. Aelius Statutus.

20. S. Applebaum, B. Isaac and Y. Landau, "Varia Epigraphica", *SCI* 4 (1978), 133, p. 134, no. 2 = *SEG* XXVIII, no. 1426 = *AE* (1984), no. 903.

    Hared near Kuneitra. AD 293/305.

    Tetrarchs (fragmentary). λίθον [δ]ιορί[ζον]τα ἄγρο[υς . .] or ὅρο[υς . .].

21. P. Porat, "A New Boundary Stone from the Southern Golan", *SCI* 10 (1989–90), 130.

    Southern Golan. AD 293/305.

    Tetrarchs. λίθο(ν) διορίζοντα ἐν <ο> ὅροις κώ(μης) ΚΑΠΑΡΗΑΡΙ-ΒΟΥ. ΑΜ[.]Α[.]ΦΛΥΟΥ κὲ ΑΓΕΛΙΠΟΥ κηνσ(ιτόρων).

    As will be seen, the area where establishment of boundary-markers by Aelius Statutus is recorded extends further west than this, into the Huleh Valley. But, whatever the reading, two (as it seems) other *censitores* are mentioned here.

22. B. W. Bacon, "A New Inscription from Upper Galilee", *AJA* 11 (1907), 315; J. Offord, *PEFQSt* (1908), 260; L. Jalabert, *MUSJ* 3 (1908–9), 40; *AE* (1907), no. 145.

    Upper Huleh Valley, west of Banias (Caesarea Philippi). AD 293/305.

    Tetrarchs. λίθον διορίζοντα ἀγροὺς ἐποικίου ΧΡΗΣΙΜΙΑΝΟΥ. Aelius Statutus.

23(?). S. Applebaum, B. Isaac and Y. Landau, "VariaEpigraphica", *SCI* 6 (1982), 98, no. 1 = *SEG* XXXII, no. 1459.

    From Golan, exact find-spot not known. Date uncertain.

    λίθος [δι]ορίζω(ν) τὰ ὅρια τοῦ Πανίου κὲ τῆς πόλεως.

    Not certain whether this is Tetrarchic.

24. Y. Aharoni, "Three New Boundary-Stones from the Western Golan", *'Atiqot* 1 (1955), p. 109, no. 1 = *AE* (1956), no. 34 = *SEG* XVI, no. 822.

    Kibbutz Shamir, on the edge of the Golan Heights, some 28 km north of the Sea of Galilee.

[Διο]κλητιανὸς καὶ
Μαξιμιανὸς Σεββ.,
Κωνστάντιος καὶ
Μαξιμιανὸς Καί-
σαρες
λίθον διορίζοντα
ἀγροὺς κω(μῶν) Γαλα-
νιας καὶ Μιγηρα-
μης στηριχθῆνε
ἐκέλευσαν φροντί-
δι Αἰλ. Στατούτου
τοῦ διασημ.

25(?). Y. Aharoni, pp. 109–110, no. 2 = *AE* (1956), no. 35 = *SEG* XVI,
no. 823.
Same area as no. 24. AD 293/305?
λίθος διορίζων ὅρια κω(μῶν) *or* κώ(μης) Μιγηραμης κὲ Γαλανιας.
For Γαλανια see nos. 24 and 31.

26(?). Y. Aharoni, p. 110, no. 3 = *AE* (1956), no. 36, = *SEG* XVI, no.
821.
Northern Huleh Valley, *circa* 1 km south of no. 22. AD 293/305?
λίθον διορίζοντα Μαμσιας κὲ Βсθ Αχων.
There is much clearer likelihood that nos. 26–28 belong to the Tetrarchic series than is the case for no. 25. See no. 29.

27. Y. Aharoni, "Two Additional Boundary-Stones from the Ḥule Valley", *'Atiqot* 2 (1959), 152, no. 13 = *SEG* XVIII, no. 620.
Same area as nos. 24–25. AD 293/305?
λίθον διορίζοντα κωμ(ης?) Δηρας καὶ Καπαρ[μ]ιγη[ραμης].
Probably the same village as named in no. 25. See also no. 29.

28. Y. Aharoni, pp. 153–154, no. 14 = *SEG* XVIII, no. 621; cf. XIX, no.
902.
Same area as nos. 24–25 and 27. AD 293/305?
λίθ[ον δι]ορίζον[τα] ἀγροὺς [κώμης?] ΩΣΕΑΣ [καὶ] [Π]ΕΡΙΣΗΣ.
See nos. 29 and 30 for the names of the villages.

29. Y. Aharoni, "Three New Boundary-Stones from the Hule Valley",
'Atiqot 3 (1961), 186, no. 15, Pl. XXVIII.1 = *SEG* XIX, no. 901.
Same area as nos. 24–25 and 27–28. AD 293/305.

Διοκλητιανὸς καὶ Μ[αξιμια]νὸς Σεββ.
Κωνστάντις καὶ Μαξι[μιανὸς Καίσαρες]
λίθον διορίζοντα ἀγροὺς [κώμ]η[ς]
Δηρας κὲ Ωσεας στηριχθῆνε
ἐκέλευσαν φροντίδι Αἰλ. Στατούτου

τοῦ διασημο.

30.   Aharoni, op. cit., 186, no. 16, Pl. XXVIII.2 = *SEG* XIX, no. 902.
        Same area as above. Almost certainly AD 293/305.
        λίθον διορίζοντα ἀγροὺς κώ[μης] Ωσεας κὲ Περισης.
        For ΩΣΕΑΣ see nos. 28–29 and for ΠΕΡΙΣΗΣ see no. 28.

31(?). Aharoni, op. cit. 187, no. 17, Pl. XXVIII.3 = *SEG* XIX, no. 903.
        Same area as above. AD 293/305?
        λίθος διορίζων ὅρια κώ[μης] Γαλανιας καὶ ὅ(ρια?) Ῥαμης.
        For Γαλανια see nos. 24–25.

BATANAEA

The boundaries, if indeed there were clear boundaries, of the area described
in antiquity as Batanaea are far from clear. It is used here as an approximate
description of the area, from which three boundary-markers are known,
which lies between Gaulanitis (the Golan Heights) to the west and the lava-
field called Trachonitis, or now Lejja, to the east. See also under nos. 33–34.
The three markers all come from a region on either side of Sanamayn, on
the present main road between Der'a and Damascus.

32.   *IGR* III, no. 1112 = *OGIS*, no. 769.
        From Agrabe, some 16 km west-north-west of Sanamayn. AD 293/
            305.

        Δεσπόται ἡμῶν
        Διοκλητιανὸς
        Μαξιμιανὸς
        Σεβαστοὶ καὶ
        Κωνστάντειος
        καὶ Μαξιμιανὸς
        Καίσαρες
        λίθον διορίζον-
        τα ὅρους μητρ-
        οκωμίας Ἀκ-
        ράβης καὶ Ἀσί-
        χων στηριχθ-
        ῆναι ἐκέλευσα-
        ν, φροντίδι
        Λουκίου καὶ Ἀ[κ?]α[κίου?]
        κηνσίτορις (κηνσιτόρ<ων>?).

For the importance of the concept of a 'mother-village' *(mētrokōmia)*
see 3.3 above. In this case also the place-name has survived as

Agrabe. There is also another village in the area called Osij. It is
probable, but not certain, that two *censitores* are named. Cf. no. 35
below.

33.   *IGR* III, no. 1252 = *OGIS,* no. 612 (variant readings).
        From Namar, a village some 15 km south-west of Sanamayn, and
             some 10 km south of Agrabe. AD 293/305. Line-divisions not
             indicated.
        Tetrarchs. λίθον διορίζοντα ὅρους κώμης Γα[σ]ιμέας καὶ Ναμαρίων
             (σ)τηρχ[θ]ῆναι ἐκέλευσαν, φροντίδι Μ. Ἀρρίου Φραιαος (*sic*) π.π.
             κη(ν)σείτορος.
        The second village named must be that referred to by Eusebius,
             Onom., ed. Klostermann, 138: καὶ νῦν ἐστι Ναμαρὰ κώμη μεγίστη
             ἐν τῇ Βαταναίᾳ. Both names have survived, the first as 'Jasem', a
             village to the south-east of Namar. The *censitor* is identified as a
             primipilaris (senior centurion).
34.   L. Jalabert and R. Mouterde, "Nouvelles inscriptions de Syrie",
             MUSJ 4 (1910), 209, on p. 222.
        From Basir, some 4 km east of Sanamayn. AD 293/305.
        Fragmentary inscription with Tetrarchs and διορ[ίζοντα λί]θον.
        This is quite possibly the place in Batanaea called Bathyra, where
             Herod settled a colony of Babylonian Jews as a protection against
             the people of Trachonitis; Josephus, *Ant.* XVII, 2, 221–222 (23–
             28), see 2.2 above. The place lies about 8 km from the edge of the
             lava-field.

THE HAURAN

35.   M. Dunand, *Syria* 7 (1926), 329 = *SEG* VII, no. 1055 (incomplete
             text). Full text in M. Dunand, *Le musée de Soueida* (1934), 75,
             no. 160, Pl. XXXII; cf. L. Robert, *Hellenica* XI–XII (1960),
             312–314.
        From Juneineh, some 5 km to the east of Maximianopolis/Shaqqa.

οἱ δεσπόται ἡμῶν
Διοκλητιανὸς καὶ
Μα[ξ]ιμιανὸς Σεββ.
καὶ Κωνστάντειος
καὶ Μαξιμιανὸς
ἐπιφανέστατοι
Καίσαρες λίθον δ-
ιορίζοντα (ἀπὸ] κώμης
Ὀρέλων ὅρον

Μαξιμιανοπόλ(εως)
στηρικθῆναι ἐκέ-
λευσαν, [φ]ροντ[ί]-
δι Λουκίου καὶ
Ἀκακίου κηνσι-
τόρων.

The earliest evidence (cf. 5.1 above) for the new city of Maximianopolis. Two *censitores* are at work, and neither will be the governor
of the province, which was almost certainly by now Arabia rather
than Syria Phoenice. The same two *censitores* are evidently named
in no. 32.

36(?). M. Dunand, "Nouvelles inscriptions du Djebel Druze et du
Hauran", *RB* 41 (1932), 561, p. 572, no. 109.

From Radeime/Rudeimeh, about 5 km west-south-west of Juneineh
(see no. 35). AD 293/305.

The beginnings (ll. 2–7) of an inscription with the names of the Tetrarchs in the nominative, laid out almost exactly as in no. 35.

The resemblance of form, along with its location a short distance
from no. 35, is the only reason for supposing, as Dunand did, that
this is a boundary-marker.

37(?). *IGR* III, no. 1278.

From Suweida. AD 293/305.

Fragmentary inscription with the names of Diocletian and Maximian, and ὅροι Διον[υσιά]δ[ος?] on one side and [ὅρ]οι
Ἀθελεν[ῶ]ν on the other.

Athelena is the village Atil in the territory of Kanatha, discussed in
11.4 above. If 'Dionysias' appears here as the name of Soada, it is
the earliest evidence for it. But it is very uncertain whether this inscription belongs among those which reflect the work of the Tetrarchic *censitores*.

DOCUMENTS FROM THE
BAR KOCHBA WAR

As noted above, there appears to be no complete hand-list of the now quite extensive range of documents, in Hebrew, Aramaic and Greek, from within the area controlled by the rebels. This appendix therefore sets out to provide one, beginning with texts which are clearly dated, and then listing the others.

Nearly all the documents, which with one exception are written on papyrus, come from caves on the sides of wadis in the Judaean Desert which run down to the Dead Sea. One major group comes from the Wadi Murabba'at, some 11 km north of Engeddi. The caves there were first explored clandestinely by the local Bedouin in 1951, and then by an expedition led by the late R. de Vaux in 1952; the relevant documents were published along with other written material from there in *Documents from the Judaean Desert* II (1961). The other major group comes from the Naḥal Ḥever, a wadi which runs into the Dead Sea some 4.5 km south of Engeddi. An Israeli expedition, led by the late Y. Yadin in 1960 and 1961, discovered in the same cave, on the northern side of the wadi and some 5.5 km from the Dead Sea, both a series of documents from the Bar Kochba war and the 'archive of Babatha' from the immediately preceding period: documents in Nabataean, Aramaic and Greek covering the years from AD 94 to 132 (August 19). The Greek, but not the Nabataean and Aramaic, texts from this archive have now been published by N. Lewis, *The Documents from the Bar Kochba Period in the Cave of Letters: Greek Papyri* (1989), abbreviated as *P. Yadin*. The documents from the period of the war itself were surveyed, and some extracts of preliminary readings printed, in *Israel Exploration Journal* 11 (1961) and 12 (1962). But until his death in 1984 Prof. Yadin made no further progress with publication, and three decades after the initial discovery the majority have remained unpublished. One papyrus of unknown prove-nance, found among Prof. Yadin's papers, was published in *IEJ* 36 (1986); see no. 12 below. Further comment on this extremely discreditable record would be superfluous.

The Aramaic documents, insofar as published, have been included in two separate collections, both of which sometimes give apparently indepen-dent readings whose origin is not made clear. These are the collections by Beyer and by Fitzmyer and Harrington listed below. Some were also repro-duced and discussed in Koffmahn, *Doppelurkunden*.

Since, as mentioned, a number of the documents carry explicit dates, par-alleling the dates by Year One and Year Two on the coinage of the revolt (see L. Mildenberg, *The Coinage of the Bar Kochba War*, 1984, and 3.3 above), it is of some significance to relate these to datings by the Christian era. For the most detailed discussion, mainly relating to later literary sources, see P. Schaefer, *Der Bar Kochba-Aufstand* (1981), 10–28. It seems clear that the administration of the short-lived independent state will have used a calendar in which the year began in the spring with the month Nisan; this was the established pattern as reflected in Jewish works of this period; see Schürer, *HJP* I, App. III, "The Jewish Calendar". The four successive 'Years' of the 'liberation of Israel' will therefore have been counted from Ni-san (March/April) to Adar (Feb./March). Though absolute certainty is not possible, it is most likely that Year One was calculated from Nisan of AD 132, the year to which Eusebius dates the revolt. See Schürer, *HJP* I, 542, n.126, and B. Kanael, "Notes on the Dates Used during the Bar Kochba Re-volt", *IEJ* 21 (1971), 39 (speculative). In the catalogue the following dating-scheme will therefore be adopted, though it should be understood as provisional:

> Year One, Nisan-Adar: March/April AD 132–Feb./March 133
> Year Two, Nisan-Adar: March/April AD 133–Feb./March 134
> Year Three, Nisan-Adar: March/April AD 134–Feb./March 135
> Year Four, Nisan-Adar: March/April AD 135–Feb./March 136

On this view the latest explicitly dated document (no. 13), of Tišri 21, Year Four, would date to early October 135. If that is correct, either the much-quoted statement of the *Mishnah, Ta'anit* 4, 6, that Beththter fell on Ab 9 (July) has to be taken as reflecting a merely symbolic correlation with the other four disasters mentioned in the same passage, or the fall of this place did not represent the collapse of all resistance in the area to the south-east, near the Dead Sea.

The alternative possibility is that Year One was spring 131–spring 132. As such, that would mean only that the revolt broke out *within* that Jewish year, which then, taken as a whole, counted as 'Year One of the Redemption of Israel' (ŠNT ḤD' LG'LT YŠR'L). But the existence of a document (no. 1) dated to the first day of the month Iyyar (April/May) of Year One would oblige us to take it that the revolt had begun early in AD 131—though presumably not earlier than Nisan (March/April), otherwise spring 130–Spring 131 might have earned the title Year One. This seems unlikely. So the tradition that the war lasted three and a half years (see Schürer, *HJP* I, 534 and 552) seems to be confirmed: the most reasonable reconstruction is that it began in Nisan 132 and ended three and a half years later, towards the end of 135.

It should be noted that the latest dated document in the 'archive of Babatha' (*P. Yadin*, no. 27) dates to August 19, 132, therefore after the probable date of the outbreak of the revolt. But at that time Babatha was still living at Maoza in the district of Zoara, in the province of Arabia (see 3.2–3 and 11.4 above). Whoever brought the archive to the cave in the Naḥal Ḥever therefore moved only subsequently into the rebel-held zone.

ABBREVIATIONS

Aegyptus (1962) = B. Lifshitz, "Papyrus grecs du désert de Juda", *Aegyptus* 42 (1962), 240.

Beyer, *AT* = K. Beyer, *Die aramäischen Texte vom Toten Meer* (1984).

DJD II = P. Benoit, J. T. Milik and R. de Vaux, *Discoveries in the Judaean Desert* II, *Les grottes de Murabba'ât* (1961).

Fitzmyer, *PAT* = J. A. Fitzmyer and D. J. Harrington, *A Manual of Palestinian Aramaic Texts (Second Century BC–Second Century AD)* (1978).

IEJ (1961) = Y. Yadin, "The Expedition to the Judaean Desert, 1960: Expedition D", *IEJ* 11 (1961), 36, on pp. 40–50.

IEJ (1962) = Y. Yadin, "The Expedition to the Judaean Desert, 1961: Expedition D", *IEJ* 12 (1962), 227, on pp. 248–257.

IEJ (1986) = M. Broshi and E. Qimron, "A House Deed Sale from Kefar Baru from the Time of Bar Kochba", *IEJ* 36 (1986), 201.

IEJ (1990) = A. Kloner, "Lead Weights of Bar Kokhba's Administration", *IEJ* 40 (1990), 58.

Koffmahn, *Doppelurkunden* = E. Koffmahn, *Die Doppelurkunden aus der Wüste Juda* (1968).

SB = *Sammelbuch Griechischer Urkunden aus Ägypten* VIII (1967)

Appendix B

THE DOCUMENTS

DATED DOCUMENTS

Year One (March/April 132–Feb./March 133)

1. *IEJ* (1962), p. 249, no. 42.
   Aramaic; material not stated.
   > Text partially reported. Lease of land carried out by two administrators. Dated 'on the first day of Iyyar, in the first year of the redemption of Israel [by ?Simeon] bar Kosiba, Prince of Israel' (BḤD L'YR ŠNT ḤD' LG'LT YŠR'L '[L YD? ŠM'W]N BR KWSYB' NŠY' YŠR'L).
   > Date: April, 132.

2. *DJD* II, no. 22, Pls. XXXIII–XXXIV; Koffmahn, *Doppelurkunden,* p. 158.
   Hebrew; papyrus.
   > Sale of land, dated '14 Marḥešvan, Year One of the redemption of Israel' (B14 LMRḤŠWN ŠNT 'ḤT LG'WLT YŠ[R]'L).
   > Date: Oct./Nov. 132.

3. *DJD* II, no. 23, Pl. XXXIV; Koffmahn, *Doppelurkunden,* p. 163; Fitzmyer, *PAT,* no. 43; Beyer, *AT,* p. 312.
   Aramaic; papyrus.
   > Very fragmentary; possibly deed of sale. Dated '10 Shebat, Year One of the freedom [. . .]' (B10 LŠBṬ ŠNT ḤD' LḤR[WT YŠR'L?]).
   > Date: Jan./Feb. 133 (Beyer, op. cit., suggests possibly Jan./Feb. AD 67, in the First Revolt).

4. *IEJ* (1962), 249, no. 43.
   Aramaic; papyrus.
   > Briefly reported. Receipt by local administrator for 39 *denarii* paid by Eliezer son of Samuel for land(?) 'which he leased from Simeon bar Kosiba' (DY ḤKR MN ŠM'WN BR KWSYBH).
   > Date: stated to be Year One.

Year Two (March/April 133–Feb./March 134)

5. *DJD* II, no. 29, Pls. XLI–XLI *bis;* Koffmahn, *Doppelurkunden,* p. 176.
   Hebrew (with Greek signature on *verso*); papyrus.
   > Deed of sale of vines (?).
   > Dated 'on 14 Elul, Year Two of the Redemption of Israel' (B'RB'H 'SR L'LWL ŠNT ŠTYM LG'LT YŠR'L).
   > Date: Aug./Sept. 133.

6. *DJD* II, no. 24, Pls. XXXV–XXXVII.
   Hebrew; papyrus, in a number of fragments.
   Series of contracts for the lease of parcels of land, some with the condition 'until the eve of the remission' (of debts, for the Sabbatical Year)—Frag. B14: 'D SWP 'RB HŠMṬH.
   Suggested corrections in *IEJ* (1961), p. 51, and (1962), pp. 253–254.
   Dated (Frag. B, l. 1) '20 Shebat Year Two of the Redemption of Israel' ([B]'ŠRYN LŠBṬ Š[N]T ŠTY[M L]G'LT YŠR'L), probably also Frag. B, l. 1, Frag. E, l. 1 and Frag. F. l. 1 (all readings somewhat uncertain).
   Date: probably Feb. 134.

Year Three (March/April 134–Feb./March 135)

7. J. T. Milik, "Un contrat juif de l'an 134 après J.-C.", *RB* 61 (1954), 182; Fitzmyer, *PAT*, no. 51 (with subsequent bibliography); Beyer, *AT*, p. 320.
   Aramaic; papyrus (exact provenance unknown).
   Sale of house.
   Dated '20 of *either* Iyyar *or* Adar, Year Three of the Freedom of Israel' (B'SRY[N] L'YR *or* L'DR [Beyer] ŠNT TLT LḤRT YŠR'L).
   Date: *either* April/May 134 *or* Feb./March 135.

8. *IEJ* (1962), 249, no. 44, Pl. 48c.
   Hebrew; papyrus.
   Described with some extracts. Reported as distribution of lands leased from the administrator (PRNSW) of Simeon ben Kosiba, Prince of Israel. At Engeddi (B'YN GDY).
   Dated 'on 28 Marḥešvan, Year Three of Simeon ben Kosiba, Prince of Israel' (B'ŠRYN WŠMNH LMRḤŠWN ŠNT ŠLWŠ LŠM'WN BN KWSYB' NŠY' YŠR'L).
   Date: Nov. 134.

9. *IEJ* (1962), 255, no. 45.
   Hebrew; papyrus (34 lines).
   Described with extracts. Sub-lease of land leased from the administrator of Simeon ben Kosiba.
   Dated 'on 2 Kislev, Year Three of Simeon ben Kosiba, Prince of Israel, at En-Gedi' (BŠNYM LKSLW. . . as no. 8 above).
   Date: Nov. 134.

10. *IEJ* (1962), 255, no. 46.
    Hebrew; papyrus.
    Described with extracts. Acknowledgment of lease.
    Dated as no. 9.
    Date: Nov. 134.

11. *DJD* II, no. 25, Pl. XXXVIII; Koffmann, *Doppelurkunden*, p. 164; Fitz-
    myer, *PAT,* no. 44.
    Aramaic; papyrus (a number of fragments).
    Deed of sale(?) of land (or 'easement', *PAT*).
    Dated '[. . . yea]r Three of the Freedom of Jerusalem' ([. . . ŠN]T TLT
    LḤRWT YRWŠLM). Frag. 3 has LMRḤŠ[WN].
    Date: March/April 134–Feb./March 135.
12. *IEJ* (1986), 201, Pl. 26B.
    Aramaic, and apparently Hebrew; papyrus (exact provenance
    unknown).
    Deed of sale of house at Kefar Baru (KPR BRW), which the editors
    suggest (very improbably) lay east of the Dead Sea in the province of
    Arabia.
    Dated '[. . . Year] Three of the Freedom of Israel, in the days of Si-
    meon ben Kosiba, Prince of Israel' ([. . .ŠNT] TLT LḤRWT YŠ[R]'L
    'L YMY ŠM'WN BN KWSBH NŠY YŠR[']L).
    Date: March/April 134–Feb./March 135.

Year Four (March/April 135–Feb./March 136)

13. *DJD* II, no. 30, Pls. XLI *bis*–XLII *bis*; Koffmann, *Doppelurkunden*,
    p. 182.
    Hebrew; papyrus.
    Deed of sale of land.
    Dated (l. 8) 'on 21 Tishri, Year Four of the Redemption of Israel'
    (B'ŠRYM W'ḤD LTŠRY ŠNT 'RB' LG'WLT YŠR'L).
    Date: Sept./Oct. 135.

UNDATED LETTERS

14. *DJD* II, no. 42, Pl. XLV.
    Hebrew; papyrus.
    Letter from the administrators of Bet-Mašiko (HPRNSYN ŠL BYT
    MŠKW) to Yešua ben Galgula, 'chief of the camp' (RWŠ
    HMḤNYH), confirming ownership of a cow.
15. *DJD* II, no. 43, Pl. XLVI.
    Hebrew; papyrus.
    Letter of Bar Kochba (ŠM'WN BN KWSBH) to the same Yešua ben
    Galgula warning him not to maltreat the Galileans (HGLL'YM) who
    are with him.
16. *DJD* II, no. 44, Pl. XLVI.
    Hebrew; papyrus.

Letter of ŠM'WN (evidently Bar Kochba) to the same Yešua ben Gal-
gula on delivery of grain, and requiring observance of Shabat.

17. *IEJ* (1961), 41, no. 1; Fitzmyer, *PAT*, no. 53; Beyer, *AT*, p. 351.
Aramaic; written on wood.
Described with extracts. Fuller text, whose origin is not stated, in
Beyer, loc. cit.
Letter of Bar Kochba (ŠM'WN BR KWSBH HNŠY 'L YŠR'L) to Ye-
honatan and Masabala, on confiscation of wheat, and threatening
punishment of men of Teqoa and arrest of YŠW BR TDMRYH.

18. *IEJ* (1961), 42, no. 2; Fitzmyer, *PAT*, no. 54.
Aramaic; papyrus.
Brief report of fragmentary letter from Bar Kochba.

19. *IEJ* (1961), 42, no. 3; *Aegyptus* (1962), 240, no. 1; *SB*, no. 9843.
Greek; papyrus.
Letter of Soumaios to Iōnathēs son of Baianos and Masabala (see no.
17) requiring delivery of wooden bars and citrus-trees (branches?)
'for the laying of citrus-branches of (the) Jews', that is, Tabernacles
(Josephus, *Ant.* XIII, 13, 5, 372).
The writer explains that he has written *Helēnesti (sic)* because of the
lack either of the 'impulse' ([ὁρ]μάν) or the opportunity ([ἀφορ]μάς)
to write *Hebraesti* or of a person, Hermas, to do so. See G. Howard
and J. C. Shelton, "The Bar-Kochba Letters and Palestinian Greek",
IEJ 23 (1973), 101; D. Obbink, *BASP* 28 (1991), 51.

20. *IEJ* (1961), 43, no. 4; Fitzmyer, *PAT*, no. 55; Beyer, *AT*, p. 351.
Aramaic; papyrus.
Short letter, published in full, of Bar Kochba (ŠM'WN BR KWSBH)
to Yehonatan son of Ba'aya (see no. 19), telling him to help one
Elisha.

21. *IEJ* (1961), 44, no. 6 = *Aegyptus* (1962), 248, no. 2 = *SB*, no. 9844.
Greek; papyrus.
Short letter from Annanos to Iōnathēs referring to help ordered by
Simōn Chōsiba (Σίμων Χωσιβᾶ).

22. *IEJ* (1961), 44, no. 7.
Aramaic; papyrus.
Brief report of badly damaged papyrus, evidently containing letter
from ŠM'WN BR [KWSBH].

23. *IEJ* (1961), 44, no. 8; Fitzmyer, *PAT*, no. 56; Beyer, *AT*, p. 351.
Aramaic; papyrus.
Letter of Bar Kochba (whose name is here spelled ŠM'WN BR
KŠBH) to Yehonatan bar Ba'ayan and Masabala bar Šimon (see nos.
19–20 and 25–27) on despatch of El'azar. Ends with attestation by
scribe: ŠM'WN BR YHWDH KTBH.

24. *IEJ* (1961), 45, no. 10; Fitzmyer, *PAT*, no. 57.
    Aramaic; papyrus.
    Four-line letter to Yehonatan and Masabala (nos. 19, 20, 22 above), partially reported.

25. *IEJ* (1961), 46, no. 11; Fitzmyer, *PAT*, no. 58; Beyer, *AT*, p. 352.
    Aramaic; papyrus.
    Description with extracts of letter of Bar Kochba to Yehonatan and Masabala (nos. 19, 20, 22 above and 26–27 below), referring to the 'Romans' (RHWM'H) and ordering the bringing of a person called TYRSYS BR TYNYNWS.

26. *IEJ* (1961), 46, no. 12.
    Hebrew; papyrus.
    Description, with quotation of first four lines, of fourteen-line letter from Bar Kochba (ŠM'WN BR KWSB') reproaching the men of En-geddi and Masabala and Yehonatan (nos. 19, 20, 22, 24 above and 27 below) for indifference.

27. *IEJ* (1961), 47, no. 14; Fitzmyer, *PAT*, no. 59; Beyer, *AT*, p. 352.
    Aramaic; papyrus.
    Description, with quotations, of letter of Bar Kochba to Yehonatan and Masabala—here spelled MŠBL' (nos. 19, 20, 22, 24, 25 above).

28. *IEJ* (1961), 48, no. 15; Fitzmyer, *PAT*, no. 60; Beyer, *AT*, p. 352.
    Aramaic; papyrus.
    Complete(?) text of five-line letter of Bar Kochba to Yehuda bar Menashe ordering the sending of two men and two donkeys to Yehonatan and Masabala for the delivery of palm-branches and citrus (LLBYN W'TRGYN) while Yehuda should send myrtles and willows.
    Note: For other fragmentary texts which may be letters from the Bar Kochba war, see *DJD* II, nos. 45–52, and *IEJ* (1961), 43–47, nos. 5, 9 and 13.

Lead Weights

29. *IEJ* (1990), 58.
    Lead weight discovered in 1987 at Ḥorvat Alim, some 3 km north of Beth Guvrin (Eleutheropolis). Side A is inscribed on the four margins of the rectangular weight with the words BNKSB', NŠY, YŠR'L, WPRNŠW and in the interior PRS. Side B has ŠM'WN, KWSB', YŠR'L and NŠY.
    Other possibly parallel weights are also alluded to in the paper.

    Note: for a further document of Year Two see M. Broshi and E. Qimron, *Eretz Israel* 20 (1989), 256, with revisions by P. Segal, *Tarbis* 60 (1991), 113.

APPENDIX

C

MATERIALS FOR THE HISTORY
OF ROMAN EDESSA AND OSRHOENE,
AD 163–337

What follows represents only a selection of the material, designed for the use of anyone approaching the study of this area from the history of the Roman Empire. I am very grateful to Sebastian Brock for much supplementation and correction, and to Steven Ross, University of California, Berkeley, for corrections.

BIBLIOGRAPHY

A. von Gutschmid, *Untersuchungen über die Geschichte des Königreichs Os-roene* (*Mém. Acad. Imp. Sc. de St Pétersbourg*, VII ser., 35.1, 1887).

R. Duval, *Histoire d'Èdesse* (1892).

R. Duval, *La littérature syriaque*³ (1907).

A. Baumstark, *Geschichte der syrischen Literatur* (1922).

A. R. Bellinger, "The Chronology of Edessa", YCS 5 (1935), 142.

E. Kirsten, "Edessa", *RAC* IV (1959), 552ff.

J. B. Segal, *Edessa: 'The Blessed City'* (1970).

A. H. M. Jones, *Cities of the Eastern Roman Provinces*2 (1971), ch. 9, "Mesopotamia and Armenia".

R. Murray, *Symbols of Church and Kingdom: A Study of Early Syriac Tradition* (1975).

H. J. W. Drijvers, "Hatra, Palmyra und Edessa", ANRW II.8 (1977), 799, on pp. 863ff.

S. P. Brock, "An Introduction to Syriac Studies", in J. H. Eaton (ed.), *Horizons in Semitic Studies* (1980), 1.

H. J. W. Drijvers, *Cults and Beliefs at Edessa* (1980).

H. J. W. Drijvers, "Edessa", *Theologische Realenzyklopädie* IX.1/2 (1981), 277.

M. Mundell Mango, "The Continuity of the Classical Tradition in the Art and Architecture of Northern Mesopotamia", in N. Garsoian, T. F. Mathews and R. W. Thomson (eds.), *East of Byzantium: Syria and Armenia in the Formative Period* (1982), 115.

J. Wagner, "Provincia Oshroenae *(sic):* New Mesopotamian Finds Illustrating the Military Organisation under the Severan Dynasty", in S. Mitchell (ed.), *Armies and Frontiers in Roman and Byzantine Anatolia* (BAR Int. Ser. 156, 1983), 103.

J. Wagner, *Die Römer an Euphrat und Tigris (Die Antike Welt, Sondernummer, 1985).*

W. Cramer, "Harran", *RAC* XV (1986), 634.

F. Millar, "Empire, Community and Culture in the Roman Near East: Greeks, Syrians, Jews and Arabs", *JJS* 38 (1987), 143, esp. 159–162.

D. Feissel and J. Gascou, "Documents d'archives romains inédits du Moyen Euphrate (IIIe siècle après J.-C.)", *CRAI* (1989), 535.

F. Millar, "The Roman *Coloniae* of the Near East: A Study of Cultural Relations", in H. Solin and M. Kajava (eds.), *Roman Eastern Policy and Other Studies in Roman History* (1990) 7, esp. pp. 38–39, 46–50.

J. Teixidor, "Deux documents syriaques du troisième siècle provenants du Moyen Euphrate", *CRAI* (1990), 144.

DOCUMENTS

SYRIAC INSCRIPTIONS (ON STONE AND MOSAIC)

H. J. W. Drijvers, *Old-Syriac (Edessean) Inscriptions* (1972). Note esp.:

   1. Birecik, AD 6 (trans. Segal, *Edessa,* p. 23, n.3).
   2. Serrin, AD 73 (trans. Segal, *Edessa,* p. 23, n.4).
   23. Sumatar Harabesi, AD 165: "Ruler of 'Arab".
   27. Edessa, Citadel (Segal, *Edessa,* Pl. 29a): MʿNW PṢGRB'.
   45. Edessa. Funerary mosaic (Segal, *Edessa,* Pl. 17a); now in Istanbul museum.
   47. Edessa. Family portrait mosaic (Segal, *Edessa,* Pl. 1).
   48. Edessa. Tripod mosaic (Segal, *Edessa,* Pl. 3).
   49. Edessa. Phoenix mosaic (Segal, *Edessa,* Pl. 43); AD 235/236.
   50. Edessa. Orpheus mosaic (Segal, *Edessa,* Pl. 44); AD 228.
   51. Edessa. Funerary couch mosaic (Segal, *Edessa,* Pl. 2); ?AD 277/278.

H. Pognon, *Inscriptions sémitiques de la Syrie, de la Mésopotamie et de la région de Mossoul* (1897), 104 (Mar Yakoub, near Edessa; Greek/Syriac bilingual tomb inscription).

J. Leroy, "Mosaiques funéraires d'Édesse", *Syria* 34 (1957), 306.

J. Pirenne, "Aux origines de la graphie syriaque", *Syria* 40 (1963), 101.

H. J. W. Drijvers, "Some New Syriac Inscriptions and Archaeological Finds from Edessa and Sumatar Harabesi", *BSOAS* 36 (1973), 1. N.B. p. 12, Pls. xi–xii, mosaic inscription of AD 224.

H. J. W. Drijvers, "Ein neuentdecktes edessenisches Grabmosaik", *Antike Welt* 12.3 (1981), 17.

H. J. W. Drijvers, "A Tomb for the Life of a King: A Recently Discovered Edessene Mosaic with a Portrait of King Abgar the Great", *Le Muséon* 95.1–2 (1982), 167.

J. B. Segal, "A Note on a Mosaic from Edessa", *Syria* 60 (1983), 107.

K. Parlasca, "Das Mosaik von Mas'udije aus dem Jahre 228/229 n. Chr.", *Dam. Mitt.* 1 (1983), 263 (bilingual, Greek/Syriac mosaic inscription from east bank of Euphrates).

GREEK AND LATIN INSCRIPTIONS

Osrhoene

AE (1984), no. 919: (Kizilburc, between Zeugma and Edessa, AD 195): 'C. Iulius Pacatianus, proc(urator) Aug(usti), inter provinciam Osrhoenam et regnum Agbari fines posuit'.

AE (1984), no. 920: (ibid., AD 205): '(Severus, Caracalla and Geta) viam ab Euphrate usque ad fines regni Sept. Ab(g)ari a novo munierunt per L. Aelium Ianuarium proc. Aug. prov. Osrhoenam *(sic)*'.

Rome

CIL VI, no. 1797 = *ILS* no. 857:
'd.m./ Abgar Prahates / filius, rex / principis(?) Orrhenoru,/ Hodda coniugi bene / merenti fec.'

IGR I, no. 179 = Moretti, *IGUR*, no. 1142:
Ἄβγαρος . . . τύμβον δ' Ἀντωνεῖνος ἑῷ θέτο τοῦτον ἀδελφῷ· οἷσιν ὁ πρὶν Βασιλεὺς Ἄβγαρος ἦν γενέτης.

SYRIAC PARCHMENTS

Contract of sale of AD 243, found at Dura (*P. Dura*, no. 28).

A. R. Bellinger and C. B. Welles, "A Third-Century Contract of Sale from Edessa in Osrhoene", *YCS* 5 (1935), 93.

C. B. Welles, R. O. Fink and J. F. Gilliam, *Excavations at Dura-Europus, Final Report V.1, The Parchments and Papyri* (1959), no. 28.

J. Goldstein, "The Syriac Deed of Sale from Dura-Europos", *JNES* 25
(1966), 1.
F. Rosenthal (ed.), *An Aramaic Handbook* II.1 (1967), 25–7 (text).
Drijvers, *Inscriptions,* pp. 54–57 (text).

Syriac parchments from Mesopotamia (found as part of archive, with
Greek papyri, some with Syriac subscriptions, from Middle
Euphrates; see Feissel and Gascou, op. cit. above).

J. Teixidor, "Les derniers rois d'Édesse d'après deux nouveaux documents
syriaques", *ZPE* 76 (1989), 219.
J. Teixidor, "Deux documents syriaques du IIIe siècle après J.-C. provenants
du Moyen Euphrate", *CRAI* (1990), 144.
A. Dec. 18, 240. Acknowledgment of receipt of debt.
B. Sept. 1, 242. Lease of land (heading only published so far).

GREEK PAPYRUS

P. Oxy. 3053, ll. 14–16 (AD 252): purchase of slave in Tripolis, Syria
Phoenice:

παρὰ Μάρκου Αὐρηλίου Δε. των . . . Σιλβανοῦ Ὀσροηνοῦ δούλην
ὀνόματι Βαλσαμέαν γένει Ὀσροηνὴν Μεσοποταμήν.

COINS

E. Babelon, "Numismatique d'Édesse en Mésopotamie", *Mélanges Numis-
matiques* II (1893), 209.
G. F. Hill, "The Mints of Roman Arabia and Mesopotamia", *JRS* 6 (1916),
135.
G. F. Hill, *BMC Arabia, Mesopotamia and Persia* (1922), lxcivff.
H. Gesche, "Kaiser Gordian mit dem Pfeil in Edessa", *Jahrb. f. Num. n.
Geldg.* 19 (1969), 47.

LITERARY SOURCES

CONTEMPORARY SYRIAC WORKS

1. *Epistle of Mara bar Serapion*
W. Cureton, *Spicilegium Syriacum* (1855): text; English trans. pp. 70–76.
Cf. F. Schulthess, "Der Brief des Mara bar Sarapion", *ZDMG* 51 (1897),
365.

K. E. McVey, "A Fresh Look at the Letter of Mara bar Serapion to his Son",
    V. Symposium Syriacum 1988 (Or. Chr. Anal. 236, 1990), 257.

2. *Oration of Meliton the Philosopher before Antoninus Caesar*
Cureton, op. cit.; English trans. pp. 41–51.
J. B. Pitra, *Spicilegium Solesmense* II (1855), xxxviiiff. (Syriac text and
    Latin translation.) No subsequent edition or detailed treatment.

3. Bardesanes/Bardaisan, *Book of the Laws of Countries*
F. Nau, *Bardesanes, Liber Legum Regnorum (Patrologia Syriaca* II, 1907),
    492–657.
F. Nau, *Bardesane, le livre des lois des pays2* (1931).
H. J. W. Drijvers, *The Book of the Laws of Countries: Dialogue on Fate of
    Bardaisan of Edessa* (1965). Text and facing English trans.
    Extracts in Greek: Eusebius, *Praep. Ev.* VI, 9, 32—10, 4.8.
    Extracts in Latin: *Clem. Recog.* IX, 19–29 (*GCS, Pseudoklementinen*
    II, ed. B. Rehm, 1965, pp. 270–317).
Cf. H. J. W. Drijvers, *Bardaisan of Edessa* (1966).

4. (?) *The Odes of Solomon*
J. H. Charlesworth, *The Odes of Solomon* (1973); text, trans. and notes.

5. (?) *Acts of Thomas*
A. F. J. Klijn, *The Acts of Thomas* (1962); discussion and trans. E. Hen
    necke, *New Testament Apocrypha* II (1974), 425ff.

6. *Martyract of Shmona and Guria*
F. C. Burkitt, *Euphemia and the Goth* (1913), esp. 90ff. (trans.); Syriac text
    ad fin., pp. 1–25.

7. *Martyract of Habib the Deacon*
P. Bedjan, *Acta Martyrum et Sanctorum* I (1890), 144.
Burkitt, op. cit., esp. 112ff. (trans.); Syriac text *ad fin.,* pp. 26–43.
On these and the martyracts of Sharbil and Barsamya (below), see Susan
    Ashbrook Harvey, "The Edessan Martyrs and Ascetic Tradition", *V. Sym-
    posium Syriacum 1988. (Or. Chr. Anal.* 236, 1990), 195.

SYRIAC CHRONICLES

See esp. S. P. Brock, "Syriac Historical Writing", *Journal of the Iraqi Acad-
    emy (Syriac Corporation)* 5 (1979–80), 1, repr. in *Studies in Syriac
    Christianity* (1992).

1. *Chronicle of Edessa.* Sixth century. Brief entries covering 132 BC–AD 540, all relating to Edessa, beginning (out of order) with longer narrative of flood of AD 201 (English trans. in Segal, *Edessa*, pp. 24–25). Following entries to AD 343 trans. in 12.3 above.

L. Hallier, *Untersuchungen über die edessenische Chronik mit dem syrischen Text und einer Übersetzung (Texte und Untersuchungen* IX, 1892), 84ff. (trans.); 145ff. (text).

I. Guidi, *Corpus Scriptorum Christianorum Orientalium* I, *Scriptores Syri.* 1, *Chronica Minora* (1903, repr. 1960), 1ff. (Syriac text).

I. Guidi, *CSCO, Scriptores Syri* ser. III.4 (1903), 3ff. (Latin trans.).

F. Rosenthal (ed.), *An Aramaic Handbook* II.1 (1967), 23–25 (text of flood narrative).

English trans. of whole chronicle by B. H. Cowper, *Journ. Sac. Lit.* 5 (1864), 28.

2. Ps-Dionysius of Tell-Mahre, *Chronicle.* Syriac world-chronicle of *circa* AD 775 known from single manuscript (Vat. syr. 162, ninth century). Includes scattered entries relating to Edessa and its kings. No complete translation into any modern language. Referred to above (12.3 and 5) as the *Chronicle of Zuqnin.* There is, however, a French translation of the whole of the latter part (the sixth century onwards) by R. Hespel (*CSCO* 507, *Scriptores Syri* 213, 1989), and an English translation of extracts is in preparation by W. Witakowski. See pp. 559–562 below.

J.-B. Chabot, *Incerti Auctoris Chronicon pseudo-Dionysianum vulgo dictum* I (*CSCO* 91, *Scriptores Syri* 43, 1927). Syriac text.

J.-B. Chabot, *CSCO* 121, *Scriptores Syri* 66 (1949). Latin trans.

See W. Witakowski, *The Syriac Chronicle of Pseudo-Dionysius of Tel-Mahre: A Study in the History of Historiography* (1987).

See esp. von Gutschmid, *Untersuchungen,* above; now in need of revision in view of subsequent documentary discoveries).

3. Elias of Nisibis, *Opus Chronologicum* I. Eleventh century. Scattered entries on kings of Edessa.

E. W. Brooks, *CSCO* 62, *Scriptores Syri* 21 (1910). Syriac text.

E. W. Brooks, *CSCO* 63, *Scriptores Syri* 23 (1910). Latin trans.

4. Michael the Syrian, *Chronicle.* Twelfth century.

J. B. Chabot, *Chronique de Michel le Syrien* I–IV (1899–1910); text and French trans. Christian world-history; Bk. V, 5 (French trans., pp. 119–120), has a summary of the history of Edessa from the second century BC to the third century AD. See p. 466 above.

SYRIAC SEMI- OR PSEUDO-HISTORICAL NARRATIVES

1. *Martyracts of Sharbil and Barsamya* (set under Trajan).
W. Cureton, *Ancient Syriac Documents* (1864), 41ff. (trans.); Syriac text
   ad fin., 41ff. See pp. 464 and 487 above.

2. *Doctrina Addai* (expanded version of legend of Jesus and King Abgar,
   written *circa* AD 400).
G. Phillips, *The Doctrine of Addai the Apostle* (1876), text and trans.
G. Howard, *The Teaching of Addai* (1981), text and trans.

GREEK AND LATIN SOURCES

1. Iulius Africanus, *Kestoi* I, 20, 28–65 (Bardesanes, King Abgar and his
   son Mannos); see J.-R. Vieillefond, *Les 'Cestes' de Julius Africanus*
   (1970).
2. Cassius Dio LXXVII, 12, 1a–12 (Caracalla's deposition of a king Abgar
   for cruelty, ?AD 212, 213).
   Cassius Dio LXXIX, 16, 2 (a king Abgar's visit to Rome under Septimius Severus).
3. (?)Hippolytus, *Refutatio* VII, 31 (a reference to a work directed πρὸς
   [B]αρδησιάνην τὸν Ἀρμένιον.
4. Herodian III, 9, 2 (Abgar and Septimius Severus).
5. Porphyry, *On the Styx,* qu. by Stobaeus, *Anth.* I, 3, 56 (*FGrH* 719 T 1;
   Bardesanes and Indian embassy to Caracalla; also *de abst.* IV, 17).
6. Eusebius, *HE* I, 13 (Judas Thomas' despatch of Thaddaios to Edessa;
   correspondence between Jesus and King Abgar as reportedly translated
   from Syriac archives at Edessa).
   Eusebius, *HE,* IV, 30 (Bardesanes).
7. Epiphanius, *Panarion* 56 (Bardesanes).
8. Sozomenus, *HE* III, 16 (Bardesanes and his son Harmonios).
9. Procopius, *Bell.*, II, 12 (the legend of Abgar, Augustus and Jesus).
10. *Itinerarium Egeriae* 19–21 (trans. J. Wilkinson, *Egeria's Travels*[2] [1981],
    115ff.; Christian Edessa and Carrhae in the 380s).

A RECONSTRUCTION OF THE KING-LIST OF
EDESSA/ORHAI IN THE PERIOD OF
ROMAN DOMINATION

The following table presents in summary form a hypothetical list of the later
kings of Edessa/Orhai based on that given in the *Chronicle of Zuqnin* (p.

558 above), but corrected in the light of contemporary documents and literary evidence.

I owe the English text of the extracts, as so much else, to the kindness of Sebastian Brock. It will be seen that the anonymous chronicler of the late eighth century, often confusingly referred to as Pseudo-Dionysius of Tel-Mahre, dates (in the relevant sections) by successive 'years of Abraham'. Exactly what, in terms of the years of the Christian era, he will have meant by this is not perfectly clear, and it is by no means certain that he will have been consistent; or, if he were, that the manuscript will have reproduced his figures accurately. He in fact deploys three different eras (plus occasional references to others): that of the Creation, that of Abraham, and the Seleucid era starting from October 312 BC (see Witakowski, *Syriac Chronicle*, 119ff.).

Fortunately, however, he does at the relevant point identify the Nativity as having occurred in year 2015 of Abraham and year 309 'of Alexander the Macedonian' (in our terms 4/3 BC). If the chronicler was consistent, the first of the entries in the table below, given as the year (of Abraham) 2130, should be the Seleucid year 424, or AD 112/113. Ma'nu son of Ma'nu should therefore have reigned, for twenty-four years, until 136/137, before a two-year reign of Wa'el son of Sahru, consistently placed by the chronicler in year 2154 (= Seleucid year 448, AD 136/137). Something must have gone wrong, for we are told by Cassius Dio that the ruler of Osrhoene during Trajan's Parthian war was called Abgar (LXVIII, 18, 1; 21, 1).

Though certainty is impossible, it is clear from the coins of Wa'el that he was a contemporary of Vologaeses IV (148–193), and from those of *a* Ma'nu, or Mannos, that he was a contemporary of Marcus Aurelius (see 12.5 above). The simplest hypothesis therefore is that the sequence of kings as given by the chronicler, while remarkably accurate in itself, is chronologically displaced: as a sequence it is some twenty-six years too early. If this hypothesis is applied to the list, it becomes perfectly consistent with the contemporary documents. The chronology presented below, obviously enough, remains hypothetical.

The 'years of Abraham' and their Seleucid equivalents are given on the left side; then the text of each entry, in Sebastian Brock's translation; then the proposed dates AD; and then key items of contemporary evidence.

Year of Abraham	Seleucid Year	Chronicle	AD (corrected by adding 26 years)	Contemporary Evidence
2130	424	The year 2130: Ma'nu son of Ma'nu reigned over Orhai for 24 years; and he crossed into Roman territory (BT RWMY ').	138/139–162/163	
2154	448	The year 2154: Wa'el son of Sahru reigned over Orhai for 2 years and after him Ma'nu son of Izat (Ma'nu?) reigned, having returned from Roman territory, for 12 years.	162/163–164/165	Coins of W'L MLK' with Vologaeses IV
		The total of his entire reign was 36 years, excluding the years he was in Roman territory.	164/165–176/167	Coins of ΒΑΣΙΛΕΥΣ ΜΑΝΝΟΣ ΦΙΛΟΡΩΜΑ(ιος) with Marcus Aurelius (161–180)
2169	463	Abgar son of Ma'nu reigned over Orhai for 35 years (strict addition of 26 years here seems to produce one year too many, see below).	176/177–211/212(?)	(a) Coins of ΑΒΓΑΡΟΣ ΒΑΣΙΛΕΥΣ with Commodus (180–192) and Septimius Severus (193–211)
				(b) *AE* (1984), no. 919 (AD 195): 'regnum Abgari'; no. 920 (AD 205): 'fines regni Sept. Ab(g)ari'
				(c) *Chron. Edess.* 1: Seleucid year 513 (AD 201/202), reign of Severus and King Abgar son of Ma'nu
2203	497	. . . And over Orhai Abgar Severus (SWRWS) reigned with his son for 1 year and 7 months.	211/212–212/213?	Coins of Caracalla and (Abgar?) ΣΕΟΥΗ(ρος), *BMC Mesop.,* p. 96

Year of Abraham	Seleucid Year	Chronicle	AD (corrected by adding 26 years)	Contemporary Evidence
		And after him Maʿnu his son reigned for 26 years.	212/213–238/239 144): Maʿnu PṢGRYBʾ, son of Abgar the king	Syriac Parchment A (*CRAI* 1991,
		[No further entries relating to kings]	[239/240 (Sel. 551)	Syriac Parchment A: year 1 of Aelius Septimius Abgar, king]
			240/241 (Sel. 552)	Syriac Parchment A: year 2 of Aelius Septimius Abgar, king, and year 3 of Gordian III (238–244)
				Coins of ΑΒΓΑΡΟΣ ΒΑΣΙΛΕΥΣ and Gordian III

Syriac Parchment B shows that the Seleucid year 553 (AD 241/242) was year 30 of the 'liberation' of the *colonia,* and *P. Dura,* no. 28, that Seleucid year 554 (AD 242/243) was year 31. Year 1 was therefore AD 212/213, and it will have been in this year that a king Abgar was deposed by Caracalla, and colonial status given to Edessa/Orhai.

Syriac Parchment A shows that the king Aelius Septimius Abgar, whose first regnal year will have been the Seleucid year 551, AD 239/240, was the son of Maʿnu PṢGRYBʾ ('crown-prince' or 'heir-apparent'), and that he in turn was the son of a king Abgar. The twenty-six years given to Maʿnu by the chronicler therefore fit exactly into 212/213–238/239. His father, 'Abgar the king', could have been either the Abgar Severus of 211/212–212/213 or Abgar 'the Great'. Iulius Africanus, *Kestoi* I, 20, 28–65, confirms that *a* king called Abgaros had a son called Mannos, but does not serve to determine which. Since Abgar 'the Great' began to rule, as it seems, in AD 176/177, it is perhaps unlikely that a son of his was still 'ruling', as 'crown-prince', sixty years later. But the question need not be decided.

MAPS

The twelve maps which follow are designed solely to assist comprehension of the text of the book. Map I is an outline map of the Near East, with indications of the areas covered in the following maps. Map II covers most of the Roman Near East, and is intended as a guide to the main sites and most important geographical features, above all mountain-ranges and rivers. Maps III–XII cover the various sub-regions of the Roman Near East, with in some cases smaller or larger degrees of overlap.

While every attempt has been made to represent physical features accurately, the small scale means that inevitably the maps have something of the character of sketch-maps. They should give a useful impression of the relationships between individual sites and their geographical contexts. But they should not be used for reading off precise distances.

Where there are modern place-names which are in general use—for instance Jerusalem, Tyre or Antioch—these are used. Otherwise ancient names are given in their Latin form and in capitals. No attempt has been made to indicate the full complexity of changing official titles, for instance those of places which became Roman *coloniae*. In some of the many instances where places changed their names, both names have been given, where space allows. Where necessary for clarity, and to make it easier to relate the maps to the text, modern names, in simplified form, have been given in lower case.

It should be emphasized that the maps make no attempt to indicate all the known ancient sites, still less to give an impression of overall settlement-patterns, and are designed solely to make it possible to locate, directly or by reference to other places, all the sites and regions mentioned in the text.

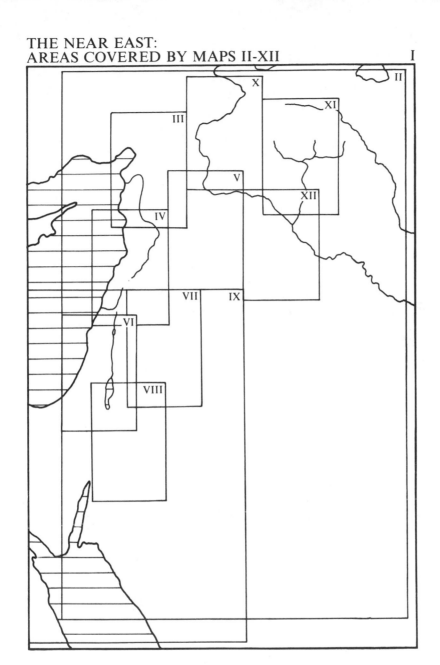

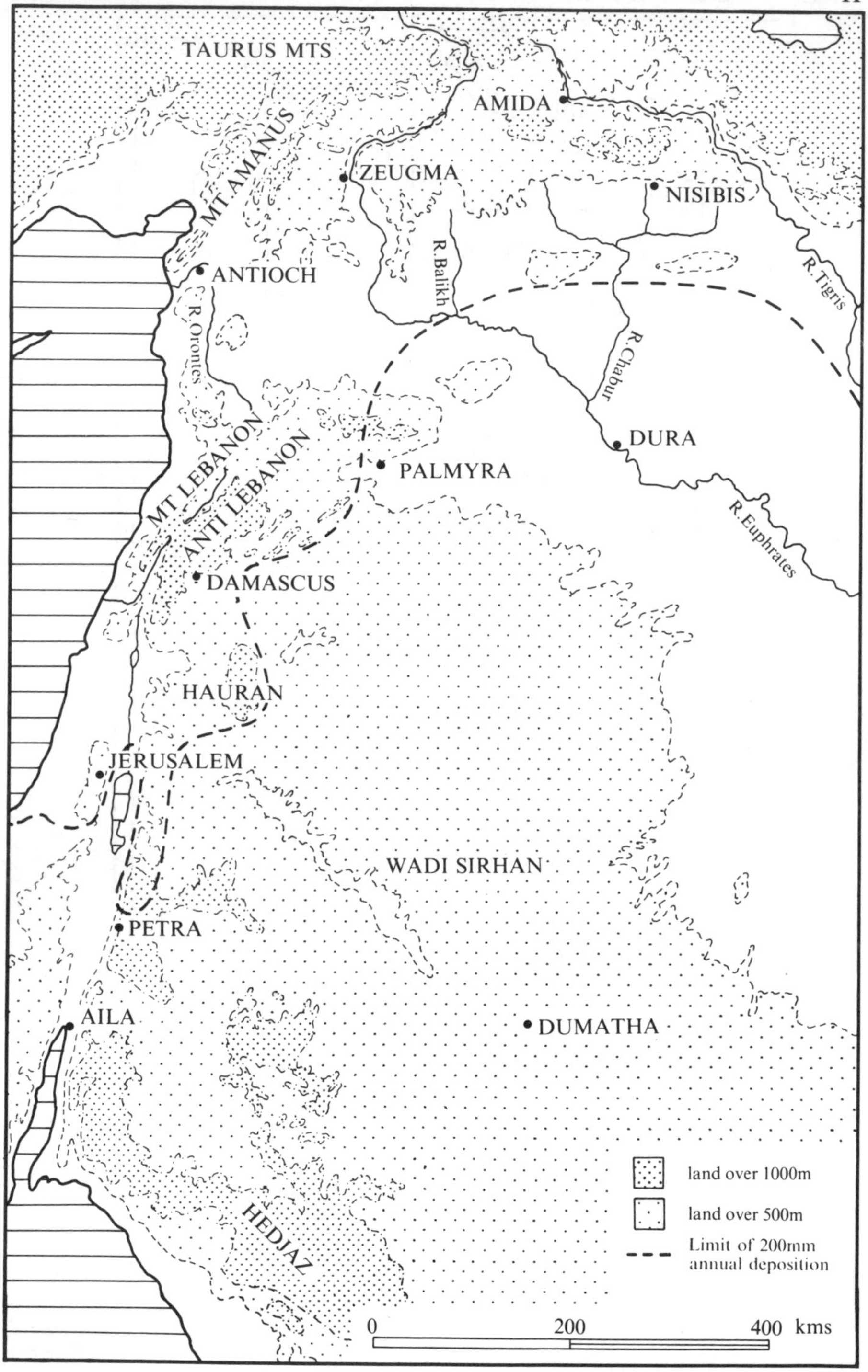

TAURUS MTS

AMIDA

ZEUGMA

NISIBIS

MT AMANUS

R.Balikh

R.Tigris

ANTIOCH

R.Orontes

R.Chabur

DURA

MT LEBANON

ANTI LEBANON

PALMYRA

R.Euphrates

DAMASCUS

HAURAN

JERUSALEM

WADI SIRHAN

PETRA

AILA

DUMATHA

HEDJAZ

land over 1000m

land over 500m

Limit of 200mm
annual deposition

0   200   400 kms

TAURUS MTS

● GERMANICIA

COMMAGENE

MT AMANUS

DOLICHE ●

CILICIA

● NICOPOLIS

R.Kara Su

R.Afrin

● CYRRHUS

● RHOSUS

GINDARVS ●

● Qalaat Seman

● IMMAE

Jebel Sheikh Barakat ●

Dehes ●

● ANTIOCH

● LITARBAE

● SELEUCIA

● BEROEA

MT KASIOS

Limestone Massif

● CHALCIS AD BELUM

MONS BARGYLUS?

R.Orontes

● LAODICEA

Jebel Ansariyeh

● APAMEA

● Qasr Ibn Wardan

GABALA ●

PALTUS ●

● LARISSA

BALANEAE

SELEUCIA
AD BELUM ●

0

100 kms

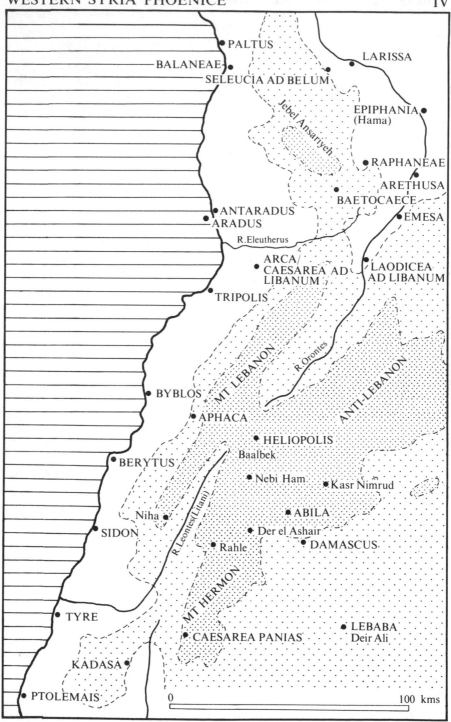

THE CENTRAL SYRIAN STEPPE,
PALMYRA AND THE EUPHRATES

V

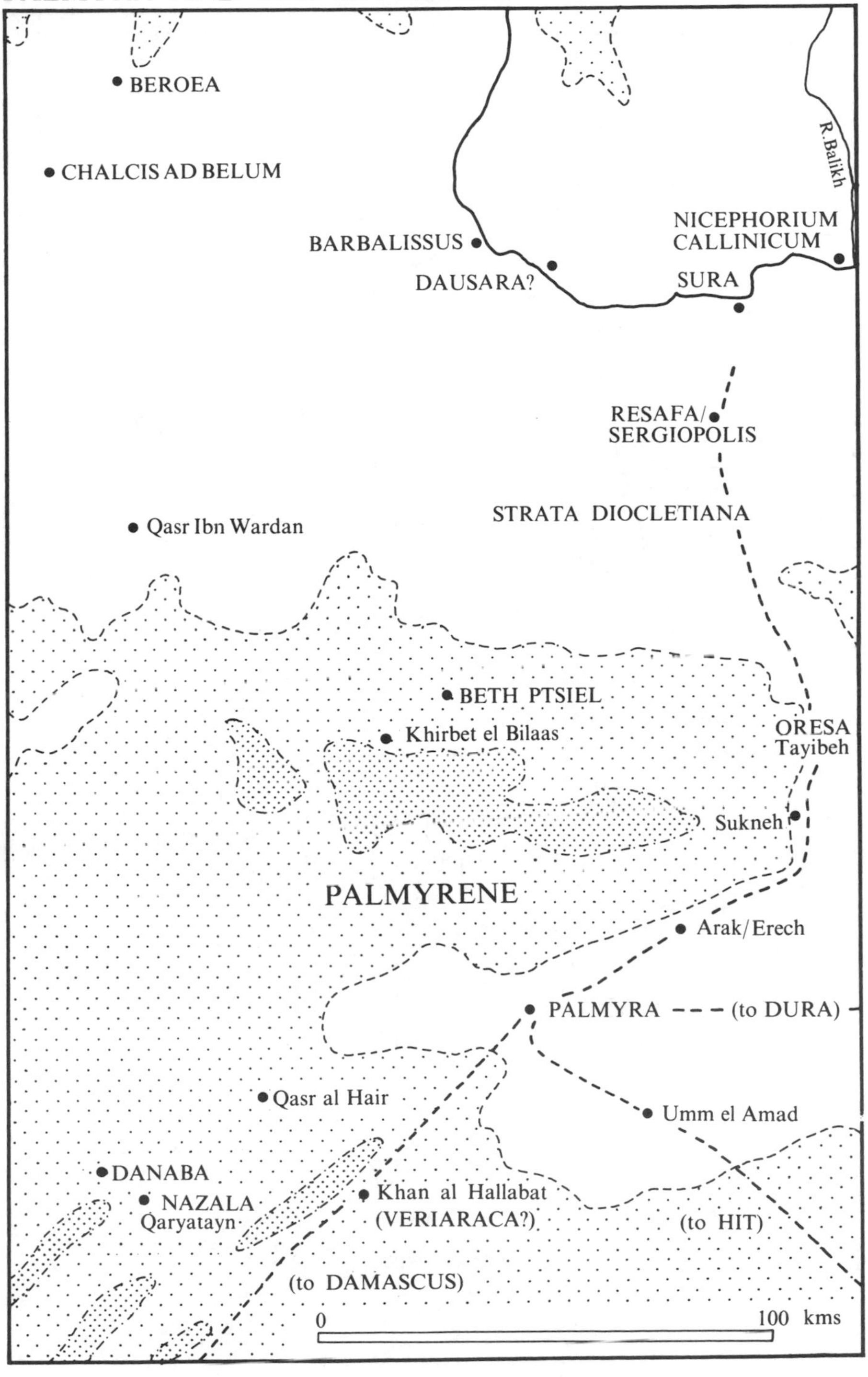

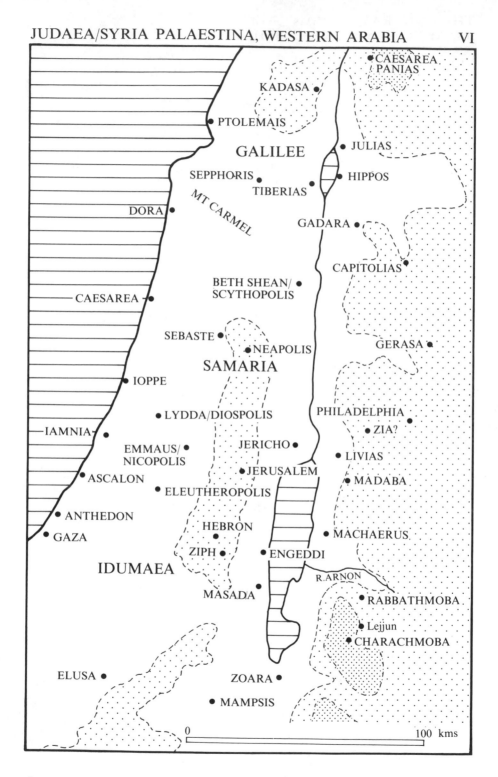

CAESAREA PANIAS

KADASA

PTOLEMAIS

GALILEE

JULIAS

SEPPHORIS

HIPPOS

TIBERIAS

DORA

MT CARMEL

GADARA

CAPITOLIAS

BETH SHEAN/ SCYTHOPOLIS

CAESAREA

SEBASTE

GERASA

NEAPOLIS

SAMARIA

IOPPE

LYDDA/DIOSPOLIS

PHILADELPHIA

IAMNIA

ZIA?

EMMAUS/ NICOPOLIS

JERICHO

LIVIAS

JERUSALEM

ASCALON

MADABA

ELEUTHEROPOLIS

ANTHEDON

HEBRON

MACHAERUS

GAZA

ZIPH

ENGEDDI

IDUMAEA

R.ARNON

MASADA

RABBATHMOBA

Lejjun

CHARACHMOBA

ELUSA

ZOARA

MAMPSIS

0   100 kms

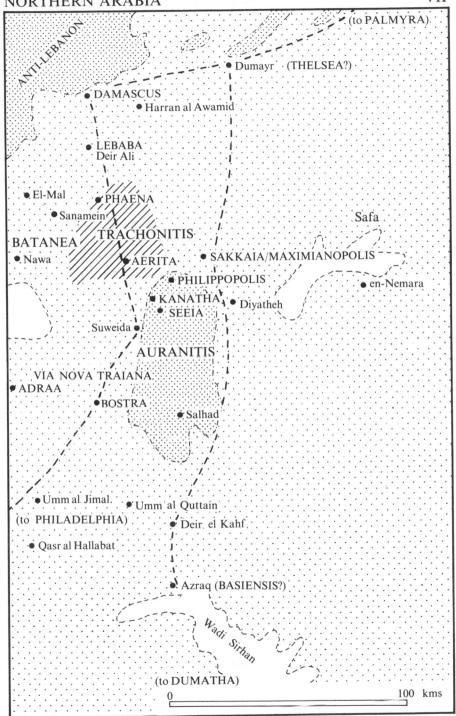

(to PALMYRA)

ANTI-LEBANON

Dumayr (THELSEA?)

● DAMASCUS
● Harran al Awamid

● LEBABA
Deir Ali

● El-Mal
● PHAENA
● Sanamein

Safa

BATANEA
TRACHONITIS
● Nawa
● AERITA
● SAKKAIA/MAXIMIANOPOLIS

● PHILIPPOPOLIS
● en-Nemara

● KANATHA
● Diyatheh
● SEEIA
Suweida ●

AURANITIS

VIA NOVA TRAIANA
● ADRAA
● BOSTRA
● Salhad

● Umm al Jimal.
● Umm al Quttain
(to PHILADELPHIA)
● Deir. el Kahf.

● Qasr al Hallabat

● Azraq (BASIENSIS?)

Wadi Sirhan

(to DUMATHA)

0   100 kms

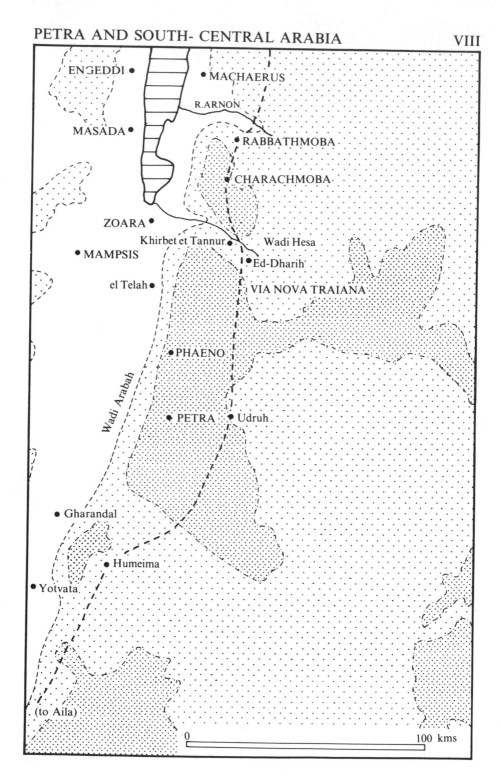

ENGEDDI

MACHAERUS

R. ARNON

MASADA

RABBATHMOBA

CHARACHMOBA

ZOARA

Khirbet et Tannur

Wadi Hesa

MAMPSIS

Ed-Dharih

el Telah

VIA NOVA TRAIANA

PHAENO

Wadi Arabah

PETRA

Udruh

Gharandal

Humeima

Yotvata

(to Aila)

0   100 kms

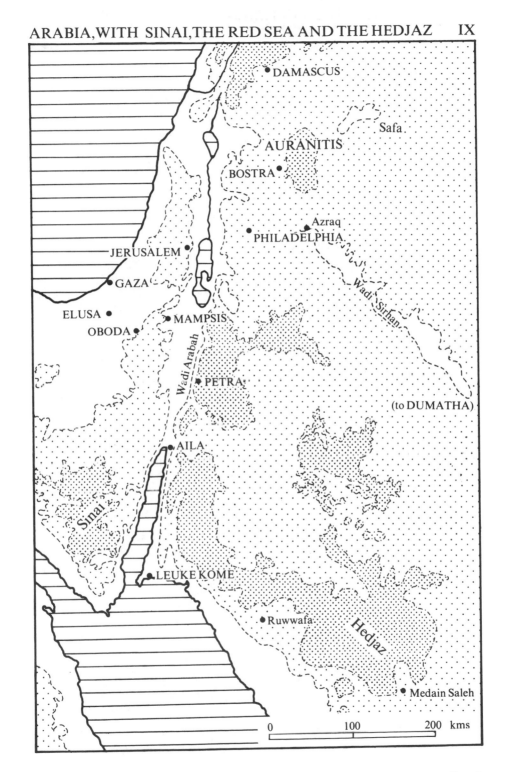

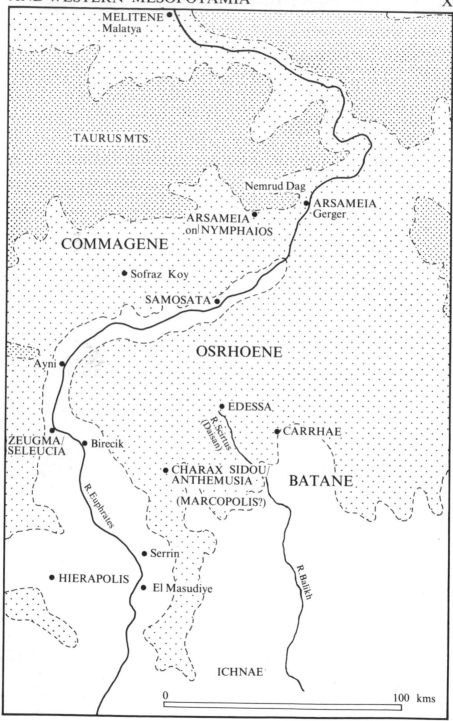

MELITENE
Malatya

TAURUS MTS.

Nemrud Dag

ARSAMEIA
Gerger

ARSAMEIA
on NYMPHAIOS

COMMAGENE

Sofraz Koy

SAMOSATA

OSRHOENE

Ayni

EDESSA

R. Scirtus
(Daisan)

CARRHAE

ZEUGMA/
SELEUCIA

Birecik

CHARAX SIDOU/
ANTHEMUSIA

BATANE

(MARCOPOLIS?)

R. Euphrates

R. Balikh

Serrin

HIERAPOLIS

El Masudiye

ICHNAE

0   100 kms

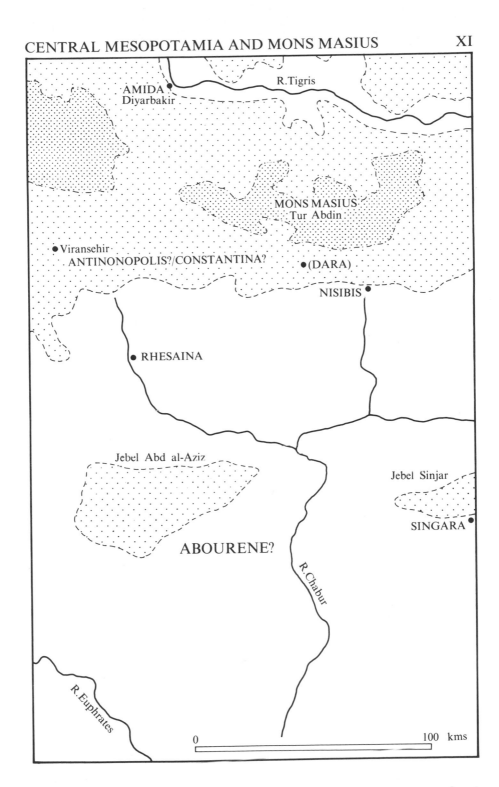

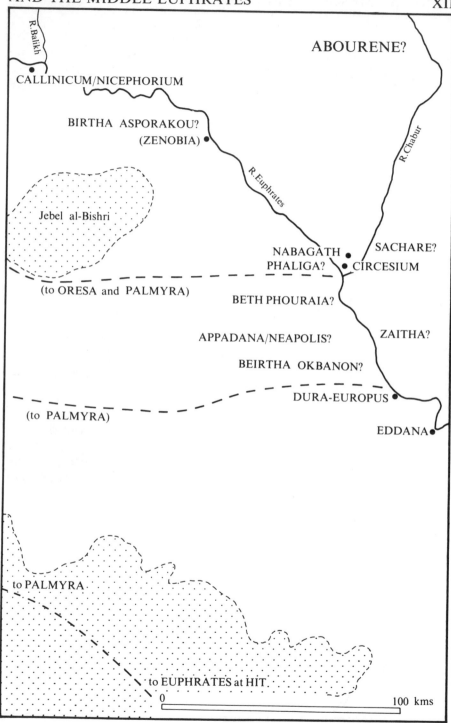

GENERAL INDEX

Achilles Tatius, *Leucippe and Clitophon*, on
Sidon, 286

Aco. *See* Ptolemais

Adiabene: possibly short-lived Trajanic province of 'Assyria', 101; kingdom, language and culture, 493–494

Aelia Capitolina (Jerusalem): refounded as *colonia* (130s AD), 106–107; Constantine's church-building at, 215 216, 350; expulsion of Jews from territory of, 348–349; Christian pilgrimage to, 385

agōnes, Greek: prevalence of, 234, 259, 523–524; in province of Arabia, 425

Agrippa I of Judaea, kingdom of, 57–58, 59–61, 63

Agrippa II of Judaea: rule over Chalcis and right to appoint High Priests (AD 50), 63; rule over Batanaea and neighbouring districts (AD 53), 66; over parts of Galilee and Peraea (AD 54), 66; forces in Jewish War, 71–72, 75; death, provincialisation of his territories (90s AD), 91–92

Alexander, imitation of by Emperors, 142–143

Allat, temple of at Palmyra, 326

altars, as cult-objects, 12–13, 253–255

Amida (Diyarbakir), fortification under Constantine, 209

Ammianus Marcellinus, account of Near Eastern provinces, 211–212

Antioch: Germanicus dies at, 53–54; relations with Titus (AD 70), 79; Roman canalization at (70s AD), 86–90; earthquake at (AD 115), 104–105; as capital of Pescennius

Niger, 120–121; made *kōmē* in the territory of Laodicea by Severus (?), 123; inscription from honouring *Praefecti Praetorio* (AD 336), 210–211; made *colonia* by Caracalla, 143, 258; evidence for internal functioning, 259–260

Apamea: attacked in Civil Wars (45–44 BC), 28; Roman forces at in third century, 146, 159; geographical setting, 238; Semitic language spoken at (?), 241; villages in territory of, 250–251; character of city, 256–263; Numenius (Neo-Platonist) from, 518

Aphaca, destruction by Constantine of cult-centre at, 215

'Arab' (as ethnic description): legendary descent from Ishmael and Hagar, 8, 11; Palmyrenes identified as (?), 221, 333; Nabataeans characterised as, 400; self-description by man from Kanatha, 419–420; Imru'l-qais as 'king of all the Arabs' (MLK' 'L 'RB KLH) (?), 434–435; 'Arabes' in Mesopotamia, 456; 'ruler of Arab', 495; problems of 'Arab' role in Near East, 512–515; 'Arab' ancestors of Palmyrenes, 525

Arabia: formation of province of, 92–97; *census* in, 97–98; forts in in Tetrarchic period, 184–189; southern part transferred to Palaestina, 192–193, 387–436; distinct variety of Christian belief in (?), 519

Arabic language, 4; inscription from Oboda with two lines in, 402-403; inscription of AD 328 in from en-Nemara, 434–435, 514

'Arabicus': as victory-title of Severus and Caracalla, 141; of Vaballathus, 171, 221, 333

[577]

INDEX OF LITERARY SOURCES

INDEX OF DOCUMENTS